Free Stuff For Busy Moms

by

Matthew Lesko

and

Mary Ann Martello

Researchers
Zsuzsa Beres; Giovina Taraschi
Melanie Coltan; Nancy Gibson
Mary Courtney Ore; Amy Hollingsworth
Allison Mays; Caroline Pharmer
Cindy Owens; Marcelle McCarthy
Bradley Sowash; Emily Subler;
Marty Brinkman, Laura Difore, Jennifer Maier

Production
Beth Meserve

Marketing
Kim McCoy

Support
Mercedes Sundeen

Cover
Steve Bonham

FIRST EDITION

Library of Congress Cataloging-in-Publication date
    Lesko, Matthew
    Martello, Mary Ann

Free Stuff For Busy Moms

ISBN # 1-878346-49-0

Most books by Matthew Lesko are available at special quantity
discounts for bulk purchases for sales promotions, premiums, fund-
raising or educational use. Special books or book excerpts also can be
created to fit specific needs.

For details, write Information USA, Special Markets, Attention: Kim
McCoy, P.O. Box E, Kensington, MD 20895; or 1-800-797-7811,
Marketing; {www.lesko.com}.

Dedication

To all Moms who are not fully recognized by our society for their important contributions

Table of Contents

FREE STUFF FOR YOUR HOME

FREE CHILD CARE RESOURCES

HELP WITH THE KIDS

FREE MONEY TO SEND YOUR CHILD TO PRIVATE KINDERGARDEN THRU HIGH SCHOOL

FREE CHILD SUPPORT

YOUR MONEY, INSURANCE AND CONSUMER HELP

GET EXTRA CASH FINDING LOST MONEY AND SURPLUS PROPERTY **231**

FREE MONEY TO PAY LEGAL FEES, FREE LAWYERS, AND FREE LEGAL HELP

FREE SERVICES TO HELP FIND YOUR LOST LOVER OR CHECK OUT A NEW ONE

FREE RESOURCES FOR YOUR HEALTH

FREE MONEY AND HELP FOR YOUR BUSINESS

OVER 100 GOVERNMENT GRANTS
FOR YOUR BUSINESS 462

EDUCATION PROGRAMS

FEDERAL JOB TRAINING PROGRAMS 564

STATE JOB TRAINING PROGRAMS 581

Appendix **658**

Real Women Get Government Money

FREE STUFF FOR BUSY MOMS

Government data show that when a married woman goes to work outside the home, she will increase the family income by an extra 93%[1] and when she does, her husband will increase his share of the housework by an extra one hour a week.[2]

Come on, guys, admit it! When we do something around the house, we feel that we should be flown to Washington and receive the Congressional Medal of Honor. We feel we're doing a lot around the house because we're doing so much more than our fathers ever did. But it's easy to forget that our mothers probably didn't work.

But that's not the only place where women are the underdogs:

- When a woman changes from working as a homemaker to working in the work force her total work schedule expands at least 20 hours a week[3]
- For women, gaining just a husband adds 4.2 hours of domestic work per week[4]

- Employed mothers spend 85 hours at work and housework[5]
- Women represent 2/3 of all poor adults[6]
- 50% of senior women are in poverty versus only 20% of senior men[7]
- Despite advancement in technology, the amount of time a full time housewife devotes to her work remained unchanged since 1910[8]
- 8 million women are raising children with no dad[9]
- Only 50% of women get full child support[10]
- Women work more in the U.S. than in any other developed country[11]
- The number of women experiencing stress-related diseases has exploded[12]
- Sleep researchers say women are living on 60-90 minutes less sleep a night than they should for optimum performance[13]
- For each extra hour a woman works outside the home, her work inside the home reduces by only 30 minutes[14]

Information USA, Inc.

- Working moms do 2/3 as much housework and child care as non-working moms[15]
- The average divorced woman will LOWER her standard of living by 27% but a divorced man will RAISE his by 10%[16]
- 70% of the informal care given to the elderly is done by women, 29% are daughters and 9% are sons[17]
- Women are 250% more likely to baby-sit grandkids than men[18]
- Women householders with no husband present earn an average of $23,040, male householders with no wife present earn an average $36,634[19]

At first glance it appears our society fails to honor mom's efforts the way it should. For example, tax laws allow you to deduct more for raising horses than for raising children. Maybe that's why our country is a leader in raising great racehorses, and also a leader, among wealthy nations, in raising kids in poverty. In the United States, 20% of the children live in poverty, in Canada it's 9%, in Germany 4%, and in Japan 2%.

> **In the United States, 20% of the children live in poverty. In Canada it's 9%, in Germany 4%, and in Japan 2%.**

Here's another telling tale on government data. When a man marries his housekeeper, the total value of goods and services produced in our country (Gross Domestic Product) goes down. Government statistics include the income earned by the housekeeper doing housework, but when a housekeeper marries her boss, the value of her work is no longer considered part of our country's economic well being.

Moms need help! They need to be honored, and it's all right here in this book. Thousands of government and nonprofit organizations offer free services, free information, free essentials, free fun stuff, and even free money to help moms and their families, no matter what their age or income level.

All you have to do is know where to go, and who to ask.

This Book Is Out Of Date!

I'm sorry to say this, but once we publish a book it is out of date. But don't despair! The whole world is that way. By the time anybody publishes anything, it's out of date. Your Yellow Pages phone book sitting in your home is out of date. The brand new book you picked up at the bookstore discussing the latest treatments for cancer is out of date, because it won't contain the latest treatment announced in yesterday's newspaper. And even today's newspapers have trouble keeping current with the latest developments in some Washington scandal. That's why you can turn on the TV and watch the 24-hour scandal channel.

Life in the new millennium means learning how to live in a world with out-of-date information. In our swiftly moving society, everything seems to be changing every day. The only thing that will remain constant in our life is change. But learning how to deal with change is easy. . . if you're ready for it. If you try to contact a source listed in this book and instead you get a Domino's Pizza delivery service, then someone has moved. But most likely the organization is still there. It's just at a different location.

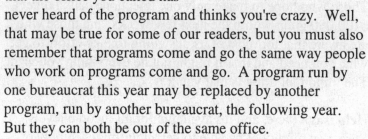

Or maybe you contact a listed source looking for a specific program only to find that the office you called has never heard of the program and thinks you're crazy. Well, that may be true for some of our readers, but you must also remember that programs come and go the same way people who work on programs come and go. A program run by one bureaucrat this year may be replaced by another program, run by another bureaucrat, the following year. But they can both be out of the same office.

Your job in the new millennium, if you choose to accept it, is to realize that because a particular office doesn't have the exact program you are looking for, it may have a similar program under a different name or may know of another organization that may also be of help. **YOU HAVE TO ASK!**

I feel our changing world makes books like this one more valuable than ever. Most books tell you that they will provide you with answers. This book doesn't tell you the answers, it tells you the sources that have the latest answers. The answers are changing all the time, but sources that keep track of the latest answers change less frequently. The person studying the latest cures for cancer is less likely to change as quickly as a report professing to contain the latest cures.

You Won't Get Everything, But It's Important To Try

There will be two types of people who read this book. Those who hope to make only one telephone call and get a $100,000 grant within the next few weeks, and those who are aware that for most of us, it's going to take effort to get what you need and it still might not be everything you want. The important thing is that you try.

Help is out there, and it's available for all income levels. Sure, you might not be able to get an unlimited supply of free medications because you make over $40,000 a year, but you can still be eligible for free cancer surgery from the

National Institutes of Health, even if you are a millionaire. That's what ABC News reporter Sam Donaldson did.

Sure, you may not be able to qualify for a free or low-cost automobile, but you may be able to get free transportation for you mom or grandma who needs a ride back and forth to the doctor. Or sure, you may not be able to get all the money you need to quit your job today and go back to school full-time maintaining your current style of life. But you can start going back to school part-time, or simplify your lifestyle and put together enough grants and loans and part time jobs to complete the education you need to do the kind of work you always dreamed of doing.

Help is out there, and it's available for all income levels

Try, try and try again! There are always exceptions. You only need one. If you don't ask, nothing will happen. Even though programs say they have certain requirements that you don't meet, ask how you can be an exception. All rules are not set in stone. Many bureaucrats in charge of the money or help have the power to bend the rules. And if they won't or can't, ask them who can. If you really need help, money, or information, don't worry about what people think about you or your tactics. Because most of these programs are from government sources or non-profits, you have a right to them as much as anyone else.

Sure, nothing works all the time. But nothing works at all
unless you try.

We Exaggerate!

The media made me do it! It's always nice to blame
someone else for my faults, and the media seems to be the
country's favorite whipping boy at the moment, so I might
as well use them too. Like most people in our society who
are trying to communicate to others I use the media. And
the media is bombarding the public with so much news,

information and
entertainment that it is
becoming increasingly
difficult to get anyone's
attention.

Titles and headlines are used
to try and cut through the
noise and get your attention. It can be a 10 second teaser
for your local news that will state something like
"Mysteries of Life Solved, Highlights At 11." Or the photo
on the front page of the newspaper at the checkout stand
showing a baby with 8 heads! Nobody says they read those
newspapers but one tabloid sells about 2.5 million copies a
week and claims a readership of over 15 million.

Headlines are also used to entice you into the door to give
something a try. Like a book title that says "Thinner
Thighs In 30 Days." Would you still be interested in the

book if it used a non-exaggerated title like "Here's A Book That Shows You How You May, Or May Not, Trim Your Thighs After A Long Period Of Hard Exercising And Hard Dieting." Not destined for the best seller list, is it?

Most people are smart enough to know that titles and headlines are often exaggerated, and I apologize to readers who are offended by such hyperbole. But I also think that it is important to use exaggerations and hyperbole in order to be as inclusive as possible in our work. If we are limiting in our titles, you may not investigate how to take advantage of certain programs. If our title says that this program does not apply to you so don't bother, you may not get the help you need.

A Lot Of Money Goes Unused

It does sound ridiculous, but it's true. Each year millions of Americans are eligible for extra money from the government and they never apply for it. If rich people hire high priced attorneys to make sure they take advantage of every tax benefit the government has to offer, why shouldn't the rest of us do all we can to take advantage of all the benefits that are offered to us? In case you're not aware, this is a rhetorical question.

During our research for this book I've uncovered studies that have shown:

- Over 6 million children who are living in families that are eligible for financial assistance don't receive it.[20]
- Over 4.7 million children are eligible for the government new Children's Health Insurance Program and are not enrolled. Almost every state now has a Children's Health Insurance Program (CHIPS) which extends medical coverage to many children.[21]
- 3 Million Seniors & Disabled Don't Apply for Their Free $1,000 For Health Care for their Medicare Premiums. Each year over 3 million eligible seniors and people with disabilities fail to apply for a little-known health care benefit.[22]

And I believe that this is just the tip of the iceberg. I feel quite certain that there must be millions of moms who are unaware that even with incomes up to $40,000, they are eligible for free prescription drugs for themselves or their children, as well as free mammograms and cancer treatments. A benefit that can greatly enhance the quality of a mom's life must be a lot more important than a tax break for a vacation rental property! My guess is that all the people with vacation rental property know all the tax breaks that are available to them, but all the women eligible for free mammograms are not likely to know of the benefits to which they are entitled.

Matthew Lesko

[1] Income data from Bureau of the Census, Money Income in the United States: 1997, p 60-200

[2] *The Overworked American*, Juliet B. Schor, Basis Books, New York, 1992, p 38

[3] *The Overworked American*, Juliet B. Schor, Basis Books, New York, 1992, p 8

[4] *The Overworked American*, Juliet B. Schor, Basis Books, New York, 1992, p 38

[5] *The Overworked American*, Juliet B. Schor, Basis Books, New York, 1992, p 73

[6] U.S. Bureau of the Census, 1997 Poverty Statistics

[7] *Women and Children Last*, Ruth Sidel, Penguin Books, New York 1992, p 158

[8] *The Overworked American*, Juliet B. Schor, Basis Books, New York, 1992, p 8

[9] *Women and Children Last*, Ruth Sidel, Penguin Books, New York 1992, p 104

[10] *Women and Children Last*, Ruth Sidel, Penguin Books, New York 1992, p 104

[11] *The Overworked American*, Juliet B. Schor, Basis Books, New York, 1992, p 8

[12] *The Overworked American*, Juliet B. Schor, Basis Books, New York, 1992, p 11

[13] *Cheating on Sleep: Modern Life Turns America Into the Land of the Drowsy*, The New York Times, May 15, 1990, p. C8

[14] *The Overworked American*, Juliet B. Schor, Basis Books, New York, 1992, p 36

[15] *The Overworked American*, Juliet B. Schor, Basis Books, New York, 1992, p 103

[16] *Kidding Ourselves*, Rhona Mahone, Basic Books, New York, 1995, p 18

[17] *Kidding Ourselves*, Rhona Mahone, Basic Books, New York, 1995, p 81

[18] *Kidding Ourselves*, Rhona Mahone, Basic Books, New York, 1995, p 81

[19] Income data from Bureau of the Census, Money Income in the United States: 1997, p 60-200

[20] *Keeping Women and Children Last*, Ruth Sidel, Penguin Books, New York, p 89

[21] *Help for Children Who Need Health Insurance, Food and Nutrition Service*, U.S. Department Of Agriculture; {www.fns.usda.gov/fns/MENU/WHATSNEW/CHIP/chipfns.htm#Background}

[22] *Shortchanged: Billions Withheld From Medicare Beneficiaries*, Families USA Publications, Washington, DC (www.familiesusa.org/SHTCHGPR.HTM)

I NEED TRANSPORTATION

*A Ride, a Taxi, a Bus, a New Car,
or Money To Fix Up an Old One*

Free Cars...
You Heard It Here First

There's a program in Tennessee giving out free cars and
even a free year's worth of insurance coverage. Another
program in Pennsylvania gives out free cars but makes you
pay for the insurance. A program in North Carolina makes
you pay $50 a month for only one year. That's only $600
bucks and you get a great car.

Other programs give out cars at book value and tell you to
pay when you can, with no interest or finance charges.
Some programs even provide free AAA Service for tows
and jump starts. Such
programs are normally
called
*"Wheels to
Work"* and
they are
popping up all over the country.
The government knows that if a mom has to drop off a
child at day care, pick up food at the store and get back and

forth to work (or school) on time, there are very few places you can do that on public transportation. If women don't have a car, they can wind up on welfare.

All of the programs look at your need for a car, and many require that you be an active participant in a welfare-to-work program. These programs are local and hard to find, but they are growing. You won't know if you're eligible for a car unless you ask.

To start looking for programs like this in your area, contact your local congressman's office or your local social service agency. You can also look in the state-by-state Appendix listing under *Transportation Department* for starting places. They won't know about all the programs but can probably give you some starting places.

Get $65 a Month Free From Your Boss For Commuting To Work

Your employer can give you $65 a month to help pay for bus, train, ferry, or vanpool commuting expense and neither you nor the employer has to pay taxes on this money. Contact your local transit authority for more details on the program called *Tax Free Qualified Transportation Fringe Benefits*, or contact: Commuter Check Services Corporation, 401 S. Van Brunt Street, Englewood, NJ 07631; 201-833-9700; Fax: 201-833-8704; {www.commutercheck.com}.

States Offer Money For: Cars, Bus Fare, Auto Repairs, Insurance and Drivers Ed

The following are examples of what just some of the states are offering in transportation assistance for those who have serious transportation needs. Transportation is a growing concern in the workforce and programs are being added and changed every day. Be sure to contact your state transportation agency listed in the appendix for the latest benefits your state has to offer.

- ☑ **Alaska:** $85 a month towards transportation
- ☑ **Arizona:** $5 a day towards transportation
- ☑ **Arkansas:** $200 for car repairs
- ☑ **Colorado:** Free cars and 3 months of insurance
- ☑ **Delaware:** 30 free transit ride tickets with a new job
- ☑ **Florida:** Money for gas, repairs and insurance
- ☑ **Illinois:** $60 a month for gas or $88 a month to take the bus
- ☑ **Kansas:** $30 a month for gas and money for car repairs
- ☑ **Kentucky:** $60 a month for gas and $300 to get a drivers license, pay for auto registration, taxes or repairs, and $900 to move to another city to get a job
- ☑ **Louisiana:** $100 a year for auto repairs
- ☑ **Massachusetts:** $150 a month towards transportation
- ☑ **Michigan:** Money for auto repairs and insurance
- ☑ **Mississippi Provides Door to Door Service**
- ☑ **Nebraska:** Money for insurance, auto repairs; $2,000 to buy you a car; 3 months of auto insurance, $500 for taxes, licensing, etc.
- ☑ **New Hampshire:** $130 a month for transportation; $240 a year for auto repairs; and money to take drivers education
- ☑ **New Jersey:** $500 for car repairs
- ☑ **New York:** $500 for car repairs
- ☑ **Oklahoma:** Money for auto repairs and insurance
- ☑ **Pennsylvania:** $200 for auto repairs
- ☑ **South Dakota:** Money for auto repairs
- ☑ **Vermont:** $200 for auto repairs
- ☑ **Washington:** $546 a month for transportation
- ☑ **Wisconsin:** $1600 interest free to buy a car or repay with community service

FREE TAXI SERVICE
To Work, School, or Day Care

One county in Oregon has a program that picks up you and your child, taking your child to day care and you to work. It doesn't charge you anything, and doesn't even ask your income.

North Carolina has programs where counties are given vans to transport people back and forth to work, with lower fees charged to those in welfare-to-work programs.

Mississippi has a program that will pick you up at your house, almost anywhere in the state and take you back and forth to work if you are working to get off welfare.

Some communities, like Fairfax County in Virginia, maintain a database that helps locate the necessary transportation for work and day care needs. And Kentucky operates an 800 hotline that tries to solve any work-related transportation need, and soon they will have a separate hotline for each county. Do these people want you to get to work, or what?

To start looking for programs like this in your area, contact your local congressman's office or your local social service agency. You can also look in the state-by-state Appendix listing under *Transportation* for starting places. They won't know about all the programs but can probably give you some starting places. You should also find out about local vanpool and rideshare programs. Your local chamber of commerce or library should have this kind of information for you.

More Free Pubs About Car Buying, Repairing and Renting

1. *Gas Saving Products* - find out why most don't work
2. *Car Ads: Reading Between The Lines*
3. *Buyers Guide* - shows your rights with used car dealers
4. *Renting A Car*
5. *Taking The Scare Out of Auto Repair*

These 5 publications are available from Public Reference, Room 130, Federal Trade Commission, Washington, DC 20580; 202-326-2222 or download them from:
{www.ftc.gov/bcp/conline/pubs02.htm}

Money For Auto Repairs, Car Insurance, Driver's Ed, Or Just A Tank Of Gas

Whatever it takes to keep you on the road! There are federal programs as well as state programs to help people with limited incomes keep their vehicles on the road so that they can get back and forth to work, focusing on those trying to get off welfare.

Twice As Many Women Don't Drive Than Men

14% of women and only 5% of men ages 18+ say they don't drive

Source: About Women and Marketing, May 1, 1998, About Women Inc., Boston MA

Some states will even give you money for driver's education or to pay for a driver's license. The issue, like the programs for free cars, is to **help people make it to work**. Illinois and Kentucky offer $60 a month for gas money. New York and New Jersey give people up to $500 for car repairs. Pennsylvania and Vermont only give $200 for car repairs. But Washington

State provides people up to $546 a month for their transportation.

Limousines anyone? These programs are organized like a patchwork quilt in most areas involving federal, state, county and non-profit organizations.

Here is just a *SAMPLING* of the Wheels to Work programs that we found:

Wheels to Work
Forsyth County
Department of Social
Services
P.O. Box 999
Winston-Salem, NC 27102
910-727-2175

Cooperative Ministry
Art Collier
P.O. Box 1705
Columbia, SC 29202
803-799-3853

New Leaf Services
3696 Greentree Farms Dr.
Decatur, GA 30034
404-289-9293

Charity Cars
1980 North Cameron Ave.

Sanford, FL 32771
407-324-5050

Cars for Work
Good Will and Crisis
Assistance Ministry
2122 Freedom Dr.
Charlotte, NC 28266
704-332-0291

Wheels to Work
Resource Conservation &
Development Council
240 Oak St., Suite 101
Lawrenceville, GA 30245
770-339-6071

First Wheels
Warren County DHS
1200 Belmont Dr.
McMinnville, TN 37110
615-473-9633

To start looking for programs like this in your area, contact your local congressman's office or your local Social Services. You can also look in the state-by-state Appendix listing under *Transportation* for starting places. They won't know about all the programs but can probably give you some starting places.

One Month of Free Bus Passes

Detroit's **Suburban Mobility Authority for Regional Transportation (SMART)** has a

"Get a Job/ Get a Ride" Program

program called "Get a Job/Get a Ride" that gives a month's worth of free rides to anyone in the Detroit area who gets a job.

The only requirement is that you started a new job within the last 30 days. You can be making $100,000 a year and they'll still give you the free passes. New Jersey will give a free one-month pass to those on low income that get a job or are going to training.

Check with your local Chamber of Commerce, Transit Authority, or look in the state-by-state Appendix listing under *Transportation Department*.

CARS AT 3-PENNIES ON $100

The government estimates that their auctions give them 3 cents for every $100 they spend on the original item. I've never seen those Jeeps for $1 advertised in the back of magazines, but one official said that he has seen vehicles with less than 3,000 miles being sold for well under $1,000. Cars and trucks can go for as little as $100. The price of cars varies depending upon who attends the auctions.

The two major agencies that sell vehicles at auctions are the *General Services Administration* and the *Department of Defense*. To find the auctions nearest to you contact:

US General Services Administration
Property Management Division
1941 Jefferson Davis Highway

Arlington, VA 22202
703-305-7841
www.fss.gsa.gov

Defense Reutilization and Marketing Service
74 N. Washington Avenue
Battle Creek, MI 49017
1-888-352-9333
www.drms.dla.mil

Free Legal Help To Fight A Car Dealer Or Repair Shop

When you can't get satisfaction from the manager or owner, then it is time to bring in the big guns:

✦ Your state attorney general's office, listed in the state-by-state section in the Appendix, is set up to handle automobile complaints. Sometimes all you have to do is send a letter to the attorney general with a copy to the business owner.

✦ Automotive Consumer Action Program (AUTOCAP) is a complaint handling system

sponsored by the
automobile
industry for new
or used car
purchases from
NEW car dealers
only. To find a
source in your
area, contact:

> ## Automotive Consumer Action Program
>
> **www.nada.org/ consumer/resolve. htm**

National Automobile Dealers Association, 8400
Westpark Drive, McLean, VA 22102; 703-821-7000;
{www.nada.org/consumer/resolve.htm}

✦ Better Business Bureau (BBB) Auto Line is a
FREE, out-of-court arbitration program, paid for by the
business community to handle automobile complaints
between consumers and most auto manufacturers.

> ## Better Business Bureau Auto Line
>
> **www.bbb.org/ complaints/ BBBautoline.html**

Contact your local
Better Business
Bureau or BBB Auto
Line, Dispute
Resolution Division,
Council of Better
Business Bureaus,
Inc., 4200 Wilson
Blvd, Suite 800,
Arlington, VA
22202; 800-955-
5100; {www.bbb.org/complaints/
BBBautoLine.html}.

FREE AND LOW COST SEMINARS ON HOW TO BUY A CAR

You can't just go on color alone! You need to become savvy as to what options to look for and how to negotiate with the dealer.

60% Of All Car Buyers Will Be Women By The Year 2000

Source: Estimate from Leggs Corp. at www.leggs.com

Do you really need rust proofing? What is the difference between the invoice and the sticker price? How can I find out what the dealer paid for the car?

Don't be intimidated by salesmanship. The dealer wants your money, so they don't want you to leave without signing on the bottom line. Many different organizations and groups offer classes on how to buy a car. Contact your county cooperative extension service, your local adult education department, or women's organizations in your area to see what they may have to offer.

Finding the Best Rate for an Auto Loan

You got your car, but now, how are you going to pay for it? Obviously, the dealer is going to want you to finance the car through the dealership. More money for them, right?

Before you sign on the dotted line, check the dealer's rate against banks, credit unions, savings and loan institutions, and other loan companies. Because interest rates vary, shop around for the best deal, comparing the annual percentage rates (APR).

Sometimes, dealers offer very low financing rates for specific cars or models, but may not be willing to negotiate on the price of these cars. Before you do anything, check out:

✤ *Buying a New Car and Car Ads: Reading Between the Lines*, free from the Federal Trade Commission, Public Reference Room 130, Washington, DC 20580; 202-326-2222; {www.ftc.gov}.

✤ Check out the BanxQuote website that provides auto
financing rates for new and used cars in all 50 states at
{www.banx.com}.

GET YOUR CAR
REPAIRED FOR FREE

June Rapp of Massachusetts took her family van into a
dealer to have it fixed and they wanted to charge her over
$1000 to make the repairs. She called the U.S. Department
of Transportation and found out that her problem was part
of a manufacturer recall. Recalls have to be fixed for free
and the repair shop didn't know that. To find out about
recalls for any car, contact:

Auto's Top Consumer Complaints

**Top 5 consumer complaints from Maryland State
Attorney General's Office:**

#1: New Car Dealers
#2: Automobile Repair and Body Shops
#3: Sweepstakes
#4: Landlord Tenant Relationships
#5: Mail Order Forms

❏ **Auto Safety Hotline**, US Dept. of Transportation, NEF-11.2HL, 400 Seventh St., SW, Washington, DC 20590; 888-327-4236; {www.nhtsa.dot.gov/cars/problems/recall/recmmy1.cfm}

❏ The **Consumer Report** people have a searchable database for car recall information. Contact Consumers Union, 101 Truman Ave., Yonkers, NY 10702; 800-208-9699; {consumerreports.org}.

What's Your Old (or New) Car Worth?

As much as someone will pay for it... But there are books that will give you the trade-in or retail value of almost any car. Or you can look in the local papers for the prices of similar cars that are advertised for sale. You can also take your car into a few used car dealers who sell your car new or seem to have a lot of your model on hand and ask them what they would pay you. Here are the books.

★ *NADA Official Used Car Guide* gives you the high, average, and low retail value of used cars. The book can be found in most libraries and is available from the publisher or bookstores for $9.95. NADA, 8400 Westpark Dr, McLean, VA 22102; 800-544-6232; {www.nada.org}. Their website contains no pricing information.

★ The Consumer Edition of the *Kelly Blue Book* provides suggested retail and trade in value. The book is available in your local library, most bookstores for about $9.95, or the information is free on their website; {www.kbb. com}.

> **85% Of New Car Buyers Haggle Over Prices With Car Salesmen**
>
> Source: "Haggle Over Car Prices? Yes please." Brenda M Eisenhauer, American Demographics, April 1995

★ Edmond Publications, *Used Car and Truck Prices & Reviews* provides the information for free on their website or is available in bookstores or from the publisher for $13.99. Edmund Publications, P.O. Box 338, Shrub Oaks, NY 10588; 914-962-6297; {www.edmunds.com}.

What Is the Best Car To Buy?

Buying a new car is usually the second most expensive purchase you make, after the purchase of your home. So getting the most for your money is important. Knowing what car model and options you want and how much you are willing to spend before you walk into a dealer's showroom will help you get the best deal.

There are several buying guides and publications available to help you choose the car that is right for you. The most common resource guide is *Consumer Reports*. They publish automobile review guides that are available at your local library.

Consumer Reports Online allows you to search through the past two years worth of reports. In the "Cars and Trucks" section, you may search for a car that contains the features you require. It also lists product recalls and has a listing of manufacturers. For a fee, they provide a new and used car price service, providing you with the invoice, sticker price, and more for a particular make and model. Contact Consumers Union, 101 Truman Ave., Yonkers, NY 10702; 800-208-9699; {consumerreports.org}

∗ *New Car Buying Guide* and *Buying A Used Car* are available free from Federal Trade Commission, Public Reference, Room 130, Washington, DC 20580; 202-326-2222; {www.ftc.gov}

∗ *Your Money, Your Car* is free from National Automotive Dealers Association, 8400 Westpark Dr., McLean, VA 22102; 800-544-6232; {www. nada.org}

✻ Two websites that provide car shopping information, car reviews, maintenance articles, and more include {www.womanmotorist.com} and {www.womenautohelp.com}.

What's The SAFEST Car To Drive?

Let the crash test dummies help you learn the safest car to drive. The U.S. Department of Transportation (DOT) has been using these guys for years to analyze the crash protection of various automobiles.

Men Are Three Times More Likely Than Women To Be Killed In Car Crashes

...according to researchers at the Johns Hopkins Schools of Medicine and Public Health

Source: **Health Letter on the CDC, CW Henderson, Atlanta, GA, June 29, 1998**

The DOT operates the *Auto Safety Hotline* that distributes the Vehicle Crash Test report showing the crash protection provided to front-seat occupants in accidents for all new cars each year. It also lists types of protection available in the cars, such as air bags or anti-lock brakes.

An interesting feature of the Hotline is that you can search the *Technical Service Bulletins* by make and model to see what kinds of problems or issues have come up for the car you are considering. You can also search the consumer complaint listings and recall information as well.

If you are having a problem with your car, register your complaint with the hotline. Yours may be just the call they need to start a recall!

For your free copy and more information, contact National Highway Traffic Safety Administration, U.S. Department of Transportation, Auto Safety Hotline, NEF-11.2HL, 400 Seventh St., SW, Washington, DC 20590; 888-327-4236; {www.nhtsa.dot.gov/hotline}.

SHOULD YOU BUY OR LEASE A CAR?

"A New Car with No Money Down" may sound enticing but beware of the fine print when you are considering leasing your next car.

The Attorney General in the state of Maryland warns that a couple returned their Chevrolet at the end of a 5-year lease in good condition but received a bill for $3,251 for reconditioning. An Annapolis consumer was surprised to learn that every time she took her car in for repair she was charged a $50 deductible.

Leasing may be an interesting option if you like changing cars often and you like making car payments forever. But be sure you get all the facts before you decide:

☞ "Consumer Guide to Vehicle Leasing" and "Look Before You Lease" are available free from Federal Trade Commission, Public Reference Room 130, Washington, DC 20580; 202-326-2222; {www.ftc. gov}

☞ "Reality Checklist for Auto Leasing for New Cars" is available free from Attorney General, Richard Blumenthal, 55 Elm Street, Hartford, CT 06106; 860-808-5318, fax: 860-808-5387, email Attorney. General@po.state.ct.us; {www.cslnet.ctstateu.edu/attgenl/reality2.htm}

> **Other helpful websites:**
>
> **www.buyerpower.com/ Articles/buylease.htm**
>
> **www.wa.gov/ago/CPD/ leases.html**
>
> **www.bog.frb.fed.us/ pubs/leasing/**

Contact your state attorney general's office listed in the state-by-state Appendix. Most have free publications and website material to help you with your decision.

What Are The Best Tires To Buy?

The government has established a tire grading systems that lets you compare Firestone with Sears. It's called the Uniform Tire Quality Grading System (UTQGS). It provides three grades, treadwear, traction, and temperature resistance.

Now it's easy for you to see if a $65 tire is really that much better than one for $42.50. The grades are normally on a paper label affixed to the tread or molded into the sidewalls.

You can receive a free report showing you the grades for most popular tires by contacting: National Highway Traffic Safety Administration, U.S. Department of Transportation, Auto Safety Hotline, NEF-11.2HL, 400 Seventh St., SW, Washington, DC 20590; 888-327-4236, or download the report from {www.nhtsa.dot.gov/hotline}.

FREE AND LOW COST SEMINARS ON HOW TO FIX UP A CAR

What do you do if you are driving on a freeway and you get a flat tire? How often should you change the oil and can you do it yourself? How do you jump a car? It is better to plan ahead for emergencies, but where do you go for help?

Many different organizations and groups offer classes on how to fix up a car. Begin by contacting your local car insurance company, automobile road service company, or department of motor vehicles. I have even seen classes being offered by automobile dealerships. Once you are there, maybe they can sell you a new car as well.

Other places to check include your county Cooperative Extension Service, your local adult education department, or women's organizations in your area. You can save yourself worry, stress, and money if you are prepared and knowledgeable regarding your car.

GRANDMA NEEDS A RIDE TO THE DOCTOR

Many seniors have to give up driving their cars, perhaps because of the cost or illness. But then how do they get to the doctor or the bank or the store? Many rely upon their friends and children to solve their transportation needs, but there are times when you need to come up with another alternative.

The Eldercare Locator provides access to an extensive network of organizations serving older people at state and local community levels. This service can connect you to information sources for a variety of services including transportation.

Eldercare Locator

www.aoa.dhss.gov

For more information, contact Eldercare Locator, National Association of Area Agencies on Aging, 1112 16th St., NW, Washington, DC 20024; 800-677-1116 between 9 a.m. and 8 p.m. EST; {www.aoa.dhss.gov}.

I Don't Have A Car & My Child Is Sick At School

DISCOUNTS on Buses, Trains and Subways

If you are a senior citizen, you can usually ride most forms of transportation for about half-price. Amtrak and Greyhound offer discounts of 10-15% for the senior set. Children even get to take advantage of discount programs, with the youngest group often getting a free ride.

Don't forget to ask about a variety of reduced fare programs, including student and military discounts. Often job training programs will compensate you for your travel, so before you begin training, inquire about support services such as transportation and child care.

Suppose your child is sick at school and needs you in the middle of the day, but you don't have a way to get there because you go to work most days by some other way than using your car.

Don't panic. You can probably get a free ride, taxi, or free rental car from the local *"Guaranteed Ride Home Program"*.

You can also use the service for most family emergencies if your normal ride falls through, or if you have to work late unexpectedly. Call your local carpool or vanpool service to see if they have a similar program. Most of these programs require that you pre-register, but it is always best to plan ahead for emergencies anyway.

If you do a computer search using the terms (including the quotes) "guaranteed ride home program," you will find a listing of many of the programs offered. You can also look in the state-by-state Appendix listing under *Transportation* for starting places.

Free & Discounted
Child Safety Seats

It's easy to spend $100 on a child's car seat, so look for the deals. There are hospitals that give out free child safety seats as you leave with your new baby, with no questions asked and no income requirements.

Local police and fire departments inspect child safety seats to see that they are in proper order and properly installed, and sometimes provide free seats to those whose current equipment is not considered safe.

Local organizations, like the Easter Seals Society were part of a federal program that gives out millions of dollars worth of free seats because of a settlement the U.S. Department of Transportation made with General Motors. Other groups will lend you a seat for as little as $5. The state of Minnesota alone has over 225 such programs.

Are You Using The Right Child Safety Seat?

Free publication from National Highway Traffic Safety Administration, 1-800-424-9393 or {www.nhtsa.dot.gov}

To find a program near you, contact your local police or fire department. Or contact your state information operator listed in the state-by-state Appendix and ask them for your state office for Highway Safety or Traffic Safety. These national organizations may also be able to give you a local source:

■ *National SAFEKIDS Campaign*, 1301 Pennsylvania Ave., NW, Suite 1000, Washington, DC 20004; 202-626-0600; fax 202-393-2072; {www.safekids.org}

■ *National Highway Traffic Safety Administration*, U.S. Department of Transportation, 400 Seventh St., SW, Washington, DC 20590; 800-424-9393; {www.nhtsa.dot.gov}

Cheap Air Fare To See A Sick Relative

Not free, but at least you don't have to pay full price. When a family member is very ill or has died, families have to make last minute airline reservations. Obviously you lose out on the 21-day advance purchase rates, but almost all airlines offer *bereavement* or *compassion* fares for domestic travel.

Generally the fares are available to close family members, and the discount on the full-fare rate varies from airline to airline. Many require that you provide the name of the deceased and the name, address and phone number of the funeral home 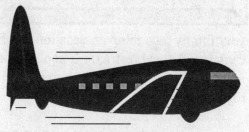 handling arrangements. In the case of a medical emergency, the name and address of the affected family member and the name, address and phone number of the attending physician or hospital are required.

Contact the airline of your choice to learn more about the "Bereavement/Compassion Fares." Full fare rate varies from airline to airline, but you could save up to 50%.

Free Cars and Air Fare To Go On Vacation

Not quite as easy as it sounds, but there are programs out there to help people move their cars. Most of the cars need to be driven across the country and in exchange, many car

moving companies offer free gas and airline travel home.

This is not to say that you can take your family on a minivan vacation across the country. Certain rules and restrictions apply. But I have known many a college kid that has gotten to drive across the U.S. for free.

Obviously, you do not get to pick your make and model, and you need to be flexible as to the departure time and destination, but this is one way to see America. Contact local moving companies to see what they have to offer. There is even a website for those interested in having their cars moved at {www.movecars.com}, and they may be able to provide you with information.

Air courier services operate the same way, but you are required to have a valid passport. Most air freight services don't do enough business to send a plane overseas each day.

As a courier, you carry a package checked as baggage to an overseas destination. There have been no incidences of contraband problems, and customs is familiar with this service.

You deliver the package to a company representative in the customs section of the airport, then you are on your own. In exchange, you get to fly to exotic ports for FREE or cheap. Children are not allowed to accompany couriers.

Contact companies listed in the air courier section of your phone book, do a web search using the terms "air courier service," or contact the Air Courier Association at 800-282-1202; or online at {www.aircourier.org}.

Discounts on Car Rentals

You never should pay full-price for car rentals and there are deals aplenty if you keep your eyes opened. AAA and AARP membership will save you a few bucks, as will many other membership programs. Car rental agencies also often offer discounts to senior citizens (check what age they consider "senior"). Many times, if you book your flight and car rental at the same time, you can get a discount rate, plus get miles added to your frequent flyer program. All you have to do is ask!

The free brochure, *Renting a Car*, outlines some points to consider and questions to ask when you reserve a rental car. You can learn how to choose a rental car company and understand the terms they use for insurance and charges.

For your copy, contact Public Reference, Room 130, Federal Trade Commission, Washington, DC 20580; 202-326-2222; or online at {www.ftc.gov}.

The Bank Messed Up My Car Loan

If you can't get satisfaction from the bank, then go to those who can put the bank out of business. Contact your state banking agency listed in the state-by-state section in the Appendix or contact Federal Deposit Insurance Corporation (FDIC), Office of Consumer Affairs, 550 17th St., NW, Washington, DC 20429; 800-934-FDIC; {www.fdic.gov}.

$65/Mo Bus Money or $170/Mo Parking Money From Your Boss

Your employer can give you $65 a month to pay for going to work in a bus, van or metro, or give you $170 a month for parking. You get the money tax free, and the employer gets to take a tax deduction. Everybody wins!

It's called the *Qualified Transportation Fringe Benefit* or *Transit Benefit Program*. Get a copy of IRS Publication 535, *Business Expenses* and show your boss the section entitled "Qualified Transportation Fringe". The publication is available from your local IRS office or from 800-TAX-FORM or from their web site at {www.irs.ustreas. gov}.

Oh No....
They're Repossessing My Car!

There is not a whole lot you can probably do about this unless the repo-man somehow "breaches the peach" when he takes back your car, like, maybe, going into your garage, or climbing over a gate, or causing some other disturbance.

Tax Deductions For Your Car

You can deduct:

- 31 1/2 cents per mile if you use your car for business (IRS Publication 463, Travel Entertainment, Gift, and Car Expenses)
- 12 cents per mile if you use your car during charity work (IRS Instructions for Schedule A, Itemized Deductions)
- 10 cents per mile if you use your car for medical care (IRS Instructions for Schedule A, Itemized Deductions)
- 10 cents per mile if you use your car to move to a new job (IRS Publication 521, Moving Expenses)

These publications are free from your local IRS office, by calling 1-800-829-3676 or download from {www.irs.ustreas.gov}

To know more about your rights in dealing with the repo-
man, get a copy of "Vehicle Repossession" from Public
Reference, Room 130, Federal Trade Commission,
Washington, DC 20580; 202-326-2222 or download from
{www.ftc.gov/bcp/conline/pubs/autos/auto.htm}. Or
you can contact your state attorney general's office listed in
the state-by-state Appendix.

Your Child Has A Doctor's Appointment and Your Car Won't Work

The Federal Transit Administration provides over $50
million a year to over 1,000 local organizations to provide
free non-emergency transportation for people who are old
or have a disability. But the groups who get this federal
money can also provide free transportation services to
moms who are in a jam.

The regulations state that the vehicles can also be used to
"serve the transportation needs of the general public on an
incidental basis". You may have to do some educating to
get a local group to give you a ride.

Tell them to see Circular FTA C9070, 1D, for Section 5310
Program, Chapter V, Program Management, paragraph 3b.
It's available from the U.S. Federal Transit Administration

or on the web at {www.fta.dot.gov/library/
policy/circ9070/
chapter5.html}.

To find groups in
your area who
receive these FTA
Section 5310
grants for Elderly
and Persons With
Disabilities,
contact your state
department of
transportation or
the U.S. Federal
Transit
Administration,
Office of Program
Management, Office of
Resource Management
and State Programs, 400 7th
St., SW, Washington, DC 20590; 202-366-4020.

Women Feel More Unsafe In Their Cars Than Men

Women 27% and men 19% said that sometimes they feel unsafe.

Source: About Women and Marketing, May 1, 1998, About Women Inc., Boston MA

FREE STUFF FOR YOUR HOME

FREE MONEY FOR CLOSING COSTS AND A DOWN PAYMENT

Houston has a program that offers $4,000 in down-payment and closing costs through their First-Time Homebuyers Program.

Iowa offers up to $2,750 in grants for a down-payment. You can be earning up to $65,000 a year and still be eligible for the money in their Down Payment/Closing Cost Grant Program.

Many cities, like Minneapolis, will offer interest free loans, called Equity Participation Loans, for up to 10% of the cost of the home. You pay back the money when you sell the house.

Programs vary from state to state and city to city. Contact your city government, your county government, and your local community development office to learn about local programs. If you have trouble locating your local community development office, the following organizations may be able to help:

❑ National Association of Housing and Redevelopment Officials, 630 I St, NW, Washington, DC 20001; 202-289-3500, Fax: 202-289-8181; {www.nahro.org}

❑ Information Center, Office of Community Planning and Development, P.O. Box 7189, Gaithersburg, MD

Free Housing Books

- *A Consumer's Guide to Mortgage Settlement Costs*

- *Home Mortgages: Understanding the Process*

- *A Consumer's Guide to Mortgage Refinancings*

- *Consumer Handbook on Adjustable Rate Mortgages*

For your copies, contact Board of Governors of the Federal Reserve System, Publications Services, MS-127, Washington, DC 20551; 202-452-3244;

{www.bog.frb.fed.us}.

20898; 800-998-9999, Fax: 301-519-5027;
{www.comcon.org}

❑ Also be sure to contact your state housing office listed
in the Appendix.

"WOW!
...The Government Will Pay My Mortgage"

You'd never have thought to
ask, would you?

There are now programs that
will make your mortgage
payments for you when you get
into financial trouble. For
example, Pennsylvania law, 35 P.S.
§ 1680.401 et seq., states it will
provide "*mortgage assistance
payments to homeowners
who are in danger of
losing their homes through
foreclosure and through no fault
of their own and who have a
reasonable prospect of resuming
mortgage payments within the prescribed time frame.*"

Pennsylvania calls it the *"Homeowners' Emergency Mortgage Assistance Program."*

One of the best ways to find out if there are programs like this in your area is to contact the local HUD approved Housing Counseling agencies. To find your closest agency, contact your state housing office listed in the Appendix, the Housing Counseling Center locator at 1-800-569-4287; {www.hud.gov/hsgcoun.html}, or Housing Counseling Clearinghouse, P.O. Box 9057, Gaithersburg, MD 20898; 800-217-6970; Fax: 301-519-6655.

Free Mortgage Publications

The Federal Trade Commission understands this, so they have compiled several brochures to get you started. Some of the titles include:

Home Financing Primer, Mortgage Servicing, Mortgage Discrimination, and more.

To receive your copies, contact Public Reference, Room 130, Federal Trade Commission, Washington, DC 20580; 202-326-2222;

{www.ftc.gov}

If your local agency doesn't have money to pay your mortgage, they will certainly help you work out other arrangements with your mortgage company.

Make Money Going To Housing Classes

A HUD-approved housing counseling agency in Philadelphia offers $1,000 in settlement costs to certain people who attend pre-purchase house counseling sessions. A counseling agency in Boston offers new home buyers access to special low down-payment mortgages if they attend pre-housing classes.

Who Qualifies As A First Time Homebuyer?

Most government programs define a first time homebuyer as someone who has not owned a home during the past 3 years or who is legally separated or divorced.

There are over 350 HUD-approved counseling agencies that offer free classes and help in housing related issues including:

> "The Best Way To Buy And Finance A Home"
> "Is A Reverse Mortgage For You?"
> "Foreclosure and Eviction Options"
> 'The Best Way To Finance A Home Fix-Up"

These non-profit agencies are trained and approved by the U.S. Department of Housing and Urban Development (HUD).

To find your closest agency, contact your State housing office listed in the Appendix, the Housing Counseling Center locator at 1-800-569-4287; {www.hud.gov/ hsgcoun.html}, or Housing Counseling Clearinghouse, P.O. Box 9057, Gaithersburg, MD 20898; 800-217-6970, Fax: 301-519-6655.

Free Home Owner Calculators at {www.homepath.com/calcs.html}

- How Much Is Your Monthly Payment?

- How Much House Can You Afford?

- What Monthly Payment Is Needed for a House with a Specific Sales Price?

- How Much House Can You Afford with a Specific Monthly Payment?

- Is Now A Good Time To Refinance?

"Get The Lead Out"
And Get Your House Or Apartment Painted For Free

If you are living in a house or apartment that was built before 1978, you, or even your landlord, may be eligible for grant money and other assistance to make sure that you do not suffer the effects of lead poisoning from lead-based paint.

Chips or dust from this type of paint can be highly dangerous to humans, especially children. The U.S. Department of Housing and Urban Development spends over $60 million a year helping home owners and apartment owners eliminate the problems that may be caused by lead paint.

Contact your state department of housing listed in the Appendix to see if your state has money for lead paint removal.

Here are a few *HOME REPAIR* programs we found that were available at the time we were doing research. Things change, but make sure to contact local agencies to see what may be available to you!

City of Sunnyvale
Housing Division
P.O. Box 3707
Sunnyvale, CA 94088
408-730-7451
www.ci.sunnyvale.ca.us/community-dev/housing/
index.htm

Tacoma Community Redevelopment Authority
747 Market St., Room 1036
Tacoma, WA 98402
253-591-5230
www.ci.tacoma.wa.us/CityHall/cbcdesc.
htm#Redevelopment

Community Development
City of Canton
218 Cleveland Ave., SW
Canton, OH 44702
330-489-3040
www.canton-ohio.com/canton/homerep.html

Minneapolis Community Development Agency
Crown Roller Mill
105 Fifth Ave. S, Suite 200

Minneapolis, MN 55401
612-673-5286

Los Angeles Housing Department
400 S. Main St.
Los Angeles, CA 90013
213-847-7368; 800-994-4444
www.cityofla.org/LAHD

Department of Housing and Community Development
P.O. Box 3136
Greensboro, NC 29402
336-373-2144
www.ci.greensboro.nc.us/HCD/index.htm

Metropolitan Development and Housing Agency
701 S. 6th St.
Nashville, TN 37202
615-252-8530
www.nashville.org/mdha

Department of Community Development
Neighborhood Conservation Services Division
602 E. 1st St.
Des Moines, IA 50309
515-283-4787

Low-Income Weatherization Program
Housing Authority and Community Services Agency
177 Day Island Rd.
Eugene, OR 97401
541-687-3999
www.hacsa.org

How Lead Paint Can Affect Your Kids

Houses and apartments built before 1978 may contain lead contaminated surface dust and paint chips, which, if consumed by children, can result in reduced intelligence, behavioral problems, learning disabilities, and even permanent brain damage.

Government sponsored programs can help you inspect your home for lead paint and even get a blood test for your children for potential problems. To find out more about these programs or the effects of lead-based paint, contact the following:

☞ *National Lead Information Center*, 1019 19th St., NW, Suite 401, Washington, DC 20036; 800-532-3394; {www.nsc.org/ehc/lead.htm}.

☞ *Office of Lead Hazard Control*, U.S. Department of Housing and Urban Development, 451 7th Street, SW, Room B-133, Washington, DC 20410; 202-755-1785; Fax: 202-755-1000; {www.hud.gov/lea/leapboff.html}.

CUT YOUR RENT BY 50%

Studies show that people with less income pay a higher portion of their salary on housing than people in higher income categories. It is not unusual for a single mom to pay 70% of her salary in rent.

The government has a program called Section 8 Rental Assistance Program that offers vouchers and direct payments to landlords. This will, in turn, cut your rent down to only 30% of your income.

Of course, there are income requirements for this program. For example, in Arlington Country, VA, a one-person household with

$4,000 Grant To Paint Your Home

That's what Canton, Ohio offers to very low-income residents — grants to paint their house or put on new siding. They feel that an investment like this improves the value of all the properties in the area.

Sunnyvale, California offers some of their residents $400 in grant money to paint their homes. And if you're over 60 or have a disability, you can get a $1,200 grant.

See if your city or state offers a program like this.

an income of $23,000 qualifies for the program. Arlington County also has housing grant rental assistance for low-income elderly, disabled, and working families with children. Some of these programs have waiting lists, but it could be worth the wait.

To apply for these federal programs, contact your state housing authority listed in the appendix, your local housing authority, or a community services agency. If you have trouble getting the help you need, you can contact Information Center, Office of Community Planning and Development, P.O. Box 7189, Gaithersburg, MD 20898; 800-998-9999, Fax: 301-519-5027; {www.comcon.org}.

Free Money To Fix Up Your Home

States, cities, and counties, as well as local community development agencies are providing grants, loans, and even supplies and technical assistance for homeowners who want to fix up the inside or outside of their homes. Many of these have income requirements you must meet. Others offer forgivable loans if you stay in the house a certain number of years. Here are some examples of what communities are offering to their residents:

☞ *Sunnyvale, CA*: $2,000 grant for disabled homeowners to fix up anything through the Home Access Grant Program.

☞ *Houston, TX*: loans and grants for major repairs through their Housing Assistance Program for the Elderly and Disabled.

☞ *Tacoma, WA*: Up to $3,500 loan at 0% interest with no monthly payments through the Major Home Repair Program.

☞ *Minneapolis, MN*: $15,000, no interest, and no payments until you sell in their Deferred Rehabilitation Loans.

☞ *Baton Rouge, LA*: $20,000 grant to fix up your home through the Housing Rehabilitation Grant Program.

☞ *Los Angeles, CA*: Free help with roofing, plumbing, electrical and heating work, painting, deadbolt locks, smoke alarms, screens, windows, and yard maintenance for seniors or disabled persons through the Handy Worker Program.

☞ *Michigan*: $1,000 to $10,000 at zero interest, to be paid back when you sell your home through the Rehabilitation Assistance Program.

☞ *Nashville, TN*: $18,000 at 3% to fix up your home.

☞ *Lane County, OR*: offers grants for weatherization assistance for weatherstripping, storm doors and windows, and insulation.

☞ *Des Moines, IA*: offers emergency repair loans.

☞ *Greensboro, NC*: has low interest loans for people with incomes over $30,000 and $8,500 grants for people with incomes up to $20,000.

Programs vary from state to state and city to city. Contact your city government, your county government, and your local community development office to learn about local programs.

$ & Help To Fix-Up A Home For A Senior

The Home Modification Action Project at:

http://www.usc.edu/ go/hmap/index.html

If you have trouble locating your local community development office, the following organizations may be able to help:

❏ National Association of Housing and Redevelopment Officials, 630 I St., NW, Washington, DC 20001; 202-289-3500, Fax: 202-289-8181; {www.nahro.org}

❏ Information Center, Office of Community Planning and Development, P.O. Box 7189, Gaithersburg, MD 20898; 800-998-9999, Fax: 301-519-5027; {www.comcon.org}

❏ Also be sure to contact your state housing office listed in the Appendix.

Your Rich Uncle Will Cosign A Loan To Buy or Fix Up a Home

Both the U.S. Department of Housing and Urban Development (HUD) and the Rural Housing Service of the U.S. Department of Agriculture offer loan guarantees to lending agencies around the county. A loan-guarantee assures the lending agency that the government will pay for the loan if you can't.

In addition, the Rural Housing Service has a direct loan program that provides loans to lower income families to buy, build, repair, renovate, or relocate their home. This is called the Section 502 Program.

To investigate the programs available in your area, contact your local HUD office listed in the blue pages of your telephone book, or U.S. Department of Housing and Urban Development (HUD), P.O. Box 6091, Rockville, MD 20850; 800-245-2691; {www.hud.gov}.

To find your local Rural Housing Service, look in the blue pages of your telephone book, or contact Single Family Housing Programs, USDA Rural Housing Service, 1400 Independence Ave., SW, Washington, DC 20250; 202-720-5177; {www.rurdev.usda.gov/agency/rhs/rhs. html}.

In addition, you may contact your state housing office located the Appendix.

Money For Seniors And Those With A Disability To Buy or Fix Up A Home

The city of Houston offers $5,000 fix up money for the disabled and elderly in their Emergency Repair Program. Minneapolis offers home repair grants of $10,000 to people with disabilities who have incomes under $18,000. Nebraska has a special low interest loan program to help people with disabilities buy a home.

The Rural Housing Service of the U.S. Department of Agriculture offers special grants through their Section 504 program of up to $7,500 if you're over 62, and need to fix up your home. Programs vary from state to state and city to city, and obviously, many have eligibility requirements.

Contact your city government, your county government and your local community development office to learn about local programs. If you have trouble locating your local community development office, contact *National Association of Housing and Redevelopment Officials*, 630 I St., NW, Washington, DC 20001; 202-289-3500, Fax: 202-289-8181; {www.nahro.org}, or *Information Center, Office of Community Planning and Development*, P.O. Box 7189, Gaithersburg, MD 20898; 800-998-9999, Fax: 301-519-5027; {www.comcon.org}.

To find your local *Rural Housing Service*, look in the blue pages of your telephone book, or contact Single Family Housing Programs, USDA Rural Housing Service, 1400 Independence Ave., SW, Washington, DC 20250; 202-720-5177; {www.rurdev.usda.gov/agency/rhs/rhs.html}. In addition, you may contact your state housing office listed in the Appendix.

$83,000 / YR Income and The Government Considers You Needy?

Many of the government housing programs, especially the grant and low interest programs, may have income requirements. But don't let a good salary stop you from investigating the opportunities. The first time home buyer program in Illinois has income requirements that go up to $83,000.

Money To Buy Or Fix Up A Mobile Home

The city of Sunnyvale, Ca will lend you up to $7,500 at 0-5% interest for a mobile home. New York State offers loans to help you buy a mobile home park or the land your mobile home sits on through their *Manufactured Home Cooperative Fund Program.* And the U.S. Department of Agriculture has what is called *Section 504 funds* that allow loans of up to $20,000 to fix a mobile home or to move it from one site to another.

Here is how to contact the major programs for manufactured (mobile) homes.

VA-Guaranteed Manufactured Home Loan

Contact your local office of the Department of Veterans Affairs, or U.S. Department of Veterans Affairs, 1120 Vermont Avenue, Washington, DC 20420; 800-827-1000; {www.va.gov/programs.htm}.

FHA Insured Title I Manufactured Home Loan

Contact your local office of Housing and Urban Development listed in the blue pages of your telephone book, or your state housing office listed in the Appendix, or the Housing Counseling Clearinghouse, P.O. Box 9057,

Gaithersburg, MD 20898; 800-217-6970;
{www.hudhcc.org}

Section 504 Rural Housing
Loans and Grants

To find your local Rural Housing Service, look in the blue
pages of your telephone book, or contact Single Family
Housing Programs, USDA Rural Housing Service, 1400
Independence Ave., SW, Washington, DC 20250; 202-720-
5177; {www.rurdev.usda.gov/agency/rhs/rhs.html}.

HUD-man Goes After The
Mobile Home Salesman

If your mobile home is not all that was promised, call
HUD. The U.S. Department of Housing and Urban
Development regulates the construction of mobile homes
and investigates complaints about their performance.

Contact: Manufactured Housing and Standards, Office of
Consumer and Regulatory Affairs, U.S. Department of
Housing and Urban Development, 451 7th St., SW, Room
9152, Washington, DC 20410; 800-927-2891, Fax: 202-
708-4231; e-mail: mhs@hud.gov; {www.hud.gov/fha/sfh/
mhs/mhshome.html}.

Money For Buying a Condo Or Co-op

In 1999 the U.S. Department of Housing and Urban Development will finance about $9 billion for people to buy condominiums. This is almost double the amount financed in 1997. The program is called *Mortgage Insurance — Purchase of Units in Condominiums (234c)*. They also have a special program for units in co-op buildings called *Mortgage Insurance — Single Family Cooperative Housing (203n)*.

Lead Poisoning and Your Children

This publication is free along with three fact sheets, and a list of state and local contacts for additional information. Specific lead questions can be answered by an information specialist at 800-424-LEAD.

For more information, contact National Lead Information Center, 1019 19th St., NW, Suite 401, Washington, DC 20036; 800-532-3394; {www.nsc.org/ehc/lead.html}.

Information USA, Inc.

Contact your local office of Housing and Urban
Development listed in the blue pages of your telephone
book, or your state housing office listed in the Appendix, or
the Housing Counseling Clearinghouse, P.O. Box 9057,
Gaithersburg, MD 20898; 800-217-6970;
{www.hudhcc.org}.

Free Houses

Well, maybe they're not free, but they can cost you as little
as a few hundred dollars a month. And
maybe they're not in good
shape, but many of the
programs will also offer you a
low interest loan to fix up
the house.

Some states refer to the
program as an *Urban
Homesteading Act*.
The idea of the program
is that the government
gets you a home for next to nothing
and you agree to live there for a certain number of years.

Minnesota has a program. Baltimore had a very active
program for many years. Davenport, Iowa purchases
homes, completely rehabs them, and then offers the houses
in a lottery each May. You must get a mortgage, but your

monthly payments are under $400 a month for a completely rebuilt house!

Free Housing Books

- A Consumer's Guide to Mortgage Settlement Costs

- Home Mortgages: Understanding the Process

- A Consumer's Guide to Mortgage Refinancings

- Consumer Handbook on Adjustable Rate Mortgages

For your copies, contact Board of Governors of the Federal Reserve System, Publications Services, MS-127, Washington, DC 20551; 202-452-3244;

{www.bog.frb.fed.us}.

There are some states, like Alaska, that still offer wilderness land for homesteading. Because the houses are so cheap, there is usually a lottery for eligible buyers. Contact your city government, your county government and your local community development office to learn about local programs.

If you have trouble finding your local community development agency, the following organizations may be able to help:

✦ National Association of Housing and Redevelopment Officials, 630 I St., NW, Washington, DC 20001; 202-289-3500, Fax: 202-289-8181; {www.nahro.org}

✦ Information Center, Office of Community Planning and Development, P.O. Box 7189, Gaithersburg, MD 20898; 800-998-9999; fax: 301-519-5027; {www.comcon.org}

✦ You can also contact your state housing office located in the Appendix.

Free Legal Help For Renters and Home Buyers

It's illegal for landlords, realtors, bankers and others to discriminate against you because of your race, religion, sex, family status, or handicap. Landlords also have rules to follow in dealing with you as a tenant. With the proper free help you can find out how to:

* Stop paying the rent if your toilet doesn't work.
* Get the government to sue your landlord for discriminating against your child.
* Break a lease and not pay a penalty.
* Get your eviction stopped.
* Force a bank to give you a loan for a new home.

✳ Get your landlord to widen your doorways to fit your wheelchair.
✳ Get a third party to fight your landlord for you.

To file a complaint or to learn more about your rights in dealing with landlords and people in the housing industry, contact any of the following:

Your state housing office

Your state Attorney General's office in the Appendix

Fair Housing and Equal Opportunity, U.S. Department of Housing and Urban Development, Room 5204, 451 Seventh St, SW, Washington, DC 20410; 800-669-9777; {www.hud.gov/hdiscrim.html}

John Marshall Law School Fair Housing Legal Support Center, 315 South Plymouth Court, Chicago, IL 60604; 312-786-2267; {www.jmls.edu/housing/fhcenter.html}

National Fair Housing Advocate Online, Tennessee Fair Housing Council, 719 Thompson Lane, Suite 324, Nashville, TN 37206; 800-254-2166; {www.fairhousing. com}.

Get Money For Down Payments And Closing Costs Here

The following are examples of financial assistance programs offered by states, cities and counties at the time we were doing our initial research for this book. Be aware that these programs are constantly changing and all have some form of eligibility requirements, but don't let that stop you! New ones are added and old ones may be discarded.

To be sure that you are aware of all the programs available in your area, contact your state office on housing (listed in the Appendix), your city housing office, your county housing office, as well as any local community development offices that may be in your area. If you need help locating your community development office, the following may be of assistance: National Association of Housing and Redevelopment Officials, 630 I St., NW, Washington, DC 20001; 202-289-3500; Fax: 202-289-8181: {www.nahro.org}.

✓ *Houston*: $3,500 to help with a down payment and closing costs in the First-Time Homebuyers Program.

✓ *Iowa*: 5% of your mortgage in grant money for a down payment and closing costs through Down Payment/ Closing Cost Grant Program.

✓ *Minneapolis, MN*: $3,000 at 0% interest due when you sell the home

✓ *Michigan*: $5,000 at 0% interest and no monthly payments

✓ *Baton Rouge, LA*: $10,000 at 0% interest and no payments for 20 years through Home Buyers Assistance Program.

✓ *Georgia*: $5,000 for a down payment at 0% interest through Own HOME Program.

✓ *Hawaii*: $15,000 loans at 3% for down payments, but you only pay interest for the first 5 years in the Down Payment Loan Program.

✓ *Kansas*: You only need $500 and Kansas will assist with down payment, closing costs, and legal fees in First Time Homebuyers Downpayment Assistance Program.

✓ *Maine*: Buy a house with only $750, and finance your down payment at 0% through Down Home Program.

✓ *La Miranda, CA*: 10% loan for down payment for first time homebuyers in the Down Payment Assistance Program.

✓ *Tacoma, WA*: A $5,000 loan for your down payment and settlement costs in Down Payment Assistance Program.

✓ *Indianapolis, IN*: Put 1% down and your closing costs go into a 2nd mortgage in Good Neighbor II Loan Program.

✓ *Los Angeles, CA*: 2% forgivable loan for closing costs money, plus $35,000 loan for repairs with no payments for 30 years or until the house is sold through Home WORKS! Program.

✓ *New York State*: 0% down payment in Low Down Payment, Conventional Rate Program.

✓ *Walnut Creek, CA*: Get a second mortgage for half of the closing costs and 2% of down payment with nothing due until you sell or refinance.

✓ *Washington County, OR*: $19,300 loan with no interest and no payment for the first 5 years in First-Time Home Buyer Program.

✓ *Michigan*: Move into a $60,000 home with only $600 in your pocket in the Down Payment Assistance Program.

✓ *New Hampshire*: $5,000 low interest loan for closing costs through HELP Program.

✓ *Nashville, TN*: Nashville Housing Fund provides down payments, closing costs and low interest loans for first time home buyers.

✓ *Tucson, AZ*: $3,000 loan for down payment and they will pay all closing costs with the Tucson Metropolitan Ministry.

✓ *Oregon*: $500 to $6,000 grant for closing costs, down payment, or minor repairs in their First-Time Homebuyer Program.

✓ *Missouri*: Move into a home with only $750 through Down Payment Assistance for Homebuyers.

✓ *Canton, OH*: Renters can apply for $5,000 loan for first time home buyers that's forgiven after 5 years through the Down Payment Assistance Program.

✓ *South Carolina*: Loans for SINGLE PARENTS for a down payment and closing costs in their Single Parent Program.

Use Your Sweat as a Down Payment and Get a No-Interest Loan

One of the biggest providers of this type of program is the non-profit organization called **Habitat for Humanity**. You've probably seen them in the news with Ex-President Jimmy Carter helping them build houses. They have even received government money to help support their program.

The typical arrangement is for people with incomes between $9,000 and $30,000. You and your family work an average of 300 to 500 hours building your home or other people's homes, and in return you get a home with no down-payment and a very low mortgage payment.

Because people provide free labor to build the home, you only pay about $60,000 for a $100,000 home, and you get the money interest free. A typical bank loan can cost you over $700 per month, but through this program you pay only about $200 a month.

Other local or national organizations may run similar programs in your area, with or without government financing. To find programs in your area, you can contact:

⇨ Habitat for Humanity International, 121 Habitat Street, Americus, GA 31709; 912-924-6935; {www.habitat. org}. To find a local affiliate, call 912-924-6935, ext. 2551 or ext. 2552

⇨ Information Center, Office of Community Planning and Development, P.O. Box 7189, Gaithersburg, MD 20898; 800-998-9999, Fax: 301-519-5027; {www.comcon.org}.

Staying Clear Of Deadly Radon Gases

Nowadays when you buy a home, you often have a radon level reading taken, but what do the numbers mean?

The *National Radon Information Hotline* has a free brochure that explains what radon is, how to test for it, and more.

National Radon Information Hotline 800-767-7236 (SOS-RADON)

There is also a Radon FIX-IT Program operated by the Consumer Research Council, a nonprofit consumer organization that provides free guidance and encouragement to consumers who are trying to fix their homes that have elevated radon levels. The Program operates from noon to 8 p.m. EST and has information on reducing elevated radon levels, referrals to experts, and names of contractors who are qualified to help.

For more information, contact National Radon Information Hotline at 800-767-7236 (SOS-RADON) and the Radon

Fix-It Program at 800-644-6999; or Indoor Air Quality Information Clearinghouse, IAQ Info, P.O. Box 37133, Washington, DC 20013; 800-438-4318; {www.epa.gov/iaq/iaqinfo.html}.

Is Your Drinking Water Safe?

According to the National Consumer Water Survey, 75% of those surveyed have concerns about the quality of the water they drink. Many people are purchasing bottled water or water purification devices for drinking water, but is it a wise use of your money?

The *Safe Drinking Water Hotline* can answer any question or concern you may have regarding drinking water, and can provide you with publications such as: *Is Your Drinking Water Safe?, Home Water Testing, Home Water Treatment Units, Bottled Water* fact sheet, and more. Contact Safe Drinking Water Hotline, U.S. Environmental Protection Agency, 401 M St., SW, Washington, DC 20460; 800-426-4791; {www.epa. gov/OGWDW}.

How To Save Up To $650/Year On Fuel Bills

The average family spends close to $1300 a year on their home's utility bills, and a large portion of that energy is wasted. By using a few inexpensive energy efficient measures, you can reduce your energy bills by 10% to 50%.

With the publication, *Energy Savers: Tips on Saving Energy and Money at Home*, you can go step by step through your home to learn energy saving tips. Topics covered include insulation/ weatherization, water heating, lighting, appliances, and  more. There is even a major appliance shopping guide that explains the energy labels on appliances and shows you how to choose the best one for you.

The Energy Efficiency and Renewable Energy Clearinghouse can answer your questions on all these topics and has publications and easy to understand fact sheets. Contact the Energy Efficiency and Renewable and Energy Clearinghouse, P.O. Box 3048, Merrifield, VA 22116; 800-363-3732; {www.eren.doe.gov}.

Will Fix Up Your (Or Your Mom's) Home For Free

Many service organizations have begun to organize community service days, where the town is beautified along with certain homes in need of repair.

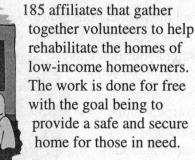

Christmas in April is a national organization with over 185 affiliates that gather together volunteers to help rehabilitate the homes of low-income homeowners. The work is done for free with the goal being to provide a safe and secure home for those in need.

An example of a program in the Dallas area is the Volunteer Home Repair and Weatherization Program. This program provides home repairs that improve the health, safety, and energy efficiency of a home for low-income homeowners.

Contact your city government, your county government and your local community development office to learn about local programs.

✓ In the Dallas area, contact Volunteer Home Repair and Weatherization Program, Center for Housing

---

Resources, 3103 Greenwood, Dallas, TX 75204; 214-828-4380, Fax: 214-828-4412; {www.chrdallas.org}

✓ Christmas in April, 1536 Sixteenth St., NW, Washington, DC 20036; 202-483-9083; {www.pdi. com/cina-usa/index.html}.

GOVERNMENT FORECLOSED HOMES AT BARGAIN PRICES

No, they are not giving away the kitchen sink, but you may be able to find some good deals nonetheless.

The government sells foreclosed homes all across the country, and even in your neighborhood. You don't need to know someone to get in on these deals. All are sold through real estate agents.

Contact your agent, ask about government repossessed homes and they can do a search for you. These are not just HUD homes, but also those from the V.A., Fannie Mae, IRS, Federal Deposit Insurance Corporation, and more.

I want to be able to say that they give you these houses at 50% off, but I can't. Most want fair market value, but the government does not want to carry the real estate taxes for all these houses either. You can make a deal that works out best for everyone.

For more information, contact HUD USER, P.O. Box 6091, Rockville, MD 20850; 800-245-2691; {www.hud. gov/homesale.html} (Note: this website has links to all the major government home sale programs); U.S. Department of Veterans Affairs, 810 Vermont Ave., NW, Washington, DC 20420; 800-827-1000; {www.va.gov}.

How To Keep Your Air Clean Of Asbestos, Carbon Monoxide, and Second Hand Smoke

You don't need to hire some high priced consultants to find how to keep the air in your home clean of pollution and other toxic substances. The Indoor Air Quality Information Clearinghouse is the expert on all forms of indoor air pollution. They have publications and information on second hand smoke, asbestos, carbon monoxide, air cleaners, and more. You can contact them at Indoor Air Quality Information Clearinghouse, IAQ Info, P.O. Box 37133, Washington, DC 20013; 800-438-4318; {www.epa.gov/iaq/iaqinfo.html}.

MONEY TO PAY YOUR
HEATING BILL

Storm windows, insulation, and even weatherstripping, can help reduce your fuel bill. Families can receive assistance to weatherize their homes and apartments at no charge if you meet certain income guidelines. States allocate dollars to nonprofit agencies for purchasing and installing energy-related repairs, with the average grant being $2,000 per year. The elderly and families with children get first dibs.

Contact your State Energy Office or the Weatherization Assistance Programs Branch, EE44, U.S. Department of Energy, 1000 Independence Ave., SW, Washington, DC 20585; 202-586-4074; {www.eren.doe.gov/buildings/state_and_community/}.

> ## FREE HOUSING EXPERTS
>
> The HUD website includes text of over 20 helpful guides, such as: *How To Buy a Home, How to Get A Mortgage,* and *Hud-approved Lenders,* as well as listings of government homes for sale. These are not just HUD homes, but also those from the Department of Veteran Affairs, General Services Administration, and more. Although the houses are not steals, you can find some great deals. For housing information, call HUD USER, P.O. Box 6091, Rockville, MD 20850; 800-245-2691; {www.hud.gov}.

50% Discount
On a New Heating System

The California Energy Commission offers residences and small businesses up to 50% of the cost of a new heating or air conditioning system if it meets their standards for "emerging renewable technologies," like solar heating, but more. Their program is called Emerging Renewables Buy-Down Program.

FREE NUTRITION COUNSELING AND CLASSES

Nutrition counseling, menu planning, cooking instruction and comparison shopping is available from your local County Cooperative Extension Service. Group instruction is free of charge, but persons requesting individual lessons are asked to pay for the lesson materials.

They also help neighborhoods establish and maintain community gardens, which provide fresh vegetables to area residents. To find an office near you, look in the blue pages of your local telephone book under county government for County Cooperative Extension Service, or contact the state lead office listed in the Appendix.

Information USA, Inc.

To learn more, contact California Energy Commission, Energy Call Center, 1516 North St., MS-25, Sacramento, CA 95814; 800-555-7794; {http://energy.ca.gov/ greengrid/index.html}. Check with your state utility commission in the Appendix to see if your state offers similar programs.

$2,000 GRANTS OR 2% INTEREST LOAN TO FIX UP YOUR HOME

A family of 4 can be making close to $30,000 year and still be eligible for a 2% interest loan from local Community Action Agency. Some agencies also offer grants or are aware of other local organizations that provide grants. There are about 1,000 of them around the country to help neighborhoods.

To find an agency near you, contact National Association of Community Action Agencies, 1100 17th St., NW, Washington, DC 20036, 202-265-7546; Fax: 202-265-8850; {www.nacaa.org}; {www.nemaine. com/whca/housing.htm}.

Free Weatherization, Fuel Bills, and Rent for Incomes Up to $50,000

If you are within a certain income and need help paying your heating bills, need money to make your house more energy efficient, or need funds for urgent repairs, call your local Community Action Agency. There are about 1,000 of them around the country to help neighborhoods. They will also come out and check if your home or apartment needs to be more energy efficient.

Community Action Agency

To find an agency near you, contact National Association of Community Action Agencies, 1100 17th St., NW, Washington, DC 20036; 202-265-7546; Fax: 202-265-8850; {www.nacaa.org}.

Also, your local utility can provide you with or refer you to other programs in your area to analyze your energy usage, recommend energy saving measures, provide fuel and utility assistance to retain or restore service, establish payment discounts based on income and usage, or establish affordable payment plans if you are in arrears. Contact your local utility company to take advantage of these services.

Information USA, Inc.

NEW HOME HELP

Here's a listing of programs we found that were available at
the time we were doing research. Don't forget to contact
state and local housing agencies to see what may be
available for you.

Nashville Housing Fund
P.O. Box 846
Nashville, TN 37202
615-780-7016
janis.nashville.org/mdha/
housing_fund.html

Washington County
Department of Housing Services-
FTHB
111 NE Lincoln St.
Suite 200-L, MS63
Hillsboro, OR 97124
503-693-4773
www.co.washington.or.us/
deptmts/ hse_serv/housemain.
htm

Indianapolis Neighborhood
Housing Partnership
3550 N. Washington Blvd.
Indianapolis, IN 46205
317-925-1400
www.inhp.org

Dept. of Community Affairs
60 Executive Parks
Atlanta, GA 30329

800-651-0597
www.dca.state.ga.us

State of New York Mortgage
Agency
641 Lexington Ave.
New York, NY 10022
800-382-HOME
www.nyhomes.org/Sonyma/
PROGRAMS.HTM

City of La Mirada
Housing Programs
13700 La Mirada Blvd.
La Mirada CA 90638
562-943-0131
www.cerritos.edu/lamirada/
housing.htm

Housing Hotline
Division of Housing
Kansas Department of Commerce
and Housing
700 S.W. Harrison, Suite 1300
Topeka, KS 66603
800-752-4422
785-296-5865
www.kansascommerce.com

Homes For Houston
P.O. Box 1562
Houston, TX 77251
713-868-8400
713-522-HOME
www.ci.houston.tx.us/
departme/housing/
homes_for_houston.html

Tucson Metropolitan Ministry
3127 E. Adams St.
Tucson, AZ 85716
520-322-9557
www.rtd.com/~tnn/ homebuy.htm

Iowa Finance Authority
100 E. Grand Ave., Suite 250

Des Moines, IA 50309
515-242-4990
800-432-7230
www.ifahome.com/
home_buyer.htm

MN Housing Finance Agency
400 Sibley St., Suite 300
St. Paul, MN 55101
800-710-8871
651-296-8215
www.mhfa.state.mn.us

Missouri Housing Development
Commission
3435 Broadway
Kansas City, MO 64111

Free Furniture

The Community Action Agency in Albany, New York
offers free furniture for those with a need because of fire.
or other hardship reasons. Other agencies offer free
furniture if you are moving into a Community Action
Agency's affordable housing or housing units operated
by the agency. See if your local agency offers free
furniture. There are about 1,000 of them around the
country to help neighborhoods.

To find an agency near you, contact National Association
of Community Action Agencies, 1100 17th St., NW,
Washington, DC 20036; 202-265-7546; Fax: 202-265-
8850; {www.nacaa.org}; {http://crisny.org/not-for-
profit/acoi/ furnit.html}.

816-759-6600
www.mhdc.com

Office of Community Development
P.O. Box 1471
Baton Rouge, LA 70802
225-389-3039
www.ci.baton-rouge.
la.us/dept/ocd/ Housing/
housing.htm

New Hampshire Housing Finance
Authority
32 Constitution Dr.
Bedford, NH 03110
800-640-7239
www.nhhfa.org

Oregon Housing and Community
Services Dept.
1600 State St.
Salem, OR 97301
503-986-2041
www.hcs.state.or.us

Maine State Housing Authority
353 Water St.
Augusta, ME 04330
207-626-4600
800-452-4668
www.mainehousing.org

Community Development
Department
1666 N. Main St.

Walnut Creek, CA 94596
925-943-5834
www.ci.walnut-creek.ca.us

South Carolina State Housing
Finance and Development
Authority
919 Bluff Rd.
Columbia, SC 29201
803-734-2207
www.sha.state.sc.us

Michigan State Housing Authority
401 South Washington Square
P.O. Box 30044
Lansing, MI 48909
517-373-8017
www.voyager.net/mshda

Housing Finance and
Development Corporation
677 Queen St., Suite 300
Honolulu, HI 96813
808-587-0567
www.hawaii.gov/hfdc

FREE CHILD CARE RESOURCES

MAKE $39,000 AND GET FREE CHILD CARE

In Connecticut your income can be $39,168 and you can get $640 a month for child care. Make $25,332 in Indiana  and get $1,260 a month for infant care. Earn $38,244 in Alaska and receive $583 a month for child care.

The Child Care and Development Block Grant gives money to states to help families meet their child care needs. Parents may choose from a variety of child care providers, including center-based, family child care and in-home care, care provided by relatives, and even sectarian child care providers. You can even get money to start a day care center! Income qualifications vary from state to state, and each state operates their programs slightly differently.

To find out how to take advantage of this program in your state and to learn the eligibility requirements, contact National Child Care Information Center, 243 Church St.,

Information USA, Inc.

NW, Vienna, VA 22180; 800-616-2242;
{http://nccic.org}. A listing of state Child Care and
Development Block Grant Lead Agencies is provided in the
Appendix.

Free Child Care When Training
Or Looking For A Job

Welfare reform, called *Temporary Assistance for Needy
Families (TANF),* does more to help people not wind up
on welfare. The new program includes free training,
education, child care, and transportation assistance
necessary to help you
obtain employment.

Child care is an
important part of the
program. Eligibility
requirements vary
from state to state, so
contact your TANF
office nearest you to
learn what options are
available to you.

3 Out Of 5
In Day Care

Every day, 13 million
preschoolers — including 6
million babies and toddlers —
are in child care. This is three
out of five young children.

*Source: Children's
Defense League*

For more information, contact Office of Family Assistance,
Administration for Children and Families, 370 L'Enfant
Promenade, SW, Washington, DC 20447; 202-401-9289;
{www.acf.dhhs.gov/programs/opa/facts/tanf.htm}.

$9 a Week Child Care At Local Non-Profits

Local non-profits around the country get grants from the United Way or other institutions and offer free and sliding scale day care services. The United Way spends about a third of its funds, about $1 billion a year, on programs for children and families.

For example, the Community Partnerships for Children Program in Brockton, MA provides child care for a family of 2 with weekly income of $210 for only $9.00 a week, and families of 4 with income of $1,000 a week can get care for $114 a week per child. There are about 500 local United Way Information and Referral Services around the country that can point you to local groups that can help you solve your child care problems.

Look in the phone book for your local United Way agency, or contact United Way of America, 701 N. Fairfax Street, Alexandria, VA 22314-2045; 703-836-7100; 800-411-UWAY (8929); {www.unitedway.org}.

Who Offers The Best Or Worst Child Care?

In Alabama and Ohio, the staff to child ratio for kids under 18 months in a child care center is 1:6. In New York, it is 1:4. In Connecticut the ratio for children under three years is 1:4.

States regulate the food, sanitation, play equipment, and more in an effort to provide your child with a safe and secure daycare setting. You need to ask questions about play programs, types of discipline used, first aid training, and more. Every state licenses child-care facilities, and

Questions To Ask When Looking For Mary Poppins

✔ Is the child care center licensed or regulated?
✔ What is the ratio of staff to children?
✔ Are caregivers trained and experienced?
✔ Have they participated in early childhood development classes?
✔ What about training in CPR and first aid?

For your free *5 Steps to Choosing Care* brochure and local child care referrals in your community, contact Child Care Aware, 2116 Campus Dr., SE, Rochester, MN 55904; 800-424-2246, {www.childcarerr.org}.

some day care homes. You can contact the state agency to learn if a setting has had any violations or problems, and inquire about the rules and regulations they must follow.

See the Appendix for the Day Care Licensing Agency in your state. You can also check out the day care licensing regulations for each state at the following websites:

▲ **National Resource Center for Health and Safety in Child Care** at {http://nrc.uchsc.edu/states.html}
▲ **National Network for Child Care** at {www.naccrra. net/livesite/Parents/FindChildCare.htm}.

One-Call For Choosing & Funding Child Care

There are over 600 Child Care Resource and Referral Agencies around the country that maintain local databases of information on child care providers in your area. They can give you locations, hours of care, ages of children accepted, fees and more. They can also tell you about local rules and regulations that centers have to follow, tips on choosing the best place for your child, as well as information about sources of money for paying for child care. Most of the services are free, but check if there is a fee first.

To find your local referral agency, contact Child Care Aware, 2116 Campus Dr., SE, Rochester, MN 55904; 800-424-2246; {www.childcarerr.org}.

Free Child Care For AmeriCorp and VISTA Workers

Over $10,000,000 a year is paid out to cover child care services for people working with AmeriCorps or VISTA. These programs allow you to tackle community problems on everything from disaster relief to tutoring. National Service jobs also provide a stipend, housing, and even college money; child care is a bonus.

Contact Corporation of National Service, 1201 New York Ave., NW, Washington, DC 20525; 202-606-5000; {www.nationalservice.org}.

Manicurists Get More Training Than Child Care Workers

Hairdressers and manicurists must attend 1,500 hours of training at an accredited school in order to get a license, yet 39 states and the District of Columbia do not require child care providers to have any early childhood training prior to serving children in their homes.

Source: Children's Defense League

Free Day Care Center Databases

There are services on the web that will charge you to search for child care centers in your area, or you can use the free ones like:

In Arkansas, licensed child care providers can be searched by zip code, age of child, or weekend hours at {www. state.ar.us/childcare}. Ohio lets you search by child's age and accreditation as well as location at {www.state. oh.us.scripts/odhs/cdc/query.asp}. North Carolina lets you search by city, county, or zip code at {www.dhr. state.nc.us/DHR/DCD/search/daycase.htm}. You can search five counties in Ohio at {www.ccrcinc.com}.

Check your state's web site at {www.state.statepostal abbreviation.us} to see if your state offers a free child care locator web site, or contact your state Day Care Licensing Office in the Appendix. You can also use one of the 600 Child Care Resource and Referral Agencies listed under the item entitled *One-Call For Choosing & Funding Child Care*. They too should be aware of any free databases.

A Great Baby Shower Idea

Try throwing a Baby Safety Shower and help give the baby a safe start in life. The National Child Care Information Center has a *Baby Safety Shower How-to-Kit* on their website at {www.nccic.org/pubs/babysafe.html}. You can also order it from the Office of Information and Public

50% Of U.S. Families Eligible For Child Care Subsidies

With half of America's families with young children earning less than $35,000 per year, and a sample of income eligibility requirements listed below, it's easy to conclude that 50% of U.S. families can receive child care subsidies.

Maximum Income For Which Families Are Eligible For Childcare Subsidies	
Alaska	$38,244
Connecticut	$39,168
Maine	$32,492
Nevada	$31,536
Oregon	$33,012
Pennsylvania	$31,320

Source: Administration for Children and Families, U.S. Department of Health and Human Services, and Jewish Woman International {www.jewishwomen.org/ccare-res.htm}

Affairs, U.S. Consumer Product Safety Commission, Washington, DC 20207 (CPSC Document #207); 301-504-0580. This is a fun way to help a family baby-proof their house, and everyone attending the shower will learn tips to keep children safe.

Your Child May Be Eligible For A HEAD START

Head Start is one of those government programs that has proven to actually work. It's preschool that has a great student teacher ratio and all teachers are certified in early childhood development.

It prepares the children with school readiness, and research shows that these children enter kindergarten with the skills necessary to succeed. Some Head Start programs are even home-based. There are income requirements for acceptance into the program, but the program does allow 10% of the students to have higher incomes. And 10% of the program needs to be offered to kids who have a disability.

To learn more about Head Start programs near you, contact your local board of education, the state Department of Social Services listed in the Appendix, or Administration for Children and Families, U.S. Department of Health and

Human Services, Head Start Bureau, P.O. Box 1182, Washington, DC 20013; 202-205-8572; {www.acf. dhhs.gov/programs/hsb}.

Work For Companies That Offer Free/Discount Child Care

You may be surprised at the number of daycare centers offering services right inside company office buildings. In fact the federal government may be in the lead as they have over 1,000 child care centers that are sponsored by various governmental agencies.

Talk to other moms and dads on the playground, call human resources departments, and even check with your local chamber of commerce. All may be able to direct you to companies providing this benefit.

Free Child Care For Teens With Disabilities

48 states provide a subsidy to parents who qualify for childcare for children ages 14 to 19 who are physically and/or mentally incapable of self-care. Each state sets their eligibility requirement and the amount of funds they have available for this type of care. To learn what your state has to offer, contact your state Child Care and Development Block Grant lead agency listed in the Appendix.

A directory of sites is available for $25 from the Work and Family Connection, 5197 Beachside Dr., Minnetonka, MN 55343; 800-487-7898; {www.workfamily.com}.

Another resource is your local Child Care Resource and Referral Agency, who should be aware of programs in their area. To locate your local referral agency, contact Child Care Aware, 2116 Campus Dr., SE, Rochester, MN 55904; 800-424-2246, {www.childcarerr.org}.

Besides child care centers, some employers offer a dependent care assistance plan that allows you to pay for child care out of pre-tax dollars. You get more care for your buck. Other employers offer direct subsidies to offset child care costs. Talk to your company human resources office to learn more.

How To Get Your Boss To Start A Day Care Center

U.S. corporations lose $3 billion a year because of child care issues. Many businesses recognize this and support child care. However, many more employers have not offered child care assistance, in part, because they lack good information on how to effectively establish such programs.

The Department of Labor's *Business-to-Business Mentoring Initiative on Child Care* is a program which demonstrates the value of employers investing in family-friendly policies for their workers and benefits it brings to their business' bottom line.

To learn more about this program or to receive *Employer Child Care Resources: A Guide to Developing Effective Child Care Programs* and *Policies and Meeting the Needs of Today's Workforce — Child Care Best Practices,* contact

Child Care Costs More Than College

The Children's Defense Fund surveyed costs for four-year-olds in urban child care centers nationally and found that the average exceeds $3,000 a child, rising to more than $5,000 a child in 17 states. In 15 states, tuition (in-state) for a single year of public college is less than half that of urban child care center costs. For example:

Location	Child Care Tuition	Public College Tuition
Wake County, NC	$5,068	$1,841
Honolulu, HI	$6,188	$2,298
Wahoe County, (Reno) NV	$4,420	$1,814
Kansas City, KS	$5,200	$2,223
Dane County, Wi	$6,240	$2,747
Anchorage, AK	$5,784	$2,552

Source: Children's Defense Fund
http://www.childrensdefense.org/release052998.html

the Women's Bureau, U.S. Department of Labor, 200 Constitution Ave., NW, Room S-3311, Washington, DC 20210; 202-219-4486; 800-827-5335; or {www.dol.gov/dol/wb}.

Emergency Care and Sick Child Care

When your kid is sick and can't go to daycare, the big decision is whose turn it is to take a day off work.

When you are a single parent or need to go to work, what can you do? Planning ahead is the key. Many child care centers offer programs just for this type of problem. By calling different centers or your local Child Care Referral Agency, you will be able to develop several back-up plans when an emergency strikes.

A directory of emergency care and sick child care is available for $25 from the Work and Family Connection, 5197 Beachside Dr., Minnetonka, MN 55343; 800-487-7898; {www.workfamily.com}. To find your local child care referral agency, contact: Child Care Aware, 2116 Campus Dr., SE, Rochester, MN 55904; 800-424-2246; {www.childcarerr.org}.

GET MONEY FOR YOUR OWN CHILD CARE CENTER

Child Care Works is a new partnership between the District of Columbia, eight area banks and three community organizations that make training, grants and loans available to licensed neighborhood day care providers to provide slots for 1,000 children. Maryland and Ohio provide special low-interest loans through their Department of Economic Development to fund child care centers. Even the Child Care and Development Block Grant provides money to develop child care centers and before and after school programs.

For more information, contact your state Department of Economic Development or your Child Care and Development Block Grant lead agency listed in the Appendix.

Uncle Sam Will Fight For Your Maternity Leave Rights

It is estimated that up to three million people have taken advantage of the Family and Medical Leave Act (FMLA) to take care of their new or sick child or elderly parent. What's more, if you are unfairly denied the leave, the U.S.

Department of Labor will advocate on your behalf and successfully resolve the complaint in your favor close to 90% of the time!

Over two-thirds of the work force are covered by FMLA. The Women's Bureau at the Department of Labor has information on age, wage, and pregnancy discrimination,

Over two-thirds of the work force are covered by the Family and Medical Leave Act

sexual harassment, and the Family and Medical Leave Act. They can provide you with materials for employers wanting to provide high quality child care for their employees, as well as information for childcare workers.

To learn more, contact the Women's Bureau, U.S. Department of Labor, 200 Constitution Ave., NW, Room S-3311, Washington, DC 20210; 202-219-4486; 800-959-FMLA; or {www.dol.gov/dol/wb}. To see a summary of the Family and Medical Leave Act, check out this website {www2.dol.gov/dol/wb/public/wb_pubs/fmla.htm}. It includes frequently asked questions and also lists the regional offices of the Women's Bureau.

Get $4,800 From The IRS To Pay For Child Care

Remember that the Internal Revenue Service (IRS) offers some benefits for child care costs. IRS Publication 503, *Child and Dependent Care Expenses*, outlines the rules covering this benefit and describes how to figure the benefit if your employer covers some of the cost. You may claim up to $2,400 for the care of one child (or $4,800 for two or more).

Local Listings For Child Care

Sometimes the yellow pages can seem overwhelming. The *National Child Care Association* is a nonprofit association for private child care and preschool education providers. They have a directory of their membership that you can search by city and age group of children served. The directory will provide you the address and phone number of a member's facility. Keep in mind that you need to make sure that the facility has an active license to operate in your state.

For more information, contact National Child Care Association, 1016 Rosser St., Conyers, GA 30012; 800-543-7161; {www.nccanet.org}. This website now includes federal legislative updates, and has links to other child care associations' websites.

For more information, contact the IRS Information Line at 800-829-1040; or {www.irs.gov}. In addition, 25 states and the District of Columbia offer some type of child care income tax benefit either in the form of credits or deductions. Contact your state Tax Revenue office to see what your state offers.

FREE RESEARCH ON Child CARE QUESTIONS

Sponsored by the Child Care Bureau of the U.S. Department of Health and Human Services, the National Child Care Information Center helps disseminate child care information to policy makers, parents, child care providers, and other organizations. They have publications, referrals to other organizations, and research information. They can direct you to sources of child care funding, and other resources to answer all of your child care questions and concerns.

For more information, contact National Child Care Information Center, 243 Church St., NW, Vienna, VA 22180; 800-616-2242; {http://nccic.org}.

Help When It's Dad's Turn

If dad's having trouble when it's his turn to care for the kids, here are some sources you can have him turn to for help:

1) **At-Home Dad**, 61 Brightwood Ave., North Andover, MA 01845; {www.parentsplace.com/readroom/athomedad}.
This newsletter and website descibes activities to do with your children, reading list for dads, home-based business

Free Answers to Your Day Care Concerns

Have a question or concern about your daycare setting? The Child Care Health and Safety Program has developed guidelines people can follow in child care settings. They can answer questions regarding illnesses, injuries or environmental concerns, covering such topics as lead poisoning, head lice, playground safety, and more.

You may contact the Child Care Health and Safety Program, National Center for Infectious Diseases, Centers For Disease Control and Prevention, MS-A07, 1600 Clifton Rd., NE, Atlanta, GA 30333; 404-639-3311; {www.cdc.gov/ncidod/publicat.htm}.

ideas, and more. There is information about At-Home Dad playgroups, and the At-Home Dad Network, which is a national list of at-home dads making it easier for them to contact each other. Subscriptions to the newsletter are $15 a year.

2) **National Fathers' Network**, 161290 NE 8th St., Bellevue, WA 98008; {www.fathersnetwork.org}

The website is supported by the U.S. Department of Health and Human Services, and includes a wealth of resources for fathers, including organizations that are advocates for fathers in a variety of settings, produces or posts articles dealing with fatherhood, encourages father support groups, and more.

3) **The Center for Successful Fathering**, 13740 Research Blvd., G-4, Austin, TX 78750; 800-537-0853; {www.fathering.org}. The Center sponsors education and seminars, and the website has a self-assessment test for dads, research information, books for sale, and links to other father-friendly sites.

MORE WEBSITES ON CHILD CARE

* *National Organization of Single Mothers*, P.O. Box 68, Midland, NC 28107; {www.parentsplace.com}. resources for single moms
* *CYFERNet*, Minnesota Extension Service, 340 Cofffey Hall, 1420 Eckles Ave., University of Minnesota, St. Paul, MN 55108; {www.cyfernet.org}. provides practical, research-based information on children
* *Contact I Am Your Child*, P.O. Box 15605, Beverly Hills, CA 90209; 888-447-3400; {www.iamyourchild.org}. information on child development
* *National Network for Child Care*, Family Life Extension Specialist, Human Development and Family Studies, 1322 Elm Hall, Suite 1085, Iowa State University, Ames, IA 50011; 515-294-0363; {www.nncc.org}. child nutrition and child development
* *The Families and Work Institute*, 330 Seventh Ave., 14th Floor, New York, NY 10001; 212-465-8637; {www.familiesandwork.org}. Child care, elder care, flextime, maternity leave, and more
* *Online Family Magazine* {www.family.com}. Fun for the whole family, sponsored by Disney

LearnChildCareHealthAndSafety

The *ABCs of Safe and Healthy Child Care*, is a 139 page spiral bound book that includes information on how disease is spread and recommends policies and practices that should be instituted in child care settings to prevent disease, injury, and environmental exposures. It also includes one to two page fact sheets on many common childhood illnesses and conditions, a first aid chart, a resource guide for obtaining additional information (many with 800 numbers), and a list of the poison control centers throughout the United States.

This is a great resource for child care providers. To order your copy of *ABCs of Safe and Healthy Child Care* ($19.00; PB97-104723), contact National Technical Information Service, 5285 Port Royal Rd., Springfield, VA 22161; 800-CDC-1824; or you can view it for free online at {www.cdc.gov/publications.htm}.

Free Books On Child Care

"Talking With Kids"

– How to discuss the tough issues like sex, AIDS, Drugs, etc. Children Now, 1212 Broadway, Suite 530, Oakland, CA 94612; 510-763-2444; also free on their website {www.childrennow.org}. The complete text of "Talking with Kids" is available on this website.

"Media Violence and Children: A Guide for Parents"

- National Association for the Education of Young Children, 1509 16th St., NW, Washington, DC 20036; 202-232-8777; 800-424-2460; {www.naeyc.org}.

"Video Games: Research, Ratings Recommendations"
"Loneliness in Young Children"
"Helping Young Children Deal With Anger"
"Early Childhood Violence Prevention"
"The Debate Over Spanking"
"Child Care Consumer Education on the Internet"

- Clearinghouse on Elementary and Early Childhood Education, University of Illinois at Urbana-Champaign, Children's Research Center, 51 Gerty Dr., Champaign, IL 61820; 800-583-4135; {http://ericeece.org}.

"Baby Safety Checklist"
"The Safe Nursery"
"Home Playground Safety Tips"
"A Grandparents Guide"
"The Super Sitter"
"Poison Look Out Checklist"

- Office of Information Services, Consumer Product Safety, Commission, Washington, DC 20207; 301-504-0000; {www.cpsc.gov}.

HELP WITH THE KIDS

Elementary and secondary schools are eligible for up to 90% discounts on Internet connections according to the Passage of the Snowe-Rockefeller-Exon-Kerry Amendment Universal Service section of the Telecommunications Act of 1996. See if your school is eligible by contacting: Federal Communications Commission, 1919 M Street, NW, Washington, DC 20554; 888-203-8100; {www.fcc.gov/learnnet/}.

Free Computers For "Homeschoolers"

Not only home schools, but any school or community group that are trying to educate kids from pre-K through grade 12, can be eligible to receive used computers from the government through its surplus property program. Contact Computers for Learning, P.O. Box 4410,Washington, DC 20026-4100; 888-362-7870; {www.computers.fed.gov/property/pm1.htm}.

Free Computer Chips and Video For Learning Computers

Educators can get everything they need to know about the inner workings of a computer including lesson plans, student materials, overheads, colorful posters of a Pentium Processor, as well as an actual silicon wafer, a microprocessor, processor chips, transistors, diodes, connecting wires and batteries for hands-on use.

This free package is available to teachers for grade five through nine. Homeschoolers are also eligible for this program! Get your kid's teacher to get one. Just like a computer, free upgrades are also available.

Contact The Journey Inside: The Computer, Education Programs; P.O. Box 5937; Denver, CO 80217; 800-346-3029; {www.intel.com/education/k12/resources/index.htm}.

FREE COMPUTERS FOR EDUCATORS

There are a number of organizations that offer free, second hand computers to educational or non-profit organizations. See a bunch of them at:

{www2.edc.org/ctcnet/ctcweb. asp?webcat=parecy}.

Science Websites

Need an answer to the question about the size of the sun? Want to find a cool experiment for the science fair? You just need to go online and all your science questions will be answered.

{www.ipl.org/youth/projectguide}

{www.biologylessons.sdsu.edu/index.html}

{www.neat-schoolhouse.org/science.html}

{www.eecs.umich.edu/~coalitn/sciendoutreach/ funexperiments/agesubject/age.html}

{http://rampages.onramp.net/~jaldr/chemtchr.html}

{www.exploratorium.edu/snacks}

{http://step.sdsc.edu/personal/vanderschaegen/ homelinks.html}

Families Can Get Free Computers and Training

In 1997, over 75% of those with incomes over $75,000 have a home computer but only 23% of those making less than $25,000 have home computers according to the National Telecommunications & Information Administration {www.ntia.doc.gov/ntiahome/ net2/charts.html}.

There are hundreds of organizations helping families so they will not fall through the net. Tech Corps of Georgia (2801 R. N. Martin St., East Point, GA 30344; 404-768-9990; {www.techcorpsga.org}) provides refurbished computers and training to low income families with school age children for a very low cost. Mindshare Collaborative in Massachusetts recycles computers for non-profits who work with kids, those physically impaired or adults trying to get a job {www.citysource.com/mindshare/}.

If you have trouble finding a local center near you, there is an association of these organizations called: Community Technology Centers' Network, 55 Chapel Street, Newton, MA 02158; 617-969-7100, ext. 2727; Fax: 617-332-4318; {www.ctcnet.org}.

Computer Repair and Training

Tech Corps is a non-profit organization designed to address the technology needs of the K-12 education group. There are branches in 42 states where volunteers train teachers and students in computer technology. They also repair and install computers, offer seminars, and work with teachers to improve use of computers in the classroom.

For more information, contact Tech Corps, P.O. Box 832, Sudbury, MA 01776; 781-687-1100; {www.ustc.org}.

FREE LEARNING GUIDE
To Ellis Island

What would you bring to America? How would it feel to travel in steerage? What do all the symbols on the Statue of Liberty mean?

These and other questions are answered in activity sheets distributed by the National Park Service. In addition educators can request a two week free loan of "Park In A Pack" which is a kit containing a teacher's guide, several videos, and educational activities dealing with Ellis Island.

For more information, contact Statue of Liberty National Monument, Liberty Island, New York, NY 10004, Attn: Superintendent; 212-363-7620; {www.nps.gov/stli/prod02.htm}.

Free Gifts And Letters From The President

Speak your mind and let the President know how you feel about the issues! Whether it's about more money for your school or your solution to problems with the environment, all you need to do is send a note to the White House.

You will receive a response on official White House stationary that will also include a picture of the President. Or you can simply write and ask for an 8x10 of the President and/or First Lady. Just make sure to include the name and address of where the note or pictures should be sent. You would never guess how many people forget to do that!

If the mail is not quite fast enough for you, then check out the White House website. You can e-mail the President, Vice-President, or First Lady. If you can't make the trip to Washington, you can take a virtual tour of the White House, as well as view pictures and biographies of past presidents. There is even a special White House web page for kids!

Contact The White House, 1600 Pennsylvania Ave., NW, Washington, DC 20500; {www.whitehouse.gov}.

Stamp It!

Dolls, monsters, airplanes, football stars. Whatever your interests may be, there is a stamp for you.

Stamp collecting is the most popular hobby throughout the world, and now is your chance to get in on the ground floor. The U.S. Postal Service (USPS) has a wonderful program for kids that explains how to start a stamp collection, the history of stamps, and stamp trivia. When you sign up for the *United Stampers of America*, you will receive free items such as *Stampers* magazines, posters, book covers, and other educational items to help you start your very own stamp collection!

For more information, contact Stampers Cool-lectibles, U.S. Postal Service, 8300 NE Underground, Pillar Q10, Kansas City, MO 64144; 888-STAMP-FUN; {www.stampsonline.com}.

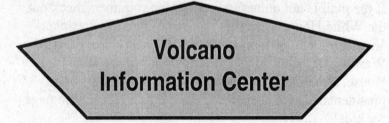

Volcano Information Center

Volcanoes can erupt at any time, and are one of the most destructive forces on Earth. Why and where they erupt, and what happens is the focus of extensive research and scientific observation.

You can request several free publications from the U.S. Geological Survey that describe volcanoes and volcanic activity, including;

- *Volcanoes*
- *Volcanoes of the United States*
- *Volcano Information for General Public*

These publications are also available online at the addresses below. With a visit to the website, you can download how to make a paper volcano, and you can be connected with the volcano observatories in Alaska, the Cascade Mountains, and Hawaii.

For more information, contact U.S. Geological Survey, P.O. Box 25286, Denver, CO 80225; 800-USA-MAPS; {http://volcanoes.usgs.gov}; {www.usgs.gov/education/learnweb.html}.

Money, Money, Money

Did you know that 95% of the notes printed each year are used to replace notes already in circulation; and that 48% of the notes printed are $1 notes? You can learn a lot about your money from the Bureau of Engraving and Printing. Some information sheets available include:

- *Changes in $1 From July 1929*, that describes the value of $1
- *Engravers and Engraving*, that gives the history of the printed dollar
- *Fun Facts about Dollars*, that contains money trivia
- *The Story of Money*

All these are free and may help when the kids argue for a raise in their allowance. Contact Bureau of Engraving and Printing, U. S. Department of the Treasury, 14th and C Sts., SW, Washington, DC 20228; 202-874-3019; {www.bep.treas.gov}.

ENDANGERED SPECIES

The time that threatened or endangered plants or species have left in this world is limited, but there are steps you can take to help them continue. The cutting down of forests, loss of habitat, pollution, and pesticides all impact upon plant and animal life, as do natural disasters such as volcanic eruptions. It is important to teach children about endangered animals, so they can learn how their actions effect wildlife, as well as how to protect these animals from extinction.

The U.S. Fish and Wildlife Service has several publications that explain how a plant or animal becomes endangered, and what is being done to protect them. Publications include *Endangered Species* and *Why Save Endangered Species*?

For your copies or more information, contact Publications Unit, U.S. Fish and Wildlife, National Conservation Training Center, Rt. 1, Box 166, Shepherdstown, WV 25443; 304-876-7203; {http://endangered.fws.gov/endspp.html}.

Everything Kids Want To Know About Earthquakes

The chance of an earthquake occurring somewhere in the world today is almost a sure thing. The National Earthquake Information Center (NEIC) locates approximately 20,000 earthquakes each year, but these are only the most important of the many million earthquakes that are estimated to occur each year.

National Earthquake Information Center (NEIC)

To learn more about epicenters, the Richter scale, and seismology, contact the NEIC, as it is the foremost collector of rapid earthquake information in the work and is responsible for publications and dissemination of earthquake data. You can learn where the largest earthquakes occurred in the U.S. and the world, as well as receive free publications on the severity of earthquakes and safety and survival in an earthquake.

For more information, contact National Earthquake Information Center, U.S. Geological Survey, Box 25046, MS 967, Denver, CO 80225; 303-273-8500; {http:// quake.wr.usgs.gov} or {wwwneic.cr.usgs.gov}.

Free Coloring Books

Teach your kids about the environment in a fun way.

The U.S. Environmental Protection Agency has several coloring books to help you increase your child's awareness of the Earth and recycling. Titles include: *The Adventures of the Garbage Gremlin* **and** *Save Our Species*, **as well as others.**

For your copies, contact National Center for Environmental Publication and Information, P.O. Box 42419, Cincinnati, OH 45242; 800-490-9198; {www.epa.gov/kids}.

Ask A Geologist

The Earth is made of rock, from the tallest mountains to the floor of the deepest ocean. Thousands of different types of rocks and minerals have been found on Earth. By studying how rocks form and change, scientists have built a solid understanding of the Earth we live on and its long history. The U.S. Geological Survey has several publications that explain rocks and fossils, including:

- *Collecting Rocks*
- *Fossils, Rocks, and Time*

The online address listed below also has a wonderful feature where you can ask a geologist a question by e-mail, although it does state that they will not write your class report for you! You can request and view these publications by contacting U.S. Geological Survey online {http://geology.usgs.gov/gip.html}.

How Things Fly

Do your kids always wonder how airplanes lift off the ground or question you about the effects of gravity?

Check out the National Air and Space Museum. They have wonderful activities to help explain the science of flight, including air pressure and buoyancy.

How Things Fly: Science Activities for Families is available by writing Educational Service Center, National Air and Space Museum, MRC 305, Washington, DC 20560; {www.nasm.edu/nasm/edu}.

Preschool Choices

Many parents worry about what elementary or high school their child will attend, but don't overlook the importance or preschool. These are very important developmental years and a wonderful preschool can help your child grow emotionally, socially, and intellectually.

The National Academy of Early Childhood Programs is an accrediting organization of early childhood programs. The accreditation process looks at the teacher training, planned activities, teacher-child ratios, environment, communication with parents, and more.

To locate early childhood accredited programs in your area or for more information contact National Association for

CHOOSING THE RIGHT PRESCHOOL AND SCHOOL

- *How To Choose A Good Early Childhood Program*
- *A Good Primary School for Your Child*
- *A Good Kindergarten for Your Child*
- *A Good Preschool for Your Child*

For your copies or more information, contact National Association for the Education of Young Children, 1509 16th St., NW, Washington, DC 20036; 202-232-8777; 800-424-2460; {www.naeyc.org}.

the Education of Young Children, 1509 16th St., NW, Washington, DC 20036; 202-232-8777; 800-424-2460; {www.naeyc.org}.

Why Do Leaves Change Colors?

Kids ask the best questions. *Why Leaves Change Color* booklet can be used to learn why leaves change to yellow, orange, and red each fall. It also contains instructions on how to copy leaves with crayons and how to make leaf prints with a stamp pad.

For more information, contact Forest Service, U.S. Department of Agriculture, 12th and Independence Aves., SW, P.O. Box 96090, Washington, DC 20090; 202-205-0957; {www.fs.fed.us}.

Free Poster On How Things Grow

The poster "How A Tree Grows" teaches about photosynthesis, enzymes, and the various parts of a tree. There is also a booklet that goes along with the poster that explains more about a tree's growth.

For more information, contact Forest Service, U.S. Department of Agriculture, 12th and Independence Aves., SW, P.O. Box 96090, Washington, DC 20090; 202-205-0957; {www.fs.fed.us}.

Free Coloring Books On
Water Safety

Spending a lot of time on your boat this summer? Make sure you follow all the boating safety rules, so your fun-filled summer is accident free.

To help educate your kids on water and boating safety  without sounding like you are lecturing, contact the *Boating Safety Hotline*. They have two coloring books for kids called *Water 'N Kids* and *Boats 'N Kids* that explain the basic concepts of water and boat safety. You can even sign them up for very inexpensive boating classes.

For more information, contact Boating Safety Hotline, Consumer and Regulatory Affairs Branch, (G-NAB-5), Auxiliary, Boating and Consumer Affairs Division, Office of Navigation Safety and Waterways Services, U.S. Coast Guard 2100 2nd St., SW, Room 1109, Washington, DC 20593; 800-368-5647; {www.uscgboating.org}.

Information USA, Inc.

What is Water?

How much water does the average person use each day?
How many baths could I get from a rainstorm?

The U.S. Geological Survey has developed a Water Science
for Schools webpage at {wwwga.usgs.gov/edu//} that
provides a wealth of information on the Earth's water,
water basics and more. They have also developed a series
of posters for grades K-5 and grades 6-9 that provide basic
knowledge of water
resources and cover
topics such as
wastewater,
wetlands,
groundwater, water
quality, and
navigation.

Contact: U.S.
Geological Survey,
Branch of
Distribution, Box
25286, Denver
Federal Center,
Denver, CO 80225;
800-435-7627;
{http://water.usgs.
gov/public/
outreach/order.
html}.

What Does The Coast Guard Do?

Our Day With The Coast Guard provides a fun way to learn about the U.S. Coast Guard. This coloring book allows you to learn what it's like to be in the Coast Guard. It includes activities such as a maze and connect-the-dots.

Contact Public Affairs, U.S. Coast Guard, U.S. Department of Transportation, Washington, DC 20593; 202-267-2596.

Have Your Kids Do A Family Oral History

Words of wisdom make more of an impression when you get them directly from the source. *The Grand Generation: Interviewing Guide and Questionnaire* ($1.50) lists guidelines for collecting folklore and oral history from older tradition-bearers. It includes a general guide to conducting interviews, a list of sample questions, and examples of ways to preserve and present findings.

Gifts That Are Flown Over The U.S. Capitol

If you are at a loss as to what to give someone, then what about purchasing an American flag? These flags are flown over the Capitol and cost between $14.05-25.30 depending upon the size and material. The flags also come with a certificate, listing name of the person for whom the flag was flown and the date. You can request a specific day, such as a birthday, anniversary, or even the day someone was discharged from the military.

The flags are available for purchase through your representatives in the House or Senate. Contact your senators or representative, The Capitol, Washington, DC 20510; 202-224-3121.

Family Folklore Interviewing Guide and Questionnaire ($1.75) is a guide to collecting family folklore, including background information on the importance of recording it, details on techniques and presentation, and a sample questionnaire. There is $4 shipping charge total per order.

Contact Smithsonian Institution Traveling Exhibition Services (SITES), Publications Department, Department 0564, Washington, DC 20073; 202-357-3168 ext. 117; {www.si.edu/organiza/offices/sites/start.htm}.

How To Create Your Own Family Tree

There is nothing like bringing a family together and showing them they all share the same roots. The Archives maintains ship passenger arrival records dating back to the 1820s, and its staff will even do research for you if you supply some basic information, such as the port of entry, passenger name, and date of arrival. If they find your ancestor, they will send you a notice.

The manifests consist of 2-by-3 foot sheets, listing passengers' age and occupations, and if after 1906 the information will include amount of money, language spoken, even height and weight. If you want to purchase a copy of the page of the manifest, the cost is $10.

For more information or a copy of Form 81 titled "Order for Copies for Ship Passenger Arrival Records," contact Reference Services Branch, National Archives and Records Administration, Eighth St. and Pennsylvania Ave., NW, Washington, DC 20408; 202-501-5400; {www.nara.gov}.

We The People

We all had to memorize the Preamble of the Constitution during our school years. It might be

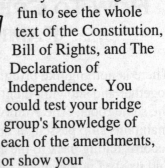

fun to see the whole text of the Constitution, Bill of Rights, and The Declaration of Independence. You could test your bridge group's knowledge of each of the amendments, or show your grandchildren how our nation was formed.

The documents can be found on the United States Information Agency's website. Their mission is to teach other countries about the United States, and their website provides a wealth of information. To view the documents, go to the United States Information Agency's website at {www.usia.gov/usa/usa.htm}.

More Than Just Digging In The Dirt

If archeology is your thing, then check out the National Park Service. They have the Archeology and Ethnography Program that has developed fascinating materials about our country's past and can help spur on your interest.

Want to know what to read or where to visit? What about archeology sites in a particular area of the country? They have several publications available including *Participate in Archeology* and *Archeology and Education*, and the website includes links to other archeology resources.

For more information, contact Publications, Archeology and Ethnography Program (2275), National Park Service, 1849 C St., NW, Washington, DC 20240; 202-343-4101; {www.cr.nps.gov}.

Homework Helpers Online

Stumped by "new math"? Need to know all the presidents and vice-presidents? The following websites provide answers and resources to help your kids correctly complete their homework and have fun doing it!

Kidinfo
www.kidinfo.com

Homework Helper
www.homeworkhelper.com

WKBW Homework Home Page
www.wkbw.com/homework/homework.html

Homework Central
www.homeworkcentral.com

Baltimore County Public Library
www.bcpl.lib.md.us/centers/education/
homework.html

Online Homework Helpers
www.searchgateway.com/
online_homework_helpers.htm

Homework Helpers
www.radix.net/~mschelling/homework.html

Yahooligans
www.yahooligans.com/School_Bell/
Homework_Help/

Schoolwork UGH
www.schoolwork.org

Libraries Online

Of course your daughter forgot to tell you about the research paper due tomorrow! And naturally your local library is closed or been completely wiped out of insect books by the rest of the class. Never fear, the Internet is here! The library is as close as your fingertips. All you need to know are the following web addresses and click away!

Internet Public Library
www.ipl.org

Library in the Sky
www.nwrel.org/sky

Study Web
www.studyweb.com

WWW Virtual Library
http://vlib.stanford.edu/Overview2.html

Library Spot
www.libraryspot.com

Awesome Library
www.awesomelibrary.org

Kids Web
www.npac.syr.edu/textbook/kidsweb

Information Please
www.infoplease.com

Homework Help
www.startribune.com/homework/

Encyclopedia.com
www.encyclopedia.com

Encarta Online
http://encarta.msn.com

Multnomah County Library
www.multnomah.lib.or.us/lib/kids

Ask An Expert

Sometimes the questions your kids ask are too technical or complicated to answer. We have searched the web and found experts on a variety of topics who will gladly answer kids questions by e-mail. Visit the following websites and submit your question to the appropriate expert.

National Park Service, American History:
www.cr.nps.gov/history/askhist.htm

Math:
www.flieger.com/mathman.htm

Dr. Math:
http://forum.swarthmore.edu/dr.math/

Grammar:
www.grammarlady.com

Construction:
www.siue.edu/ENGINEER/CONSTRUCT/conclub.htm

Health:
www.goaskalice.columbia.edu/index.html

Science:
http://sln.fi.edu/tfi/publications/askexprt.html

Zoo Animals:
www.imon.com/mgzoo/pages/ask.htm

Earth Scientist:
www.soest.hawaii.edu/GG/Ask/askanerd.html

Energy:
www.eren.doe.gov/menues/energyex.html

Bill Nye:
http://nyelabs.kctx.org/ask/email/index.html

Science
Whatzit: www.omsi.edu/online/whatzit

Astronomer:
http://image.gsfc.nasa.gov/poetry/ask/askmag.html

Mad Scientist:
www.madsci.org

Geologist:
http://walrus.wr.usgs.gov/docs

Amish:
http://padutch.welcome.com/askamish.html

Ask Jeeves:
www.askjeevesforkids.com

Free CD-ROM Full Of Kid Activities

Floods, wildfires, hurricanes, tornadoes, earthquakes, and winter storms are all natural disasters. What can you do to prepare your family, children and pets before the disaster strikes? Contact FEMA, the Federal Emergency Management Agency.

Information USA, Inc.

FEMA has fact sheets, informational brochures, posters and more to help your children learn the warning signals and develop their own disaster survival kit. They even have a wonderful free CD-ROM of their FEMA for Kids website that has games, quizzes, coloring pages, resources, and more designed just for kids!

For your copies, contact Federal Emergency Management Agency, 500 C St., SW, Washington, DC 20472; 800-480-2520; {www.fema.gov/kids}.

BRING A CAST-IRON UMBRELLA

You don't want to get wet. *Acid Rain: A Student's First Sourcebook* is a great way to teach kids about the environment and what needs to be done to protect it.

Designed for grades 4-8 and their teachers, the sourcebook describes the effects of acid rain, solutions, experiments, and activities. The website also has links to other acid rain resources.

For more information, contact Acid Rain Division, U.S. Environmental Protection Agency, 401 M St., SW, 6204J, Washington, DC 20460; 202-564-9620; {www.epa.gov/teachers/curriculumair.htm}.

The Next Thomas Edison

If your kid loves to take things apart and create new things, then he/she has the inventor's spirit. Project XL is an outreach program designed to encourage the inventive thinking process through the creation of unique inventions or innovations. The Patent and Trademark Office has developed an educator's resource guide, video, and a special curriculum.

WETLANDS AND WATER

What are wetlands and why are they so important? Wetlands play an important role in the food web with many birds and mammals relying on wetlands to provide food, water and shelter.

To learn more the role of wetlands contact the Wetland Hotline and request several free publications including: *EPA Wetlands Fact Sheets*; *Wetlands are Wonderlands Student Activity Packet*; *Wetlands Reading List*; and *The Young Scientist's Introduction to Wetlands*.

Contact Wetlands Protection Hotline, Office of Wetlands, Oceans, and Watersheds, 1355 Beverly Rd., Suite 250, McLean, VA 22101; 800-832-7828; {www.epa.gov/ OWOW}. Check out the kid's website at {www.epa.gov/wetlands/scinfo. html#Kids} for resources, links, games, and more!

To request your free copy of the Inventive Thinking
Project, contact Office of Public Affairs, Patent and
Trademark Office, U.S. Department of Commerce, 2011
Crystal Dr., Room 208B, Washington, DC 20231; 703-
305-8341.

Help Students Clean-Up

Kids intuitively grasp recycling and the need to keep the
earth green and clean, so what's with their own rooms?

*Let's Reduce and Recycle: Curriculum for Solid Waste
Awareness* provides lesson plans for
grades K-12, and includes activities,
skits, bibliographies,
and other resources.
Other booklets
include *A Resource
Guide of Solid Waste
Educational Materials*;
*School Recycling
Programs*; *Recycle
Today!;* and more.

For these publications
or more information, contact RCRA/Superfund Hotline,
Office of Solid Waste, U.S. Environmental Protection
Agency, 401 M St., SW, Washington, DC 20460; 800-424-
9346; {www.epa.gov/epaoswer/osw/teacher.htm}.

Free Videos On Famous Artists

You don't need to leave the comfort of your home or school to view great works of art. The National Gallery of Art's Extension Program is an attempt to develop awareness in the visual arts and make its collections accessible to everyone, no matter how far away from the Gallery they may live.

The Gallery offers free loans of over 150 videos, slide sets, films, teaching packets, and videodiscs, covering a wide variety of topics and time periods. The Gallery's website also lets you tour the gallery and hear audio recordings regarding many of the works.

Contact Department of Education Resources, Education Division, National Gallery of Art, 4th St. and Constitution Ave., NW, Washington, DC 20565; 202-842-6875; {www.nga.gov}.

Learn About Solar Energy

With the right stuff, the sun can power your Playstation and many calculators already come solar equipped. You can learn more about alternative sources of energy through the Energy Efficiency and Renewable Energy Clearinghouse.

They have many publications just for kids including: *Learn About Renewable Energy*; *Solar Heating*; *Learn About Saving Energy*; and even *Solar Power Science Experiments*. For more information and other links contact Energy Efficiency and Renewable Energy Clearinghouse, P.O. Box 3048, Merrifield, VA 22116; 800-363-3732; {www.eren.doe.gov/kids.html}. The website even has a link where you can ask an energy expert your tough questions!

FREE COURSE MATERIAL
FOR TEACHING ENERGY

Want to learn about energy conservation, renewable energy, energy sources, or earth science? The Energy Information Administration's National Energy Information Center can help.

Its publication, *Energy Education Resources: Kindergarten Through 12th Grade*, is an annual directory of low-cost or no-cost energy information resources. The current edition has 160 entries ranging from curriculum guides, fact sheets, brochures, films, kits, tours, and software. The publication is also available online.

For more information, contact National Energy Information Center, EI-30, Energy Information Administration, Forrestal Building, Room 1F-048, Washington, DC 20585; 202-586-8800; {www.eia.doe.gov}.

Sprocket Man!

Your kids may be too young to drive a car, but they can easily go 20mph on their bikes. So there are risks involved when your child is bike riding. In fact, over 500,000 emergency room visits are for bicycle related injuries.

How can you help your child ride safely? The U.S. Consumer Product Safety Commission has several free publications targeting bicycle use. *Sprocket Man* is a comic book that teaches your child how to ride safely and provides important tips on dealing with traffic and pedestrians. *Ten Smart Routes To Bicycle Safety* gives ten rules everyone should follow while riding. *Kids Speak Out On Bike Helmets* provides facts on bike safety and the importance of wearing a helmet. And *Bicycle Safety: Message to Parents, Teachers and Motorists* is a two page fact sheet urging parents and teachers to teach proper bicycle riding skills and habits to children.

For your free copies, contact the U.S. Consumer Product Safety Commission, Washington, DC 20207; 800-638-2772; {www.cpsc.gov}.

FREE OR LOW-COST ROCKS

Lots of fourth graders across the U.S. study about rocks and minerals. How do you help your kids grasp the subject with some enthusiasm?

Contact your state geologist located in your state capital. They have informational sheets, brochures, videos, slides, and activities designed to bring rocks alive to kids. Some states even have field trips for teachers and kids to learn more about the rock and mineral sin their region. Many states, like Ohio, offer free rock samples to give kids that hands-on experience at rock and mineral identification and classification.

Go To Mars

Not actually, but the Mars Millennium Project provides a poster and activity kit that challenges students to design a community for the planet Mars. This project will connect educators, community leaders and professionals to weave the arts, sciences and humanities into an exploration of their own communities.

For information on how to participate in the project and to receive your poster and activity kit, contact Mars Millennium Project, c/o U.S. Department of Education Publications Center, P.O. Box 1398, Jessup, MD 20794; 877-4-ED-PUBS; {www.mars2030.net}.

If you have trouble locating your state geologist, the Association of American State Geologists has a website that will link you directly to your geologist. Visit them at {www.kgs.ukans.edu/AASG}.

Free Information On Outer Space

Want to help your child build a solar system? "Solar System Puzzle Kit" is an activity where kids are asked to assemble an eight-cube paper puzzle, and when solved, they can create a miniature solar system.

Information on rockets, the moon, all the planets, current Space Shuttle information, space exploration, and more is available through NASA's incredible educational resources system for educators and students. You can download hundreds of publications, chat with experts, and look at the latest pictures from space. Each state has an Educators Resource Center that can provide you with information as well.

To learn more, contact NASA Education Division, Code FEO, NSAS Headquarters, Washington, DC 20546; {http://spacelink.nasa.gov}.

Take Your Kids On an Archeology Expedition

Never liked staying on the sidelines? Well then, dig in. "Passport In Time" helps you open a window to the past by allowing you to join activities such as archaeological excavation, site mapping, drafting, laboratory and art work, collecting oral histories, restoration, and much more. Projects vary in length and there is no registration fee. Kids are allowed on many of the projects.

For information on upcoming opportunities, contact Passport In Time Clearinghouse, P.O. Box 31315, Tucson, AZ 85751; 800-281-9176.

The History Of The Automobile

Yes there were cars in the olden times. Henry Ford built the Model T and the Model A, and was instrumental in developing the mass production of the automobile. His goal was to produce the largest number of cars at the lowest cost.

For information on Ford history and the evolution of the automobile, contact Ford Motor Company, Educational Affairs Department, P.O. Box 1899, Dearborn, MI 48121; 313-322-3000; {www.ford.com}.

Look What Followed Me Home!

When a child wants a dog, he or she may promise to walk him and feed him, but do they really know what's involved in caring for a pet?

Backyard Conservation

Want to bring wildlife into your backyard? *Backyard Conservation* is a free booklet where you can learn how to help improve the environment, help wildlife, and more just in your own backyard. You can learn about composting, attracting birds and butterflies, backyard ponds, and other ideas to help improve your yard, as well as your community.

For your free copy, contact Backyard Conservation, USDA NRCS, 7515 NE Ankeny Rd., Ankeny, IA 50021; 888-LANDCARE: {www.nrcs.usda.gov}.

A household pet needs special care, and no one knows this better than the Center for Veterinary Medicine. For this reason, they have published several fact sheets that help explain to children how to care for pets properly. So, write today. You're dog (cat or even horse) will thank you.

Contact Center for Veterinary Medicine, Food and Drug Administration, 7500 Standish Place, HFV-12, Rockville, MD 20855; 301-594-1755; {www.fda.gov/cvm}.

Weather Happens

Whether you like it or not! High pressure, low pressure, barometric pressure; if you feel the pressure to explain the differences to your little meteorologist, let the experts at the National Oceanic and Atmospheric Administration help.

They can provide you with information on keeping a weather log, weather warnings, and much more! *Watch Out...Storms Ahead! Owlie Skywarns' Weather Book*, is a fun way to learn about different weather conditions. Publications also include information on hurricanes, tornadoes, floods, and other weather disasters.

You can contact your local weather service office for information, or Educational Programs Branch, National Oceanic and Atmospheric Administration, 1325 East West Highway, Silver Spring, MD 20910; 301-713-0090, ext. 118; {www.nws.noaa.gov}.

Hoot, Man!

One of America's most beloved mascots is now one of America's most beloved authors! *The Woodsy Owl Activity Guide* is jam-packed with ideas for classroom activities, list of kid's books, coloring pages, and more!

Contact Smokey Bear-Woodsy Owl Center of Excellence, 402 SE 11th St., Grand Rapids, MN 55744; {www.fs.fed.us/spf/woodsy}.

Bring The Birds To You

Kids love to look at pictures of birds in books. Why not teach them to go outside and look at the real thing?

The U.S. Fish and Wildlife Service has published the booklet, *For the Birds*. It details various types of bird food, nests, and plants that attract birds.

For your copy, contact Publications Unit, U.S. Fish and Wildlife Service, National Conservation Training Center, Rt. 1, Box 166, Shepherdstown, WV 25443; 304-876-7203; {www.fws.gov}.

International Studies

What is the leading export from Ireland? How many people live in Ethiopia?

The federal government has two websites that can provide enough information for a two page country report, and it doesn't even involve going to the library! Check out {http://lcweb2.loc.gov/frd/cs/cshome.html#about} and {www.state.gov/www/backgound_notes/index.html}.

Free Speakers
For Your School

Need someone to help bring your study unit alive? Have an astronaut come to your class, or a Peace Corps volunteer, or even an endangered species specialist.

Many of the government programs offer speakers to schools and other groups to help with their education mission. All you need to do is ask.

To locate a speaker, contact any of the listings above and ask for the address and phone number of the office in

What To Read

Sometimes choosing a book is difficult, and sometimes kids need a little encouragement to keep reading. The Sylvan Learning Foundation has a website where you can plug in a child's reading level, types of books the child finds interesting, and the computer will do a search for you.

You will be able to print a list of books, including grade level and subject focus, to take with you to the library. Your kids can take quizzes on books they read, as well as earn points and prizes. To sign up, check out Sylvan Learning Foundation at {www.bookadventure.com/index.html}.

charge of your state. Each government office has a regional and state office that is responsible for their area. You can also look in the blue pages of your phone book. Kids love to hear from the experts!

HELP YOUR DAUGHTERS GAIN SELF-ESTEEM THROUGH SPORTS

Studies have shown that most women who hold leadership positions in the workplace have at one time participated in sports. Sports instill a sense of discipline, teamwork and the development of strong communication and leadership skills. However, girls should also participate in sports because it is fun!

Currently, YWCAs around the country provide opportunities for girls to develop their social, athletic and leadership skills through various sports programs, focusing on tennis, soccer, softball, field hockey, aquatics, artistic and rhythmic gymnastics. The YWCA/NIKE Sports Program presently implements over 30 basketball and over 15 volleyball programs throughout the country. The program targets girls of diverse backgrounds, ages 9-14, as girls in this age group are more likely to drop out of sports due to outside influences.

The YWCA/NIKE Sports Program provides an alternative to negative influences such as teenage pregnancy, or becoming involved with gangs or drugs.

YWCA/NIKE Sports Program

The program has been successful in providing girls with the opportunity to discover their potential, make friends and have fun. Contact your local YWCA or YWCA of the U.S.A., Empire State Building, Suite 301, 350 Fifth Avenue, New York, NY 10118; 212-273-7800; Fax: 212-465-2281; {www.ywca.org}.

Make Cyberspace A Safe Place For Your Kids!

If you're concerned for your children's well being on the Information Super Highway, get a free copy of *Parents Guide to the Internet,* or read it on the Internet. The American Academy of Pediatrics worked with the U.S. Department of Education to develop this brochure, which showcases the Internet as an educational tool and gives tips on Internet safety for children, and highlights web sites for families and parents.

Contact: American Academy of Pediatrics, 141 Northwest Point Boulevard, Elk Grove Village, IL 60007-1098; {www.aap.org}; 800-USA-Learn – for free booklet; {www.ed.gov/pubs/parents/internet} – to download booklet.

Toys For You

Children like to have new toys to play with and you may even want to see if they like something before you invest your hard-earned dollars.

Many communities have toy lending libraries like the one listed here for some areas of California {www.childcarelinks.org/toylending/toylendi.html}. Contact your local library or child care resource agency to learn what may be available to you.

Find Your Child & Get Free Transportation and Lodging To Go Pick Them Up

If your child ran away from home or is missing for some other reason, you can get immediate help from the *National Center for Missing and Exploited Children (NCMEC)*. Whether desperate parents are seeking help to find their child, a police officer needs case assistance, or a citizen is asking for information on child safety, all it takes is one call, to the *High-Tech Search Network* of NCMEC. United States and Canada: 800-THE-LOST (800-843-

5678); Mexico: 001-800-843-5678; Europe: 00-800-0843-5678.

This is a 24-hour Hotline that operates every day of the week. They will also assist your family in the reunification process by arranging for free transportation and lodging, once a missing child is found. NCMEC's private-sector partners, American Airlines, Greyhound, and Choice Hotels International provide these services free of charge to the families in need of financial assistance when picking up their child, and the programs are coordinated exclusively through NCMEC.

Free Help For Kids To Overcome Crisis

KidsPeace has a set of parenting brochures, including:

- *7 Standards for Effective Parenting,*
- *15 Ways to Help Your Kids Through Crisis,*
- *24 Ways You Can Prevent Child Abuse* and
- *What Every Preteen Really Wants You to Know... But May Not Tell You*

To receive your FREE set, please print out the form on the KidPeace website, and mail to: KidsPeace Fulfillment Department, 5100 Tilghman Street, Suite 028, Allentown, PA 18104; 800-8KID-123; {www.kidspeace.org}.

Contact: National Center for Missing & Exploited Children, 2101 Wilson Boulevard, Suite 550, Arlington, VA 22201-3077; 703-235-3900. Fax: 703-235-4067.

The NCMEC Hotline has also successfully established a system of networking calls to the National Runaway Switchboard (NRS) in Chicago, IL. Call them toll free at 800-621-4000; 800-621-0394 (TDD) for the hearing impaired. This sharing of information ensures that both agencies talk with the caller about the runaway child.

GRANTS AND LOANS FOR ADOPTIONS

The National Adoption Foundation (NAF) is a national non-profit organization dedicated to providing financial support, information, and services for adoptive and prospective adoptive families. They recently announced the expansion of its programs to include home equity loans, as well as unsecured loans and grants for adoption expenses. A grant program to cover adoption expenses is also available on a limited basis for prospective adoptive parents.

National Adoption Foundation (NAF)

Other sources of money for adoption include:

- Ask your employer for employee adoption assistance benefits. Approximately 65 percent of Fortune 500 companies now offer some kind of adoption benefit.

- Take advantage of the new adoption expense tax credit in advance by modifying your income tax withholding to reflect your tax savings when you file your return. This frees up cash for adoption expenses due now.

Contact: National Adoption Foundation, 1415 Flag Ave., So. , Minneapolis, MN 55426; 800-448-7061; 203-791-3811; Fax: 612-544-6698; {Email: SFreivalds@aol.com}.

FREE MONEY TO SEND YOUR CHILD TO PRIVATE KINDERGARDEN THRU HIGH SCHOOL

Private Voucher Clearinghouse

CEO (Children's Educational Opportunity Foundation) serves as a national clearinghouse for privately funded voucher programs that provide everything from support services to new programs on videotapes for K-12 grades. These private tuition grants and tax funded options give families the power to choose the K-12 school that will best accomplish their needs.

The website has a map of the U.S. Just click on the area of the program that is located near or in your hometown. For example, click on Phoenix, AZ and the next screen will pop up indicating who is the contact person for AZ, the total amount invested in the voucher program, as well as other information. The website also gives you a history about school choice legislation, school choice research, and some testimonies on how you can make a difference in the program.

Contact: CEO America, P.O. Box 330, Bentonville, AR 72712; 501-273-6957; Fax: 501-273-9362; {www. ceoamerica.org}.

TUITION ASSISTANCE FOR BLACK STUDENTS

The Black Student Fund has provided financial assistance and support services to African American students and their families in the Washington, DC area for over 34 years. All financial assistance is based on a sliding scale. During the last several years, their scope has broadened to provide services to families in the greater Washington, DC area and the nation.

Black Student Fund

Contact them at Black Student Fund, 3636 16th Street, NW, 4th Floor, Washington, DC 20010; 202-387-1414; {www.blackstudentfund.org}; {E-mail: mail@ blackstudentfund.org}.

40,000 Scholarships For Kids From K to 8th Grade

That's how many scholarships were given out in 1999 by the Children's Scholarship Fund, but at press time it was not clear when the scholarships will be available again. The scholarships averaged $1,100 for children from K through 8th grade to attend private schools. There were income requirements, but the income level can go up to $44,415 for a family of 4. The awards are based on a lottery process.

To keep in touch to see when this program will be available again, contact Children's Scholarship Fund, 7 West 57th St. 3rd Floor, New York, N Y 10019; 212-751-8555; {www.scholarshipfund. org}.

Dentist Offers Scholarships for Elementary School Children

For several years Dr. Albert Landucci has sponsored awards and scholarships to the less fortunate. Scholarships are based on academic excellence, community service, volunteering, science and mathematics excellence and dental assisting.

Scholarships are offered in the San Mateo Elementary
School District at:

Abbott	Laurel
Audubon	Laurel's Highly Gifted Program
Bayside	Meadow Heights
Baywood	Nesbit
Beresford	North Shoreview
Borel	Notre Dame
Bowditch	Park
Brewer Island	Parkside
Central Elementary	Ralston
Cipriani	St. Gregory
Fiesta Gardens International	St. Matthew
Foster City	St. Timothy
Fox	Sandpiper
George Hall	Sunnybrae
Highlands	Turnball Learning Academy
Horrall	All the high schools in San Mateo
Immaculate Heart of Mary	County College of San Mateo

For more information about the awards, scholarships and to
see if your school is in the district, visit Dr. Landucci's
website. Contact: Albert O. J. Landucci, D.D.S, 2720
Edison Street, San Mateo, CA 94403-2495; 650-574-4444;
650-574-4441 (voice mail); {www.Dr.Landucci.com}; {E-
mail: Dr.Landucci@aol.com}.

$1,400 FOR ELEMENTARY STUDENTS IN NEW YORK CITY

The School Choice Scholarships Foundation provides funds to cover the annual tuition costs up to $1,400 maximum per child and it is guaranteed for at least three years.

Scholarships are only for elementary school children who are currently enrolled in a New York City's public schools, and meet the income levels requirements. Students are selected by a lottery drawing with priority given to children who attend the lowest performing schools.

Contact: School Choice Scholarships Foundation, Inc., 730 Fifth Avenue, 9th Floor, New York, NY 10019; 212-338-8711; Fax: 212-307-3230; {www.nygroup. com}; {E-mail: scsf@ nygroup.com}.

$1,700 Washington Scholarship Fund, Inc.

The Washington School Fund provides financial assistance for children to attend either private or parochial schools in the Washington, D.C. area for grades K through 8th. The maximum amount received per child is $1,700, and families of 4 with incomes up to $35,802 are eligible to apply.

Contact: Washington Scholarship Fund, Inc., 1133 15th Street, NW, Suite 600, Washington, DC 20005; 202-293-5560; Fax: 202-293-7893; {www.wsf-dc.org}.

Free Private Schools For Kids of Color

A Better Chance's mission is work with minority students from the 6th grade through college to open opportunity doors that otherwise would not be open without a helping hand. There are several programs that include helping students receive financial aid for attending private local schools, boarding schools, or summer programs to help prepare for college.

Contact: A Better Chance, 419 Boylston St., Boston, MA 02116-3382; 800-562-7865; 617-421-0950; Fax: 617-421-0965; {www.abetterchance.org}.

MONEY FOR FUTURE WRITERS

For those future award-winning writers, Amelia Magazine awards $200 for a high school student's first publication. First publications can be a previously unpublished poem, a nonfiction essay or a short story. Deadline for the contest is May 15.

Write or call for further information. Amelia Student Award, Amelia Magazine, 329 East Street, Bakersfield, CA 93304; 805-323-4064.

EDUCATION LOANS UP TO $20,000 FOR GRADES K THRU 12

As with college loans, there are many financial institutions that provide loans for families to send their children to private or parochial schools at the elementary and secondary school levels. Listed below are some of the organizations that are providing these types of loans. Be sure to be aware that you can always contact your state

$2,000 FOR CHILDREN IN ARIZONA

Arizona children in K-12, with incomes up to $29,693 (for family of 4) can receive up to $2,000 per child per school year with a minimum three-year commitment to qualified children.

Contact: Arizona Scholarship Fund, P.O. Box 2576, Mesa, AZ 85214; 602-497-4564; Fax: 602-832-8853; {E-mail: ChamBria@ Azscholarships. org}; or Arizona Scholarship Fund, P.O. Box 31354, Tucson, AZ 85751-1354; 502-886-7248; {E-mail: ChamBria@ Azscholarships. org}; {www. azscholarships. org}.

banking commissioner by calling your state capitol operator listed in the Appendix.

1) **Key Education Resources**
   745 Atlantic Ave., Suite 300
   Boston, MA 02111
   800-225-6783 (toll free)
   617-348-0010
   Fax: 617-348-0020
   {www.key.com}

2) **USA Group Tuition Payment Plan**
   P.O. Box 6145
   Indianapolis, IN 46206-6145
   800-348-4607
   Fax: 317-951-5889
   {www.usagroup.com}

3) **The Education Resources Institute (TERI)**
   800-255-TERI
   {www.teri.org}

4) **First Marblehead Corporation**
   30 Little Harbor
   Marblehead, MA 01945
   781-639-2000
   Fax: 781-639-4583
   {www.pregate.com}

5) **FACTS SCHOLAR Loan Program**
   P.O. Box 67037
   100 N. 56th Street, Suite 306

Lincoln, NE 68504
800-624-7092
402-466-1063
Fax: 402-466-1136
{www.factsmgt.com}

$ 10,000
for a 7th Grade Essay

The 53-year-old contest is open to parochial, private and home schooled 7th and 8th graders. Students should submit a 300-400 word, typed essay based on a patriotic theme established by VFW.

Contact your school counselor or principal to apply, or contact the VFW listed and they will tell you where your local chapter is located. First place national winners receive a $10,000 savings bond, 2nd place winners receive a $6,000 savings bond and 3rd place winners receive $5,000 savings bond.

Contact: VFW Voice of Democracy Essay Contest, Veterans of Foreign Wars of the United States, VFW Building, 406 West 34th Street, Kansas City, MO 64111;

816-756-3390; Fax: 816-968-1149; {www.vfw.org};
{E-mail: Harmer@vfw.org}.

$3,000 for Artists

Any high school students that need help with furthering
their education can enter the VFW Ladies Auxiliary
National Patriotic
Creative Art
Competition. Students
should submit their entry
through the VFW Ladies
Auxiliary Local Chapter
first.

Finalists from the local
chapters are selected for
the grand prize
competition. First place
grand prize winners
receive $3,000, and an
all expense paid trip to
the VFW Ladies
Auxiliary Conference
for Community Service
in Washington, DC.
Second place winners
receive $2,000, 3rd place winners receive $1,500, 4th place
winners receive $1,000 and 5th place winners receive $500.

Money For Young Writers

Contestants receive a
cash award for writing a
short story that
promotes brotherhood
and is 4,000 words
maximum. The money
can be used for
anything. For more
information, contact
Aim Magazine Short
Story Contest, 7308 S
Eberhart, Chicago, IL
60619.

Contact: VFW Ladies Auxiliary National Patriotic Creative
Art Competition, Ladies Auxiliary to the VFW National
Headquarters, 406 West 34th Street, Kansas City, MO
64111; 816-561-8655; Fax: 816-931-4753;
{www.ladiesauxvfw.com}.

$1,500 For Young Science Types

Each year General Learning Communication with Dupont
sponsors a science essay contest for children in grades 7-

12. First place
winners of each
division receive
$1,500, and an
expense paid trip to
Space Center
Houston with their
parents. This trip
includes airfare,
hotel and an allowance. Second place winners receive a
$750 prize, 3rd place winners a $500 prize and honorable
mentions receive $50. The deadline for the contest is
January 29. Write or visit the website to obtain the entry
application and mail first class in a 9x12 envelope.

Contact: Dupont Science Challenge, Science Essay Awards
Program , c/o General Learning Communications, 900
Skokie Blvd, Suite 200, Northbrook, IL 60062; 847-205-
3000; Fax: 847-564-8197; {www.glcomm.com/dupont}.

$150 For Young Artists

American Automobile Association (AAA) awards prizes up to $150 for children in K to 12th grade and $5,000 for college students in their *School Traffic Safety Program*. In the K-12 division, children submit posters. In the senior high division, students can submit essays, brochures, and even creative videos.

Contact your local AAA office and ask for the School Traffic Safety Division. You may also contact AAA School Traffic Safety Poster Program, Poster Program Manager, American Automobile Association (AAA), 1260 Fair Lakes Circle, Fairfax, VA 22033; 407-444-7916; Fax: 407-444-7956.

$1,000 FOR 13-21 YEAR OLDS

Seventeen Magazine's writing contest offers first place winners $1,000, 2nd place winners $500, and 3rd place winners $250. Honorable Mentions receive $50.

Writers must be between the ages of 13-21. Contestants should submit a double-spaced manuscript copy of their fiction writing and the copy should be no more than 4,000 words, which is approximately 16 pages. Deadline date is April 30.

Contact: Seventeen Magazine, 850 3rd Avenue, New York, NY 10020; 212-407-9700.

Students in Grades 6-12 Can Win $20,000

Each year the **NSTA (National Science Teachers Association)** sponsors a scholarship competition for students in grades 6-12, who compete either individually or in pairs. The first place winner in the grades 6-9 receive a $20,000 savings bond, two 2nd place winners receive one $10,000 savings bonds each, and each 3rd place winner (5) receives one $3,000 savings bonds. The same awards disbursement will be done for grades 10-12. Deadline for the competition is in January.

$10,000 For Young Inventors

Craftsman sponsors a program where students either invent or modify a tool independently. Two winners from grades 3-5 and 6-8 will receive a $10,000 savings bond. Ten finalists, five from each grade will receive a $5,000 savings bond. The teachers of these winners and their schools will receive prizes from Sears. Every contestant will receive a gift and certificate of appreciation.

Contact: Craftsman/NSTA Young Inventors Awards Program, National Science Teachers Association, 1840 Wilson Boulevard, Arlington, VA 22201; 888-494-4994 (toll free); {E-mail: younginventors@ nsta.org}.

Six teachers from the 1st and 2nd place winners will receive a $2000 gift certificate towards computer equipment. Ten teachers from the third place winners will receive a $200 certificate for NSTA publications. Contact: Duracell/NSTA Scholarship Competition, 1840 Wilson Blvd., Arlington, VA 22201; 888-255-4242 (toll free); {www.nsta.org}.

$1,000 For Writing About Technology

Students in K-12 from the U.S. and Canada can use their imagination and creative writing and illustrating skills to compose a ten page or less essay to indicate what technology would be like 20 years from now. There are four categories for students to participate: grades K-3, grades 4-6, grades 7-9 and grades 10-12. Final first place winners receive a $10,000 savings bond, second place winners receive a $5,000 savings bond, and teachers receive Toshiba prizes.

Contact: Toshiba/NSTA Explora Vision Awards Program, 1840 Wilson Boulevard, Arlington, VA 22201; 800-397-5679 (toll free); 703-243-7100; {E-mail: exploravision@nsta.org}.

$1,000 a Year for 3 Years In Kentucky

School Choice Scholarships Inc. (SCSI) in Jefferson County, Kentucky awards its kids with 100 new partial-scholarships per year in addition to the 325 scholarships awarded just last year! If your Jefferson County child is in K-6 and your family meets the Federal School Lunch regulations, you can be awarded 50%-60% of all tuition (up to $1000) for THREE YEARS! SCSI is willing to make a three-year commitment to making sure your child can enjoy the freedom of school choice! Contact: SCSI, P.O. Box 221546, Louisville, KY 40252-1546; 502-254-7274.

$1,250 FOR 4 YEARS IN CONNECTICUT

CEO Connecticut offers your K-5 child, living in either Hartford or Bridgeport, CT, the extra help needed to attend any chosen private school in the area. Just meet the Federal School Lunch Program guidelines, apply, and you could be awarded up to half the tuition for four years (up to $1250). Just last year, CEO Connecticut awarded 200 four-year scholarships in Hartford and another 106 in Bridgeport! Plus, they're happy to help families stay together by making use of a sibling policy! Contact: CEO Connecticut, P.O. Box 6364, Bridgeport, CT 06606; 203-334-3003; Fax: 203-334-7358.

$1,200 in Arizona

Arizona School Choice Trust (coupled with the Childrens Scholarship Fund) will grant 25%-75% towards your child's choice of educational institution (up to $1200). If you live in Maricopa County, meet the Federal School Lunch Program guidelines, and your child is in a grade from K-8, you are eligible to apply!

The Arizona School Choice Trust has awarded more than 500 four-year awards and through tax-deductible donations adds more students to the program each year. To ensure your child's success in the program, ASCT requires that while enrolled, your student must maintain a 90% attendance rate.

Up to $1,800 in Michigan

The Educational Choice Project assist K-8 students eligible for the Federal School Lunch Program by offering to pay half of the tuition needed to attend the child's school of choice (up to $1800). Last year alone, 149 students from Calhun County gladly accepted this generous opportunity! Contact: The Educational Choice Project, 34 W. Jackson, One River Walk Center, Battle Creek, MI 49017-3505; 616-962-2181; Fax: 616-962-2182.

Contact: Arizona School Choice Trust, Inc., 3737 E. Broadway Rd., Phoenix, AZ 85040-2966; 602-454-1360; Fax: 602-454-1362; {www.asct.org}.

$1,450 For Families In TEXAS

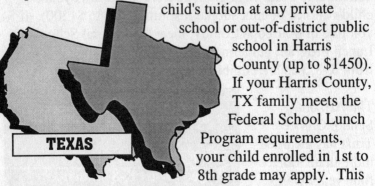

The Childrens Educational Opportunity Foundation is a private scholarship program that will pay one-half of a child's tuition at any private school or out-of-district public school in Harris County (up to $1450). If your Harris County, TX family meets the Federal School Lunch Program requirements, your child enrolled in 1st to 8th grade may apply. This year, the Foundation hopes to award 550 students with the ability to practice school choice!

Contact: The Childrens Educational Opportunity Foundation, 952 Echo Lane, Suite 350, Houston, TX 77024; 713-722-8555; Fax: 713- 722-7442; {www.hern.org/ceo/index.html}.

Over $5 Million More For Texas Children

The Today Foundation of Dallas, Texas joins with the Childrens Education Fund and the Childrens Scholarship Fund (CSF) to be able to grant Dallas students in grades K-8 with help to attend their schools of choice. Just recently, the CSF agreed to donate 5 million dollars (over four years) to help these students (who must also be eligible for the Federal School Lunch Program).

Already, the Today Foundation has been able to award 500 students with half of their school choice tuition and due to this amazing gift from the CSF, many more students will be given a very special opportunity. For more information, contact Childrens Education Fund, P.O. Box 225748, Dallas, TX 75214; 972-296-1811; Fax: 972-296-6369; {www.TodayFoundation.org}.

Childrens Education Fund

$2,000 For Elementary Students In Colorado

Educational Options for Children offers your K-6 Denver student the opportunity to get up to 65% of private school tuition paid for four years! (You must also meet the criteria of the Federal School Lunch Program.) Every 2 years, another 50-60 four year partial-tuition opportunities (up to $2000) are available!

EOC is a non-profit organization. For more information, contact Linda Tafoya, Executive Director or Sheryl Glaser, Program Administrator at c/o Adolph Coors Foundation, 3773 Cherry Creek North Dr., Denver, CO 80209; 303-380-6481; Fax: 303-477-9986.

Save 50% On Elementary School Tuition

Gateway Educational Trust offers to pay half of your child's tuition (up to $1000) for up to three years to elementary school children. Your child must be entering K-4, live or attend school in St. Louis, and meet the regulations of the Federal Reduced Price Lunch Program. That's it! Simple!

If you'd like an application mailed to you, call 314-771-1998 and leave your name and address. For more information, you may contact Irene Allen, the Executive Director at Gateway Educational Trust, 7716 Forsyth Blvd., St. Louis, MO 63105-1810; 314-721-1375; Fax: 314-721-1857; {E-mail: ager2@aol.com}.

FREE CHILD SUPPORT

Legal Help For Millionaires

No matter what your income, you can get the most powerful organization in the world, *your government*, to fight for you to:

1) Establish paternity;
2) Set up a court order for child support;
3) Track down a missing parent and collect your child support; and even
4) Get the courts to adjust child support orders when circumstances change.

Actually I lied. There are a few states that may charge you up to $25.00. So the maximum you will pay is $25.00. So, why hire an attorney, who may or may not know the law, and will charge you up to $200 an hour, when you can call someone who wrote the law, whose duty is to enforce it for you, and who is free?

Contact your state Child Support Enforcement Office listed in the Appendix, or contact Office of Child Support Enforcement, U.S. Department of Health and Human Services, 370 L'Enfant Promenade, SW, Washington, DC 20447; 202-401-9383; {www.acf.dhhs.gov/programs/cse/}.

Why You Should Not Use
A Child Support Collection Service

Understand that we are biased. We've spent an entire career telling people how not to spend money on services when they can get them free.

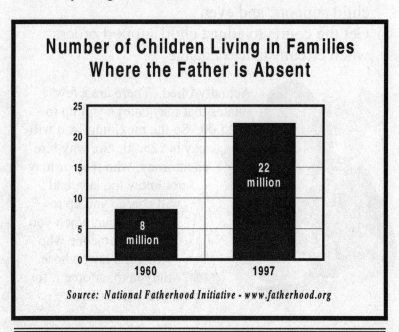

Number of Children Living in Families Where the Father is Absent

Source: National Fatherhood Initiative - www.fatherhood.org

Most of these organizations will charge you at least 30% of any recovered money whether they are responsible for getting it or not. Do you want to share 30% of something that you thought the government was initially responsible for getting?

They also do not have access to one of the best sources of getting your support money, the IRS. Only the government can use the IRS to get your support money. You will also have to pay an application fee and may never get any help.

Nearly 40 percent of children under the age of 18 in America live apart from their biological fathers.

Source: Pennsylvania's Fatherhood Initiative Project

If you are dying to hire someone, it is a lot safer to hire a private attorney. Or, if you are just trying to locate a non-custodial parent, be sure to first use the following free services:

1) *The Federal Parent Locator* at your state Child Support Enforcement Office listed in the Appendix, and

2) *The Association for Children for Enforcement and Support (ACES) Locator* at ACES, 2260 Upton Avenue, Toledo, OH 43606; 800-537-7072; fax 419-472-5943; {www.childsupport-aces.org}.

And if these sources fail, it will still be a lot cheaper to hire a private investigator to locate someone. An investigator may only cost you $100 or so. Contact ACES listed here if you need further assistance on this process.

FINDING DEADBEATS WHO CHANGE JOBS OR SKIP TOWN

In order to locate and withhold wages from child support obligors who have taken a job in another state, each state now collects information on all new employees from businesses. The state then transmits the information to the U.S. Department of Health and Human Services, placing the data into the National New Hire Reporting System.

This data is matched against delinquent parent information that is sent in by the states. When matches are discovered,

Half Don't Get Their Child Support

49% of custodial parents who have court orders for child support don't receive it all in a given year.

Source: *Trends in the Well-Being of America's Children & Youth*, 1997 Office of Assistant Secretary for Planning and Evaluation, U.S. Department of Health and Human Services

that information is returned to the state so that a **WAGE GARNISHMENT** order may be issued and sent to the delinquent parent's employer. In the first 6 months, the program located 60,000 delinquent parents. Talk about Big Brother! You can run, but you can't hide.

Federal Parent Locator Service

The government can also locate non-custodial parents for child support payments by accessing information in the *Federal Parent Locator Service*. This database includes information from some of the best sources in the world, including:

1) Social Security Administration

2) Internal Revenue Service

3) Department of Defense / Office of Personnel Management

4) Federal Bureau of Investigation

5) Department of Veterans Affairs

Contact your state Child Support Enforcement Office listed in the Appendix if you need to access this information to collect your child support.

The IRS and Others Will Get Your
Child Support Money

Almost two out of every three dollars collected from child support agencies comes from employers through wage garnishment. But under new laws, local child support agencies now have the power to take any refund money that a deadbeat may be getting from the IRS. In 1995 alone, over $1 billion was collected from IRS refunds and sent to 1.2 million families.

The government also has the power to collect child support money from:

Taxes On Alimony and Child Support

	For the Recipient	For the Payer
Child Support	Tax Free	Not Deductible
Alimony	Taxed	Is Deductible

See: 1997 IRS Publication 17, *Your Federal Income Tax* (Chapter 20, and page 92, and page 144)

Information USA, Inc.

- ✦ state unemployment benefits
- ✦ disability insurance payments
- ✦ lottery winnings
- ✦ interest and dividend income

- ✦ worker's compensation payments
- ✦ public or private retirement funds

The government can also:

- ✦ report your name as a bad credit risk to credit agencies;
- ✦ get the state to deny you a driver's license, a hunting license, or a professional or business license; or
- ✦ seize your assets.

They can also stop you from getting a government loan, a loan guarantee or loan insurance to buy a house, start a business or get an education. And in some cases, they can require community service for failure to pay.

Every state operates a little differently. Check what your state can do by contacting your state Child Support Enforcement Office listed in the Appendix.

$5,000 In Unpaid Child Support Can Get You 6 Months

And $10,000 can get you two years! The Deadbeat Parents Punishment Act of 1998 creates two new categories of felonies, with penalties of up to two years in prison for more egregious child support evaders:

1) Traveling across state or country lines with the intent to evade child support payments will now be considered a felony if the obligation has remained unpaid for a period longer than one year or is greater than $5,000.

2) When the obligation has remained unpaid for a period of longer than two years or is greater than $10,000, willful failure to pay child support to a child residing in another state will be considered a felony.

Contact your state Child Support Enforcement Office listed in the Appendix.

Forgive Us Our Past Child Support

There are programs like the one offered by the Indianapolis District Attorney's Office that offers low-income fathers "forgiveness" of a certain portion of the money owed in back child support in exchange for participation in job training or education programs. Localities that use this type of program report an increase in fathers' participation in the child support program.

To see if your state offers such a program, contact your state Child Support Enforcement Office listed in the Appendix.

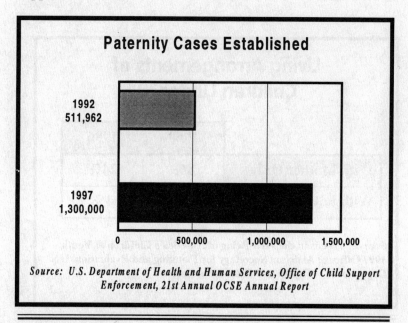

Paternity Cases Established

Year	Cases
1992	511,962
1997	1,300,000

Source: U.S. Department of Health and Human Services, Office of Child Support Enforcement, 21st Annual OCSE Annual Report

Get Updates On Your Case By Phone

If your lawyer is handling your child support case, it may be hard to reach her by phone. But if the government is handling it, there are states like Massachusetts and Montana where you can follow your case on an automated recording system.

It can tell you what payments have been received, what enforcement action has been taken, tell you about court actions, or even genetic testing appointments. Non-custodial parents can even pay support by phone using a credit card.

Living Arrangements of Children Under 18

	1960	1996
With Mother Only	8%	24%
With Father Only	1%	4%

Source: Trends in the Well-Being of America's Children & Youth, 1997 Office of Assistant Secretary for Planning and Evaluation, U.S. Department of Health and Human Services

See what's available from your state Child Support
Enforcement Office listed in the Appendix.

They'll Put Up Your Picture In The Post Office

If you are a non-custodial
parent owing child support, you
may be right there next to the
FBI's most wanted in your local
post office.

The U.S. Postal Service is
working with each state's Office
of Child Support Enforcement to
display "Wanted Lists" of parents
who owe child support. It will
be nice for your friends to see
the next time they are waiting in
line for stamps!

Many states are also posting photos of deadbeats on the
Internet. Check out California at {www.childsup.
cahwnet.gov/mostwntd.htm} and Massachusetts at
{www.ma-cse.org/htdocs/Wanted-Campaigns/
tenmostwanted.htm}

See if someone you know is listed on your state's website!

More Free Legal Services

You don't have to go to your neighbor's brother's cousin's kid who is an attorney, unless you want to pay for his legal advice. Uncle Sam has set up law offices all across the country to help those who cannot afford standard legal fees.

It is the Legal Services Corporation's job to give legal help to low-income individuals in civil matters. These offices are staffed by over 6,400 attorneys and paralegals. Each program follows certain guidelines as to what cases it accepts and specific financial eligibility that possible clients must meet.

33% of All Women Murdered in the US are Killed by their Husbands, Former Husbands or Boyfriends

Source: Center for Policy Alternative
www.cfpa.org/publications/index.html

To learn about the program nearest you, look in the blue pages of your phone book, or contact Legal Services Corporation, 750 First St., NE, 11th Fl., Washington, DC 20002; 202-326-8800.

Free Child Support Handbook

The Office of Child Support Enforcement has developed a booklet titled, *Handbook on Child Support Enforcement*, that answers questions regarding locating a non-custodial parent, enforcing the support order, and how to collect payments across state lines. Included is a listing of **State Child Support Enforcement Offices** and a form for enforcement record keeping.

Deadbeats Put Kids Into Poverty

➡ **50% of all white children growing up in a single parent households who do not receive support, live at or below the poverty level**

➡ **60% of all Hispanic children growing up in single parent households, live at or below the poverty level**

➡ **70% of all black children growing up in single parent households live at or below the poverty level**

Source: Association for Children for Enforcement of Support (ACES)

For your free copy, contact Office of Child Support
Enforcement, U.S. Department of Health and Human
Services, 370 L'Enfant Promenade, SW, Washington, DC
20447; 202-401-9383; {www.acf.dhhs.gov/programs/
cse/}.

Divorce Isn't So Difficult Online

For some, divorce is a smooth process with a few forms to
sign. For others, it is a long
protracted battle. You need to
know what issues you are
going to face.

Divorce Source is an
online website "which
provides divorce
information pertaining
to child custody, child
support, alimony,
counseling, visitation,
and more." There are chat
rooms on different topics,
divorce and family law publications,
and other resources right at your fingertips.

Need help finding a divorce lawyer? A search feature
allows you to locate the one nearest you. Even they say

that the information provided should in no way be considered legal advice, but at least you can use the information as points of discussion with your own attorney.

Visit Divorce Source at {www.divorcesource.com}.

Online Support Learning

Need some basic information about child support? The Divorce Support website answers your child support questions and has links to various states' statutes.

There are close to fifty chapters of easy to understand information about child support written by an attorney. There is a search feature if you are looking for a professional to help you with child support issues, chat rooms, state law resources, visitation issues, and more. Obviously, this does not take the place of getting your own legal advice, but it will provide you with a basic understanding of the issues involved.

Visit the website at {www.divorcesupport.com}.

YOUR MONEY, INSURANCE AND CONSUMER HELP

Top 10 Ways
To Beat The Clock and
Prepare For Retirement

If you can put aside $2,000 a year for retirement and get only 4% interest a year, you will get back $112,170 at age 60.

Learn nine more ways to save from this free report from: Pension & Welfare Benefits Administration Request Line, U.S. Dept. of Labor, 200 Constitution Ave., NW, Washington, DC 29210; 800-998-7542;

{www.dol.gov/dol/pwba/public/pubs/topten/top10txt.htm}.

Find Out What Social Security Owes You When You Retire

More importantly, this publication will help you figure out how to qualify to receive the maximum amount when you retire.

Get a free copy of your *"Personal Earnings and Benefit Statement"* today by phone or on the internet. Contact Social Security Administration, Office of Public Inquiries, 6401 Security Blvd., Room 4-C-5 annex, Baltimore, MD 21235; 800-772-1213; {www.ssa.gov}.

Where To Bitch About What

You can get even without hiring a high priced lawyers. Find the government office that regulates the offending party and contact them about getting even for free.

- **Professionals - Doctors, Lawyers,**
- **Utilities - Gas, Electric, Phone, Cable, etc**
- **Businesses -**
- **Health Care - Hospitals, HMO's etc**
- **Money People - Banks, Brokers, Realtors**

Get An Estimate of Your
Retirement Needs

Get a Ballpark Estimate of Your Retirement Needs

www.asec.org/ bpk-comp.htm

The seventh annual Retirement Confidence Survey shows that only 36% of workers have tried to determine how much they'll need to save for retirement. And of those that tried, 24% still don't know.

Get a free copy of *"Get a Ballpark Estimate of Your Retirement Needs"* from American Savings Council, 2121 K St., NW, Suite 600, Washington, DC 20037; 202-659-0670; {www.asec. org/bpk-comp.htm}.

Is Your Stockbroker A Bad Person?

You can find out if any disciplinary actions have been taken from securities regulators and criminal authorities by contacting: National Association of Securities Dealers, Inc (NASD), 1735 K Street, NW, Washington, DC 20006; 800-289-9999; {www.nasdr.com}.

You can call directly or search on the internet by your broker's individual name or company's name. And like plumbers or contractors you can contact your state government to see if your broker is licensed to do business in your state. Contact your state security regulator listed in the Appendix.

10 Questions To Ask When Choosing A Financial Planner

How do they charge, where do I find one, and how do you check out their background are the kinds of answers you'll find in this free publication from: Certified Financial Planner Board of Standards, 1700 Broadway, Suite 2100, Denver, CO 80290; 888-CFP-MARK; {www.cfp-board.org/index.html}.

A Guide To Understanding Mutual Funds

Although it may be biased because it's brought to you by the association of mutual fund people, this publication does explain the industry jargon and it is free from Investment Company Institute, 1401 H Street, NW, Washington, DC 20005; 202-326-5800; {www.ici.org/pdf/g2 understanding. pdf}.

Make $500 Turning In Annoying Telephone Solicitors

The Federal Communications Commission's (FCC) Consumer Protection Act says that you can collect $500 or more from telephone solicitors if:

✦ they call two or more times within a 12 month period after you tell them to stop

✦ they call you with a pre-recorded voice message to your home

✦ they call you at home before 8am or after 9pm

✦ they send you an unsolicited advertisement on your fax machine

✦ they tie up two or more lines on a multi-line business system with an automatic dialing machine

For more details on stopping telephone solicitors or how to collect your money, contact:

Federal Communications Commission, Common Carrier Bureau, Consumer Complaints, Mail Stop 1600A2, Washington, DC 20554; 888-CALL-FCC; {www.fcc.gov/ccb/consumer_news/unsolici.html}.

You can get your telephone number taken off many of the major telephone solicitation lists by sending your name and telephone number to:

Telephone Preference Services, Direct Marketing Association, P.O. Box 9014, Farmingdale, NY 11735; {www.the-dma.org/topframe/index1.html}.

Free Credit Repair

It always seemed strange to me that if you're in debt enough to need help with credit repair, why in the world would you spend more money on a credit repair services? You can do it for free, yourself!

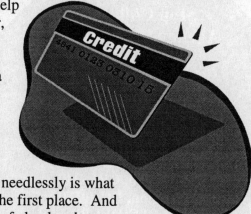

Spending money needlessly is what got you there in the first place. And more importantly, federal and state regulators have been warning consumers against using credit counseling companies. Companies, lawyers and others will charge you $300 to $1000 for something you can do for free.

Here are some of the free reports you can get from the Federal Trade Commission:

- ❏ *Credit Repair: Self-Help May Be The Best*
- ❏ *Knee Deep in Debt*
- ❏ *How To Dispute Credit Reporting Errors*
- ❏ *How To Deal With Credit Problems*
- ❏ *How to Dispute Credit Report Errors*

For your copies, contact Public Reference, Room 130, Federal Trade Commission, Washington, DC 20580; 202-326-2222; 877-FTC-HELP; {www.ftc.gov}.

Stop Collection Agency Harassment!

Get free copies of "Credit and Your Consumer Rights" and Fair Debt Collection" from Consumer Response Center, Federal Trade Commission, CRC-240, Washington, DC 20580; 877-FTC-HELP; {www.ftc.gov}.

If you don't want to do it ALL yourself, you can ask for **FREE HELP**. The following non-profit and government organizations provide free, or low-fee credit counseling services. You can contact them to find the office nearest you.

Some of these offices are financed by the bank and credit card industry, who are biased toward having you pay all your bills without using the bankruptcy option. So be sure that they explain your bankruptcy options.

❑ *National Foundation for Consumer Credit*, 8611 Second Avenue, Suite 100, Silver Spring, MD 20910; 800-388-2227; Spanish: 800-68AYUNDA; {www.credit.org}.

❑ Free internet credit counseling services from the non-profit organization, *Credit Counseling Center of America*, P.O. Box 830489, Richardson, TX 75083-0489; 800-493-2222; {www.cccamerica.org}.

❑ *County Cooperative Extension Service*: to find your local office see the state-by-state listing in the Appendix.

GET FREE COPIES OF YOUR CREDIT REPORT

You can get a free copy of your credit report if:

★ you have been denied credit, insurance, or employment within the last 60 days
★ you're unemployed and plan to look for a job within 60 days
★ you're on welfare, or
★ your report is inaccurate because of fraud.

Otherwise they can charge you up to $8 for a copy of your report. For copies of your report, contact the credit reporting agencies listed in the yellow pages of your telephone book, or contact the three major national credit bureaus:

Equifax
PO Box 740241, Atlanta, GA 30374; 800-685-1111
Experian (formerly TRW)
PO Box 949, Allen, TX 75013; 800-682-7654
Trans Union
760 West Sproul Road, Springfield, PA 19064; 800-916-8800

If you have trouble getting satisfaction from a credit reporting agency contact: Consumer Response Center, Federal Trade Commission, CRC-240, Washington, DC 20580; 877-FTC-HELP; {www.ftc.gov}.

Dress For Success For Free

Looking for work and can't afford the right wardrobe? There are about 50 non-profit organizations around the country that provide women with two separate outfits for free. One can be used to go to an interview and the other can be used once you get the job.

The following organization acts as a clearinghouse for similar opportunities around the country. Bottomless Closet, 445 North Wells, Chicago, IL 60610; 312-527-9664; Fax: 312-527-4305; {www.bottomlesscloset.org}.

Free Books On Your Money

✓ *A Consumer's Guide To Mortgage Lock-Ins*
✓ *A Consumer's Guide To Mortgage Settlement Costs*
✓ *A Consumer's Guide To Mortgage Refinancing*
✓ *Consumer Handbook on Adjustable Rate Mortgages*
✓ *Consumer Handbook to Credit Protection Laws*
✓ *A Guide to Business Credit for Women, Minorities and Small Business*
✓ *Home Mortgages, Understanding the Process and Your Right to Fair Lending*
✓ *How To File a Consumer Complaint about a Bank*
✓ *Keys to Vehicle Leasing*
✓ *Making Deposits: When Will Your Money Be Available*
✓ *SHOP: The Card You Pick Can Save You Money*
✓ *When Your Home Is On the Line: What You Should Know about Home Equity Lines of Credit*

Free from: Publications Services, MS-127, Board of Governors of the Federal Reserve System, Washington, DC 20551; 202-452-3244; Fax: 202-728-5886;
{www.bog.frb.fed.us/pubs/order.htm}.

HOW BAD IS YOUR INSURANCE COMPANY?

There are state insurance offices that will rate all the insurance companies in the state by the amount of complaints filed against them. For example, here are the three worst private passenger automobile insurance companies from Missouri's Department of Insurance 1994-1996 Complaint Index. The number 100 is normal. Higher is bad and lower is good.

- Atlanta Casualty Co.   628
- Metropolitan Property & Casualty
  Insurance Co.   248
- Gateway Insurance Co.   247

This information is obviously very helpful when choosing an insurance company or an HMO. You don't want to sign on with an insurance company that has people standing in line waiting to complain. Contact your state insurance office listed in the Appendix to see if they rate companies.

Investigate A Company Before You Invest

http://www.sec. gov/edgarhp.htm

How To Get the Cheapest/Best Insurance Policy?

If you are a single female in St. Louis with a 1995 Ford F250 2WD, you can get a standard auto insurance policy from United Services Automobile Association for $439, or pay $1698 from American Family Mutual. The rates for 10 different companies are analyzed by the Missouri Department of Insurance, P.O. Box 690, Jefferson City,  MO 65102; 800-726-7390; {www. insurance.state.mo. us/consumer/index.html}.

A single person, living in Baltimore looking for comprehensive standard health benefit plan, can pay $145 a month under a Kaiser HMO, or $191 with a company called PHN-HMO, Inc. The rates for 15 HMO plans are analyzed by Maryland Insurance Administration, 501 St. Paul Place, Baltimore, MD 21202; 800-492-6116; {www.gacc.com/mia/}.

Company by company comparisons and individual consultation is available to help you purchase an insurance policy. Insurance companies have to file all their rate information with the state government, so analysts at the state insurance commissioner's office can help find the right plan for you. Contact your state insurance office listed in the Appendix to see what they have to offer.

GET EVEN
With A Nasty Insurance Company

Missouri helps its residents collect over $5 million a year from insurance companies that don't treat their people right. And they don't charge a dime to do it.

If you have a complaint against an action taken by an insurance company, don't call a lawyer. Call your state insurance commissioner's office. They are more powerful than a lawyer because they can put an insurance company out of business. See the state-by-state listing in the Appendix for your State Insurance Commissioner's Office.

Free Help Fighting a High
ELECTRIC BILL
Or Stopping A TURN-OFF

The state utility commissions can help you fight high gas or electric bills. Some will even come out and make sure that your meter is not over charging you.

They don't have money to pay for your bills, but they can negotiate payment arrangements with the company for you or suggest non-profit organizations that may have emergency funds to help. For example Maryland suggests the Fuel Fund for Central Maryland or the Maryland Energy Assistance program.

The office can also force the utility not

Check For A $100 Heating Bill Tax Credit

The state of Michigan offers a home heating bill tax credit (that means you pay less in taxes) for people who are low income, receiving public assistance or unemployment.

Call your state department of taxation to learn about tax credits available to you. Michigan Department of Treasury, Lansing, MI 48956; 800-487-7000; {www.treas.state.mi.us/formspub/forms/indtax/MCR717.pdf}.

to cut off your service because of medical emergencies or cold weather. Contact your state utility commission listed in the Appendix for further assistance.

$200 To Pay Your Phone Bill

The Salvation Army's Universal Telephone Assistance Program provides up to $200 to continue or restore telephone services. While the service is available to persons with limited income, expenses compared to income are evaluated on a case by case basis to ensure telephone access is available for emergencies, medical appointments and other needs.

Universal Telephone Assistance Program

For information or to apply, consult your telephone directory for the local Salvation Army office or contact Salvation Army National Headquarters, 615 Slaters Lane, P.O. Box 269, Alexandria, VA 22313; 703-684-5500; Fax: 703-684-3478; {www.salvationarmy.org}.

Free Voice Mail

If you are unemployed and the phone company cut off your phone, how does a potential employer get in touch with you? Free voice mail.

You can get set up with your own personalized greeting, as well as get a security code and instructions on how you can retrieve your messages 24 hours a day. The program is available in over 27 cities and is growing.

See if you're eligible for your area by contacting Community Technology Institute, P.O. Box 61385, Seattle, WA 98121; 206-441-7872; Fax: 206-441-4784; {www.cvm.org/home.html}.

GET AN $84 REDUCTION ON YOUR TELEPHONE BILL

Link-Up and *Lifeline* are two government programs that offers up to $84 a year in discounts on your monthly bill and a 50% reduction for your hook-up service, or $30 which ever is less. These programs have income requirements that vary from state to state.

Ask your phone company about them or contact your state Utility Commissioner listed in the Appendix or Federal Communications Commission, 1919 M Street, NW, Washington, DC 20554; 888-CALL-FCC; {www.fcc.gov}.

"Ticked Off" by Nasty Dry Cleaners, Accountants, Pest Control Operators, Pharmacists, Real Estate Brokers, Lawyers, Etc., Etc., Etc.?

It seems that everyone nowadays needs a license to do business. Maybe because it's a good way for the state to raise money and for professionals to limit the competition.

But licensing is good for consumers. Your state licensing office is a good place to turn to when someone gives you a bad time. No one in business wants to mess with a government regulator because if they mess up, they could wind up out of business. The state licensing office allows them to do business in the state, so it's a powerful office.

Top 10 Scams

The following are the top 10 scams identified by the State of California Department of Consumer Affairs

1. Sweepstakes
2. Travel Scams
3. Gemstones
4. Recovery Rooms - Get Your Money Back From Another Scam
5. Business Opportunities
6. Charitable Solicitations
7. Advance Fee Loans
8. Toner Rooms - Great Deals On Office Supplies
9. Work At Home
10. Credit Repair

Next time you have trouble with a professional or local business, see if they require a license from the state to do business. Contact your state licensing office listed in the Appendix.

Don't Let Your Ex Destroy Your Credit

If you have recently been through a divorce — or are contemplating one — you may want to look closely at issues involving credit. You may discover unanticipated problems.

On joint charge accounts, both spouses are responsible for all debts incurred. In fact, even if the divorce decree states that your ex is responsible for paying off the balance on the credit cards, if he neglects to do so, you are still responsible for paying and your credit will suffer accordingly if those debts are left unpaid. An important tip is to make sure that any joint accounts or accounts in which your former spouse was an authorized user be closed.

Women Make 80% of Consumer Decisions

Source: Center for Policy Alternative
www.cfpa.org/publications/index.html

For more information on how you can protect your credit rating, request the free publication *Credit and Divorce* by contacting Public Reference, Room 130, Federal Trade Commission, Washington, DC 20580; 202-326-2222; 877-FTC-HELP; {www.ftc.gov}.

It's Illegal To Be Denied Credit Because You're a Woman?

Each year, many women are denied credit because they cannot prove themselves good credit risks. A good credit history is the way most companies predict your future success in using credit.

Your payment on credit cards, charge accounts, installment loans, and other credit accounts is your "track record." It gives a creditor evidence that you are a good risk. But what are your rights and what are easier ways for you to obtain credit?

In the publication, *Women and Credit Histories*, you can find out about the Equal Credit Opportunity Act and the Fair Credit Reporting Act that ensure your rights under the law. If you've never had credit in your own name, a "no file" report can cause your application to be rejected. A newly married woman may have the same problem if she changes her name.

There are steps you can take to fill an empty file with your past credit history or to build the file with new information. You can even learn the questions to ask if you have been denied credit.

For your free copy, contact Public Reference, Room 130, Federal Trade Commission, Washington, DC 20580; 202-326-2222, 877-FTC-HELP; {www.ftc.gov}.

Credit For Seniors

Securing credit is as important for older Americans, as it is for younger. Yet, older consumers and particularly older women may find they have special problems with credit.

For example, if you've paid with cash all your life, you may find it difficult to open a credit account because you have "no credit history." If you now are living on a lower salary or pension, it might be harder to obtain a loan because you have "insufficient income." Or, if your spouse dies, creditors may try to close credit accounts that you and your spouse once shared.

Uncover ways to apply for credit, check your credit history, learn what can happen if a spouse should die, and more. For your copy of *Credit and Older Americans*, contact Public Reference, Room 130, Federal Trade Commission, Washington, DC 20580; 202-326-2222, 877-FTC-HELP; {www.ftc.gov}.

$800 FOOD MONEY

You don't get the cash, but you do get it in the form of
Food Stamps. The Food Stamp
Program was designed to help low-
income families buy the food
they need to stay healthy and
productive.

The amount of Food Stamps
you get each month is
determined by the number of
people in your family and by the
household income. The average benefit is about $71
dollars a month, but a 4-person household could get up to
$408 a month. There are obviously income requirements
you must meet.

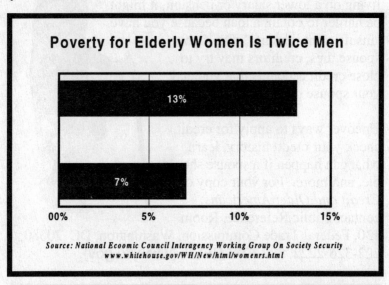

Poverty for Elderly Women Is Twice Men

13%

7%

00%   5%   10%   15%

Source: National Ecoomic Council Interagency Working Group On Society Security
www.whitehouse.gov/WH/New/html/womenrs.html

To apply for the Program, look in the blue pages of your telephone book under "Food Stamps," "Social Services," or "Public Assistance." You can also find more information by contacting U.S. Department of Agriculture, Food and Nutrition Service, 3101 Park Ctr. Dr., Park Office Center Bldg., Alexandria, VA 22302; 703-305-2276; {www.fns.usda.gov/fsp}.

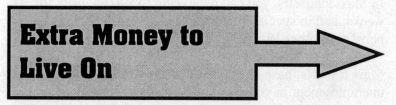

Extra Money to Live On

Struggling to pay bills because you or your child are disabled? Supplemental Security Income (SSI) provides funds to individuals who are 65 or older, or blind, or have a disability and who don't own much or have a lot of income.

SSI isn't just for adults. Monthly checks can go to disabled and blind children. There are income requirements you must meet and you or your child's disability will be screened. But it could mean an extra $400 a month and that could help a great deal!

For more information, contact Social Security Administration, Office of Public Inquiries, 6401 Security Blvd., Room 4-C-5 Annex, Baltimore, MD 21235; 800-772-1213; {www.ssa.gov}.

Social Security Administration

{www.ssa.gov}

Money When You're Out Of Work

In Massachusetts, you can receive up to $402 a week for 30 weeks, and in special circumstances they will extend the benefits another 18 weeks.

Mass lay-offs, base closings, trade agreements, and high unemployment in your state, all affect your ability to find and keep a job. If you are out of work, take advantage of unemployment insurance. This is the government's first line of defense against the ripple effects of unemployment.

Getting It Free At Check Out

Consumer studies show that checkout scanners can have error rates up to 9% of the time. Some store will simply adjust the price while others will offer you the product free if a checkout error occurs. Check out the facts. Free copy of Making Sure the Scanned Price is Right from Consumer Response Center, Federal Trade Commission, CRC-240, Washington, DC 20580; 877-FTC-HELP; {www.ftc.gov}.

All states are required to provide benefits up to 26 weeks and some extend them further. If your state has very high unemployment, you may be eligible for 13 additional weeks of compensation. If you lost your job because of an increase in imports, you may qualify to have your benefits extended up to an extra 52 weeks if you are in a job-retraining program.

Your weekly benefit amount depends upon your past wages within certain minimum and maximum limits that vary from state to state. Many states also will add additional funds depending upon the number of dependents. If you are denied benefits, learn about the appeal process, as your chances of winning are good.

For more information, contact your state Unemployment Insurance office listed in the Appendix.

$500 For Seniors and Disabled

The state of Pennsylvania offers up to $500 for seniors and people with disabilities who pay property taxes or rent. If you live in Pennsylvania, contact Department of Aging, 555 Walnut St., 5th Floor, Harrisburg, PA 17101; 717-783-1549. If you live elsewhere, contact your state Office on Aging listed in the Appendix, or your state Department of Revenue.

Walk away or hang up when you hear the following:

..... "Sign now or the price will increase;"

..... "You have been specially selected...;"

..... "You have won...;"

..... "All we need is your credit card (or bank account) number--for identification only;"

..... "All you pay for is postage, handling, taxes...;"

..... "Make money in your spare time-- guaranteed income...;"

..... "We really need you to buy magazines (a water purifier, a vacation package, office products) from us because we can earn 15 extra credits...;"

..... "I just happen to have some leftover paving material from a job down the street...;"

..... "Be your own boss! Never work for anyone else again. Just send in $50 for your supplies and...;"

..... "A new car! A trip to Hawaii! $2,500 in cash! Yours, absolutely free! Take a look at our...;"

..... "Your special claim number entitles you to join our sweepstakes...;" or

..... "We just happen to be in your area and have toner for your copy machine at a reduced price."

FINDING INFO
ABOUT A COMPANY

Before you work for, or do business with, a company, you can find out a lot about its financial condition as well as how it treats people from a number of public and private sources. If you are interviewing for a job, you will sound like an expert by gathering information from all of these sources.

☎ ***Better Business Bureau (BBB)*** is a private non-profit organization supported by business and professional groups. It provides Business Reports that tell how long a company has been in business, complaint patterns and government enforcement activities. BBB also has information on consumer warnings, dispute resolution, scam alerts, and consumer buying guides. Look in the phone directory for the office nearest you, or contact Council of Better Business Bureaus, 4200 Wilson Blvd., Suite 800, Arlington, VA 22203; 703-276-0100; {www.bbb.org}.

☎ ***State Attorney General's Office*** is the primary consumer advocate for the state against fraudulent practices by businesses operating within the state. So, if the company you are investigating is selling consumer services or products, it would be worth the effort to check with this office. Look in the Appendix for your state Attorney General's Office.

☎ ***The Security and Exchange Commission*** has information on companies that have their securities traded publicly. The registration and financial statements include a description of the company's properties and businesses, description of the securities offered for sale, information about the management of the company, and certified financial statements. For more information contact U.S. Securities and Exchange Commission, Office of Consumer Affairs, 450 5th St., NW, MS 11-2, Washington, DC 20549; 800-SEC-0330 (publications only); 202-942-7040; {www.sec.gov}.

> **County Cooperative Extension Service Women Run Businesses Index**
>
> **The Bloomberg Women.Com Index is an index of publicly-traded U.S. companies run by female chief executive offices and/or chairmen.**
>
> **On the web at: www.womenswire.com/ 30index/companyIndex. html**

☎ ***Your State Office of Corporations*** can provide you with information on companies incorporated within the state. You can find out corporate names, date of incorporation, names of officers and directors and their addresses, location of the company, and more. See the Appendix for a listing of State Office of Corporations.

☎ ***Your local library and local newspapers*** have a wealth of information dealing with companies in their area. You can search the newspapers or magazines for relevant articles, and the library often has a section of local interest materials.

Free Help In Writing A Will

Estate planning is not something that people often relish doing, but it is extremely important. It is difficult enough when a loved one dies, but then to have to search through papers trying to find information about insurance, or investments  is often too much. When children are involved, estate planning is essential. Who will take care of the children and how can you secure their financial future?

Your local Cooperative Extension Service often offers classes or publications on estate planning. The time to plan ahead is now. Look in the blue pages of your phone book for the nearest Cooperative Extension office, as they are in almost every county across the country. The Appendix has a listing of the main state office to help you in your search.

Learn To Manage Your Own Finances

The YWCA of the U.S.A. has launched a national partnership with Citigroup to provide low-income women with the business and technical know-how to achieve financial security and independence. The Program will focus on developing your financial management and asset development skills, and providing training on PCs and on-line banking software. This program will help you to better manage your household budgets, and will give you skills that are in demand in the workplace.

The program will pilot at the YWCA of Greater Miami and Dade County, in Miami; the YWCA of New Castle County, in Wilmington, DE; the YWCA of Rochester and Monroe, in Rochester, NY; and the YWCA of the National Capital Area, in Washington, D.C. Contact: YWCA of the U.S.A., Empire State Building, Suite 301, 350 Fifth Avenue, New York, NY 10118; 212-273-7800; Fax: 212-465-2281; {www.ywca.org}.

$700 Discount
On Your Utility Bills

The legislature in Massachusetts passed a law giving
discounts up to $700 on heating bills for families making
up to $30,000, along with up to 40% discount on electric
bills, $108 off telephone bills, and $100 off oil
bills. It's in the Massachusetts Budget for
FY 99 (Line Item 4403-2110). Also:

✿ **Mason County** in the state of
   Washington offers a utility bill
   discount of $13.00 a month for
   seniors making less than $18,000, and
   disabled people at 125% of poverty.
   Contact Public Utility District #3, 307 W.
   Cota St., Shelton, WA 98584; 800-424-
   5555; {www.olywa.net/maspud3/
   bill.htm}.

✿ **Phoenix, Arizona** offers discounts on utility bills,
   discounts on phone bills and even help paying utility
   deposits and heating repairs for low-income residents
   through the Arizona Public Service Energy Support
   Program, P.O. Box 6123-086Z, Phoenix, AZ 85008;
   800-582-5706; {www.azstarnet.com/azinfo/
   ag997.htm}.

✿ **Ameritech in Illinois** gives a 100% discount on
   connection charges and $5.25 off the monthly bill to

low-income residents. To sign up, call Ameritech at 800-244-4444; {www.ameritech.com/media/releases/releases-1630.html}.

✿ **Ohio** offers reduced or free phone hook up service and possibly $8.00 a month off your phone bill for low-income residents. Contact Public Utilities Commission, 180 E. Broad St., Columbus, OH 43215; 800-686-7826; {www.puc.state.oh.us}.

✿ **Pennsylvania Bell Atlantic** offers free telephone hook up and $9.00 monthly discount to low-income residents through Lifeline and Universal Telephone Assistance Programs. To sign up, call 800-272-1006.

Contact your state's utilities office in the Appendix to find out about special discounts on your gas, electric, cable or telephone in your state.

Money Matters For the Single Parent

- *Consumer Protection When Selecting a Home Water Treatment System*
- *Should You Buy or Rent*
- *Credit Wise*
- *Manage Your Money To Get What You Want*
- *How and Ways To Save Money*

www.ces.ncsu.edu/depts/fcs/docs/index.html#strenghts

Stop Paying For Overpriced
Dial-a-Porn

All major phone companies have agreed with the Federal Communications Commission stand that if a customer complains about bill from a Dial-a-Porn company, the phone company will side with the consumer and not the Dial-a-Porn company.

This only works when the charge occurs on your bill for the first time. So, if you have any unauthorized calls to such numbers, call the phone company and get them removed. Not every local telephone company cooperates, but most do.

Free Hair Cuts and Coloring

By participating as a model for training classes at salons and cosmetology schools, you can receive quality services for free. Check your yellow pages for salons and schools in your area.

If you have trouble, you can contact Federal Communications Commission, Common Carrier Bureau, Informal Complaints & Inquiries Branch, Enforcement Division, Stop Code 1600A2, Washington, DC 20554; 888-CALL-FCC; {www.fcc.gov}.

What To Do, Before and After, Your Bank Does You Wrong

Before choosing a bank or credit union, check the institution's financial health. Request a copy of the bank's annual report, which will provide a great deal of information regarding a bank's stability and assets.

**National
Banks
Savings and
Loans
FDIC Insured**

Be sure to check out the bank's fees for services! ATM, maintenance, and checking account fees can vary widely from bank to bank. Almost all banks offer credit card services, and may waive the annual fee for those with savings at a certain level.

Different banks are governed by different agencies, but all take complaints and make efforts to assist customers. Your state Banking Commissioner handles complaints dealing with state chartered banks, and a listing can be found in the Appendix.

For banks with the "national" or "N.A." in its name:
Comptroller of the Currency
Compliance Management
U.S. Department of the Treasury
250 E St., SW
Washington, DC 20219
202-622-2000

800-613-6743
{www.occ.treas.gov}

For Savings and Loans:
Office of Thrift Supervision
U.S. Department of the Treasury
1700 G St., NW
Washington, DC 20552
202-906-6000
{www.ots.treas.gov}

For FDIC Insured:
Federal Deposit Insurance Corporation
Office of Consumer Affairs
550 17th St., NW, Room F-130
Washington, DC 20429
800-934-3342
{www.fdic.gov}

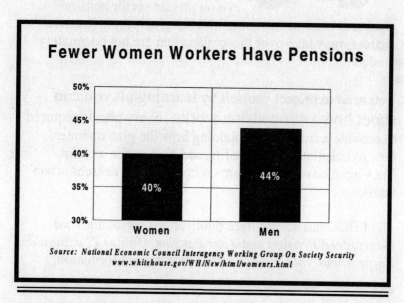

Fewer Women Workers Have Pensions

Source: *National Economic Council Interagency Working Group On Society Security*
www.whitehouse.gov/WH/New/html/womenrs.html

WHEN TO CALL IN THE

PENSION POLICE

You are putting in your years with the company, but you better make sure you will get what you are due when you retire.

Over 42 million workers and retirees are covered by employer-sponsored pension plans. The **Pension Benefit Guaranty Corporation (PBGC)** keeps an eye on private sector pension plans and in some instances involving corporate financial distress, may take over those plans that are not adequately funded.

You need to protect yourself by learning all you can about how your pension works. Every plan is required to provide a summary explaining how the plan operates, how to calculate your benefits, and how to file a claim. They even have information on how divorce decrees affect pensions.

The PBGC has several free publications including *Your Guaranteed Pension* and *Your Pension: Things You Should Know About Your Pension Plan.* For more information,

contact the Pension Benefit Guaranty Corporation, 1200 K
St., NW, Washington, DC 20005; 800-400-7242;
{www.pbgc.gov}.

Free Tax Help
With Your Pension

No need to pay an attorney money to interpret the
tax issues surrounding retirement and pension
plans. You can talk to the guys who wrote the
law!

The Internal Revenue Services operates a hotline
service that allows you to speak to tax attorneys
specializing in retirement and pension plan
issues. They are available Monday through
Thursday, from 1:30 p.m. to 3:30 p.m. (EST).

They can be reached at Employee Plans
Technical and Actuarial Division, Internal
Revenue Service, U.S. Department of Treasury,
Room 6550, CP:E:EP, 1111 Constitution Ave., NW,
Washington, DC 20224; 202-622-6074 or 6075.

 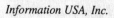

Free Help To Fight The IRS

If you are having problems dealing with the IRS, you don't have to fight the battle without reinforcements.

The Taxpayer Advocate administers the *Problem Resolution Program (PRP)* that has the authority to cut through red tape. They will keep you informed of your case's progress. PRP can usually help with delayed refunds, unanswered inquiries, and incorrect billing notices.

For more information, request Publication 1546, *How To Use The Problem Resolution Program of the IRS*. To get in contact with the program, call the IRS at 800-829-1040; {www.irs.gov}.

A Hot List of Tax Deductions For Seniors

We all feel like we pay, and we pay, and we pay. Now here is someone who is looking out for your needs for a change.

If you are a senior citizen or know someone who is, it is important to get a copy of a free publication titled, *Protecting Older Americans Against Overpayment of*

Income Taxes. Designed to ensure that older Americans claim every legitimate income tax deduction, exemption, and tax credit, this publication is very easy to understand and provides many examples and checklists.

Send a request on a postcard to Special Committee on Aging, U.S. Senate, Senate Dirksen Bldg. G31, Washington, DC 20510; 202-224-5364; {www.senate. gov/~aging}.

free Tax Help for Seniors

It is nice to get special treatment every now and then, and tax time is no exception.

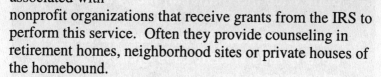

The Tax Counseling for the Elderly program was designed to provide free taxpayer assistance to those ages 60 and above. The staff usually consists of retired individuals associated with nonprofit organizations that receive grants from the IRS to perform this service. Often they provide counseling in retirement homes, neighborhood sites or private houses of the homebound.

For information on the Tax Counseling for the Elderly program near you, contact your local IRS office, call the hotline at 800-829-1040; {www.irs.gov}.

Beware Of Ads For Weight Loss

The Federal Trade Commission has brought nearly 140 enforcement actions against weight loss companies. Listed below are just some of the companies and products that have been caught by the long arm of the law for false advertising. Before you try a new dieting product or service get a free copy of "Facts About Weight Loss Products and Programs" and "Skinny on Dieting" from Consumer Response Center, Federal Trade Commission, CRC-240, Washington, DC 20580; 877-FTC-HELP; {www.ftc.gov}.

- Amerfit, Inc - Fat Burners and Fast Burners
- Dean Distributors - Food for Life Weight Management System and Cambridge Diet
- Slim America, Inc
- NordicTrack,Inc
- The Diet Workshop, Inc. settled with FTC on charges of deceptive advertising
- Body Wise International, Inc - Future Perfect, Right Choice AM
- Doctors Medical Weight Loss Centers, Inc.
- Beverly Hills Weight Loss Clinics International, Inc.
- Jenny Craig Weight Loss Program
- Weight Watchers International, Inc

Buy Your Safety First

Product safety is enormously important when deciding on a purchase. The Consumer Product Safety Commission has information on toy and bicycle safety, children's furniture, electrical and fire safety, and more.

The hotline can also inform you of recalled items and accepts complaints about specific products. Receiving similar complaints on a particular product may force the company to recall it.

For more information on products or publications, contact U.S. Consumer Product Safety Commission, Office of Information and Public Affairs, Washington, DC 20207; 800-638-2772; 301-504-0051 (fax-on-demand); {www.cpsc.gov}.

Volunteers Get a 50% Discount On Food

It's called the Self-Help and Resource Exchange (SHARE), and it distributes food at 50% discounts to 5,415 community-based organizations, which in turn give it to individuals. The only catch is that you have to volunteer your time in the community for at least 2 hours a month. You can coach little league or help fix up a playground.

To find a SHARE affiliate near you, contact SHARE, 6950 Friars Road, San Diego, CA 92108; 888-742-7372; Fax: 618-686-5185; {www.worldshare.org}.

Government Supported Agencies Offer Free Money And Help When You Don't Know Where To Turn

If you need emergency money to pay a bill, or for housing, training, health care, or just additional support, these organizations can be of service and they are likely to have an office near you. Although these are private organizations, they do receive a portion of their funds from your favorite Uncle Sam.

17% of Funeral Homes Violate Consumer Law

An investigation by the Federal Trade Commission of funeral homes in Grand Rapids, Michigan found that 7 out of 42 violated consumer pricing laws.

Get a free copy of "Funeral: A Consumer Guide" from Federal Trade Commission, Consumer Response Center, Room 130, 6th Street and Pa Ave, NW, Washington, DC 20580; 877-FTC-HELP; {www.ftc.gov}.

1) Community Action Agencies

Nearly 1,000 agencies around the country received funds from the U.S. Government's Community Services Block Grants to offer education, counseling, employment, training, food packages, vouchers, weatherization and utility assistance, life skills, affordable housing, transportation, furnishings, recreation, emergency services, information and referral services. To locate an agency serving your area, contact: National Association Of Community Action Agencies. 1100 17th St., NW, Washington, DC 20036; 202-265-7546; Fax: 202-265-8850; {www.nacaa.org}.

2) Catholic Charities

Over 14,000 local organizations offer a variety of services for many different communities including: child care, elderly services, emergency financial services, emergency shelter, food pantries, housing assistance, job training, out-of-home care, parenting education, youth services, rental assistance, utility assistance, and health care. For an office near you, contact Catholic Charities USA, 1731 King Street #200, Alexandria, VA 22314; 703-549-1390; Fax: 703-549-1656; {www.catholiccharitiesusa.org}.

3) Salvation Army

Families in need can receive a wide range of services including: utility assistance, transitional housing, emergency food, furnishings, Section 8 tenant counseling, counseling, rent or mortgage assistance, and even clothing.

Most services are for households who are below 150% of the poverty level (about $24,000 for family of 4). For an office near you, contact Salvation Army National Headquarters, 615 Slaters Lane, P.O. Box 269, Alexandria, VA 22313; 703-684-5500; Fax: 703-684-3478; {www.salvationarmy.org}.

FREE DIRECTORY/OPERATOR ASSISTANCE IF YOU HAVE A DISABILITY

Directory assistance can cost up to 95 cents per request and an additional 50 cents for the connection. To assist persons with visual, hearing, or other disabilities, local telephone companies offer directory and operator assistance exemptions.

Simply request and complete a form from the local telephone company and have your physician complete the appropriate section. When you return the form to the phone company, you'll be eligible for the exemptions. Contact the business office of your local telephone company.

GET EXTRA CASH FINDING LOST MONEY AND SURPLUS PROPERTY

Make $2,000 in 45 minutes. That's what the author, Mary Ann Martello, did when she searched state databases looking for old forgotten utility deposits and bank accounts set up by grandparents. Every state has an office that collects money in that state that has been abandoned, forgotten, or left unclaimed, including:

- ✓ Savings and checking accounts
- ✓ Uncashed payroll or cashiers checks
- ✓ Money orders and travelers checks
- ✓ Certificates of deposit
- ✓ Customer deposits or overpayment
- ✓ Paid up life insurance policies
- ✓ Health and accident insurance payments
- ✓ Uncashed death benefit checks
- ✓ Gift certificates and Christmas club accounts
- ✓ Stock and dividends
- ✓ Utility deposits
- ✓ Oil and gas royalty payments

The money could be a savings account that grandma set up for you when you were born. Or it could be a Christmas fund Great Aunt Rose contributed to before she passed away. Your father may have even had a safe deposit box he never told you existed.

According to reports, state agencies across the U.S. may be holding over $8 billion dollars in abandoned money. Although the rules vary from state to state, generally after two or more years without activity on an account (no deposits or withdrawals), the bank will try to contact you. If their efforts fail, the property is considered abandoned and transferred to the state of your last known address.

To locate funds, contact the unclaimed property office in the state (usually part of the state treasurer's department) where you or your benefactors have lived or conducted business. Most state agencies have websites, and many have searchable databases.

You can contact the National Association of Unclaimed Property Administrators, P.O. Box 7156, Bismarck, ND 58507; {www.unclaimed.org}. Not only does the website give you a listing of state offices, it also links you to those that have existing websites. A listing of state Unclaimed Property Offices is also listed in the Appendix.

Real Estate Property As Low As $500

Failed commercial banks often own businesses, land, or real estate that they must sell. Although a booklet of all available properties is not available, the Federal Deposit Insurance Corporation (FDIC) makes an effort to keep their website up-to-date showing available properties under the button, "**Asset Info**".

You can search the site for a specific location, business, price parameter, and more. A contact number is available for each listing. Look under *Special Sales, FDIC Bargain Properties*, for the deals that go as low as $500. Property sales are handled through each regional FDIC office.

For more information on asset sales, contact Federal Deposit Insurance Corporation, 550 17th St., NW, Washington, DC 20429; 800-934-FDIC; {www.fdic.gov}.

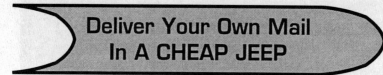

Deliver Your Own Mail In A CHEAP JEEP

Well, not the actual mail, but you could be seen touring your town in a postal jeep.

The U.S. Post Office sells used postal vehicles, including jeeps, sedans, trucks, buses, tractor-trailers, and more.

These vehicles are sold through the more than 200 vehicle maintenance facilities throughout the country. Contact your local post office to find out which vehicle maintenance facility serves your area. Vehicles are put up for sale, and occasionally, several facilities will get together and hold an auction.

For more information, contact Vehicle Maintenance Facility, U.S. Postal Service, 475 L'Enfant Plaza, SW, Washington, DC 20260.

Seized Property DO AGAIN

The U.S. Customs and Treasury Department confiscate seized property and then sell it at regularly scheduled auctions, held approximately every nine weeks, at sales centers across the United States. Examples of property offered for sale include cars, boats, airplanes, real estate, commercial real estate opportunities, carpets, electronics, industrial goods, jewelry, and wearing apparel.

Contact EG&G, 3702 Pender Dr., Suite 400, Fairfax, VA 22030; 703-273-7373; {www.treas.gov/auctions/customs}.

Toys, Books, Videos, CDs, TVs, VCRs, & Infomercial Products

Did you ever wonder what happens to undeliverable mail? The U.S. Postal Service auctions it to willing buyers. Everything from the Christmas sweater you never received from grandma to the latest infomercial diet craze that never found its rightful dieter. Some people attend these auctions and collect bundles of items that they then resell for a profit at flea markets, garage sales, or retail stores.

Contact the Mail Recovery Centers listed below to learn more about the auctions in your area. You can be put on a mailing list to receive advance notice about the auctions. These auctions are held every six to eight weeks, with lots of similar goods being offered together. Although what is available varies from auction to auction,

you will generally find anything that can be mailed — from
CDs to televisions and books to jewelry and clothes. Call
ahead to find out about payment procedures. Some require
cash only, while others allow checks for those pre-
approved.

Central Region
U.S. Postal Service Mail Recovery Center, 443 E. Fillmore
Ave., St. Paul, MN 55017-9617; 612-293-3083. Includes
Minnesota, Michigan, Wisconsin, North Dakota, South
Dakota, Nebraska, Iowa, Illinois, Northern New Jersey,
New Hampshire, Maine, Vermont, Rhode Island,
Massachusetts, Kansas, Missouri, Connecticut, and New
York.

Western Region
U.S. Postal Service Mail Recovery Center, 390 Main St.,
4th Floor, San Francisco, CA 94105; 415-543-1826.
Includes Alaska, Oregon, Idaho, California, Washington,
Nevada, Utah, Arizona, New Mexico, part of Texas,
Hawaii, Wyoming, Colorado, Montana, Guam, and Samoa.

Southern Region
U.S. Postal Service Mail Recovery Center, 730 Great
Southwest Parkway, Atlanta, GA 30336; 404-344-1625;
Includes Georgia, Florida, Louisiana, Tennessee, Arkansas,
Mississippi, Oklahoma, part of Texas, Alabama,
Mississippi, Virgin Islands, Puerto Rico, Pennsylvania,
Southern New Jersey, Maryland, Delaware, Ohio,
Kentucky, Indiana, Virginia, West Virginia, North
Carolina, and South Carolina.

Crime Does Pay:
Get Discount Boats, Limos, or Airplanes From The Bad Guys

The U.S. Marshals Service offers property for sale to the public that has been forfeited under laws enforced by the U.S. Department of Justice, the Drug Enforcement Administration, Federal Bureau of Investigation, and the Immigration and  Naturalization Service. More than 6,000 items of forfeited real and personal property are sold annually with gross sales of $195 million.

The property offered for sale consists of residential and commercial real estate, business establishments, and a wide range of personal property such as motor vehicles, boats, aircraft, jewelry, art, antiques, collectibles, and livestock. The U.S. Marshals Service does not maintain a list of forfeited property for sale, nor a mailing list to notify prospective buyers of upcoming sales. The sales are handled through contract service providers.

The U.S. Marshals Service website provides information on the company/agency names, locations, and telephone numbers. This listing is also available by fax at 202-307-9777. For those without a fax or computer, the listing is available for 50 cents from the Consumer Information Center.

To learn how to order a copy, call the Federal Information Center at 800-688-9889. For more information on the sales, contact U.S. Marshals Service, Seized Assets Division, U.S. Department of Justice, 600 Army-Navy Dr., Arlington, VA 22202; 202-307-9237; {www.usdoj.gov/marshals/nsl.html}.

The Gov't Buys For $1.00 And Sells To You For 2¢

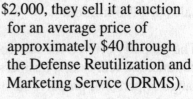

If the U.S. Department of Defense buys a computer for $2,000, they sell it at auction for an average price of approximately $40 through the Defense Reutilization and Marketing Service (DRMS).

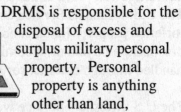

DRMS is responsible for the disposal of excess and surplus military personal property. Personal property is anything other than land, buildings, and real estate. It includes items such as tools, office furniture, camping equipment, appliances, furniture, computers, electronics, and much more.

DRMS offers four types of sales. Businesses can buy property in large quantities through the DRMS National Sales Office in Battle Creek, Michigan. Property is sold by auction, sealed bid sales, and in special circumstances, negotiated sales. These sales include such items as aircraft parts, ships, hazardous property, electronics, scrap bearing and hardware, and other property having wide commercial application.

National Sales Office
Regional Sales
Retail Sales Outlet Stores
www.drms.com

Regional Sales offer deals for smaller businesses by selling smaller quantities of property through auction or sealed bids. This property includes vehicles and vehicular parts, furniture, appliances, material handling equipment, tools, and other property of interest.

DRMS also maintains DRMS Retail Sales Outlet Stores, where property is offered at a fixed price. You can also purchase items via the World Wide Web. Sales schedules, catalogs, and bid submissions information can be found on the website.

For more information on any of these items, contact the Defense Reutilization Marketing Service (DRMS), Federal Center, 74 N. Washington, Battle Creek, MI 49107; 800-GOVT-BUY; 888-352-9333; {www.drms.com}.

Checking Into Your Retirement Check

Did you work some place twenty years ago that is no longer in business? What about an old pension fund that was in financial trouble?

Don't give up. The Pension Benefit Guaranty Corporation (PBGC) monitors and sometimes takes over private sector-defined benefit plans. These are traditional pensions that promise a specified monthly benefit at retirement.

The PBGC operates a Pension Search Directory to find people who are owed pensions from the plans PBGC now controls. You can search by name, company worked for, or by state where the company is/was headquartered. In the last eighteen months, the directory found 1,400 people owed more that $4 million with the average benefit being

$4,100. There is still $13 million just waiting to be claimed.

For more information, contact Pension Benefit Guaranty Corporation, Pension Search Program, 1200 K St., NW, Washington, DC 20005; 800-326-LOST; {www.pbgc.gov}.

MISSING MORTGAGE MONEY MEANS MORE MOULA$

If you ever purchased a home using a HUD/FHA insured mortgage, you may be eligible for a refund on part of your insurance premium or a share of the earnings. There are certain requirements you have to have met.

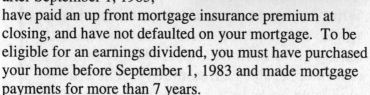

To be eligible for a premium refund, you must have purchased your home after September 1, 1983, have paid an up front mortgage insurance premium at closing, and have not defaulted on your mortgage. To be eligible for an earnings dividend, you must have purchased your home before September 1, 1983 and made mortgage payments for more than 7 years.

Many people known as "Tracers" are locating this money for people and charging a finder's fee. HUD does state that people can do this for free, but many people are unaware that they are due a refund! You can search by a person's name or case number on the website.

For more information, contact U.S. Department of Housing and Urban Development, P.O. Box 23699, Washington, DC 20026; 800-697-6967; {www.hud.gov/wsrefund/html/page1.html}.

The IRS Has "GOOD NEWS" For 100,000 Taxpayers

Seems impossible, doesn't it? Close to 100,000 taxpayers are due a refund, yet their checks have been returned to the tune of over $62.6 million. The average check is $627.

What do you do if you think you or someone you love is missing a check? Contact the IRS toll-free hotline at 800-829-1040 and talk to a customer service representative. They can plug your name in the computer and see if your name pops up on their screen.

165,000 Unclaimed Social Security Checks

Social Security checks go out to 92% of those over the age of 65, so once in awhile a check may go astray. If you think you are missing some checks, or if you find un-negotiated checks, contact your local Social Security Administration office. They can reissue the checks to the person or to the estate.

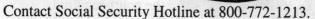

Social Security assures me that this occurs rarely, as they send out 612 million payments with only 165,000 checks that were not endorsed. Contact Social Security Hotline at 800-772-1213.

The same deal holds true with the Veterans Affairs Administration. If you feel you are missing checks or find checks that have not been endorsed, contact your local Veterans Affairs office so that checks can be reissued to you or to the estate of a loved one. Contact Veterans Affairs at 800-827-1000.

FREE MONEY TO PAY LEGAL FEES, FREE LAWYERS, AND FREE LEGAL HELP

Money For Battered Women To Fight Their Legal Problems

Legal Aid For Abused Women (LAAW) provides legal aid for women and men trying to remove themselves from an abusive situation. Legal aid is often necessary to secure restraining orders, obtain child support, settle child custody issues, initiate separation and divorce proceedings, and collect the court-required documentation of the emotional, sexual and physical abuse.

LAAW provides a revolving fund for legal aid where recipients pay back or if they can't, they can volunteer their time to assist others affected by domestic violence. Legal aid is provided regardless of race, nationality, gender, or social status.

Contact: Legal Aid for Abused Women, 3524 S. Utah St., Arlington, VA 22206; 703-837-8993; Fax: 703 820-7968; {http://ourworld.compuserve.com/homepages/ LAAW/}.

Free Legal Help If Your Child Is Suspended or Expelled From School

"Zero Tolerance" and other school system disciplinary practices can place your child's education in jeopardy if you are not aware of your rights. Your first meeting with the principal on such matters can actually serve as a trial for your child's future.

The School House Legal Services of Baltimore, Maryland provides free attorneys and paralegals to represent Maryland families in

School House Legal Services

these matters. Maryland has an income limit for representation that is about $30,000 for a family of four, but information about the process is free.

If you don't live in Maryland, contact your local Legal Services Office or your State Department of Education listed in the Appendix for more information and help. School House Legal Services can be reached at 34 Market Place, 5th Floor, Baltimore, MD 21202; 410-547-9200; Fax: 410-547-8690; {www.acy.org}.

Get Rid of Neighborhood Troublemakers Without the Police, For FREE

Some states allow local community groups to get tenants or property owners thrown out of the neighborhood — under civil laws, not criminal laws — if they are involved with drugs or are a nuisance to the community. It's easier to enforce a civil law than a criminal law. Which is probably why O.J. Simpson lost his civil trial, but won his criminal trial.

Community Law Center in Maryland

The Community Law Center in Maryland provides free legal assistance to communities in Maryland to enforce these laws. Their services are free to non-profit community groups who seek to rid their neighborhood of troublemakers.

To find out if your community has similar services, contact your state Attorney General's office listed in the Appendix. The Community Law Center can be reached at 2500 Maryland Avenue, Baltimore, MD 21218; 410-366-0922; Fax: 410-366-7763; {clawc@aol.com}.

Free Legal Help With Family, Consumer, Housing, Income, Work, Children and Senior Citizen Issues

Legal Services Corporation is a collection of over 269 government supported local offices that provide free legal services in their area. Over 5000 attorneys and paralegals are available to individuals and families that are under certain income limits. The maximum income can be up to

10,000 Lawyers That Work For Free

If your income is less than $32,000 (for a family of 4), it's worth checking out the pro bono legal services that are available in your state. And even if your income is more, it's worth checking because some of these services have flexible requirements depending upon your situation and the problem involved. Every year tens of thousands of lawyers volunteer their services to people who need help with almost any kind of problem.

For a listing of pro bono organizations in your state, contact your state bar association listed in your state capitol. The state capitol operator listed in the Appendix can provide you with a number, or you can contact: American Bar Association 750 N. Lake Shore Dr., Chicago, IL 60611; 312-988-5000; {www.abanet.org/legalservices/probono}.

$30,000 for a family of four, or even more depending on certain financial obligations.

To find an office near you, contact your state capitol operator listed in the Appendix and ask for the Legal Services Office or contact: Legal Services Corporation, 750 First Street NE, 10th Floor, Washington, DC 20002; 202-336-8800; {www.lsc.gov}.

Help For Families Fighting For Veterans Benefits

Through low cost publications, training courses and other services, for 25 years the **National Veterans Legal Services Program** has been helping veterans get their due. Current publications include: *VA Claims, Agent Orange,* and *Veterans Family Benefits.*

Contact: National Veterans Legal Services Program, P.O. Box 753, Waldorf, MD 20604-0753; 301- 638-1327; 800-688-5VET; Fax 301-843-0159; {www.nvlsp.org}.

FREE LAWYERS WILL FIGHT FOR YOUR RIGHTS

We've all heard of the *American Civil Liberties Union (ACLU)*. They have over 300 offices around the country and handle close to 6,000 cases a year.

The ACLU has more than 60 staff attorneys who collaborate with at least 2,000 volunteer attorneys in handling cases. They have appeared before the Supreme Court more than any other organization except the U.S. Department of Justice. If you feel that your civil liberties have been violated, they may take your case.

> **If you feel that your civil liberties have been violated, they may take your case.**

The kinds of issues they are most currently active in include: woman's rights, reproductive freedom, workplace rights, AIDS, arts censorship, capital punishment, children's rights, education reform, lesbian and gay rights, immigrants' rights, national security, privacy and technology, prisoners' rights, and voting rights.

Contact the local ACLU office listed in your telephone directory or the main office website can provide you with a local contact: ACLU - American Civil Liberties Union, 125 Broad Street, 18th Floor, New York, NY 10004-2400; {www.aclu.org/action/chapters.html}.

FREE LEGAL HELP WITH SEXUAL HARASSMENT AT WORK OR SCHOOL

Free assistance to women and girls who are facing sex, or race discrimination, sexual harassment at work or at school, pregnancy, discrimination, or problems with family medical leave and other employment issues related specifically to women. The staff offers information and answers questions, and occasionally can draft "demand" letters, demanding that an employer or other person or organization stop doing something. In some circumstances, they can help you pursue internal grievance or

Your Family's Rights Under the New Fair Housing Law: Protecting Families with Children from Discrimination

This book is written by one of the country's leading advocates for children's rights. It shows how to tell if families with children have been discriminated against in housing and what to do about it! A great guide for parents, as well as advocates who work with families.1990 (ISBN: 0-938008-74-9. $4.75, plus $2.00 postage). Contact: Children's Defense Fund, CDF Publications, 25 E Street NW, Washington, DC 20001; 202-628-8787; Fax: 202-628-8333; {www.childrensdefense.org}.

administrative procedures, and in some precedent-setting cases, they will provide legal representation.

Contact: Equal Rights Advocates, 1663 Mission Street, Suite 550, San Francisco, CA 94103; 415-621-0672; Fax: 415-621-6744; Advice and Counseling Line: 800-839-4ERA; {www.equalrights.org}.

Help For You Or Your Child With A Learning Or Physical Disability

The disability laws not only cover people with disabilities that everyone can see. It's also for children who aren't getting the education they need from the local school, or for the cancer patient who feels discriminated against at work.

A free hotline will help you learn about your rights, help you enforce them, and will even handle some high impact legal cases. Contact: Disability Rights Education and Defense Fund, Inc., 2212 Sixth Street, Berkeley, CA 94710; 510-644-2555 V/TTY; Fax: 510-841-8645; {edf@dredf.org}; {www.dredf.org}.

FREE LEGAL HELP FOR BREAST CANCER PATENTS

If you are a breast cancer patient living in California, you maybe eligible to receive free legal assistance on issues such as:

★ Debt collection problems with hospital and doctor bills.

★ Barriers to access to diagnosis and treatment.

★ Negotiations with insurance carriers for coverage and payment options.

★ Housing discrimination.

★ Employment discrimination.

★ Temporary guardianships or modification of custody arrangements.

If you don't live in California, ask them if they are aware of similar services in your area.

Breast Cancer Legal Project

Contact: Breast Cancer Legal Project, California Women's Law Center, 3460 Wilshire Blvd., Suite 1102, Los Angeles, CA 90010; 213-637-9900; Fax: 213-637-9909; {cwcl@cwcl.org}; {www.cwlc.org/BCLC.intro.html}.

FREE WOMEN'S LAW CENTERS

Rich or poor, women in **Maryland** can get free telephone help in filling out the forms to represent themselves in family court matters that are simple and uncontested. The hotline number is *800-845-8550* and it operates Tuesdays and Thursdays 9:30 am to 4:30 pm. Or women can call the hotline for information on family law issues, such as, how to obtain a separation, child custody, child support, and how to escape domestic violence. Contact: The Women's Law Center of Maryland, Inc., 305 West Chesapeake Ave., Towson, MD 21205; 410-321-8761; {info-flc@ wlcmd.org}; {www.wlcmd.org}.

Women in the state of **Washington** can call a free legal *Information and Referral line* that is staffed with attorneys and paralegals to respond to questions about family law or employment. They

Free Legal Assistance For Domestic Violence Problems

Seven days a week, 24 hours a day, you can call the hotline and not only get access to sources that will solve your immediate problem, but also get information and sources in your area that can explain your legal options and get you through the legal process. Contact: National Domestic Violence Hotline, P.O. Box 161810, Austin, TX 78716; 800-799-SAFE; TTY: 800-787-3224; {ndvh@ ndvh.org}; {www.ndvh.org}.

also can receive legal rights publications including *Sexual Harassment in Employment and Education*; *Family Law in Washington State: Your Rights and Responsibilities*; and *Grandparents Raising Grandchildren; A Legal Guide for Washington State*. You can also attend free legal workshops, or receive help in filling out legal forms, and free legal consultations in domestic violence cases. Contact: Northwest Women's Law Center, 119 South Main St., Suite 410, Seattle WA 98104-2515; 206 682 9552; Fax: 206 682 9556; Legal Information and Referral: 206-621-7691; {NWWLC@nwwlc.org}; {www.nwwlc.org}.

Free Help With Welfare Rights

Over 157 local organizations around the country fight for the rights of low-income people on welfare. These organizations can be a good place to turn to insure that you are getting the proper benefits, and for knowing your rights in dealing with the bureaucracy.

Welfare Law Center

You can contact your local social services agency to locate an office near you or the website for the Welfare Law Center that contains a directory of all the organizations. Contact: Welfare Law Center, 275 Seventh Ave., Suite 1205, New York, NY 10001; 212-633-6967; {dirk@ welfarelaw.org}; {www.lincproject. org/lid/lid.html}.

Free Legal Help To Fight For Your Home Schooling Rights

The Home School Legal Defense Association (HSLDA) provides legal help for members on home schooling issues. Families receive legal consultation by letter and phone, and representation for negotiations with local officials, and court proceedings.

HSLDA also takes the offensive, filing actions to protect members against government intrusion and to establish legal precedent. On occasion, HSLDA will handle precedent-setting cases for non-members, as well.

Contact: HSLDA, P.O. Box 3000, Purcellville, VA 20134; 540-338-5600; Fax: 540-338-2733; {www.hslda.org}.

Free Legal Help To Fight Your Union At Work

If you feel your rights have been violated by compulsory unionism, or you simply have a question about your Right to Work, legal experts are available for free to help answer your questions. Contact: The National Right to Work Legal Defense Foundation, 8001 Braddock Rd., Springfield, VA 22160; 800-336-3600; {www.nrtw.org}.

Free Legal Rights For Women's Issues

The National Organization for Women Legal Defense and
Education Fund (NOW LDEF)
has a hotline that provides free
information and referrals on
women's issues including
reproductive rights, violence
against women, economic justice,
and gender equity in education.
They also provide low-cost legal
guides, some of which are
available free on the Internet,
on the following topics:

➡ *A Guide to Court Watching in Domestic Violence and
  Sexual Assault Cases*
➡ *Divorce and Separation*
➡ *Domestic Violence and Child Custody*
➡ *Employment Sexual Harassment & Discrimination*
  (Spanish)
➡ *Incest and Child Sexual Abuse*
➡ *Pregnancy & Parental Leave*
➡ *Sexual Harassment in Housing*
➡ *Sexual Harassment in the Schools*
➡ *Sexual Harassment in the Schools: A Blueprint for
  Action* (Spanish)
➡ *Stalking*
➡ *Violence Against Women*
➡ *How to Find a Lawyer* (free)

Contact: NOW LDEF, 395 Hudson Street, New York, NY 10014; 212-925-6635 (9:30 a.m. to 11:00 p.m. EST); Fax: 212-226-1066; email your question to {astrubel@ nowldef.org}; {www.nowldef.org}.

Free Consulting Services In Sex Discrimination Law Suits

If, as a woman, you feel discriminated against in higher education, the Legal Advocacy Fund (LAF) of the American Association of University Women (AAUW) may be able to help by providing financial support for sex discrimination lawsuits. LAF organizes a network of volunteer attorneys and social scientists who consult with

Free Legal Help For Pregnant Teens Discriminated In Honors Society

Feminists for Life of America, along with the ACLU, got the a federal court to rule that two high school seniors, whose school denied them National Honor Society membership because they became pregnant and chose to give birth, must be admitted into the society. For free legal information on these kinds of issues, contact Feminists for Life of America, 733 15th St. NW, Suite 1100, Washington, DC 20005; 202-737-FFLA; {www.serve.com/fem4life/index.htm}.

women on legal strategy, informational resources, and the strength of current or potential lawsuits.

To find out if you're eligible, please contact: AAUW Legal Advocacy Fund, Dept. LAF.INT., American Association of University of Women, 1111 16th St., NW, Washington, DC 20036; 800-326-AAUW; Fax: 202-872-1425; TDD: 202-785-7777; {E-mail: info@aauw.org}; {www.aauw.org}.

Legal Assistance for Overseas Teachers

Free legal aid is available for teachers employed in U.S. Department of Defense schools overseas and are members of the *Federal Education Association (FEA)*. The FEA legal staff conducts arbitration and other legal actions to insure the rights and benefits of teachers.

Contact: Federal Education Association, 1201 16th St. NW, Washington, DC 20036; 202-822-7850; Fax: 202-822-7867 (legal/president); {FEA_Legal/Pres@odedodea.edu} (legal office, president); {www.feaonline.org}.

Free Legal Help On Civil Liberties and Rights

The Rutherford Institute defends people who have been denied civil and human rights without charging them for such services. The issues they cover include civil liberties, religious freedom, parental rights, and sexual harassment. You may remember them from their involvement in the Paula Jones case.

If you need legal help, contact The Rutherford Institute, Legal Department, P.O. Box 7482, Charlottesville, VA 22906; 804-978-3888; {www.rutherford.org}.

FREE HELP COLLECTING CHILD SUPPORT

An association of concerned parents helps others learn about their rights and the remedies available for collecting what is due to them. Some services are free, others are for those who join for only $20. They can show you that you don't need to use a professional collection agency, and they will even contact officials on your behalf.

Contact: Association for Children for Enforcement and Support (ACES), 260 Upton Ave., Toledo, OH 43006; 800-537-7072; Fax: 419-472-5943; {www.childsupport-aces.org}.

Free Legal Help for Lesbians, Gay Men and People With HIV/AIDS

Lambda carries out carries out legal work on issues such as discrimination in employment, housing, public accommodations, and the military; HIV/AIDS-related discrimination and public policy issues; parenting and relationship issues; equal marriage rights; equal employment and domestic partnership benefits; "sodomy" law challenges; immigration issues; anti-gay initiatives; and free speech and equal protection rights. If you are seeking assistance with a legal matter, contact one of the offices listed below. They can guide you to a solution or help you directly:

National Headquarters
Lambda
120 Wall Street, Suite 1500
New York, NY 10005-3904
212-809-8585
Fax: 212-809-0055

Western Regional Office
6030 Wilshire Boulevard
Los Angeles, CA 90036-3617

323-937-2728
Fax: 323-937-0601

Midwest Regional Office
11 East Adams, Suite 1008
Chicago, IL 60603-6303
312-663-4413
Fax: 312-663-4307

Southern Regional Office
1447 Peachtree Street, NE, Suite 1004
Atlanta, GA 30309-3027
404-897-1880
Fax: 404-897-1884

Lambda's website is {www.lambdalegal.org}.

FREE LEGAL LATINO HELP

The Mexican American Legal Defense and Educational Fund (MALDEF) is a national nonprofit organization whose mission is to protect and promote the civil rights of the more than 29 million Latinos living in the United States in the areas of education, employment, political access, and more. They take cases to court and provide other legal help for the Latino community. Contact: MALDEF, 634 South Spring St., 11th Floor, Los Angeles, CA 90014; 213-629-2512; Fax: 213-629-0266; {www.maldef.org}.

Paralegals Offer Legal Work at 75 % Discount

The only things a paralegal can't do that a lawyer can, is give legal advice and represent you in court. That means they can file uncontested divorce papers, family court petitions, wills and probate, power of attorney, bankruptcy, incorporation. etc.

There are states where paralegals can represent clients in cases like those involving evictions or government agencies. And if you are seeking a legal opinion from an attorney, you may want to get a paralegal to research the law for you, so that you can make your own decisions.

Remember 50% of all lawyers lose their cases in court. So why pay $200 an hour for a lawyer, when you can get a lot of the same services done for less than $50 and hour.

Paralegals are in the yellow pages and you can contact your state or local paralegal association by contacting the national association that can give you a local contact. For more information, contact National Federation of Paralegal Associations, P.O. Box 33108, Kansas City, MO 64114; 816-941-4000; Fax: 816-941-2752; {www.paralegals. org}.

Fight Your Bank, Credit Card Company, Etc.

Finding the right bank, savings and loan, or credit union means figuring out your own needs first. How much money can you keep on deposit and how many checks will you write?

Examine your future loans and savings needs, as well as look at the convenience of the financial institution, its service charges, fees, and deposit and loan interest rates.

Discrimination Because You're A Woman, Pregnant, Person of Color, etc.

There's no need to take harassment or bullying on the job. Here is your chance to fight back.

If you believe you have been discriminated against by an employer, labor union, or employment agency when applying for a job or while on the job because of race, color, sex, religion, national origin, age, or disability, you may file a charge with the Equal Employment Opportunity Commission (EEOC). For more information, contact Equal Employment Opportunity Commission, 1801 L St., NW, Washington, DC 20507; 800-669-4000; {www.eeoc.gov}.

You can contact one of the following offices to learn more. These offices will also help you if you think the bank is messing with your money.

National Banks (banks that have the word "National" in their names or the intitals "N.A." after their names)
> Comptroller of the Currency
> U. S. Department of the Treasury
> Customer Assistance Group
> 1301 McKinner St.
> Suite 3710
> Houston, TX 77010
> 800-613-6743
> {www.occ.reas.gov}

FDIS-Insured Banks
> Office of Consumer
> Affairs
> Federal Deposit Insurance Corporation
> 550 17th St., NW
> Room F-130
> Washington, DC 20429
> 202-898-3542
> 800-934-3342
> {www.fdic.gov}

Savings and Loans
> Office of Thrift Supervision
> U.S. Department of Treasury
> 1700 G St., NW
> Washington, DC 20552
> 202-906-6237

800-842-6929
{www.ots.treas.gov}

State Banks

Contact your State Government Banking Commissioner
located in your state capital (look in the blue pages of
your phone book or contact your state capitol operator
listed in the Appendix).

Retailers, Mail Order Companies, Auto Dealers, Contractors, Etc.

You go to a store to get the best price on the gift for Uncle
George, only to learn that the store is out of stock despite
the product being advertised in the paper. Did the salesman
try to get you to buy a higher priced item? You could be
the victim of the old bait
and switch scam.

> The number one complaint heard is about problems dealing with your car dealership or car repair shop.

Is the paint peeling off
of the new toy doll you
bought your daughter?
Problems dealing with
your car dealership or
car repair shop? (This
is the number one complaint heard.) What about the
contractor that has yet to finish the job?

There are ways to deal with all these problems and get
them resolved to your satisfaction. You just need to pull in
the big guns. The States' Attorney General's Offices (listed

in the Appendix) have Consumer Protection Offices, and
many also have separate offices that handle only car
complaints. They will take your complaint and try to help
you get the satisfaction you deserve. For other problems
contact:

◆ *Defective Products* — contact Consumer Product
   Safety Commission, 5401 Westbard Ave., Washington,
   DC 20207; 800-638-2772; {www.cpsc.gov}.
◆ *Contractor or Licensed Professional Problems*
   — contact the state Licensing Board for the profession
   located in your state capitol. You can contact the state
   operator listed in the Appendix for assistance in finding
   the office.

Housing Discrimination

Buying your first home is a very exciting time. But
for many, house shopping is more than an eye
opening experience. Some people are not shown
houses in particular neighborhoods or are denied a
home because of their sex, race, or living
arrangement.

If you feel you have been treated unfairly, contact
office of Fair Housing and Equal Opportunity, U.S.
Department of Housing and Urban Development,
451 7th St., SW, Room 5100, Washington, DC
20410; 202-708-4252; 800-669-9777;
{www.hud.gov}.

♦ ***Mail Order Problems*** — contact the U.S. Postal Service, Public Affairs Branch, 475 L'Enfant Plaza, SW, Room 3140, Washington, DC 202060; 202-268-5400; {www.usps.gov}.

♦ ***Fraud Issues*** — contact Federal Trade Commission, Public Reference, CRC-2480, Washington, DC 20580; 202-382-4357; {www.ftc.gov}.

Lawyers, Accountants, Pharmacists, Doctors, Real Estate Agents, and Other Professionals

Lawyer over-charging you? Do you feel you have been mistreated by your doctor?

These issues and more are handled by the agency or board that licenses that particular profession. Whether it is your accountant, real estate agent, doctor, dentist, or other professional, you can contact the licensing board directly to file a grievance. These boards will then help you to resolve the problem.

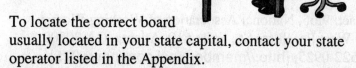

To locate the correct board usually located in your state capital, contact your state operator listed in the Appendix.

Where to Get Help to Stop Sexual Harassment

Call **"9 to 5"** if you experience any of the following at work:

> ➥ Suggestive comments about your appearance
> ➥ Unwanted touching or other physical contact
> ➥ Unwanted sexual jokes or comments
> ➥ Sexual advances

Sexual harassment is not only offensive, it's against the law. It is illegal even if the harasser is not your boss, even if he is not threatening that you will lose your job if you don't go along. 9to5's **toll free job problem hotline** and trained job counselors give information and support to thousands of working women.

If you decide to pursue a legal remedy, contact your state discrimination agency or the federal Equal Employment Opportunity Commission (look in your phone book for the field office closest to you). The federal agency covers workplaces of 15 or more. State law covers workplaces with fewer employees.

Contact: 9to5, National Association of Working Women, 1430 West Peachtree St., Suite 610, Atlanta, GA 30309; 800-522-0925; {http://members.aol.com/naww925}.

HOW AN ABUSER CAN DISCOVER YOUR INTERNET ACTIVITIES
(And what you can do about it)

The *American Bar Association's (ABA) Commission on Domestic Violence* has issued a warning concerning possible threats to you if an abuser has access to your e-mail account and thus may be able to read your incoming and outgoing mail. If you believe your account is secure, make sure you choose a password he or she will not be able to guess. If an abuser sends you threatening or harassing e-mail messages, they may be printed and saved as evidence of this abuse. Additionally, the messages may constitute a federal offense.

For more information on this issue, contact your local United States Attorney's Office. For more information about what you can do, and the efforts of the ABA's Commission on Domestic Violence, please contact American Bar Association Commission on Domestic Violence, 740 15th Street, NW, 9th Floor, Washington, DC 20005-1022; 202-662-1737/1744; Fax: 202-662-1594, {E-mail: abacdv@abanet.org}; {www.abanet.org}.

Emergency Shelter, Housing & Counseling For Violence Victims

If violence is ripping your life apart, you have nowhere to go, and you do not know how to reclaim your life, the YWCA, the nation's leading provider of shelter and services to women and their families can help you!

YWCA of the U.S.A

In the United States, more than 650,000 people come to the YWCA each year for services and support overcome violence. For more information about the services offered in your state, contact your local YWCA.

The YWCA takes a holistic approach to helping women escape, recover from and prevent violence in their lives and the lives of their families. Many local YWCAs offer programs and services including emergency shelter for women and children, transitional housing, support to victims of rape and sexual assault, individual and group counseling, peer support, self-defense training, programs for batterers and legal advocacy.

Contact: YWCA of the U.S.A., Empire State Building, Suite 301, 350 Fifth Ave., New York, NY 10118; 212-273-7800; Fax: 212- 465-2281; {www.ywca.org}. National Domestic Violence Hotline 800-799-SAFE; hearing impaired 800-787-3224.

Lawyer's Referral Service

The *American Bar Association's* lawyer referral service is designed to assist you in finding the appropriate service-provider to help you solve your legal problem. There are two steps to this process: first, helping you determine whether you need to see a lawyer, and second, referring you to a lawyer who handles your type of case or to an appropriate community or governmental agency 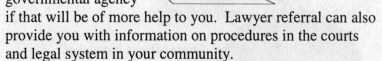 if that will be of more help to you. Lawyer referral can also provide you with information on procedures in the courts and legal system in your community.

When you contact lawyer referral, be prepared to briefly describe your situation so that the consultant can determine what kind of help you need. Lawyer Referral does not offer legal advice or free legal services. If you are referred to an attorney, you are entitled to a half-hour initial consultation at no charge, or for a nominal fee that goes to fund the lawyer referral service's operation. If additional legal services are required, you may choose to hire the lawyer. It is important to discuss legal fees and costs with the lawyer. We strongly recommend that you and the lawyer sign a written fee agreement, so that there is no question about what services the lawyer will perform, and what those services will cost you.

Contact your state Bar Association listed in your state capitol or The American Bar Association, 750 N. Lake Shore Dr., Chicago, IL 60611; 312-988-5000; {E-mail: info@abanet.org}; {www.abanet.org}.

WHEN ALL ELSE FAILS

People forget that they can turn to their representative or senators for help resolving a complaint. You vote these people into office, and most of them want to stay there. They know that if they can help you, then you and your family will vote for them in each and every election.

Their offices have case managers whose job is to cut the red-tape and push your case through quickly. Look in your phone book for their local office or you can call U.S. House of Representatives, Washington, DC 20515; 202-224-3121; {www.house.gov}; or U.S. Senate, Washington, DC 20510; 202-224-3121; {www.senate.gov}.

FREE SERVICES TO HELP FIND YOUR LOST LOVER OR CHECK OUT A NEW ONE

SOCIAL SECURITY WILL SEND THEM YOUR NOTE

Close to 92% of senior citizens receive social security checks each month. As a gesture of kindness, the Social Security Administration will forward letters to recipients for humanitarian reasons.

The letter you want forwarded must be sent unsealed, and must include a letter explaining why the enclosed letter should be sent. You need to supply the name and social security number of the recipient, or the person's date and place of birth. Send to Office of Public Inquiries, Room 4100, Annex Building, Social Security Administration, Baltimore, MD 21235; 410-965-2736.

If They Vote, You Get Their Address & Party

How a person votes is confidential information, but their voting registration form is a matter of public record. Contact the county Board of Elections (also called the Registrar of Voters). They can do a search to see if the person is registered to vote in their district.

The registration form can provide verification of the person's full name, date of birth, current address, political party affiliation, and sometimes, even the person's telephone number.

Cities With The Biggest Number of Unmarried Men

Jacksonville, NC	1:224
Killeen-Temple, TX	1:123
Fayetteville, NC	1:118
Brazoria, TX	1:117
Lawton, OK	1:116
State College, PA	1:113
Clarksville-Hopkinsville, TN-KY	1:113
Anchorage, AK	1:112
Salinas-Seaside-Monterey, CA	1:112
Bryan-College Station, TX	1:111

Source: Bureau of the Census

Information USA, Inc.

FIND YOUR LOVER
WHILE STUCK IN TRAFFIC

Want to know that good looking
driver who pulled up next to
you in a traffic jam? What
about a listing of all Jaguar
owners in your area?

Driver's license and car
registration information is
public record in almost all
states. This information can
be obtained by contacting your
state Department of Motor
Vehicles located in your state
capital.

Each state has different requirements about the information
they need to conduct a search. Some require the person's
full name and date of birth, while others may also need a
driver's license number. You may need to put your request
in writing and include a small fee.

The information you can obtain includes the person's name
and birthdate, driving record, date the license was issued,
and more. If you begin your search with a license number,
you can receive the name and address of the vehicle's
owner, insurance information, and make and model of the
car.

Sending The Right Letter Will Still Work

People say that letter writing is a lost art. But if you are looking for a lost friend, then a letter may be the answer to your question.

In the past, the Post Office would provide you with a person's forwarding address if they had moved within the past year. A privacy law was passed which now forbids the Post Office from releasing this information. But don't give up hope yet! You can send a letter to the last known address and write in bold letters "Do not forward. Address correction requested." Your letter will be returned to you with the person's forwarding address.

How To Get Birth, Death, & Marriage Records

Want to know when someone was born? Want to be sure your ex-husband is truly dead? What about whether or not someone got married?

 Information USA, Inc.

Each state and county has Offices of Vital Records, which consist of birth, death, and marriage records. Most of this information is available to the public. When writing your request, make sure to include the full name of the person (or couple), relevant dates, the purpose for which a copy of the record is needed, and your relationship to the person whose record is being requested. There is usually a small fee (under $5) to process the request. It is best to call ahead to find the correct address and fee information.

Contact the Office of Vital Records located in your state capital for more information.

The Military Will Fight To Find Your Man

One source of valuable information on locating people is the U.S. military. If you think you've hit a dead end in your search for someone, you should look into the possibility that the individual is serving, or has served at one time, in the military. If so, their personnel records might hold the answer to where they are currently located.

Each branch of the service does things a little differently, and some charge a fee. All stated that they do not have up-

to-date addresses on retired personnel, but can try to
forward a letter for you. Each branch's website can also
direct you to veteran organizations and publications where
you can post your search request.

Army: {www.army.mil}
Army Worldwide Locator
U.S. Army Enlisted Records and Evaluation Center
8899 E. 56th St.
Indianapolis, IN 46249
703-325-3732
Active Personnel: Include the soldier's full name and social
security number or date of birth with your request for an
address. The fee is $3.50 with the check made out to
Finance Office. This fee is waived for immediate family
members.

Retired Personnel: The Army will not release addresses,
but is willing to forward a letter to the last known address
for you. Write a letter to the soldier and place it in a sealed

Top Six States For Millionaires

California	1,303 millionaires
New York	235 millionaires
Florida	131 millionaires
Texas	72 millionaires
New Jersey	59 millionaires
Pennsylvania	55 millionaires

Source: Internal Revenue Service

and stamped envelope. Be sure to include your full name
and return address on the envelope. Write another letter
requesting assistance with your search. Include the service
member's name, serial number or social security number,
and date of birth, if available. Place both letters in one
envelope addressed to:

 National Personnel Records Center
 9700 Page Blvd.
 St. Louis, MO 63132-5200.

Marine Corps: {www.usmc.mil}
Headquarters
U.S. Marine Corps
Personnel Management
Support Branch (MMSB-17)
2008 Elliot Rd.
Quantico, VA 22134
703-784-3942

U.S. Coast Guard: {www.uscg.mil}
U.S. Coast Guard
2100 2nd St., SW
Washington, DC 20593
202-267-0581

Navy: {www.navy.mil} {www.bupers.navy.mil}
Active and Retired: Send a written request including full
name, social security number, grade/rank, and last known

duty station if possible. Correspondence will be forwarded, if possible, to retirees. Send to:

Navy Worldwide Locator
Bureau of Naval Personnel
Pers-312
5720 Integrity Dr.
Millington, TN 38055-3120
901-874-3388

Air Force: {www.af.mil}

Active duty, Reservists, Guardsmen, and Retirees write to:

Air Force Worldwide Locator
AFPC/MSIMDL
550 C St., W, Suite 50
Randolph AFB, TX 78150-4752
210-652-5774 (recorded message)
210-652-5775
Send check for $3.50 made payable to DAO-DERAFB

HOW TO REPLACE A MISSING BIRTH CERTIFICATE

Did the hospital or clerk's office lose your record of birth? Happens to the best of us. But what if you need a passport or need proof of birth for Social Security?

A birth certificate is required, but in place of that, the Census will conduct an "Age Search Service." They can search the confidential records from the Federal population censuses of 1910 to 1990 and issue an official transcript of the results. This information can be released only to the named person, his/her heirs, or legal representatives.

Individuals can use these transcripts, which may contain information on a person's age, sex, race, state or country of birth, and relationship to the householder, as evidence to qualify for social security and other retirement benefits, for passport applications, to prove relationship in settling estates, and more. The fee for the search is $40 made payable to Commerce-Census.

Age Search Service

Request Transcript Application Form BC-600 from Personal Census Search Unit, Bureau of the Census, P.O. Box 1545, Jeffersonville, IN 47131; 812-218-3046.

FIND OUT IF YOUR LOVER'S DOING TIME

The government's Inmate Locator Hotline will give you the address of a loved one who is incarcerated in a federal correctional institution. These inmates have been convicted of, or are awaiting trial for violating Federal laws. Those convicted of violating state or local laws are sent to state or local prisons.

The website provides the phone number for each state's Department of Corrections to help you with your search at those prisons. You can learn the prisoner's name, age, and registration number, as well as sentencing and confinement data.

For information on Federal inmates released before 1982, write to Office of Communications and Archives, Federal Bureau of Prisons, 320 First St., NW, Washington, DC 20534; Attn: Historic Inmate Locator Request. For those from 1982 to the present, contact Inmate Locator Hotline, Bureau of Prisons, U.S. Department of Justice, 320 First St., NW, Washington, DC 20536; 202-307-3126; or online at {www.bop.gov}.

The Right Data Increases The Odds Of Finding Mr. Right

No sense wasting your time in a town where all the single men are already taken. Check out the singles scene anywhere in the country by contacting the Bureau of the Census, that keeps some interesting figures regarding the population, such as the ratio of total number of single men to single women in metro areas. Give them a call to find out what areas of the country will improve your chances of finding that special someone.

Contact Fertility and Family Statistics Branch, Population Division, Bureau of the Census, Bldg. 3, Room 2353, Washington, DC 20233; 301-457-2465.

How To Find A Rich Man

Money isn't everything, remember? But you can do a little research before you begin looking for Mr. Right.

The government has information about county and metro areas that have the highest per capita income. In fact, they have even posted the highest and lowest 250 areas on their

THE CITIES WITH THE RICHEST MEN IN THE U.S.

San Francisco, CA
New Haven-Bridgeport-Stamford-Danbury-Waterbury, CT
West Palm Beach-Boca Raton, FL
San Jose, CA
Bergen-Passaic, NJ
Naples, FL
Middlesex-Sommerset-Hunterdon, NJ
Trenton, NJ
Newark, NJ
Nassau-Suffolk, NY

website. Unfortunately, they cannot break the data down into single versus married, so that has been left up to you.

For more information, contact Bureau of Economic Analysis, U.S. Department of Commerce, 1441 L St., NW, Washington, DC 20230; 202-606-5360; {www.bea.doc.gov, then go to regional data}.

Make Sure You Get 50% Of What's Yours

Think your ex may be hiding or not claiming property during your divorce settlement? Just go to the source to find out for sure. The county clerk's office can tell you who owns what property, the location of the property, the address of the owner of the property, and when the property was purchased. If your ex suddenly buys a mansion after he claimed he couldn't afford child support, I'd take him back to court to re-examine his finances.

How To Make Sure He's Divorced

Sometimes it may not be clear if your new boyfriend has finalized his divorce from bride number 1. Rather than get in the middle of a nasty divorce scene, you can go check things out with the records in civil court.

Divorce records are not open in every state, but those records that are open can provide you with a better understanding of your boyfriend's past. These records can tell you when and where the couple was married, the reason for the divorce, whether or not they had children, the division of their property, and the date the divorce was finalized. There may be a small fee involved, but it could be worth it.

How Much Does Your New Beau Owe?

Any public or private company, organization, and for that matter, individual, that borrows money and offers an asset as collateral, must file with the state at the Office of Uniform Commercial Code (UCC). A filing is made for each loan and each of the documents is available to the public.

To obtain these documents is a two-step process. The first step is to request a search to see if there are any filings for a certain company or person. The fee for such a search usually is under $10. You will next want to request copies of each of these documents. The cost for each document averages only a few dollars.

The Office Of Uniform Commercial Code is part of the state government and usually is located near or in the same office as the Office of Corporations which falls under the Secretary of State. Contact your state information office, or the Office of Corporations for your state (listed in the Appendix).

Find Out What He's Worth

Want to know if that guy you're going out with really owns that house he brags about? Then you just need to make a visit to the county tax assessor's office. Not only can they tell you who owes a house, they can tell you the amount of money he has to pay in property taxes each year, the address of the owner, and the value of the property.

Cities With The Ten Areas With The Lowest Per Capita Personal Income

Bryan-College Station, TX
Sumter, SC
Jacksonville, NC
Provo-Orem, UT
Yuma, AZ
Las Cruces, NM
El Paso, TX
Brownsville-Harlingen-San Benito, TX
Laredo, TX
McAllen-Edinburg-Mission, TX

Source: Bureau of Economic Analysis, U.S. Department of Commerce

---

If He Says He's A Professional, Check Him Out

One way is to think about his occupation. Doctor, lawyer, physical therapist? Over one hundred occupations must be licensed with a state or professional licensing board or organization. You can search to find out if a person has an active license, the address of the licensee, license number and expiration date, and the current standing of the license. It is an easy way to track someone who is living in another state.

How To Marry A Millionaire

The first step is to get yourself to a good state. The Internal Revenue Service compiles statistics on which states have the most millionaires. Unfortunately, they can't tell you if they are available. They have to leave something for you to do!

To get your hands on some interesting statistics, contact Statistics of Income, Internal Revenue Service, P.O. Box 2608, Washington, DC 20013; 202-874-0410; {www.irs.gov}.

Check to See If He Really Has A Ph.D

You may have forgotten the team mascot or school song, but you can be sure the school didn't forget you. Almost every college, university, and high school has alumni associations, whose job is to raise funds for the school.

Their main task in this endeavor is to keep up-to-date addresses for all past students, and it could be a great source of information when searching for your lost love. Many will give out the address upon request.

Find a Missing Person For $25

The Salvation Army Mission Person Bureau can assist in locating immediate blood relatives. The Bureau can conduct searches in all 50 states and in countries overseas which have a Salvation Army site. A one-time processing fee of $25 is required and the full name, name of parents, and date of birth of the relative must be provided. Searches are not conducted for spouses, friends, adoption or foster care.

Salvation Army Mission Person Bureau

For further information or to initiate a search, contact the office nearest you:

Salvation Army Western Territory, 30840 Hawthorne Blvd, Rancho Palos Verdes, CA, 90724; 310-541-4721; Fax: 310-544-1674

Salvation Army Central Territory, 10 West Algonquin Road, Des Plaines, IL 60016; 847-294-2000; 847-294-2000; Fax: 847-294-2299

Salvation Army Southern Territory, 1424 Northeast Expressway, Atlanta, GA 30329; 404-728-1300; Fax: 404-728-1331

Salvation Army Eastern Territory, 440 West Nyack Road, West Nyack, NY 10994; 914-620-7200; 800-315-7699; Fax: 914-620-7466; National web address {www.salvationarmy.org}.

WEBSITES TO HELP YOU FIND LOST LOVES

www.infoseek.com
www.search.com
www.whowhere.com
www.switchboard.com
www.yahoo.com
www.worldemail.com
www.databaseamerica.com
www.anywho.com
http://search.bigfoot.com
www.teldir.com
www.hotbot.com
www.altavista.com

FREE RESOURCES FOR YOUR HEALTH

TEENS CAN GET CONFIDENTIAL GYN EXAMS FOR $5.00

In Montgomery County, MD, teenage girls can get gynecological exams, breast exams and even birth control counseling at the local Planned Parenthood Clinic for only $5.00. All they need to have is a note from the school nurse.

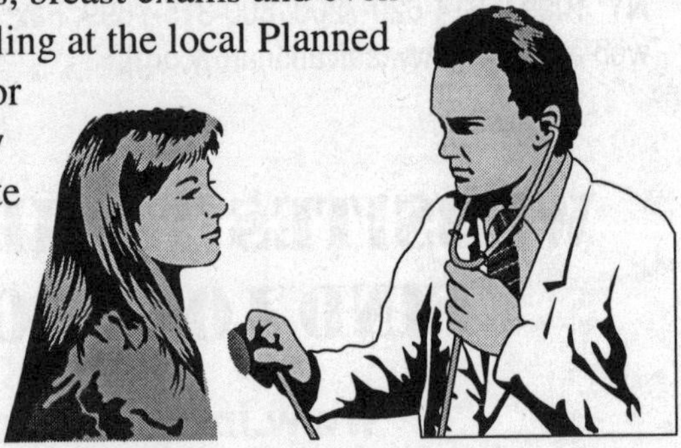

Planned Parenthood has 900 clinics around the country and services vary according to local laws and funding sources. To investigate what your local clinic offers call 1-800-230-PLAN.

THINGS YOU SHOULD KNOW ABOUT QUALITY MAMMOGRAMS

This free publication is available in English or Spanish from Publications Clearinghouse, Health Care Policy and Research, P.O. Box 8547, Silver Spring, MD 20907; 800-358-9295; {www.ahcpr.gov}.

Contact Planned Parenthood Federation of American, 810 Seventh Avenue, New York, NY 10019; 212-541-7800; Fax: 212-245-1845; {www.plannedparenthood.org}.

3 Million Seniors & Disabled
Don't Apply for Their Free $1,000 For Health Care

Each year over 3 million eligible seniors and people with disabilities fail to apply for a little-known program that will give them up to an extra $1,051 in their Social Security check. That's how much the government deducts from their Social Security to pay for their Medicare premiums. It amounts to $87.60 a month for couples and $43.80 for individuals. There are three basic programs:

1) *Pays for Medicare premiums, deductibles and co-payments under the Qualified Medicare Beneficiaries (QMBs) plan.*
2) *Pays for Medicare Part B premiums under the Specified Low-Income Medicare Beneficiaries (SLMBs) plan.*
3) *Pays for Medicare Part B premiums under the Qualified Individuals Plan for people with incomes up to $14,892.*

Studies show that only 5,000 of the 500,000 eligible apply for this program. With so few eligible people applying, it's understandable that many people don't know about this program.

Here's where to go. Contact your local Social Security Office. If they don't know, contact your state Office of Social Services listed in the Appendix. You can also contact the Medicare Hotline and request the publication, *Guide to Health Insurance for People With Medicare.* Contact Medicare Hotline at 800-638-6833; {www.medicare.gov}.

Discounts On Dental And Vision Care

If you live near a university that has a dental or optometry school, then you may be in luck. Many of these schools offer reduced fee services for dental care or vision screening. You will receive treatment from students, but they will be supervised by some of the best people in the field.

These schools also often conduct research studies, so you if you qualify, you may be able to receive treatment for free. My eleven-year-old daughter gets glasses, contacts, plus free contact solution for three years, because she is part of a study on nearsightedness in children. Not a bad deal! To locate schools near you, you can contact American Association of Dental Schools, 1625 Massachusetts Ave., NW, Suite 60, Washington, DC 20036; 202-667-9433;

[www.aads.jhu.edu]. You can also contact American Optometric Association, 243 N. Lindbergh Blvd., St. Louis, MO 63141; 314-991-4100; [www.aoanet.org].

Abortions Starting At $250

Some of the 900 Planned Parenthood clinics offer abortions during the first 11 weeks of pregnancy starting at $250 for those not covered by health insurance. In some cases they even have special funds to help women pay for services.

To investigate what your local clinic offers, call 1-800-230-PLAN. You can also contact Planned Parenthood Federation of America, 810 Seventh Avenue, New York, NY 10019; 212-261-4647; Fax: 212-261-4560; {www.plannedparenthood.org}.

There is another consumer hotline that can also handle your abortion related questions: Contact The National Abortion Federation, 1755 Massachusetts Ave., NW, Washington,

H-E-A-L-T-H-F-I-N-D-E-R

This is a gateway consumer health information web site from the U.S. government that can lead you to online publications, clearinghouses, databases, web sites, and support and self-help groups, as well as government agencies and non-profit organizations that produce reliable information for the public: {www.healthfinder.org}.

DC 20036; 800-772-9100 or in Canada 800-424-2282, weekdays from 9:00 to 7:00 EST; {www.prochoice.org/index.html}.

Free Flu Shots

Who should get flu shots? The U.S. Center for Disease Control recommends it for

- adults over 65
- residents of nursing home
- persons over 6 months of age with chronic cardiovascular or pulmonary disorders, including asthma
- persons over 6 months of age with chronic metabolic diseases including diabetes, renal dysfunction, hemoglobinipathies, immunosupressive or immunodeficiency disorders
- women in their 2nd or 3rd trimester of pregnancy during flu season
- persons 6 months to 18 years receiving aspirin therapy
- groups, including household members and care givers who can infect high risk persons

Almost anyone can get free or low cost ($10-$15) flu shots from their county health office or other community sources. Some doctors, like Dr. Donald McGee in New Hampshire {www.drmcgee.com}, offer free shots in their office. Medicare Part B also pays for flu shots.

Contact your county office of public health listed in your telephone book or your state Department of Health listed in the Appendix. If you have trouble finding a local low cost source, or would like more information on the flu vaccine contact the National Immunization Information Hotline at 800-232-2522 (English); 800-232-0233 (Spanish); {www.cdc.gov/nip}.

Is Your Food Safe?

E-coli, Salmonella, and Listeria Monocytogenes

Fungi, viruses, parasites, and bacteria in foods are estimated to account for 6.5 to 33 million cases of human illness and up to 9,000 deaths in the United States each year.

Since 1992, when E coli contaminated hamburger in a fast-food restaurant in Washington and made 500 people ill,

Free Nutrition Analysis Tool

Allows you to analyze the foods you eat for various different nutrients. Developed by the Department of Food Science and Human Nutrition, University of Illinois, Urbana-Champaign at {http://spectre.ag.uiuc.edu/~food-lab/nat/}.

consumers seem to be more aware of the potential problems with food safety. Now the Center for Disease Control and Prevention estimates as many as 20,000 cases of E coli infections happen every year. And many people even know that the nitrates in your water may cause "blue baby syndrome."

If you need the facts on food safety, contact the government's main information center on the topic: USDA/FDA Foodborne Illness Education Information Center, National Agricultural Library/ USDA, Beltsville, MD 20705; 301-504-5719; fax: 301-504-6409; {foodborne@nal.usda.gov}.

Grants Up To $2,500 and Loans To Finance Adoptions

The National Adoption Foundation helps arrange loans and provides limited grants for parents to cover expenses before and after adoption. They also provide information on sources of other financial help like the 325 Fortune 500 companies who offer an average cash reimbursement of $4,000 for their employees who adopt, or the new adoption expense tax credit that is available from the IRS. Contact: National Adoption Foundation, 100 Mill Plain Rd, Danbury, CT 06811; 203-791-3811.

The following organizations also provide free publications, referral services and advice on adoption and searching for birth relatives:

★ **National Adoption Information Clearinghouse**, 330 C Street, NW, Washington, DC 20447; 888-251-0075; 703-352-3488; {www.calib.com/naic}.

★ **National Adoption Center**, 1500 Walnut St, Suite 701, Philadelphia, PA, 19102; Answer Line: 215-735-9988; {www.adopt.org}.

★ **National Council For Adoption**, 1930 17th Street, NW, Washington, DC 20009; 202-328-8072; fax: 202-332-0935; {www.ncfa-usa.org}.

Free Plastic Surgery For Children

Austin Smiles provides free reconstructive plastic surgery, mainly to repair cleft lip and palate, to the children around Austin, Texas. They do about 75 surgeries a year. Austin Plastic Surgery Foundation, P.O. Box 26694, Austin, TX 78755-0694; 512-451-9300; Fax: 512-451-9312; {www. main.org/smiles/}.

To see if similar services are available anywhere near you contact Cleft Palate Foundation, 104 S. Estes Dr., Suite 204, Chapel Hill, NC 27514; 800-24-CLEFT; 919-933-9044; {www.cleft.com/ cpf.htm}.

AN EXTRA $6,000 A YEAR IF YOU CAN'T WORK

Is your check too small to live on? If so, don't be
discouraged. If you don't qualify for Social Security, or if
your benefits are very low, you may qualify for
Supplemental Security Income (SSI).

This program was established to help poor seniors over 65,
as well as the blind
and disabled, meet
basic living needs.
To qualify, you
must meet a
maximum monthly
income test. Some
of the income and
services you receive
are excluded when
they calculate your
monthly income in
relation to your personal expenses.

Women Without Health Insurance

15% of all adult women have no
insurance
500,000 pregnant women have no
insurance

Source: Center for Policy Alternative
www.cfpa.org/publications/index.html

Those who meet SSI's eligibility usually automatically
qualify for Medicaid coverage and food stamp benefits.
Studies have found that only between 40 and 60 percent of
those who qualify for SSI actually receive benefits under
the program. To find out if you qualify, contact your local
Social Security office or call the Social Security Hotline at
800-772-1213.

Emergency Help From Domestic Violence

If you or someone you know is being emotionally or physically abused, call the National Domestic Violence Hotline. This hotline is supported with funds from the Violence Against Women Act, which also gives money for local governments to hire more prosecutors to enforce domestic violence laws, and to improve domestic violence training among prosecutors, police officers, and health and social services professionals.

Contact: National Domestic Violence Hotline, P.O. Box 161810, Austin, TX 78716; 800-799-SAFE; TTY 800-787-3224; {www.ndvh.org}.

A Woman's Chance of Violence

- 18% of all women will be a victim of rape or attempted rape
- 54% of rapes occur to women under 17
- over 50% of women will be physically assaulted during their lives
- 76 % of rapes occur by a current or former husband, a cohabiting partner, or a date

Source: U.S. Center for Disease Control, National Center for Injury Prevention and Control; {www.hhs.gov/press/1998pres/98117a.html}

Free Speech Therapy For Toddlers

It doesn't matter how much money you earn. You can have your child tested to see if any speech problems are developing and even get free speech therapy.

It's part of the U.S. Individuals with Disabilities Education Act (IDEA) to make sure that children in need receive special education beginning on their third birthday, and in some states, like Virginia, it starts at age 2.

The program is run through your local school district, so check with them first, or your state Department of Education listed in the Appendix. You can also contact Division of Educational Services, Office of Special Education Programs, U.S. Department of Education, 330 C St., SW, Washington, DC 20202; 202-205-9172; {www.ed.gov/offices/OSERS/OSEP/osep.html}.

Free Nutritional Quiz

Take the online "Rate Your Plate" nutritional quiz from the American Dietetic Association and find out how you can make your diet a healthier one. Contact American Dietetic Association 216 W. Jackson Blvd., Chicago, IL 60606-6995; 312-899-0040; 800-366-1655; {E-mail: hotline@ eatright.org}; {www.eatright.org/nuresources. html} (Rate Your Plate).

Free Help • At Your Home, • Every Day • For The First 3 Weeks After Childbirth

The Healthy Families America Project operates 300 programs in 40 states. It helps new mothers cope with the pressures of being a new parent by offering volunteer home visitors who come to your home for the first three weeks after birth. They are trained to show you how to deal with the physical, emotional and financial strains of a new baby. First time mothers and older mothers are among those considered for the program.

15% of Adult TV Characters are identified as parents of minor children, in real life it's 32%

34% of Adult TV WOMEN Characters are working for pay, in real life it's 67%

Source: National Partnership for Women & Families; {www.womenandfamilies.org}

To see if there is a program in your area and if you qualify, contact National Committee to Prevent Child Abuse, 200 S. Michigan Ave., 17th Floor, Chicago, IL 60604; 312-663-3520; Fax: 312-939-8962; {www.childabuse.org}.

Camp Wheezeaway Is Free For Kids With Asthma

Every year, about 80 kids with asthma, between 8 and 12 years of age, can go to summer camp for free in Jackson Cap, Alabama. For information on how to apply, contact American Lung Association of Alabama, 900 South 18th St., Birmingham, AL 35205; 205-933-8821.

For more information on other camps for children with asthma, or other questions concerning asthma, contact The American Lung Association, 1740 Broadway, New York, NY 10019; 212-315-8700; 800-LUNG-USA; {www.lungusa.org}.

Kids Get Free Expert Care At 22 Hospitals

Children suffering from orthopedic injuries, diseases of the bones, joint and muscles, or burns can get free treatment from one of the 22 Shriners Hospitals. The requirements for admission are that the child is under the age of 18, and there is a reasonable possibility the condition can be helped.

For more information, contact Shriners Hospitals, P.O. Box 31356, Tampa, FL 33631; 800-237-5055 (in Canada 800-361-7256); {www.shrinershq.org}.

Find Out How Long You'll Live & Save $50

A free, personalized, confidential Health Risk Assessment is available online from a health care consulting firm called Greenstone Healthcare Solutions in Kalamazoo, Michigan.

From the information you provide through a questionnaire, they process the data instantly against a database of statistics showing what kind of behavior shortens your life.

HOTLINE LOCATES WANDERING ALZHEIMER'S PATIENTS

Alzheimer's patients are known to wander away and even wind up in other cities. My father, in his later years, went for a drive that took him into someone's back yard.

Safe Return is a national clearinghouse that helps police and private citizens locate and return lost Alzheimer's patients. Contact The Alzheimer's Association, 919 N. Michigan Ave., Suite 1000, Chicago, IL 60611; 800-272-3900; {www.alz.org}.

Your instant report shows you how many years you can add by changing your behavior.

I took the test and it showed that my health is six years younger than my age, but I can still add two years to my life. Such assessments usually cost from $10 to $50. But here, it's free. Contact Greenstone Healthcare Solutions at {www.youfirst.com}.

Top 10 States With Largest % of Children Without Health Insurance

State	Children Uninsured
Texas	46%
New Mexico	43%
Louisiana	43%
Arkansas	42%
Mississippi	41%
District of Columbia	39%
Alabama	38%
Arizona	38%
Nevada	37%
California	37%
Total US	**33%**

Of the children who lacked insurance, 89% lived in households where the parents worked.

Source: One Out Of Three Kids Without Health Insurance 1995-1996, Families USA Foundation {http://tap.epn.org/families/kwohi.htm}.

Head Lice Hotline

Anywhere from 6 to 10 million kids a year get head lice. That's one of the reasons why the U.S. Federal Trade Commission made three large producers of head lice treatment shampoos change their false advertising claims. They claimed that their shampoos eliminated head lice 100% of the time. They don't.

To get the facts about head lice treatments or to report outbreaks, treatment failures, or adverse reactions to treatments, contact The National Pediculosis Association, P.O. Box 610189, Newton, MA 02161; 800-446-4672; 781-449-6487; Fax: 781-449-8129; {www.headlice.org}.

Free Private Eye and Mediation For Missing Children

Besides location and investigative services, as well as mediation services for families estranged by parental abduction, you can also get free kidnapping prevention programs and referral and support services.

Contact Find-A-Child of America, Inc., P.O. Box 277, New Paltz, NY 12561; 800-I-AM-LOST; 914-255-1848; 800-A-WAY-OUT (for mediation and support); {www.childfindamerica.org}.

Law Gives Kids With ADD Free Special Classes

The nonprofit organization, *Children and Adults with Attention Deficit Disorder (CHADD),* identifies a number of federal laws that require the government to provide children with this disorder special educational services. It is only recently that these children became eligible for such services, so many eligible children may not be receiving what they deserve.

To learn more about these free educational services, or to find out more and how to treat a child with ADD, or what's good and bad about available treatments, contact: CHADD, 8181 Professional Place, Suite 201, Landover, MD 20785; 800-233-4050; Fax: 301-306-7090; {www.chadd.org}.

Grant Money For Parents of Children With Hearing Loss

If your child is under 6 and has a moderate to profound hearing loss, you can apply for money to pay for intervention, educational and/or rehabilitation services. There is also money available for children with hearing loss between the ages of 5 and 19 to attend art or science courses during the summer, weekends, or even after school.

Contact: Alexander Graham Bell Association for the Deaf, 3417 Volta Place, NW, Washington, DC 20007; 202-337-5220 (voice and TTY); {www.agbell.org}.

$1,300 Worth Of Dental Care For Seniors and Disabled

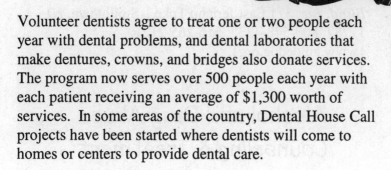

The National Foundation of Dentistry for the Handicapped started the Donated Dental Services program to help disabled and elderly persons who are low-income by matching them with volunteer dentists. Homeless and mentally ill people are also helped.

Volunteer dentists agree to treat one or two people each year with dental problems, and dental laboratories that make dentures, crowns, and bridges also donate services. The program now serves over 500 people each year with each patient receiving an average of $1,300 worth of services. In some areas of the country, Dental House Call projects have been started where dentists will come to homes or centers to provide dental care.

To learn where services are located in your area, contact National Foundation of Dentistry for the Handicapped, 1800 15th St., Unit 100, Denver, CO 80202; 303-534-5360, Fax: 303-534-5290.

Sightless Get Free Seeing Eye Dogs, Training, Travel and Air Fare

Pilot Dogs gives its trained animals to the blind at absolutely no charge. They also include four weeks of training in using the dog and will pay for room and board, all equipment, and round trip transportation. Other groups provide similar services:

✳ *Pilot Dogs, Inc.*, 625 West Town Street, Columbus, OH 43215; 614-221-6367; fax: 614-221-1577; {www.pilotdogs.org/index.shtml}.

✳ *Guide Dog Foundation for the Blind, Inc*, 371 East Jericho Tpke., Smithtown, NJ 11787; 800-548-4337; 516-265-2121; {www.guidedog.org}.

Alcohol and Drug Abuse Counseling & Treatment

Georgia provides outpatient counseling services, short-term residential programs, and even school student assistance programs. Florida provides substance abuse treatment programs through a partnership with 102 public and private not-for-profit community providers. Delaware contracts with private organizations around the state to provide screening, outpatient counseling, and detoxification, as well as short term and long term treatment. Contact your state Department of Health, listed in the Appendix, to see what your state has to offer.

There are also nonprofit organizations who, by themselves, offer free treatment to people, like the Center for Drug-Free Living in Orlando, Florida (5029 N. Lane, Suite 8, Orlando, FL 32808; 407-245-0012; {www.cfdfl.com}).

Finding A Doctor In A Hay Stack

650,000 doctor practices are online at {www. ama-assn.org}. You can search by name, specialty, and get reference info on all major diseases and conditions.

If your state can't help you get the information or treatment you need, one or both of the following hotlines should be able to help:

■ *National Drug and Treatment Routing Service*, Center for Substance Abuse Treatment, National Institute on Alcohol Abuse and Alcoholism (NIAAA), 600 Executive Blvd, Willco Bldg., Bethesda, MD 20892; 800-662-HELP; {www.niaaa.nih.gov}.

■ *The National Clearinghouse for Alcohol and Drug Information*, 11426 Rockville Pike, Suite 200, Rockville, MD 20852; 800-729-6686 24 hours a day; 301-468-2600 TDD; {www.health.org}.

Free Wheelchairs

Easter Seals, the American Cancer Society and other helpful organizations provide free wheelchairs and other medical related equipment, like walkers, commodes, bathtub rails, bathtub chairs, crutches, transfer benches, electric wheelchairs and scooters, on a short- or long-term basis. Some programs require deposits that are completely refundable.

Check with your local office of Easter Seals and the American Cancer Society. You can also contact your state Department of Health listed in the Appendix.

- *American Cancer Society, Inc.*, 1599 Clifton Road, NE, Atlanta, GA 30329; 800-ACS-2345; {www.cancer.org}.

- *Easter Seals*, 230 West Monroe Street, Suite 1800, Chicago, IL 60606; 800-221-6825; 312-726-6200; fax: 312-726-1494; {www.seals.com}.

MAKE $40,000 & GET FREE PRESCRIPTION DRUGS — EVERYTHING BUT VIAGRA

Valium, Prozac, Dilantin are just a few of the medications you can get FREE directly from the drug companies themselves. That's right: drug companies don't want everybody to know this, but they will give certain people who can't afford their medications their drugs free of charge.

So what's the catch? It sounds too easy. The drug companies require that you participate in their "indigent patient programs." Your doctor needs to write them a note stating that you cannot afford the drugs that you need. Your doctor is the one that needs to call the drug manufacturer. Once the forms are filled out, you will be able to pick up your drugs directly from your doctor's office.

Call the Pharmaceutical Research and Manufacturers of America hotline to receive a listing of the drug companies and their programs. Contact Pharmaceutical Research and Manufacturers of America, 1100 15th St., NW, Washington, DC 20005; 800-PMA-INFO; {www.phrma.org}.

Make $38,657 And Get Free Health Care For Your Kids

Over 4.7 million children are eligible for this program and are not enrolled. Almost every state now has a Children's Health Insurance Program (CHIPS) which extends medical coverage to many children who may not be covered.

Report Bad Burgers

Or any other food, for that matter, that makes you, or someone you know, sick. Your local public health officials will take immediate action. They'll get you treated and make sure the problem does not spread. Contact your county office of public health listed in your telephone book, or your state Department of Health listed in the Appendix.

A family of four living in Connecticut can make up to $38,657 and get free health care for their children up to 18 years of age. For a family of two, it's $25,487. And a family of four making $49,350 will pay only $30 a month for insurance. Contact Department of Social Services, State of Connecticut, 25 Sigourney St., Hartford, CT 06105; 877-CT-HUSKY (toll-free); {www.huskyhealth.com/qualify.htm}.

A family of four living in Virginia and making up to $30,000 can get free coverage. Contact Department of

Medical Assistance Services, 600 E. Broad St., Suite 1300, Richmond, VA 23219; 877-VA-CMSIP (toll free); {http://dit1.state.va.us/~dmas/cmsip.htm}.

Maryland's program covers pregnant women of any age and children up to 19 if the family of four have an income below $32,900. Their program includes dental and vision care. Contact Health Choice, Maryland Department of Health and Mental Hygiene, W. Preston St., Room L, Baltimore, MD 21201; 800-456-8900; {www.dhmh.state. md.us/healthchoice/html/maqanda3.htm}.

Contact your state Department of Health listed in the Appendix to see what version of the CHIPS program is offered in your area. It is usually part of the state's Medicaid program. A new government hotline can also help you locate free health care for kids. Call toll-free 877-KIDS-NOW (877-543-7669).

Access To Your Health Records

In Minnesota, you have access to your health records. If a patient asks in writing, the provider must give copies of records or a summary of the information. They can charge 90 cents per page and $11.91 for time spent retrieving and copying records and actual cost of x-rays.

Free Care
Even If You Don't Qualify

You or your child may still be able to get free health care from local government programs even if you don't qualify.

Many local health offices have the authority to stretch the rules if they see fit. Others have set up special arrangements with the local medical society for people who don't qualify for their programs. These offices can direct you to local nonprofit organizations or groups that can give you the care you need at the price you can afford.

Over-the-Counter Birth Control Made Easy

Find out the cost and what's good and bad about using over-the-counter products like foam, suppositories, vaginal film, sponge, and the male and female condom for birth control. Check out the web page of the Feminist Women's Health Center at {www.fwhc. org}.

Contact your county office of public health listed in your telephone book or your state Department of Health listed in the Appendix. If you cannot get satisfaction from these offices, contact your local office of your state or federal elected official.

Morning After Hotline: Eliminate A Pregnancy Within Three Days After Unprotected Intercourse

When all else fails, the Emergency Contraceptive Pills (ECP) taken within 72 hours after having unprotected intercourse, with a second dose 12 hours after the first, increases your chances of NOT getting pregnant by 75%.

The hotline describes the procedures and will direct you to four local offices and clinics that offer these pills. For women who already have birth control pills, the clinic will instruct her on how to use them correctly as emergency contraception. If you don't already have pills, you can get a prescription for emergency contraception.

Call the hotline operated by the Office of Population Research at Princeton University at 800-584-9911; {http://opr.princeton.edu/ec/}.

FIGHT BACK — What to Do When Your HMO Says No

This booklet is free from The Center for Patient Advocacy, 1350 Beverly Road, Suite 108, McLean, VA 22101; 800-846-7444; {www.patientadvocacy.org}.

Emergency Contraceptive Pill Available Without A Prescription

Call **1-888-NOT-2-LATE** in the state of Washington and you can find a local pharmacist who can directly prescribe Emergency Contraceptive Pills (ECP).

Going directly to a pharmacist allows women to skip the process of going to a clinic or doctor or a prescription and provides access to pharmacies on evenings, weekends and holidays. The use of such pills within 72 hours after unprotected intercourse reduces the risk of pregnancy by about 75%.

"The Facts About Weight Loss Products and Programs"

" Infertility Services" - how to choose a good one

"The Skinny on Dieting" - the facts about weight loss claims

All free from Federal Trade Commission, Public Reference, Room 130, Washington, DC 20580; 202-326-2222; {www.ftc.gov}.

Normally 8 in 100 women who have unprotected intercourse once during the second or third week of their menstrual cycle will become pregnant. Taking ECPs will reduce this to 2 out of 100.

For more information about the programs, contact: Program for Appropriate Technology in Health, 4 Nickerson Street, Seattle, WA 98109; 206-285-3500; Fax: 206-285-6619; {www.path.org}.

Free Mammograms / Free Tests For Breast and Cervical Cancer

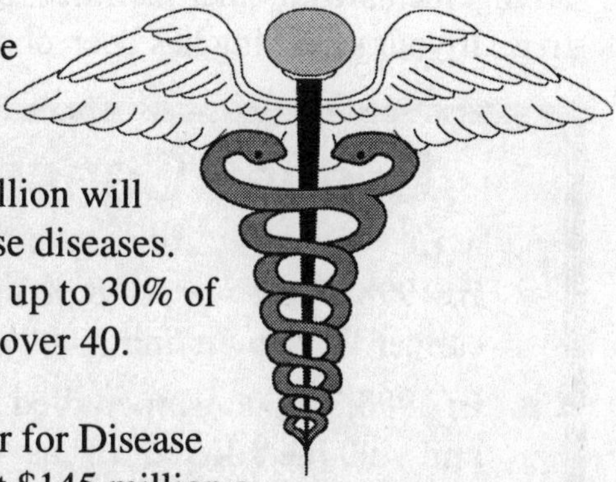

An estimated 2 million American women will be diagnosed with breast or cervical cancer in the 1990s, and half a million will lose their lives from these diseases. Screening could prevent up to 30% of these deaths for women over 40.

The government's Center for Disease Control will spend about $145 million a year to maintain a state-by-state program to establish greater access to screening and follow-up services. Each state runs their program a little differently. Most states have the following requirements:

➜ women starting 40 or 50 years old,
➜ are underinsured or have no insurance
➜ have income below a certain level (usually $32,000 or $40,000 for family of 4)

Some states can adjust eligibility requirements for special cases. States vary in the array of services covered but they normally include:

→ breast and cervical cancer screening
→ mammograms
→ treatment if diagnosed with cancer
→ breast reconstruction or prosthesis

States that don't have direct funds for treatment often make arrangements with other facilities to provide treatment for free. If your screening has been done elsewhere, you can

Breast Cancer Facts

∗ In 1998, there were 178,00 new cases of breast cancer in women and 1,600 new cases in men.

∗ In 1998, 43,500 women died from breast cancer, and 400 men died of breast cancer. 97% of women diagnosed with cancer have survived 5 years , in 1940 it was only 72%.

∗ 67% of women diagnosed with breast cancer survive 10 years.

∗ 57% of women diagnosed with breast cancer survive 15 years.

∗ By age 40 one in 217 women are diagnosed with breast cancer.

∗ By age 70 one in 14 women are diagnosed with breast cancer.

Source: American Cancer Society {www.cancer.org},
U.S. Dept of Health and Human Services Press Office
{www.hhs.gov/news/1998pres/981125.html}.

still receive free treatment under this program. Men diagnosed with breast cancer can also receive free treatment.

Contact your county office of public health listed in your telephone book or your state Department of Health listed in the Appendix. You can also contact the main office of this program at Division of Cancer Prevention and Control, National Center for Chronic Disease Prevention and Health Promotion, Center for Disease Control and Prevention, 4770 Buford Highway, NE, MS K-64, Atlanta, GA 30341, 770-488-4751; {www.cdc.gov/nccdphp/dcpc/nbccedp/index.htm}.

More Free Mammograms

Not all insurance companies pay for mammograms, and not every woman is eligible for the government's program described earlier. The following organizations can help you identify free and low cost mammograms in your area.

1) *The American Cancer Society*: contact your local office the national office at 800-ACS-2345.
2) *YMCA's Encore Plus Program*: contact your local office or the national office at 800-95-EPLUS
3) *National Cancer Institute*: 800-4-CANCER
4) *State Office of Breast and Cervical Cancer*: contact your state Department of Health listed in the Appendix

5) *October is National Breast Cancer Awareness Month*: many mammogram facilities offer their services at special fees during this period. Call and see what kind of deal you can get.

6) *Medicare coverage of mammograms*: call 800-638-6833

For a free copy of *How To Get A Low Cost Mammogram*, contact National Alliance of Breast Cancer Organizations, (NABCO) 9 East 37th Street, 10th Floor, New York, NY 10016; 800-719-9154; {www.nabco.org}.

Free Hospital Care

Don't have money for your gall bladder surgery? What about that hospital visit you had two months ago? You might not have to pay a cent. Call the Hill-Burton Hotline.

Under this program, certain hospitals and other health care facilities provide free or low-cost medical care to patients who cannot afford to pay. You may qualify even if your income is up to double the Poverty Income Guidelines. That's $32,900 for a family of four! You can apply before or after you receive care, and even after the bill has been sent to a collection agency.

Information USA, Inc.

Call the Hotline to find out if you meet the eligibility requirements and to request a list of local hospitals who are participating. For more information, contact Hill-Burton Hotline, Health Resources and Services Administration, 5600 Fishers Lane, Room 11-19, Rockville, MD 20857; 800-638-0742; 800-492-0359 (in MD); {www.hrsa.dhhs. gov/osp/dfcr/about/aboutdiv.htm}.

Free Food At School For Your Kids

A 1998 Tufts University study states: "Children who participate in the U.S. Department of Agriculture's School Breakfast Program were shown to have significantly higher standardized achievement test scores than eligible non-participants. Children getting school breakfasts also had significantly reduced absence and tardiness rates."

Your child can get a free breakfast at one of the 70,000 participating schools at one income level ($21,385 for family of 4) and at a reduced fee at another level ($30,433 for family of 4). Families who pay full price still get a bargain. Over 6.9 million kids participate and 5.9 million get it for free or at a reduced rate.

Lunch is also available under the U.S. Department of Agriculture's National School Lunch program at 95,000 schools serving 26 million children. The same general requirements apply to both programs.

Ask your school if they participate, or contact your local School Food Service Authority in your school system. If all this fails, contact your state Department of Education listed in the Appendix.

Check out the Food and Nutrition Services web page at {www.usda.gov/fcs}. *Note*: website will change to {www.usda.gov/fns} in the near future.

Legal Aid For Abused Women Who Are Not Eligible For Free Legal Services

If you have been turned down from state-offered services, and cannot afford a lawyer on your own, you can apply to *Legal Aid For Abused Women (LAAW),* a nonprofit organization that helps people when no other means are available.

LAAW can help you find a lawyer. LAAW provides a revolving fund for legal aid. Recipients reimburse up to 100% of the monetary assistance provided and/or volunteer their time to assist others affected by domestic violence.

Legal aid is provided regardless of race, nationality, gender, social status, orientation, or education level.

Contact: Legal Aid For Abused Women, 3524 S. Utah St., Arlington, VA 22206; 703 820-8393; Fax: 703 820-7968; {E-mail: 75700.655@ compuserve.com}; {http://ourworld.compuserve.com/homepages/laaw}.

Rich Kids Pay 2 Cents For Half-Pint of Milk

Milk at this price is available to students, no matter what the family income, at over 8,000 schools, 1,400 summer camps, and 500 non-residential child care institutions. The program is called the U.S. Department of Agriculture's **Special Milk Program** and is available to institutions that do not use the School Breakfast Program or the National School Lunch program.

Ask your school if they participate, or contact your local School Food Service Authority in your school system. If all this fails, contact your state Department of Education listed in the Appendix. If you cannot get satisfaction from these offices, contact your local office of your state or federal elected official.

Free Immunizations For Your Kids

Only 78% of children receive their full recommended vaccinations that protect them against polio, diphtheria, mumps, whooping cough, German measles, tetanus, spinal meningitis, chicken pox, and hepatitis B. An increasing number of children are exposed to diseases in day-care settings and elsewhere.

Almost any child, no matter what their income, can receive free or very low cost immunizations in their local area.

You Can Get Free Medical Care and Food But Not Welfare

Welfare reform laws have caused local governments to actively try to discourage people from applying for welfare payments. But, by federal law, they cannot discourage anyone from immediately applying for free medical care (Medicaid) and food assistance (Food Stamps). They are completely separate programs, and officials in Washington, DC believe that many eligible people are not applying for these services because local officials don't tell them their rights. It's the law. You have the right to apply.

Source: New York Times, November 22, 1998, Section 4, page 4

Contact your county office of health listed in your telephone book, or your state Department of Health listed in the Appendix. If you have trouble, call the National Immunization Information Hotline at 800-232-2522 (English); 800-232-0233 (Spanish); {www.cdc.gov/nip}.

Low Cost Immunizations for Travelers

In order to prevent contracting diseases like Yellow Fever, Cholera or Japanese Encephalitis when traveling in other countries, the government's Center for Disease Control recommends that certain vaccines would eliminate your risk of infection. Some local Public Health offices offer these vaccines at a fraction of what you would pay at a doctor's office.

To find your local county office of health, look in your telephone book or contact your state Department of Health listed in the Appendix. For more information about disease and vaccines for travel, contact: Center for Disease Control and Prevention, National Center for Infectious Diseases, Division of Quarantine, 1600 Clifton Road, MS E-03, Atlanta, GA 30333; 404-638-8100; Fax: 404-639-2500; {www.cdc.gov/travel/index.htm}.

How To Fight Your Doctor, Hospital, Or Insurance Company — Call The Marines

Well, not the actual Marines from the Department of Defense, dressed in fatigues and armed with high tech weapons. But you can call other government offices and advocacy groups that will do your fighting for you or give you the needed weapons to do your own fighting. Before you call a lawyer, call these free offices first:

♦ *State Insurance Commissioner*: will help you learn your legal rights regarding insurance.

♦ *State Medical Boards*: will review your complaint (including billing issues) and help resolve disputes.

♦ *State HMO boards*: will review your complaint (including billing issues) and help resolve disputes.

♦ *The Center for Patient Advocacy*, 1350 Beverly Road, Suite 108, McLean, VA 22101; 800-846-7444; {www.patientadvocacy.org}: provides free advice and publications on how to fight the system, also does advocacy work for patients rights on Capitol Hill)

♦ *Center for Medicare Advocacy, Inc*, P.O. Box 350, Willimantic, CT 06226; 860-456-7790; {www.medicareadvocacy.org}. Attorneys, paralegals, and technical assistants provide legal help for elderly and disabled who are unfairly denied Medicare coverage in the states of Connecticut and

New York. They will send materials to people in other states to learn how to fight for themselves.

♦ *American Self Help Clearinghouse*, Northwest Covenant Medical Center, 25 Pocono Road, Denville, NJ 07834; 973-625-9565; Fax: 973-635-8848; TTD 973-625-9053; {www.cmhc.com/selfhelp}: makes referrals to self-help organizations world wide and helps people interested in starting their own self help group.

♦ *National Self-Help Clearinghouse*, c/o CUNY, Graduate School and University Center, 25 West 43rd St., Room 620, New York, NY 10036; 212-354-8525; Fax: 212-642-1956; {www.selfhelpweb.org}: makes referrals to self-help groups nationwide.

National Immunization Information Hotline

This hotline tells you where you can go locally to get **Free Immunization** shots for your kids or flu shots for yourself. Immunizations for children can run as much as $335 per child.

This program is run by the U.S. Government's Center for Disease Control, which can answer almost any question you have about shots over the telephone or send you free publications. In most areas of the country, immunizations are available FREE for children. Adult services may be free or very low cost. Call 800-232-2522 (English); 800-232-0233 (Spanish); {www.cdc.gov/nip}.

Free Hepatitis B Shots
To Children

Oswego County Health Department offers free shots for children 18 and younger. The same with Buena-Vista County in Iowa, but people 19 and over are charged $31.75 for the shot. However, you won't be turned away if you cannot pay.

Hepatitis can cause serious liver disease, cancer and even death. About 1 in 20 people in U.S. have been infected, and over 4,000 a year die. To find out about services in your area, contact the county office of health listed in your telephone book or your state Department of Health listed in the Appendix.

30% of All Families Eligible For Free Health Services — Others Pay Sliding Scale

Many services provided by county governments are free and persons who don't qualify for free services are charged on a sliding scale based on income.

A typical fee chart is the one below from Denton, Texas. The data is based on 1996 Federal Poverty Rates from the

Bureau of the Census. Denton also states that *NO ONE WILL BE REFUSED SERVICES FOR INABILITY TO PAY*, which is typical for most counties. **REMEMBER**, if you don't qualify for free services, everyone qualifies for services on a sliding scale.

Estimated Income Limits For Free Service			
Service	Single Person	Family of 2	Family of 4
Food Vouchers and Nutritional Info (185% of poverty)	$14,893	$20,073	$30,433
Prenatal Care During Pregnancy (200% of poverty)	$16,100	$21,700	$32,900
Child Medical Care (200% of poverty)	$16,100	$21,700	$32,900
Adult Health Care (150% of poverty)	$12,075	$16,275	$24,675
Dental Care (150% of poverty)	$12,075	$16,275	$24,675
HIV Counseling & Testing	No limits, $10.00 donation requested		
Sexually Transmitted Disease Clinic	No limits, $10.00 donation requested		
Tuberculosis	No limits, $4.00 for testing		
Overseas Vaccinations	No limits, $5.00 to $50.00		
Immunizations	No limits, up to $30 per family, no one refused		
Substance Abuse Screening & Referral	No limits, Free		

Estimate of Families Living At Poverty Levels

% Of Poverty Level	Number of Families	% of Total Families
100%	12,594,000	12.3%
150%	21,055,000	20.0%
185%	28,174,000	27.4%
200%	30,078,000	29.3%

(Poverty Data from Census Report P60-198 1996 ----One Person = $7,995,
Two Persons = $ 10,233, Four Persons = $16,063,
Household Income Data from Census Current Population Reports, P60-200)
(Poverty Data 7/1/98 USDA {www.usda.gov/fcs/cnp/ieg98-99.htm}
1=$8,050, 2=$10,850, 3=13,650, 4=16,450, 5=19,250, 6=22,050, 7=24,850, 8=27,650

Cheap Air Fare to See a Sick Relative

Not free, but at least you don't have to pay full price. When a family member is very ill or has died, families have to make last minute airline reservations. Obviously you lose out on the 21-day advance purchase rates, but almost all airlines offer *bereavement* or *compassion* fares for domestic travel.

Generally the fares are available to close family members, and the discount on the full-fare rate varies from airline to airline. Many require that you provide the name of the deceased and the name, address and phone number of the funeral home handling arrangements. In the case of a medical emergency, the name and address of the affected family member and the name, address and phone number of the attending physician or hospital are required.

Contact the airline of your choice to learn more about the *"Bereavement/Compassion Fares."* Full fare rates vary from airline to airline, but you could save up to 50%.

Grants and Fundraising Help For Transplant Patients

Organizations like The National Foundation for Transplants and National Transplant Assistance Fund assist patients, their families, and friends in raising significant amounts of money for the patient's transplant care when there is no public or private insurance that will cover all the costs. They also provide grants to help pay for medications required after a transplant, or money for transplant-related emergencies, and one-time assistance grants of $1,000.

Other transplant related non-profits, like the Liver Foundation's Liver Transplant Fund, provide services and help for patients and families to raise money for an organ transplant.

☐ *National Foundation for Transplants*, 1102 Brookfield, Suite 200, Memphis, TN 38119; 800-489-3836, 901-684-1697, Fax: 910-684-1128; {www.transplants.org}.

☐ *National Transplant Assistance Fund*, 6 Bryn Mawr Avenue, P.O. Box 258, Bryn Mawr, PA 19010; 800-642-8399; Fax: 610-527-5210; {www.transplantfund. org}.

☐ *American Liver Foundation*, 75 Maiden Lane, Suite 603, New York, NY 10038; 800-GO LIVER; {www.liverfoundation.org}.

Working People With Disabilities Can Get Cheap Health Insurance

A change to the Balanced Budget Act of 1997 passed by Congress allows states to offer Medicaid to individuals who are working and who have a disability. Prior to this, states could only offer Medicaid to people with disabilities who were NOT working. The income limits goes up to $40,000 and the state can charge premiums on an income-related sliding scale.

Everything You Need To Know On Any Women's Health Topic: HOTLINE

This hotline sends out free publications and makes referrals to other organizations and groups on women related health topics. Contact National Women's Health Information Center, Office on Women's Health, U.S. Department of Health and Human Services, 200 Independence Ave., SW, Room 730B, Washington, DC 20201.

800-944-WOMEN; {www.4women.gov}.

Contact your state Department of Health listed in the Appendix to identify your Medicaid office. You can contact the local office of your congressman or senator for more information on the law. You can also check out the website of the Bazelon Center at {www.bazelon.org}.

Free Audio Tapes Describe Medicare Benefits To Disabled

If you have use of a high speed cassette player (talking book reader), you can learn about Medicare benefits with free audio copies of:

1) Medicare Home Health
2) Medicare and Medicaid Guide To Choosing a Nursing Home
3) Medicare Hospice Benefits
4) Medicare Managed Care
5) Medicare Savings for Qualified Beneficiaries
6) Medicare & Other Health Benefits: Who Pays First?

Contact your local Medicare office, order from 800-318-2596, or order online at {www.medicare.gov}.

$5 For SEXually Transmitted Diseases Tests

If you are worried that you may have contracted a Sexually Transmitted Disease (STD) or even HIV, you can get tested and even treated for free or for very low cost at one of your local public health clinics, or other public and private clinics around the country. Contact your county office of health listed in your telephone book or your state Department of Health listed in the Appendix.

If you need more help in identifying local help or need further information about HIV or an STD, contact one of the following, run by the U.S. Department of Health and Human Service's Center For Disease Control:

- *STD Hotline* 1-800-227-8922; {www.cdcnpin.org/}

- *National AIDS Hotline* 1-800-342-AIDS; {www.cdcnpin.org/}.

- *National Herpes Hotline* 1-919-361-8488; {www.cdc.gov/nchstp/dstd/dstdp/html}

These hotlines can answer questions over the phone, send out educational literature about a wide variety of sexually transmitted diseases and prevention methods, and provide referrals to free and low cost clinics nationwide.

Free Transportation
To Medical Appointments For Your Mom

Mom has to get to a doctor's visit in the middle of the day and you can't take her. Or you have a disability that may cause you to miss an appointment if someone else doesn't drive. You  may be able to get free transportation and escort services provided by either your local health office or local office on aging. Some communities even provide very low cost door-to-door services for seniors to go anywhere.

If you can't find your local area agency on aging or public health office in your telephone book, contact your state

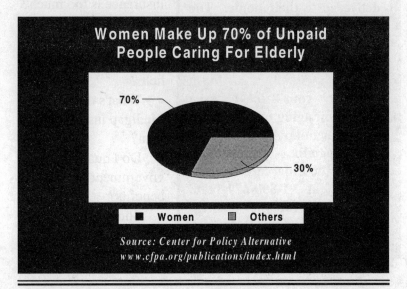

Women Make Up 70% of Unpaid People Caring For Elderly

70%

30%

■ Women   ▨ Others

Source: Center for Policy Alternative
www.cfpa.org/publications/index.html

Department of Aging or Health listed in the Appendix. If that fails, contact the Eldercare Locator Hotline at 1-800-677-1116. They are available to help anyone identify services for seniors.

Free Health Insurance Counseling

Free Take Out Taxi For Seniors

People 60 and over who are homebound because of illness, incapacity, or disability, or who are otherwise isolated can receive hot meals delivered to their home. The program is funded in every state by the Older Americans Act.

Contact your local area agency on aging or your state Department on Aging listed in the Appendix. If that fails, contact the Eldercare Locator hotline at 1-800-677-1116. They are available to help anyone identify services for seniors.

Free one-on-one counseling is available to seniors and, in most areas, people with disabilities, to answer questions like:

- How much insurance is too much?
- If something sounds like fraud, where can I go for help?
- What's the best Medigap insurance plan?
- Do I qualify for government health benefits?
- Should I buy long-term care insurance?

The program is called

Health Insurance Counseling and Advocacy Program (HICAP) and is sponsored by the U.S. Health Care Financing Administration. In most states, it is usually run by the state Department on Aging or the State Insurance Commissioner's office. The office for each state is listed in the Appendix. If that fails, contact the Eldercare Locator hotline at 1-800-677-1116. They can give you the local number.

Low Cost Home Health Care

Montgomery County in Maryland provides home health care free or on a sliding scale, depending on income, through the local public health office. You don't have to be a senior to qualify.

A survey by the Center for Disease Control reports that about half of all local public health agencies provide similar services. To see what is available in your area, contact your county office of health listed in your telephone book or your state Department of Health listed in the Appendix. If

---

Free Video Describes What Medicare Covers For In-Home Health Care

Get a free VHS copy of *Home Health Care* from your local Medicare office or from 800-318-2596 or order on-line at {www.medicare.gov}.

---

you cannot get satisfaction from these offices, contact your local office of your state or federal elected official.

For similar services for seniors, contact your local area agency on aging or your state Department on Aging listed in the Appendix. If that fails, contact the Eldercare Locator hotline at 1-800-677-1116. They are available to help anyone identify services for seniors.

$$$$$ Money To Buy A Van, A Talking Computer Or Rubber Door Knob Grips

People with disabilities now have a place to turn to learn everything they need to know about how the latest in technology can improve their lives. It can be a specially equipped van, a talking computer, a special kitchen or eating aid, or adaptive toys for children. Or it may be a student with learning disabilities who needs special help getting through school.

A project funded by the U.S. Department of Education, called Technical Assistance Project has established an office in each state that can provide:

▲ *Information Services*: will help you identify the special products that are available to help you cope with your disability.

▲ *Equipment Loan Program*: allows people to borrow new technology devices for a number of weeks before they purchase them.

▲ *Recycling Program*: matches up people with needs for products with people who want to sell or donate products.

▲ *Funding Information*: collects information on the various sources of funding for this equipment from public and private sources.

▲ *Loans*: many states are offering special loans to help people purchase the necessary equipment; Ohio offers low interest loans up to $10,000, California has loans up to $20,000, North Carolina up to $15,000.

Easter Seals In Arizona Offers Free Computers to People With Disabilities

Washington State chapter has a free loan program, and the chapters in Missouri offer computer classes. Contact you local Easter Seals Society to see what they may offer in the way of computers and computer skills for people with disabilities. If you can't find your local office, contact: Easter Seals, 230 West Monroe Street, Suite 1800, Chicago, IL 60606; 800-221-6825; 312-726-6200; fax: 312-726-1494; {www.seals.com}.

Contact your state capitol operator listed in the Appendix and ask for your state Office of Social Services or Vocational Rehabilitation. They should be aware of your state Assistance Technology Office.

If you have trouble locating your state office, you can contact the office that coordinates all state activities: Rehabilitation Engineering and Assertive Technology Society of North America, (RESNA), 1700 North Moore Street, #1540, Arlington, VA 22209; 703-524-6686; Fax: 703-524-6630; TTY: 703-524-6639; {www.resna.org}.

Free & Low Cost Dental Care for Kids, Seniors, and Certain Incomes

Many of the local health offices provide dental services to children and to income-eligible adults on a sliding fee scale. Contact your county office of health listed in your telephone book or your state Department of Health listed in the Appendix.

Many states have special free or discount services just for seniors. Contact your local Area Agency on Aging or your state Department on Aging listed in the Appendix. If that fails, contact the Eldercare Locator Hotline at 1-800-677-1116.

Do You Need A Break As A Caregiver?

If you're the only caregiver for a sick child or relative and get frustrated because you cannot leave the patient alone, you can get someone to take over for a few hours or a few days while you get rest or run errands.

Respite Care

The service is called Respite Care and depending on your income you can get this care for free or low cost through a number of different agencies:

★ *Your local public health services* : Contact your county office of health listed in your telephone book or your state Department of Health listed in the Appendix

★ *Your local office on aging*: Contact your local Area Agency on Aging or your state Department on Aging listed in the Appendix. If that fails, contact the Eldercare Locator hotline at 1-800-677-1116

★ *Easter Seals office* or Easter Seals, 230 West Monroe Street, Suite 1800, Chicago, IL 60606; 800-221-6825; 312-726-6200; Fax: 312-726-1494; {www.seals.com}. This organization charges on ability to pay, but no person is refused service

★ *Respite Locator Service*: National Resource Center or Respite & Crisis Care, 800 Eastowne Drive, Suite 105, Chapel Hill, NC 27514; 800-7 RELIEF; {www.chtop. com/locator.htm}.

INFERTILITY HELP LINE

Resolve is a non-profit organization that provides information, support and advocacy on the issues surrounding infertility. Their help line will help non-members with physician referrals, insurance questions, local support groups, and some free publications.

HELPLine hours are: Monday thru Friday 9am to noon, and 1pm to 4pm Eastern Standard Time and Tuesday evenings 4pm to 9pm. Contact Resolve, Inc., 1310 Broadway, Somerville, MA 92144; 617-623-1156; fax: 617-632-0252; HELPLine: 617-623-0744; {www.resolve.org}.

Discounts On Bicycle Helmets

The Department of Health in Mesa County Colorado offers discounts on bicycle helmets for children in the county. Check with your local office of health to see if there are any programs like this in your area.

If not, you can start one with a free *Toolkit for Organizers of Bicycle Helmet Programs* from Bicycle Helmet Safety Institute, 4611 Seventh Street South, Arlington, VA 22204; 703-486-0100; Fax 703-486-0576; {www.helmets.org}. This organization will also send you a free copy of *A Consumer's Guide to Bicycle Helmets*.

Choosing An Option

Deciding to have a child or children is an important step in anyone's life. Choosing a method of birth control is another big decision.

The Food and Drug Administration has several free publications dealing with specific types of birth control methods, along with a general overview of the different types of contraceptive methods. A good general overview publication is titled, *Protecting Against Unintended Pregnancy: A Guide to Contraceptive Choices*.

For your copies, contact Office of Communications, Food and Drug Administration, 5600 Fishers Lane, HFI-40, Rockville, MD 20857; 888-463-6332 (toll-free); {www.fda.gov}.

Join a Parkinson's Support Group - Or Start One!

The National Parkinson Foundation (NPF) has over 900 active support groups throughout the United States and Canada. If you are interested in starting a group or just want to find out about events in your area, contact: National Parkinson Foundation, Inc., 1501 NW 9th Ave, Miami, FL 33136; 305-547-6666; Fax 305-243-4403; 800-327-4545; 800-433-7022 (in FL); {E-mail: mailbox@npf.med.miami.edu}.

Work Out With Your Own Personal Trainer

You don't need to spend a fortune having someone coming to your house to motivate you to exercise. The President's Council on Physical Fitness and Sports has several free publications to spark your new exercise program.

Some titles include: *Fitness Fundamentals, Exercise and Weight Control*, and *Walking for Exercise and Pleasure*. Each of these titles provides technique guides, motivational tips, and more to get you up and moving.

For these publications and more information contact President's Council on Physical Fitness and Sports, HHH Bldg., Room 738H, 200 Independence Ave., SW, Washington, DC 20201; 202-690-9000; {www.indiana. edu/~preschal}.

Choosing a Safe and Successful Weight-Loss Program
Very Low-Calorie Diets
Weight Loss for Life.

Weight-Control Information Network, 1 Win Way, Bethesda, MD 20892; 301-984-7378; 800-WIN-8098; {www.niddk.nih.gov}.

Hot Flash Hotline

Menopause doesn't have to be the hormonal hurricane women faced in the past. Taking estrogen and progesterone can help relieve the problems of menopause, although they may not be without problems of their own.

A free booklet entitled *Menopause* can answer many of your questions and outlines different forms of treatment. Contact: Information Center, National Institute on Aging, P.O. Box 8057, Gaithersburg, MD 20898; 800-222-2225; {www.nih.gov/nia}.

BLADDER PROBLEMS

Wetting the bed affects many young people, although it usually disappears over time. No matter when it happens or how often it happens, incontinence causes great distress. That's why it is important to understand that occasional incontinence is a normal part of growing up and that treatment is available for most children who have difficulty controlling their bladders.

Urinary Incontinence in Children is a free publication that looks at the causes of daytime and nighttime incontinence and describes treatments available and additional resources. For your copy, contact National Kidney and Urologic Diseases Information Clearinghouse, 3 Information Way, Bethesda, MD 20892; 301-654-4415; {www.niddk.nih.gov}.

DYSLEXIA

Has the school talked with you about some problems your child is having? Do they suspect a learning disability? *Facts About Dyslexia* is a free publication that describes what dyslexia is, how it is diagnosed, and what you can do to help your child.

For your free copy, contact National Institute for Child Health and Human Development, 31 Center Dr., Room 2A32, MSC 2425, Bethesda, MD 20892; 301-496-5133; {www.nih.gov/nichd}.

Plain Talk About Stress
Plain Talk About Adolescence
Plain Talk About Dealing with the Angry Child

For the above free publications, contact Public Inquiries, National Institute of Mental Health, Room 7C-02, 5600 Fishers Lane, Rockville, MD 20857; 301-443-4513; {www.nimh.nih.gov}.

EAR INFECTIONS

There is not too much you can do at two in the morning when your child is crying because of an ear infection. You try to make the child as comfortable as possible and wait for the doctor's office to open.

Ear infections are a common problem for children, but one they usually outgrow by the time they are six. The National Institute on Deafness and Other Communication Disorders has an *Ear Infection Packet* they can send to parents, explaining how these infections occur and current treatment options.

For more information, contact National Institute on Deafness and Other Communication Disorders Clearinghouse, P.O. Box 37777, Washington, DC 20013; 800-241-1044; {www.nih.gov/nidcd/}.

Average Home Has 3-10 Gallons of Hazardous Materials

And 92% of human poisonings reported to U.S. poison control centers took place in the home

Source: Children's Health Environmental Coalition Network, Malibu, CA {www.checnet.org/ chec/index.html}.

ATTENTION DEFICIT

It seems as though there has been an increase in the diagnosis of Attention Deficit Disorder. Are we becoming more aware of this disorder or are we over-diagnosing it?

The National Institute of Mental Health funds research on a variety of learning disabilities and has published several helpful brochures and information packets on attention deficit disorder and learning disabilities in general.

Attention Deficit Hyperactivity Disorder describes symptoms, co-existing conditions, and possible causes, as well as treatment and education options. *Learning Disabilities* describes treatment options, strategies for coping, and sources of information and support.

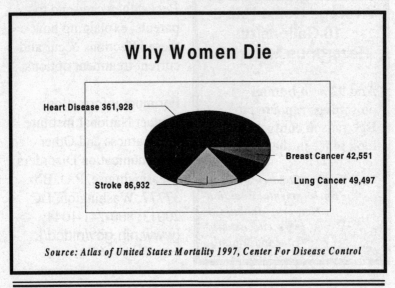

Why Women Die

Heart Disease 361,928

Breast Cancer 42,551

Stroke 86,932

Lung Cancer 49,497

Source: Atlas of United States Mortality 1997, Center For Disease Control

For more information, contact National Institute of Mental Health, 5600 Fishers Lane, Room 7C-02, Bethesda, MD 20892; 301-443-4513; {www.nimh.nih.gov}.

Diabetes During Pregnancy

Approximately 3-5 percent of all pregnant women in the United States develop gestational diabetes while pregnant. Gestational diabetes disappears after delivery, but careful control of blood sugar levels is necessary in order to manage and prevent complications.

Understanding Gestational Diabetes: A Practical Guide to a Healthy Pregnancy answers questions about diet, exercise, measurement of blood sugar levels, and general medical and obstetric care for women with gestational diabetes. Questions addressed include: Will gestational diabetes hurt your baby? How will it affect labor and delivery? What foods help keep blood sugar levels normal? And how much weight should you gain?

For your free booklet, contact National Institute of Child Health and Human Development, National Institutes of Health, Building 31, Room 2A32, 9000 Rockville, Pike, Bethesda, MD 20892; 301-496-5133; {www.nih.gov/nichd}.

Dear Diary

Following your development — and that of your baby — can be fun with this free booklet entitled, *Health Diary: Myself, My Baby.* Divided into two sections, the "Myself" section provides several pages for documenting your own health history, prenatal care, diet, weight gain and special memories of your pregnancy. Chock-full of information about labor and delivery, there's even a pull-out chart illustrating your baby's week-by-week development from birth to 24 months.

---

1 Out Of 4 Women Who Show Breast Cancer Don't Have It

A study published in the April 16, 1998 issue of The New England Journal of Medicine shows suggests that almost 25% of women will have a false-positive result at some point in 10 years of clinical breast exams.
{www.cancer.org/ bottomjoining.html}

You'll find spaces for snapshots of your newborn, information about caring and feeding, and a schedule for taking your baby to the doctor. There's also a section on treating minor problems, as well as spaces to record illnesses and notes following each doctor's visit. Contact National Maternal and Child Health Clearinghouse, 2070 Chain Bridge Rd., Suite 450, Vienna, VA 22182; 888-434-4MCH, 703-356-1964; {www.nmchc.org}.

Service Organizations

Need help with child care, elderly services, substance abuse treatment? What about youth programs or disaster assistance? Many large service organizations have local offices that provide all this and more. Services vary depending upon the needs of the community, but before you fight your battles alone, contact these main offices to find out about local programs:

✦ *Catholic Charities USA*, 1731 King St., #200, Alexandria, VA 23314; 703-549-1390; {www.catholiccharitiesusa.org}.
✦ *Salvation Army*, 615 Slaters Lane, P.O. Box 2696, Alexandria, VA 22313; 703-684-5500; 800-SAL-ARMY; {www.salvationarmyusa.org}.
✦ *United Way of America*, 701 N. Fairfax St., Alexandria, VA 22314; 800-411-UWAY; {www.unitedway.org}.

E-Mail A Friend Healthy Heart Greetings!

Create very special e-cards for those you love. Choose from lots of great images, heartwarming sayings and heart-healthy hints provided by the American Heart Association. And you can add your own personal message. You can send your free Heart to Heart e-card immediately, or schedule it to be sent any time during the ensuing twelve months. To create and send a free e-card, surf to: {www.americanheart.org/ecard/index.html}.

Help Is Just A Phone Call Away

No child, no matter if his parents are rich or poor, should be denied a healthy start to life. Under Title V of the Social Security Act, all families with young children and expecting mothers whose incomes fall near the federal poverty guidelines receive Medicaid. Poverty thresholds for 1997 were $7,890 for one person, $10,610 for two, $13,330 for three, and $16,050 for a family of four.

In addition, many prenatal and infant care services are often available to these low income families. These services include:

- Prenatal care clinics
- Home visiting services
- Translation services and other culturally focused services
- Parenting classes
- Programs for smoking cessation
- Male support programs
- Substance abuse treatment programs
- Help obtaining assistance such as Medicaid, food stamps, and WIC (supplemental food program for Women, Infants, and Children).

Information USA, Inc.

Begun in 1997, a new toll-free hotline funded by the U.S. Department of Health and Human Services will link callers from anywhere in the United States to prenatal and infant health services located nearest them. Call **800-311-BABY (2229)**. For Spanish speaking people, call **800-504-7081**.

Hospice Care

Sometimes, there is nothing to be done for a terminally ill patient other than to keep him or her comfortable. Hospice can help your loved one live their remaining days fully and comfortably.

To find a hospice provider near you, contact your doctor or local hospital for a referral. The National Hospice Organization is a non-profit organization dedicated to

Your Rights In The Health Care Industry

In 1998 the President's Advisory Commission on Consumer Protection and Quality in the Health Care Industry released their report showing consumers what they should demand when dealing with the health care industry.

For a free copy of the report contact: Consumer Bill of Rights, Box 2429, Columbia, MD 21045; 800-732-8200; {www.hcqualitycommission.gov}.

hospice care and can connect you to over 2,400 hospices across the United States. You may contact the National Hospice Organization, 1901 North Moore St., Suite 901, Arlington, VA 22209; 703-243-5900; {www.nho.org}.

Emergency Rooms Have To Take You

If you walk into an emergency room, do they have to treat you? Emergency rooms are now required to provide an initial screening to assess a patient's condition, which is designed to stop the automatic transfer of people unable to

pay. Emergency rooms must also treat emergency situations until they are stabilized, then they can refer you to other hospitals or clinics for further treatment.

If your health plan offers coverage for emergency services, your insurance must cover legitimate emergency department visits. You will not be required to obtain prior authorization for emergency services. Health plans are required to cover and pay for emergency care based upon the patient's presenting symptoms, rather than the final diagnosis.

If you feel you have been denied service, contact Health Care Financing Administration, 7500 Security Blvd., Baltimore, MD 21244; 410-786-3000;{www.hcfa.gov}.

Free Care By the Best Doctors In The World

Bob Dole knew where to go when he had his cancer surgery — The National Institutes of Health (NIH). Each year, close to 75,000 patients receive free medical care by some of the best doctors in the world.

Medical research professionals receive millions of dollars each year to study the latest causes, cures, and treatments to various diseases or illnesses. If your health condition is being studied somewhere, you may qualify for what is called a "clinical trial" and get the treatment for free.

There are several ways to find out about ongoing clinical trials across the nation. Your first call should be to the

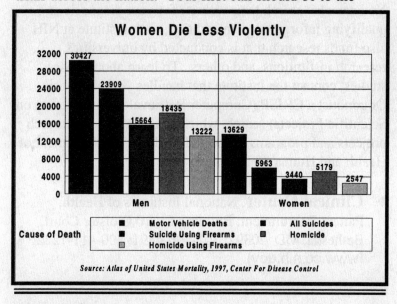

Women Die Less Violently

Cause of Death:
- Motor Vehicle Deaths
- Suicide Using Firearms
- Homicide Using Firearms
- All Suicides
- Homicide

Source: Atlas of United States Mortality, 1997, Center For Disease Control

National Institutes of Health Clinical Center. NIH is the federal government's focal point for health research. The Clinical Center is a 325-bed hospital that has facilities and services to support research at NIH. Your doctor can call the Patient Referral Line to find out if your diagnosis is being studied and to be put in contact with the primary investigator who can then tell if you meet the requirements for the study.

Women Make 3/4ths of the Health Care Decisions In America and Spend 2 Out of Every 3 Health Care Dollars

Source: Society for the Advancement of Women's Health Research; {www.womens-health.org}

You can also search their website for your diagnosis and qualifying information. In addition, each Institute at NIH also funds research that is conducted by universities, research institutions, and others. To learn about those studies, contact the Institute that handles your diagnosis. Or conduct a CRISP (Computer Retrieval of Information on Scientific Projects) search, which is a database of research projects and programs supported by the U.S. Department of Health and Human Services.

♦ **Clinical Center**, National Institutes of Health, Patient Recruitment, Building 61, 10 Cloister Court, Bethesda, MD 20892; 301-496-4891; 800-411-1222; {www.cc.nih.gov}.

♦ **National Institutes of Health**, Office of Communications, Building 1, Room 344, 1 Center Dr., MSC0188, Bethesda, MD 20892; 301-496-4000; {www.nih.gov}.

♦ **CRISP**, Office of Reports and Analysis, Office of Extramural Research, 6700 Rockledge Dr., Room 3210, Bethesda, MD 20892-7772; 301-435-0656; {www-commons.cit.nih.gov/crisp/}.

Free Eye Care

If you or someone you love needs eye care, but cannot afford it, the following organizations can help:

♥ For those 65 and older: *National Eye Care Project*, American Academy of Ophthalmology (AAO), P.O Box 429098, San Francisco, CA 94142; 415-561-8500; 800-222-3937; {www.eyenet.org}.

♥ For low-income families and children, applications are accepted on a first come-first serve basis in January with treatment following later in the year: *VISION USA*, American Optometric Association, 243 North Linbergh Blvd., St. Louis, MO 63141; 314-991-4100; 800-766-4466; {www.aoanet.org}.

♥ *Lions Clubs International*, 300 22nd St., Oak Brook, IL 60523; 630-571-5466; {www.lionsclubs.org}.

♥ *Glaucoma 2001*, American Academy of Ophthalmology (AAO), P.O Box 429098, San Francisco, CA 94142; 415-561-8500; 800-391-EYES; {www.eyenet.org}.

ARE YOU ELIGIBLE?

Health insurance can be quite confusing. What exactly do you qualify for?

Medicare is a health insurance program, generally for people age 65 or older who are receiving *Social Security* retirement benefits. You can also receive Medicare if you are under 65 and receive Social Security or Railroad Board disability benefits for 24 months, or if you are a kidney dialysis or kidney transplant patient.

Medicaid is a federal program administered by each state, so eligibility and benefits vary from state to state. The program is administered by a state welfare agency, and it provides health insurance to people with low income and limited assets.

Do You Smoke?

You Can Quit Smoking Consumer Guide is a free publication that tells you how you can improve your chances of quitting and overcoming your addiction to nicotine. Agency for Health Care Policy and Research, P.O. Box 8547, Silver Spring, MD 20907; 800-358-9295; {www.ahcpr.gov}.

To determine your eligibility, contact your state Office of Social Services listed in the Appendix. For Medicare eligibility, contact Medicare Hotline, Health Care Financing Administration, 6325 Security Blvd., Baltimore, MD 21207; 800-638-6833; {www.medicare.gov}.

Get Money While You're Waiting For Government Money

General Public Assistance or just Public Assistance (it is known by many different names) is a welfare program offered in 42 states. This is a program of last resort for people either waiting to qualify for other government programs such as disability benefits, or who do not qualify for any programs, yet need money to live.

The program eligibility and benefit levels vary within and across state lines. In some states, this benefit is only available in certain areas. There are strict income and asset levels that you must meet to qualify.

In Kansas, General Assistance pays families $278 per month while they are waiting for other government money. In California, the benefit is $225. Contact your local welfare office, your state Department of Social Service, or your state Temporary Assistance to Needy Families office listed in the Appendix to see what your state offers and the eligibility requirements.

National Institute's of Health Toll-Free Information Lines

AIDS Clinical Trials	800-TRIALSA
AIDS Treatment Information Service	800-HIV-0440
National Institute on Aging Information Center	800-222-2225
Alzheimer's Disease Education and Referral Center	800-438-4380
Cancer Information Service	800-4-CANCER
Patient Recruitment and Public Liaison Office	800-411-1222
National Institute of Child Health and Human Development	800-370-2943
National Diabetes Outreach Program	800-438-5383
National Institute on Deafness and Other Communication Disorders	800-241-1044
National Clearinghouse for Alcohol and Drug Information	800-729-6686
EnviroHealth: Information Service of the National Institute of Environmental Health Sciences	800-643-4794
National Heart, Lung, and Blood Institute Information Line	800-575-WELL
National Institute of Diabetes and Digestive and Kidney Diseases Bladder Control for Women Campaign	800-891-5388
National Institute of Mental Health Anxiety	888-8-ANXIETY

National Institute of Mental Health
    Depression   800-421-4211
National Institute of Mental Health Panic   800-64-PANIC
National Network of Libraries of
    Medicine   800-338-7657
National Institute of Neurological
    Disorders and Stroke Information   800-352-9424
National Center for Complementary and
    Alternative Medicine   888-NIH-6226
NIH Ovulation Research   888-644-8891
Osteoporosis and Related Bone Diseases   800-624-BONE
Weight-Control Information Network   800-WIN-8098

FREE HEALTHY HELPLINES

The following government and non-profit organizations are experts in their specific areas and will help you online or on the telephone line with free expertise, publications and referrals.

Women's Health

National Women's Health Information Center, U.S. Public Health Service, Office on Women's Health, 1600 Clifton Rd., NE, Atlanta, GA 30333; 800-944-WOMEN; {www. 4women.gov}.

Any Health Topic

National Health Information Center, P.O. Box 1133, Washington, DC 20013; 800-336-4797; 301-565-4167; Fax: 301-984-4256; {http://nhic-nt.health.org/}

Adoption

National Adoption Information Clearinghouse, 330 C St, NW, Washington, DC 20447; 703-352-3488; Fax: 703-385-3206; {www.calil.com/naic}.

National Adoption Center, 1500 Walnut St, #701, Philadelphia, PA 19102; 800-TO-ADOPT; 215-735-9988; Fax: 215-735-9410; {www.adopt.org/adopt}.

Aging

National Aging Information Center, U.S. Administration on Aging, 330 Independence Ave., NW, Room 4656, Washington, DC 20211; 202-619-7501; Fax: 401-7620; {www.aoa.dhhs.gov/naic/}.

National Institute on Aging Information Center, P.O. Box 8057, Gaithersburg, MD 20898; 800-222-2225; 301-587-2528; TDD: 800-222-4225; Fax: 301-589-3041; {www.nih.gov/nia}.

American Association of Retired Persons (AARP), 601 E St., NW, Washington, DC 20049; 800-424-3410; {www.aarp.org}.

AIDS

CDC National AIDS Clearinghouse, P.O. Box 6003, Rockville, MD 20849; 800-458-5231; Fax: 301-738-6616; TDD:800-243-7012; AIDS Clinical Trials: 800-874-2572; Fax-Back Service: 800-458-5231; HIV/AIDS Treatment: 800-448-0440; 301-519-0459; {www.cdcbac.org}.

Allergies

National Institute of Allergy and Infectious Diseases, Office of Communications, Building 31, Room 7A50, 900 Rockville Pike, Bethesda, MD 20892; 301-496-5717; {www.niaid.nih.gov}.

Alternative Medicine

National Center for Complementary and Alternative Medicine Clearinghouse, P.O. Box 8218, Silver Spring, MD 20907; 888-644-6226 (toll-free); 800-531-1794 (Fax-back); {http://altmed.od.nih.gov/ncccam/clearinghouse/}.

Alzheimer's Disease

Alzheimer's Disease Education and Referral Center, National Institute on Aging, P.O. Box 8250, Silver Spring, MD 20907; 800-438-4380; {www.alzheimers.org}.

Alzheimer's Association, 919 N. Michigan Ave., Suite 1000, Chicago, IL 60611; 800-272-3900; {www.alz.org}.

Arthritis

National Arthritis and Musculoskeletal and Skin Diseases Information Clearinghouse, 1 AMS Circle, Bethesda, MD 20892; 301-495-4484; 301-881-2731 (Fax-back service); {www.nih.gov/niams}.

Arthritis Foundation, 1330 W. Peachtree St., Atlanta, GA 30309; 404-872-7100 ext. 6350; 800-238-7800; {www.arthritis.org}.

Birth Defects

March of Dimes Birth Defects Foundation, 1275 Mamaroneck Ave., White Plains, NY 10605; 888-MODIMES; 914-428-7100; {www.modimes.org}.

Cancer

Cancer Information Service, National Cancer Institute; 31 Center Dr., MSC2580; Bldg. 31, Room 10A07; 800-4-CANCER; {http://cis.nci.nih.gov}.

Child Abuse

National Clearinghouse on Child Abuse and Neglect Information, 330 C St., SW, Washington, DC 20447; 800-FYI-3366; 703-385-7565; {www.calib.com/nccanch}.

Child Care

National Child Care Information Center, Administration For Children and Families, 243 Church St., NW, 2nd. Floor, Vienna, VA 22180; 800-616-2242; {http://nccic.org}.

Child Health

National Institute on Child Health and Human Development, National Institutes of Health, 31 Center Dr., MSC2425, Room 2A32, Bethesda, MD 20897; 301-496-5133; {www.nih.gov/nichd}.

Deafness

National Institute on Deafness and Other Communication Disorders Information Clearinghouse, 1 communication Ave., Bethesda, MD 20892; 800-241-1044; 800-241-1055 (TTY); {www.nih.gov/nidcd}.

Depression

National Mental Health Association, Public Information, 1021 Prince St., Alexandria, VA 22314; 703-684-7722; 800-969-6642; {www.nmha.org}.

National Institute of Mental Health, National Institutes of Health, 9000 Rockville Pike, MSC 80-30; Bethesda, MD 20892; 301-443-4513; 800-421-4211; 800-64-PANIC (panic disorder hotline); 888-8-ANXIETY (anxiety disorders hotline); {www.nimh.nih.gov}.

Diabetes

National Diabetes Information Clearinghouse, 1 Information Way, Bethesda, MD 20892; 301-654-3327; {www.niddk.nih.gov/health/diabetes/ndic.htm}.

American Diabetes Association, 1660 Duke St., Alexandria, VA 22314; 800-232-3472; {www.diabetes.org}.

Juvenile Diabetes Foundation International, 120 Wall St., 19th Floor, New York, NY 10005; 212-785-9500; 800-223-1138; {www.jdfcure.org}.

Digestive Disorders

National Digestive Diseases Information Clearinghouse, 2 Information Way, Bethesda, MD 20892; 301-654-3810; {www.niddk.nih.gov}.

Disabilities
National Rehabilitation Information
Center, National Institute on
Disabilities and Rehabilitation
Research, 8455 Colesville Rd., Suite
935, Silver Spring, MD 20910; 301-
588-9284; 301-495-5626 TTY; 800-
346-2742; {www.cais.com/naric}.

National Information Center for Children and Youth with
Disabilities, P.O. Box 1492, Washington, DC 20013; 800-
695-0285; {www.nichcy.org}.

Domestic Violence
National Domestic Violence Hotline, P.O. Box 161810,
Austin, TX 78716; 512-453-8117; 800-799-SAFE;
{www.ndvh.org}.

Food and Drug Information
Food and Drug Administration, Office of Consumer
Affairs, 5600 Fishers Lane, HFE-88, Rockville, MD
20857; 888-463-6332; {www.fda.gov}.

Heart Disease
American Heart Association, 7272 Greenville Ave., Dallas,
TX 75231; 214-706-1200; 800-242-8721;
{www.americanheart.org}.

National Heart, Lung, and Blood Institute, Information
Center, P.O. box 30105; 301-251-1222; 800-575-WELL;
{www.nhlbi.nih.gov/nhlbi/infcntr/infocent.htm}.

Immunizations

Centers for Disease Control and Prevention, Mail Stop D25, 1600 Clifton Rd., NE, Atlanta, GA 30333; 800-CDC-SHOT; {www.cdc.gov}.

Kidney Disease

National Kidney and Urologic Diseases Information Clearinghouse, 3 Information Way, Bethesda, MD 20892; 301-654-4415; {www.niddk.nih.gov/health/kidney/nkudic.htm}.

Lead

National Lead Information Center, 8601 Georgia Ave., Suite 503, Silver Spring, MD 20910; 800-424-LEAD (clearinghouse); 800-LEAD-FYI (hotline); {www.epa.gov/lead/nlic/htm}.

Medicare

Medicare Hotline, Health Care Financing Administration, 6325 Security Blvd, Baltimore, MD 21207; 800-638-6833; {www.medicare.gov}.

Nutrition

Food and Nutrition Information Center, U.S. Department of Agriculture, 10301 Baltimore Ave., Room 304, Beltsville, MD 20705; 301-504-5719; {www.nal.usda.gov/fnic}.

American Dietetic Association, 216 W. Jackson Blvd., Suite 800, Chicago, IL 60606; 312-899-0040; 800-366-1655; {www.eatright.org}.

Weight-Control Information Network, National Institute of Diabetes and Digestive and Kidney Diseases, 1 Win Way, Bethesda, MD 20892; 301-984-7378; 800-WIN-8098; {www.niddk.nih.gov/health/nutrit/win.htm}.

Oral Health

National Oral Health Information Clearinghouse, 1 NOHIC Way, Bethesda, MD 20892; 301-402-7364; {www.aerie.com/nohicweb}.

Osteoporosis

Osteoporosis and Related Bone Diseases National Resource Center, 1150 17th St., NW, Suite 500, Washington, DC 20036; 800-624-BONE; 202-223-0344; {www.osteo.org}.

Pregnancy

International Childbirth Education Association, P.O. Box 20048; Minneapolis, MN 55420; 800-624-4934; {www.icea.org}.

National Maternal and Child Health Clearinghouse, Health Resources and Services Administration, 2070 Chain Bridge Rd., Suite 450, Vienna, VA 22182; 703-356-1964; {www.circsol.com/mch}.

Postpartum Support International, 927 North Kellog Ave., Santa Barbara, CA 93111; 805-967-7636; {www.iup.edu/an/postpartum}.

La Leche League International, 1400 North Meacham Rd., P.O. Box 4079, Schaumburg, IL 60168; 800-LALECHE; {www.lalecheleague.org}.

Product Safety

U.S. Consumer Product Safety Hotline, Washington, DC 20207; 800-638-2772; {www.cpsc.gov}.

Rural Information

Rural Information Center Health Service, National Agricultural Library, Room 304, 10301 Baltimore Blvd., Beltsville, MD 20705; 800-633-7701; {www.nal.usda.gov/ric/richs}.

Sleep Disorders

National Center on Sleep Disorders Research, 2 Rockledge Center, 6701 Rockledge Dr., MSC 7920, Bethesda, MD 20892; 301-435-0199; {www.nhlbi.nih.gov/nhlbi/sleep/sleep.htm}.

Smoking

Office on Smoking and Health, National Center for Chronic Disease Prevention and Health Promotion, Centers For Disease Control and Prevention, Mail Stop K-50, 4770 Buford Hwy, NE, Atlanta, GA 30341; 770-488-5705; 800-CDC-1311; {www.cdc.gov/nccdphp/osh}.

Substance Abuse

National Clearinghouse for Alcohol and Drug Information, P.O. Box 2345, Rockville, MD 20847; 800-729-6686; {www.health.org}.

PRIDE, National Parent's Resource Institute for Drug Education, 3610 Dekalb Technology Parkway, Suite 105; Atlanta, GA 30340; 770-458-9900; 800-853-7433; {www.prideusa.org}.

National Substance Abuse Helplines, 164 W. 74th St., New York, NY 10023; 800-COCAINE; 800-DRUGHELP; 800-RELAPSE; {www.drughelp.org}.

ASK-AN-EXPERT WEBSITES

The following is a list of websites where you can ask experts in the medical field your health questions. These websites are designed to help educate you on a wide range of health topics.

Go ahead and ask them anything. Some questions include: Can I travel by air in my seventh month of pregnancy? What can be done for excessive snoring? Are the herbal medicines sold in health food stores really safe? Can the new cartilage transplant surgery help my arthritic knee?

Allergies: {www.allernet.com}

Aneurysms: {www.westga.edu/~wmaples/doc.html}

Arthritis: {www.arthritis.org/forms/ask_help.shtml}

Asthma: {www.asthmacentre.com/ask_the_doctor.
html}

Attention Deficit Disorder: {www.erols.com/
drleeb/}

Bipolar Mood Disorder: {www.mhsource.com/
bipolar/expert.html}

Blood Vessels: {www.visi.com/~irm/}

Bones and Joints: {http://bunny.lek.net/~fed/}

Brain and Nervous System: {www.surgery.
missouri.edu/ns/Services/nurse.html}

Cancer: {www.cancercareinc.org/services/
referral2.htm}
_ {www.cancerhope.com/ask_a_doctor/
question.html}
_ {http://143.111.212.41/cancerinfoask_doc.thm}

CPR: {www.learncpr.org/askdoctor.html}

Dentist: {www.the-toothfairy.com}

Diabetes: {www.childrenwithdiabetes.com/
dteam/d_0d004.htm}

Diet: {www.drdiet.com}

Eyes: {www.visioncare.com/ask.htm}
{www.magrudereye.com/home2.htm}

General Health: {www.mercyhealthsystem.org/
ASKNURSE/askartcl.htm}
_ {www.intelihealth.com/IH/}
_ {www.ahooo.com/health/Ask_the_Nurse}
_ {www.harthosp.org/questions/}

_ {www.dreamtek.com/doctor.html}

_ {www.coloradohealthnet.org/COPD/
copd_ask.html}

_ {www.bethisraelny.org/interactive/askdoctor.htm}

Grief: {www.death-dying.com/experts/index.html}

Heart Disease: {www.sacheart.com/ask_the_docs.
html}

Infertility: {www.fetilitext.org/Question.htm}

Kidneys: {www.dreamscape.com/kidneycny/}

Knee Problems: {www.knees.com/}

Medications: {www.wilmington.net/dees/ask.html}

Men's Health: {http://methodisthealth.com/Urology/
ask.htm}

Mental Health: {www.mhsource.com/expert.html}
{www.brylin.com}

Muscles: {www.openmri-southtexas.com/
askthe.html}

Muscular Dystrophy: {www.mdausa.org/experts}

Neonatology: {www.neo.tch.tmc.edu/}

Neurology: {www.dr-neurosurg.com/index.html}
_ {www.bih.harvard.edu/neurology/docbag.htm}

Orthodontics: {www.bracesrus.com/}

Pain: {www.pain.com/defaultcon.cfm?direct=dr}

Parenting: {www.mbnet.mb.ca/crm/granny/
granny.html}

Pediatric Urology: {http://peds-www.bsd.uchicago.
edu/sections/urology/index.html}

Pediatrics: {www.drplaintalk.org}
_ {www.mindspring.com/~drwarren/wpsl.htm}

_ {www.drs4kids.com/index.html}
_ {www.med.virginia.edu/cmc/emailsrv.html}

Plastic Surgery: {www.ariyan.com/index.html}
_ {www.phudson.com/WELCOME/form.html}

Pregnancy: {www.abilene.com/armc}
_ {www.modimes.org/rc/help.htm}

Radiology: {http://telescan.nki.nl/SecondOpinion/index.html}

Skin Conditions: {www.facefacts.com/doctork.htm}

Spinal Problems: {www.orthospine.com/questions_entrance.html}

Sports Medicine: {www.kyclinic.com}

Surfing Ailments: {www.mavsurfer.com/riptide/index.html}

Thyroid Disease: {www.thyroid.com/index.html}

Veterinarian: {www.prah.com/ask.htm}
{www.k9shrink.com/html/askdoc.html}

Whiplash: {www.whiplash101.com/discussion/}

Women's Health: {www.womenshealth.org}
{www.healthywomen.com/asknp/index.htm}

Note: Obviously, this is not meant to replace seeing a doctor, but to educate you to be a more informed health consumer.

FREE FOR SENIOR MOMS AND THOSE TAKING CARE OF SENIOR MOMS

Get Presidential Honors For A Deceased Veteran

You can help commemorate the honor of a deceased veteran by requesting a *Presidential Memorial Certificate*, a parchment certificate with a calligraphic inscription expressing the nation's recognition of the veteran's service. The veteran's name is inscribed and the certificate bears the signature of the President.

Eligible recipients include next of kin, other relatives and friends. The veteran may have died at any time in the past. VA regional offices can assist in applying for certificates or obtaining the necessary documents.

For more information, contact Department of Veterans Affairs, 810 Vermont Ave., NW, Washington, DC 20420; 800-827-1000.

Travel Tips For Older Americans

What do you do if you lose your passport or have a health emergency? Is it safe to travel to a particular country? What about your medications?

Travel Tips for Older Americans explains all this and more, and can be viewed for free online at {http://travel.state.gov} or you can order the publications for $1.25 (044-000-02459-4) at Superintendent of Documents, U.S. Government Printing Office, Washington, DC 20406; 202-512-1800.

A Great Gift For An Old Sea Dog

For those who spent their military years on a ship or in service to the Navy, pictures are available to help you remember those exciting times. The U.S. Naval Institute has over 450,000 photographs (a limited number are in color), chronicling the Navy's ships, battles, and major events.

You can purchase an 8x10 photograph of a specific ship or subject matter for $12 for black and white and $18 for color. There is a $3.50 shipping and handling charge. The more information you can supply with your photo request, the better. Ship name, hull number, and year of service are helpful.

If you request a photo of a ship, make sure to ask for a free two-page history of the vessel to be included with the picture. It normally takes 4-6 weeks to process the order. For more information, contact U.S. Naval Institute, 118 Maryland Ave., Annapolis, MD 21402; 410-295-1022.

LOCATING HELP FOR SENIORS

Looking for the local meals on wheels programs, or need a home health aide for mom? The *Eldercare Locator* searches their database for the services for seniors in any area of the country. These can include transportation, legal assistance, housing options, recreation and social activities, adult daycare, senior center programs, and more.

Contact the Eldercare Locator, National Association of Area Agencies on Aging, 1112 16th St., NW, Washington, DC 20036; 800-677-1116 (9 a.m.- 8 p.m. EST); {www.n4a.org}.

Free Exercise Book For Seniors

Exercise: A Guide from the National Institute on Aging will get you moving. It describes the benefits of exercise, safety tips, nutritional information, and motivational tips, to help you start an exercise program that is right for you. You can see illustrated examples of exercises that you can do in your home.

For your copy, contact National Institute on Aging, Information Center, P.O. Box 8057, Gaithersburg, MD 20898, 800-222-2225; {www.nih.gov/nia}.

Vet Services Hotline

The Department of Veterans Affairs hotline can provide you with information on such programs as life insurance, comprehensive dental and medical care, nursing homes, home loan programs, burial services, and more.

Contact Department of Veterans Affairs, 810 Vermont Ave., NW, Washington, DC 20420; 800-827-1000; {www.va.gov}.

Free Hospital Care

If you are having trouble paying your hospital bill, or need an operation but don't have the funds, contact the Hill-Burton Hotline. Under this program certain hospitals and other health care facilities provide free or low-cost medical care to patients who cannot afford to pay. You can apply before or after you receive care, and even after the bill has been sent to a collection agency.

Call the Hotline to find out if you meet eligibility requirements and to get a list of local hospitals that participate in the program. Contact Hill-Burton Hotline at 800-638-0742.

50% Discount On Telephone Service

Under the Federal Communication Commission's Link-Up America and Lifeline programs, low-income households seeking telephone service are given a 50% discount on local connection charges, and may be able to pay installment payments on the remaining charge. These programs are available in most states.

To sign up for this service, contact the customer service representative at your local telephone company.

IT'S LESS TAXING
FOR SENIORS

The *Tax Counseling for the Elderly* program was designed to provide free taxpayer assistance to those age 60 and above. The staff usually consists of retired individuals associated with non-profit organizations that receive grants from the IRS to perform this service. Often they provide counseling in retirement homes, neighborhood sites or private houses of the homebound.

For information on the Tax Counseling for the Elderly program near you, contact your local IRS office or call the hotline at 800-829-1040. Information is also available online at {www.irs.gov}.

Special Tax Help

The tax guys thought only of you when they wrote the *Older Americans' Tax Guide* (Publication 554). It answers all those specific tax questions about your filing status, retirement benefits, life insurance proceeds, and more.

Other publications of interest include *Credit for the Elderly or Disabled* (Pub. 524); *Pension and Annuity Income* (Pub. 575); and *Medical and Dental Expenses* (Pub. 502). For

your copies, contact the IRS Forms Line at 800-829-3676;
{www.irs.gov}.

A List of Senior Tax Deductions

A free publication titled, *Protecting
Older Americans Against
Overpayment of Income Taxes* is
designed to ensure that older
Americans claim every
legitimate income tax deduction,
exemption, and tax credit. It's very easy to
understand and provides many examples and checklists.

Send a request on a postcard to Special Committee on
Aging, U.S. Senate, Senate Dirksen Bldg. G31,
Washington, DC 20510; 202-224-5364;
{www.senate.gov/~aging}.

Free Help With Pension Tax Questions

No need to pay an attorney money to interpret the tax issues
surrounding retirement and pension plans. You can talk to
the guys who wrote the law!

The Internal Revenue Services operates a hotline service
that allows you to speak to tax attorneys specializing in
retirement and pension plan issues. They are available
Monday through Thursday, from 1:30 p.m. to 3:30 p.m.

(EST). They can be reached at Employee Plans Technical and Actuarial Division, Internal Revenue Service, U.S. Department of Treasury, Room 6550, CP:E:EP, 1111 Constitution Ave., NW, Washington, DC 20224; 202-622-6074 or 6075.

Extended Care Database

Access the *National Directory of Health-Care Services Providers* when an elderly relative is too frail to live alone but too healthy for hospitalization. It lists over 33,000 acute rehabilitation providers, retirement communities, home health-care agencies and more.

Nursing Home Shopping List

Learn what to ask and check for with your free copy of *Choosing a Quality Nursing Home* from American Association of Homes and Services for the Aging, 901 E St., NW, Suite 500, Washington, DC 20004; 301-490-0677; 800-508-9442; {www.aahsa.org}.

You may search by city, state, county provider name or provider type. The listings display provider's name, address, telephone number, number of beds and rooms, and the type of care available. It's not an all-inclusive list, but it can be good starting ground, especially for those searching from miles away.

Visit the website for Extended Care Information Network Inc. at {www.extendedcare.com}.

When Alzheimer's Strikes

Caring for someone with Alzheimer's can be emotionally, physically, and financially stressful. There may come a time when you will need to find a place for your loved one to live or at least somewhere they can receive respite care.

Many nursing homes have special Alzheimer's units where the staff receives special training and where they can accommodate the special needs of your loved one. The Alzheimer's Association provides information about Alzheimer's disease and links families with local chapters that are familiar with community resources.

Free Help With Nursing Home Problems

If a problem with a nursing home is not resolved to your satisfaction, you can then contact your state's Nursing Home Ombudsman. They will investigate and resolve your complaint for you. They act as mediators, but they are not enforcement agencies. But it is in the best interest of the nursing home to work with you before you refer your complaint elsewhere.

To locate the Nursing Home Ombudsman in your state, look in the blue pages of your phone book or contact your State Department of Aging, listed in the Appendix.

For more information, contact Alzheimer's Association, 919 North Michigan Ave., Suite 1000, Chicago, IL 60611; 800-272-3900; {www.alz.org}.

FREE EYE CARE

The *National Eye Care Project Helpline* puts callers in touch with local ophthalmologists who have volunteered to provide medical eye care at no out-of-pocket expense. Individuals must be 65 or older and not have had access to an ophthalmologist within the past three years. The emphasis of this program is to help disadvantaged people.

For more information, contact National Eye Care Project Helpline, American Academy of Ophthalmology, P.O. Box 429098, San Francisco, CA 94142-9098; 800-222-3937 (8 a.m.- 4 p.m. PST); {www.eyenet.org}.

Free Help For Cancer Families

Local chapters of the American Cancer Society sponsor a wide range of services for cancer patients and their families, including self-help groups, transportation programs, and lodging assistance for those who must travel far for treatment. To find your local chapter or for more information on cancer detection, prevention and treatment, contact American Cancer Society, 1599 Clifton Rd., NE, Atlanta, GA 30329; 800-ACS-2345; {www.cancer.org}.

Give Your Heart A Chance

The American Heart Association sponsors public education programs on the prevention and control of heart diseases. They have a division called *The Stroke Connection* at the American Heart Association that offers support to stroke survivors, their families, and caregivers.

To locate your local chapter, contact American Heart Association, 7272 Greenville Ave., Dallas, TX 75231; 800-242-8721; Stroke Connection is 800-553-6321; {www.amhrt.org}.

DIABETES HELPLINE

If you're looking for information on diabetes cures, treatments, free screenings, support groups or other help contact American Diabetes Association, 1660 Duke St., Alexandria, VA 22314; 800-DIABETES; {www.diabetes.org}.

Arthritis Information

The Arthritis Foundation's mission is to support research, prevention, and find a cure for 100 forms of arthritis, and to improve the quality of life for people with arthritis. They have chapters nationwide that offer health education programs in local communities, including arthritis self-help courses, aquatic programs, exercise programs, support groups, public forums, and more. They have publications, videos, and other resources that are available for free or at minimal cost.

For more information, contact Arthritis Foundation, 1330 W. Peachtree St., Atlanta, GA 30309; 800-283-7800; {www.arthritis.org}.

Parkinson's Help

The United Parkinson Foundation is a nonprofit organization that provides supportive services to patients and their families. The Foundation can provide background information on Parkinson's, exercise materials, a newsletter, and more.

For more information, contact United Parkinson Foundation, 833 West Washington Blvd., Chicago, IL 60607; 312-733-1893; {Email:upf_itf@msn.com}.

Money For New Hearing Aids

You can get information on different types of hearing loss, lists of hearing professionals, and information on locating financial assistance for assistive hearing devices by calling The Better Hearing Institute, P.O. Box 1840, Washington, DC 20013; 800-EAR-WELL; {www.betterhearing.org}.

Caring For Your Parents

Many of us are finding that it is our turn to provide care and assistance to our parents. We do it willingly, but at times we need help ourselves. Where do we turn?

Children of Aging Parents is a nonprofit organization that provides information and emotional support to caregivers of older people. They are a national information and referral service, and can help you locate needed services or information ranging from respite care to elder attorneys to nursing homes.

For more information, contact Children of Aging Parents, 1609 Woodbourne Rd., Suite 302A, Levittown, PA 19057; 800-227-7294; {www.experts.com}.

GET PAID TO HELP YOUR COMMUNITY

Low-income seniors can volunteer to serve as mentors, tutors, and caregivers for children and young kids with special needs, and can also work in schools, hospitals, and recreation centers in their communities. Volunteers work twenty hours per week, and receive a small paycheck and other benefits.

For more information on this program, contact National Senior Service Corps, 1201 New York Ave., NW, Washington, DC 20525; 800-424-8867; {www.cns.gov}.

Get Paid To Help A Fellow Senior

The *Senior Companion Program* pays seniors to take care of other seniors who want to remain at home but need a little extra help. What a great way to help or get the help you need, remain in dependent and also get a friend!

Contact National Senior Service Corps, 1201 New York Ave., NW, Washington, DC 20525; 800-424-8867; {www.cns.gov}.

Share Your Know-How

You've got forty years of business experience out there and you're on the golf course during your retirement. There are hundreds of businesses and even nonprofit groups starting up each day run by people who have the energy, but not the experience that you possess.

You can lend your expertise to those who need your help the most. The ***Retired Senior Volunteer Program*** gives retired people a chance to continue using their professional experience by working with local service organizations doing such things as conducting employment workshops and acting as consultants to nonprofit

Spend Your Vacation As A Moose Crossing Guard At Old Faithful

Each year the National Parks use 80,000 volunteers, 15,000 of whom are in the over 50 crowd! Contact your nearest park to discover an interesting way to spend your free time or to receive a free brochure, contact Office of Public Inquiries, National Park Service, U.S. Department of the Interior, 1849 C St., NW, Washington, DC 20240; 202-208-4747; {www.nps.gov}.

organizations. You can even work in schools, libraries, hospitals, and other community service centers.

For more information, contact National Senior Service Corps, 1201 New York Ave., NW, Washington, DC 20525; 800-424-8867; {www.cns.gov}.

Get Out Of The House And Into the Woods

If you prefer saving spotted owls and counting woodchucks to playing bridge with the girls, you can be a volunteer with the Forest Service and be a nature hike leader or help with fascinating research.

Contact your nearest national forest. For a list of national forests nearest you, contact U.S. Forest Service, U.S. Department of Agriculture, Human Resource Programs, P.O. Box 96090, Washington, DC 20090; {www.fs.fed.us}.

Travel The World And Save It Too, For Free

Provide business assistance in Poland. Teach school in Nepal. These are just two examples of how over 500 seniors spent their time with the Peace Corps.

As a volunteer, you serve for two years, living among the native people and becoming part of the community. The Peace Corps sends volunteers throughout most of the world to share their expertise in education, agriculture, health, economic development, the environment, and more.

To learn how you can serve, contact Peace Corps, 1990 K St., NW, Washington, DC 20526; 800-424-8580; {www.peacecorps. gov}.

Make Your Local Businesses Run Better

Retired business professionals can make the world run better by volunteering their experience to the next generation of business owners. You can be one of the 12,400 SCORE volunteers at the U.S. Small Business Administration by contacting SCORE, 409 Third St., SW, Washington, DC 20024; 202-205-6762; 800-634-0245; {www.score. org}.

10-50% OFF
HOTEL ROOMS

Almost all major hotel chains offer discounts from 10-30% off the cost of rooms. Some require that you belong to AARP or AAA, so it is best to call ahead and ask.

Three hotel chains, Ramada, Hilton, and Red Roof Inns offer special deals to seniors who frequent their hotels. Ramada's Best Years Club charges $15 for a lifetime membership fee. The fee entitles you to 25% off regular two double bed room rates, plus you receive points redeemable for travel and prizes (800-672-6232; available at most Ramadas).

Hilton Senior HHonors program charges $50 ($40 annual renewal fee), and seniors receive up to 50% off rooms and 20% off hotel restaurants (800-492-3232).

Red Roof has a lifetime Redicard for seniors that costs $10. The card gets you 10% off rooms, plus 3 $5 off coupons for lodging (800-843-7663).

10% Off
Your Airline Tickets

Every airline offers discounts to seniors amounting to
usually 10%. What happens, though, is that some of the
airlines' special offers may be exempt from the discount. It
is best to see what the lowest available rate is and then
inquire about the discount.

All the major airlines also offer coupon books for seniors
that are four round-trip tickets good for wherever the airline
flies. The price of the coupon books is around $540. In

10-15% OFF
WHEN YOU TRAVEL

All car rental chains offer senior discounts, but
again AARP or AAA membership may be required.
The amount of discount varies from location to
location, but usually is 10%. You should call ahead
to see if a discount is available. Some chains also
require reservations 24 hours in advance.

For those that prefer to leave the driving to others,
two other discount programs include AMTRAK and
Greyhound. Amtrak offers 15% off any fare
available to those 62 and older (800-USA-RAIL).
Greyhound has an 8% discount for people 55 and
over (800-231-2222).

many instances, the airline only requires that one person meet the age requirement for a discount, so your companion can receive the lower rate as well.

Free (Or Cheap) Hunting and Fishing Licenses

Practically every state has a special license rate for seniors. States such as Alabama, Alaska, Delaware, Georgia, Kansas, and others do not require that people age 65 and over to carry a fishing and hunting license. Other states offer seniors, on average, half off the cost of licenses.

Inquire where you usually purchase these licenses to learn what age you need to be to receive the discount and the specific details.

50% Off Camping

Almost all states offer discounts to seniors at state parks. Entrance fees are usually waived for seniors, or states like Illinois offer 50% off camping fees. Eighteen states have no residency requirements to receive the discount, so if you are planning a cross country camping trip, contact the state Parks Department to find out about eligibility criteria.

For those wanting to camp in the National Forest, the Golden Age Passport is available to those 62 and over. For $10 you receive free lifetime admission to the parks, plus 50% off on camping and many other services. The Passport is available at all National Forests.

5-10% Off When You Shop

Banana Republic offers seniors age 62 and older 10% off every day, while Ross, Stone & Thomas, and Glik's offer 10% off to seniors on specific days during the week. Other stores like Wal-mart and May Co. frequently offer advertised senior specials. Sears and Montgomery Ward have discount cards or clubs you can join for a fee that entitles you to discounts and other services.

10% OFF AT RESTAURANTS

The Early Bird specials can happen all day once you hit a certain age. Many restaurant chains offer special deals for seniors. Most restaurant chains are independently owned and operated, but they usually follow the recommendations from the headquarters.

Places like Denny's, Bob Evan's, and International House of Pancakes frequently offer seniors a reduced price menu. Other chains, such as Applebee's, Kentucky Fried Chicken, and Wendy's, often give seniors a 10% discount on their meals. It never hurts to ask if a discount is offered.

Ask at the main offices of stores where you shop to see what may be available to you. Even grocery stores are getting into the act!

10%-100% Off
On Your Glasses

Pearle Vision Centers offer 50% off either the lenses or frames when you purchase a complete set of glasses to people 50-59, 60% off to those 60-69, 70% to those 70-79, and so on until seniors reach 100 and they give them 100% off either the lenses or frames when they purchase a complete set of glasses. Lens Crafters and Eye Glass Factory also offer a 10% discount to seniors, and Sears Optical Centers give 15% off to AARP members. Now it makes seeing clearly less costly.

Save Money When You Bank

First Citizens Bank has **Senior Quest Accounts** where customers 60 and over receive unlimited check writing, no per check charge, interest bearing checking, no monthly service charge, free safe deposit box, no ATM fees, free cashier's checks, travelers' checks, and money orders. They even offer special rates on 6 and 12 month CD's, no annual fee credit card, free direct deposit and discount brokerage fees, with some of these services requiring a minimum balance. Not a bad deal. Other banks offer similar services, with most offering free checks, no minimum balance, and unlimited check writing.

FREE SENIOR YELLOW PAGES

No matter what the medical condition, activity or even hobby, *The Resource Directory for Older People* will identify a non-profit or government organization that will offer support, services, information and sometimes even money to help seniors remain independent.

To receive your free copy (while supplies last), call National Institute on Aging Information Center, P.O. Box 8057, Gaithersburg, MD 20898; 800-222-2225; {www.nih.gov/~nia}.

HELPING MOM WITH MONEY PROBLEMS

Over 92% of American seniors receive Social Security check each month, and a portion have them directly deposited into their checking accounts.

There may come a time when you or your loved one can no longer handle all the responsibilities of managing your own finances. When it involves handling your Social Security check, you need to designate a person as the Representative

Payee. This will allow the person to receive your Social Security check, so that they can in turn pay your bills for you. A person can petition the courts to be designated a Representative Payee if their loved one cannot do so themselves due to a physical or mental condition.

To learn more about direct deposit or about becoming a Representative Payee, contact your local Social Security office, or you may call the Social Security Hotline at 800-772-1213; {www.ssa.gov}.

What's Covered Under Medicare?

Did you know that 80% of all care given to seniors is done by family members and friends? Medicare has been helping people meet the costs of health care for over 30 years, but there are still questions about what is covered.

The *Medicare Handbook* is a free booklet published every year that explains Medicare in easy to understand terms. You can learn how to apply for Medicare, the difference between Part A and Part B, what things are covered such as flu shots and mammographies, and more. Also included is information about HMOs and

Medigap insurance. If Medicare denies a claim, the booklet explains how to appeal Medicare's decisions.

A *Medicare Handbook* is sent when a person first signs up for Medicare, but you should call and request a new booklet each year to keep on top of the changes in coverage. Contact your local Social Security Office, or Medicare Hotline, Health Care Financing Administration, 6325 Security Blvd., Baltimore, MD 21207; 800-638-6833; {www.medicare.gov}.

Free Retraining for Over 55

The *Senior Community Service Employment Program* offers part-time training and employment opportunities for eligible low-income persons 55 years of age and older in a variety of public and private non-profit community service settings, such as senior centers, nutrition programs, social service agencies, and many others.

To learn where in your area this program is offered contact your state Department of Labor listed in the Appendix, or Division of Older Worker Programs, U.S. Department of Labor, Employment and Training Administration, 200 Constitution Ave., NW, Room N4641, Washington, DC 20210; 202-219-5901; {www.wdsc.org/owprog/index.html}.

Help with Getting Mom to the Doctor

Many seniors have to give up driving their cars, maybe because of the cost or illness. But then how do they get to the doctor or the bank or the store? Many rely upon their friends and children to solve their transportation needs, but there are times when you need to come up with another alternative.

The *Eldercare Locator* provides access to an extensive network of organizations serving older  people at state and local community levels. This service can connect you to information sources for a variety of services including transportation.

For more information, contact Eldercare Locator, National Association of Area Agencies on Aging, 1112 16th St., NW, Washington, DC 20024; 800-677-1116 between 9 a.m. and 8 p.m. EST; {www.aoa.dhss.gov}.

Information USA, Inc.

GET MOM'S ROOF FIXED FOR FREE

Need money to widen your doorway for wheelchairs, install ramps or grab bars, or even put on a new roof? There's a free money program that awards grants of at least $1000 to help a senior citizen fix up and repair their home.

As part of the HOME Investment Partnership Program, the *HOME Repair/Modification Programs for Elderly Homeowners* program makes funds available

Free Courses On How To Choose A Nursing Home

The decision to enter a nursing home is never an easy one, but with some preparation, the move can go smoothly. Many County Cooperative Extension offices offer pamphlets or workshops on choosing a nursing home, or planning for it financially. Some local offices have information on estate planning and the pros and cons of nursing home insurance.

To learn more about what your local county Cooperative Extension office has for seniors, look in the blue pages of your phone book for the office nearest you, or contact the Cooperative Extension lead office listed in the Appendix.

to low-income individuals for home repair services. Money is distributed through over 500 sites, so to locate the closest program and application information, contact the Community Connections, P.O. Box 7189, Gaithersburg, MD 20898; 800-998-9999.

350 COLLEGES MOM CAN GO TO FOR FREE

Believe it or not, more than 350 colleges and universities all across the country have special programs for seniors who are interested in going back to school. This often means free or low-cost tuition, discounts on fees and books, and even special deals on housing, if you feel like living in a dorm and blasting your Benny Goodman records to all hours of the night!

Anyone interested should contact the school they wish to attend to find out how to apply for a discount or waiver. Some limitations and restrictions may apply, such as residency, and space availability.

$5,000
Extra Spending Money

If your check is too small to live on, don't be discouraged.
If you don't qualify for Social Security, or if your benefits
are very low, you may qualify for
supplemental Security Income
(SSI).

This program was established
to help poor seniors over 65
and the blind and disabled meet
basic living expenses. To
qualify you must meet a
maximum monthly
income test. Some of
the income and services
you receive are excluded
when they calculate
your monthly income
in relation to your
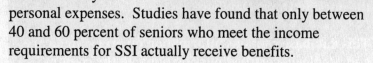
personal expenses. Studies have found that only between
40 and 60 percent of seniors who meet the income
requirements for SSI actually receive benefits.

To find out more about the program contact your local
Social Security office or contact the Social Security Hotline
at 800-772-1213.

$800 MONEY FOR FOOD

Not in cash, but in Food Stamps that is. Contact your local social service agency listed in the blue pages of your local telephone book and ask about the Food Stamp Program. Senior citizens are given special consideration. For example, seniors unable to go to the food stamp office to be interviewed may request a phone or home interview instead. Seniors can even be living with others and still qualify as a separate household in order to receive this assistance.

Contact U.S. Department of the Agriculture, Food and Nutrition Service, Public Information Office, 3101 Park Ctr., Dr., Alexandria, VA 22302; 703-305-2286; {www.usda.gov/fcs/stamps/fs.htm}.

Nursing Home Reports

Want to know how a nursing home did on their last inspection? Check out the Medicare website that has the nursing Home Database.

This database contains information on every Medicare and Medicaid certified nursing home in the country. The website allows you to get information about nursing homes and the results of its most recent survey. Publications are also available on the site to help you choose the right nursing home. For more information, contact {www.medicare.gov}.

FREE MONEY AND HELP FOR YOUR BUSINESS

MONEY TO START A BUSINESS WHEN YOU'RE OUT OF WORK

There are literally hundreds of programs around the country that provide training and money to out-of-work and low-income people who want to start their own businesses. Most of these organizations are nonprofit and obtain money from a variety of sources, including government grants. The target population of many of these programs is women.

The *Self-Employment Loan Fund* in Phoenix, AZ, has helped over 350 people get training and money to start their own businesses. For information, contact Self-Employment Loan Fund, Inc., 201 North Central Ave., Suite CC10, Phoenix, AZ 95073; 602-340-8834; {www.onlinewbc.org/docs/wbcs/AZPhoenix.html}.

Iowa has the *Self-Employment Loan Program*, which provides low interest loans to people with low income or disabilities. For more information, contact Iowa Department of Economic Development, 200 E. Grand Ave., Des Moines, IA 50309; 800-245-IOWA; {www.smart.state.ia.us/financial.htm#selp}.

Many of these programs offer business loans to people who are at or below the poverty level. These programs may be identified though your state Office of Economic Development located in the Appendix. You may also try contacting the state Office of Social Services listed in the Appendix.

The Aspen Institute keeps track of many of these organizations and sells a directory called *Directory of U.S. Microenterprise Development Programs* for $15.00. To order a copy, contact Aspen Institute, 1333 New Hampshire Ave., NW, Suite 1070, Washington, DC 20036; 202-736-5800.

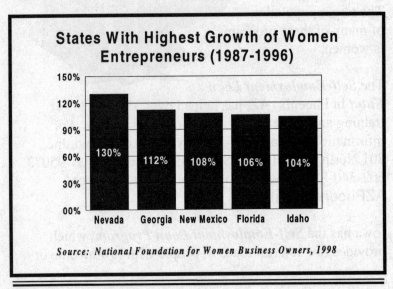

States With Highest Growth of Women Entrepreneurs (1987-1996)

Source: National Foundation for Women Business Owners, 1998

Money For Entrepreneurs
With Disabilities

Entrepreneurs with disabilities can apply for up to $50,000
from the Minority, Woman and Disabled Participation
Loan Program in Illinois through the Department of
Commerce and Community Affairs.

Iowa offers
grants up to
$15,000
through a
program
called
Entrepreneurs
with
Disabilities
from the Iowa
Department of
Economic Development. Iowa
also offers low interest loans to those with disabilities
through its Self-Employment Loan Program.

Connecticut has laws that make sure entrepreneurs with
disabilities (and other minorities) get up to 25% of state
government contracts through the Set-Aside Unit of the
Department of Administrative Services.

Maryland even has venture capital set aside for the disabled
in its Equity Participation Program of the Maryland Small
Business Development Financing Authority.

The U.S. Small Business Administration used to have a special program for people with disabilities, but now includes them in its major loan program. See what your state has to offer by contacting your state Office of Vocational Rehabilitation or the Office of Economic Development listed in the Appendix.

Money To Start A
Day Care Center

You can always apply to the traditional state loan programs and the Small Business Administration for money to start or expand a day care center, but you should also keep in mind special programs at the state level.

Ohio has a Child Day Care Loan program offered through the Ohio Department of Development. Tennessee offers a

Top Reasons
Women Start Businesses

Reason #1:   Improve things for themselves and family

Reason #2:   Do for themselves what they did for their employer

Reason #3:   Fulfill long-time dream

Source: National Foundation for Women Business Owners, 1998

loan of up to $250,000 to start a day care center through the Economic and Community Development Department, and $5,000 in grant money to train your employees through the Department of Labor. Virginia has a loan program called Child Day Care Financing through the Virginia Small Business Financing Authority, and Maryland has three loan programs for day care facilities through the Maryland Department of Business and Economic Development.

Contact your state Office of Economic Development listed in the Appendix to begin exploring the opportunities in your state.

Free Help In Starting a Business, Plus $800, If You Lose Your Job From A Dirty Company

Free entrepreneurial training is available if you lost your job because of a company's compliance with the Clean Air Act. The program was initiated from the Environmental

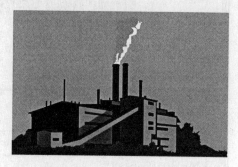

Protection Agency's Clean Air Act, which amended the Department of Labor's Job Training Partnership Act (Title III). So it's the U.S. Department of Labor that runs the training program.

Are you confused yet?

There is also money in this program to get $800 to move to another city to look for a job. It may be hard to find at the state level, which get grants from the Feds to run the program. The state of Illinois runs it out of their Department of Commerce.

Contact your state Department of Labor listed in the Appendix. You can also locate your state contact by contacting the Office of Worker Retraining and Adjustment Programs, Employment and Training Administration, U.S. Department of Labor, Room N5426, 200 Constitution Ave., NW, Washington, DC 20210; 202-219-5577; {www.wdsc.org/layoff/title3.htm}.

Two-Thirds Want Their Own Business

When asked which would be more personally fulfilling:

Working way to top of large organization	24%
Starting own successful small business	67%
No difference	7%
Don't know or refused	2%

Source: Luntz Research Company, September 1997

When Your Business Fails: Get Free Money, Child Care and Training

The U.S. Department of Labor provides money to states under a program called *The Economic Dislocation and Worker Adjustment Assistance (EDWAA) Act*. Although the money is primarily meant for people who lose their jobs because of layoffs, the money can also be used for people who are out of work because their small business failed or because they are a displaced homemaker as a result of a divorce.

Under this act, you can receive free courses and training for a new career, emergency financial aid, child care money, travel money for getting to work or training, and even relocation money if you have to move for a new job.

Contact your state Department of Labor listed in the Appendix and ask for the office that is designated as the state's Dislocated Worker Unit. If you have trouble contacting your local office, you may contact the Office of Worker Retraining and Adjustment Programs, Employment and Training Administration, U.S. Department of Labor, Room N-5426, 200 Constitution Ave., NW, Washington, DC 20210; 202-219-5577; {www.wdsc.org/layoff/title3.htm}.

Free Seminars

On How to Sell Your Stuff Overseas

Kentucky offers free half-day seminars on how to sell and finance your products overseas. They may charge a fee if it's a full day program, but it's usually only $25 to cover the lunch.

They will bring in bankers and government money officials to show you how you can make deals and get them financed. The program is offered through the International Trade Office of the Department of Community Development.

Women-Owned Firms Account for 36% of All US Businesses

Source: National Foundation for Women Business Owners, 1998

Most states will offer training to help you generate business overseas whether you are a first time exporter/importer or an old pro. Contact your state Office of Economic Development listed in the Appendix and ask for the office that helps businesses sell overseas.

Show Investors How They Can Get A
$37,500 Tax Break
For Investing In Your Company

If you want to start a high tech company in the state of
Ohio, you can show potential investors how they can get a
tax credit up to $37,500 for their investment. It's called the
Technology Investment Tax Credit Program and is offered
through the Ohio Department of Development.

See if your state offers a similar program that you can use
to help raise money for your idea. Contact your state
Office of Economic Development listed in the Appendix.

One Page Gets You A $150,000 Business Loan

A one-page form is all you have to fill out to apply for a
loan of up to $150,000 for your business through the
government's LOWDOC Loan Guarantee program. Contact
your local office of the U.S. Small Business Administration
to learn more about the steps necessary to apply for the
loan.

Contact U.S. Small Business Administration, 409 Third St.,
SW, Washington, DC 20416; 800-8ASK-SBA;
{www.sba.gov}. Here's what the application looks like.

U.S. SMALL BUSINESS ADMINISTRATION
APPLICATION FOR LOWDOC LOAN

OMB Approval No. 2245-0016
Expiration Date: 10/31/98

A. BORROWER   Please Print Legibly or Type **(ALL BLANKS MUST BE COMPLETED, Use "N/A," if Blank is Not Applicable)**

Business Name _____
Trade Name (if different) _____
Type: Proprietorship ☐ Partnership ☐ Corporation ☐ LLC ☐ Other ☐
Address _____
City _____ State _____ County _____ Zip _____
Mailing Address (if different from above) _____
City _____ State _____ County _____ Zip _____
Phone _____ IRS Tax ID # _____
Business Bank _____ Checking Balance $ _____

Nature of Business _____
Date Business Established _____
Date Current Ownership Established _____
Number of employees _____
Number of affiliate(s) employees _____
Total number of employees after Loan _____
Exporter? Yes ☐ No ☐   Franchise? Yes ☐ No ☐
Franchise Name _____

B. LOAN REQUEST

AMOUNT $ _____ Maturity: _____ Purpose: _____
Have you employed anyone to prepare this application? Yes ☐ No ☐   If Yes, how much was paid? $ _____ How much do you owe? $ _____
Name of Packager _____ Packager's Tax ID No. or Social Security No. _____

C. INDEBTEDNESS: Furnish information on ALL BUSINESS debts, contracts, notes and mortgages payable. Indicate by an (*) items to be paid by loan proceeds.

To Whom Payable	Orig. Amount	Orig. Date	Cur. Balance	Int. Rate	Maturity Date	Pmt. Amt.	Pmt Frequency	Collateral	Status

D. PRINCIPALS: Submit all information in this section, for each principal of the business. Use separate attachments for each principal.

D1 Full Name _____ Phone _____ Social Security Number _____ Title _____
Address _____ City _____ State _____ Zip _____
Date of Birth _____ Place of Birth (City, ST or Foreign Country) _____ U.S. Citizen? Yes ☐ No ☐ If No, Alien reg # _____

D2 Percentage Owned _____ % Veteran *: Non-Veteran ☐, Vietnam Era Veteran ☐, Other Veteran ☐   Gender *: Female ☐ Male ☐
Race*: African American ☐, Puerto Rican ☐, Native American ☐, Hispanic ☐, Asian/Pacific Islander ☐, Eskimo & Aleuts ☐, Caucasian ☐, Multi-Ethnic ☐

*This data is collected for statistical purposes only. It has no bearing on the credit decision. Disclosure is voluntary.

D3 PERSONAL FINANCIAL STATEMENT: Complete for all principals with 20% or more ownership.

Liquid Assets $ _____ Ownership in Business $ _____ Real Estate $ _____ Assets Other $ _____ Total Assets $ _____
Liabilities Real Estate $ _____ Liabilities Other $ _____ Total Liabilities $ _____ Net Worth (less value of business) $ _____
Annual Salary $ _____ Other Source of Repayment $ _____ Source _____ Residence: Own ☐ Rent ☐ Other ☐ Mthly Housing $ _____

D4 PREVIOUS SBA OR OTHER GOVERNMENT FINANCING: For all owners, principals, partners, and affiliates.

Borrower Name	Name of Agency	Loan No.	Date	Amount	Balance	Status

D5 ELIGIBILITY AND DISCLOSURES:

I.   Are you or your business involved in any pending lawsuits? Yes ☐ No ☐   If Yes, provide the details as Exhibit A.

II. Do you or your spouse or any member of your household, or anyone who owns, manages, or directs your business or their spouses or members of their households work for the Small Business Administration, Small Business Advisory Council, SCORE or ACE, any Federal Agency, or the participating lender? Yes ☐ No ☐
If Yes, please provide the name and address of the person and the office where employed. Label this Exhibit B.

III. Affiliations. Do you or the applicant business have any interest in any other business as owner, principal, partner or manager? Yes ☐ No ☐ If Yes, please provide details as Exhibit.

IV. Are you (a) presently under indictment, on parole or probation, Yes ☐ No ☐ or (b) have ever been charged with or arrested for any criminal offense other than a minor motor vehicle violation (including offenses which have been dismissed, discharged, or nolle prosequi) Yes ☐ No ☐ or (c) convicted, placed on pretrial diversion, or placed on any form of probation including adjudication withheld pending probation for any criminal offense other than a minor vehicle violation? Yes ☐ No ☐
If Yes to any "IV" question, Lender must submit application to local SBA Office for processing under the regular 7(a) program.

If you knowingly make a false statement or overvalue a security to obtain a guaranteed loan from SBA you can be fined up to $10,000 and/or imprisoned for not more than five years under 18 U.S.C.1001; if submitted to a Federally insured institution, under 18 USC 1014 by imprisonment of not more than twenty years and/or a fine or not more than $1,000,000. I authorize the SBA's Office of Inspector General to request criminal record information about me from criminal justice agencies for the purpose of determining my eligibility for programs authorized by the Small Business Act, as amended.

V. Principal Signature _____ Date _____

E. BORROWER SIGNATURE   (Principal(s) should sign in Section "D," above)

I authorize SBA/Lender to make inquiries as necessary to verify the accuracy of the statements made and to determine my creditworthiness. I agree that if SBA approves this loan application I will not, for at least two years, hire as an employee or consultant anyone that was employed by the SBA during the one year period prior to the disbursement of the loan. And, I hereby certify that (1) as consideration for any Management, Technical, and Business Development Assistance that may be provided, I waive all claims against SBA and its consultants, (2) all information contained in this document and any attachments is true and correct to the best of my knowledge, and

(3) I have received and read SBA Form 1261, STATEMENTS REQUIRED BY LAW AND EXECUTIVE ORDER _____ (Applicant initials)

Print Name _____ Date _____
Signature _____ Title _____
If Corporation, Attested By: _____
Signature of Corporate Secretary

SBA Form 4-L (3-98) Previous Editions are Obsolete   This form was electronically produced by Elite Federal Forms, Inc.

Don't Pay Taxes For 15 Years

That's what the state of Michigan lets you do if you start a
business in one of their 11 Renaissance Zones. Michigan is
the first state in the nation to create these **Tax-Free
Renaissance Zones,** in the belief that lowering tax
barriers is the best way to stimulate economic growth. The
program is offered through the Michigan Jobs Commission.

See what your state has to offer in the way of tax breaks for
your business by contacting your state Office of Economic
Development listed in the Appendix.

$4,000 To Improve Your Productivity

The mission of the Manufacturing Extension Partnership of
Illinois is to improve the productivity and competitiveness
of small manufacturing firms located in Illinois. They help
companies develop affordable realistic plans for growth
and competitiveness. An onsite team provides an objective
analysis, identifying your company's strengths, weaknesses,
opportunities and threats.

For more information, contact Illinois Manufacturing
Extension Center, 403 Jobst Hall, Bradley University,
Peoria, IL 61625; 800-MEPI-MFG.

Access To 20,000 FREE Experts To Increase Your Profits

I used to have a business that charged $100 an hour to get information from free government experts, so that my Fortune 500 clients could use the information to make billion dollar decisions.

Don't call high priced consultants when you need information. Go direct, and call the government yourself. The government has 9 experts on Saudi Arabia, 5 experts on vitamins, 17 on radiation, 19 on productivity and technology, and even experts on sewing machines, toys, VCRs, soap, and zoonoses.

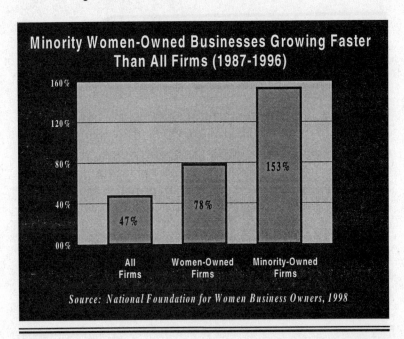

Minority Women-Owned Businesses Growing Faster Than All Firms (1987-1996)

- All Firms: 47%
- Women-Owned Firms: 78%
- Minority-Owned Firms: 153%

Source: National Foundation for Women Business Owners, 1998

There are even offices that will help find the experts for you and they'll do it for free. A good place to start is the Federal Information Center at 800-688-9889; {http://fic.info.gov}.

Free Classes on How To Do Business Taxes

Don't pay an accountant $100 an hour to do your taxes when you can learn how to do them yourself for free.

The Connecticut's Department of Revenue Services offers a 2 1/2 hour class in understanding small business taxes and over 2,500 business owners have taken advantage of this free course. Nevada's Department of Business and Industry offers free small business workshops on accounting and taxes.

The IRS offers free courses called Small Business Tax Workshops and even an instructional video called "Small Business and Taxes", which follows that story of a young woman who, after losing her job, learns all about starting up her own small business from a friend. They discuss record keeping and accounting methods.

To learn more, contact your state Office of Economic Development listed in the Appendix, your state office of taxation, or your local IRS office. You can also contact Internal Revenue Service, U.S. Department of the Treasury, 1111 Constitution Ave., NW, Washington, DC 20224; 800-829-1040; {www.irs.ustreas.gov/prod/bus_info-bus_help.html}.

Lots of Loan Money,
Some At 0% Interest

The U.S. Small Business Administration runs the government's most popular loan program. Well, it's actually a loan guarantee program. This means that the government will tell a bank that they will pay back the loan if you can't.

U.S. Small Business Administration

About 70,000 loans a year are made through this program. But there are dozens, even hundreds, of other government loan and loan guarantee programs. The U.S. Department of Agriculture has direct loans and loan guarantees to entrepreneurs living in small towns. They even have programs that offer grants to nonprofit organizations, which in turn lend the money to small businesses.

And the states are loaded with loan programs for businesses. Maryland, for example, has about 10 loan programs at the state level and has 11 more business loan programs at the county level. It's not unusual for some of these loans to be low interest or even 0% interest. Start with your state Office of Economic Development listed in the Appendix and go from there. And don't stop!

Loans and Grants
To Start Businesses in Small Towns

The U.S. Department of Agriculture has 6 different programs worth over $1 billion to start or expand businesses in small towns:

- Business and Industry Guaranteed Loans - $1 billion
- Business and Industry Direct Loans - $50 million
- Intermediary Relending Program - $35 million
- Rural Business Enterprise Grants - $38 million
- Rural Economic Development Loans - $25 million
- Rural Economic Development Grant - $11 million

Some of this money is given to local non-profits which in turn is lent out to small businesses at 0% interest. Many states also have money programs set aside for small town entrepreneurs.

Contact your state Office of Economic Development, your local office of the U.S. Department of Agriculture (USDA) or headquarters at USDA Rural Development, Stop 0705, 1400 Independence Ave. SW, Washington, DC 20250; 202-720-1400; Fax: 202-690-0311; {www.rurdev. usda.gov}.

Sell Overseas at Government Expense

The U.S. Department of Agriculture's Foreign Market Development Cooperation Program grants over $3 million a year to companies and cooperatives to sell their products overseas. The Indiana's Trade Show Assistance Program offers grants up to $5,000 to attend a trade show in a foreign country.

Wisconsin also offers $5,000 to party overseas. I mean, to attend a trade show. Many states also offer special money programs to help finance your sales overseas through the Office of Economic Development.

The Export-Import Bank of the United States provides working capital to small businesses to finance their exports as well as Export Credit Insurance, Direct Loans and Loan Guarantees. Contact Export-Import Bank of the U.S., 811 Vermont Ave., NW, Washington, DC 20571; 800-565-EXIM; {www.exim.gov}.

The Overseas Private Investment Corporation (OPIC) also provides financing and insurance to small businesses to sell their goods and services overseas. Contact Investment Services Director, Program Development, Investment Development Department, 1100 New York Ave., NW, Washington, DC 20527; 202-336-8621; {www.opic.gov}.

Overseas Marketing

The government offers free market studies about your product overseas. Our Embassies and Consulates around the world will check out potential customers for you anywhere in the world. State governments even have offices overseas to sell your products.

A good starting place is your state Office of Economic Development listed in the Appendix, and the Trade Information Center, U.S. Dept. of Commerce, Washington, DC 20230; 800-USA-TRADE; {http://infoserv2.ita.doc.gov/tic.nsf}.

Get Paid To Attend Entrepreneur Classes

If you lost your job and are eligible for unemployment, contact your local Unemployment Office and find out how you can collect your employment money while you are attending classes on how to set up your own business. You can't collect while you are starting a business, but you can collect while you are learning **how** to start a business.

This is very new and exciting program to help those who are unemployed develop their own jobs. Maryland, Delaware, California, New York, New Jersey, Oregon,

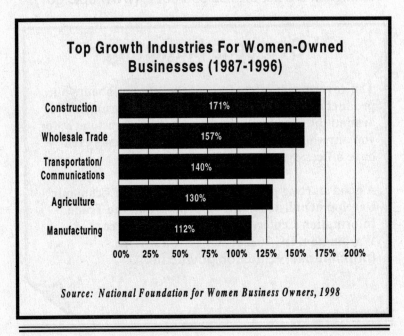

Top Growth Industries For Women-Owned Businesses (1987-1996)

Industry	Growth
Construction	171%
Wholesale Trade	157%
Transportation/ Communications	140%
Agriculture	130%
Manufacturing	112%

Source: National Foundation for Women Business Owners, 1998

Information USA, Inc.

Maine, and Pennsylvania run programs, and there are likely to be more. In 1998, the congress passed HR 4558 that extended this program and allowed all states to be eligible to provide similar programs.

Contact your state Unemployment Insurance office in your state capital (listed in the Appendix) and ask if they are participating in any self-employment programs.

Money To Start A Woman-Owned Business In A High Unemployment Area

The Economic Development Administration makes grants to local communities with high unemployment, that in turn make business loans to small entrepreneurs who can create jobs. This is done through the revolving loan fund of the Economic Adjustment Program.

Women Businesses Growing Twice All Businesses	
Growth In Women-Owned Businesses 1987-1991	**78%**
Growth In All Businesses 1987-1991	**47%**

Source: National Foundation for Women Business Owners, 1998

The Buffalo, New York area recently used this program to make loans to 182 companies targeting start-ups as well as minority and women-owned businesses.

Find out where in your area there may be revolving loan programs from your state Office of Economic Development listed in the Appendix, or contact the Economic Development Administration, U.S. Dept. of Commerce, 14th & Constitution Ave, Room 7800B, Washington, DC 20230; 202-482-5081; {www.doc.gov/eda}.

$75,000 Grant If Hurt By Imports, and Loans If Hurt By Defense Cutbacks

If your business suffers a loss due to imports, you may be eligible to receive up to $75,000 to pay for consultants to develop a new business plan to put you back on the road to success.

The program is called Trade Adjustment Assistance, and there are 12 regional offices around the country that help businesses apply for this help. These offices also help businesses with assistance and loans when they have been hurt by defense cutbacks.

Contact: Planning and Development Assistance Division, Economic Development Administration, Room H7315,

Washington, DC 20230; 202-482-2127; Fax: 202-482-0466; {www.doc.gov/eda}.

Mother & Daughter Get Community $ To Open Natural Cotton Store

They got the money to open Common Threads from the city of Burlington, VT, who got the money from the U.S. Department of Housing And Urban Development's Community Development Block Grant program. This program gives over $3 billion a year to local communities who can use the money to start businesses or create jobs.

- Springfield, MO uses the money to give out small business loans at 5% through the Small Business Development Loan program.
- Middletown, CT uses it for micro loans up to $50,000 through the JOBS LOAN Program.

More Women Than Men Start Businesses Around A Personal Interest

	Women	Men
% who start a business unrelated to previous job	56%	31%
% who start a business around a personal interest	42%	2%

Source: National Foundation for Women Business Owners, 1998

- Lowell, MA uses it to finance small companies who want to move into the area, expand, or even startup through the Lowell Development and Financial Corporation.
- Biloxi, MS uses it in a Revolving Loan Fund program that provides low-interest loans to start businesses, including loaning a single mom $15,000 to start a real estate business.

Contact your local city and county Office of Community Development and ask who is getting the Community Development Block Grant money. If you get lost, you can contact the main Office of Block Grant Assistance, Office of Community Planning and Development, Entitlement Communities Division, 451 7th St. SW, Washington, DC 20410; 202-708-1577; {www.hud.gov/whatwork.html}; or Community Connections at 800-998-9999.

$20,000 Grant For Horse Lovers

The Virginia Horse Industry Board offers grants to groups and individuals with good ideas on how to promote Virginia's Horse industry. Contact Virginia Horse Industry Board Office, Virginia Department of Agriculture and Consumer Services, 1100 Bank Street, Room 1004, Richmond, VA 23219; 804-786-5842; Fax: 804-371-7786; {www.vhib.org/VHIB.html}.

Money If You Start A Business In Certain Zip Codes

Connecticut will give your business a grant of up to $2,250 per employee if your business is in certain enterprise zones. Plus, you pay only 50% in corporate taxes and only 20% in property taxes.

Locating your business in certain areas of Chicago will get you an exception of income taxes on money made from the area, low interest rate loans and a big break on your sales and property taxes. The federal government has designated over 100 areas around the country as enterprise areas and offers special low interest loans, $3,000 tax credit for every employee you have and an extra $20,000 tax deduction for capital investments, as well as a boat load of other services and money incentives.

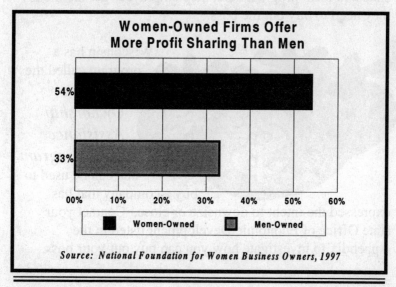

Women-Owned Firms Offer More Profit Sharing Than Men

54%

33%

00% 10% 20% 30% 40% 50% 60%

■ Women-Owned   ▨ Men-Owned

Source: National Foundation for Women Business Owners, 1997

Enterprise zones, also called empowerment zones, have been established in order to generate jobs and economic development in certain rural and urban areas around the country. Contact your state Office of Economic Development listed in the Appendix to identify the zones in your area; or contact U.S. Department of Housing and Urban Development, 451 7 St., SW, Washington, DC 20410; 202-708-1577; {www.hud.gov/ezeclist.html}.

Money To Buy Out The Boss

The government doesn't want your boss to move your company or close it down. So the government has set up state and local programs that help employees get the money they need to buy out the boss.

Wisconsin has a program called the *Employee Ownership Assistance Loan Program* that can be used to buy a company that has expressed the intent to downsize or close. Contact your state Office of Economic Development listed in the Appendix to investigate how you can buy out your boss.

Save $2,000 On
Preparing A Business Plan

Why spend thousands on attorneys, accountants, and
management consultants when you are putting together
your business idea? You can get some of the best help
available to develop a business plan, marketing plan,
financial plan, management plan, etc. for nothing or next to
nothing by contacting your local Small Business
Development Center.

Next to Social Security, this is probably one of the most
valuable services Uncle Sam has ever offered. You can
find your local office by contacting your state's main Small
Business Development Center office listed in the
Appendix.

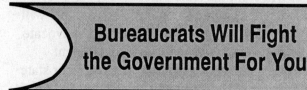

Bureaucrats Will Fight
the Government For You

You don't have to hire a hot shot "Washington Insider" at
$200 an hour to fight a government regulation that you feel
is unfair, or to fight an agency who is taking too long to pay
a legitimate bill, or to suffer from a fine imposed by a
government official that you feel is not justified. You can
call *"BUREAUCRACY MAN"*. There are actually a

number of government bureaucrats that will fight other
bureaucrats for you:

★ The **Small Business Administration** has set up an
office that will investigate complaints and help you get
equitable settlements. They will even show you how to
sue the government and
get attorney's fees and
costs. Contact Office of
the National Ombudsman,
U.S. Small Business
Administration, 500
West Madison, Suite
1240, Chicago, IL
60661; 312-353-0880;
fax: 312-353-3426; 888-
REG-FAIR;
{www.sba.gov/regfair}.

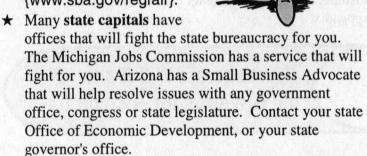

★ Many **state capitals** have
offices that will fight the state bureaucracy for you.
The Michigan Jobs Commission has a service that will
fight for you. Arizona has a Small Business Advocate
that will help resolve issues with any government
office, congress or state legislature. Contact your state
Office of Economic Development, or your state
governor's office.

★ The **IRS's Problem Resolution Center** has offices
around the country that will fight the IRS for you after
your efforts prove futile. They are listed in the blue
pages of your telephone book under U.S. Department of
the Treasury.

★ Your **elected official**, in both Washington and your state capital, is probably the only government office with a real motive to help you with a problem. They want your vote to keep their job. All the rest of the officials will keep their job whether they make you happy or not.

$10,000

For Your 10-Year-Old To Start A Business

The U.S. Department of Agriculture (USDA) has a program that loans money to kids between the ages of 10 and 21, who live in small towns, to start a business.

Nebraska runs entrepreneur camps for teenagers through their Center For Rural Affairs. The Pennsylvania Department of Agriculture gives out loans to people starting at 18 years of age. Harris County in Texas has $10,000 to invest in

Government Will Recruit and Hire Your Employees

State governments are so eager for you to hire people, many will set up their local Department of Labor Office into an employment agency just for you. They will recruit, interview and qualify potential employees. Contact your state Office of Labor listed in the Appendix.

youth entrepreneurs, and the City of Minneapolis has a
program that trains youth in entrepreneuring by having
them run a retail store that sells property confiscated by the
police department.

For the USDA program, contact your local Farm Service,
or the Farm Service Agency, Loan Marketing Division, Ag
Box 0522, Washington, DC 20250; 202-720-1632;
{www.fsa.usda.gov/}. For other local programs, a good
place to start is your local County Cooperative Extension
Service, listed under County Government in your phone
book. The main state office is listed in the Appendix.

Loans For Failures and Bad Credit Risks

That's what it sounds like when you investigate your local
Capital Access Program (CAP).

Capital Access Program (CAP)

Banks offering this program are
more likely to lend to people who
are less than credit worthy, because, if
for some reason you can't pay back
the bank, your state government will.

It's just another way for state
government to encourage you to start
and grow your business. New Hampshire, California,
Virginia, Pennsylvania, Indiana and many more were
offering the program the last time I checked. Contact your
state Office of Economic Development listed in the
Appendix to see if the program is offered in your state.

Free Money For Inventors

People pay good money for good ideas, especially, the government. There is even government grant money available to work on ideas, either your own or the ones that the government has. Here is how some state governments give money to inventors:

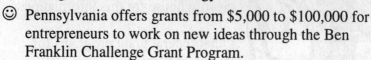

- ☺ North Dakota gives inventors up to $100,000 to work on new ideas through Technology Transfer, Inc.

- ☺ Rhode Island offers grant money to develop new products using the ocean, (how about seaweed cereal), through the Ocean Technology Center.

- ☺ Pennsylvania offers grants from $5,000 to $100,000 for entrepreneurs to work on new ideas through the Ben Franklin Challenge Grant Program.

- ☺ Delaware offers inventors up to $25,000 in venture capital to write business plans and get patents, and then up to $250,000 to do marketing, as part of the Delaware Innovation Fund.

☺ North Carolina grants up to $25,000 to develop ideas to eliminate wood waste through the Solid Waste Reduction Assistance Grant.

☺ Wisconsin gives out grants for new ways of recycling in their Recycling Early Planning Grant Program.

☺ Ohio and Indiana have grants for inventors who have new ideas on what to do with old tires.

Contact your local state Office of Economic Development listed in the Appendix to investigate what your state has to offer inventors.

Other Inventing Grants

Some states also offer grant money to inventors who are working on getting government grants for their ideas. The largest source of these grants is the Small Business Innovative Research Grants that offer over $1 billion from 10 different agencies. The Small Business Administration acts as a clearinghouse for this information.

Other federal grant programs for inventors include:

✪ The Inventions and Innovation Program, managed by the U.S. Department of Energy, provides grants for ideas that result in the more efficient use of energy.

❂ The Advanced Technology Program gives $200 million a year in grants for developing new technology from the U.S. Department of Commerce's National Institute of Standards and Technology.

❂ The U.S. Department of Energy's National Industrial Competitiveness through Energy, Environment and Economics (NICE3) offers grants up to $400,000 to develop ideas that save energy.

You can find these programs in a government book in your library called *The Catalog of Federal Domestic Assistance* or by contacting your local Federal Information Center at 800-688-9889; {http://fic.info.gov}.

Get The Government To Pay Half Your Employees' Wages

If you hire some people who have had trouble getting a job, the IRS will give you back up to 35% of the first year's salary, and up to 50% of the second year's salary. You can get up to $2,400 back in tax credit for hiring someone from certain zip codes.

Tax Credits for New Employees

There are states, like Mississippi, that will give you up to $2,000 a year for five years in credits for new employees, or 50% back on any child care expenses you pay for your employees. There are many areas of the country where an employer can get back $2,400 just for creating A JOB for anyone.

You wouldn't believe the types of tax credits available! There are even tax credits just for people in the wine business in Missouri.

Contact your state Office of Economic Development listed in the Appendix to see what kind of credits are available to you.

Free Help Selling Your Arts And Crafts

The Kentucky Craft Marketing Program can get your studio, shop or work listed in directories or on the web and can get you into fairs to sell your work. They also offer help to train you in other ways to market and sell your work.

Check with your state arts council located in your state capital for the kind of help you can get in your state. Illinois has a free *Art Fair Directory* showing you where you can display your work. Also, check into the American Folklife Center, Library of Congress, 101 Independence Ave., SE, Washington, DC 20540; 202-707-5510; {http://lcweb.loc.gov/folklife}.

Lots of Free Money Available To Train Your Employees

Training is the business buzzword for the year 2000. Almost every state has money to help companies in their state train new or existing employees. Most of it is in the form of grant money that you don't have to pay back.

States like Connecticut, Tennessee and Kentucky will give grants from $3,000 to $25,000 to train your employees. Indiana will go as high as $200,000 in grant money. Wisconsin will pay for 50% of your training costs. And in Louisiana and Iowa, you can send your employees to the state's vocational schools and community colleges for free. Virginia even offers free video production so that you can produce your own training films.

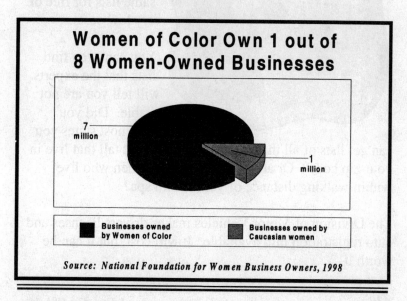

Women of Color Own 1 out of 8 Women-Owned Businesses

7 million

1 million

■ Businesses owned by Women of Color   ■ Businesses owned by Caucasian women

Source: National Foundation for Women Business Owners, 1998

Contact your state Office of Economic Development listed in the Appendix for information about training help for your company.

WHERE TO GET A
FREE LIST OF CUSTOMERS

You can look in the Yellow Pages under mailing lists or marketing consultants and spend thousands of dollars for customer lists. Or, you can search the government and find many of the same lists for free or very low costs.

You can even find lists that the experts will tell you are not available. Did you know that in most states you can get lists of all the rich men over six feet tall that live in your zip code? Or all the overweight women who live within walking distance of your health spa?

The Division of Motor Vehicles makes drivers licenses and auto registration info available. It will cost, but it can be worth it.

You can also get a list of all the new businesses that open up in your area with the name, address, and phone number of the owners. When a business starts up, they have to register at the state Office of Corporation.

Or how about a list of physical trainers, sports agents, dry cleaners, lawyers, hearing aid dealers, day care centers, or insurance agents? All these people have to register with the state to get a license. Yea for public information!

Contact your state Capitol Operator listed in the Appendix to see where to go in your state for your mailing list needs.

Uncle Sam Is Getting A Sex Change

It wasn't very long ago that most small businesses in this country used to be headed by men. Now, 2 out of every 3 new businesses that start are headed by women.

The government's lead office for supporting small business, The Small Business Administration, has wised up and now has special staff in almost every area of the country that cater strictly to the specific needs of women entrepreneurs. They can help you network with other women business owners, learn where to find financial assistance, or how to obtain government procurement contracts.

To locate the nearest Women's Business Ownership Representative, contact Office of Women's Business Ownership, U.S. Small Business Administration, 409 3rd St., SW, Washington, DC 20416; 202-205-6673; 800-8ASK-SBA; {www.sba.gov}.

Women's Online Business Help

Have a thousand questions and no answers? All you need to do is go to the Online Women's Business Center created by the U.S. Small Business Administration and several major corporations.

This online site provides answers to all your questions, including information on how to get a business started, classes in determining whether you really want to start a business, and more. This is a one-stop shopping site where you can find information about everything from how to start your business to how to operate in the global market place.

They have the most current information on business principles and practices, management techniques, mentoring, networking, and business resources. There is a link to important internet sites, an information exchange section, and a listing of Women's Business Centers.

For more information, visit the Online Women's Business Center at {www.onlinewbc.org}.

60 Places To Get A Little Help From Your Friends

Sometimes you just need someone to show you the way. The Women's Demonstration Program has 60 sites across the country where women are trained and counseled in the skills necessary to launch their own businesses.

These sites get money from the government to offer financial, management, marketing, and technical assistance to current and potential women business owners.

Women Balance Better Than Men

	Women	Men
Entrepreneurs who say they deserve "A" for achieving healthy balance between work and family	37%	17%

Source: Nation's Business, August 1998 v86 n8 p38(1)

Contact your local Small Business Administration office to find a site near you, or contact U.S. Small Business Administration, 409 3rd St., SW, Washington, DC 20416; 202-205-6673; 800-8-ASK-SBA; {www.sba.gov}.

Entrepreneur Mentors:
Someone Just To Watch Over You

When a tough question or problem arises, it is nice to have someone to turn to for guidance. That is the goal for the Women's Network for Entrepreneurial Training (WNET).

This program matches successful mentors with aspiring women business owners. Offered through the Small Business Administration district offices and other organizations, the program is designed to improve women entrepreneurs' prospects for success by linking them to experienced women business owners. Meeting regularly over a period of one year, mentors guide proteges through the challenges of growing a business, smoothing their path to success.

For more information on the program, contact your local Small Business Administration Office, or Office Of Women's Business Ownership, U.S. Small Business

Administration, 409 3rd St., SW, Washington, DC 20416;
202-205-6673; 800-8-ASK-SBA; {www.sba.gov}.

Texas Women-Owned Businesses Get $586,740 In Free Training Money

Each year the state of Texas gives out about $27 million in grant money to help state businesses train their employees. Below is a list of the women-owned businesses in Texas that received free money from this program:

Company	Grant Amount
Arctic Breeze, Canutilli, TX	$20,000
Arnott & Associates, Grapevine, TX	$11,420
Certified Data Services, Inc., Houston, TX	$68,525
Computer Station Corporation, Houston	$27,411
Environmental Technologies, Inc., Magnolia, TX	$10,040
General Truck Body Mfg., Houston, TX	$78,527
Greystone House, Houston, TX	$19,950
Hairston & Associates Insurance, Houston, TX	$14,431
Laboratories for Genetic Services, Inc Houston, TX	$57,258
NTCS, Inc., Denton, TX	$101,019
Tarlton Supply, Co., Brenham, TX	$178,068

Contact your state Office of Economic Development in the Appendix to look for information on a similar program in your state. For more information in the Texas program contact: Smart Jobs Fund, Texas Dept. of Economic Development, P.O. Box 12728, Austin, TX 78711; 512-936-0500; {www.tded.state.tx.us/commerce/bizsrv/annual/spage10.htm}.

The Feds Have To Give You 5%

The Federal Acquisition Streamlining Act of 1994 establishes a 5 percent government-wide goal for contract awards to small businesses owned by women. One way the Small Business Administration is helping to ensure that these new goals are achieved is through the Women-Owned Business Procurement Pilot Program.

Each of the following eleven federal agencies has designated a women-owned business advocate to act as a liaison. Each provides outreach, training, and marketing assistance to women-owned businesses. The Small Business Administration and the liaisons from each of the

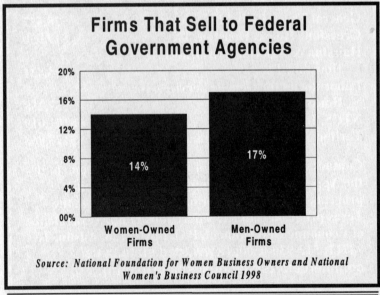

Firms That Sell to Federal Government Agencies

Women-Owned Firms: 14%
Men-Owned Firms: 17%

Source: National Foundation for Women Business Owners and National Women's Business Council 1998

agencies meet regularly to assess the progress of the program, resolve problems, and develop new initiatives.

For more information on this program, you may contact your local Small Business Administration Office, or Office of Women's Business Ownership, U.S. Small Business Administration, 409 3rd St., SW, Washington, DC 20416; 202-205-6673; 800-8-ASK-SBA; {www.sba.gov}.

Procurement Pilot Program Contacts

Ms. Sharon Harris
U.S. Department of
Agriculture
Office of Small and
Disadvantaged Business
Utilization
14th St. and Independence
Ave., SW
Room 1323 South Bldg.
Washington, DC 202050
202-720-7117

Ms. Janet Koch
U.S. Department of Defense
Office of Small and
Disadvantaged Business
Utilization
Room 2A338
3061 Defense Pentagon
Washington, DC 20301
703-695-1536

Ms. Gloria Smith
U.S. Department of Energy
Office of Impact
1000 Independence Ave., SW

Washington, DC 20585
202-586-8383

Ms. Y. Angel Graves
U.S. Department of Health and
Human Services
Office of Small and
Disadvantaged Business
Utilization
Washington, DC 20201
202-690-6670

Mr. Joseph Piljay
U.S. Dept. of Housing and
Urban Development
Office of Small and
Disadvantaged Business
Utilization
Washington, DC 20582
202-708-1428

Mr. Joseph Bryan
U.S. Department of Justice
Office of Small and
Disadvantaged Business
Utilization

ARB Room 3235
Washington, DC 20530
202-616-0521

Ms. June Robinson
U.S. Department of Labor
Office of Small Business and
Minority Affairs
200 Constitution Ave., NW
Room C2318
Washington, DC 20210
202-219-9148

Ms. Margie Wilson
Environmental Protection
Agency
Office of Small and
Disadvantaged Business
Utilization

401 M St., SW
Mail Code 1230C
Washington, DC 20460
703-305-7305

Ms. Elizabeth Ivey
General Services
Administration
18th and F Sts.
Washington, DC 20405
202-501-4466

Ms. Rae Martel
National Aeronautics and
Space Administration
Headquarters
Washington, DC 20546
202-358-0640

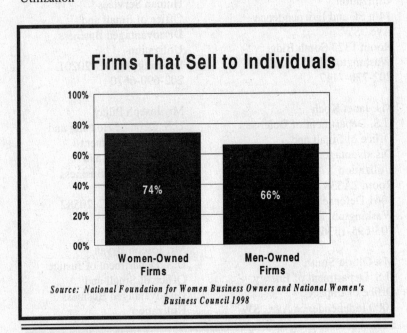

Firms That Sell to Individuals

Women-Owned Firms: 74%
Men-Owned Firms: 66%

Source: National Foundation for Women Business Owners and National Women's Business Council 1998

Government Regulations Say A Little-Bitsy Loan Is $25,000

The U.S. Small Business Administration's (SBA) Microloan Program was developed for those times when just a small loan can make the real difference between success and failure. Under this program, loans range from less than $100 to a maximum of $25,000.

SBA has made these funds available to nonprofit organizations for the purpose of lending to small businesses and they can also provide intense management and technical assistance. A microloan must be repaid on the shortest term possible — no longer than six years, depending on the earnings of the business. The interest

State Contracts And Marketing Help For Women

Many state governments also have regulations that require them to give a percentage of their contracts to small and women owned businesses. They also have offices that train small businesses on how to get contracts from the federal or state governments.

Call your state Office of Economic Development listed in the Appendix and tell them you want to learn how to get government contracts. You want to help the government make their quota.

rates on these loans will be competitive and based on the cost of money to the intermediary lender.

This program is currently available in 44 states. To learn which nonprofit organizations in your area offer this program, contact your local Small Business Administration Office, or U.S. Small Business Administration, 409 3rd St., SW, Suite 8300, Washington, DC 20416; 800-8-ASK-SBA; 202-205-6490; {www.sba.gov}.

Women Pre-Qualified Loans Cut Down On Banker Stress

Need help filling out your loan application package? The Women's Pre-Qualification Pilot Loan Program was developed to promote the Small Business Administration's business loan programs to current and prospective women small business owners. It also provides specialized  support and assistance with the agency's loan application process.

This program uses nonprofit organizations as intermediaries to assist prospective women borrowers in developing a viable loan application package. The program focuses on the applicant's character, credit, experience, and reliability — not just her assets.

Eligible businesses must be at least 51 percent owned, operated, and managed by women. The loan guarantee is for $250,000 or less. The application can be submitted directly to the Small Business Administration for expedited consideration of a loan pre-qualification.

Currently, this program is available in 16 states. For more information on this program, you may contact your local Small Business Administration Office, or Office of Women's Business Ownership, U.S. Small Business Administration, 409 3rd St., SW, Washington, DC 20416; 202-205-6673; 800-8-ASK-SBA; {www.sba.gov}.

Money To Change From Welfare Mom To Entrepreneur Mom

It is not easy breaking the welfare cycle. But if owning your own business is a goal, then help is on the way.

The Job Opportunities for Low Income Individuals (JOLI) program gives grants to organizations that offer training and technical assistance to welfare recipients and other low income women who want to become their own boss. These sites are located across the country.

To find an organization near you, contact U. S. Department of Health and Human Services, Office of Community Services, 370 L'Enfant Promenade, SW, Fifth Floor, Washington, DC 20447; 202-401-9347.

1997 Grant Recipients

African American Unity
Center
Curtis Owens
5300 S. Vermont Ave.
Los Angeles, CA 90037
213-789-7300

Institute for Social and
Economic Development
John Else
1901 Broadway, Suite 313
Iowa City, IA 52240
319-338-2331

Grace Hill Neighborhood
Services
Rodney Wead
2600 Hadley St.
St. Louis, MO 63106
314-539-9506

WSOS Community Action
Commission
Don Stricker
109 S. Front St.
P.O. Box 590
Fremont, OH 43420
419-334-8911

People for People, Inc.
Rev. Herbert Lusk

714 North Broad St.
Philadelphia, PA 19130
215-235-2340

Centros Sor Isolina Ferre, Inc.
Hecto Cruz
P.O. Box 213
Ponce, Puerto Rico 00734
787-841-1058

Innercity Community
Development Corp.
Linda Jordan
2503 Martin Luther King
Dallas, TX 75215
214-426-5657

Wider Opportunities for
Women
Lina Frescas Dobbs
815 15th St., NW
Washington, DC 20005
202-638-3143

Peoples Involvement
Corporation
Andrea Gandy
2146 Georgia Ave., NW
Washington, DC 20001
202-797-3900

Promoting Economic
Advancement and Career
Education
Michael McLaughlin
3665 Thomasson Crossing Dr.
Triangle, VA 22172
703-221-6610

Virginia Eastern Shore
Economic Empowerment and
Housing Corporation
Arthur Carter
P.O. Box 814
Nassawadox, VA 23413
757-442-4509

2,000 Productivity Specialists Offer Free Analysis

Lorrie Browing got help to find the best way to move her homemade beef jerky business out of her kitchen and into a real facility. A Texas wood products company turned their $35,000 loss in disposing of saw dust into a $15,000 profit by selling it as animal bedding for horse stable floors.

The U.S. Department of Commerce has established 70 not-for-profit centers that will analyze your program and help you determine the best way to solve your problem. The analysis is free, but there is a charge for follow up work.

These centers have been established to help small and medium size manufacturers increase their potential for success. They can help companies cope with a changing environment, decrease manufacturing costs, or discover ways to use new technology.

To identify your local center, contact Manufacturing Extension Partnership, National Institute of Standards and Technology, Gaithersburg, MD 20899; 800-637-4634; {www.mep.nist.gov}.

MONEY FOR WOMEN RUNNING A TAXI COMPANY OR THE AIRLINE CATERING BUSINESS

Actually, the money can be used by women in almost any kind of transportation related business. The U.S. Department of Transportation works hard at trying to help women succeed by helping them get contracts as well as offering short term working capital loans at prime interest rates while working on transportation related contracts.

In order to help spread the word about these and other opportunities, the U.S. Department of Transportation conducts trade fairs around the country. To learn more about these programs, contact National Information

Clearinghouse, U.S. Department of Transportation, 400 7th St., SW, Room 9414, Washington, DC 20590; 800-532-1169; {http://osdbuweb.dot.gov}.

Short Term Lending Program Banks

Cathay Bank
777 North Broadway
Los Angeles, CA 90012
212-625-4709
States: AK, AZ, CA, CO, HI, ID, MT, NV, OR, UT, WA, WY

Hamilton Bank, NA
8750 NW 87th Ave.
Miami, FL 33178
305-717-5726
States: AL, CT, DE, FL, GA,

KY, ME, MD, MA, MS, NH, NJ, NY, NC PA, RI, SC, TN, VT, VA, WV, Puerto Rico, US Virgin Islands

NAB Bank
4928 North Broadway
Chicago, IL 60640
773-561-2300
States: AR, IA, IL, IN, KS, LA, MI, MN, MO, ND, NE, NM, OH, OK, SD, TX, WI

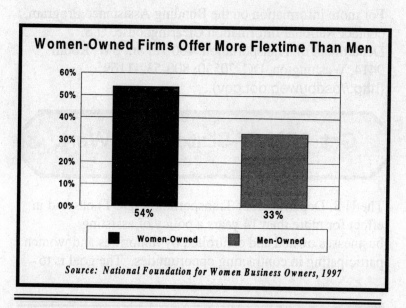

Women-Owned Firms Offer More Flextime Than Men

54% — Women-Owned
33% — Men-Owned

Source: National Foundation for Women Business Owners, 1997

Get Yourself Covered

The U.S. Department of Transportation has a Bonding Assistance Program that offers certified minority, women-owned, and disadvantaged business enterprises an opportunity to obtain bids, payment, and performance bonds for transportation-related projects.

The Program provides an 80% guarantee against losses on contracts up to $1,000,000. They will even help you fill out the application package.

For more information on the Bonding Assistance Program, contact National Information Clearinghouse, U.S. Department of Transportation, 400 7th St., SW, Room 9414, Washington, DC 20590; 800-532-1169; {http://osdbuweb.dot.gov}.

Get 10% Of State Road Work

The U.S. Department of Transportation (DOT) has had in effect for more than 14 years a policy of assisting businesses owned and controlled by minorities and women participating in contracting opportunities. The goal is to ensure that at least 10% of the funds authorized for contracts go to Disadvantaged Business Enterprises (DBE).

State and local transportation agencies that receive U.S. Department of Transportation federal financial assistance must have goals for the participation of disadvantaged entrepreneurs and certify the eligibility of these firms to participate in DOT-assisted contracts.

For more information about Disadvantaged Business Enterprises, and to learn how you can be certified as a DBE and get state and local transportation contracts, contact National Information Clearinghouse, U.S. Department of Transportation, 400 7th St., SW, Room 9414, Washington, DC 20590; 800-532-1169; {http://osdbuweb.dot.gov}.

Free Software for Starting a Business

The Small Business Administration lets you download free shareware that will help you write a business plan, developing your idea or help you plan a whole new career. Visit the site at (www.sba.gov/shareware/starfile. html).

Your Government Contact

Need some help marketing your product or service to the government? The Procurement Assistance Offices are attuned to the federal procurement process, and can help you draw up a sensible business plan that will be successful. They can match the product or service you are selling with the appropriate agency, and then help you market your wares effectively.

Several programs even have online bid matching services. They can obtain specifications, get your name on solicitation mailing lists, and more. These Offices are located throughout the country. These offices are partially funded by the Department of Defense to assist businesses with Defense procurement.

To find the office nearest you, contact Small and Disadvantaged Business Utilization Office, Cameron Station, Room 4B110, Defense Logistics Agency, Alexandria, VA 22304; 703-767-1661; {www.dla.mil} then to the small business site.

Give Women Entrepreneurs Credit: Banks Are Starting To Get It

To encourage credit availability for women, the Federal Reserve Bank of Chicago recently issued a guide to lenders and women owners of small businesses entitled, *Access to Credit: Women, Lenders, and Small Business Loans*.

This free 41 page publication contains suggestions that can help lenders comply with fair lending guidelines when handling credit applications from women owners of small businesses. It offers suggestions for both lenders and women business owners seeking credit.

WOMEN MORE SUCCESSFUL THAN MEN

	Women Businesses	All Businesses
Companies who started in 1991 and are still in business in 1994	75%	67%

Source: *Nation's Business, August 1998 v86 n8 p38(1)*

For your copy, contact Federal Reserve Bank- Chicago, Public Information, 230 S. LaSalle St., Chicago, IL 60604; 312-322-5112; {www.frbchi.org}.

Franchise French Fries

Franchises are big businesses in today's marketplace. But before you sign on the dotted line, learn the questions you need to ask and what the franchiser needs to tell you.

The Federal Trade Commission has several pamphlets that will help you learn your way through the franchise business. Some titles include: *Before You Buy*, *Your Legal Rights*, and *State Disclosure Requirements*. The FTC can also provide you with the Franchise Rule, as well as information on franchise fraud.

For your copies, contact Correspondence Branch, Federal Trade Commission, Washington, DC 20580; 202-326-2222; {www.ftc.gov}.

Small Businesses Can Get Large Contracts

Every Federal government department has an Office of
Small and Disadvantaged Business Utilization (OSDBU)
that provides procurement assistance to small, minority,
8(a), and women-owned businesses. Their primary
function is to ensure that small and disadvantaged
businesses receive their fair share of U.S. Government
contracts.

These offices are the contacts for their respective agencies
and are excellent sources of information. Contact the

MONEY FOR SMALL BUSINESSES HURT BY DEFENSE CUTBACKS

The U.S. Department of Defense and the Small
Business Administration have established a SBDC
Defense Economic Transition Assistance program
that offers loans up to $1.5 million. The money is for
businesses who get at least 25% of their sales from
defense contracts and have been hurt by defense
cutbacks.

Contact [www.defensedollars.com/delta. html]
or find your local Small Business Development
Center from your state Lead Small Business
Development Center listed in the Appendix.

federal government department directly, or for a listing of offices, contact U.S. Small Business Administration, 409 3rd St., SW, Washington, DC 20416; 202-205-6673; 800-8-ASK-SBA; {www.sba.gov}.

Free Accounting Services For Non-Profits and Small Businesses

There are a number of organizations around the country that provide free accounting services to help non-profits, small businesses, and even needy individuals get the accounting help they need. They can help with bookkeeping instruction, system analysis, preparation of 990 forms, preparation for audits and free publications. A minimal one-time cost may be required.

Community Accountants in Philadelphia provides volunteers to assist non-profits with one-on-one help to:

1) Establish a bookkeeping system
2) Set up an easy payroll system
3) Help provide the financial information needed for IRS Application for Tax Exempt Status
4) Free Hotline and E-mail service for accounting questions

To find free accounting help in your area, contact Accountants for the Public Interest, University of

Baltimore, Thurnel Business Center, Room 155, 1420 North Charles Street, Baltimore, MD 21201; 410-837-6533; Fax: 410-837-6532; {www.accountingnet. com/asso/api/index.html}.

If this source doesn't work, contact your state association of Certified Public Accountants (CPA). Many of these associations should be able to identify a volunteer CPA who would be willing to help. Contact your state capitol operator listed in the Appendix or call your local public library.

Free Computers for "Good Guy" Lawyers

The American Bar Association donates used computers to nonprofit organizations who provide legal services to the poor.

Contact Technology Exchange Project, American Bar Association Standing Committee on Legal Aid and Indigent Defendants, 1459 Clayton, Denver, CO 80206; 303-329-2091, Fax: 303-329-0362; [www.ta.doc.gov/go4it/programs/00/14.htm].

OVER 100 GOVERNMENT GRANTS FOR YOUR BUSINESS

One of the biggest frustrations we hear is from people looking for *FREE MONEY* from the government for their business. By free money, they usually mean grants or other programs where they don't have to pay back the money they receive.

Many people will contact the **Small Business Administration** asking about free money programs and will be told that there is no such thing. Well, they are right and wrong. They are right, because the Small Business Administration does not offer grants. They specialize in loans and loan guarantees. But, they are wrong because there are dozens of other government organizations that do offer grants to businesses. The real good stuff in life is never the most plentiful and always takes extra effort and sometimes ingenuity to uncover it.

Information USA, Inc.

The following is a list of a number of national and local government organizations which offer grants or other forms of money you don't have to pay back, like venture capital. It is in no way a complete list, because programs always come and go in our fast changing society. But it certainly does offer you an idea of the opportunities that are out there waiting, and dispels the myth that there are no government grants for business. Just ask **Paul Newman** when you see him. He received government grant money from the U.S. Department of Agriculture to help sell his salad dressing overseas.

U.S. Government Federal Information Center

To locate the federal programs listed below, contact your local U.S. Government Federal Information Center listed in the Appendix, or contact the agencies directly in Washington. Each of these agencies also has websites describing their programs. For more information about the state programs, contact the appropriate state Department of Economic Development listed in the Appendix.

State Departments of Economic Development

GRANTS AND VENTURE CAPITAL PROGRAMS OFFERED BY GOVERNMENT AGENCIES

1. $1 billion a year in *Small Business Innovation Research* grants (coordinated through the Small Business  Administration) is awarded to small businesses from ten different agencies to work on new ideas.

   2. The *Small Business Technology Transfer Program* provides grants to small businesses to work on new ideas with nonprofit organizations and is coordinated through the Small Business Administration.

3. The *Inventions and Innovation Program*, managed by the U.S. Department of Energy, provides grants to individuals and small businesses to work on ideas that result in more efficient use of energy.

4. Grants are available to cover the cost of consultants to expand your business after being hurt by imports, from the Economic Development Administration's Trade *Adjustment Assistance Program* of the U.S. Department of Commerce.

Information USA, Inc.

5. $50,000,000 in grants is available to airlines that service small towns from the Federal Aviation Administration's *Payments for Essential Air Services.*

6. The U.S. Department of Agriculture's *Foreign Market Development Cooperator Program* grants over $3 million a year to companies and cooperatives to sell their products overseas.

7. Over 111,000 businesses have received venture capital through the Small Business Administration's *Small Business Investment Company* program.

8. Over $200 million a year in grants, with half going to small business, is available for developing new technology from the *Advanced Technology Program* at the U.S. Department of Commerce's National Institute of Standards and Technology.

9. The U.S. Department of Energy's *National Industrial Competitiveness through Energy, Environment, and Economics (NICE3)* offers grants of up to $425,000 to small and large businesses to develop ideas that save energy.

10. North Dakota *Women's Business Program* offers an incentive grant program.

11. Entrepreneurs can get up to $100,000 in venture capital from North Dakota's *Technology Transfer, Inc.* to work on their ideas.

12. Massachusetts has its own *Venture Capital Fund* that gives out $100,000 to $300,000 through the Massachusetts Office of Business Development.

13. An 80% discount on the cost of energy consultants is offered through the Massachusetts *Energy Advisory Service* of the Massachusetts Division of Energy Resources.

14. Grants to train your employees are available from the Rhode Island *Economic Development Set-Aside Program* of the Rhode Island Economic Development Corporation.

15. Rhode Island's Competitiveness Improvement Program offers $25,000 grants to upgrade your employees' skills from the Rhode Island *Economic Development Corporation*.

16. $5,000 is available for employees in Rhode Island to learn new technology through *Project Upgrade Grant* from the Rhode Island Economic Development Corporation.

17. Grants up to $2,250 are available for every job your business creates in certain zip codes in Connecticut through the *Enterprise Zone Program* of the Department of Economic and Community Development.

18. Up to $500,000 in venture capital is available from the *Small Business Technology Investment Fund Program* of the New York Empire State Development.

19. Pennsylvania's *Ben Franklin Seed Venture Program* offers venture capital from the Department of Community and Economic Development.

20. $5,000 to $100,000 for new products or new companies from Pennsylvania's *Ben Franklin Challenge Grant Program* of the Department of Community and Economic Development.

21. Pennsylvania's *Opportunity Grant* programs gives out $25 million a year for job training and working capital from the Department of Community and Economic Development.

Job Training Grants

22. Grants to fix up property are available from Pennsylvania's *Industrial Site Reuse Program* of the Department of Community and Economic Development.

23. Pennsylvania *Customized Job Training Grants* from the Department of Community and Economic Development can be used for new employees

24. Grants from Pennsylvania's *Office of Pollution Prevention and Compliance Assistance* are available to convert gas vehicles to alternative fuels.

25. $150,00 to $250,000 is available from Maryland's *Enterprise Investment Program* for technology-driven companies.

26. Venture capital for low-income entrepreneurs and people with disabilities is offered through Maryland's *Equity Participation Investment Program.*

27. Pollution control grants are available from Virginia's *Department of Environmental Quality.*

28. The *Virginia Horse Industry Board* offers grants to those who develop projects that will benefit Virginia's horse industry.

29. Delaware has three *venture capital funds* offering from $150,000 to $42 million.

30. $50,000 is available for inventors waiting for government money from Delaware's *SBIR (Small Business Innovation Research) Bridge Grant Award.*

31. North Carolina's *Pollution Challenge Grants* offer $20,000 for ideas on how to reduce waste.

32. $25,000 is available through the North Carolina's *Wood Waste Reduction Grants* from North Carolina Division of Pollution Prevention and Environmental Assistance.

33. Up to $250,000 in venture capital is available from North Carolina *Innovation Research Fund* from the North Carolina Technological Development Authority.

34. Florida's *Technology Investment Fund* offers $25,000 to $250,000 from Enterprise Florida.

35. *Cypress Equity Fund* of Florida makes $35 million available.

36. Tennessee offers $5,000 to *train employees* in the area of health and safety.

37. *Valley Management* in Tennessee gives out $100,000 in venture capital to disadvantaged businesses.

38. The *Commerce Capital Venture Fund* provides up to $3 million to growing businesses in Tennessee.

39. Entrepreneurs with new products or services can apply for up to $500,000 in venture capital from Tennessee *Venture Alliance Capital Fund*.

40. Money to train your employee is available from Kentucky's *Bluegrass State Skills Corporation*.

41. Ohio's *Scrap Tire Loan and Grant Program* offers money to entrepreneurs who want to recycle tires.

42. Ohio's *Industrial Training Program Grant* offers $250,000 through the Ohio Department of Development.

43. Grants to start your business are available from Ohio's *Business Development Account* from the Ohio Department of Development.

44. *West Virginia Capital Company* offers money to small businesses.

45. $10,000 to develop alternative fuel technology is available from Indiana's *Alternative Energy Systems Program* of the Indiana Department of Commerce.

46. Grants to improve energy efficiency are offered through Indiana's *National Industrial Competitiveness Through Energy, Environment and Economics Grant* of the Indiana Department of Commerce.

47. Indiana's *Recycling Market Development Program* offers $40,000 to develop products from used tires through the Indiana Department of Commerce.

Trade Show Assistance Program

48. $5,000 to attend a trade show in a foreign country is available through Indiana's *Trade Show Assistance Program* of the Indiana Department of Commerce.

49. Indiana's LYNX Capital Corporation offers venture capital to minority owned businesses through the *Cambridge Capital Management Corporation.*

50. Up to $200,000 in grants is available for training new or existing employees through Indiana's *Job Training Programs* through the Indiana Department of Commerce.

51. The *Manufacturing Extension Partnership* of Illinois offers money to improve your business' productivity.

52. $1.6 million in training grants went to 340 companies in Illinois through the *Industrial Training Program* of the Illinois Department of Commerce and Community Affairs.

53. Illinois offers grants in their *Used Tire Recovery Program* of the Department of Commerce and Community Affairs.

54. Grants to purchase equipment to make products from recycled materials are available from the Illinois *Market Development Program* of the Bureau of Energy and Recycling.

55. Grants to recycle solid waste are available from the Illinois *Recycling Industry Modernization Program.*

56. Michigan offers *Economic Development Job Training Grants* from $500 to $1000 for each employee through the Michigan Jobs Commission.

57. Wisconsin's *Brownfields Grant Initiative* offers grants for environmental cleanup through Wisconsin Department of Commerce.

58. Up to $10,000 in grant money is available for every new job created from Wisconsin's *Commerce/DVR Job Training Program* through Wisconsin Department of Commerce.

59. Wisconsin pays 50% of training costs in their *Customized Labor Training Fund* through Wisconsin Department of Commerce.

60. The *Rural Economic Development Early Planning Grant Program* in Wisconsin offers grants up to $15,000 to start a new business.

61. Entrepreneurs with disabilities can get grants from Wisconsin's *Business Development Initiative.*

62. Minority entrepreneurs can get grants from Wisconsin's *Minority Business Early Planning Grants Program.*

63. Grant money for recycling ideas is available from Wisconsin's *Recycling Market Development Education Grant Program.*

64. Grants to get into the recycling business are available from the Wisconsin *Recycling Early Planning Grant Program.*

65. The Wisconsin *Trade Project Program* offers $5,000 to attend a foreign trade show.

66. Wisconsin gives out grants to develop new products from its *Wood Utilization Program.*

67. $4,000 for technical assistance is available from Minnesota's *Microenterprise Assistance Grants* from the Trade and Economic Development Office.

68. The Missouri Market Development Program gives grants up to $75,000 to market recycled products through *Environmental Improvement and Energy Resources Authority.*

69. Arkansas grants up to $50,000 to retrain your employees in its *Existing Workforce Training Program* of the Economic Development Commission.

70. Louisiana has 4 different Venture Capital Funds through the Louisiana *Economic Development Corporation.*

71. Over 22,000 employees a year get grants to be trained from Texas' *Smart Jobs Program* of the Texas Department of Economic Development.

72. Oklahoma gives money back to business through its *Quality Jobs Program* of the Oklahoma Department of Commerce.

73. Small businesses can get grant money from Oklahoma's *Small Employer Quality Jobs Program* of the Oklahoma Department of Commerce.

74. $25,000 for training grants is available from the Iowa *Industrial New Jobs Training Program* of the Iowa Department of Economic Development.

75. Two businesses can get $50,000 to train their employees together from Iowa's *Business Consortia Training Project* of the Department of Economic Development.

Quality Jobs Programs

76. The *Forgivable Loan Program* gives out training money through the Community Economic Betterment Account of the Iowa Department of Economic Development.

77. Iowa's *Innovative Skills Development Program* gives grants to learn new technology skills.

78. Grants for training, childcare and transportation are available from Iowa's *Career Link*.

79. Five or more businesses can train their employees together with Iowa's *Business Network Training Project Grants*.

80. Grants for new agricultural products are available from Iowa's *Value Added Products and Processes Financial Assistance Program.*

81. $15,000 is available from Iowa's *Entrepreneurs with Disabilities Program.*

82. Iowa's *Capital Corporation* offers $250,000 in venture capital.

83. $125,000 to work on new products is available from the Kansas *Applied Research Matching Fund* from the Kansas Technology Enterprise Corporation.

84. The Kansas *Attraction Development Grant* gives money to develop a new tourist attraction.

85. Grant money to train employees is offered through the Kansas *High Performance Incentive Program* of the Kansas Department of Commerce and Housing.

86. Venture capital is available from the Kansas *Innovation and Commercialization Corporation.*

87. The Kansas *Electric Power Corporation* offers grants for entrepreneurs in small towns.

88. The Kansas *Ad Astra Seed Capital* offers venture capital from the Kansas Technology Enterprise Corporation.

89. $3,500 to sell overseas is available from the Kansas *Trade Show Assistance Program* of the Kansas Department of Commerce and Housing.

90. Kansas has *venture and seed capital* available from the Kansas Department of Commerce and Housing.

91. The Kansas *Invention Development Assist Program* offers a $1,000 grant to start your invention from the Kansas Technology Enterprise Corporation.

92. $5,000 to prepare a grant proposal is available from the Kansas *Small Business Innovation Research Matching Grant Program* of the Kansas Technology Enterprise Corporation.

93. The *Workforce Development Program* in South Dakota gives grants for employee training through the Governor's Office of Economic Development.

94. New Mexico's *Industrial Development Training Program* gives grants that cover costs and wages for employee training through the New Mexico Economic Development Department.

95. The *Job Skills Program* in Washington grants up to 50% of the cost of training employees and is offered through the Workforce Training and Education Coordinating Board.

96. Venture capital is available from the Oregon *Resource and Technology Development Fund.*

97. Oregon's *Workforce Development* offers grants to train employees and is offered through the Oregon Economic Development Department.

98. *Colorado First* offers grants for new and existing employees through Colorado's Office of Business Development.

99. Venture Capital is available from the Colorado *Capital Alliance*.

100. Grants are available from the Colorado *Institute for Research in Biotechnology*.

101. Alaska offers grants to provide *child care* through their Department of Community and Regional Affairs.

102. $3 million a year in grants are given to small *coal mine operators* to clean up their mess from the U.S. Department of Interior's Regulation of Surface Coal Mining and Surface Effects of Underground Coal Mining.

103. Maine's *Market Development Center* will pick up 50% of the cost of a marketing consultant for some businesses.

104. *Marketing and Utilization grants* are available to sell agricultural related products from North Dakota's Agricultural Products Utilization Commission.

105. *Delaware Innovation Fund* provides up to $25,000 in matching grants (sweat equity counts!) to develop business plans and get patents.

106. Grants to Indian-owned businesses in North Dakota's *Native American Program*.

107. $2,000 per employee from the *Idaho Workforce Training Program.*

108. $100,000 grant to move your business to Utah from the *Industrial Assistance Fund* of the Department of Community and Economic Development.

109. Utah's *Short Term Intensive Training grants* cover new employees.

110. Grants to small businesses who are hurt by defense cutbacks are available from Colorado's *Office of Statewide Defense Initiatives.*

EDUCATION PROGRAMS

Learn Entrepreneuring For Free

There are programs at the state level like the Self-Employment Investment Development Program in Minnesota that offer free small business training, technical assistance and in many cases, small business loans to lower income individuals who want to start their own businesses. Check your state Department of Social Services listed in the Appendix to begin your search for programs like this in your area.

You can also contact your state Small Business Development Center listed in the Appendix to identify your local Small Business Development Center. Many of these offices also offer free or low cost training courses for entrepreneurs.

Help for African-Americans Going To College

The National Urban League helps African-Americans and first generation college students get through the maze of information for applying to Historically Black Colleges as well as mainstream institutions. They also help with identifying scholarships for minorities.

Contact: Black Excel, 28 Vesey Street, Suite 2239, New York, NY 10007; 718-527-8896; {http://cnct/com/home/ijblack/BlackExcel.shtml}.

College Is Possible

What do you need to do to prepare your child for college? What classes should they take in high school? How much do you need to save?

All these questions and more are answered on the *College Is Possible website* at {www.CollegeIsPossible.com}. A resource library is there to peruse and there are links to hundreds of other resources. This website is operated by a coalition of organizations with the hope of making college possible for every student.

Getting Your GED

Bill Cosby, Mary Lou Retton, and 10 million other people famous and not so famous have obtained their GED.

GED stands for General Educational Development, and consists of tests in five different areas. Once you pass these tests, you earn your GED diploma, which is the equivalent of a high school diploma.

GED tests are given all across the U.S. You can contact your local Board of Education to learn about the tests and any adult education classes they may offer to prepare for the test. You can also contact the GED Information Hotline at 800-62-MY-GED. The tests are administered by American Council on Education, P.O. Box 81826, Lincoln, NE 68501; {www.acenet.edu./calec/GED/home.html}.

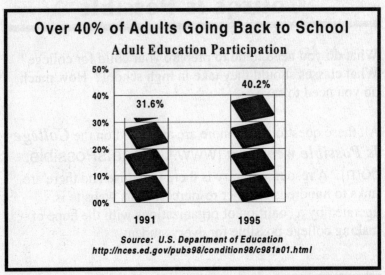

Over 40% of Adults Going Back to School

Adult Education Participation

Source: U.S. Department of Education
http://nces.ed.gov/pubs98/condition98/c981a01.html

College Grants For Workers Who Make a Lot of Money

In 1999 the Vice President of the United States informed the U.S. Department of Education to allow colleges to provide Pell Grants to dislocated workers (people out of work) even though their income the previous year would otherwise make them ineligible.

Contact the college financial aid office, or Federal Student Aid Information Center, U.S. Department of Education, P.O. Box 84, Washington, DC 20044; 800-4-FED-AID.

Pell Grants can also be used for working adults enrolled in part time programs leading toward a degree. If they don't believe you, contact the White House and get a copy of "Vice President Gore Announces New Efforts To Prepare America's Workers and Employers for the 21st Century" at {www.vpskillsummit.org/media3.asp}.

Clearinghouse of Free Education Services for Those With Disabilities

Free help is available if you have a disability and are looking for the right school or education program that is best suited for you.

Contact: HEALTH Resource Center, 1 Dupont Circle, Suite 800, Washington, DC 20036; 202-939-9320; 800-544-3284; Fax 202-833-4760; {www.healthy.net/pan/cso/cioi/HRCACE.HTM}.

Training For Displaced Defense Workers

San Diego State University offers people laid off from their job because of the cutback in defense contracts free career counseling, job search assistance, internships, and free 6 to 9 month retraining courses.

Free E-Mail Mentors For Women Science Students

Undergraduate and graduate women students studying science or engineering are paired with professionals already working in industry. Free at {www.mentornet.net}.

Contact San Diego State University Foundation, 5250 Campanile Drive, San Diego, CA 92182; 618-594-4524; Fax: 619-594-8915; {www.foundation.sdsu.edu}. OR for local programs in your area, contact your state Labor Department listed in the Appendix and ask for the state Employment and Training Office.

Free Tuition, Day Care and Transportation

- Low income
- Receive some kind of government assistance like unemployment insurance
- Laid off because of company closure or mass layoffs

You may be eligible to receive money for tuition, books, transportation, and even day care. There are a number of federal, state and local programs that offer such services.

Review the programs listed under "Government Training Programs" in this book and contact your state Departments of Education, Labor and/or Social Services listed in the Appendix.

Women Over 55 Can Go To College For Free

There are over 350 colleges and universities that offer free or very low cost courses for seniors beginning at age 55 or 60. You can take a computer course, an art course or become a doctor or lawyer. Remember at 55 or 60 you have a good chance of living another 30 years. You can begin a whole new career.

Most state supported colleges and junior colleges offer senior discounts, as well as many private colleges. Contact your local college admission office and ask. If you have trouble locating colleges in your area, your state Department of Education is listed in the Appendix.

CHEAP CHILD CARE

Think you can't afford to go to school and pay for child care? Talk to the child care center at your college.

Ohio State University has five day a week pre-school offered on a sliding fee scale and staffed with mostly four-year early childhood degree teachers. Columbus State University has a two-day a week preschool for $48. Check with your school to see what they have to offer.

The Higher Education Information Center in Boston has a listing of Massachusetts' colleges that offer child care facilities (700 Boylston St., Copley Square, Boston, MA 02116; 617-536-0200; 800-422-1171-in MA; {www.heic.org/childcar.htm}). Check with your state's Office of Higher Education listed in the Appendix to see if

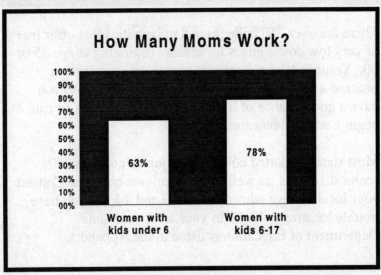

How Many Moms Work?

Women with kids under 6: 63%
Women with kids 6-17: 78%

they offer a similar service. You can also contact the Child Care and Development Block Grant contact for your state (listed in the Appendix) to learn what child care subsidies are available to you.

SAT Prep

If you want to go to college, you can't avoid the SAT or ACT test. What you can do is prepare for them, as they could help you get into the college of your choice.

There are several books and preparation classes you can take. California just passed SB-1697 law that allows school districts to offer preparation courses for college admission examinations through the College Preparation Partnership Program. Many school districts offer similar programs through their adult education classes. Talk to your high school or local board of education to see what is available in your area.

Websites offering SAT tips include:

- {www.testprep.com/satmenu.html}
- {www1.kaplan.com/view/article/0,1275, 1680,00.html}
- {www.powerprep.com/classmap.htm}

COLLEGE CREDIT FOR $5

California offers low-income students the chance to take Advanced Placement tests to earn college credit or advanced academic standing for only $5. You must be an economically disadvantaged student or attend a high school where at least 75 percent of the students are eligible for a free or reduced lunch program. Contact your local board of education to see what is offered in your area.

WHAT SHOULD MY MAJOR BE?

It is hard to make a career choice at age eighteen. What are the hot jobs for the future? When should you start planning for college?

Federal Money For School Starting Place:

Federal Student Aid Information Center, U.S. Department of Education, P.O. Box 84, Washington, DC 20044; 800-4-FED-AID.

Boston has the Higher Education Information Center (700 Boylston St., Copley Square, Boston, MA 02116; 617-536-0200; 800-422-1171-in MA; {www.heic.org}) where you can find free information, counseling, financial aid resources, and career information. Many states operate similar services through the state Office of Higher Education. Contact your state office listed in the Appendix. A listing of many programs is available at {www.heic.org/callist.htm}.

Similar programs include:

- ***Education and Employment Information Center***, Connecticut Department of Higher Education, 61 Woodland St., 3rd. Floor, Hartford, CT 06105; 800-842-0229; {www.ctde.commnet.edu/dheweb/eeic.htm}.
- ***New Hampshire Higher Education Resource Center***, 4 Barrel Ct., P.O. Box 877, Concord, NH 03302; 800-525-2577 ext. 119; {www.nhheaf.org}.
- ***Vermont Student Assistance Corporation***, P.O. Box 200, Champlain Mill, 4th Floor, Winooski, VT 05404; 802-655-9602; 800-642-3177; {www.vsac.org}.

Get Help If You're On Public Assistance And Can't Finish College

Hundreds of thousands of women have been juggling child rearing, class schedules and studies while trying to survive economically on a small Temporary Assistance to Needy Family (TANF) Check. Some states let you finish college while collecting assistance and some don't.

If your local Health and Welfare agency is trying to force you to quit your studies and get a job under the new Welfare Reform Laws, you can get information and help from College and TANF, LINC Project, c/o Welfare Law

Center, 275 Seventh Ave., Suite 1205, New York, NY 10001; 212-633-6967; {www.lincproject.org/college. html#anflinks}.

AT HOME ONLINE LEARNING

Sit home and learn. That's the trend. It's now called distance learning.

72% of the Fastest Growing Jobs, With Above Average Pay, Require At Least A Bachelors Degree

Source: Bureau of Labor Statistics; http://stats.bls.gov/ oco/oco2003.htm

You can take an on-line course on Recreation Therapy from the Kansas City Community College {www. recreationtherapy. com/distant.htm}. Or get a Ph.D. in Psychology from Honolulu University {www.honolulu-university.net}.

Investigate your local colleges for distance learning programs or find more than you ever wanted to know on the subject from Distance Education and Training Council, 1601 18th St, NW, Washington, DC 20009; 202-234-5100; Fax: 202-332-1386; {www.detc.org}.

Displaced Homemakers

Single mothers deserve respect, as does any woman who suddenly needs to become a principal breadwinner for her family. It's a leap of faith, but looking for career opportunities has never been easier for women than it is today.

Women Work! is a national network of over 1300 programs that provide support networks, skills training, job placement assistance, education and training, workshops, and more designed to help women enter the workforce. You can learn computers in New York, plumbing in Illinois, truck driving in Arizona. There is something waiting for you!

To learn what is available in your state, contact Women Work!, National Network for Women's Employment, 1625 K St., Suite 300, Washington, DC 20006; 800-235-2732; [www.womenwork.org}.

Call The Fair Pay Hotline

If you need help or information about removing sex or race discrimination in pay policies at work, call the U.S. Department of Labor's Fair Pay Clearinghouse at 1-800-347-3741 or {www.dol.gov/dol/wb/public/programs/fpc.htm}.

Free 24-Hour Career Advisor and Job Search

Choose the *Best Career* by accessing American's Career InfoNet at {www.acinet.org}. You'll learn:

★ the fastest and slowest growing jobs in the future

★ the best and worst jobs in your state

★ the salary level for any job in any state

★ the names, address, and phone of businesses in any city that hire people with your kind of skills

★ details about the duties and responsibilities for any career

★ sources of information on education, training and financial aid

Choose the *Best Available Job* by accessing America's Job Bank at {www.ajb.dri.us}. You can search:

✦ by any category, a list of 800,000 available jobs in the US with over 5,000 new jobs added every day

✦ employment, real estate and auto classified ads in newspapers anywhere in the country

✦ job openings from hundreds of private employment agencies across the country

✦ only new job openings that fit your requirements

Get Your Resume Seen by accessing America's Talent Bank at {www.ajb.dni.us/htmlatb_home.html} and you can:

▲ have your resume seen by employers in any area of the country you choose

Get the Education You Need by accessing America's Learning Exchange at {www.alx.org}. You can:

☑ find schools or organizations in any area of the country that offer courses or training that match your interest and career goals

☑ find out how to verify if a school is accredited and has a good reputation

---

LET YOUR STATE PAY YOUR WAY

$3,000 to become a nurse! Money to become a vet or landscape architect! Money for teachers! Every state offers scholarships and grants to students to go to college. Some are income specific, grade specific, and even degree specific, but others are designed to help any student attend college both in-state and out-of-state.

Contact your state Office of Higher Education listed in the Appendix to see what scholarship, grant, and loan programs your state has to offer.

Go To One-Stop Career Centers For Free Money And Help

Over 1,000 centers around the country offer free telephones, fax machines, photocopiers, computers, Internet access, help with day care, job search, resume preparation, free education and training money and more. It's a place that job seekers should start with to begin the process of finding out how you can get help to improve your career.

Each community has tailored their own system to meet the needs of its citizens. In Nevada, you will find the **Career Information System** whose resources include Discover Your Career Options and how to establish long-term career goals. The employment services staff at the **Ohio Job Net** will match you to the job that fits your skills. Idaho's **Job Search Workshops** teach

Get Free Computer Training When You Lose Your Job

People in Connecticut can be trained for free in computer repair, computer-aided design, or even customer relations, or go to a one year technical college. Contact: The WorkPlace, Inc. 350 Fairfield Avenue, Bridgeport, CT 06604; 203-576-7030; Fax 203-335-9703; {http:// workplace.org}. Check your area for similar programs by contacting your state Department of Labor listed in the Appendix.

techniques on how to target employers, interview, and get a job by employment experts.

The number of centers is growing every day. To find a center near you contact your local employment office; look in the Appendix for your state Department of Labor; or online at {www.ttrc.doleta.gov/onestop/pdf/1stop.pdf}

Free Computer Classes & Jobs For Liberal Arts Majors

Liberal arts graduates with no computer skills can get free computer training through a program offered by employers and The American University in Washington, DC. The companies pay for the training and employ the graduates.

Contact the universities in your area to learn of local programs like this or TurnKey Technical Training, American University, 4400 Massachusetts Ave., NW, Washington, DC 20016; 202-885-2629; fax: 202-885-3453; {www.american.edu/training/}.

Should You Study Acting or Accounting?

Minimum wage for dancing on Broadway is about $1,040 a week. And a new graduate with a bachelor's degree in accounting earns about $600 a week. But before you decide you may want to also know about the 1) Nature of the Work, 2) Working Conditions, 3) Employment , 4) Training, Other Qualifications and Advancement, 5) Related Occupations, and 6) Sources of Additional Information.

Companies Get Government Grants To Train You For Free

Technical schools that normally charge large fees for their training services also provide their services for free to people who are out of work. The Institute for Industrial and Engineering Technology (IIET) in Connecticut gets federal block grant money to train out of work people in new skills. IIET, 185 Main Street, New Britain, CT 06051; 860-827-7966; Fax: 860-827-7025; {www.ta.doc.gov/go4it/programs/00/16.htm}. Check your area for similar programs by contacting your state Department of Labor listed in the Appendix.

You can find out all this information on 250 occupations in the *Occupational Outlook Handbook*. It's available in any library or you can order it for $42 from U.S. Bureau of Labor Statistics, Publications Sales Center, P.O. Box 2145, Chicago, IL 60690; 312-353-1880. Or look at all of it for free on the web at {http://stats.bls.gov/ocohome.htm}.

$2,000
For Computer or Health Care Training

Michigan gives out over 10,000 scholarships worth $2,000 each for people who get an associate degree or a certificate in a high demand technical field like computers or health care. If you live in Michigan, contact Governor's Career Scholarship Program, 201 N Washington Square, 5th Fl. Lansing, MI 48913; 517-373-9808; Fax: 517-241-0559;

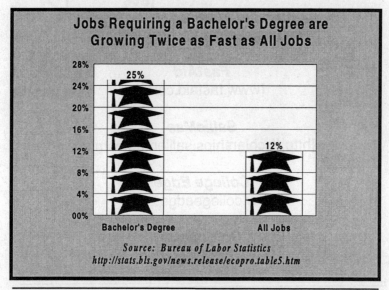

Jobs Requiring a Bachelor's Degree are Growing Twice as Fast as All Jobs

Bachelor's Degree: 25%
All Jobs: 12%

Source: *Bureau of Labor Statistics*
http://stats.bls.gov/news.release/ecopro.table5.htm

{www.state.mi.us/mjc/ceo/stats/overview/agenda.htm}. If you don't live in Michigan, contact your state Department of Labor listed in the Appendix.

Save Your Money

Don't spend money on something you can do yourself! Search for scholarships on the web using any of these search engines for FREE!

Free Scholarship Information Service
{www.freschinfo.com}

The Scholarship Page
{www.iwc.pair.com/scholarshipage}

FastAid
{www.fastaid.com}

SallieMae
{http://schlarships.salliemae.com}

College Edge
{www.collegeedge.com}

Go College
{www.gocollege.com}

FastWEB
{www.fastweb.com}

ASIS Arkansas Scholarship Information Service
{http://scholarships-ar-us.org}

Grip Magazine
{www.gripvision.com}

SRN Express Search
{www.rams.com/srn/execsrch.htm}

College Planning Web Site
{http://collegeplan.org}

College Net
{www.collegenet.com}

OSAD Scholarship Search
(online study abroad directory)
{www.istc.umn.edu/osad/scholarship-search.html}

Purdue Scholarship Search System
{www.purdue.edu/DFA/schinst.htm}

Arkansas Student Loan Authority
{www.asla.state.ar.us/search/index.htm}

P.L.A.T.O.
{www.plato.org}

FREE PUBS

*Ouch...Students Getting Stung Trying to Find
   $$$ For College Alert
$cholarship $cams Campaign*

Available from: Federal Trade Commission, 6th and Pennsylvania Ave., NW, Washington, DC 20580; 202-326-2222; {www.ftc.gov}.

FTC has taken action against the following companies

- Career Assistance Planning, Inc.
- Christopher Ebere Nwaigwe (Higher Education Scholarship Program, National Health Scholarship Program, National Scholarship Program, National Law Scholarship Program, National Science Program, and National Management Scholarship Program)
- Students Assistance Services, Inc.
- College Assistance Services, inc.
- Student Aid Incorporated
- National Scholarship Foundation
- Deco Consulting Services, Inc.
- Student Financial Services
- National Grant Foundation

Source: Federal Trade Commission

Websites For Overseas Studies

Want to study overseas, but are not sure how to do it? Here are websites that offer courses overseas. Some have a particular focus, while others want to offer the experience of living in a different country.

www.afs.org
www.overseasjobs.com
www.studyabroad.com
www.umabroad.umn.edu
www.transabroad.com
www.eiworldwide.com
www.lionsclub.org
www.aspectworld.com
www.iie.org
www.ciee.org

Getting Ready For College Early

Preparing Your Child For College
Funding Your Education
Looking For Student Aid
The Student Guide

Available from: U.S. Department of Education, 600 Independence Ave., SW, Washington, DC 20202; 800-USA-LEARN; {www.ed.gov/pubs/parents}.

FASTEST GROWING JOBS
BY 2006

Occupation	Education/ Training Required	Estimated Salary*
Database administrator/ computer scientists	Bachelor's degree	$39,722 starting
Computer engineers	Bachelor's degree	$39,722 starting
Systems analysts	Bachelor's degree	$39,722 starting
Personal & home care aides	Short-term OTJ training	$15,600 starting
Physical therapy assistants	Moderate-term OTJ training	$24,000 starting
Home health aides	Short-term OTJ training	$15,600 starting
Medical assistants	Moderate-term OTJ training	$18,720 starting
Desktop publishing	Long-term OTJ training	N/A
Physical therapists	Bachelor's degree	$39,364 average
Occupational therapy aide	Moderate-term OTJ training	$14,560 starting

Information USA, Inc.

FASTEST GROWING JOBS BY 2006
(CONTINUED)

Occupation	Education/ Training Required	Estimated Salary*
Paralegals	Associate's degree	$29,300 starting
Teachers, special education	Bachelor's degree	$37,900 average
Human services workers	Moderate-term OTJ training	$20,000 starting
Data processing equipment repairs	Post-secondary	N/A
Medical records technicians	Associate's degree	$31,200 average
Speech-language pathologists and audiologists	Master's degree	$43,500 average
Dental hygienists	Associate's degree	$39,468 average
Amusement and recreation attendants	Short-term OTJ training	N/A
Physician assistants	Bachelor's degree	$52,116 starting
* Salary data is for 1997 and is for either average salary for those in the profession or the starting salary for those new to the profession		
Source: U.S. Bureau of Labor Statistics; http://stats.bls.gov/ocohome.htm		

$1,000 Plus Free Training
To Become A Child Care Provider

Earn money as you provide valuable service to your community as a child care provider! The Child Care Works program of the Center for Policy Alternatives (CPA) wants to help dedicated people become licensed child care providers.

Child Care Works

Child Care Works is a partnership that combines public and private resources to provide child care providers with the know-how and money for starting or expanding a child care business. Child Care Works is designed to help existing and potential child care providers who may need start-up and operating funds, business advice, and/or training to meet licensing agreements.

For more information about Child Care Works, contact Washington Child Development Council, 2121 Decautor Place, NW, Washington, DC 20008; 202-387-0002; or ARCH Family Service, 2208 Martin Luther King, Jr. Ave., SE, Washington, DC 20020; 202-610-0096; or H Street Community Development Corporation, 2002 Rhode Island Avenue, NE, Washington DC 20018; 202-635-2445; or CPA Center for Policy Alternatives, 1875 Connecticut Ave., NW, Suite 710, Washington, DC 20009; 202-387-6030; 800-935-0699; Fax: 202 986 2539; {www.cfpa.org}; {E-mail: info@cfpa.org}.

Money Clearinghouse For Students With Disabilities

The HEATH Resource Center of the American Council on Education operates a FREE national clearinghouse on postsecondary education for individuals with disabilities. Their *Financial Aid for Students with Disabilities* publication provides information on U.S. federal student aid programs and other financial aid programs for students

Get Ahead In Washington With Free Clothing

Suited for Change is a Washington, DC-based nonprofit organization, that provides professional clothing and ongoing career education to low-income women to help boost their chances of employment, job retention and economic independence. Services provided by Suited for Change are available free of charge and by referral only to low-income women who have completed job training and/or readiness programs and are seeking employment. Since its founding, Suited for Change has helped nearly 3,000 women in the transition from welfare to work in the District of Columbia, suburban Maryland and Northern Virginia.

Contact: Suited for Change, 1712 I Street, NW, Suite B-100, Washington, DC 20006; 202-293-0351; Fax: 202-293-035; {E-mail: suitedforchange@ erols.com}; or {E-mail: sfc2@erols.com}.

with disabilities. It also includes a list of 29 sponsors of scholarships specifically designated for students with disabilities.

Disabled students may also wish to request a copy of *Vocational Rehabilitation Services — A Postsecondary Student Consumer's Guide*. Contact: HEATH, One Dupont Circle, Suite 800, Washington, DC 20036-1193; 800-544-3284; 202-939-9320 (both numbers voice/TTY); Fax: 202-833-4760.

Employment Training and Job Placement For Women and Girls

If you need better qualifications and training to better provide for yourself and your family, the YWCA may be 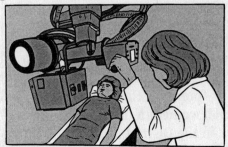 able to help you! The YWCA's spectrum of offerings in this area include basic lifeskills training, English courses, GED courses, adult education, welfare to work programs, structured training curricula, training for non-traditional employment, career counseling, entrepreneurial workshops, job clubs and more. Local YWCAs tailor their programs and services to meet the needs of the women, families and employers in their local communities.

For more information about this program, please contact your local YWCA. Contact: YWCA of the U.S.A., Empire State Building, Suite 301, 350 Fifth Ave., New York, NY 10118; 212-273-7800; Fax: 212-465-2281; {www.ywca.org}.

Free Internet Access and Internet Training

Many libraries and community centers such as community colleges, Y's, job training centers and cable television public access stations offer free or low-cost Internet access and instruction. Try calling your local public library; it may have free access or may know where you can get it. Also, contact the Community Technology Centers Network 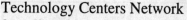 for a list of over 25 community centers in the United States that offer free or low-cost access to computers/Internet.

Contact Community Technology Centers Network, 55 Chapel St., Newton, MA 02158; 617-969-7100 ext. 2727; {www.ctcnet.org}.

Grown Ups Don't Take SATs

A survey of the 14 colleges in the Washington/Baltimore Maryland area showed that only 3 out of the 14 colleges required those over 25 to take the Scholastic Aptitude Test (SAT) as part of their entrance requirements.

College	Requires SAT For Over 25
Bowie State University	YES
Coppin State College	NO
Frostburg State University	NO
Salisbury State University	NO
University of Baltimore	NO
University of Maryland Baltimore	NO
University of Maryland College Park	NO
Morgan State University	NO
College of Notre Dame of MD	YES
Goucher College	NO
Hood College	NO
Johns Hopkins University	YES
Baltimore City Community College	NO
Montgomery Community College	NO

Information USA, Inc.

66 FEDERAL MONEY PROGRAMS WORTH $30 BILLION

Most people have heard of the Federal government's largest money programs for students like the Pell Grant program and the Guaranteed Student Loan program. But did you know that the Federal government is the single largest source of money for students — whether they show financial need or not?

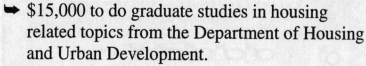

It's true, but very few people are aware of the many grant programs in place and just waiting to give money to those students smart enough to find out about them. These little known programs can provide students with:

➡ $15,000 to do graduate studies in housing related topics from the Department of Housing and Urban Development.
➡ Money to finance a graduate degree in criminal justice from the Department of Justice
➡ $14,000 to get a graduate degree in foreign languages from the Department of Education
➡ $8,800 plus tuition and expenses to be a nurse from the Department of Health and Human Services

How To Apply

Requirements and application procedures vary widely from program to program. Some programs accept applications once a year, while others award money on a year round basis. Some programs require you to apply directly to the main funding office in Washington, DC, while other programs distribute the money to local organizations that then distribute funds to individuals. Many of the programs give the money directly to the schools, and then the schools distribute it. For those, you need to request a listing of the schools that receive the funds.

All these federal programs are listed in the Catalogue of Federal Domestic Assistance, which is available in most libraries. The Catalog lists all the grant and money programs offered by the Federal government. The program name and number in parenthesis refers to this publication.

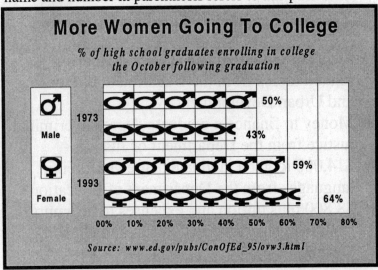

Source: www.ed.gov/pubs/ConOfEd_95/ovw3.html

Get Loans Directly From Your School (Federal Direct Loan 84.268)

Contact: Federal Student Aid Information Center, P.O. Box 84, Washington, DC 20044; 800-433-3243; or U.S. Department of Education, Direct Loan Payment Center, P.O. Box 746000, Atlanta, GA 30374; 800-557-7394; {www.ed.gov/DirectLoan/fact.html}.

$4,000 Grants For Students Having Trouble Paying Tuition (Federal Supplemental Education Opportunity Grants 84.007)

Federal Direct Loans

Contact: Federal Student Aid Information Center, P.O. Box 84, Washington, DC 20044; 800-433-3243; or Student Financial Assistance Program, Office of the Assistant Secretary for Post-Secondary Education, U.S. Department of Education, 400 Maryland Ave., SW, Washington, DC 20202; 202-708-8242; {www.ed.gov}.

Money For a Foreign Language Degree (National Resource Centers and Fellowships Program for Language and Area or Language and International Studies 84.015)

Contact: International Studies Branch, Center for International Education, Office of Postsecondary Education, U.S. Department of Education, Seventh and D Sts., SW, Washington, DC 20202; 202-401-9783; {www.ed.gov/office/OPE/OHEP/iegps/flas.html}.

Money For Students And Teachers To Travel Overseas (Fulbright-Hays Training Grants — Group Projects Abroad 84.021)

Contact: Office of Assistant Secretary for Postsecondary Education, U.S. Department of Education, 600 Independence Ave., SW, Washington, DC 20202; 202-708-7283; {www.ed.gov/offices/OPE/OHEP/iegps/index.html}

Money For Ph.D Students To Do Research Overseas (Fulbright-Hays Training Grants — Doctoral Dissertation Research Abroad 84.022)

Contact: Karla Ver Bryck Bloc, Advanced Training and Research Branch, Center for International Education, Office of Assistant Secretary for Postsecondary Education, U.S. Department of Education, 600 Independence Ave., SW, Washington, DC 20202; 202-

---

Financial Aid Facts

* $60 Billion Available To Students Every Year
* 7 out of 10 Full Time Students Receive Financial Aid
* The Average Student At A Private College Receives $9,000/Yr in Financial Aid

Source: The Coalition of America's Colleges and Universities {www.collegeispossible.org/paying/myths.htm}

401-9774; {www.ed.gov/offices/OPE/OHEP/
iegps/index.html}.

Loans To Go To School (Federal Family Education Loans 84.032)

Contact: Division of Policy Development, Policy,
Training and Analysis Service, Office of Assistant
Secretary for Postsecondary Education, U.S.
Department of Education, Washington, DC 20202;
202-708-8242; {www.ed.gov/offices/OPE}.

Work-Study Program Pay For School (Federal Work-Study Program 84.033)

Work Study Programs

Contact: Federal Student Aid
Information Center, P.O. Box 84,
Washington, DC 20044; 800-
433-3243; or Division of Policy Development, Student
Financial Assistance Programs, Office of Assistant
Secretary for Postsecondary Education, 400 Maryland
Ave., SW, Washington, DC 20202; 202-708-9167;
{www.ed.gov/offices/OPE}.

Low-Interest Student Loans (Federal Perkins Loan Program 84.038)

Contact: Federal Student Aid Information Center, P.O.
Box 84, Washington, DC 20044; 800-433-3242; or
Division of Policy Development, Student Financial
Assistance Programs, Office of Assistant Secretary for
Postsecondary Education, U.S. Department of
Education, 600 Independence Ave., SW, Washington,

DC 20202; 202-708-8242; {www.ed.gov/offices/
OPE}.

Get Help To Study (Upward Bound 84.047)

Contact: Division of Student Services, Education
Outreach Branch, Office of Postsecondary Education,
U.S. Department of Education, 600 Independence Ave.,
SW, Room 5065, Washington, DC 20202; 202-708-
4804; {www.ed.gov/offices/OPE}.

$2,700 Grants To Go To School (Federal Pell Grant Program 84.063)

Contact: Federal Student Aid
Information Center, P.O. Box
84, Washington, DC 20044;
800-433-3243; or Division of Policy
Development, Student Financial Assistance Programs,
Office of Postsecondary Education, U.S. Department of
Education, 600 Independence Ave., SW, Washington,
DC 20202; 202-708-8242; {www.ed.gov/offices/
OPE}.

Aid For Students Who Want To Help The Deaf (Training Interpreters For Individuals Who Are Deaf and Individuals Who Are Deaf-Blind 84.160)

Contact: Deafness and Communicative Disorders
Branch, Rehabilitation Services Administration, U.S.
Department of Education, 600 Independence Ave., SW,
Washington, DC 20202; 202-205-9152; 202-205-8352

TTY; {www.ed.gov/offices/OSERS/RSA/PGMS/
RT/scholrsp.html}.

$30,000 To Study The Humanities (Promotion of the Humanities — Fellowships and Stipends 45.160)

Contact: Fellowships and Stipends, Division of
Research and Education, National Endowment for the
Humanities, Room 318, Washington, DC 20506; 202-
606-8466; {www.neh.gov}.

Money For Students Interested In Helping People With Disabilities (Rehabilitation Training 84.129)

Contact: Rehabilitation Services Administration, Office
of Special Education and Rehabilitation Services, U.S.
Department of Education, Washington, DC 20202;
202-205-8926; {www.ed.gov/offices/OSERS/RSA/
PGMS/RT/scholrsp.html}.

$25,400 Per Year For Graduate Study (Jacob K. Javits Fellowships 84.170)

Jacob K.
Javits
Fellowships

Contact: Federal Student Aid Information Center, P.O.
Box 84, Washington, DC 20044; 800-4-FED-AID; or
Higher Education Programs, Office of Postsecondary
Education, U.S. Department of Education, Washington,
DC 20202; 202-260-3574; {www.ed.gov/offices/
OPE/OHEP/iegps/javits.html}.

$1,500 Per Year For College (Robert C. Byrd Honors Scholarships 84.185)

Contact: U.S. Department of Education, Office of Student Financial Assistance, Office of the Assistant Secretary for Postsecondary Education, Division of Higher Education Incentive Programs, The Portals, Suite C-80, Washington, DC 20024; 202-260-3394; {www.ed.gov}.

Money For Graduate Study (Graduate Assistance In Areas Of National Need 84.200)

Contact: International Education and Graduate Programs Service, Office of Postsecondary Education, U.S. Department of Education, 600 Independence Ave., SW, Washington, DC 20202; 202-260-3608; {www. ed.gov/offices/OPE/OHEP/iegps/gaann.html}.

Grants For Those Who Have Trouble Paying Tuition (Ronald E. McNair Contact: Post Baccalaureate Achievement 84.217)

U.S. Department of Education, Division of Student Services, Office of Postsecondary Education, 600 Independence Ave., SW, Washington, DC 20202; 202-708-4804; {www.ed.gov/offices/OPE/OHEP/hepss/mcnair.html}.

Money For Public Service Students (Harry S. Truman Scholarship Program 85.001)

Contact: Louis Blair, Executive Secretary, Truman Scholarship Foundation, 712 Jackson Place, NW,

Washington, DC 20006; 202-395-4831;
{www.truman.gov}.

Part-Time Jobs In The Government (Student Temporary Employment Program 27.003)

Part-Time Jobs in the Government

Contact: Employment Service, Office of Personnel Management, 1900 E St., NW, Washington, DC 20415; 202-606-0830; {www.usajobs.opm.gov}.

Internships For Graduate Students To Work AT 54 Government Agencies (Presidential Management Intern Program 27.013)

Contact: Office of Personnel Management, Philadelphia Service Center, Federal Building, 600 Arch St., Philadelphia, PA 19106; 215-597-7136; Career America Hotline at 912-757-3000; {www.usajobs. opm.gov}.

Spend A Semester In A Department Of Energy Lab (Science and Engineering Research Semester 81.097)

Contact: Sue Ellen Walbridge, Office of Laboratory Management, U.S. Department of Energy, Washington, DC 20585; 202-586-7231; or ERULF, ORISE 36, P.O. Box 117, Oak Ridge, TN 37831; 423-576-2478; {www.orau.gov/doe_erulf}.

Money For Minority Students At Junior Colleges Who Are Energy Majors (Minority Technical Education Program 81.082)

Contact: The Minority Energy Information Clearinghouse, Minority Economic IMPACT, Office of Economic Impact and Diversity, U.S. Department of Energy, Forrestal Building, Washington, DC 20585; 202-586-5876; {www.hr.doe.gov/ed/index.html}.

Money for Health Profession Students (Health Professions Student Loans 93.342)

Contact: Health Professions Student Loan Program, Division of Student Assistance, Bureau of Health Professions, Health Resources and Services Administration, Public Health Service, U.S. Department of Health and Human Services Administration, Parklawn Building, Room 8-34, 5600

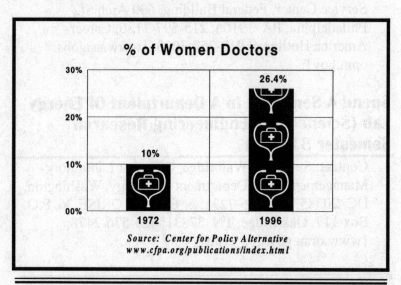

% of Women Doctors

30%

26.4%

20%

10%

10%

00%

1972   1996

Source: Center for Policy Alternative
www.cfpa.org/publications/index.html

Fishers Lane, Rockville, MD 20857; 301-443-4776;
{www.hrsa.dhhs.gov/bhpr}.

Money For Primary Care Students (Health Professions Student Loans, Including Primary Care Loans 93.342)

Contact: Division of Student Assistance, Bureau of
Health Professions, Health
Resources and Services
Administration, Public
Health Service, U.S.
Department of Health and
Human Services
Administration, Parklawn
Building, Room 8-34, 5600
Fishers Lane, Rockville,
MD 20857; 301-443-
4776; {www.hrsa.dhhs.
gov/bhpr}.

Loans For Disadvantaged Health Profession Students (Loans for Disadvantaged Students 93.342)

Contact: Division of Student Assistance, Bureau of
Health Professions, Health Resources and Services
Administration, Public Health Service, U.S.
Department of Health and Human Services
Administration, Parklawn Building, Room 8-34, 5600
Fishers Lane, Rockville, MD 20857; 301-443-4776;
{www.hrsa.dhhs.gov/bhpr}.

Money For Nursing Students
(Nursing Student Loans 93.364)

Contact: Division of Student Assistance, Bureau of
Health Professions, Health Resources and Services
Administration, Public Health Service, U.S.
Department of Health and Human Services
Administration, Parklawn Building, Room 8-34, 5600
Fishers Lane, Rockville, MD 20857; 301-443-4776;
{www.hrsa.dhhs.gov/bhpr}.

Money For Faculty Loan Repayments
(Disadvantaged Health Professions Faculty
Loan Repayment Program 93.923)

Contact: Division of Student Assistance, Bureau of
Health Professions, Health Resources and Services
Administration, Public Health Service, U.S.
Department of Health and Human Services
Administration, Parklawn Building, Room 8-34, 5600
Fishers Lane, Rockville, MD 20857; 301-443-1503;
{www.hrsa.dhhs.gov/bhpr}.

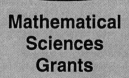

Mathematical
Sciences
Grants

Opportunity To Receive
College Tuition From NSA
(Mathematical Sciences
Grants Program 12.901)

Contact: National Security
Agency, Manager, Undergraduate
Training Program, Attn: S232R (UTP), 9800 Savage
Rd., Suite 6840, Ft. Meade, MD 20755-6840; 800-669-
0703; {www.nsa.gov}.

Scholarships For Disadvantaged Health Profession Students (Scholarships For Health Profession Students From Disadvantaged Backgrounds 93.925)

Contact: Division of Student Assistance, Bureau of Health Professions, Health Resources and Services Administration, Public Health Service, U.S. Department of Health and Human Services Administration, Parklawn Building, Room 8-34, 5600 Fishers Lane, Rockville, MD 20857; 301-443-4776; {www.hrsa.dhhs.gov/bhpr}.

Money For American Indians Who Want To Be Health Care Professionals (Health Professions Recruitment Program For Indians 93.970)

Indian Health Service

Contact: Indian Health Service, Division of Health Professions Support, 12300 Twinbrook Parkway, Suite 100, Rockville, MD 20852; 301-443-4242; {www.ihs.gov}.

Health Professions Scholarships For American Indians (Health Professions Pregraduate Scholarship Program for Indians 93.123)

Contact: Indian Health Service, Scholarship Program, 12300 Twinbrook Parkway, Suite 100, Rockville, MD 20852; 301-443-6197; {www.ihs.gov}.

Money For American Indians Who Need Extra Studies For Health Care Program (Health Professions Preparatory Scholarship Program for Indians 93.971)

Contact: Indian Health Service, Scholarship Program, 12300 Twinbrook Parkway, Suite 100, Rockville, MD 20852; 301-443-6197; {www.ihs.gov}.

Scholarships For Health Care Professionals (Health Professions Scholarship Program 93.972)

Contact: Indian Health Service, Scholarship Program, 12300 Twinbrook Parkway, Suite 100, Rockville, MD 20852; 301-443-6197; {www.ihs.gov}.

Grants For Nurse Anesthetists (Grants For Nurse Anesthetist Faculty Fellowships 93.907)

Contact: Bureau of Health Professions, Health Resources and Services Administration, Public Health Service, Room 9-36, Parklawn Building, 5600 Fishers Lane, Rockville, MD 20857; 301-443-6193; {www.hrsa.dhhs.gov/bhpr}.

Money For Dental Students For Advanced Residency Training (Residency Training And Advanced Education in General Practice Of Dentistry 93.897)

Contact: Public Health and Dental Education Branch, Division of Associated Dental and Public Health

Professions, Bureau of Health Professions, Health
Resources and Services Administration, Public Health
Service, U.S. Department of Health and Human
Services, 5600 Fishers Lane, Rockville, MD 20857;
301-443-4832; {www.bphc.hrsa.dhhs.gov}.

Health Careers Opportunity Program (Health Careers Opportunity Program 93.822)

Contact: Division of
Disadvantaged
Assistance, Bureau of
Health Professions,
Health Resources and
Services Administration, Public Health Services, U.S.
Department of Health and Human Services, Room 8A-
09, 5600 Fishers Lane, Rockville, MD 20857; 301-
443-4493; {www.hrsa.dhhs.gov/bhpr}.

Health Careers Opportunity Program

Money For Nursing Students To Repay Their Loans (Nursing Education Loan Repayment Agreements For Registered Nurses Entering Employment At Eligible Health Facilities 93.908)

Contact: Loan Repayment Programs Branch, Division
of Scholarships and Loan Repayment, Bureau of
Primary Health Care, Health Resources and Services
Administration, 4350 East-West Highway, Rockville,
MD 20857; 301-594-4400; 800-435-6464;
{www.bphc.hrsa.dhhs.gov}.

Money For Health Professionals Who Want To Be In Public Health (Public Health Traineeships 93.964)

Public Health Traineeships

Contact: Division of Associated, Dental, and Public Health Professions, Bureau of Health Professions, Health Resources and Services Administration, Public Health Service, Parklawn Bldg., Room 8C-09, 5600 Fishers Lane, Rockville, MD 20857; 301-443-6041; {www.hrsa.dhhs.gov/bhpr}.

Scholarships For National Health Service Corps (National Health Service Corps Scholarship Program 93.288)

Contact: National Health Service Corps Scholarships, Division of Scholarships and Loan Repayments, Bureau of Primary Health Care, Health Resources and Services Administration, Public Health Service, U.S. Department of Health and Human Services, 4350 East-West Hwy., 10th Floor, Bethesda, MD 20814; 301-594-4410; 800-638-0824; {www.bphc.hrsa. dhhs.gov/nhsc}.

Grants For Graduate Training In Family Medicine (Grants For Graduate Training In Family Medicine 93.379)

Contact: Division of Medicine, Bureau of Health Professions, Health Resources and Services Administration, Public Health Service, U.S.

Department of Health and Human Services, Room
9A27, 5600 Fishers Lane, Rockville, MD 20857; 301-
443-1467; {www.hrsa.dhhs.gov/bhpr}.

Money To Train To Be A Professional Nurse (Professional Nurse Traineeships 93.358)

Contact: Division of Nursing, Bureau of Health
Professions, Health Resources and Services
Administration, Public Health Service, U.S.
Department of Health and Human Services, 5600
Fishers Lane, Rockville, MD 20857; 301-443-6193;
{www.hrsa.dhhs.gov/bhpr}.

Money For Job Safety and Health Training (Occupational Safety and Health — Training Grants 93.263)

Occupational
Safety and
Health
Training
Grants

Contact: National Institute for Occupational Safety and
Health (NIOSH), Centers for Disease Control and
Prevention, Public Health Service, U.S. Department of
Health and Human Services, 1600 Clifton Rd., Atlanta,
GA 30333; 404-639-3525; {www.cdc.gov/niosh}.

Money For Health Care Training In Rural Areas (Interdisciplinary Training For Health Care For Rural Areas 93.192)

Contact: Division of Associated, Dental and Public
Health Professions, Bureau of Health Professions,
Health Resources and Services Administration, Room
8C-26, Parklawn Building, 5600 Fishers Lane,

Rockville, MD 20857; 301-443-6867; {www.hrsa.dhhs.gov/bhpr}.

Grants For Podiatric Training (Grants For Podiatric Primary Care Residency Training 93.181)

Contact: Division of Medicine, Bureau of Health Professions, Health Resources and Services Administration, Public Health Service, U.S. Department of Health and Human Services, Room 8C-26, Parklawn Building, 5600 Fishers Lane, Rockville, MD 20857; 301-443-6880.

Money For Disadvantaged Students To Study Nursing (Nursing Education Opportunities For Individuals From Disadvantaged Backgrounds 93.178)

Contact: Division of Nursing, Bureau of Health Professions, Health Resources and Services Administration, Public Health Services, U.S. Department of Health and Human Services, Room 8C-26, Parklawn Building, 5600 Fishers Lane, Rockville, MD 20857; 301-443-6880; {www.hrsa.dhhs.gov/bhpr}.

Get Your Loans Paid Through Indian Health Service (Indian Health Service Loan Repayment Program 93.64)

Contact: Indian Health Service, Loan Repayment Program, 12300 Twinbrook Parkway, Suite 100, Rockville, MD 20852; 301-443-3369; {www.ihs.gov}.

Money To Repay Loans (National Health Service Corps Loan Repayment 93.162)

Contact: National Health Service Corps Scholarships, Division of Scholarships and Loan Repayments, Bureau of Primary Health Care, Health Resources and Services Administration, Public Health Service, U.S. Department of Health and Human Services, 4350 East-West Hwy., 10th Floor, Bethesda, MD 20814; 301-594-4410; 800-435-6464; {www.bphc.hrsa.dhhs.gov/nhsc}.

Money For Minorities Pursuing a Health Professions Education (Programs of Excellence In Health Professions Education For Minorities 93.157)

Contact: Division of Disadvantaged Assistance, Bureau of Health Professions, Health Resources and Services

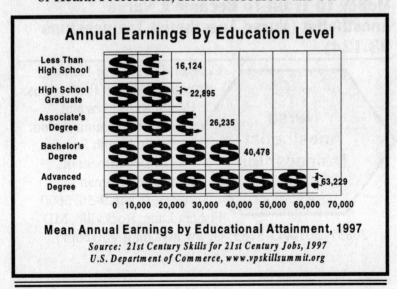

Annual Earnings By Education Level

Less Than High School	16,124
High School Graduate	22,895
Associate's Degree	26,235
Bachelor's Degree	40,478
Advanced Degree	63,229

0 10,000 20,000 30,000 40,000 50,000 60,000 70,000

Mean Annual Earnings by Educational Attainment, 1997

Source: 21st Century Skills for 21st Century Jobs, 1997
U.S. Department of Commerce, www.vpskillsummit.org

Administration, Public Health Service, U.S. Department of Health and Human Services, Room 8A-09, Parklawn Building, 5600 Fishers Lane, Rockville, MD 20857; 301-443-4493; {www.hrsa.dhhs.gov/bhpr}.

Financial Assistance For Disadvantaged Health Professions Students (Financial Assistance For Disadvantaged Health Professions Students 93.139)

Contact: Division of Student Assistance, Bureau of Health Professions, Health Resources and Services Administration, Public Health Service, U.S. Department of Health and Human Services, Room 8-34, 5600 Fishers Lane, Rockville, MD 20857; 301-443-4776; {www.hrsa.dhhs.gov/bhpr}.

Money To Train To Become A Nurse Anesthetist (Nurse Anesthetist Traineeships 93.124)

Nurse Anesthetist Traineeships

Contact: Division of Nursing, Bureau of Health Professions, Health Resources and Services Administration, Public Health Service, U.S. Department of Health and Human Services, Room 9-36, 5600 Fishers Lane, Rockville, MD 20857; 301-443-5763; {www.hrsa.dhhs.gov/bhpr}.

Money To Study Food (Food and Agricultural Science National Needs Graduate Fellowship Grants 10.210)

Contact: Grants Program Manager, Office of Higher Education Programs, CSREES, U.S. Department of Agriculture, Administrative Building, Room 338A, 14th and Independence Ave., SW, Washington, DC 20250; 202-720-1973; {www.reeusda.gov/serd/hep/index.htm}.

Money To Help Math Students and Summer Scientists (Independent Education and Science Projects and Programs 11.449)

Contact: Tony Tafoya, NOAA/Environmental Research Laboratories, R/Ex-4, 325 Broadway, Boulder, CO 80303; 303-497-6731; {www.etl.noaa.gov}.

Money To Study Community Planning and Development (Community Development Work-Study Program 14.512)

Contact: U.S. Department of Housing and Urban Development, Community Planning and Development, Office of University Partnerships, 451 7th St., SW, Room 8130, Washington, DC 20410; 202-708-1537 ext. 218; {www.huduser.org}.

Money To Study Housing Issues (Doctoral Dissertation Research Grant Program

Contact: Division of Budget, Contracts, and Program Control, Office of Policy Development and Research, U.S. Department of Housing and Urban Development, 451 7th St., SW, Room 8230, Washington, DC 20410; 202-708-0544; {www.huduser.org}.

Money For Members Of Indian Tribes To Go To College (Indian Education-Higher Education Grant Program 15.114)

Contact: Bureau of Indian Affairs, Office of Indian Education Programs, Code 522, Room S 3512-MIB, U.S. Department of the Interior, 1849 C St., NW, Washington, DC 20240; 202-219-1127; {http://shaman.unm.edu/oiep/home.htm}.

Money For Criminal Justice Majors (Criminal Justice Research and Development — Grant Research Fellowships 16.562)

Criminal Justice Research and Development

Contact: NIJ Research Plan from the National Criminal Justice Reference Service, Box 6000, Rockville, MD 20850; 800-851-3420; or National Institute of Justice, 633 Indiana Ave., SW, Washington, DC 20531; 202-307-2942; {www.ncjrs.org}.

Money To Study The Break Up Of The USSR (Russian, Eurasian, and East European Research and Training 19.300)

Contact: Eurasian and East European Research and Training Program, INR/RES, U.S. Department of State; 2201 C St., NW, Room 6841, Washington, DC 20520; 202-736-4572; {www.state.gov/www/regions/mis/grants}.

$3,000 A Year To Be A Merchant Marine (State Marine Schools 20.806)

> **State Marine Schools**

Contact: Office of Maritime Labor and Training, Maritime Administration, U.S.. Department of Transportation, 400 7th St., SW, Washington, DC 20590; 202-366-5755; {http://marad.dot.gov}.

All Expenses Plus $558 A Month To Be A Merchant Marine

Contact: Office of Maritime Labor and Training, Maritime Administration, U.S. Department of Transportation, 400 Seventh St., SW, Washington, DC 20590; 202-366-5755; {http://marad.dot.gov}.

Money For Social, Behavioral, And Economic Sciences Students (Social, Behavioral, and Economic Sciences 47.075)

Contact: Assistant Director, Social, Behavioral, and Economic Research, National Science Foundation, 4201 Wilson Blvd., Arlington, VA 22230; 703-306-1710; {www.nsf.gov}.

Money For Disabled Veterans To Go To College (Vocational Rehabilitation For Disabled Veterans 64.116)

Contact: Department of Veterans Affairs, Central Office, Washington, DC 20420; 800-827-1000; {www.va.gov}.

Money For Spouses And Children Of Deceased Or Disabled Veterans To Go To School (Survivors and Dependents Educational Assistance 64.117)

Contact: Department of Veterans Affairs, Central Office, Washington, DC 20420; 800-827-1000; {www.va.gov}.

Money For Vietnam Veterans To Go To School (Post-Vietnam Era Veterans' Educational Assistance 64.120)

Contact: Department of Veterans Affairs, Central Office, Washington, DC 20420; 800-827-1000; {www.va.gov}.

Money For Retired Veterans To Go To School (All-Volunteer Force Educational Assistance 64.124

Contact: Department of Veterans Affairs, Central Office, Washington, DC 20420; 800-827-1000; {www.va.gov}.

Volunteer And Earn Money To Pay For School (AmeriCorps 94.006)

Contact: Corporation for National Service, 1201 New York Ave., NW, Washington, DC 20525; 202-606-5000 ext. 474; {www.americorps.org}.

$15,000 For Graduate Students To Study Overseas (Educational Exchange — Graduate Students 82.001)

Contact: Institute of International Education, 809 United Nations Plaza, New York, NY 10017; 212-984-5330; {www.iie.org}.

Average College Tuition

For the 1998-99 academic year, average tuition charges for a full-time undergraduate before student aid was deducted were as follows:

Public Community Colleges	$1,633
Public University	$3,243
Private College or University	$14,508

Source: The Coalition of America's Colleges and Universities {www.collegeispossible.org/paying/myths.htm}

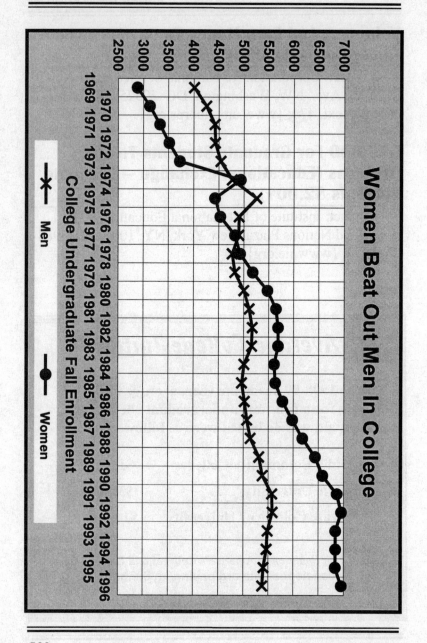

Women Beat Out Men In College

College Undergraduate Fall Enrollment

Men ──✕──   Women ──●──

SCHOLARSHIP PROGRAMS

Organizations are continuously initiating, ending or
changing scholarship
programs. We have
attempted to gather
information on some
scholarships available,
but because of the
perpetual changes you
will want to check directly
with the organization for details
and the most up-to-date information. When possible,
we have included the website of the organization offering
the scholarship for your convenience.

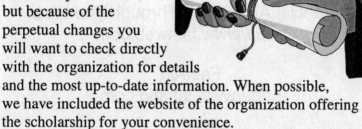

USE THE INTERNET!

Half the battle of scholarships is FINDING them! Thanks
to the advent of the Internet, it has become increasingly
easy to find scholarships and financial aid information.

If you have Internet access, you will want to consider
exploring the following websites first. All allow free
searches of their databases. Some allow you to "save" your
search results, others automatically notify you of new or
updated scholarship offerings, and some provide excellent
advice on how to improve your odds of winning
scholarships. To maximize your information, it is

recommended that you try all of them because each database offers different information and services.

FreSch!
The Free Scholarship Information Service
http://www.freschinfo.com

FastWeb:
Financial Aid Search Through The Web
http://www.fastweb.com

FastAid
http://www.fastaid.com

SallieMae
http://scholarships.salliemae.com

CollegeEdge
www.CollegeEdge.com/FA/

GoCollege
www.gocollege.com

SRN Express Search
http://www.rams.com/srn/search.htm

ExPan Online
http://www.collegeboard.org/fundfinder/bin/
fundfind01.pl

CollegeNet
http://www.collegenet.com

Molis Scholarship Search for Minority
Students
http://www.fie.com/molis/scholar.htm

OSAD Scholarship Search for Study Abroad
http://www.istc.umn.edu/osad/scholarship-
search.html

IUPUI Scholarship Database
http://www.iupui.edu/~creation/scentral.html

For those of you with AOL access, try *RSP Funding* by
going to **KEYWORD: RSP**

GENERAL FINANCIAL AID
INFORMATION WEBSITES

FinAid
http://www.finaid.org

The Financial Aid Resource Network
http://www.theoldschool.org

EMPLOYERS

If you have a job, ask your own human resources department if they offer scholarships or tuition reimbursement programs. If you are still in high school, have your parents ask their employers.

PROFESSIONAL OR SOCIAL ORGANIZATIONS

What professional or social organizations are you or your parents involved with? 4H, JayCees, Lions Club? Association for Internet Addiction?

If you or your parents are a member of an organization, ask them and see if they offer any kind of scholarships. If you are NOT a member of any organizations, the next thing to check is organizations that represent what you are planning on studying.

Many such organizations offer scholarships to students who are studying what they support, even if you are not a member. For example, the American Medical Record Association offers several scholarships for those planning on making a career in Medical Record Administration, but there is no requirement that you be a member. Many organizations that do permit non-members to apply for scholarships, however, do expect you to join the organization after receiving the scholarship.

LABOR UNIONS

Are you or your parents a member of a union? All the major labor unions offer scholarships for members and their dependent children (AFLCIO, Teamsters, etc.)

CHURCH

Check with your church. Your local parish may or may not have any scholarships for their members, but the diocese or headquarters may have some available. And if you have been very active in your local church, they may be able to help you in other ways.

HIGH SCHOOL

If you are still in high school, it is very important that you speak with your guidance counselor or administration office and ask about scholarships that are available to students at your school.

COLLEGE

If you are already attending college, or are planning on attending, the financial aid office at your college can be an excellent resource for scholarships and financial aid. You will also find applications for most of the state and federal level aid programs available at your financial aid office.

> The following is a listing of scholarship opportunities. Each has their own requirements, eligibility, and deadlines. When writing for information, include a self-addressed stamped envelope.
> *Happy money hunting!*

$1,000 + Job From Microsoft

Contact: Mary Blain, National Women's Technical Scholarship Application or National Technical Scholarship Application, Microsoft Corporation, One Microsoft Way, Redmond, WA 98052; {www.microsoft.com/college/scholarship.htm}

$5,000 for Minorities in Science and Engineering

Contact: Xerox Corp., Corporate Employment and College Relations, Technical Minority Scholarship Program, 800 Phillips Rd., Webster, NY 14580; {www.xerox.com/employment/scholar.htm}.

Women In Science and Engineering Scholarship Program

For more information, contact {www.intel.com/intel/community/scholars.htm}.

Scholarships For Mature Women

Contact: Women's Opportunity Award, Soroptimist International of the Americas, Two Penn Center Plaza, Suite 1000, Philadelphia, PA 19102.

Scholarships For Composers

Contact: BMI Foundation, 320 West 57th Street, New York, NY 10019; 212-586-2000.

Scholarships for Smart Business Majors

Contact: State Farm Companies Foundation, One State Farm Plaza, SC-3, Bloomington, IL 61710; 309-766-2039/2161; E-mail: {Nancy.Lynn.gr3o@statefarm.com}; {www.statefarm.com}.

$1000 Scholarships For Smart Women Pursuing Science Majors

Contact: Association For Women In Science (AWIS), AWIS National Headquarters, 1200 New York Ave., NW, Suite 650, Washington, DC 20005; 202-326-8940; 800-886-AWIS; E-mail: {awis@awis.org.}

$1500 Scholarships For Children Of Air Force Members

Contact: Air Force Aid Society (AFAS), Education Assistance Department, 1745 Jefferson Davis Hwy., Suite 202, Arlington, VA 22202-3410; 202-692-9313.

Garden Club Awards Up To $4000/Year

Contact: The Garden Club Of America (GCA), 14 East 60th Street, New York, NY 10022; 212-753-8287; {www.gcamerica.org}.

$2000 For Library Science Graduate Students

Contact: Medical Library Association (MLA), 6 North Michigan Ave., Suite 300, Chicago, IL 60602-4805; 312-419-9094.

Money For Physical Therapy Doctoral Students

Contact: Foundation For Physical Therapy, 1111 North Fairfax Street, Alexandria, VA 22314-1488; 706-684-5984; 800-875-1378; E-mail: {foundation@apta.org.}

Up To $1500 For Federal Employees And Dependents

Contact: Federal Employee Education And Assistance Fund, 8441 W. Bowles Ave., Suite 200, Littleton, CO 80123-3245; 303-933-7580; 800-323-4140; {www.fpmi.com/ FEEA/ FEEAhome.html}.

Up To $4000 For A Health And Nutrition Major

Contact: ODWALLA, 120 Stone Pine Road, Half Moon Bay, CA 94019; 650-726-1888; {www.Odwalla.com}.

$1500 For Women Over 35 Years Of Age Pursuing Below Graduate Level Education

Contact: Jeanette Rankin Foundation, PO Box 6653, Athens, GA 30604; 404-543-8733; {www.wmst.unt.edu/jrf/}.

Up To $5000 For Health Information Management

Contact: American Health Information Management Association (AHIMA), 919 N. Michigan Ave., Suite 1400, Chicago, IL 60611-1683; 312-787-2672, ext. 302.

Money For Female Artists And Writers

Contact: Money For Women, P.O. Box 630125, Bronx, NY 10463.

Up To $10,000 For RN's To Pursue Graduate Nursing Education

Contact: Nurses Educational Fund, Inc., 555 West 57th Street, New York, NY 10019; 212-399-1428.

Scholarships For Medical And Dental Assistant Studies

Contact: American Medical Technologists, 710 Higgins Road, Park Ridge, IL 60068-5765; 847-823-5169.

$1000 For Students Interested In Medical Assisting

Contact: American Association Of Medical Assistants (AAMA), 20 North Wacker Drive, Suite 1575, Chicago, IL 60606-2903; 312-899-1500; 800-228-2262.

$1000 For A Woman In Surveying And Mapping

Contact: American Congress On Surveying And Mapping, 5410 Grosvenor Lane, Suite 100, Bethesda, MD 20814; 301-493-0200; E-mail: {lillym@ mindspring.com}.

$500 Available For Masters And Doctoral Level Health Education

Contact: American Association For Health Education (AAHE), 1900 Association Drive, Reston, VA 20191-1599; 703-476-3437.

Creative Mothers Can Win Money!

Contact: American Mothers Inc., The Waldorf Astoria, 301 Park Avenue, New York, NY 10022; 212-755-2539; {www.americanmothers.org}.

Money For Women Builders

Contact: National Association Of Women In Construction (NAWIC), 327 South Adams, Fort Worth, TX 76104; 817-877-3943; {www.nawic.org}.

Get $1,000
Going Back To School

The IRS's new Lifetime Learning Credit gives you up to $1,000 back on your taxes every year you are going to school. Income eligibility for this deduction goes up to $100,000. In the year 2002, the refund goes up to $2,000. Call IRS Helpline at 1-800-829-1040, get publication number 970 or {www.irs. ustreas.gov/prod/hot/not97-602.html}

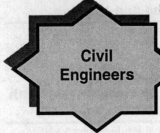

$1500-$5000 Available For Civil Engineers

Contact: American Society Of Civil Engineers (ASCE), Member Scholarships and Awards, 1801 Alexander Bell Drive, Reston, VA 20191-4400; 800-548-2723; {www.asce.org/peta/ed/cssf_hm.html}.

Creative Women Over 35 Are Eligible For $1000 Award

Contact: The National League Of American Pen Women, Scholarship Chairman-Mrs. Mary Jane Hillery, 66 Willow Road, Sudbury, MA 01776-2663.

Bright Broadcasters Eligible For $1250-$5000 In Scholarships

Contact: Broadcast Education Association, 1771 N St., NW, Washington, DC 20036-2891; 202-429-5354; {www.beaweb.org} or E-mail: {fweaver@nab.org}.

$1000 For Women In Advanced Agriculture Or Horticulture Study

Contact: Women's National Farm And Garden Association, Inc., Mrs. Elmer Braun, 13 Davis Drive, Saginaw, MI 48603; 517-793-1714.

Up To $1500 For Veterinarian Students

Contact: American Association Of Equine Practitioners, 4075 Iron Works Pike, Lexington, KY 40511; 606-233-0147.

$2500 Available For Technical Communication Students

Contact: Society For Technical Communication (STC), 901 N. Stuart Street, Suite 904, Arlington, VA 22203-1854; 703-522-4114; {www.stc-va.org}

Money Available For Business Majors

Contact: Kemper Foundation, 1 Kemper Drive, Long Grove, IL 60049-0001.

Scholarships Starting At $2000 For Physician Assistants Students

Contact: American Academy Of Physician Assistants, 950 N. Washington St., Alexandria, VA 22314-1552; 703-836-2272; E-mail: {aapa@aapa.org}.

Creative Kids Can Win Up To $20,000 In U.S. Savings Bonds

Contact: DURACELL/NSTA Scholarship Competition, 1840 Wilson Boulevard, 3rd Floor, Arlington, VA 22201-3000; 888-255-4242; E-mail: {duracell@ nsta.org}.

$500-$2500 Available For Architectural Students

Contact: The American Institute Of Architects and The American Architectural Foundation, 1735 New York Ave., NW, Washington, DC 20006-5292; 202-626-7511.

Many Opportunities For Orthopedic Nurses

Contact: National Association Of Orthopedic Nurses (NAON), NAON Foundation, East Holly Avenue, Box 56, Pitman, NJ 08071-0056; 609-256-2310.

Up To $5000 In Grants Available For English Teachers

Contact: National Council Of Teachers Of English (NCTE), 1111 W. Kenyon Road, Urbana, IL 61801-1096; 217-328-3870.

$1500 Available For Students Pursuing Critical Care

Contact: American Association Of Critical-Care Nurses, Educational Advancement Scholarship, AACN, 101 Columbia, Aliso Viejo, CA 92656-1491; 800-899-2226; {www.aacn.org}.

$500-$1500 Scholarships Available To Court Reporting Students

Contact: National Court Reporters Association (NCRA), 8224 Old Courthouse Road, Vienna, VA 22182-3808; 703-556-6272; 800-272-6272.

Opportunity To Receive College Tuition From NSA

Contact: National Security Agency, Manager, Undergraduate Training Program, Attn: S232R (UTP), 9800 Savage Rd., Suite 6840, Ft. Meade, MD 20755-6840; 800-669-0703; {www.nsa.gov}.

Opportunity For An RN To Win $3000 Toward Occupational Health Education

Contact: American Association Of Occupational Health Nurses (AAOHN), AAOHN Foundation, Suite 100, 2920 Brandywine Road, Atlanta, GA 30341-4146; 770-455-7757; {www.aaohn.org}.

Opportunity For $600-$12,000 For Manufacturing Engineering Students

Contact: Society Of Manufacturing Engineers (SME), Education Foundation, One SME Drive, PO Box 930, Dearborn, MI 48121-0930; 313-271-1500; {www.sme.org/foundation}.

Money Available For Therapists

Contact: AMBUCS Scholarship Committee, P.O. Box 5127, High Point, NC 27262; 336-869-2166; {www.ambucs.com}.

$200-$5000 Available For Smart Women Engineers

Contact: Society Of Women Engineers (SWE), 120 Wall Street, 11th Floor, New York, NY 10005-3902; 212-509-9577; {www.swe.org}; E-mail: {hq@swe.org}.

Opportunity For Pharmacy Students To Get $250-$5000 Scholarships

Contact: American Society of Health-System Pharmacists (AHSP), 7272 Wisconsin Ave., Bethesda, MD 20814; 301-657-3000; {www.ashp.org}.

Funeral Service Scholarship Opportunities Available

Contact: National Funeral Directors Association (NFDA), 13625 Bishop's Drive, Brookfield, WI 53005-6607; 414-789-1880; {www.nfda.org}; E-mail: {nfda@nfda.org}.

75% of All Working Women Earn $25,000/Year or Less

Source: Women's Bureau Fair Play Clearinghouse; {www.dol.gov/dol/wb/public/programs/fpc.htm}

$4000 Scholarship For Communication Science Graduate Student

Contact: American Speech-Language-Hearing Foundation, 10801 Rockville Pike, Rockville, MD 20852; 301-897-5700.

$1000 Scholarship Opportunity For Women In Business Or Economic Education

Contact: Phi Chi Theta Foundation, Scholarship Committee, 8656 Totempole Dr., Cincinnati, OH 45249.

Daughters Of A Career Officer Eligible For Scholarships

Contact: Daughters Of The Cincinnati, Scholarship Program, 122 East 58th Street, New York, NY 10022; 212-319-6915.

$5000 Grant Opportunity For Midwifery Students

Contact: Maternity Center Association (MCA), 281 Park Avenue South, 5th Floor, New York, NY 10010; 212-777-5000; {www.maternity.org}; E-mail: {macbirth@AOL.com}.

$500-$1500 Scholarship Opportunities For Federal Employees And Their Family Members

Contact: Federal Employee Education & Assistance Fund, FEEA, Suite 200, 8441 West Bowles, Littleton, CO 80123; 800-323-4140.

Scholarship Of $2500 Available To High School Seniors With Inter-Scholastic Sports

Contact: Sports Leadership, ESPN Sportsfigures Scholarship, P.O. Box 630, Hartford, CT 06142-0630.

Money To Study The Earth And Sky

Contact: American Meteorological Society (AMS), 45 Beacon Street, Boston, MA 02108; 617-227-2426 #235; {www.ametosoc.org/AMS}; E-mail: {armstrong@ametsoc.org}.

Scholarships For Licensed Radio Amateurs, Females Preferred

Contact: Foundation For Amateur Radio (FAR), P.O. Box 831, Riverdale, MD 20738.

$300 Available For Geographic Education

Contact: Women In Geographic Education Scholarships, NCGE Central Office, Indiana University of Pennsylvania, Leonard Hall, Room 16A, 421 North Walk, Indiana, PA 15705; 724-357-6290.

$2,000 For High School Female Golfers

Contact: Women's Western Golf Foundation, Director of Scholarship, Mrs. Richard W. Willis, 393 Ramsay Road, Deerfield, IL 60015.

$3000-$5000 For Family And Consumer Science Students

Contact: American Association Of Family And Consumer Sciences, 1555 King Street, Alexandria, VA 22314-2752; 703-706-4600; {www.aafcs.org}; E-mail: {staff@aafcs.org}.

Daughters Of The US Army Offers Scholarships

Contact: Society Of Daughters Of The United States Army, c/o Janet B. Otto, Chairman, DUSA Memorial & Scholarship Funds, 7717 Rockledge Court, Springfield, VA 22151-3854.

Scholarships To Students Who Have Hearing Impairment Or Loss

Contact: Optimist International, 4494 Lindell Blvd., St. Louis, MO 63108; 314-371-6000.

Scholarships For Young Black Women

Contact: National Association Of Negro Business & Professional Women's Clubs, Inc., 1806 New Hampshire Avenue, Washington, DC 20009-3298; 202-483-4206.

California Courses Online

The California Virtual University connects you with hundreds of online courses through this website:

{www.california.edu}

$2000 Scholarships For Spouses And Children Of Blind Veterans

Contact: Blinded Veterans Association, 477 H Street, Northwest, Washington, DC 20001-2694; 202-371-8880.

$4000 Scholarship For Industrial Engineering

Contact: United Parcel Service Scholarship For Female Students, Institute of Industrial Engineers, 25 Technology Park/Atlanta, Norcross, GA 30092-2988; 770-449-0461; 800-494-0460.

$300-$1000 Scholarship For Chemistry Students

Contact: Iota Sigma Pi, c/o Dr. Lily Ng, Chemistry Dept., Cleveland State University, Cleveland, OH 44115; {www-

chem.ucsd.edu/Faculty/sawrey/ISP/}; E-mail: {I.ng@popmail.
csuohio.edu}.

Legally Blind Eligible For $300-$10,000

Contact: National Federation Of The Blind, 805 Fifth Ave.,
Grinnel, IA 50122; 515-236-3366.

Scholarships For Lutheran Women

Contact: Women Of The Evangelical Lutheran Church In America,
8765 W. Higgins Road, Chicago, IL 60631-4189; 773-380-2730;
800-638-3522 ext. 2730; E-mail: {womnelca@elca.org}.

Musicians Eligible For Awards

Contact: National Federation Of Music Clubs (NFMC), 1336
North Delaware Street, Indianapolis, IN 46202-2481; 317-638-
4003.

Scholarships For Female Jocks

Contact: Women's Sports Foundation,
Eisenhower Park, East Meadow, NY 11554;
800-227-3988; {www.lifetimetv.com/
WoSport}; E-mail: {WoSport@aol.com}.

Smart Science Majors Scholarships

Contact: The Clare Boothe Luce Program, The
Henry Luce Foundation, Inc., 111 West 50th Street, New York,
NY 10020; 212-489-7700; {www.hluce.org}.

$1500 For Engineering Students

Contact: The Society Of Automotive Engineers, 400 Commonwealth Drive, Warrendale, PA 15096-0001; 724-772-8534.

Up to $5000 For Aspiring Journalists

Contact: National Association Of Hispanic Journalists, 1193
National Press Building, Washington, DC 20045-2100; 888-346-
NAHJ; {www.nahj.org}.

$1000-$5000 For Broadcast Journalism Majors

Contact: Radio And Television News Directors Foundation,
RTNDF Scholarships, 1000 Connecticut Ave., NW, Suite 615,
Washington, DC 20036; {www.rtndf.org}.

$6000 For Women Pursuing Sports Administration

Contact: The National Collegiate Athletic Association, 6201
College Boulevard, Overland Park, KS 66211-2422; 913-339-
1906.

$1000 For Female With A Love Of Flying

Contact: Nancy Horton "Touch The Face Of God" Scholarship,
4466 N.E. 91st Ave., Portland, OR 97220.

$1000-$2500 For Students Studying Real Estate

Contact: George M. Brooker Collegiate Scholarship For
Minorities, Institute of Real Estate Management, Attn: Brooker
Scholarship, 430 N. Michigan Ave., Chicago, IL 60611-4090;
312-329-6008; E-mail: {gohlson@irem.org}.

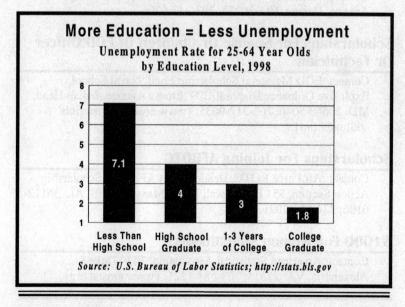

More Education = Less Unemployment
Unemployment Rate for 25-64 Year Olds
by Education Level, 1998

Source: U.S. Bureau of Labor Statistics; http://stats.bls.gov

Women Pursuing CEO Or CFO Positions Eligible For Scholarships

Contact: The Karla Scherer Foundation, 737 North Michigan Avenue, Suite 2330, Chicago, IL 60611; 312-943-9191; {http://comnet.org/kschererf}.

$5000 For Students With Disabilities

Contact: Electronic Industries Foundation (EIF), Scholarship Award Committee, 2500 Wilson Boulevard, Suite 210, Arlington, VA 22201-3834; 703-907-7408.

Up To $4000 Female Medical Students

Contact: American Medical Women's Association Foundation (AMWA), 801 North Fairfax Street, Suite 400, Alexandria, VA 22314; 703-838-0500; E-mail: {mglanz@amwa-doc.org}.

$5000 For Training In Field Of Water Supply And Treatment

Contact: American Water Works Association, 6666 W. Quincy Avenue, Denver, CO 80235; 303-347-6206.

Scholarships For Spouse Or Children Of EOD Officer Or Technician

Contact: EOD Memorial Scholarship Fund, Naval School, Explosive Ordnance Disposal, 309 Strauss Avenue, Indian Head, MD 20640-5040; 703-317-0635; {www.erols.com/ncerino/eodfund.html}.

Scholarships For Joining AFROTC

Contact: Air Force ROTC, Headquarters AFROTC Scholarship Action Section, 551 E. Maxwell Blvd., Maxwell AFB, AL 36112-6106; 334-953-2091.

$1000 For Women Statisticians

Contact: American Statistical Association, 1429 Duke St., Alexandria, VA 22314; 703-684-1221; {www.amstat.org}.

Money For Grandmas

Contact: The Thanks Be To Grandmother Winifred Foundation, P.O. Box 1449, Wainscott, NY 11975; 516-725-0323.

Up to $2,500 For Respiratory Care Majors

Contact: American Respiratory Care Foundation, 1030 Ables Lane, Dallas, TX 75229; 972-243-2272; {www.aarc.org}.

Respiratory Care Majors

Money For Midwives To-Be

Contact: American College of Nurse-Midwives, 818 Connecticut Ave., NW, Suite 900, Washington, DC 20006; 202-728-9860; {www.midwife.org}.

Add Up Your Money Women Accountants

Contact: The Educational Foundation for Women in Accounting, Administrative Office, P.O. Box 1925, Southeastern, PA 19399; 610-407-9229; {www.efwa.org}.

A Total of $15,000 For Women Accounting Majors

Contact: American Society of Women Accountants, 60 Revere Dr., Suite 500, Northbrook, IL 60062; 800-326-2163; {www.aswa.org}.

Money For Human Resource Majors

Contact: Society for Human Resource Management, 1800 Duke St., Alexandria, VA 22314; 703-548-3440; {www.shrm.org}.

$1000 For Real Estate Appraisers

Contact: Appraisal Institute, 875 North Michigan Ave., Suite 2400, Chicago, IL 60611; 312-335-4121; {www.appraisalinstitute.org}.

Count On Accounting

Contact: National Society of Public Accountants, 1010 North Fairfax St., Alexandria, VA 22314; 703-549-6400; {www.nsacct.org}.

AT&T Labs Fellowship Program for Women & Minorities in Science & Tech

Contact: AT&T Labs Fellowship Administrator, Room C103, 180 Park Ave., Florham Park, NJ 07060; {www.att.com/attlabs/people/fellowships.html}.

$500-$1,500 for Smart Business Women

Contact: American Business Women's Association, 1891 Poplar Ridge Rd., Pasadena, MD 21122; 301-255-1067; {www.abwahq.org}.

Money for Smart Business Women

Contact: Business and Professional Women's Association, 2012 Massachusetts Ave., NW, Washington, DC 20036; 202-293-1200.

$500 for Meteorologists and Atmospheric Science Majors

Contact: American Geophysical Union, American Geophysical Union, 2000 Florida Ave., NW, Washington, DC 20009; {earth.agu.org} or {www.agu.org}; 202-462-6903.

$1,000 for Engineering, Math and Science Students

Contact: Brookhaven Women in Science, P.O. Box 183, Upton, NY 11973; 516-344-7226.

$2000 for Smart Engineering Women

Contact: National Society of Professional Engineers, 1420 King St., Alexandria, VA 22314; 703-684-2858; {www.nspe.org}.

$1,000 for Smart Journalism Women

Contact: National Federation of Press Women, 4510 W. 89th St., Prairie Village, KS 66207-2282; 913-341-0165.

$500-$5,000 for Daughters of the Railroad

Contact: John Edgar Thomson Foundation, The Rittenhouse Claridge, Suite 318, Philadelphia, PA 19103; 215-545-6083.

Up to $2000 for Women in Broadcasting

Contact: Opportunities for Women in Broadcasting, c/o The Citizen's Scholarship Foundation of America, 326 S. Minnesota Avenue, St. Peter, MN 56082; 507-931-1682; 507-931-8034.

Up to $1000 for Landscape Architects

Contact: Landscape Architecture Foundation, 4401 Connecticut Ave., NW, Suite 500, Washington, DC 20008; 202-686-0068.

Up to $1,000 for Medical Women

Contact: American College of Medical Practice Executives, 104 Inverness Terrace East, Englewood, CO 80112; 303-799-1111; {www.ache.org}.

$6,000 for Graduate Women In Aerospace Studies

Contact: Zonta International Foundation, 557 W. Randolph St., Chicago, IL 60661; 312-930-5848.

Money for Women Ministers

Contact: Disciples of Christ Church, P.O. Box 1986, Indianapolis, IN 46206.

Money for Women in Oregon

Contact: Oregon State Scholarship Commission, 1500 Valley River Dr., Suite 100, Eugene, OR 97401-7020.

Over $1 Million Available for Farmers

Contact: Future Farmers of America, Inc., Scholarship Office, P.O. Box 68960, Indianapolis, IN 46268-0960; {www.ffa.agriculture. com/activities/activitiessectionpg.html}.

Tuition and up to $13,500 for Smart Graduate Students

Contact: The A.W. Mellon Fellowship in Humanities, Woodrow Wilson National Fellowship Foundation, CN 5329, Princeton, NY 08543-5329; 609-452-7007; {www.wwnff.org}.

Money for Dietetic Technicians

Contact: American Dietetic Association, 216 W. Jackson Blvd., Suite 800, Chicago, IL 60606-6995; 312-899-0040; {www.eatright.org}.

Up to $1,500 for Dental Hygienists

Contact: American Dental Hygienists Association, 444 N. Michigan Ave., Suite 3400, Chicago, IL 60611; 312-440-8944; {www.adha.org}.

$2,500 for Nurses

Contact: The American Legion, Attn: Eight and Forty Scholarships, P.O. Box 1055, Indianapolis, IN 46206; {www.legion.org/educasst.htm}.

50% of Graduate Students Receive An Average Of $9,814 In Financial Aid

Source: U.S. Department of Education {http://nces.ed.gov/pubs97/97570.pdf}

Up to $5,000 for Food Service Experience

Contact: National Restaurant Association Educational Foundation,
250 S. Wacker Drive, Suite 1400, Chicago, IL 60606-5834; 800-
765-2122 x760; {www.foodtrain.org}.

Up to $2,500 for Respiratory Care

Contact: American Respiratory Care Foundation, 11030 Ables
Lane, Dallas, TX 75229-4593; 972-243-2272; {www.aarc.org}.

Up to $1,500 for Returning Students

Contact: P.E.O. Sisterhood, 3700 Grand Avenue, Des Moines, IA
50312-2899, Attn: Executive Office.

$1,000 for Young Feminists

Contact: Spinsters Ink, ATTN: Claire Kirch, 32 East First St. #330,
Duluth, MN 55802; 218-727-3222; 800-301-6860;
{www.spinsters-ink.com}.

Money for Texas Women Returning to School

Contact: Association for Women in Communications, San Antonio
Professional Chapter, P.O. Box 780382, San Antonio, TX 78278;
210-231-5799; E-mail: {jones@texas.net}.

Money for Arkansas Single Parents

Contact: Arkansas Single Parent Scholarship Fund, 614 East
Emma Avenue, Suite 119, Springdale, AR 72764; 501-927-1402.

Money for Palo Alto, California Women

Contact: Peninsula Community Foundation, 1700 South El Camino
Real, Suite 300, San Mateo, CA 94402-3049; 650-358-9369.

Money for Mathematical Woman

Contact: American Mathematical Society, Attn: Executive
Director, P.O. Box 6248, Providence, RI 02940-6248; 401-455-
4000; 800-321-4AMS; E-mail: {ams@ams.org}; {www.ams.org}.

$3,000 for Sports Journalism

Contact: Freedom Forum, 1101 Wilson Boulevard, Arlington, VA 22209; 703-284-2814; E-mail: {gpolicinski@freedomforum.org}; {www. freedomforum.org/}.

3M Engineering Awards

Contact: National Action Council for Minorities in Engineering, 350 Fifth Avenue, Suite 2212, New York, NY 10118-2299; 212-279-2626; {www.nacme.org}.

Money For Graphic Communication Majors

Contact: National Scholarship Trust Fund of the Graphic Arts, Attn: Scholarship Competition, 200 Deer Run Road, Sewickley PA 15143-2600; 412-741-6860; 800-910-GATF; E-mail: {info@gatf.org}; {www.gatf.org}.

$1,000 for Naval Academy Children and Women

Contact: Naval Academy Women's Club, P.O. Box 826, Annapolis, MD 21404-0826.

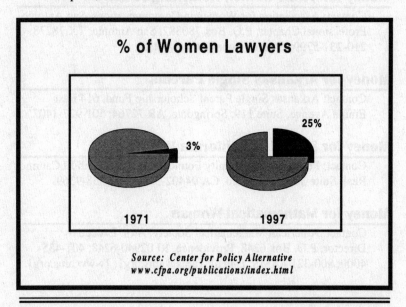

% of Women Lawyers

3%   1971

25%   1997

Source: Center for Policy Alternative
www.cfpa.org/publications/index.html

Money for Future Homemakers

Contact: Future Homemakers of America, Inc., 1910 Association Drive, Reston, VA 20191-1584; 703-476-4900; 800-234-4425; E-mail: {natlhdqtrs@ fhahero.org}; {www.fhahero.org}.

Money for Smart Women

Contact: American Mensa, 1229 Corporate Drive West, Arlington, TX 76006-6103; 817-607-0060; {www.us.mensa.org}.

Up to $8000 for Nebraska Women in English

Contact: Willa Cather Foundation, 326 N. Webster, Red Cloud, NE 68970; 402-746-2653.

Up to $2,000 for California Real Estate Students

Contact: California Association of Realtors, 525 S. Virgil Ave., Los Angeles, CA 90020; 213-739-8200.

Money for Welding Women

Contact: The American Welding Society, 550 N.W. LeJeune Rd., Miami, FL 33126; 800-443-9353; {www.aws.org}.

Money for Horse Racers

Contact: Harness Horse Youth Foundation, 14950 Greyhound Ct., Suite 210, Carmel, IN 46032; 317-848-5132; {www. hhyf.org}.

Up to $2,500 for Architectural Women in California

Contact: Association for Women in Architecture, 2550 Beverly Blvd., Los Angeles, CA 90057; 213-389-6490.

Money for Petroleum Women

Contact: Desk and Derrick Educational Trust, 4823 S. Sheridan, Suite 308A, Tulsa, OK 74145; 918-622-1675.

Up to $10,000 for Executive Women

Contact: Executive Women International, 515 S. 700 East, Suite 2E, Salt Lake City, UT 84102; 801-355-2800.

Money for Ham Radio Women

Contact: American Radio Relay League, 225 Main St., Newington, CT 06111; 203-666-1541; {www.arrl.org}.

Up to $1,000 for Dental Women

Dental Women

Contact: American Association of Women Dentists, 401 N. Michigan Ave., Chicago, IL 60611; 312-527-6757.

Up to $10,000 for Heating, Refrigerating and Air Conditioning

Contact: American Society of Heating, Refrigerating and Air Conditioning Engineers, Inc., 1791 Tullie Circle, NE, Atlanta, GA 30329-1683; 404-636-8400; {www.ashrae.org}.

Up to $3,000 for Logistics

Contact: SOLE-The International Logistics Society, 8100 Professional Pl., Suite 211, New Carrollton, MD 20785; {www.sole.org}.

$1,500 for Safety Engineers

Contact: American Society of Safety Engineers Foundation, 1800 E. Oakton, Des Plaines, IL 60018; 847-699-2929.

$1,000 for Food Technology

Contact: Institute of Food Technologists, 221 N. LaSalle St., Suite 300, Chicago, IL 60601; 312-782-8424.

Up to $1,000 for African American Nurses

Contact: National Black Nurses Association, Inc., 1511 K St., NW, Suite 415, Washington, DC 20005.

Up to $2,500 for Oncology Nurses

Contact: Oncology Nursing Foundation, 501 Holiday Dr., Pittsburgh, PA 15220; 412-921-7373; {www.ons.org}.

Up to $4,000 for Physical Therapy and Occupational Therapy Women

Contact: Allied Resources, 810 Regal Drive, Huntsville, AL 35801; 800-217-7870.

Up to $1,000 for Jewelry and Gems

Contact: Gemological Institute of America, 5345 Armada Dr., Carlsbad, CA 92008-4698; 760-603-4005.

Up to $3,000 for Travel Agents

Travel Agents

Contact: American Society of Travel Agents, Scholarship Foundation, 1101 King St., Suite 200, Alexandria, VA 22314-2187; 703-739-2782; {www.astanet.com}.

Money for Girl's Club Members

Contact: Reader's Digest Foundation, 1230 W. Peachtree St., NW, Atlanta, GA 30309.

Up to $10,000 for Non-Traditional Michigan Women

Contact: Center for the Education of Women, 330 E. Liberty St., Ann Arbor, MI 48104-2289; 734-998-7210.

$1,000 for Sculpture

Contact: National Sculpture Society, 1177 Avenue of the Americas, 15th Floor, New York, NY 10036; 212-764-5645.

Money for Non-Traditional Native Americans

Contact: Association on American Indian Affairs, Inc., P.O. Box 268, Sisseton, SD 57262; 605-698-3998.

Money for Flight Attendants

Contact: Association of Flight Attendants, P.O. Box 212, Warrenton, VA 22186.

Up to $2,000 for Short People

Contact: Billy Barty Foundation, 929 W. Olive Avenue, Suite C, Burbank, CA 91506; 800-891-4022; 818-953-5410.

Up to $1,500 for Theater Women

Contact: Lotta M. Crabtree Trusts, 11 Beacon St., Suite 1110, Boston, MA 02108; 617-742-5920.

Up to $2,000 for Jewelry Women

Contact: Women's Jewelry Association, 333B Route 46 W., Suite B201, Fairfield, NJ 07004; 201-575-7190.

Money for Hispanic Nurses

Contact: National Association of Hispanic Nurses, 1501 16th St., NW, Washington, DC 20036; 202-387-2477.

Up to $2,000 for Travel and Tourism Women

Contact: National Tourism Foundation, 5546 E. Main St., P.O. Box 3071, Lexington, KY 40596-3071; 606-226-4444.

$1,000 or more for Women Grocers

Contact: Women Grocers of America, 1825 Samuel Morse Dr., Reston, VA 20190-5317; 703-437-5300.

$2,500 for Diabetes Women

Contact: Lilly For Learning, Diabetes Scholarship Program, Eli Lilly and Company, Lilly Corporate Center, Drop Code 1625, Indianapolis, IN 46285; 800-88LILLY; {www.lilly.com/diabetes.scholarship/index.htm}.

$2000 for Graduate Historical Women

Contact: State Historical Society Of Wisconsin, 816 State St., Madison, WI 53706; 608-264-6464.

$2,000 for Women in Massachusetts

Contact: General Federation Of Women's Clubs Of Massachusetts, Box 679, Sudbury, MA 01776-0679; 508-443-4569.

Up to $1,000 for New York Business Women

Contact: Business and Professional Women's Clubs, New York State Chapter, 7509 State Route 5, Clinton, NY 13323-3632; 315-735-3114.

$4000 for Bowling Women

Contact: Young American Bowling Alliance, 5301 S. 76th St., Greendale, WI 53129.

$1,000 for African American Writing Women

Contact: Women On Books, 879 Rainier Ave. N., Suite A105, Renton, WA 98055; 206-626-2323.

Up to $5,000 for Minority Women in Technology

Contact: National Technical Association, Inc., 6919 North 19th St., Philadelphia, PA 19126-1506; 215-549-5743; {www.huenet.com/nta}.

Money for Flying Women

Contact: International Society Of Women Airline Pilots, 2250 E. Tropicana Ave., Suite 19-395, Las Vegas, NV 89119-6594.

$3,500 for Medical Women

Contact: Cartland Shackford Medical Fellowships, c/o Wellesley College, Secretary, Graduate Fellowships, Career Center, Wellesley, MA 02181; 617-283-3525.

Money for Women in Sports Journalism

Contact: Sports Journalism Institute, Sports Illustrated, 1271 Avenue of the Americas, New York, NY 10020-1393; 212-522-6407.

Up to $10,000 for Texas Women

Contact: Houston Livestock Show and Rodeo, P.O. Box 20070, Houston, TX 77225-0070; 713-791-9000; {www.hlsr.com}.

Money for Chiropractic Women

Contact: International Chiropractors Association, 1110 N. Glebe Rd., Suite 1000, Arlington, VA 22201; 703-528-5000.

Up to $3000 for Women in Technology

Contact: AFCEA Educational Foundation, 4400 Fair Lakes Ct., Fairfax, VA 22033-3899; 703-631-6149; 800-336-4583 ext. 6149; E-mail: {scholarship@ afcea.org}; {www.afcea.org}.

Up to $4,000 for Journalism Women

Contact: F. Ward Just Scholarship Foundation, c/o Kennedy, 805 Baldwin Ave, Apt. 308, Waukegan, IL 60085-2359.

Up to $10,000 for Smart Women

Contact: AdamsVision USA Scholar-Leadership Award, 440 Louisiana, Suite 1250, Houston, TX 77002; 888-294-4969; E-mail: {avision@hic.net}, {www.adamsvision.com}.

Up to $10,000 for Women with Community Service

Contact: Target All-Around Scholarship, c/o Citizens' Scholarship Foundation of America, Inc., 1505 Riverview Rd., P.O. Box 297, St. Peter, MN 56082; 800-537-4180.

Over 27% of Families Making Over $100,000 Get $5,536 for College

% of Dependent Undergraduates Receiving Financial Aid in 1996

Family Income	%
Less Than $20,000	70.2
$20,000 to $39,999	60.3
$40,000 to $59,999	47.4
$60,000 to $79,999	42.5
$80,000 to $99,999	37.6
$100,000 and more	27.5

Average Amount of Financial Aid Received by Dependent Undergraduates in 1996

Family Income	Avg. Financial Aid
Less Than $20,000	$5,799
$20,000 to $39,999	$5,111
$40,000 to $59,999	$6,009
$60,000 to $79,999	$6,809
$80,000 to $99,999	$5,945
$100,000 and more	$5,536

Source: U.S. Department of Education
{http://nces.ed.gov/pubs97/97570.pdf}

FEDERAL JOB TRAINING PROGRAMS

In today's economy, training is the key to advancement in the work world. How do you get the training you need? Let the government provide it at no cost to you! Uncle Sam knows that we need a skilled work force to compete with other developed countries, and so he wants to help. The following is a listing of the major federal job training programs designed to provide you with the skills you need to succeed.

Become A Journeyman

Getting a good job does not always mean that you must attend college or trade school, but no one will readily admit that. There are apprenticeship programs all over the country that will provide free on-the-job training, and you will learn while you earn. Apprentices learn each skill of a job by carrying it out step by step under the close supervision of a skilled craft worker.

An apprenticeship involves planned, day-by-day supervised training on the job, combined with technical instruction. Length of training varies depending on the job and is determined by standards adopted by a particular industry. The minimum term of apprenticeship is one year, but can be as long as four. Currently there are over 800 apprenticeable occupations, including cook, air craft mechanic, electrician, computer programmer, tool maker, and welder.

Currently there are over 800 apprenticeable occupations

For more information, look in the blue pages of your phone book for the Bureau of Apprenticeship located in your state, or you may contact Bureau of Apprenticeship and Training, U.S. Department of Labor, 200 Constitution Ave., NW, Room N4649, Washington, DC 20210; 202-219-5921; {www.doleta.gov/indiv/apprent.htm}.

Free Training If You Are Laid Off

If you have found yourself on the losing end of a plant closing or mass layoff, apply for money and re-training under the Economic Dislocation and Worker Adjustment Assistance Act. The program is administered by each state, and because of that, the program differs from state to state. Under certain circumstances, states may also authorize service for displaced homemakers.

Workers can receive classroom, occupational skills, and/or on-the-job training to qualify for jobs in demand. Basic and remedial education, entrepreneurial training, and instruction in literacy or English-as-a-second-language may be provided.

For more information, contact your state Department of Labor in the blue pages of your phone book, or you may contact Office of Worker Retraining and Readjustment Programs, U.S. Department of Labor, Room N-5426, 200 Constitution Ave., NW, Washington, DC 20210; 202-219-5577; (www.doleta.gov/programs/factsht/edwaa.htm}.

Free Training If You Lose Your Job From Increased Imports

Ever notice how so many products have gotten less expensive over the last ten years? Shirts that once cost $30 are now sold for $15. Televisions and VCRs — not to mention computers — have never been cheaper.

Almost everything we now buy in the U.S. is being made overseas. If you lost your job because of imports, you can get help looking for a new job or get paid to get more training. The Trade Adjustment Assistance program will help you learn more marketable job skills, so you can move to greener employment pastures. You can receive up to 104 weeks of on-the-job and classroom training; you can receive 52 weeks of benefits after your unemployment expires if you are part of a job training program; you can receive $800 to travel for job hunting purposes; $800 to relocate for a job; and transportation expenses to job training programs.

For more information, contact your local employment services office in the blue pages of your phone book, or Office of Trade Adjustment Assistance, Employment and Training Assistance, U.S. Department of Labor, Room C4318, 200 Constitution Ave., NW, Washington, DC 20210; 202-219-5555; {www.doleta.gov}.

FREE TRAINING FOR THOSE WHO LOSE THEIR JOBS BECAUSE OF INCREASED TRADE WITH MEXICO OR CANADA

NAFTA is not a dirty word, but a lot of U.S. workers swear it is a plan to put them out of work and ship their jobs where labor costs are cheaper — Canada, but more significantly to Mexico and other Latin American countries. In a dog-eat-dog global economy, there are no real borders.

North American Free Trade Agreement (NAFTA)

If you were laid off or lost your job because of the North American Free Trade Agreement (NAFTA), the government wants to help you find a new one, and probably one that pays you more than your last job. The NAFTA Transitional Adjustment Assistance Program is like a job skills and retraining SWAT team geared to provide rapid and early response to the threat of unemployment.

The program includes on-site services to let workers know they are eligible; assessment of skills; financial and personal counseling; career counseling; job placement assistance; child care; transportation; income support for up to 52 weeks after the worker has exhausted unemployment compensation while the worker is enrolled in training; relocation allowance; and more.

For more information, contact your local employment services office in the blue pages of your phone book, or Office of Trade Adjustment Assistance, Employment and Training Assistance, U.S. Department of Labor, Room C4318, 200 Constitution Ave., NW, Washington, DC 20210; 202-219-5555; {www.doleta.gov}.

44 Million Adults Can't Read To Their Children.....

or struggle with a job application or are left on welfare rolls because they lack basic skills.

Source: National Adult Literacy Study
{www.vpskillsummit.org/media3.asp}

Free Training For Teens And Unemployed Adults

The Job Training Partnership Act (JTPA) provides job-training services for disadvantaged adults and youth, dislocated workers, the elderly, and others who face significant employment barriers. Free services include an assessment of an unemployed individual's needs and abilities and a strategy of services, such as classroom training, on-the-job training, job search assistance, work experience, counseling, basic skills training, and support services, such as transportation and child care.

There are hundreds of JTPA sites across the U.S. To locate your nearest one, look in the blue pages of your phone book or contact Office of Employment and Training Programs, U.S. Department of Labor, 200 Constitution Ave., NW, Room N4469, Washington, DC 20210; 202-219-6236; {www.doleta.gov}.

Job Training Partnership Act (JTPA)

Free Job Training And Education For Kids And High School Dropouts

Are you or is someone you love a high school drop out? Need some help sticking with a program? Job Corps may be for you.

This is the nation's largest residential education and training program for disadvantaged youth. There are 111 centers in 46 states, the District of Columbia and Puerto Rico. It is a full-time year-round residential program that offers a comprehensive array of training, education and supportive services, including supervised dormitory housing, meals, medical care, and counseling. The job training covers a variety of occupational trades and more.

Your Interest On Educational Loans Is Deductible

Under the Taxpayer Relief Act of 1997, you are allowed to deduct the yearly interest you pay on an educational loan. You can deduct up to $2,500 worth of interest a year, but your adjusted gross income can not be over $75,000. Call IRS Helpline at 800-829-1040 or {www.irs.ustreas.gov/prod/hot/tax-law.html}.

To learn about Job Corps, contact Office of Job Corps, U.S. Department of Labor, 200 Constitution Ave., NW, Room N4510, Washington, DC 20210; 202-219-8550; 800-733-JOBS; {www.jobcorps.org}.

Free Training for Workers Laid Off Because Their Factories Complied With Air Pollution Laws

First, federal air pollution laws on the books are certainly better than none at all. Look at Mexico City, where they are laying the groundwork for respiratory fatalities due to industrial smoke.

Even though the government has shut down your factory because of pollution or environmental questions, Uncle Sam will help you get back on your feet with free training programs and unemployment services. Those eligible for this program include dislocated workers who are unlikely to return to their previous industries or occupations, and who have been terminated or laid off due to a decision to reduce employment as a result of a company's compliance with the requirements of the Clean Air Act.

For more information, contact your state Department of Labor in the blue pages of your phone book, or Office of Worker Retraining and Adjustment Programs, Employment and Training Administration, U.S. Department Labor, Room N5426, 200 Constitution Ave., NW, Washington, DC 20210; 202-219-5577; {www.doleta.gov}.

FREE TRAINING IF YOU ARE LAID OFF DUE TO DEFENSE CUTBACKS

Thousands of communities around the country have felt the fallout of the end of the Cold War. And the fallout has been economic, not nuclear. Base closings mean no jobs — pure and simple.

Defense Conversion Adjustment (DCA) Program

Fortunately, the Defense Conversion Adjustment (DCA) Program provides retraining and other assistance for workers hurt by defense cutbacks. The DCA Program offers retraining and readjustment services, tailored to meet each individual participant. Long-term training, including educational and occupational, is encouraged. Those eligible include workers who lose their jobs because of plant closings or mass layoffs due to reduced U.S. defense expenditures or closed military facilities.

For more information, contact your state Department of Labor in the blue pages of your phone book, or Office of Worker Retraining and Adjustment Programs, Employment and Training Administration, U.S. Department Labor, Room N5426, 200 Constitution Ave., NW, Washington, DC 20210; 202-219-5577; {www.doleta.gov}.

Free Training If You Are Laid Off By A Defense Contractor

If you have been laid off or fired because the company you worked for was on the wrong end of cutbacks at the U.S. Department of Defense, you may qualify to be retrained for another job.

The Defense Diversification Program (DDP) provides retraining and readjustment assistance to workers and military personnel dislocated by defense cutbacks and base closings, as well as career planning support and assistance.

Those eligible for the program include civilian employees of the Department of Defense, Department of Energy, and defense contractors who have been terminated or laid off, or have a notice of termination or layoff.

For more information, contact your state Department of Labor in the blue pages of your phone book or Office of Worker Retraining and Adjustment Programs, Employment and Training Administration, U.S. Department Labor, Room N5426, 200 Constitution Ave., NW, Washington, DC 20210; 202-219-5577; {www.doleta.gov}.

How To Make A High School Diploma Worth More

The School-to-Work program provides money to states and local partnerships of business, labor, government, education, and community organizations to develop school-to-work systems. School-to-Work is based on the concept that education works best and is most useful for future careers when students apply what they learn to real life, real work situations.

School-to-Work has three core elements: School-based learning, Work-based learning, and Connecting Activities. School-to-Work looks different in each state and locality. Contact your state office to learn more.

State offices can be located by contacting National School-To-Work Learning and Information Center, 400 Virginia Ave., SW, Room 210, Washington, DC 20024; 800-251-7236; {www.stw.ed.gov}.

Free Training For Dead Beat Dads

No one likes a dead beat dad, but Uncle Sam understands that many fathers fall behind in child support not because they're evil, wicked, mean, and nasty. Some just don't have a job and not much training to make them qualified for many jobs.

Parents Fair Share Program

The Parents Fair Share Program was a demonstration program of the Administration for Children and Families (part of the U.S. Department of Health and Human Services), and was designed to help parents get the training they need to get a paycheck to help with child support. The demonstration program has since ended, but many of the sites continue to provide job readiness and job skills training. For more information, contact one of the sites below:

California:
Los Angeles County Fair Share, Bureau of Family Support Operations, 5770 South Eastern Ave., Commerce, CA 90024; 323-889-2954.

Florida
Duvall County Parents' Fair Share, Employment and Training Security, Department of Labor, 421 W. Church St., Jacksonville, FL 32202; 904-798-4720.

Massachusetts
Massachusetts JOBS Parents' Fair Share Project, Springfield
Employment Resource Ctr., Inc., 140 Wilbraham Ave.,
Springfield, MA 01109; 413-737-9544.

Michigan
Non-Custodial Parent Program, 385 Leonard NE, Grand Rapids,
MI 49503; 616-458-6350.

New Jersey
Operation Fatherhood, Union Industrial Home For Children, 4
N. Broad St., Trenton, NJ 08608; 609-695-3663.

Ohio
Options for Parental Training and Support, Montgomery County
Department of Human Services, 14 W. Fourth St., Dayton, OH
45402; 937-225-4077.

Triple Your Salary With Job Training For Migrant And Farmworkers

Migrant workers and seasonal laborers are some of the
hardest working people in America. Yet when the crops
are all picked or the economy sags, they are some of the
first to be out of a job. And most of these people live just
at the poverty level to begin with.

Fortunately, the government has a special job training
program to help them find less backbreaking work.
Participants can receive a weekly allowance at the current

minimum wage and learn new work skills in classroom and on-the-job training programs, work experience in new employment areas, job development and placement services, relocation and education assistance, and more.

For more information, contact your local job training office, or U.S. Department of Labor, Office of Special Targeted Programs, Division of Migrant and Seasonal Farmworker Programs, Room N-4641, 200 Constitution Ave., NW, Washington, DC 20210; 202-219-5500; {www.wdsc.org/msfw}.

Free Jobs and Training for Dropouts Interested in Construction Careers

Bottom line: most construction jobs pay really well. If you like the work, training in the construction industry can fatten the paycheck even further. If you get the itch, you might even want to become an engineer — or-better yet- become someone who gets to use the wrecking ball.

Young men and women can get experience in the construction trades, while helping to build housing for the homeless under the Youthbuild program.

Participants get hands-on training in the rehabilitation and construction of housing, as well as valuable off-site education. Low income kids between the ages of 16 and 24 are eligible to participate.

Free Job Training and More For Foster Care Teens

All kinds of free help is out there for teenagers in foster care — and young adults who have been raised in foster homes — to get the job skills they need to make a good life on their own.

The Independent Living program provides help for foster care youth between the ages of 16 and 21, help in getting a GED or a driving permit, even assistance in filling out college applications. Those who live out in the country can even get free transportation to job training programs that can assure them of a good paying career track.

For more information, contact your foster care worker, or to learn your state contact for the Independent Living program contact Division of Child Welfare, Children's Bureau, Administration for Children and Families, P.O. Box 1182, Washington, DC 20013; 202-205-8740; {www.acf.dhhs.gov/programs/cb/programs/index.htm}.

For more information about sites across the country, contact Office of Economic Development, Community Planning and Development, U.S. Department of Housing and Urban Development, Washington, DC 20410; 202-708-2035.

FREE JOB TRAINING, GED COURSES, AND GUARANTEED JOBS FOR HIGH SCHOOL KIDS AND POVERTY ZONE DROP OUTS

Growing up in poverty today isn't what it was earlier this century. In years past, a life of poverty was much harder. There was no government assistance, no food stamps, no volunteer organizations willing to spend time helping anyone out.

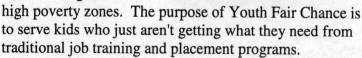

Youth Fair Chance is a new community based program that gives money directly to areas where problems for kids are greatest — high poverty zones. The purpose of Youth Fair Chance is to serve kids who just aren't getting what they need from traditional job training and placement programs.

Some of the special kinds of help kids can receive include: employment and training, help staying in school, assistance in dealing with drug and gang involvement, participation in sports and recreation, family support, and more. Kids and young adults between 14-30 years of age who reside in rural and urban communities are eligible.

For more information on the program or to locate the site nearest you, contact Office of Policy and Research, Employment and Training Administration, U.S. Department of Labor, 200 Constitution Ave., NW, Washington, DC 20210; 202-219-8668; {www.doleta.gov}.

STATE JOB TRAINING PROGRAMS

Each state offers a variety of job training programs to encourage their residents to get employment or upgrade their job skills. Here is a listing of both national and state programs to get you started.

To give you an idea of what is available, The Single Parent/ Homemaker Project Services in Greensburg, IN and the Center for Displaced Homemakers in Shreveport, LA provide vocational education, job training, career counseling, job placement, and life management training, as well as support groups for single parents. The Institute of Social and Economic Development in Iowa City, IA and the Grand Rapids Opportunities for Women in Grand Rapids, MI want to encourage self-sufficiency through the growth of a small business and will provide services to help you begin your endeavor. Hard Hatted Women in Cleveland, OH and Tradeswomen of Purpose in Philadelphia, PA allow women to learn the construction trades through various apprenticeship and training programs. Don't forget to also contact your local One-Stop Career Center and your state Department of Labor office listed here to learn more about job training programs near you.

National

America's Learning eXchange

American Association of Community Colleges is
partnering with the US Department of Labor to support
learners, employers, and training suppliers. The vehicle is
America's Learning eXchange. ALX connects people to the
training and education they need. ALX is the breakthrough
resource for workers entering the job force, people
interested in lifelong learning, and employers looking for
enhanced performance. Web-based ALX is your one-stop
electronic marketplace for lifelong learning resources. ALX
links you instantly to tens of thousands of training offerings
and providers--everything from continuing education
courses to Internet-based training, from traditional
classroom-based courses to CD-ROM and video
instruction. Check out {www.alx.org/}.

LEARN SKILLS ONLINE

Does your lifestyle or location prevent you from
entering a conventional learning center? This one is
a cyber university for women! Women's
International Electronic University promotes the
empowerment of women online by facilitating access
to training in skills such as information technology,
health promotion and living skills. They have no
physical address, so visit their website to learn more
at {www.wvu.edu/~womensu/}.

Considering a Nontraditional Career?

The Institute for Women in Trades, Technology & Science (IWITTS) is dedicated to integrating women into the full range of trades, technology and science careers in which they are underrepresented: from engineer to police officer, pilot, automotive technician, electrician and web master, to name just a very few. To accomplish this mission, IWITTS serves as a resource nationally to the education and job-training systems and employers. Contact them at Institute for Women in Trades, Technology & Science (IWITTS), 3010 Wisconsin Ave., NW, Suite E-10, Washington, DC 20016; 202-686-7275; {Email: iwitts@aol.com}; {www.serve.com/iwitts}.

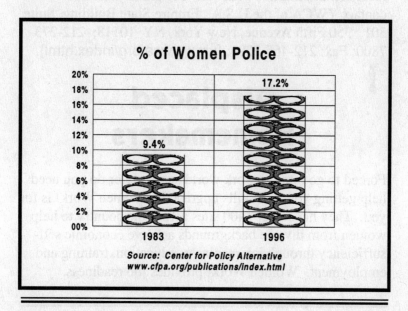

% of Women Police

17.2%

9.4%

1983   1996

Source: Center for Policy Alternative
www.cfpa.org/publications/index.html

THE OLD RELIABLE

The YWCA has long been committed to providing women and girls with the education, training, and support they need to provide for themselves and their families. The YWCA's spectrum of offerings in this area include basic life skills training, English courses, GED courses, adult education, welfare to work programs, structured training curricula, training for non-traditional employment, career counseling, entrepreneurial workshops, job clubs and more.

Local YWCAs tailor their programs and services to meet the needs of the women, families and employers in their local communities. To find the YWCA in your area contact YWCA of the U.S.A., Empire State Building, Suite 301, 350 Fifth Avenue, New York, NY 10118; 212-273-7800; Fax: 212-465-2281; {www.ywca.org/index.html}.

Displaced Homemakers

Forced to go into the work world suddenly or do you need help getting your job skills upgraded? Women Work! is for you. They have over 1400 sites across the country to help women from diverse backgrounds achieve economic self-sufficiency through job readiness, education, training and employment. Women Work! provides job readiness, education and training, and employment services through a network of programs in every state. Women Work! also takes on the toughest women's employment issues and fights for them in Congress and in state legislatures.

For more information on Women Work! or to find a location near you, contact Women Work!, 1625 K Street NW, Suite 300, Washington, DC 20006; 800-235-2732; 202-467-6346; Fax: 202-467-5366; {Email: womenwork@womenwork.org}; {www.womenwork.org/}.

Network With Other Businesswomen

The mission of the American Business Women's Association is to bring together businesswomen of diverse occupations and to provide opportunities for them to help themselves and others grow personally and professionally through leadership, education, networking support and national  recognition. ABWA believes education and training are key to helping women grow personally and professionally.

The Association supports education by providing continuing education programs and products, which enhance members business skills. Members receive discounts on a variety of products and services, including career-focused books and audiotapes, seminars by national seminar providers and computer application classes.

For more information, contact American Business Women's Association, 9100 Ward Parkway, P.O. Box 8728, Kansas City, MO 64114-0728; 816-361-6621; Fax: 816-361-4991; {E mail:abwa@abwahq.org}; {www.abwahq.org/}.

YOU CAN BUILD IT

An association of women in construction industry, the National Association of Women in Construction (NAWIC) enhances members' careers. With more than 204 chapters in the United States and Canada and over 6200 members employed in all phases of the industry, NAWIC committees provide resources for continuing education, legislative awareness, employment referral, business ownership, and networking with others who share the same interests and goals. The organization publishes a membership directory and publications, and sponsors regional conferences and annual conventions.

The NAWIC Education Foundation offers three construction education programs. Membership is open to women employed in diverse aspects of the construction industry and women students pursuing a degree of certification related to the construction industry. Contact National Association of Women in Construction, 327 South Adams, Fort Worth, TX 76104; 800-552-3506; 817-877-5551; {http://nawic.org}.

Free Job Training and Part-Time Jobs For Those Age 55 And Over

The Senior Community Service Employment Program offers part-time training and employment opportunities for eligible low-income persons 55 years of age and older in a variety of public or private nonprofit community service settings, such as senior centers, nutrition programs, social service agencies, libraries, environmental projects, and many others. The program provides seniors with income and the opportunity to learn new skills or improve the ones they already have.

There are sites in every state that offer training and employment. To learn about the site nearest you, contact Division of Older Worker Program, Employment and Training Administration, U.S. Department of Labor, 200 Constitution Ave., NW, Room 4641, Washington, DC 20210; 202-219-5904; {www.wdsc.org/owprog/index.html}.

State Job Training Programs

Alabama

One-Stop Career Center: Department of Industrial Relations, 649 Monroe St., Montgomery, AL 36131; 334-242-8846, Fax: 334-242-8843; {www.dir.state.al.us}; {Email: webmaster@ dir.state.al.us}.

Department of Labor: Alabama Department of Economic Security, P.O. Box 6123, Montgomery, AL 36130-3500; 334-242-3460.

Women's Business Assistance Center, Kathryn Cariglino, Director, 1301 Azalea Road, Suite 201A, Mobile, AL 36693; (Mailing Address: P. O. Box 6021, Mobile, AL 36660); 334-660-2725; 800-378-7461; Fax: 334-660-8854; {Email: wbac@ceebic.org}; {http://ceebic. org/~wbac}.

Alabama Women Work!, Linda Waide, President, Northwest Shoals Community College, PO Box 2545, Muscle Shoals, AL 35662; 256-331-5321.

Alaska

One-Stop Career Center: Alaska Job Center Network, Department of Labor, P.O. Box 21149, Juneau, AK 99802; 907-456-2700; {www.jobs.state.ak.us}.

Alaska Department of Labor: P.O. Box 21149, Juneau, AK 99802; 907-456-2700; {www.labor.state.ak.us/}.

WOMEN$ Fund, A Program of the YWCA of Anchorage, 245 West Fifth Avenue, P. O. Box 102059, Anchorage, AK 99510-2059; 907-274-1524; Fax: 907-272-3146; {Email: ywcaak@alaska.net}.

Alaska Tradeswomen Network, P.O. Box 240712, Anchorage, AK 99524-0712; 907-566-2200.

Alaska Women's Environmental Network, Martha Levensaler, 750 W. 2nd Ave. #200, Anchorage, AK 99501; 907-258-4810; Fax: 907-258-4811; {Email: levensaler@ nwf.org}.

Alaska Human Resource Investment Council, 3610 C Street, Suite 380, Anchorage, AK 99503; 907-269-7489; Fax: 907-269-7489; {Email AHRIC@gov.state.ak.us}.

Division of Community and Rural Development, Department of Community and Regional Affairs, P.O. Box 112100, Juneau, AK 99811-2100; 907-465-4863; Fax: 907-465-3212; {Email: kbrown@ ComRegAf.state.ak.us}.

Jobs Program, 350 Main St., Room 310, P.O. Box 110640, Juneau, AK 99811-0640; 907-465-3349; 907-465-5154; {health.hss.state.ak.us/htmlstuf/pubassis/jobs/job. htm}.

Arizona

One Stop Career Center: Arizona Department of Economic Security, 1717 West Jefferson, Phoenix, AZ 85007; 602-542-4296; {www.de.state.az.us/osoc}; {Email: webmaster@ de.state.az.us}.

Department of Labor: Arizona Department of Economic Security, 1717 West Jefferson, Phoenix, AZ 85007; 602-542-4296; {www.de.state.az.us}.

AWEE-AZ Women's Education and Employment, 640 N. 1st Ave., Phoenix, AZ 85003; 602-223-4338.

Self-Employment Loan Fund, Inc. (SELF), 201 North Central Avenue, Suite CC10, Phoenix, AZ 85073-1000; 602-340-8834; Fax: 602-340-8953; {Email: self@ uswest.net}.

Food Stamp Employment & Training Policy Specialist, JOBS Administration, 1789 West Jefferson, SC-720A, Phoenix, AZ 85007-3202; 602-542-6542; Fax: 602-542-6310.

Arizona Department of Education, 1535 West Jefferson, Bin #39, Phoenix, AZ 85007; 602-542-5142; Fax: 602-542-3818; {Email: stewar@mail1.ade.state.az.us}; {Email: dpawlak@mail1.ade.state. az.us}.

STEP Program AZ Western CC, P.O. Box 929, Yuma, AZ 85366-0929; 520-344-7699/23; Fax: 520-344-7730.

Working in New Directions (WIND), Central AZ CC, Superstition Mt. Campus, 273 Old West Hwy., Apache Junction, AZ 85219; 602-288-4033; Fax: 602-288-4038.

Working in New Directions (WIND), Central AZ CC, Main Campus, 8470 N. Overfield Rd., Coolidge, AZ; 85228; 520-426-4422; Fax: 520-426-4234.

Single Parent Program, Cochise CC, 901 N. Colombo, Sierra Vista, AZ 85635; 520-364-0223; 520-515-5410; Fax: 520-364-0236.

Self PRIDE Program, Coconino CC, 3000 N 4th St., #17, Flagstaff, AZ 86004; 520-527-1222; 800-350-7122, ext. 323; Fax: 520-526-1821.

$1,500 Of Your Taxes Can Pay Your Tuition

Beginning in 1998, students during their first 2 years of higher education can get up to $1,500 back on their taxes under the HOPE Scholarship Credit. Income eligibility for this deduction goes up to $100,000. This can't be used in the same year as the Lifetime Learning Credit. So use this the first two years and Lifetime Learning Credit for the rest. Call IRS Helpline at 1-800-829-1040, or {www.irs.ustreas.gov/prod/hot/not97-601.html}.

Single Parents/Homemakers Eastern, Arizona Community College, 600 Church St., Thatcher, AZ 85552; 520-428-8317; Fax: 520-757-0850.

Re-Entry And Change (REACH), Mohave CC, 1971 Jagerson Ave., Kingman, AZ 86401; 520-757-0850; Fax: 520-757-0896.

REACH, Mohave CC North Campus, P.O. Box 980, Colorado City, AZ 86021-0980; 520-875-2799; Fax: 520-875-2831.

REACH, Mohave CC Valley Campus, 3400 Hwy 95, Bullhead City, AZ 86442; 520-758-3926; Fax: 520-758-4436.

Re-Entry And Change (REACH)

REACH, Mohave CC Lake Havasu Campus, 1977 W Acoma Blvd, Lake Havasu, AZ 8 6403; 520-855-7812; Fax: 520-453-1836.

Women in Progress, WIP Pima Community College Downtown Campus, 1255 N. Stone, Tucson, AZ 85709-3000; 520-206-6293/6135; Fax: 520-206-6201.

New Directions, Yavapai CC, 601 Blackhills, Clarkdale, AZ 86324; 520-634-6528, Fax: (520) 634-6549.

AWEE-North, 914 E Hatcher, #135, Phoenix, AZ 85021; 602-371-1216; Fax: 602-534-2773.

AWEE-Prescott, 161 S. Granite, Suite C, Prescott, AZ 86303; 520-778-3010; Fax: 520-778-0737.

Center for New Directions, 1430 N. 2nd St., Phoenix, AZ 85004; 602-252-0918; Fax: 602-253-2628.

Center for New Directions East Valley, 943 S. Gilbert, Suite 204, Mesa, AZ 85204; 602-507-8619; Fax: 602-507-8618.

Center for New Directions West Valley, 6010 W. Northern, #304, Glendale, AZ 85301; 602-435-8530; 602-435-2392.

Adult Vocational Training Project (AVTP), Pima County AVTP, 1630 S. Alvernon, Suite 104, Tucson, AZ 85711; 520-327-8733; Fax: 520-327-8904.

Project for Homemakers in Arizona Seeking Employment (PHASE), University of Arizona PHASE, 1230 N. Park Ave., #209, Tucson, AZ 85721; 520-621-3902; Fax: 520-621-5008.

Transition Works, NAU, P.O. Box 6025, Flagstaff, AZ 86011-6025; 520-523-4564; Fax: 520-523-6395.

Career Success Program, Yavapai Community College, Prescott Valley Business Center, 6955 Panther Path, Prescott Valley, AZ 86314; 520-772-8368; Fax: 520-772-8861.

Arizona Women's Education and Employment, Inc., 755 E. Willeta, Phoenix, AZ 85006; 602-223-4333.

Arkansas

One-Stop Career Center: Arkansas Career Development Network, Employment Security Department, #2 Capitol Mall, Room 506, ESD Building, Little Rock, AR 72201; 501-682-2121; Fax: 501-682-2273; {www.state.ar.us/esd/}.

Arkansas Department Of Labor: 10421 West Markham, Little Rock, AK 72205; 501-682-4500; {www.ark.org/ labor}.

Garland County Community College, 101 College Drive, Hot Springs, AR 71913-9174; 501-760-4243; 501-760-4244 {Email: dmurphy@admin.gcc.ar.us}.

Crowley's Ridge, Technical Institute, P.O. Box 925, Forrest City, AR 72335; 870-633-5411.

Northwest Technical Institute, PO Box Drawer A, Springdale, AR 72765-1301; 501-751-8824.

Pulaski Technical College, 2020 W. Third, Suite 520, Little Rock, AR 72205; 501-372-7261.

Phillips Community College of U of A, P.O. Box 427, Dewitt, AR 72042; 870-946-3506.

Southern Arkansas University Tech, 133 Jackson St., Camden, AR 71701; 870-777-0117.

Southern Arkansas Development Council, Inc., P.O. Box 574, Hope, AR 71801; 870-777-8892.

Westwark Community College, P.O. Box 3649, Fort Smith, AR 72913; 501-452-8994.

Arkansas Public Administration Consortium, Library Room 523, University of Arkansas at Little Rock, 2801 South University Avenue, Little Rock, AR, 72204; 501-569-3090; Fax: 501-569-3021; {Email: apacprog@ualr.edu}; {www.ualr.edu/~iog/APAC.html}.

Karen Mellon, Work Place Coordinator, Conway Adult Education Center, 615 E. Robins Street, Conway, AR 72032; 501-450-4810; Fax: 501-450-4818; {Email: k.mellon@conwaycorp.net}; {www.caec.org/}.

Single Parent/Homemaker Program, Department of Workforce Education, No. 3 Capital Mall, Little Rock, AR 72201; 501-682-1508.

California
One-Stop Career Center: One-Stop Office, P.O. Box 826880, MIC 77, Sacramento, CA 94280-0001; 916-654-9995; Fax: 916-654-9863; {www.sjtcc.cahwnet.gov/ SJTCCWEB/ ONE-STOP/}; {Email: onestop@edd. ca.gov}.

Department of Labor: California Employment Development Department, 800 Capital Mall, Sacramento, CA 95814; 916-227-0300; {wwwedd.cahwnet.gov/ eddhome.htm}.

Women Work! Regional Representative, Region IX, Joanne Durkee, Displaced Homemaker Program, Mt. Diablo Adult Education, 1266 San Carlos Avenue, Concord, CA 94518; 510-685-7340, ext. 2786; Fax: 510-687-8217.

Center for Employment
Training Corporate Offices,
701 Vine St., San Jose, CA
95110; 408-287-7924; 800-
533-2519; {Email:
cfet@best.com};
{www.best.com/~cfet/
main.htm}.

Women's Enterprise Development Corporation, 100 West Broadway, Suite 500, Long Beach, CA 90802; 562-983-3747; Fax: 562-983-3750; {Email: wedc1@aol.com}; {www.wedc.org/}.

Women's Enterprise Development Corporation, 2301 Campus Drive, Suite 20, Irvine, CA 92715; 310-983-3747; Fax: 310-983-3750.

Los Angeles County/South Central One-Stop Career Center, 9230 W. Imperial Highway, Ingelwood, CA 90303; 213-779-2199; Fax: 213-779-2856; {1stop.co. la.ca.us/sc/text-only/about.html}.

Women's Initiative for Self Employment (WI), 450 Mission Street, Suite 402, San Francisco, CA 94105; 415-247-9473; Fax: 415-247-9471; {Email: womensinitsf@igc.apc.org}; {Oakland Site: wioakland@igc.apc.org}; {Spanish Site: wialas@igc.apc.org}.

Brady JobNet, 717 S. Brady Avenue, Los Angeles, CA 90022; 213-722-4495.

Career Encores, 3700 Wilshire Blvd., Suite 200, Los Angeles, CA 90010; 800-833-6267.

Chicana Service Action Center - Los Angeles, 134 East First Street, Los Angeles, CA 90012; 213-253-5959.

Chinatown Service Center, 767 N. Hill Street, Suite 400, Los Angeles, CA 90012; 800-733-2882.

Forty Plus of Southern California, 3450 Wilshire Boulevard, Suite 510, Los Angeles, CA 90010; 213-388-2301.

Jewish Vocational Services, 5700 Wilshire Boulevard #2303, Los Angeles, CA 90036; 323-761-8888.

Pacific Asian Consortium in Employment (PACE)

L.A. Central Job Service, Employment Development Department, 158 W. 14th Street, Los Angeles, CA 90015; 213-744-2244.

LA Works, 5200 Irwindale, Ave., Suite130, Irwindale, CA 91706; 626-960-3964.

Los Angeles County Regional Occupational Programs, 20122 Cabrillo Lane, Cerritos, CA 90703; 562-403-7382.

Los Angeles Urban League, 3450 Mount Vernon Drive, Los Angles, CA 90008; 213-299-9660.

Maxine Waters Employment Preparation Center, Los Angeles Unified School District Skills Centers, 10925 S. Central Avenue, Los Angeles, CA 90059; 213-564-1431.

Mexican American Opportunity Foundation, 401 N. Garfield Avenue, Montebello, CA 90640; 213-890-9600.

Pacific Asian Consortium in Employment (PACE), 1541 Wilshire Blvd., Suite 407, Los Angeles, CA 90017; 213-389-2373.

Southeast L.A. County Private Industry Council, 10900 E. 183rd St., #350, Cerritos, CA 90703; 562-402-9336.

Southern California Indian Center, 3440 Wilshire Blvd., Los Angeles, CA 90010; 213-387-5772.

Verdugo Private Industry Council, 706 W. Broadway, Suite 202, Glendale, CA 91204; 818-409-0476.

Women at Work, 50 North Hill Avenue, Suite 300, Pasadena, CA 91106; 626-796-6870.

Women Business Owners Corporation, Kathleen Schwallie, President, 18 Encanto Drive, Palos Verdes, CA 90274-4215; 310-530-7500; Fax: 310-530-1483.

Job Training Network, 228 W Carrillo St # C, Santa Barbara, CA 93101-6159; 805-882-3675; {www. jtnwinjobs. org/}.

Norwalk-LaMirada Adult School, 12820 Pioneer Blvd., Norwalk, CA 90650; 562-868-0431.

Ebony Shakoor-Akbar, Women In Nontraditional Employment Roles, P.O. Box 90511, Long Beach, CA 90809-0511; 310-590-2266; {www.ttrc.doleta.gov/ wanto/}.

Training & Employment Center, 2447 Old Sonoma Road, Napa, CA 94558; 800-289-1872.

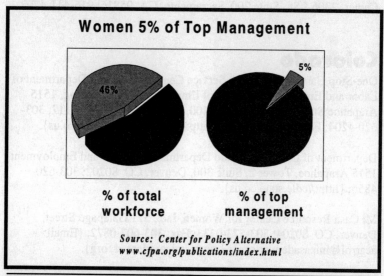

Women 5% of Top Management

46%

5%

% of total
workforce

% of top
management

Source: Center for Policy Alternative
www.cfpa.org/publications/index.html

North Valley Private Industry Council, 505 W. Olive Avenue, #550, Sunnyvale, CA 94086; 408-730-7232; (TDD) 408-730-7501.

Opportunities Industrialization Center West (OICW), 1200 O'Brien Drive, Menlo Park, CA 94025; 650-322-8431.

San Jose Job Corps Center, 3485 East Hills Drive, San Jose, CA 95127; 408-254-5627.

Santa Clara County Office of Education, 575 W. Fremont Avenue, Sunnyvale, CA 94087; 408-733-0881.

Community Services and Employment Training, Inc., 909 W. Murray, Visalia, CA 93291; 559-732-4194.

Mission Valley Regional Occupational Program, 40230 Laiolo Rd., Fremont, CA 94538; 510-657-6124.

Women in the Skilled Trades, Oakland Private Industry Council, 2229 Poplar St., Oakland, CA 94607; 510-891-0666.

Women's Employment Services and Training, Sacramento Women's Center, 2306 J St., Suite 200, Sacramento, CA 95816; 916-441-4207.

Colorado

One-Stop Career Center: Job Service Centers, Colorado Department of Labor and Employment, Office of Employment and Training, 1515 Arapahoe Street, Tower 2, Suite 400, Denver, CO 80202-2117; 303-620-4204; Fax: 303-620-4257; {http://navigator.cdle.state.co.us}.

Department of Labor: Colorado Department of Labor and Employment, 1515 Arapahoe, Tower 2, Suite 300, Denver, CO 80202; 303-620-4856; {http://cdle.state.co.us}.

Mi Casa Resource Center for Women, Inc., 571 Galapago Street, Denver, CO 80204; 303-573-0333; Fax: 303-607-0872; {Email: acarrol@micasadenver.org}; {www. micasadenver. org}.

Northeast Women's Center, 4821 E. 28th Ave., Denver, CO 80207; 303-355-3486.

Connecticut

One-Stop Career Center: Connecticut Works, Connecticut Department of Labor, 200 Folly Brook Boulevard, Wethersfield, CT 06109; 860-263-6785; {www.ctdol. state.ct.us/ctworks/ ctworks.htm}; {Email: dol.help@ po.state.ct.us}.

Connecticut Department of Labor: 200 Folly Brook Blvd., Wethersfield, CT 06109-1114; 860-566-7980; {www. ctdol. state.ct.us}.

American Woman's Economic Development Corporation, 2001 W. Main Street, Suite 140, Stamford, CT 06902; 203-326-7914; Fax: 203-326-7916.

Workforce Connection, 249 Thomaston Ave., Waterbury, CT 06702; 203-574-6971.

Connecticut Permanent Commission on The Status of Women, 18-20 Trinity St., Hartford, CT 06106; 860-240-8300.

Preliminary Awareness of Construction Trades Training, National Association of Women in Construction (NAWIC), Hartford Chapter, 125 Silas Deane Highway, Hartford, CT 06109; 860-291-8917.

Hartford Area Training Center, Inc., Art Helfgott, Vocational Counselor, 56 Coventry St., Hartford, CT 06112; 860-286-9202.

Displaced Homemakers Program
Region I: Ansonia/Waterbury, Danbury/Torrington, Bridgeport/Stamford, Norwalk, Greenwich
• YWCA of Eastern Fairfield County, Job Readiness Program, 753 Fairfield Avenue, Bridgeport, CT 06604; 203-334-6154; Fax: 203-579-8882.

- YWCA of Greenwich, New Horizons, 259 East Putnam Avenue, Greenwich, CT 06830; 203-869-6501, ext. 218.

  - YWCA of Darien/Norwalk, Beginning Again, 49 Old Kings Highway North, Darien, CT 06820; 203-655-2535.

    - YWCA of Waterbury, Step by Step, 80 Prospect Street, Waterbury, CT 06702; 203-754-5136, ext. 3311.

    Region II: New Haven, Meriden, Middletown
    - YWCA of Meriden, Open Door, 169 Colony Street, Meriden, CT 06450; 203-235-9297; Fax: 203-237-7571.
    - New Transitions Program, c/o Red Cross Building, 703 Whitney Ave., New Haven, CT 06511; 203-776-8453.

Region III: Hartford, New Britain, Bristol
- Hartford College for Women of the University of Hartford, Look Forward, 50 Elizabeth Street, Hartford, CT 06105; 860-768-561; Fax: 860-768-5680.
- YWCA of New Britain, Look Forward, 22 Glen Street, New Britain, CT 06051; 860-225-4681, ext. 288; Fax: 860-826-7026.

Region IV: Northeast: Willimantic/Danielson Southeast: Norwich/New London
- ACCESS Agency, Incorporated, 1315 Main St., Willimantic, CT 06226; 860-450-7400, ext. 749; Fax: 860-450-7477.
- ACCESS-Multiservices, 16H Maple St., Danielson, CT 06239; 860-774-0418; Fax: 860-450-7477.
- ACCESS-Multiservices, 106 Truman Street, New London, CT 06320; 860-442-4630; Fax: 860-447-1826; {www.ctdol.state.ct.us/progsupt/jobsrvce/ discjt.htm}.

Delaware

One-Stop Career Center: Delaware Career Network, Department of Labor, Employment and Training, 4425 North Market St., Wilmington, DE 19809-0828; 302-761-8102; Fax: 302-761-6617; {www.vcnet.net}; {Email: rclarkin@state.de.us}.

Delaware Department of Labor: 4425 North Market St., Wilmington, DE 19802; 302-761-8029; {www. harvellinteractive.com/dol}.

Workforce Development, Delaware Economic Development Office, 99 Kings Highway, Dover, DE 19901; 302-739-4271; {Email: bennis@ state.de.us}.

The Virtual Career Network at {www.vcnet.net/}.

District of Columbia

One-Stop Career Center: DOES One-Stop Career Center, Department of Employment Services, 500 "C" Street, NW, Washington, DC 20001; 202-724-7100; {http://does.ci. washington.dc.us/ one_stop.html}.

Department of Labor: Department of Employment Services, 500 "C" Street, NW, Washington, DC 20001; 202-754-7054; {http://does.ci.washington.dc.us}.

National Women's Business Center, 1250 24th St., NW, Suite 350, Washington, DC 20037; 202-466-0544; 202-466-0581; {www.womenconnect.com/ womensbusinesscenter}.

D.C. Central Kitchen, 425 Second Street, NW, Washington, DC 20001; 202-234-0707; Fax: 202-986-1051; {Email: dccentralkitchen. org}; {www. dccentralkitchen.org/ Job_Training.html}.

Harrison Center for Career Education, 624 9th Street, NW, Washington, DC 20001; 202-628-5672.

Florida

One-Stop Career Center: Workforce Florida, Department of Labor and Employment Security, Division of Jobs and Benefits, 2012 Capital Circle SE, Suite 303, Hartman Building, Tallahassee, FL 32399-2152; 850-922-7021; {www.floridajobs.org/jb/initiatives/ onestop}.

Department of Labor: Florida Department of Labor and Employment Security, 2012 Capital Circle SE, Suite 306, Tallahassee, FL 32399-2156; 850-481-1927; {www.state. fl.us/dles}.

Women's Business Development Center (WBDC), 10555 West Flagler Street, Room 2612, Miami, FL 33174; 305-348-3951, 305-348-3903; Fax: 305-348-2931; {Email: obermann@fiu.edu} (Program Coordinator); {Email: rojasm@fiu.edu} (Financial Consultant).

Center for Employment and Training, 301 Southwest 14th Ave., Delray Beach, FL 33444; 561-265-1405; Fax: 561-243-2596; {Email: mailto:d_gainer@cetmail.cfet.org}.

Women Business Owners Of North Florida, P.O Box 551434, Jacksonville, FL 32255-1434; 904-278-9270; {www.jaxwbo.org/}.

YWCA, 325 E. Duval St., Jacksonville, FL 32202; 904-354-6681.

Single Parent/Displaced Homemaker Program, Okaloosa-Walton Community College, 100 College Boulevard, Niceville, FL 32578; 850-729-5291; 850-678-5111; {www.owcc.cc.fl.us/departs/ cont_ed/ programs/ single_displaced_home.html}.

Displaced Homemaker Program, Valencia Community College Foundation, P.O. Box 3028, Orlando, FL 32802-3028; 407-317-7950; Fax: 407-317-7956; {Email: Valencia3@aol.com}; {www.valencia. org/442.html}.

Edison Community College, Single Parent/Displaced Homemaker/Single Pregnant Woman Program, Howard Hall 125, Fort Myers, FL 33919-5598; 941-489-9005; {www.edison.edu/ departments/ supportserv/ singleparent.htm}.

Florida Community College Jacksonville, Gender Equity Program, FCCJ Downtown Campus 101 W. State St., Jacksonville, FL 32202; 904-633-8390 Fax: 904-633-8496.

Gateway to Health, Health Education Center, 7200 66th Street North, Pinellas Park, Fl 33781; 813-341-3687; {http://hec.spjc.cc.fl.us/}.

Displaced Homemaker Program, 1000 Coconut Creek Blvd., Bldg. 41, Coconut Creek, FL 33066; 305-973-2398.

Resource Center for Women Inc., 1301 Seminole, Blvd., Suite 150, Largo, FL 33770; 727-586-1110.

When Entering New Directions, Brevard Community College, Room U12, 1519 Clearlake Rd., Cocoa, FL 32922; 407-632-1111, ext. 65516.

Woman Working Program, Orange County Public Schools, Mid Florida Tech, 2900 West Oak Ridge Rd., Orlando, FL 32809; 407-855-5880, ext. 2294.

New Options Center, 5603 34th St., West, Bradenton, FL 34210; 941-751-7922.

Equity, Dade County Public School, Robert Morgan Vocational Technical Institute, 18180 SW 122 Ave., Miami, FL 33177; 305-253-9920.

Sex Equity Program, Haney Vocational-Technical Center, 3016 Highway 77, Panama City, FL 32405; 850-747-5500, ext. 559.

Georgia

One-Stop Career Center: Department of Labor, Employment Services, 148 International Boulevard, NE, Atlanta, GA 30303-1751; 404-656-6380; Fax: 404-657-8285; {www.state.ga.us/index/gaemp. html}.

Georgia Department of Labor: 148 International Boulevard, Atlanta, GA 30303-1751; 404-656-3028, {www.dol.state. ga.us}.

Women Work! Regional Representative, Region IV, Department Of Technology and Adult Education, Loydia Webber, Director of Special Services, 1800 Century Place NE, Suite 400, Atlanta, GA 30345; 404-679-1654; Fax: 404-679-1675.

Women's Economic Development Agency (WEDA), 675 Ponce de Leon Avenue, Atlanta, GA 30308; 404-853-7680; Fax: 404-853-7677; {Email: dorothy.fletcher@ internetmci.com}.

Goodwill Industries of Atlanta, 2201 Glenwood Ave., SE, Atlanta, GA 30116; 404-486-8400.

New Connections To Work, P.O. Box 1505, Lawrenceville, GA 30246; 770-962-7580, ext. 365.

Hawaii

One-Stop Career Center: Workforce Development, Department of Labor, Workforce Development Division, 830 Punchbowl Street, #112, Honolulu, HI 96813; 808-586-8700; Fax: 808-586-8724; {http://dlir.state.hi.us/wdd}.

Department of Labor: Hawaii Department of Labor and Industrial Relations, 830 Punchbowl Street, Honolulu, HI 96813; 808-586-8842; {www.aloha.net/~edpso}.

Hawaii Women Work!, Janet Morse, President, Hawaii Literacy, Inc., 200 N. Vineyard Blvd., Suite 403, Honolulu, HI 96817; 808-537-6706; {Email: hliteracy@aol.com}.

Idaho

One-Stop Career Center: Idaho Works, Idaho Department of Labor, 317 Main Street, Boise, ID 83735-0600; 208-334-6303; Fax: 208-332-7417; {www.idahoworks.state. id.us}.

Idaho Department of Labor: 317 Main Street, Boise, ID 83735-0600; 208-334-6252; {www.labor.state.id.us}.

Illinois

One-Stop Career Center: Illinois Employment and Training Center
(IETC) Network, Department of Employment Security, Employment
Services, 400 West Monroe Street, Springfield, IL 62704; 217-785-
5069; {www.ides.state. il.us/html/ employer.htm}.

Illinois Department of Labor: State of Illinois Building, 160 North
LaSalle, SuiteC-1300, Chicago, IL 60601; 312-793-2800;
{www.state.il.us/agency/idol}.

Women Work! Regional Representative, Region V, Displaced
Homemaker Program, Lincoln Land Community College, Shepard Rd.,
Springfield, IL 62794-9256; 217-786-2275; Fax: 217-786-2223.

Center for Employment and Training, 1307
South Wabash Ave., 3rd Floor, Chicago, IL
60605; 312-913-0055; Fax: 312-913-
0937; {Email: VFW9091@aol.com}.

Richland Community College, One
College Park, Decatur, IL 62521; 217-875-
7200; {www.richland.cc.il.us/}.

Women In Management Incorporated, 30 N. Michigan Ave # 508,
    Chicago, IL 60602-3404; 312-263-3636 and
Women-In-Management Incorporated, 2203 Lakeside Dr # B,
    Deerfield, IL 60015-1265; 847-295-0370.

Women's Business Development Center (WBDC), 8 South Michigan
Avenue, Suite 400, Chicago, IL 60603; 312-853-3477; Fax: 312-853-
0145; {Email: wbdc@aol.com}.

Displaced Homemaker/Single Parent Program, 201 Normantown Road,
Romeoville, IL 60446-1261; 815-886-3324; or 375 W. Briarcliff Road,
Bolingbrook, IL 60440-0951; 630-226-8400.

Technical Opportunity Program, Chicago Women in Trades, 220 South
Ashland, Chicago, IL 60607; 312-942-1444.

Project Impact, Southwest Women Working Together, 4051 West 63rd St., Chicago, IL 60629; 773-582-0550.

Keys to Success Program, Women Employed Institute, 22 E. Monroe, Suite 1400, Chicago, IL 60603; 312-782-3902.

Indiana

One-Stop Career Center: Workforce Development, Indiana Department of Workforce Development, Indiana Government Center, 10 North Senate Avenue, Indianapolis, IN 46204; 317-232-4259; Fax: 317-233-4793; {www.dwd. state.in.us}; {Email: workone@dwd-is.state.in.us}.

Indiana Department of Labor: Indiana Government Center-South, 402 West Washington Street, Room W 195, Indianapolis, IN 46204; 317-232-2655; {www.state. in.us/labor}.

Indiana Small Business Development Corporation (ISBD Corp.), 1 N. Capitol Ave # 1275, Indianapolis, IN 46204-2025; 317-264-2820.

Indiana Women Work!, New Directions, P.O. Box 887, Vincennes, IN 47591; 812-885-5882.

Single Parent/Homemaker Project Services, 1025 Freeland Rd, Greensburg, IN 47240; 812-663-8597; {www.treecity. com/library/ resource/ single.htm}.

McDowell Adult Education Center, Single Parent/ Displaced Homemaker Program, 2700 McKinley Avenue, Columbus, IN 47201; 812-376-4451; {http:// columbus.in. us/ iris/irisonline/Content/ Single_Parent_Displaced_ Homemaker_Program_ McDowell.html}.

Bartholomew County Division of Family & Children, 2330 Midway Street, Suite 3, P.O. Box 587, Columbus, IN 47202; 812-376-9361; {http://columbus.in.us/iris/ irisonline/Content/ Bartholomew_ County_Division_of_ Family_Children.htm}.

Columbus Area Career Connection, 2650 Home Avenue, Columbus, IN 47201; 812-376-4240; Fax: 812-376-4699; {http://columbus.in.us/ iris/irisonline/Content/C4_ Columbus_Area_Career_Connection.html}.

Certified Nursing Assistant Program - McDowell, 2700 McKinley Ave., Columbus, IN 47201; 812-376-4451.

Co-operative Office Education/Basic Office Services, 1400 25th Street, Columbus, IN 47201; 812-376-4240; {http://columbus.in.us/ iris/ irisonline/Content/ Co_operative_ Office_ Education_ Basic_Office_ Services.html}.

Computer Training (Interim), 1504 N. Lincoln, Greensburg, IN 47240; 812-379-1070; Fax: 812-663-9096; {http://columbus.in.us/ iris/irisonline/ Content/ Computer_ Training_ Interim.html}

Computer Training (Kelly), 810 Brown Street, Suite B, Columbus, IN 47201; 812-378-3757; {http:// columbus. in.us/ iris/irisonline/ Content/ Computer_ Training_ Kelly.html}.

Computer Training (Manpower), 1309 North National Road, Columbus, IN 47201; 812-376-4111; {http:// columbus.in.us/ iris/ irisonline/ Content/ Computer_ Training_ Manpower.html}.

Family Self-Sufficiency - Columbus Housing Authority, 801 McClure Road, Columbus, IN 47201; 812-376-2523; {http://columbus.in.us/ iris/irisonline/Content/Family_ Self_ Sufficiency_Columbus_Housing_ Authority. html}.

Health Careers Training, 2650 Home Ave., Columbus, IN 47201; 812-376-4240; {http://columbus.in.us/iris/ irisonline/ Content/Health_ Careers_ Training.html}.

Horizon House - Human Services, Inc., 724 Chestnut Street, P.O. Box 588, Columbus, IN 47202; 888-485-6137; {http://columbus.in.us/iris/ irisonline/ Content/Horizon_ House_Human_Services_Inc.html}.

IMPACT (Indiana Manpower Placement & Comprehensive Training), 2330 Midway St., Suite 3, Columbus, IN 47202; 812-376-9361;

{http://columbus.in.us/iris/irisonline/ Content/IMPACT__
Indiana_Manpower_ Placement___Comprehensive_ Training.html}.

Restaurant Dining-McDowell Education Center, 2700 McKinley Ave.,
Columbus, IN 47201; 812-376-4451; {http://columbus.in.us/iris/
irisonline/Content/ Restaurant_ Dining_McDowell_Education_Center.
html}.

Technology Preparation Classes, 2650 Home Ave., Columbus, IN
47201; 812-376-4240; {http:// columbus. in.us/iris/irisonline/ Content/
Technology_ Preparation_ Classes.html}.

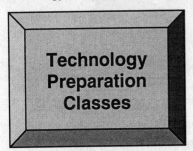

Trade and Industry, 2650 Home
Ave., Columbus, IN 47201; 812-
376-4240; {http://
columbus.in.us/iris/irisonline/
Content/Trade_and_
Industry.html}.

Transition Resources
Corporation, 220 Clifty Drive,
Unit J, Madison, IN 47250; 800-664-6066; 812-273-5451; Fax: 812-
273-1881; {http:// columbus. in.us/iris/ irisonline/ Content/Transition_
Resources_ Corporation.html}.

Single Parent/Displaced Homemaker Program, Workforce
Development Services, 2015 W. Western, South Bend, IN 46629; 219-
239-2660.

Indiana Workforce Development, 3771 South A St., Richmond, IN
47374; 765-962-8591; 800-962-8592.

New Directions Single Parent/Homemaker Program, Evansville-
Vanderburgh School Corporation, Henry Reis Education Center, 1900
Stringtown Rd., Evansville, IN 47711; 812-435-8275.

Fort Wayne Women's Bureau, 303 E. Washington Blvd., Fort Wayne,
IN 46802; 219-424-7977.

Circle Seven Training Council. Inc., 143 Green Meadows Dr., Suite 2, Greenfield, IN 46140; 317-467-0248, ext. 317.

Career Resources, North Central Indiana Private Industry Council, 36 West 5th St., Suite 102-B, Peru, IN 46970; 765-473-5571.

Iowa

One-Stop Career Center: Workforce Development, Department of Workforce Development , 1000 East Grand Avenue, Des Moines, IA 50319-0209; 515-281-5387; 800-JOB-IOWA; {www.state.ia.us/ government/ wd/}.

Department of Labor: Iowa Workforce Development, 1000 East Grand Avenue, Des Moines, IA 50319-0209; 515-281-5387; {www.state. ia.us/iwd}.

Institute of Social and Economic Development, 1901 Broadway, Suite 313, Iowa City, IA 52240; 319-338-2331; Fax: 319-338-5824.

Pre-Vocational Training Program, University of Iowa, C107 Seashore Hall Center, Iowa City, IA 52242; 319-335-0560.

Promise Jobs Program, Division of Economic Assistance, Iowa Department of Human Services, Hoover State Office Building, 5th Floor, Des Moines, IA 50319-0114; 515-281-8629.

Program for Women in Science and Engineering, Iowa State University, 210 Lab of Mechanics, Ames, IA 50011; 515-294-9964.

New Choices, Iowa Western Community College, 2700 College Rd., Box C0214, Council Bluffs, IA 51503; 712-325-3269, ext. 269.

Mentor Support Program, Commissions on the Status of Women, Iowa Department of Human Rights, Lucas State Office Building, Des Moines, IA 50319; 515-281-9052.

Indian Hills Community College, Sex Equity Coordinator, 525 Grandview, Ottumwa, IA 52501; 800-726-2585, ext. 231.

Kansas

One-Stop Career Center: Kansas Job Service Career Centers, Department of Human Resources, Division of Employment and Training, 401 SW Topeka Boulevard, Topeka, KS 66603-3182; 913-296-5000; {http://entkdhr. ink.org}.

Department of Labor: Kansas Department of Human Resources, 401 SW Topeka Boulevard, Topeka, KS 66603-3182; 785-296-5000; {www.hr.state.ks.us}.

Kansas Women Work!, Cynthia Shanley, President, New Directions-KSU, 2323 Anderson Avenue, Suite 221, Manhattan, KS 66502; 785-532-6561; {Email: shanley@ksu.edu}.

SP/DH/SPW Program, Pratt Community College & AVS, 348 NE SR 61 Pratt, KS 67124-8317; 316-672-5641, ext. 231, Fax: 316-672-5288; {Email: deannah@pcc.cc.ks.us}; {www.pcc.cc.ks.us/Dph.htm}.

Allen County Community College, Single Parent/Displaced Homemaker Program, 1801 N. Cottonwood, Iola, KS 66749; 316-65-5116, ext. 255; {Email: harvey@acccn1. allen.cc.ks.us}; {www.allen.cc.ks.us/Irc/Spdh.htm}.

Career Assistance Network, Topeka YWCA, 1129 SW Wanamaker Rd., Topeka, KS 66604; 785-273-5190.

Butler County Community College, CRC Coordinator, Augusta Resource Center, 420 Walnut St., Augusta, KS 67010; 316-775-5098.

Single Parent/Displaced Homemaker Program, Coffeyville Community College, 400 W. 11th St., Coffeyville, KS 67337; 316-251-7700.

Project Re-Entry, Colby Community College, 1255 S. Range, Colby, KS 67701; 913-462-3984, ext. 280.

Single Parent/Homemaker Program, Allen County Community College, 1801 N. Cottonwood, Iola, KS 66749; 316-365-5116.

Community Outreach Counseling Program/WRC, Women's Resource Center, Kansas City Kansas Community College, 7250 State Ave., Kansas City, KS 66112; 913-334-1100, ext. 270.

Kentucky

One-Stop Career Center: One-Stop Career Centers System, Department for Employment Services, 275 East Main Street, Frankfort, KY 40621; 502-564-5331; {www.state. ky.us/agencies/wforce/one-stop/oscc.htm}.

Department of Labor: Kentucky Cabinet for Workforce Development, 500 Mero Street, Frankfort, KY 40601; 502-564-6606; {www.state.ky.us/agencies/ wforce/index.htm}.

Kentucky Vocational Equity Re-Entry Center, 506 Johns Hill Rd., Highland Heights, KY 41099; 606-442-3536.

Family Care Center, 1135 Red Mile Place, Lexington, KY 40504; 606-288-4040.

Creative Employment Project, Center for Women and Families, 226 West Breckinridge St., Louisville, KY 40203; 502-581-7237.

Louisiana

One-Stop Career Center: Louisiana Works, Louisiana Occupational Information Coordinating Committee (L.O.I.C.C.), P.O. Box 94094, Baton Rouge, LA 70804; 504-342-5149; Fax: 504-342-5115; {www.ldol.state.la.us}.

Louisiana Department of Labor: 1001 North 23rd, P.O. Box 94094, Baton Rouge, LA 70804; {www. ldol. state.la.us}.

Women Entrepreneurs for Economic Development Inc. (W.E.E.D.), 1683 North Claiborne Ave., New Orleans, LA 70116; 504-949-8885; Fax: 504-949-8885.

Hamilton Terrace Learning Center, c/o Caddo Parish School Board, 1105 Louisiana Ave., Shreveport, LA 71101; 318-222-4518.

Southeast Louisiana Black Chamber of Commerce (SLBCC), Women's Business Center, 2245 Peters Road, Suite 200, Harvey, LA 70058; 504-365-3866; Fax: 504-365-3890; {Email: wbc200@bellsouth.net}; {www.gnofn.org/~slbcc/wbc}.

Governor's Office of Women's Services, 1885 Wooddale Blvd., 9th Floor, Baton Rouge, LA 70806, P.O. Box 94095, Baton Rouge, LA 70804-9095; 504-922-0960; Fax: 504-922-0959; {Email: owsbrcdh@cmq.com}; {www.ows.state.la.us/}.

Center for Displaced Homemakers, 752 Dalzell, Shreveport, LA 71104; 318-676-7137; Fax: 318-676-7149.

The Panther CAVE, Neosho County Community College, 800 West 14th St., Chanute, KS 66720; 316-431-2820, ext. 279; {www.neosho.cc.ks.us/cave.html}.

Building and Industrial Trades Program for Women, State Program Manager, Governor's Office of Women's Services, P.O. Box 94095, Baton Rouge, LA 70804; 504-922-0960; Fax: 504-922-2067.

Louisiana Technical College, 5200 Blair Dr., Metairie, LA 70001; 504-736-7077.

Maine

One-Stop Career Center: Maine Career Centers, Department of Labor, Bureau of Employment Services, 55 State House Station, Augusta, ME 04333-0055; 888-457-8883; TTY: 800-794-1110; {www.state.me.us/labor/ jsd/ jobserv.htm}.

Maine Department of Labor: Bureau of Employment Services, 55 State House Station, Augusta, ME 04333-0055; 207-624-6390; {www.state.me.us/labor/ jsd/observ.htm}.

Women Work! Regional Representative, Region I, Thia Hamilton, Maine Centers for Women, Work and Community, 200 Madison Ave., Skowhegan, ME 04976; 207-474-0788.

Women Unlimited, 71 Winthrop St., Augusta, ME 04330; 207-623-7576; 800-281-5259.

Coastal Enterprises Inc. (CEI), Women's Business Development Program (WBDP), 7 North Chestnut St., Augusta, ME 04330; 207-621-0245; Fax: 207-622-9739; {Email: jmr@ceimaine.org}; {Email: eat@ceimaine.org}.

Training & Development Corporation, 2 Main St, Corinna, ME 04928; 207-278-5500.

Women Unlimited

Training & Development Corporation, 1 Cumberland Pl., Bangor, ME 04401-5085; 207-945-9431.

Training & Development Corporation, 14 High St., Ellsworth, ME 04605-1706; 207-667-7543.

Training & Development Corporation, 18 School St., Bucksport, ME 04416; 207-469-6385.

Training & Development Corporation, Rt. 15, Dover Foxcroft, ME 04426; 207-564-8438.

Training & Development Corporation, 257 Harlow St. # 201, Bangor, ME 04401-4944; 207-942-9492.

ASPIRE--JOBS and JET Program, Maine Department of Human Services, Bureau of Family Independence, State House Station #11, Augusta, ME 04333-0011; 207-287-2826.

Maryland

One-Stop Career Center: CareerNet, Department of Labor, Licensing and Regulation, Employment Services, 500 North Calvert Street, Baltimore, MD 21202-2272; 410-767-2400; TTY: 410-767-2986; {www.careernet.state. md.us/ CareerNet.html}; {Email: det@dllr.state.md.us}.

Department of Labor: Maryland Department of Labor, Licensing and Regulation, 1100 N. Eutaw St., Baltimore, MD 21201-000; 410-767-2000; {www.dllr. state.md.us}.

Women Work! Regional Representative, Region III, Renew Program, Kay Shattuck, Director/ Joyce Sebian, Counselor, Carroll Community College, Room 118, 1601 Washington Road, Westminster, MD 21157; 410-876-9617; Fax: 410-876-9040; {Email: cglaeser@carroll.cc.md.us}.

AdVANtage II, Sojourner-Douglass College, 500 N. Caroline St., Baltimore, MD 21205; 410-276-9741.

Center for Employment Training, 1100 East Baltimore St., Baltimore, MD 21202; 410-962-0238; Fax: 410-962-1558; {Email: c_greene@cetmail.cfet.org}.

Women Entrepreneurs of Baltimore, Inc. (WEB), 28 East Ostend St., Baltimore, MD 21230; 410-727-4921; Fax: 410-727-4989.

New Focus Program, Howard Community College, 10901 Little Patuxent Parkway, Columbia, MD 21044; 410-772-4800; V/TDD: 410-772-4822; {www.howardcc.edu}.

Displaced Homemakers Program, 311 West Saratoga St., Baltimore, MD 21201; 410-767-7661; {www.dhr.state. md.us/transit/ts-dhp.htm}.

Montgomery County Commission for Women, 255 North Washington St., 4th floor, Nations Bank Building, Rockville, MD 20850-1703; 301-279-1800; TTY: 301-279-1034; Fax: 301-279-1318; {www.co.mo.md.us/cfw}.

Displaced Homemaker's Program, Community College of Baltimore County, 7200 Sollers Point Rd., Baltimore, MD 21222-4694; 410-285-9808; Fax: 410-285-9903; {www.dundalk.cc.md.us/}

Maryland Commission for Women, 311 W. Saratoga St., Room 232, Baltimore, MD 21201; 410-767-7137; TTY: 410-333-0017.

Mayor's Office of Employment Development, 417 Fayette St., Suite 468, Baltimore, MD 21202; 410-396-3009 (Information Line).

Baltimore County Office of Employment and Training CareerNet, 1 Investment Place, Suite 409, Towson, MD 21204; 410-887-4473; Fax: 410-887-5773.

Baltimore County Reemployment Assistance Center, 901 Dulaney Valley Rd., Suite 100, Towson, MD 21204; 410-887-4400.

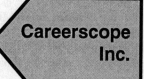

Careerscope Inc., One Mall North #216, 10025 Governor Warfield Parkway, Columbia, MD 21044; 410-992-5042.

Open Doors Career Center, Inc., 42 N. Main St., Suite 202, Bel Air, MD 21014; 410-838-1480.

Maryland New Directions, Displaced Homemaker Program, 2220 North Charles St., Baltimore, MD 21218; 410-889-6677.

Massachusetts

One-Stop Career Center: Massachusetts One-Stop Career Center Network, Division of Employment and Training, 19 Stanford Street, Boston, MA 02114; 617-727-6560; {www.masscareers.state.ma.us}.

Department of Labor: Massachusetts Division of Employment and Training, 19 Stanford Street, Boston, MA 02114; 617-727-6560; {www.detma.org}.

Massachusetts Center for Women & Enterprise Inc., Andrea Silbert, Director, 45 Bromfield St., 6th Floor, Boston, MA 02108; 617-423-3001, ext. 222; Fax: 617-423-2444; {Email: info@cweboston.org}; {Email: asilbert@cweboston.org}.

Women In the Building Trades, 555 Amory St., Jamaica Plain, MA 02130; 617-524-3010.

Apprenticeship Preparedness Program, Building and Construction Trades Council of the Metropolitan District, 12A Everclean St., Boston, MA 02122; 617-282-2242.

Michigan

One-Stop Career Center: Michigan Works!, Michigan Jobs Commission, 201 North Washington Square, Victor Office Center, 4th Floor, Lansing, MI 48913; 517-373-9808; {www.state.mi.us/mjc/ceo/ employ/employ.htm}; {Email: Customer-Assistance@state.mi.us}.

Department of Labor: Michigan Jobs Commission, 201 North Washington Square, Victor Office Center, 4th Floor, Lansing, MI 48913; 517-373-9808; {www.state.mi. us/mjc/ceo}.

Ann Arbor Community Development Corporation Women's Initiative for Self Employment (WISE), 2008 Hogback Road, Suite 2A, Ann Arbor, MI 48105; 313-677-1400; Fax: 313-677-1465; {Email: mrichards@ miceed.org}.

Grand Rapids Opportunities for Women (GROW), 25 Sheldon SE, Suite 210, Grand Rapids, MI 49503; 616-458-3404; Fax: 616-458-6557; {Email: grow@voyager.net}.

State of Michigan's Economic Development Agency, 201 N. Washington Square, Victor Office Center, 4th Floor, Lansing, MI 48913; 517-373-9808; {Email: Customer-Assistance@state.mi.us}; {www.state.mi.us/mjc/ceo/}.

Single Parent/Displaced Homemaker and Sex Equity Programs, Kirtland Community College, 10775 North St. Helen Road, Roscommon, MI 48653; 517-275-5121, ext. 252; {www.kirtland. cc.mi.us/}.

Every Woman's Place - Almond Center, 1221 W. Laketon, Muskegon, MI 49441; 616-759-7909: Fax: 616-759-8618.

Telamon Corporation, 710 Chicago Dr., Suite 310, Holland, MI 49423; 616-396-5160.

Minnesota

One-Stop Career Center: Minn WorkForce Center, Department of Economic Security, 390 N. Robert St., St. Paul, MN 55101; 888-GET-JOBS; {www.des. state.mn.us/ jseek.htm}; {Email: mdes.webmaster@ des. state.mn.us}.

Department of Labor: Minnesota Economic Security, 390 North Robert Street, St. Paul, MN 55101; 651-296-3644; {www.des.state.mn.us}.

Life-Work Planning Center has four convenient locations in four counties:

- Union Square Business Center, 201 North Broad St., Suite 100, Mankato, MN 56001; 507-345-1577; 800-369-5166; {www.lwpc.org/}.
- New Ulm WorkForce Center, 1618 South Broadway, New Ulm, MN 56073; 507-354-3138; 800-505-9073.
- 118 South Main Street, Fairmont, MN 56031; 507-238-9361; 800-433-1706.
- Relations Center, 204 Second Street NW, Waseca, MN 56093; 507-345-1577, 800-369-5166.

Minnesota Women in the Trades, Minnesota Women's Bldg., 550 Rice St., St. Paul, MN 55103; 651-228-9950.

Women in New Development (WIND), 2715 15th Street NW, P.O. Box 579, Bemidji, MN 56601; 218-751-4631; Fax: 218-751-8452; {Email: bicap@ northernnet.com}.

Minnesota Department of Economic Security/Workforce Preparation Branch, 390 North Robert Street, St. Paul, MN 55101; 651-296-6060; {Email: susan.m.johnson@ state.mn.us}.

Mainstay, Inc., 308 North Third Street, P.O. Box 816, Marshall, MN 56258; 507-537-1546; 800-554-2481; {Email: mainstay@bresnanlink.net}; {www.swmnmall. com/mainstay/}.

Women In Transition, 6715 Minnetonka Blvd., Suite 212, St. Louis Park, MN 55426; 612-924-1261.

Minneapolis Employment and Training Program, 510 Public Service Center, 250 S. 4th St., Minneapolis, MN 55415; 612-673-2907.

Working Opportunities For Women, 1295 Bandana Blvd., North, Suite 110, St. Paul, MN 55108; 651-647-9961.

Discover, Gender Equity Program Manager, Minnesota State Colleges and Universities, 700 World Trade Center, 30 E. 7th St., St. Paul, MN 55101; 612-296-9451.

Mississippi

One-Stop Career Center: Workforce, State Board for Community & Junior Colleges, 3825 Ridgewood Road, Jackson, MS 39211; 601-982-6439; Fax: 601-982-6365; {www.sbcjc.cc.ms.us/workfor.htm}.

Department of Labor: Mississippi Employment Security Commission, MESC P.O. Box 1699, Jackson, MS 31295-1699; 601-354-8711; {www.mesc.state.ms.us}.

Mississippi Women's Economic Entrepreneurial Project (MWEEP), 106 West Green St., Mound Bayou, MS 38762; 601-741-3342; Fax: 601-741-2195; {Email: jthompson@tecinfo.com}; {www.ncnw.com}.

Mississippi Women Work!, Chris Tanner-Watkins, President, SP/DH Program, Hinds Community College, Utica Campus, Utica, MS 39175; 601-885-7042; 601-885-6062.

Meridian Community College Single Parent/Displaced Homemaker Services, 910 Highway 19 North, Meridian, MS 39307; 601-484-8836; {www.mcc.cc.ms.us/online_ catalog/Single%20Parent/displace.htm}.

Itawamba Community College, 602 West Hill Street, Fulton, MS 38843; 601-862-3101; Fax: 601-862-4608; {www.icc.cc.ms.us/stu_services.htm}.

Missouri

One-Stop Career Center: Missouri Wins, Workforce Development
Transition Team, P.O. Box 1928, Jefferson City, MO 65102-1928;
573-751-7039; Fax: 573-751-0147; {www.works.state.mo.us/wfd};
{Email: workforce@ works. state.mo.us}.

Department of Labor: Missouri Department of Labor and Industrial
Relations, 3315 West Truman Boulevard, P.O. Box 58, Jefferson, MO
65102; 573-751-4091; {www.dolir. state.mo.us}.

Women Work! Regional Representative, Region VII, Cheryl Parks
Hill, 6921 N. Bales, Gladstone, MO 64119; 816-858-3723; Fax: 816-
858-3278.

NAWBO - St. Louis (National Association of Women's Business
Owners - St. Louis), 7165 Delmar, Suite 204, St. Louis, MO 63130;
314-863-0046; 888-560-9813; Fax: 314-863-2079; {Email:
nawbostl@ibm.net}; {www2. stlmo. com/nawbo/}.

Workplace Readiness for Women, Central Ozarks Private Industry
Council, 1202 Forum Drive, Rolla, MO 65401; 800-638-1401, ext.
153; Fax: 573-634-1865.

Women's Employment Network, 3521 Broadway, Suite 300, Kansas
City, MO 64114; 816-531-7055, ext. 300.

New Perspectives, Kirksville Area Vocational Technical Center, 1103
South Cottage Grove, Kirksville, MO 63501; 816-665-2865.

Outreach/Reentry Programs, Maple Woods Community College, 2601
NE. Barry Rd., Kansas City, MO 64156; 816-437-3000.

New Horizons: Nontraditional Careers, Missouri Department of
Elementary and Secondary Education, Special Vocational Services,
Mineral Area College, P.O. Box 1000, Park Hills, MO 63601; 573-431-
4593.

Changing Channels, Linn Technical College, Highway 50 East, Linn,
MO 65051; 573-897-3603.

Montana

One-Stop Career Center: Job Service Centers, Department of Labor and Industry, Workforce Development, Montana Department of Labor and Industry, P.O. Box 1728, Helena, MT 59624; 406-444-4513; {http://jsd.dli.state.mt.us}; {Email: kechapman@state.mt.us}.

Department of Labor: Montana Department of Labor and Industry, P.O. Box 1728, Helena, MT 59624; 406-444-9091; {http://jsd.dli.state.mt.us/ dli_home/dli.htm}.

Women Work! Regional Representative, Region VIII, Sharon Kearnes, Career Development Program, Miles Community College, 2715 Dickinson, Miles City, MT 59301; 406-232-3031, ext. 38; Fax: 406-232-5705.

Montana Women's Capital Fund, 54 North Last Chance Gulch, P.O. Box 271, Helena, MT 59624; 406-443-3144; Fax: 406-442-1789.

Career Training Institute and Women's Business Center (CTI), 347 North Last Chance Gulch, Helena, MT 59601; 406-443-0800, Fax: 406-442-2745; {Email: mgarrity@ ixi.net}.

Women's Opportunity & Resource Development Inc., 127 N. Higgins, Missoula, MT 59802; 406-543-3550, ext. 19; Fax: 406-721-4584; {Email: mcdc@montana.com}.

Career Transitions, Inc., 321 E. Main, Suite 215, Bozeman, MT 59715; 406-587-1721; Fax: 406-586-3249; {Email: info@ careertransitions. com}; {www.careertransitions. com/}.

YMCA of Billings, 909 Wyoming Ave., Billings, MT 59101; 406-252-6303.

Nebraska

One-Stop Career Center: Nebraska Workforce Development Centers, Department of Labor, 550 South 16th Street, Lincoln, NE 68509; 402-471-9928; Fax: 402-471-2318; {www.dol.state.ne.us}; {Email: cplager@ dol.state.ne.us}.

Nebraska Department of Labor: 550 South 16th Street, Lincoln, NE 68509-4600; 402-471-4189; {www.dol. state.ne.us}.

Blair Community Schools, Young Women in Nontraditional Careers; Blair Community Schools, 140 S. 16, P.O. Box 288, Blair, NE 68008; 402-426-4941.

Burke High School, Zoo and Nontraditional Career Academies, 12200 Burke Blvd., Omaha, NE, 68154; 402-557-3264.

Central Community College, Platte Campus, 4500 63rd St., P.O. Box 1027, Columbus, NE 68602-1027; 402-562-1265; 800-642-1083.

Central Community College, Nontraditional Careers/Single Parent, Displaced Homemaker, Hastings Campus, East Highway 6, P.O. Box 1024, Hastings, NE 68902-1024; 402-461-2480; 800-742-7872.

Central Community College, Grand Island Campus, 3134 W. Highway 34, P.O. Box 4903, Grand Island, NE 68802-4903; 308-384-5220; 800-652-9177.

Crete PS Special Programs Office, Single Parent/Displaced Homemaker, Crete Public Schools, 920 Linden Ave, Crete, NE 68333; 402-826-5228.

Grand Island YWCA, Single Parent/Displaced Homemaker, Incarcerated Women, Grand Island YWCA, 234 E. 3rd, Grand Island, NE 68801-5912; 402-384-0860.

Lincoln Public Schools, Teen Parents, 5901 'O' Street, Lincoln, NE 68510; 402-436-1817.

Lincoln YWCA, Safety Professionals, Teen Parents, 1432 'N' St., Lincoln, NE 68508; 402-434-3494.

McCook Community College, Single Parent/Displaced Homemaker, 1205 East Third St., McCook, NE 69001-2631; 308-345-6303; 800-658-4348.

Metropolitan Community College, Single Parent/Displaced Homemaker, P.O. Box 3777, Omaha, NE 68103-0777; 402-457-2319; 800-228-9553.

Mid Plains Community College, Single Parent/Displaced Homemaker, 416 N. Jeffers, North Platte, NE 69101; 308-532-8740.

FREE COMPUTER TRAINING FOR SENIORS

There are 150 centers around the country that train seniors on the use of computers to help make decisions about their health, independence and financial security as well as a tool for finding jobs and communicating with others.

To find the center near you contact the PC Empowerment Initiative at National Council on the Aging, 409 Third Street, SW, Suite 200, Washington, DC 20024; 202-479-0735; {www. nco.org/ pcempowerment/ index.html}.

Norfolk Public Schools, Nontraditional Careers/Teen Parent, Norfolk Public Schools, 512 Philip Ave., P.O. Box 139, Norfolk, NE 68702; 402-644-2516; 402-644-2500.

Nontraditional Careers/Teen Parent Program

Northeast Community College, Nontraditional Career Camp, Single Parent/Displaced Homemaker, 801 East Benjamin Ave., P.O. Box 469, Norfolk, NE 68702-0469; 402-644-0435; 402-644-0471; 800-348-9033; {www.wjag.com/nccstory.htm}.

Omaha Public Schools, Teen Parent Program, 3215 Cumming St., Omaha, NE 68131; 402-557-2615.

Omaha YWCA, 222 S. 29th, Omaha, NE 68131-3577; 402-345-6555.

Southeast Community College, RR 2, Box 35-A, Beatrice, NE 68310-9683; 402-345-6555; 800-233-5027.

Southeast Community College, Nontraditional Careers/Single Parent, Southeast Community College, 8800 'O' St., Lincoln, NE 68520-1299; 402-437-2629; 800-642-4075.

Southeast Community College, Technology Careers for Women, 600 State St., Milford, NE 68405-9397; 402-761-8202.

University of Nebraska-Lincoln, Nebraska Career Information System, Single Parent/Displaced Homemaker, NH 421, Lincoln, NE 68588-0552; 402-472-2570.

Western NE Community College, Single Parent/Displaced Homemaker, 1601 East 27th St., Scottsbluff, NE 69162, 308-635-6121; 800-348-4435.

Western NE Community College, Nontraditional Careers, 371College Drive, Sidney, NE 69162; 308-254-7414; 800-222-9682.

New Beginnings, Northeast Community College, 801 East Benjamin, P.O. Box 469, Norfolk, NE 68702; 402-644-0471.

Women in Transition, Mid-Plains Community College, Voc-Tech Campus, 1101 Halligan Dr., North Platte, NE 69101; 308-532-8740.

Nevada

One-Stop Career Center: Nevada Department of Employment, Training and Rehabilitation, 500 East Third Street, Carson City, NV 89713; 702-687-4550; {www.state.nv.us/detr/detr.html}; {Email: detrinfo@ govmail.state.nv.us}.

Department of Labor: Nevada Department of Employment, Training and Rehabilitation, 500 East Third Street, Carson City, NV 89713; 702-687-4550; {www.state.nv.us/ detr/detr.html}.

Nevada Self-Employment Trust, 1600 E. Desert Inn Road, #209, E. Las Vegas, NV 89109; 702-734-3555; Fax: 702-734-3530.

Nevada MicroEnterprise Initiative (NMI), 116 East 7th Street, Suite 3, Carson City, NV 89701; 702-841-1420; Fax: 702-841-2221; {Email: lizs@cbrcnmi.reno.nv.us}.

Center for Employment Training, 520 Evans Avenue, Reno, NV 89512; 702-348-8668 Fax: 702-348-2034; {Email: m_smith@cetmail.cfet.org}.

New Hampshire

One-Stop Career Center: New Hampshire Works, Department of Employment Security, 32 South Main Street, Concord, NH 03301-3860; 603-271-3494; {www.nhworks.state.nh.us}; {Email: webmaster@nhes. state.nh.us}.

New Hampshire Department of Labor: 95 Pleasant Street, Concord, NH 03301; 603-271-3177; {www.state.nh. us/dol/index.html}.

Women's Business Center, Inc., 150 Greenleaf Avenue, Unit 4, Portsmouth, NH 03801; 603-430-2892; Fax: 603-430-3706; {Email: wbc.inc@rscs.net}.

New Hampshire Job Training Council, 64 Old Suncook Road, Concord, NH 03301; 603-228-9500; 800-772-7001 (NH only); Fax: 603-228-8557; TDD: 800-622-9180; {Email: nhjtc@orgtheenterprise}; {www.nhti.net/}.

New Jersey

One-Stop Career Center: Workforce New Jersey, Division of Employment and Training, P.O. Box 005, Trenton, NJ 08625; 609-292-5005; {www.wnjpin.state.nj.us}.

New Jersey Department of Labor: John Fitch Plaza, P.O. Box 110, Trenton, NJ 08625; 609-292-2323; {www.state.nj.us/labor}.

New Jersey NAWBO Excel, Harriet Scooler, Project Director, 225 Hamilton St., Bound Brook, NJ 08805-2042; 732-560-9607; Fax: 732-560-9687; {Email: njawbo@njawbo.org}; {www.njawbo.org}.

Displaced Homemakers Network of NJ, Inc., Circle Branch P.O. Box 5545, Trenton, NJ 08638-5545; 732-774-3363.

The Women's Fund of NJ, 355 Chestnut Street, Union, NJ 07083; 908-851-7774; Fax: 908-851-7775; {www.wfnj.org/Displaced%20Homemakers.htm}.

Elaine Muller, County College of Morris, 214 Center Grove Road, SCC/133, Randolph, NJ 07869-2086; 973-328-5025; Fax: 973-328-5146.

Friendship Pregnancy Centers, 82 Speedwell Avenue, Morristown, NJ 07960; 973-538-0967; 888-324-6673; 888-3Choose; 973-644-2960.

Occupational Training Center, 10 Ridgedale Avenue, Cedar Knolls, NJ 07927; 973-538-8822

Green Thumb, Inc., Morris County Office, 20 Hillside Terrace, Newton, NJ 07860; 973-383-3621.

Bergen Employment Action Project (BEAP), AFL-CIO Community Services, 214 State St., Hackensack, NJ 07601; 201-489-7476.

Bergen WorkForce Center, 540 Hudson St., Hackensack, NJ 07601; 201-329-9600; {www.users.bergen. org/~margot/}.

WISE Women's Center, Room 3276 - 3rd Level, Yellow Area, Essex County College, 303 University Ave., Newark, NJ 07102; 973-877-3395.

St. Francis Counseling Service, 4700 Long Beach Blvd., Brant Beach, NJ 08008; 609-494-1554.

Center For People In Transition at Gloucester County College, 1400 Tanyard Rd. Sewell, NJ 08080; 609-464-5229.

Women's Rights Information Center, 108 West Palisade Ave., Englewood, NJ 07631; 201-568-1166.

Training for Trades and Technology, Bergen County Technical Institute, Career and Life Counseling Center, 540 Hudson St., Hackensack, NJ 07601; 201-329-9600, ext. 5200.

Training, Recruiting, Educating and Employing, Inc., Middlesex County Vocational School System, 256 Easton Ave., New Brunswick, NJ 08901; 732-745-4721.

Women Working Technical, Career and Life Counseling Center, Bergen County Technical Institute, 540 Hudson St., Hackensack, NJ 07601; 201-343-6000, ext. 2270.

New Beginnings for Displaced Homemakers, Project Self-Sufficiency,
P.O. Box 322, Sparta, NJ 07871; 201-383-5129.

New Mexico

One-Stop Career Center: New Mexico Works, Department of Labor,
401 Broadway, NE , Albuquerque, NM 87102; 505-841-2000;
{www3.state.nm.us/dol/nmworks/ default. asp}; {Email: jslowen@nm-
us.campus.cwix.net}.

New Mexico Department of Labor: 401 Broadway NE, Albuquerque,
NM 87102; 505-841-8486; {www3. state. nm.us/dol}.

New Mexico Women's Economic Self-Sufficiency Team (WESST
Corp.), 414 Silver Southwest, Albuquerque, NM 87102; 505-241-
4760; Fax: 505-241-4766; {Email: wesst@ swcp.com}.

WESST Corp., 418 Cerrillos
Road, Suite 26, Santa Fe, NM
87501; 505-988-5284; Fax:
505-988-5221; {Email:
sfwesst@ swcp.com}.

**Women's Economic
Self-Sufficiency
Team
(WESST Corp.)**

WESST Corp, Box 5007
NDCBU, Taos, NM 87571;
505-758-3099; Fax: 505-751-1575; {Email: redpath@ laplaza. org}.

WESST Corp., 200 West First, Suite 324, Roswell, NM 88201; 505-
624-9850; Fax: 505-622-4196; {Email: wesst@ rt66.com}.

WESST Corp., 691 South Telshor, Las Cruces, NM 88001; 505-522-
3707; Fax: 505-522-4414; {Email: jencraig@ zianet.com}.

WESST Corp., 500 West Main, Farmington, NM 87401; 505-325-
0678; Fax: 505-325-0695; {Email: 4business@ acrnet.com}.

New Mexico State Department of Education, Vocational-Technical and
Adult Education Unit, Education Building, 300 Don Gaspar, Santa Fe,
NM 87501-2786; 505-827-6571.

New York

One-Stop Career Center: Workforce Development System, Department of Labor, Workforce Development, Building 12, State Office Campus, Albany, NY 12240; 518-457-3584; {www.wdsny.org}.

New York Department of Labor: Building 12, State Campus, Albany, NY 12240; 518-457-5519; {www.labor. state.ny.us}.

Women Work! Regional Representative, Region II, Iren Navero Hammel, Queens Women's Network, 161-10 Jamaica Ave., Suite 416, Jamaica, NY 11432; 718-657-6200; Fax: 718-739-6974.

Center for Employment and Training, 1071 East Tremont Ave., Bronx, NY 10460; 718-893-4582; Fax: 718-893-4680; {Email: s_coaxum@ cetmail.cfet.org}; or 346 West 17th Street, 5th Floor, New York, NY 10011; 212-924-2272; Fax: 212-924-7773; {Email: CETNY@ aol.com}.

American Woman's Economic Development Corporation (AWED), Suzanne Tufts, President and CEO, 71 Vanderbilt Avenue, Suite 320, New York, NY 10169; 212-692-9100; Fax: 212-692-9296.

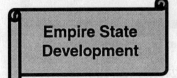

Empire State Development

Empire State Development, One Commerce Plaza, Albany, NY 12245; 518-474-7756; 800-STATE-NY; {www.empire.state.ny.us}.

Women's Venture Fund, Inc., 155 East 42nd Street, Suite 316, New York, NY 10017; 212-972-1146; Fax: 212-972-1167.

Everywoman Opportunity Center, 237 Main Street Suite 330, Buffalo, NY 14203; 716-847-1120; Fax: 716-847-1550; {Email: ewocbuf@ everywoman.org}.

Everywoman Opportunity Center, Greenacres Blvd. Room 108, 205 Yorkshire Rd., Tonawanda, NY 14150; 716-837-2260; Fax: 716-837-

0124; {Email: ewocton@ everywoman. org}; {www.everywoman. org}.

Everywoman Opportunity Center, 10825 Bennett Road, Dunkirk, NY 14048; 716-366-7020; Fax: 716-366-1925; {Email: ewocdf@ everywoman.org}.

Everywoman Opportunity Center, 800 Main St., Third Floor, Niagara Falls, NY 14301; 716-282-8472: Fax: 716-282-4868; {Email: ewocnf@ everywoman.org}.

Mary Snodgrass, Everywoman Opportunity Center, 265 N. Union Street, Olean, NY 14760; 716-373-4013; Fax: 716-373-7668; {Email: ewocol@everywoman.org}.

Agudath Israel/Fresh Start DHC, 1756 Ocean Ave., Brooklyn, NY 11230; 718-338-9200; Fax: 718-377-3151.

Bensonhurst DHC, 1708 West 10th Street, Brooklyn, NY 11214; 718-946-8570; Fax: 718-946-8572; {Email: bicdhp.erols.com}.

Bronx Community College DHC, 181 S. Street & University Ave., Gould Residence Hall, Room 309, Bronx, NY 10453; 718-289-5824; Fax: 718-289-6341.

Merble Reagon, Executive Director, Women's Center for Education & Career, Advancement, 45 John Street, Suite 605, New York, NY 10038; 212-964-8934; Fax: 212-964-0222.

Queen's Women's Network DHC, 161-10 Jamaica Ave., Suite 207, Jamaica, NY 11432; 718-657-6200; Fax: 718-739-6974.

YWCA - NYC DHC, 610 Lexington Ave., New York, NY 10022; 212-735-9729; Fax: 212-759-3158.

DHC/Suffolk Vocational Center, Bailey Hall, S. Oaks Hospital, 400 Sunrise Highway, Amityville, NY 11701; 516-598-0108; Fax: 516-264-0432; {Email: fsutherland@ fegs.org}.

Women In Self Help

S.C. Dept. of Labor, Veterans Memorial Highway, BLDG 17, North County Complex, Hauppage, NY 11788; 516-853-6620; 516-853-6510.

Women In Self Help, 503 Fifth Ave., 4th Floor, Brooklyn, NY 11215; 718-768-9700; Fax: 718-369-3192; {Email: CMarsh503@aol.com}.

Displaced Homemakers Multiservice Center, Economic Opportunity Commissions, DHMC, 134 Jackson St., Hempstead, NY 11550; 516-486-2800; Fax: 516-292-3176.

Westchester Comm. College, Project Transition, 75 Grasslands Rd., Valhalla, NY 10595; 914-785-6825; Fax: 914-785-6508; {Email: mbw@wcc.co. westchester.ny.us}.

Displaced Homemakers Women-in-Transition, Rockland Co. Guidance Ctr., Displaced Homemaker Program, 83 Main Street, Nyack, NY 10960; 914-358-9390; Fax: 914-358-4980.

Albany Displaced Homemaker Center, Albany DHC, 227 S. Pearl Street, Albany, NY 12202; 518-434-3103; Fax: 518-434-3211; {Email: adhc@albany.net}; {www.albany.net/~adhc}.

Displaced Homemakers Center Of Tompkins County, Tompkins County DHC, 315 N. Tioga Street, Ithaca, NY 14850; 607-272-1520; Fax: 607-272-2251; {Email: dhc@clarityconnect.com}.

Lifespan's Displaced Homemaker Center, Lifespan's DH Program, 79 N. Clinton Avenue, Rochester, NY 14604; 716-454-3224 Ext. 133; Fax: 716-454-3882; {Email: les1job@aol.com}.

Greater Utica Displaced Homemaker Center, Utica DHC, State Office Bldg., Room 209, 207 Genesee Street, Utica, NY 13501; 315-793-2790; Fax: 315-793-2509; {Email: dhc207@dreamscape.com}.

Syracuse Displaced Homemaker Program, Regional Learning Service DHC, 3049 East Genesee St., Syracuse, NY 13224-1644; 315-446-0550; Fax: 315-446-5869.

Displaced Homemaker Program - Schenectady Community Action Program, Schenectady/ Fulmont DHC, C/O SCAP, 433 State Street, Schenectady. NY 12305; 518-374-9181, Fax: 518-374-9190.

Project Lift, Fulton-Montgomery Community College, 2805 State Highway 67, Johnstown, NY 12095; 518-762-4651 Ext. 346; Fax: 518-762-4334; {Email: dpiurek@ fmcc.suny.edu}.

Schoharie Displaced Homemaker Program, 150 E. Main Street, Cobleskill, NY 12043; 518-234-2568, Fax: 518-234-3507; {Email: sccapinc@midtel.net}.

Access for Women

Nontraditional Employment for Women, 243 West 20th St., New York, NY 10011; 212-627-6252.

Cooperative Home Care Associates, 349 East 149th St., Bronx, NY 10451; 718-993-7104.

New York State Career Options Institute, 6 British American Blvd., Suite G, Latham, NY 12110; 518-786-3236.

Access for Women, New York City Technical College, 300 Jay Street, M 407, Brooklyn, NY 11201; 718-260-5730.

Small Contractor's Assistance Program, Coordinator/ Counselor, Borough of Manhattan Community College, City University of New York, Office of Continuing Education, 199 Chambers St., New York, NY 10007; 212-346-8100.

North Carolina

One-Stop Career Center: Joblink Career Centers, Governor's Commission on Workforce Preparedness, NC Department of Commerce, P.O. Box 29571, Raleigh, NC 27626; 919-733-4806 ext. 259; Fax: 919-733-1128; {www.joblink.state.nc.us}.

North Carolina Department of Labor: 4 West Edenton Street, Raleigh, NC 27601; 919-733-7166; {www.dol. state.nc.us/dolhome.htm}.

Joblink Career Center of Avery County, P.O. Box 939, 175 Linville St., Avery, NC 28657; 828-733-8288; Fax: 828-733-8245; {Email: Rosh.david@newcg.joblink. state.nc.us}.

The Mountain Area JobLink Career Center, P.O Box 729, Asheville, NC 28802; 828-250-4767; Fax: 828-232-4416; {Email: briggs. linda@avljt. joblink.state.nc.us}.

Edenton-Chowan JobLink Center, 1316-C North Broad St., Edenton, NC 27932; 252-482-2195; 252-482-2196; Fax: 252-482-2188.

JobLink Career Center of Cumberland County, 410 Ray Ave., Fayetteville, NC 28301; 910-486-1010, Fax: 910-323-5755; {Email: Goodman.Pauline@esc.state.nc.us}.

JobLink Career Centerof Duplin County, James Sprunt Community College, P.O. Box 398, Kenansville, NC 28349-0398; 910-296-2400; Fax: 910-296-1222; {Email: dmorrise@duplinnet.com}.

JobLink Career Center of Guilford County Guilford Technical Community College, 901 S. Main Street, High Point, NC 27260, 336-821-6473; Fax: 336-821-6462.

Employment Security Commission Office, 18 Noble Street, Smithfield, NC 27577; 919- 934-0536; Fax: 919- 934-1369.

Wake County, JobLink Career Center, Wake County, Human Services Center, 220 Swinburne St., Raleigh, NC 27620; 919- 250-3770; Fax: 919-212-7045.

JobLink Career Center of Macon County, 427 Harrison Ave., Franklin, NC 28734; 828-369-9534; Fax: 828-369-5166.

JobLink Career Center of Mitchell County, P.O. Box 365, 117 North Mitchell Street, Bakersville, NC 28705; 336-688-2175; Fax: 336-688-4940.

JobLink Career Center of Mitchell County, PO Box 827, 307 Oak Ave., Spruce Pine, NC 28777; 336-765-7758; Fax: 336-765-8552; {Email: Deyton@mitchell.dhr. state.nc.us}.

JobLink Career Center of Surry County, Surry County Community College, P.O. Box 304, 630 South Main St., Dobson, NC 27017; 336-386-8121, ext. 268; Fax: 336-386-8951; {Email: BullinA@surry.cc.nc.us}.

JobLink Career Center of Vance County, 945-G West Andrews Ave., Henderson, NC 27536; 252-438-7324; Fax: 252-438-8766; {Email: Alvarado.daniel@esc.state.nc.us}.

JobLink Career Center of Wayne County, 309 North William St., Goldsboro, NC 27534; 919-731-7950; Fax: 919-731-7967; {Email: Pate.William@esc.state.nc.us}.

JobLink Career Center of Alleghany County, P.O. Box 280, 348 South Main St., Suite C, Sparta, NC 28358; 336-372-9675; Fax: 336-372-4306.

JobLink Career Center of Beaufort County, 1 Harding Square, Washington, NC 27889; 252-946-3116; 800-799-9194; Fax: 252-946-8700; {Email: Wdorsey@coastalnet. com}.

JobLink Career Center of Burke County, 720 East Union St., Morganton, NC 28655; 828-438-6161; Fax: 828-438-6207; {Email: Pettus.Linda@esc.state.nc.us}.

JobLink Career Center of Durham County, 1105 S. Briggs Ave., Durham, NC 27703; 919-560-6880, ext. 210; Fax: 919-560-3387; {Email: Keefe.Kathy@esc.state. nc.us}.

JobLink Career Center of Hoke County, 113 E. Elwood Ave., Raeford, NC 28376; 910-875-5050; Fax: 910-875-2125.

Sampson County One-Stop Service Center, Sampson Community College, P.O. Box 318, Clinton, NC 28329; 910-592-8081.

JobLink Career Center

JobLink Career Center of Wilkes County, Wilkes Community College, P.O. Box 120, Wilkesboro, NC 28697; 336-838-6100; Fax: 336-838-6198.

JobLink Career Center of Edgecombe County, 121 Fairview Rd., Rocky Mount, NC 27802; 252-977-3306; Fax: 252-446-272; {Email: Rogers.Steve@ esc.state.nc.us}

JobLink Career Center of Martin County, 200 Green St., Williamston, NC 27892; 252-792-7816; Fax: 252-792-2479.

JobLink Career Center of Robeson County, 118 West 5th St., Lumberton, NC 28358; 910-618-5500; Fax: 910-618-5570; {Email: Jones. Anderson@ esc. state.nc.us}.

JobLink Career Center of Scotland County, 303 North Main St., Laurinburg, NC 28352; 910-276-4260; Fax: 910-277-2628; {Email: Graham. Burnest@ esc. state.nc.us}.

JobLink Career Center of Transylvania County, 40 Gaston St., Brevard, NC 28712; 828-884-3214; Fax: 828-884-3525.

JobLink Career Center of Anson County, 720 East Union St., Wadesboro, NC 28170; 704-694-655; Fax: 704-694-9070; {Email: Thomas.JoAnn@esc.state.nc.us}.

JobLink Career Center of Bladen County, P.O. Box 266, 7418 Hwy. 41W, Dublin, NC 28332; 910-862-2164, ext. 232; Fax: 910-862-7424.

JobLink Career Center, Southeastern Community College, Building-A, P.O. Box 151, 4564 Chadbourn Hwy., Whiteville, NC 28472; 910-642-7141, ext. 261, Fax: 910-642-5658; {Email: cwayne@mail.southeast.cc.nc.us}.

JobLink Career Center of Davidson County, P.O. Box 1287, 197 DCCC Rd., Lexington, NC 27295; 336-249-8186, ext. 245; Fax: 336-249-2386.

JobLink Career Center of Forsyth County, Winston-Salem JobLink Career Center, 516 N. Trade St., Winston-Salem, NC 27101; 336-727-2886; Fax: 339-748-3303; {Email: JennifeP@ci.winston-salem.nc.us}.

JobLink Career Center of Haywood County, 1511 North Main St., Waynesville, NC 28786; 828-456-6061; Fax: 828-452-1430; {Email: cooke.elizabeth@esc.state.nc.us}.

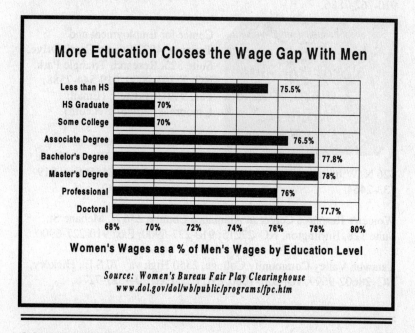

More Education Closes the Wage Gap With Men

Women's Wages as a % of Men's Wages by Education Level

Education Level	Percentage
Less than HS	75.5%
HS Graduate	70%
Some College	70%
Associate Degree	76.5%
Bachelor's Degree	77.8%
Master's Degree	78%
Professional	76%
Doctoral	77.7%

Source: Women's Bureau Fair Play Clearinghouse
www.dol.gov/dol/wb/public/programs/fpc.htm

JobLink Career Center of Lenoir County, Lenoir Community College, P.O. Box 188, Kinston, NC 28502; 252-527-6223ext 126; 252-527-7320; Fax: 252-527-7320.

JobLink Career Center of McDowell County, 35 South Main Street, Marion, NC 28752; 828-659-6001; Fax: 828-659-8733; {Email: Jbroome@ joblink. mcdowell.cc.nc.us}

JobLink Career Center of Nash County, 121 Fairview Rd., Rocky Mount, NC 27802; 252-977-3306; Fax: 252-446-2720; {Email: Rogers.Steve@ esc.state.nc.us}.

JobLink Career Center of Pitt County, Pitt Community College, P.O. Drawer 7007, Hwy 11 So. - Vernon Bldg., Room #1, Greenville, NC 27835; 252-321-4534; Fax: 252-312-4553; {Email: rogers.leslie.pitt@dcc001.ncdcc}.

North Carolina Women Work!, Lois Cook Steele, President, YWCA of Wilmington NC, Inc., 245 South 17 Street, Wilmington, NC 28401; 910-762-7886.

Center for Employment and Training, 4022 Stirrup Creek Drive, Suite 325, Research Triangle Park, NC 27703-9000; 919-544-7588; Fax: 919-361-1328; {Email: t_moore@ cetmail.cfet.com}.

North Carolina Council for Women, Merrimon-Wynne House, 526 N. Wilmington St., Raleigh, NC 27604; 919-733-2455; Fax: 919-733-2464.

Women's Resource Center in Alamance County, 236 N. Mebane St., Suite 128, Burlington, NC 27215; 910-227-6900; Fax: 910-227-6900.

Catawba Valley Community College, 2550 Highway 70 S.E., Hickory, NC 28602-9699; 704-327-7000, ext. 222; Fax: 704-327-7276.

Reach, P.O. Box 977, Murphy, NC 29806; 704-837-8064; Fax: 704-837-2097.

Cleveland County Abuse Prevention, P.O. Box 2895, Shelby, NC 28151-2895; 704-487-9325; Fax: 704-487-9325.

Southeastern Community College, P.O. Box 151, Whiteville, NC 28472; 910-642-7141; Fax: 910-642-5658.

Women's Center, P.O. Box 2384, Fayetteville, NC 28302; 910-323-3377; 800-849-8519; Fax: 910-323-8828.

Outer Banks Hotline Inc., P.O. Box 1417, Manteo, NC 27954; 919-473-5121; Fax: 919-473-4895.

Winston-Forsyth County Council for Women, 660 West 5th St., Winston-Salem, NC 27101; 910-727-8409; Fax: 910-727-2549.

N.C. Cooperative Extension Service, P.O. Box 46, Gatesville, NC 27938; 919-357-1400; Fax: 919-357-1167.

Women's Resource Center, 623 Summit Avenue, Greensboro, NC 27405; 910-275-6090; Fax: 910-275-7069.

Cooperative Extension Service, P.O. Box 37, Halifax, NC 27839; 919-583-5161; Fax: 919-583-1683.

Connie Piland, Roanoke-Chowan SAFE, P.O. Box 98, Ahoskie, NC 27910; 919-332-4047; Fax: 919-332-2155.

REACH of Jackson County, P.O. Box 1828, Sylva, NC 28779; 704-586-8968; Fax: 704-586-2155.

Mecklenburg County Women's Commission, 700 N. Tryon Street, Charlotte, NC 28202; 704-336-3784; Fax: 704-336-4449.

YWCA, 22 S. 17th Street, Wilmington, NC 28401; 910-762-7886;
Fax: 910-762-7885.

Orange County Women's Center, 210 Henderson Street, Chapel Hill,
NC 27514; 919-968-4610, Fax: 919-932-3125.

Pamlico Community College,
P.O. Box 185, Grantsboro,
NC 28529; 919-249-
1851; Fax: 919-249-
2377.

Albemarle HOPELINE,
P.O. Box 2064, Elizabeth
City, NC 27906-2064; 919-
338-5338.

Pitt County Violence Program Inc., P.O. Box 8429, Greenville, NC
27835; 919-758-4400; Fax: 919-752-4197.

Family Resources Center, P.O. Box 845, Spingdale, NC 28160; 704-
286-3411; Fax: 704-286-3417.

Tri-County Women's Resource Center, P.O. Box 1265, Mount Airy,
NC 27030; 910-789-3500; Fax: 910-789-8545.

Swain/Qualla SAFE Inc., P.O. Box 1416, Bryson City, NC 28713;
704-488-9038; Fax: 704-488-9038.

The Women's Center, 128 E. Hargett Street, Raleigh, NC 27601; 919-
829-3711; Fax: 919-829-9960.

The Women's Center, P.O. Box 1057, 210 Henderson St., Chapel Hill,
NC 27514; 919-968-4610.

North Carolina Division for Training Initiative, Division for Training
Initiative, North Carolina Department of Labor, 4 W. Edenton St.,
Raleigh, NC 27601; 919-715-0344.

North Dakota

One-Stop Career Center: Job Service North Dakota, P.O. Box 5507, Bismarck, ND 58506-5507; 800-732-9787; 701-328-2868; TTY; 800-366-6888; Fax: 701-328-4193; {www.state.nd.us/jsnd/lmi.htm}; {Email: jsndweb@ pioneer. state.nd.us}.

Department of Labor: Job Service North Dakota, P.O. Box 5507, Bismarck, ND 58506-5507; 701-328-2868; {www.state. nd.us/jsnd/lmi.htm}.

Women's Business Institute (WBI), 320 North Fifth Street, Suite 203, P. O. Box 2043, Fargo, ND 58107-2043; 701-235-6488; Fax: 701-235-8284; {Email: wbinstitute@ corpcomm.net}; {www.rrtrade.org/women/wbi}.

ND Women's Business Program, 418 East Broadway, Suite 25, Bismarck, ND 58501; 701-258-2251; Fax: 701-222-8071; {Email: holt@btigate.com}.

Community Action and Development Program, 202 East Villard, Dickinson, ND 58601; 701-227-0131; 800-359-2243.

Ohio

One-Stop Career Center: One-Stop Systems, One-Stop Employment and Training System, Bureau of Employment Services, 145 Front Street, 6th Floor, Columbus, OH 43215; 614-728-8107; Fax: 614-728-9094; {www.state.oh.us/obes/ onestop.html}.

Department of Labor: Ohio Bureau of Employment Services, 145 South Front Street, Columbus, OH 43215; 614-466-4636; {www.state.oh.us/obes}.

Western Reserve Business Center for Women, University of Akron, Community and Technical College, M/185V Polski Building, Room 185, Akron, OH 44325-6002; 330-972-5592; Fax: 330-972-5573; {Email: kdf@uakron.edu}.

Women's Organization for Mentoring, Entrepreneurship & Networking (WOMEN), 526 South Main Street, Suite 235, Akron, OH 44311-1058; 330-379-9280; 330-379-2772; Fax: 330-379-9283; {Email: cherman@womennet.org}; {www.womennet.org}.

Women's Business Resource Program of Southeastern Ohio, Ohio University, 20 East Circle Drive, Suite 155, Technology and Enterprise Building, Athens, OH 45701; 614-593-1797; Fax: 614-593-1795; {Email: aa428@ seorf.ohiou.edu}.

Micro-Business Assistance (MBA) Pyramid Career Services, 2400 Cleveland Avenue North, Canton, OH 44709; 330-453-3767; Fax: 330-453-6079; {Email: pyramid@ezo.net}.

Women Entrepreneurs Inc., Bartlett Building, 36 East 4th Street, Suite 925, Cincinnati, OH 45202; 513-684-0700; Fax: 513-665-2452; {Email: wei@eos.net}.

Glenville Development Corporation Micro-Enterprise Program, 10640 St. Clair Ave., Cleveland, OH 44108; 216-851-8724; Fax: 216-851-8941; {Email: glenville@ interax.com}.

Greater Columbus Women's Business Development Center, 37 North High Street, Columbus, OH 43215-3065; 614-225-6081; 614-225-6082; Fax: 614-469-8250; {Email: linda_steward@ columbus.org}; {www.columbus.org/ busi/sbdc/index.html}.

Ohio Women's Business Resource Network (OWBRN), 77 South High Street, 28th Floor, P. O. Box 1001, Columbus, OH 43215-1001; 614-466-2682; 800-848-1300, ext. 62682; Fax: 614-466-0829; {www.ohiobiz.com}.

Women's Development Center, 42101 Griswold Road, Elyria, OH 44035; 216-324-3688; Fax: 216-324-3689.

Enterprise Center / Women's Business Center, Ohio State University, 1864 Shyville Road, Piketon, OH 45661; 614-289-3727; 800-860-

7232; Fax: 614-292-1953; {Email: enterprise@agvax2.ag.osu.edu};
{www.ag.ohio-state. edu/~prec/}.

Women's Business Center, 42101 Griswold Road, Elyria, OH 44035;
216-324-3688; Fax: 216-324-3689.

Northwest Ohio Women's Entrepreneurial Network, Linda
Fayerweather, Director, 5555 Airport Highway, Suite 210, Toledo, OH
43615; 419-381-7555; Fax: 419-381-7573; {Email: lindafay@
primenet.com}.

EMPOWER Pyramid Career Services, 2400 Cleveland Avenue NW,
Canton, OH 44709; 330-453-3767; Fax: 330-453-6079.

Ohio Women Work! , Marilyn Mead, President, Awareness 101,
Vantage Vocational School, 818 N. Franklin Street, Van Wert, OH
45891; 419-238-5411.

The University of Toledo, Center for Women, Tucker Hall 0168,
Toledo, OH 43606-3390; 419-530-8570; Fax: 419-530-8575; {Email:
ecwomen@utnet.utoledo.edu}; {www. student-affairs.utoledo.edu/
eberly-ctr/index.html}.

Hard Hatted Women of Cleveland, 4207 Lorain Ave., Cleveland, OH
44113; 216-961-4449.

Preparation, Recruitment, Employment Program, Inc., 2261 Francis
Lane, P.O. Box 68018, Cincinnati, OH 45206; 513-221-4700.

Oklahoma

One-Stop Career Center: Oklahoma Workforce Centers, Employment
Security Commission, 218 Will Rogers Building, Oklahoma City, OK
73152; 405-557-7201; {www.oesc.state.ok.us}.

Oklahoma Department of Labor: 4001 North Lincoln Boulevard,
Oklahoma City, OK 73105-5212; 405-528-1500;
{www.oklaosf.state.ok.us/~okdol}.

Women Work! Regional Representative, Region VI, Patty McGuire, Displaced Homemaker Program, High Plains AVTS, 3921 34th Street, Woodward, OK 73801-0009; 405-571-6149; Fax: 405-571-6190.

Women's Business Center, Working Women's Money University (WWMU), 234 Quadrum Drive, Oklahoma City, OK 73108; 405-232-8257; Fax: 405-947-5388; 405-842-5067; {Email: lori@wbc-okc.org}; {Email: charlotte@wbc-okc.org}.

El Reno Center, 6505 East Highway 66, El Reno, OK 73036; 405-262-2629.

Mid-America Vo-Tech, Counseling Office, Box H, Wayne, OK 73095; 405-449-3391; Fax: 405-449-3395; {cust.iamerica.net/mavotech/service.html}.

Nontraditional/Careers Unlimited Program, Nontraditional Advisor, Francis Tuttle Vo-Tech Center, 12777 N. Rockwell, Oklahoma City, OK 73142-2710; 405-720-4356.

Single Parent/Homemaker Program, Oklahoma Dept. of Vocational and Technical Education, 1500 W. Seventh Ave., Stillwater, OK 74074-4364; 403-793-6162; 405-377-2000.

Oregon

One-Stop Career Center: Oregon Career Network, Oregon Employment Department, 875 Union Street, NE, Salem, OR 97311; 503-947-1470; {www.emp.state.or.us}; {Email: info@emp.state.or.us}.

Department of Labor: Oregon Employment Department, 875 Union Street NE, Salem, OR 97311; 503-947-1391; {www.emp.state.or.us/agency.htm}.

Women Work! Regional Representative, Region X, Sandy Nelson, The New Workforce, Chemeketa Community College, Building 20, 4000 Lancaster Dr., N.E., Salem, OR 97305-1453; 503-399-6554; Fax: 503-399-2580.

Southern Oregon Women's Access to Credit (SOWAC), 33 North
Central, Suite 209, Medford, OR 97501; 541-779-3992; Fax: 541-779-
5195; {Email: jasmith@sowac.org}; {Email: geninf@sowac.org};
{www.sowac.org}.

ONABEN - A Native American Business Network, 520 Southwest 6th
Avenue, Suite 930, Portland, OR 97204; 503-243-5015; Fax: 503-243-
5028; {Email: borunda@bonaben.org}; {www.onaben.org}.

Newmark Center: Adult Learning Skills Program, Southwestern
Oregon Community College, 1988 Newmark, Coos Bay, OR 97420;
503-888-7121; Fax: 503-888-7120; {www.teleport.com/~ctrc2004/
oww/newmar.htm}.

Building Futures in Industry and Trades (BFIT), P.O. Box 19000,
Portland, OR 97280-0880; 503-614-7255, ext. 7449.

Pennsylvania

One-Stop Career Center: Pennsylvania Works, Department of Labor
and Industry, 1720 Labor and Industry Building, Seventh and Foster
Street, Harrisburg, PA 17120; 717-783-1115; {http://pacareerlink.
state.pa.us/homeframe.asp}.

Department of Labor: Pennsylvania Department of Labor and Industry,
1700 Labor and Industry Building, Harrisburg, PA 17120; 707-787-
5279; {www.li.state.pa.us}.

Pennsylvania Women Work!, Janice Himes, New Options, Bradford
High School, 81 Interstate Parkway, Bradford, PA 16701; 814-362-
6188; {Email: jmhst88@pop.pitt.edu}.

HomeCare Associates, 1314 Chestnut St., Philadelphia, PA 19107;
215-735-0677.

Women's Business Development Center (WBDC), 1315 Walnut St.,
Suite 1116, Philadelphia, PA 19107-4711; 215-790-9232; Fax: 215-
790-9231; {Email: wbdc@erols.com}.

Community Women's Education Project, 2801 Frankford Ave., Philadelphia, PA 19134; 215-426-2200; Fax: 215-426-3284; {Email: CWEP@ nni.com}; {http://users. nni. com/ cwep}.

OPTIONS, 225 S. 15th Street, Suite 1635, Philadelphia, PA 19102-3916; 215-735-2202; Fax: 215-735-8097; {Email: Info@ optionscareers.com}.

Tradeswomen of Purpose/Women in Nontraditional Work, 2300 Alter Street, Philadelphia, PA 19146; 215-545-3700 (PA); 609-728-5931 (NJ); Fax: 215-545-8713.

Puerto Rico

Women's Business Institute (WBI), Universidad Del Sagrado Corazon, (The University of the Sacred Heart), Center for Women's Entrepreneurial Development, P. O. Box 12383, San Juan, PR 00914-0383; 787-728-1515, ext. 2560 ; 787-726-7045; Fax: 787-726-7077; {Email: womenbiz@caribe.net or carms@caribe.net}.

Rhode Island

One-Stop Career Center: NetWorkri, Department of Labor and Training, 101 Friendship Street, Providence, RI 02903-3740; 401-222-3722; Fax: 401-222-2731; {www.networkri.org}.

Department of Labor: Rhode Island Department of Labor and Training, 101 Friendship Street, Providence, RI 02903-3740; 401-277-3600; {www.det.state.ri.us}.

South Carolina

One-Stop Career Center: 1 Stop Partnership, Employment Security Commission, P.O. Box 995, 1550 Gadsden Street, Columbia, SC 29202; 803-737-9935; Fax: 803-737-0202; {www.sces.org/1stop/ 1stopmain.htm}; {Email: jobs@ sces.org}.

Department of Labor: South Carolina Department of Labor, Licensing and Regulation, Public Information Office, 110 Centerview Drive, P.O. Box 11329, Columbia, SC 29211-1329; {www.llr.state.sc.us}.

South Carolina Women Work!, Gilda Kennedy, President, South Carolina Dept. Of Social Services, 3150 Harden Street, Columbia, SC 29204; 803-737-4430.

Center for Women Entrepreneurs, Columbia College of South Carolina, 1301 Columbia College Drive, Columbia, SC 29203; 803-786-3582; Fax: 803-786-3804; {Email: susdavis@colacoll.edu or smckee@colacoll.edu}; {www.colacoll.edu}.

South Dakota

One-Stop Career Center: JobsService of South Dakota, Department of Labor, Kneip Building, 700 Governors Drive, Pierre, SD 57501-2291; 605-773-3101; Fax: 605-773-4211; {www.state.us/dol/sdjob/ js-home.htm}; {Email: infor@dol-pr.state.sd.us}.

South Dakota Department of Labor: 700 Governors Drive, Pierre, SD 57501-2291; 605-773-3101; {www.state.sd. us/dol/dol.htm}.

The Entrepreneur's Network for Women (ENW), 100 South Maple, P.O. Box 81, Watertown, SD 57201; 605-882-5080; Fax: 605-882-5069.

Watertown Area Career Learning Center, The Entrepreneur Network for Women (ENW), Career Specialist/Financial Officer, 100 S. Maple, P.O. Box 81, Watertown, SD 57201-0081; 605-882-5080; Fax: 605-882-5069; {Email: network4women@basec.net}; {www.network4women. com}.

South Dakota Women Work! , Connie Hermann, President, SP/DH Program, Northwest Area Schools Multi-District, 100 E. Utah Street, P.O. Box 35, Isabel, SD 57633-0035; 605-466-2206; {Email: conniehermann@hotmail.com}.

Career Learning Center, 1310 South Main Ave., Brookings, SD 57006; 605-688-4370.

Tennessee

One-Stop Career Center: Tennessee Career Center, Office of Workforce Development, Andrew Johnson Building, 8th Floor, 710 James Robertson Parkway, Nashville, TN 37243; 615-253-1324; Fax: 615-253-1329; {www.owd. state.tn.us/index.html}; {Email: jfite@mail.state.tn.us}.

Tennessee Department of Labor: 2nd Floor Andrew Johnson Tower, 710 James Robertson Parkway, Nashville, TN 37213-0658; 615-741-2582; {www.state.tn.us/labor}.

Women in Trades, YWCA of Greater Memphis, 1044 Mississippi Blvd., Memphis, TN 38126; 901-942-4653.

The National Association for Women Business Owners - Nashville Chapter (NAWBO), P.O. Box 101024, Nashville, TN 37224; 615-248-3474; Fax: 615-256-2706; {Email: tnwrc@bellsouth.net}.

Tennessee Women Work!, LaSherrie McKinnie, President, West Tennessee Area Health Education Center, 295 S. Belle View, Memphis, TN 38104; 901-274-9009.

Shelby State Community College New Horizons Program, Building F, Room 309, 737 Beale St., P.O. Box 40568, Memphis, TN 38174-0568; 901-544-5063; Fax: 901-544-5480; {www.jericho.org/_sscc_nh.html}.

Texas

One-Stop Career Center: Texas Workforce Information System (TWIST), Texas Workforce Commission, 101 East 15th Street, Austin, TX 78778; 512-463-6438; {www.twc. state.tx.us}; {Email: ombudsman@twc. state.tx.us}.

Department of Labor: Texas Workforce Commission, 101 East 15th Street, Austin, TX 78778; 512-463-2222; {www.twc.state.tx.us}.

Texas Center for Women's Business Enterprise (TXCWBE), Two Commodore Plaza, 13th Floor, 206 East 9th Street, Suite 13.140, Austin, TX 78701; Mailing Address: P.O. Box 340219, Austin, TX 78734-0219; 512-261-8525; 512-499-3083; {Email: txcwbe@ onr.com}; {www.onr.com/ CWE}.

Center for Employment and Training, 10102 North Loop Dr., Socorro, TX 79927; 915-859-1070; Fax: 915-860-9089; {Email: s_avila@cetmail.cfet.org}.

North Texas Women's Business Development Center Inc., 1402 Corinth Street, Suite 1536, Dallas, TX 75215-2111; 214-428-1177; Fax: 214-428-4633; {Email: women@ onramp.net}.

Texas Women Work!, Student Support Services, Central Texas College, P.O. Box 1800, Killeen, TX 76540; 254-526-1291; {Email: mlevando@ctcd.cc.tx.us}.

Richland College, Adult Resource Center, Dallas County Community College District, 12800 Abrams Road, Dallas, TX 75243-2199; 972-238-6106; {www.rlc.dcccd. edu/ ce/ARC/WorkWon. html}.

Single Parent / Displaced Homemaker Services, McLennan Community College, Career Development Office, 1400 College Drive, Waco, TX 76708; 254-299-8614; 254-299-8414.

South Central Texas Regional Training Center, Career Advancement Programs and Training, Texas Engineering Extension Service, 9350 S. Presa, San Antonio, TX 78223; 210-633-1000; or Texas Engineering

Extension Service, P.O. Box 40, San Antonio, TX 78291; 210-208-9300.

Women in Technology, P.O. Box 20500, El Paso, TX 79998; 915-831-5085.

Jobs NOW, Women's Center of Tarrant County, Inc., P.O. Box 11860, 1723 Hemphill, Fort Worth, TX 76110; 817-927-4050.

Utah

One-Stop Career Center: Career Centers, Department of Workforce Services, 140 East 300 South, Salt Lake City, UT 84111; 801-531-3780; Fax: 801-531-3785; {www. dws. state.ut.us/default.htm}; {Email: www@ dwsa. state.ut.us}.

Department of Labor: Utah Department of Workforce Services, P.O. Box 45249, Salt Lake City, UT 84145-0249; 801-526-9675; {http://dwsa.state.ut.us}.

Utah Technology Finance Corporation, 177 East 100 South, Salt Lake City, UT 84111; 801-364-1521, ext. 3; Fax: 801-364-4361.

Women's Business Center at the Chamber, Salt Lake Area Chamber of Commerce, 175 East 400 South, Suite 600, Salt Lake City, UT 84111; 801-328-5051; Fax: 801-328-5098; {Email: ramona@ slachamber. com}; {www. slachamber.com}.

Information, Utah Valley State College, 800 West 1200 South, Orem, UT 84058; 801-222-8000; {Email: info@ uvsc.edu}.

Vermont

One-Stop Career Center: One-Stop Career Resource, Department of Employment and Training, Division of Jobs and Training, 5 Green Mountain Drive, P.O. Box 488, Montpelier, VT 05602; 802-828-4000; TDD: 802-828-4203; Fax: 802-828-4022; {www.det.state.vt.us}.

Department of Labor: Vermont Department of Employment and Training, 5 Green Mountain Drive, P.O. Box 488, Montpelier, VT 05601-0488; 802-229-1157; {www.det. state.ut.us}.

Department of Economic Development, National Life Building, Drawer 20, Montpelier, VT 05620-0501; 802-828-3221, 800-341-2211; Fax: 802-828-3258; {www.state. vt.us/dca/economic/developm.htm}.

Virginia

One-Stop Career Center: Workforce Development System, Employment Commission, P.O. Box 1358, Richmond, VA 23218-1358; 804-786-4832; Fax: 804-786-6091; {www.vec.state.va.us/seeker/seeker.htm}; {Email: vaemployment@aol.com).

Department of Labor: Virginia Department of Labor and Industry, Powers-Taylor Building, 13 South Thirteenth Street, Richmond, VA 23219; 804-371-2327; {www.dli.state.va.us}.

PVCC, 501 College Drive, Room 206, Charlottesville, VA 22902 804-961-5228; Fax: 804-961-5224.

FOCUS, 1508 Grady Ave., Charlottesville, VA 22903; 804-977-5627; 804-977-2662; Fax: 804-977-3495; {Email: cpg20d@pvcc.cc.va.us}; {http://piedmontworks.org/ women.htm}.

Center for Employment and Training, 2762 Duke St., Alexandria, VA 22314; 703-461-9767; Fax: 703-461-9761; {Email: d_jroosa@cetmail.cfet.org}.

Washington

One-Stop Career Center: Washington One-Stop Career Center System, Employment Security Department, 212 Maple Park, P.O. Box 9046, Olympia, WA 98507-9046; 360-438-4611; 360-438-3224; {www.wa.gov/esd/1stop}, {Email: btarrow@esd.wa.gov}.

Department of Labor: Washington Workforce Training and Education Coordinating Board, Building 17 Airdustrial Park, Olympia, WA 98504-3105; 360-753-5662; {www.wa.gov/wtb/}.

Department of Community, Trade And Economic Development, 906 Columbia St. SW, P.O. Box 48300, Olympia, WA 98504-8300; 800-237-1233; {http://access.wa.gov}.

ONABEN - A Native American Business Network, 3201 Broadway, Suite C, Everett, WA 98201; 425-339-6226; Fax: 425-339-9171; {Email: sonya@onaben.org}; {www.onaben.org}.

Impact!, Walla Walla Community College/Clarkston Center, 1470 Bridge Street, Clarkston, WA 99403; 509-58-1716; Fax: 509-758-9512.

Lifestyles Displaced Homemaker Program

Columbia Basin College, 2600 North 20th Avenue, Pasco, WA 99301; 509-47-0511, ext. 357; Fax: 509-546-0401; {www.cbc2.org/}.

Lifestyles Displaced Homemaker Program, YWCA of Wenatchee Valley, 212 First Street, Wenatchee, WA 98801; 509-662-3531; Fax: 509-663-7721.

Southwest Washington Regional Displaced Homemaker Center, Clark College, 1800 East McLoughlin Blvd., Vancouver, WA 98663; 360-992-2321; 360-992-2366; Fax: 360-992-2878; {Email: bmerritt@gaiser.clark.edu}; {www.clark.edu/StudentServices/ StudentSupport Services/Displaced/}.

YWCA of Clark County, 3609 Main St., Vancouver WA 98663-2225; 360-696-0167; Fax: 360-693-1864

Lower Columbia College, 1600 Maple Street, P.O. Box 3010, Longview, WA 98632-0310; 360-577-3429; Fax: 360-578-5470; {http://lcc. ctc.edu/}.

Lower Columbia Community Action Council, 1526 Commerce Avenue, Longview, WA 98632; 360-425-3430; Fax: 360-425-6657.

Lifestyles Displaced Homemaker Program, YWCA of Wenatchee Valley, 212 First Street, Wenatchee, WA 98801; 509-662-3531; Fax: 509-663-7721.

Yakima Valley Community College, P.O. Box 1647 (16th and Nob Hill), Yakima, WA 98907; 509-574-4976; Fax: 509-574-4731; {www.yvcc.cc.wa.us/}.

Pierce College Women's Center, Fort Steilacoom Campus, Room 300J, 9401 Farwest Drive SW, Lakewood, WA 98498-1999; 253-964-6298; {www.pierce.ctc.edu/Users/Depts/Womenctr/main.htm}.

Turning Point, Skagit Valley College, 2405 East College Way, Mount Vernon, WA 98273; 360-416-7762; Fax: 360-416-7890.

Southwest Washington Regional Displaced Homemaker Center, Clark College, 1800 East McLoughlin Blvd., Vancouver, WA 98663; 360-992-2321; Fax: 360-992-2878.

YWCA of Clark County, 3609 Main Street, Vancouver WA 98663-2225; 360-696-0167; Fax: 360-693-1864.

Pathways for Women YWCA, 6027-208th Street SW, Lynnwood, WA 98036; 425-774-9843; ext. 223; Fax: 425-670-8510; {www.ywcaworks.org/snohomish.html} and {www.housinglink.com/}.

Edmonds Community College, 20000 68th Ave West, Lynnwood, WA 98036-5999; 425-640-1309; Fax: 425-771-3366; {www.edcc.edu/WomensPrograms.htm}.

ChangePoint, Community Colleges of Spokane, 3305 W. Ft. George Wright Drive, Spokane, WA 99224-5228; 509-533-3760; Fax: 509-533-3226.

Southwest Washington Regional Displaced Homemaker Center, Clark College, 1800 East McLoughlin Blvd., Vancouver, WA 98663; 360-992-2321; Fax: 360-992-2878.

Turning Point, Whatcom Community College, 237 W. Kellogg Road, Bellingham, WA 98226; 360-384-1541; Fax: 360-676-2171.

WA State Migrant Council, 301 N 1st Street, Sunnyside, WA 98944; 509-544-0904; 800-234-4615; Fax: 509-544-0922.

Downtown Human Services Council, 115 Prefontaine Pl. South, Seattle, WA 98104; 206-461-3865.

DSHS, Dept. of Vocational Rehabilitation, 1700 East Cherry St., Seattle, WA 98122; 206-720-3200.

El Centro de la Raza, 2524 16th Ave. South, Seattle, WA 98144; 206-329-7960.

Urban League of Metropolitan Seattle, 105 14th Ave., Seattle, WA 98116; 206-461-3792

United Indians of All Tribes Foundation, 1945 Yale Pl. SE, Seattle, WA 98102; 206-325-0070.

Women & Family Center, Millionaire Club, 113 1st Ave. North, Seattle, WA 98109; 206-301-0833.

YWCA, Employment Service, 118 5th Ave., Seattle, WA 98101; 206-461-4448 (voice mail).

YWCA, West Seattle Center, 4800 40th SW, Seattle, WA 98116; 206-461-4485.

YWCA, East Cherry, Employment Services, 2820 East Cherry, Seattle, WA 98112; 206-461-4882.

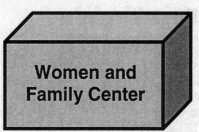

ANEW, Apprenticeship and Nontraditional Employment for Women, P.O. Box 2490, 3000 NE 4th Street, Renton, WA 98056; 206-235-2212.

Center for Career Alternatives (CCA), 901 Rainier Ave. South, Seattle, WA 98144; 206-322-9080.

Homeless Employment Project, 2106 2nd Ave., Seattle, WA 98121.

Pacific Associates, 2200 6th Ave., Suite 260, Seattle, WA 98121; 206-728-8826.

Pioneer Human Services, Pioneer Industries, 7000 Highland Parkway SW, Seattle, WA 98106; 206-762-7737.

Seattle Indian Center, 611 12th Ave. South, Suite 300, Seattle, WA 98144; 206-329-8700.

Washington Works, 616 1st Ave., Fifth Floor, Seattle, WA 98104; 206-343-9731.

Apprenticeship and Nontraditional Employment for Women, P.O. Box 2490, Renton, WA 98056; 425-235-2212.

Women in Transition: Strategies and Options for Change, Lower Columbia College, P.O. Box 3010, Longview, WA 98632-0310; 360-577-3429.

West Virginia

One-Stop Career Center: Job Service, Bureau of Employment Programs, Jobs/Job Training, 112 California Avenue, Charleston, WV 25305-0112; 304-558-1138; Fax: 304-558-1136; {www.state. wv.us/bep/jobs/default.HTM}; {Email: haydep@wvnvm.wvnet.edu}.

Department of Labor: West Virginia Bureau of Employment Programs, 112 California Avenue, Charleston, WV 25305-0112; 304-558-2630; {www.state.wv.us/bep}.

Center for Economic Options, Inc., 601 Delaware Avenue, Charleston, WV 25302; 304-345-1298; Fax: 304-342-0641; {Email: wvmcoptns@ citynet.net}; {www.centerforeconoptions.org/}.

Educational Outreach Counselor, Bluefield State College - Conley Hall Room 307, 219 Rock Street, Bluefield, WV 24701; 304-327-4500; {Email: rdishner@bscvax.wvnet.edu }; {www.bluefield.wvnet. edu/}.

Technical Schools
Putnam County Technical School, P.O. Box 640, Eleanor, WV 25070; 304-586-3494
Cabell County Vocational School, 1035 Norway Ave., Huntington, WV 25705; 304-528-5172
Monongalia County Technical Education Center, 1000 Mississippi St., Morgantown, WV 26505; 304-291-9240.

State Department of Education, Sex Equity, Bldg. 6, Room 230, 1900 Kanawha Blvd. East, Charleston, WV 25305.

Multicap Employment Training, P.O. Box 3228, Charleston, WV 25332; 304-342-6100.

Wisconsin

One-Stop Career Center: Partnership for Full Employment (PFE), Department of Workforce Development, 201 East Washington Avenue, P.O. Box 7946, Madison, WI 53707-7946; 608-266-3131; Fax: 608-261-7979; {www.dwd.state.wi.us/dwepfe/}; {Email: DWDINFO@dwd.state.wi.us}.

Department of Labor: Wisconsin Department of Workforce Development, 201 East Washington Avenue, P.O. Box 7946, Madison, WE 53707-7946; 608-267-4400; {www.dwd.state.wi.us}.

Wisconsin Women Work! , Barbara Schall, President, Moraine Park Technical College, 2151 North Main St., West Bend, WI 53090; 414-335-5770; {Email: bschall@moraine.tec.wi.us}.

Employment Options, Inc., 2095 Winnebago Street, Madison, WI 53704; 608-244-5181.

Nontraditional Employment Training Program, YWCA of Greater Milwaukee, 101 E. Pleasant, Milwaukee, WI 53212; 414-224-9080.

Wisconsin Women's Business Initiative Corporation, 2821 N. Fourth Street, Milwaukee, WI 53212; 414-263-5450; Fax: 414-263-5456; or WWBIC - Madison Office, 217 S. Hamilton Street, Suite 201, Madison, WI 53703; 608-257-7409; Fax: 608-257-7429; {Email: info@wwbic.com}; {www.wwbic.com}; {www.onlinewbc.org}.

C4 Dane County Career Center, 4513 Vernon Blvd., #208, Madison, WI 53715; Diane Kraus, Coordinator; 608-232-2870; Fax: 608-232-2866; {Email: krause@cesa2. k12.wi.us}.

Fox Cities Career Connection, 1239 Valley Fair Mall, Appleton, WI 54915; 920-831-1155; Fax: 920-831-1156; {Email: career-connection@athenet.net }.

Green Bay Careers 2000, 2740 W. Mason Street, P.O. Box 19042, Green Bay, WI 54307-9042; 920-498-6833; Fax: 920-498-6869; {Email: gbcc@netnet.net}.

Milwaukee Career Center, 219 Milwaukee Street, Milwaukee, WI
53202; 414-226-2440; Fax: 414-226-0318; {Email:
mbeers@milwjobs.com}

Northwest Career Counseling
Network, 618 Beaser Avenue,
Ashland, WI 54606; 715-682-2363;
Fax: 715-682-7244; {Email:
jeanettep@cesa12.k12.wi.us}.

Racine Career Discovery Center,
1717 Taylor Ave., Racine, WI 53403;
414-638-6432; Fax: 414-638-6782;
{Email: lland@racineco.com}.

Watertown Career Center, 825 Endeavour Dr., Watertown, WI 53098;
920-262-7515; Fax: 920-262-7545; {Email: sandbergc@watertown.
k12.wi.us}.

Waukesha County Community Career Center, 892 Main Street, Suite
C, Pewaukee, WI 53072-5811; 414-695-7848; Fax: 414-695-7865;
{Email: jpritchett@waukesha.tec.wi.us}.

Northcentral Wisconsin Career Center, 1200 W. Wausau Ave.,
Wausau, WI 54401; 715-261-3227; Fax: 715-261-3260; {Email:
jwestpha@kennedy.wausau.k12.wi.us}.

West Bend Career InfoNet, 120 North Main Street, West Bend, WI
53095; 414-338-3860; Fax: 414-338-1771; {Email:
joe@job.careernet.org }.

Western Wisconsin Career Exploration Link, WWTC, R120, 400 N.
7th St., LaCrosse, WI 54602-2908; 608-789-7890; 800-59-LINK UP,
Fax: 608-789-6320; {Email: leahyb@email.western.tec.wi.us}

Reentry Transition Program, Moraine Park Technical College, 235
North National Ave., P.O. Box 1940, Fond Du Lac, WI 54936-1940;
920-922-8611.

Women School, Creative Technology Options Workshops, Blackhawk Technical College, 6004 Prairie Rd., Janesville, WI 53547; 608-757-7752.

The Opportunity Center, Western Wisconsin Technical College, 304 N. 6th St., P.O. Box C-908, La Crosse, WI 54602-0908; 608-785-9436.

Electronics are our Future, Women's Development Center, Waukeska County Technical College, 800 Main St., Pewaukee, WI 53072; 414-691-5400.

Wyoming

One-Stop Career Center: Employment Resource Centers, Department of Employment, Employment Resource Division, 100 West Midwest, Casper, WY 82602; 307-235-3254; {http://wydoe.state.wy.us/erd}.

Department of Labor: Wyoming Department of Employment, 122 West 25th Street, Cheyenne, WY 82002; 307-777-7672; {http://wydoe.state.wy.us/}.

State of Wyoming, Workforce Development Council, Herschler Building, 2 East, Cheyenne, WY; 307-777-3465; Fax: 307-777-5857

Employment Resources Division, P.O. Box 2760, 100 West Midwest, Casper, WY 82602-2760; 307-235-3254; Fax: 307-235-3278

Department of Employment, 122 West 25th Street, Herschler Building, 2nd Floor East, Cheyenne, WY 82002; 307-777-6402; Fax: 307-777-5805; or Department of Employment, Division of Employment Resources, P.O. Box 2760, Casper, WY 82620; 307-235-3254; Fax: 307-235-3278.

Wyoming Women's Center, 1000 West Griffith, P.O. Box 20, Lusk, WY 82225; 307-334-3693; Fax: 307-334-2254; {wydoe.state.wy.us/wcwi/}.

APPENDIX

Don't know who to call or where to turn for assistance? Never fear; the Appendix is here! This is a state-by-state listing of starting places for any problem, concern, or issue you may have. We have included address, phone number and website wherever possible. Each listing should be able to either answer your question or direct you to an office near you. Happy hunting!

The *Federal Information Center* can connect you with the appropriate federal government agency that handles your topic of interest.

The *State Information Operator* can connect you to the correct state government office that can answer your question.

State Departments on Aging focus on issues and concerns of the senior population. If you are looking for nutrition, transportation, housing, financial assistance, nursing home resources, or anything else having to do with seniors, then contact this office. They will direct you to local services and resources, as well as tell you about programs offered by the state.

Attorney General's Offices have Consumer Protection Offices where you can call to complain or seek assistance for a problem dealing with a business in the state. Many of these offices have special automobile hotlines that handle car complaints.

Information USA, Inc.

Banking Commissioners are in charge of state banks. If you feel a state bank has not treated you fairly or you would like to do research on a bank before you hand over your life savings, then call the Banking Commissioner.

Child Care and Development Block Grant Agencies give money to states to help families meet their child care needs. Each state sets up their eligibility requirements and programs offered. To find out what your state provides in the way of child care assistance contact this office.

Child Support Enforcement Agencies are the people to contact if your ex has not been paying all of the child support payment. These offices can help track down your ex and get what you are owed — even across state lines.

The *Cooperative Extension Service* has offices located in almost every county across the U.S. and has a wealth of information regarding finances, child care, home economics, gardening, and more. Many operate special horticulture hotlines where you can find information concerning your garden, plants, and grass. They offer free or cheap courses and publications in cooking, sewing, financial planning and more.

Corporation Division Offices are the people that incorporate businesses in their state. If you are starting a business, you need to talk to this office. If you have a concern about a corporation in your state, they can provide you with information about the corporation's status. You can also find out who owes money to whom through the Uniform Commercial Code.

Day Care Licensing Agencies license daycare facilities in the state. Each state has their own rules the agencies must follow. Contact this agency to learn if a child care setting has had any violations or problems, and to inquire about the rules and regulations they must follow.

Economic Development Offices are a good place to start to learn about business assistance and financing programs offered through the state. Many have one-stop business assistance centers that will answer your licensing questions as well.

State Departments of Education are responsible for the elementary and secondary schools in the state. They can provide you with the amount spent per child, student-teacher ratio, test scores, experiences, and more concerning the different school districts.

The *Departments of Higher Education* are responsible for colleges and universities in the state and can tell you about accreditation concerns. This office usually has information regarding state scholarship and loan programs.

The *Health Departments* are in charge of various health programs offered by the state. They can direct you to local community services, and can answer questions regarding health statistics and other health information. If you cannot afford health insurance, this office can direct you to resources your state may have to provide coverage.

State Housing Offices have a variety of programs to help with the construction and purchase of homes. Contact this office to learn more, and to be referred to county and city offices that may have additional programs. If you are

having a problem with your housing needs, call this office
for assistance. This office can also refer you to rental
assistance programs.

Insurance Commissioners enforce the laws and regulations
for all kinds of insurance, and they also handle complaints
from consumers. If you have a complaint about your
insurance company's policies, and the company won't help
you, contact the Insurance Commission in the state. This
office can also let you know what insurance companies can
do business in the state, and most have informative
booklets to help you learn how to choose the best insurance
coverage for you.

Labor Departments are in charge of the state's work force.
They offer special job training programs to help people get
the training they need and offer incentives to companies
often in the form of training subsidies. Call this department
if you are looking for a job to see what kinds of assistance
programs your state offers.

Licensing Offices can provide you with information
concerning various licensed professionals, and can direct
you to the appropriate office for those professions covered
by other agencies or boards. If you are having trouble with
your beautician, contractor, veterinarian, or other
professional, call this office.

One Stop Career Centers are located throughout the U.S.
and offer career services to those looking for a job.
Services vary from site to site, but most include help with
resume writing, job skills training, job hunting assistance,
and more.

Security Regulators license and regulate stock brokers and investment advisers in their state, as well as the securities these people offer and sell. This office can provide information on these various professionals, such as their current standing and will accept complaints, although they will usually only investigate to make sure no laws were broken. These offices usually have information for investors for assistance in making sound investment decisions.

Small Business Development Centers are located in over 700 cities across the U.S. and offer free or very low cost consulting services on most aspects of business ownership, including how to write a business plan, sell your idea, get government contracts, and more.

Social Services Offices are the ones in charge of child care programs, welfare, Medicaid, and other programs designed to help individuals and families get back on their feet. If you are struggling to make ends meet, contact this office to be directed to resources and services in your area.

Temporary Assistance to Needy Families (TANF) is the new office that replaced Aid to Families With Dependent Children (AFDC). This program helps people who need funds to pay for basic necessities as they enter job training programs, finish their education, or care for small children. Welfare-To-Work is often part of this program.

Transportation Departments are in charge of highways, road construction, and can direct you to those in charge of transportation systems and programs throughout their state. Many of these departments offer funds to local organizations to help fill some transportation needs in the community.

Unclaimed Property Offices hold money and other valuables that go unclaimed in the state. Unclaimed funds include savings and checking accounts, certificates of deposit, health insurance payments, stock and dividends, and more. If you think you or someone in your family may have missing funds, contact this office and they can do a search for you.

Unemployment Insurance Offices are the ones that distribute unemployment checks. Contact this office if you are eligible for the checks, want to appeal a denial, or need an extension of your benefits.

Utility Commissioners are in charge of the utility companies in the state. Many companies offer discounts and other special services to seniors or those in need. Contact your local utility company or this office to learn what is available.

In almost every state, there are ***Women's Commissions*** and similar groups that provide direction or assistance to women. Missions and programs vary, but these groups all share the goal of working toward eliminating the inequities that affect women at home and in the workplace. Some commissions are simply advocacy groups, bringing attention to issues that affect women and working to bring about legislative changes that would improve situations that women face. Others provide information and referrals to help women get ahead and some even provide direct services to help women get the training, education, and financial help they need to succeed.

ALABAMA

Federal Information Center
All locations; 800-688-9889

State Information Office
334-242-8000
http://www.state.al.us

Department on Aging
Aging Commission
770 Washington Ave.
Suite 470
Montgomery, AL 36130
334-242-5743

Attorney General's Office
Office of the Attorney General
State House
11 South Union St.
Montgomery, AL 36130
334-242-7300
800-392-5658
www.e-pages.com/aag

Banking Commissioner
Superintendent of Banks
401 Adams Ave., Suite 680
Montgomery, AL 36130
334-242-3452

**Child Care and Development
Block Grant Lead Agency**
Alabama Department of Human
Resources
Division of Family and Children
Services

50 Ripley St.
Montgomery, AL 36130
334-242-1773
Fax: 334-242-0513
http://www.state.al.us/govern/dhr/
dhrmain.html

**Child Support Enforcement
Agency**
Carolyn Lapsley
Department of Human Resources
Division of Child Support
50 Ripley St.
Montgomery, AL 36130
334-242-9300
800-284-4347 (in AL)
Fax: 334-242-0606

Cooperative Extension Offices
Dr. W. Gaines Smith, Interim
Director
Alabama Cooperative Extension
Service
109 A Duncan Hall
Auburn University
Auburn, AL 36849-5612
334-844-4444
http://www.acesag.auburn.edu

Chinelle Henderson, Administrator
Alabama A&M University
Cooperative Extension Service
P.O. Box 222
Normal, AL 35762
205-851-5710

http://www.saes.aamu.edu/
exten.htm

Dr. Moore, Director
Cooperative Extension Program
U.S. Dept. of Agriculture
Tuskegee University
207 N. Main St., Suite 400
Tuskegee, AL 36083-1731
334-727-8806
http://www.tusk.edu

Corporation Division Office
Division of Corporation
Secretary of State
4121 Carmichael Rd.
Montgomery, AL 36103
334-242-5324
www.alalinc.net/alsecst/
corporat.htm

Day Care Licensing Agency
State Department of Human
Resources
Office of Day Care
50 Ripley St.
Montgomery, AL 36130
334-242-1425
http://www.state.al.us/govern/dhr/
dhrmain.html/

Economic Development Office
Alabama Development Office
401 Adams Avenue
Montgomery, AL 36104-4340
800-248-0033
334-242-0400
Fax: 334-242-0415
www.ado.state.al.us

Alabama Department of Revenue
P.O. Box 327001
Montgomery, AL 36132-7001
334-242-1170
alaweb.asc.edu

Department of Education
Alabama Department of Education
50 N. Ripley
Montgomery, AL 36130-2101
334-242-9700
http://www.alsde.edu/

Department of Higher Education
Alabama Commission on Higher
Education
P.O. Box 30200
Montgomery, AL 36130-2000
334-242-2271
Fax: 334-242-0268
www.ache.state.al.us

Health Department
Alabama Dept. of Public Health
RSA Tower
201 Monroe Street
Montgomery, AL 36104
MAILING:
  RSA Tower
  P.O. Box 303017
  Montgomery, AL 36130-3017
334-206-5300
www.alapubhealth.org
E-mail: webmaster@
alapubhealth.org

Housing Office
Alabama Housing Finance Authority
P.O. Box 230909

Montgomery, AL 36123-0909
334-244-9200

Insurance Commissioner
Insurance Commissioner
201 Monroe St., Suite 1700
Montgomery, AL 36104
334-269-3550
800-243-5463

Labor Department
Alabama Department of Economic
Security
P.O. Box 6123
Montgomery, AL 36130-3500
334-242-3460
NO WEB SITE

Licensing Office
State Occupational Information
Coordinating Community (SOICC)
401 Adams Ave.
P.O. Box 5690
Montgomery, AL 36103
334-242-2990

One-Stop Career Center
Department of Industrial Relations
649 Monroe Street
Montgomery, AL 36131
334-242-8846
Fax: 334-242-8843
www.dir.state.al.us
E-mail: webmaster@dir.state.al.us

Security Regulators
Alabama Securities Commission
770 Washington Ave., Suite 570
Montgomery, AL 36130

334-242-2984
800-222-1253

**Small Business Development
Center**
Alabama Small Business
Development Consortium
University of Alabama at
Birmingham
Medical Towers Building
1717 Eleventh Avenue South
Suite 419
Birmingham, AL 35294-4410
205-934-7260
Fax: 205-934-7645
E-mail: sandefur@uab.edu
www.asbdc.org

Social Services Offices
Alabama Department of Human
Resources
P.O. Box 304000
Montgomery, AL 36130-4000
334-242-1850
www.state.al.us/govern/dhr/
dhrmain.html

**Temporary Assistance to Needy
Families (TANF)**
Temporary Aid to Needy Families
Joel Sander
Alabama Department of Human
Resources
Gordon Persons Bldg.
50 Ripley St.
Montgomery, AL 36130
334-242-1773
www.dhr.state.al.us

Transportation Department
Sonya Rice
Alabama Department of
Transportation
1409 Coliseum Blvd.
Montgomery, AL 36130
334-242-6930
www.dot.state.al.us

William Luckerson
Alabama Department of
Transportation
1409 Coliseum Blvd.
Montgomery, AL 36130
334-242-6083
www.dot.state.al.us

Unclaimed Property Office
Unclaimed Property Division
P.O. Box 302520
Montgomery, AL 31632
334-242-9614
http://agencies.state.al.us/
treasurer/

Unemployment Insurance Office
Unemployment Compensation
Division
Department of Industrial Relations
649 Monroe St., Room 629
Montgomery, AL 36131
334-242-8025
www.dir.state.al.us/uc.htm
Weekly benefit range: $45-190
Duration of benefits: 15-26 weeks

Utility Commission
Public Service Commission
P.O. Box 991
Montgomery, AL 36101
334-242-5207
800-392-8050 (AL only)

Women's Commission
Alabama Women's Commission
P.O. Box 1277
Tuscaloosa, AL 35403
205-345-7668
Jean Boutwell, elected Secretary
Bab F. Hart, Chair
www.alawomenscommission.org

ALASKA

Federal Information Center
All locations; 800-688-9889

State Information Office
907-465-2111
http://www.state.ak.us

Department on Aging
Division of Senior Services
Commission on Aging
P.O. Box 110209
Juneau, AK 99811-0209
907-465-3250

Attorney General's Office
Office of the Attorney General
P.O. Box 110300
Juneau, AK 99811
907-465-3600
www.law.state.ak.us

Banking Commissioner
Director of Banking
Corporations and Securities
P.O. Box 110807
Juneau, AK 99811-0807
907-465-2521
http://www.commerce.
state.ak.us/bsc/bsc.htm

Child Care and Development Block Grant Lead Agency
Alaska Department of Health and
Social Services
Division of Public Assistance

P.O. Box 110630
Juneau, AK 99811-0640
907-465-3329
Fax: 907-465-5154
http://www.hss.state.ak.us

Child Support Enforcement Agency
Barbar Miklos
Child Support Enforcement
Division
550 West 7th Ave., Suite 310
Anchorage, AK 99501
907-269-6900
Fax: 907-269-6913
http://www.revenue.state.
ak.us/csed/csed.htm

Cooperative Extension Office
Hollis D. Hall, Director
Alaska Cooperative Extension
University of Alaska Fairbanks
P.O. Box 756180
Fairbanks, AK 99775-6180
907-474-7246
http://zorba.uafadm.alaska.
edu/coop-ext/index.html

Corporation Division Office
State of Alaska
Division of Banking, Securities
and Corporation
Corporation Section
P.O. Box 110808
Juneau, AK 99811

907-465-2530
www.commerce.state.ak.us/
bsc/corps.htm

Day Care Licensing Agency
Department of Health and Human
Services
Office of Day Care Licensing
P.O. Box 110630
Juneau, AK 99811
907-465-3191
http://health.hss.state.ak.us/
htmlstuf/famyouth/ table.htm

Economic Development Office
Alaska Department of Commerce
and Economic Development
P.O. Box 110800
Juneau, AL 98111
907-465-2017
800-478-LOAN
Fax: 907-465-3767
http://www.commerce.state. ak.us

Department of Education
Alaska Department of Education
Public Information
801 W. 10th St., Suite 200
Juneau, AK 99801-1894
907-465-2851
http://www.educ.state.ak.us/report/c
ontents.html

Department of Higher Education
Alaska Commission on
Postsecondary Education
3030 Vintage Boulevard
Juneau, AK 99801-7109
800-441-2962

907-465-2962
Fax: 407-465-5316
www.state.ak.us/acpe/home.html

Health Department
Alaska Department of Health &
Social Services
350 Main Street
Room 503
Juneau, AK 99801
MAILING
   P.O. Box 110610
   Juneau, AK 99811-0610
907-465-3090
Fax: 907-586-1877
http://health.hss.state.ak.us
E-mail: petern@ health.state.ak.us

Housing Office
Alaska Housing Finance
Corporation
P.O. Box 101020
4300 Boniface Parkway
Anchorage, AK 99510
907-338-6100
http://www.ahfc.state.ak.us

Insurance Commissioner
Director of Insurance
P.O. Box 110805
Juneau, AK 99811-0805
907-465-2515
http://www.commerce.state.ak.
us/insurance

Labor Department
Alaska Department of Labor
P.O. Box 21149
Juneau, AK 99802

907-456-2700
www.labor.state.ak.us/

Licensing Office
Division of Occupational Licensing
Department of Commerce and
Economic Development
State of Alaska
P.O. Box 110806
Juneau, AK 99811
907-465-2534
www.commerce.state.ak.us/
occ.home.htm

One-Stop Career Center
Alaska Job Center Network
Department of Labor
P.O. Box 21149
Juneau, AK 99802
907-456-2700
www.jobs.state.ak.us

Security Regulators
Division of Banking and Securities
P.O. Box 110807
Juneau, AK 99801
907-465-2521
www.dced.state.ak.us/bsc/
secur.htm

Small Business Development Center
Alaska Small Business
Development Center
University of Alaska Anchorage
430 West Seventh Avenue
Suite 110
Anchorage, AK 99501-3550
907-274-7232

Fax: 907-274-9524
E-mail: anjaf@uaa.alaska.edu

Social Services Offices
Alaska Department of Health and
Social Services
3601 "C" Street, Suite 578
P.O. Box 240249
Anchorage, AK 99524
907-269-2680
www.hss.state.ak.us

Temporary Assistance to Needy Families (TANF)
Temporary Aid to Needy Families
Jim Nordlund
Alaska Department of Health and
Social Services
P.O. Box 110640
Juneau, AK 99811
907-465-3347
www.hss.state.ak.us/htmlstuf/
pubassis/atap.htm

Transportation Department
Bruce Wells
Alaska Department of Transportation and Public Facilities
3132 Channel Dr., Room 200
Juneau, AK 99801
907-465-6991
www.dot.state.ak.us

Tom Brigham
Alaska Department of
Transportation and Public
Facilities
3132 Channel Dr., Room 200
Juneau, AK 99801

907-465-2171
www.dot.state.ak.us

Unclaimed Property Office
Department of Revenue
Unclaimed Property Unit
P.O. Box 110420
Juneau, AK 99811
907-465-4653
www.revenue.state.ak.us/iea/
property/index.htm

Unemployment Insurance Office
Unemployment Insurance
Program Manager
Employment Security Division
P.O. Box 25509
Juneau, AK 99802
907-465-2712

www.labor.state.ak.us
Weekly benefit range: $44-248
Duration of benefits: 16-26 weeks

Utility Commission
Public Utilities Commission
1016 W. 6th Ave., Suite 400
Anchorage, AK 99501
907-276-6222
http://www.state.ak.us/ local/
akpages/commerce/ apuc.htm

Women's Commission
Anchorage Women's Commission
P.O. Box 196650
Anchorage, AK 99519-6650
907-343-6310
Fax: 907-343-6730
www.ci.anchorage.ak.us

ARIZONA

Federal Information Center
All Locations; 800-688-9889

State Information Office
602-542-4900
http://www.state.az.us

Department on Aging
Aging and Adult Administration
Economic Security Department
1789 W. Jefferson
Phoenix, AZ 85007
602-542-4446

Attorney General's Office
Office of the Attorney General
1275 West Washington St.
Phoenix, AZ 85007
602-542-4266

Banking Commissioner
Superintendent of Banks
2910 N. 44th St., Suite 310
Phoenix, AZ 85018
602-255-4421
800-544-0708 (toll free in AZ)
http://www.azbanking.com

Child Care and Development Block Grant Lead Agency
Arizona Department of Economic Security
Child Care Administrator
Box 6123
Phoenix, AZ 85005-6123

602-542-4248
Fax: 602-542-4197
http://www.governor.state.az.us/dept/des.html

Child Support Enforcement Agency
Nancy Mendoza
Division of Child Support Enforcement
Department of Economic Security
P.O. Box 40458
Site Code 021A
Phoenix, AZ 85067
602-252-4045
800-882-4151

Cooperative Extension Office
Jim Christenson, Director
Cooperative Extension Office
University of Arizona
Forbes 301
Tucson, AZ 85721
520-621-7205
http://ag.arizona.edu/ext/coopext.html

Corporation Division Office
Arizona Corporation Commission
Secretary of State
1200 W. Washington
Phoenix, AZ 85007
602-542-3026
www.cc.state.az.us

Day Care Licensing Agency
State Department of Health
Services
Office of Child Care Licensing
1647 E. Morton St.
Suite 230
Phoenix, AZ 85020
602-674-4340
http://www.hs.state.az.us/als/
childcare/ index.html

Economic Development Office
Department of Commerce
3800 N. Central
Suite 1650
Phoenix, AZ 85012
602-280-1480
800-542-5684
Fax: 620-280-1339
www.commerce.state.az.us/
fr_abc.shtml

Department of Education
Arizona Department of Education
Research and Evaluation Division
1535 W. Jefferson
Phoenix, AZ 85007
602-542-5022
http://www.ade.state.az.us/

Department of Higher Education
Arizona Commission for
Postsecondary Education
2020 North Central
Suite 275
Phoenix, AZ 85004-4503
602-229-2591
Fax: 602-229-2599
www.acpe.asu.edu

Health Department
Arizona Department of Health
Services
Office of Women's & Children's
Health
411 North 24th Street
Phoenix, AZ 85008
602-220-6550
Fax: 602-220-6551
TDD: 602-256-7577
www.hs.state.az.us

Housing Office
Arizona Dept. of Commerce
Office of Housing Development
3800 N. Central, Suite 1200
Phoenix, AZ 85012
602-280-1365
http://www.state.az.us/ commerce

Insurance Commissioner
Director of Insurance
2910 N. 44th St., Suite 210
Phoenix, AZ 85018
602-912-8400
800-325-2548
http://www.state.az.us/id/

Labor Department
Arizona Department of Economic
Security
1717 West Jefferson
Phoenix, AZ 85007
602-542-4296
www.de.state.az.us

Licensing Office
Registrar of Contractors
800 W. Washington

Phoenix, AZ 85007
602-542-1525 ext. 7605
www.rc.state.az.us

One-Stop Career Center
One Stop Career Center
Arizona Department of Economic
Security
1717 West Jefferson
Phoenix, AZ 85007
602-542-4296
www.de.state.az.us/osoc
E-mail: webmaster@de.
state.az.us

Security Regulators
Arizona Corporation Commission
1300 W. Washington St.. 3rd Floor
Phoenix, AZ 85007
602-542-4242
www.ccsd.cc.state.az.us

**Small Business Development
Center**
Arizona Small Business
Development Center Network
Maricopa County Community
Colleges
Small Business Development
Center
2411 West 14th Street
Tempe, AZ 85281
602-731-8720
Fax: 602-230-7989
E-mail: york@maricopa.edu
www.dist.maricopa.edu/sbdc

Social Services Offices
Arizona Department of Economic
Security

1717 West Jefferson
Phoenix, AZ 85007
602-542-4296
www.de.state.az.us

**Temporary Assistance to Needy
Families (TANF)**
Temporary Aid to Needy Families
Social Services Block Grant
Linda Blessing
Arizona Department of Economic
Security
1717 West Jefferson St.
Phoenix, AZ 85007
602-542-5678
www.de.state.az.us

Transportation Department
Sam Chavez
Arizona Department of
Transportation
206 South 17th Ave.
Suite 340-B
Phoenix, AZ 85007
602-255-8956
www.dot.state.az.us

Gregg Kiely
Arizona Department of
Transportation
206 South 17th Ave.
Suite 340-B
Phoenix, AZ 85007
602-255-6736
www.dot.state.az.us

Unclaimed Property Office
Department of Revenue
Unclaimed Property Unit

1600 West Monroe
Phoenix, AZ 85007
602-542-4643
www.revenue.state.az.us/
uclprop.htm

Unemployment Insurance Office
ESA Administrator
P.O. Box 6123-910A
Phoenix, AZ 85007
602-255-3722
Weekly benefit range: $40-185
Duration of benefits: 12-26 weeks

Utility Commission
Corporation Commission
1200 W. Washington St.
Phoenix, AZ 85007
602-542-3935

800-222-7000 (AZ only)
http://www.cc.state.az.us

Women's Commission
Phoenix Women's Commission
Equal Opportunity Department
251 West Washington, 7th Floor
Phoenix, AZ 85003-6211
602-261-8242
Fax: 602-256-3389

Tucson Women's Commission
240 North Court Ave.
Tucson, AZ 85701
520-624-8318
Fax: 520-624-5599
E-mail: tctwc@starnet.com
Neema Caughran, Exec. Director
Louisa Hernandez, Chair

ARKANSAS

Federal Information Center
All Locations; 800-688-9889

State Information Office
501-682-3000
http://www.state.ar.us

Department on Aging
Aging and Adult Services Division
Box 1437, Slot 1412
Little Rock, AR 72203
501-682-2441
http://www.state.ar.us/
dhs.index2.html

Attorney General's Office
Office of the Attorney General
200 Tower Building
323 Center St.
Little Rock, AR 72201
501-682-2007
800-482-8982
www.state.ar.us/ag/ag.html

Banking Commissioner
Bank Commissioner
Tower Bldg.
323 Center St., Suite 500
Little Rock, AR 72201
501-324-9019
http://www.state.ar.us/
bank/banking1.htm/

Child Care and Development Block Grant Lead Agency
Arkansas Department of Human
Services

Division of Child Care and Early
Childhood Education
101 East Capitol, Suite 106
Little Rock, AR 72201
501-682-4891
Fax: 501-682-4897/2317
http://www.state.ar.us/dhs/
dhs1.html

Child Support Enforcement Agency
Dan McDonald
Office of Child Support
Enforcement
Division of Revenue
P.O. Box 8133
Little Rock, AR 72201
501-682-6169
800-264-2445 (in AR)
Fax: 501-682-6002

Cooperative Extension Offices
David Foster, Director
Cooperative Extension Service
P.O. Box 391
Little Rock, AR 72203
501-671-2000
http://www.uaex.edu

Corporation Division Office
Secretary of State
Corporations Division
State Capitol Bldg., Room 058
Little Rock, AR 72201
501-682-5151
www.sosweb.state.ar.us

Day Care Licensing Agency
State Department of Human
Services
Child Care Licensing Unit
P.O. Box 1437, Slot 720
Little Rock, AR 72203-1437
501-682-8590
http://www.state.ar.us/dhs/
dhs1.html

Economic Development Office
Arkansas Economic Development
Commission
1 State Capitol Mall
Little Rock, AR 72201
501-682-1121
Fax: 501-682-7341
www.aedc.state.ar.us

Department of Education
Arkansas Department of Education
Office of Accountability
4 State Capitol Mall, 204-B
Little Rock, AR 72201
501-682-4330
http://arkedu.state.ar.us

Department of Higher Education
Arkansas Department of Higher
Education
114 East Capitol
Little Rock, AR 72201
501-371-2000
Fax: 501-371-2001
www.adhe.arknet.edu

Health Department
Arkansas Department of Health
4815 West Markham

Little Rock, AR 72201
501-661-2000
800-482-5400
http://health.state.ar.us
E-mail: wbankson@
mail.doh.state. ar.us

Housing Office
Arkansas Development Finance
Authority
P.O. Box 8023
100 Main St., Suite 200
Little Rock, AR 72203
501-682-5900

Insurance Commissioner
Insurance Commissioner
1200 W. 3rd St.
Little Rock, AR 72201
501-371-2600
800-852-5494

Labor Department
Arkansas Department Of Labor
10421 West Markham
Little Rock, AR 72205
501-682-4500
www.ark.org/labor

Licensing Office
Boards and Commissions
Governor's Office
State Capitol Building
Little Rock, AR 72201
501-682-3570

One-Stop Career Center
Arkansas Career Development
Network

Employment Security Department
#2 Capitol Mall, Room 506
ESD Building
Little Rock, AR 72201
501-682-2121
Fax: 501-682-2273
www.state.ar.us/esd/

Security Regulators
Arkansas Securities Department
Heritage West Building
201 East Markham, 3rd Floor
Little Rock, AR 72201
501-324-9260

Small Business Development Center
Arkansas Small Business
Development Center
University of Arkansas at Little
Rock
Little Rock Technology Center
Building
100 South Main, Suite 401
Little Rock, AR 72201
501-324-9043
Fax: 501-324-9049
E-mail: jmnye@ualr.edu
www.ualr.edu/~sbdcdept

Social Services Offices
Arkansas Department of Human
Services
Donaghey Plaza West
Slot 3430
P.O. Box 1437
Little Rock, AR 72203
501-682-8650
www.state.ar.us/dhs/

Temporary Assistance to Needy Families (TANF)
Temporary Aid to Needy Families
Gordon Page
Division of County Operations
Arkansas Department of Human
Services
101 East Capitol
Little Rock, AR 72203
501-682-6728
www.state.ar.us/dhs/tea/plan/

Transportation Department
James Gilbert
Arkansas State Highway and
Transportation Department
P.O. Box 2261
Little Rock, AR 72203
501-569-2471
www.ahtd.state.ar.us

Unclaimed Property Office
Auditor of State
Unclaimed Property Division
1400 West 3rd, Suite 100
Little Rock, AR 72201
501-682-9174
800-252-4648
www.unclaimed.org/ar.htm

Unemployment Insurance Office
Unemployment Insurance Director
Arkansas Employment Security
Department
P.O. Box 2981
Little Rock, AR 72203
501-682-3200
Weekly benefit range: $47-264
Duration of benefits: 9-26 weeks

Utility Commission
Public Service Commission
1000 Center St.
P.O. Box 400
Little Rock, AR 72203-0400

501-682-1453
800-482-1164 (AR only)

Women's Commission
Closed 96-99

CALIFORNIA

Federal Information Center
All Locations; 800-688-9889

State Information Office
916-322-9900
http://www.state.ca.us

Department on Aging
California Department of Aging
1600 K St.
Sacramento, CA 95814
916-322-5290
http://www.aging.state.ca.us

Attorney General's Office
Office of the Attorney General
P.O. Box 944255
Sacramento, CA 94244
916-322-3360
800-952-5225
http://caag.state.ca.us

Banking Commissioner
State Banking Department
111 Pine St., Suite 1100
San Francisco, CA 94111-5613
415-263-8555
800-622-0620 (toll free in CA)
http://www.dfi.ca.gov

Child Care and Development Block Grant Lead Agency
Child Development Division
California State Department of Education

560 J St., Suite 220
Sacramento, CA 95814-4785
916-322-4240
Fax: 916-323-6853
http://www.cde.ca.gov/

Child Support Enforcement Agency
Leslie Frye
Office of Child Support
744 P St.
Mail Stop 17-29
Sacramento, CA 95814
916-654-1532
800-777-2515 (in CA)
http://www.chilsup.cahwnet.gov

Cooperative Extension Office
Kenneth Farrell, VP
University of California
Division of Agriculture and Natural Resources
300 Lakeside Dr., 6th Floor
Oakland, CA 94612-3560
510-987-0060 (programs are at county level)

Corporation Division Office
Corporations Unit
Secretary of State
1500 11th St.
Sacramento, CA 95814
916-653-2121
www.ss.ca.gov/business/business.htm

Day Care Licensing Agency
Department of Social Services
Community Care Licensing
Division
744 P St., Mail Station 19-50
Sacramento, CA 95814
916-324-4031
http://www.dss.cahwnet.gov/
default.htm

Economic Development Office
California Trade and Commerce
Agency
801 K St., Suite 1700
Sacramento, CA 95814
916-322-1394
www.state.ca.us/s/business

Department of Education
California Department of Education
721 Capitol Mall
P.O. Box 944272
Sacramento, CA 94244-2720
916-657-2676
http://goldmine.cde.ca.gov/

Department of Higher Education
California Student Aid
Commission
P.O. Box 419026
Rancho Cordova, CA 95741-9026
916-526-7590
Fax: 916-526-8002
www.csac.ca.gov

Health Department
California Department of Health
Services
Office of Women's Health

714 P Street, Room 792
Sacramento, CA 95814
906-653-3330
Fax: 916-653-3535
www.dhs.ca.gov

Housing Offices
California Housing Finance Agency
1121 L St., 7th Floor
Sacramento, CA 95814
916-322-3991
http://www.chfa.ca.gov

California Department of Housing
and Community Development
P.O. Box 952054
Sacramento, CA 94252-2054
916-322-1560
http://housing.hcd.ca.gov

Insurance Commissioner
Commissioner of Insurance
300 S. Spring St., 13th Floor
Los Angeles, CA 90013
916-492-3500 (Sacramento)
213-346-6400 (Los Angeles)
800-927-HELP (complaints)
http://www.insurance.ca.gov/
docs/index.html

Labor Department
California Employment
Development Department
800 Capital Mall
Sacramento, CA 95814
916-227-0300
wwwedd.cahwnet.gov/
eddhome.htm

Licensing Office
State of California
Department of Consumer Affairs
400 R St.
Sacramento, CA 95814
916-445-1254
800-952-5210
www.dca.ca.gov

One-Stop Career Center
One-Stop Office
P.O. Box 826880, MIC 77
Sacramento, CA 94280-0001
916-654-9995
Fax: 916-654-9863
www.sjtcc.cahwnet.gov/
SJTCCWEB/ONE-STOP/
E-mail: onestop@edd.ca.gov

Security Regulators
Department of Corporations
980 9th St., Suite 500
Sacramento, CA 95814
916-445-7205
www.corp.ca.gov

Small Business Development Center
California Small Business
Development Center
California Trade and Commerce
Agency
801 K Street, Suite 1700
Sacramento, CA 95814
916-324-5068
800-303-6600
Fax: 916-322-5084
http://commerce.ca.gov/
business/small/starting/
sb_sbdcl.html

Social Services Offices
California Department of Social
Services
Office of Community Relations
744 P Street
M.S. 17-02
Sacramento, CA 95814
916-657-3661
www.dss.cahwnet.gov

Temporary Assistance to Needy Families (TANF)
Temporary Aid to Needy Families
Eloise Anderson
California Department of Social
Services
744 P Street
Mail Station 17-11
Sacramento, CA 95814
916-657-2598
www.dss.cahwnet.gov/getser/
afdc.html

Transportation Department
Ralph Caudillo
California Department of
Transportation - CALTRANS
P.O. Box 942874
Sacramento, CA 94274
916-654-8144
www.dot.ca.gov

John James
California Department of
Transportation - CALTRANS
P.O. Box 942874
Sacramento, CA 94274
916-654-9777
www.dot.ca.gov

Unclaimed Property Office
Division of Collections
Bureau of Unclaimed Property
P.O. Box 942850
Sacramento, CA 94250
916-445-8318
800-992-4647
www.sco.ca.gov

Unemployment Insurance Office
Unemployment Insurance
Employment Development
Department
P.O. Box 826880-MIC 86
Sacramento, CA 94280
916-654-9047
wwwedd.cahwnet.gov/ uiind.htm
Weekly benefit range: $40-230
Duration of benefits: 12-26 weeks

Utility Commission
Public Utilities Commission
505 Van Ness Ave.
San Francisco, CA 94102
415-703-2782
http://www.cpuc.ca.gov

Women's Commission
California Commission on the
Status of Women
1303 J St., Suite 400
Sacramento, CA 95814-2900
916-445-3173
Fax: 916-322-9466
E-mail: csw@sna.com
www.statusofwomen.ca.gov
Eileen Padberg, Chair

COLORADO

Federal Information Center
All Locations; 800-688-9889

State Information Office
303-866-5000
http://www.state.co.us

Department on Aging
Commission For Aging and Adult
Services
Social Services Department
110 16th St., Suite 200
Denver, CO 80202
303-620-4147
http://www.aclin.org/
~sherlock/colodaas.htm

Attorney General's Office
Office of the Attorney General
Department of Law
1525 Sherman St.
Denver, CO 80203
303-866-3052
800-332-2071
www.sate.co.us/gov_dir/dol/
index.htm

Banking Commissioner
State Bank Commissioner
Division of Banking
Denver Post Bldg.
1560 Broadway, Suite 1175
Denver, CO 80202
303-894-7575

http://www.state.co.us/
gov_dir/regulatory_dir/ ban.htm

**Child Care and Development
Block Grant Lead Agency**
Office of Child Care Services
Colorado Department of Human
Services
1575 Sherman St.
Denver, CO 80203-1714
303-866-5958
Fax: 303-866-4453
http://www.cdhs.state.co.us/

**Child Support Enforcement
Agency**
Pauline Burton
Division of Child Support
Enforcement
Department of Human Services
1575 Sherman St.
Second Floor
Denver, CO 80203
303-866-5992
303-866-2214
http://www.state.co.us/ gov_dir/
human_services_ dir/ CSE/
Csenet.htm

Cooperative Extension Office
Milan Rewets, Director
Colorado State University
Cooperative Extension
1 Administrative Building
Fort Collins, CO 80523

970-491-6281
http://www.colostate.edu

Corporation Division Office
Corporate Division
Secretary of State
1560 Broadway, Suite 200
Denver, CO 80202
303-894-2251
www.state.co.us/gov_dir/sos/
index.html

Day Care Licensing Agency
State Department of Human
Services
Office of Social Services
Child Care Licensing
1575 Sherman St.
Denver, CO 80203-1714
303-866-5958
http://www.state.co.us/gov_dir/
human_services_dir/hs_home.
html

Economic Development Office
Office of Economic Development
1625 Broadway
Suite 1710
Denver, CO 80202
303-892-3840
Fax: 303-892-3848
TDD: 800-659-2656
www.state.co.us

Department of Education
Colorado Department of Education
Planning and Evaluation Unit
201 E. Colfax
Denver, CO 80203

303-866-6600
http://www.cde.state.co.us/

Department of Higher Education
Colorado Commission on Higher
Education
1300 Broadway, 2nd Floor
Denver, CO 80203
303-866-2723
www.state.co.us/cche_dir/
hecche.html

Health Department
Colorado Department of Public
Health & Environment
4300 Cherry Creek Drive South
Denver, CO 80246-1530
303-692-1000
www.state.co.us/gov_dir/
cdphe_dir/

Housing Office
Colorado Housing and Finance
Authority
1981 Blake St.
Denver, CO 80202-1272
303-297-7316
http://www.state.co.us/
gov_dir/loc_affairs_dir/ doh.htm

Insurance Commissioner
Commissioner of Insurance
1560 Broadway
Suite 850
Denver, CO 80202
303-894-7499
800-544-9181
http://www.state.co.us/gov_dir/
regulatory_dir/insurance_reg. html

Labor Department
Colorado Department of Labor
and Employment
1515 Arapahoe
Tower 2, Suite 300
Denver, CO 80202
303-620-4856
http://cdle.state.co.us

Licensing Office
Department of Regulatory
Agencies
State Services Building
1560 Broadway
Suite 1550
Denver, CO 80303
303-894-7855
www.dora.state.co.us

One-Stop Career Center
Job Service Centers
Colorado Department of Labor
and Employment
Office of Employment and
Training
1515 Arapahoe Street
Tower 2, Suite 400
Denver, CO 80202-2117
303-620-4204
Fax: 303-620-4257
http://navigator.cdle.state.co.us

Security Regulators
Division of Securities
1580 Lincoln St.
Suite 420
Denver, CO 80203
303-894-2320
www.dora.state.co.us/ Securities

**Small Business Development
Center**
Colorado Small Business
Development Center
Office of Business Development
1625 Broadway, Suite 1710
Denver, CO 80202
303-892-3809
800-333-7798
Fax: 303-892-3848
E-mail: cec.ortiz@state.co.us
www.state.co.us/gov_dir/
obd/sbdc.htm

Social Services Offices
Colorado Department of Human
Services
1575 Sherman Street
Denver, CO 80203-1714
303-866-5922
www.cdhs.state.co.us

**Temporary Assistance to Needy
Families (TANF)**
Temporary Aid to Needy Families
Sue Tuffin
Colorado Department of Human
Services
1575 Sherman St.
Denver, CO 80203
303-866-4630
www.cdhs.state.co.us/cdhs/
oss/Self_Sufficiency.html

Transportation Department
Pat Loose
Colorado Department of
Transportation
4201 East Arkansas Ave.

Room 212
Denver, CO 80222
303-757-9769
www.dot.state.co.us

Unclaimed Property Office
Unclaimed Property Division
1560 Broadway, Suite 1225
Denver, CO 80202
303-894-2443
www.treasurer.state.co.us

Unemployment Insurance Office
Office of Unemployment
Insurance
1515 Arapahoe St.
Tower 2, Suite 400
Denver, CO 80202
303-620-4712
http://unempben.cdle. state.co.us
Weekly benefit range: $25 -272
Duration of benefits: 13-26 weeks

Utility Commission
Public Utilities Commission
1580 Logan St.

Logan Tower, Office Level 2
Denver, CO 80203
303-894-2000
800-888-0170 (CO only)
http://www.puc.state.co.us

Women's Commission
Denver Women's Commission
303 West Colfax
Suite 1600
Denver, CO 80204
303-640-5826
Fax: 303-640-4627
www.denvergov.org/
Marilyn Ferran, Chair

Fort Collins City Commission on
the Status of Women
c/o Human Resources
City of Ft. Collins
P.O. Box 580
Fort Collins, CO 80522
970-221-6871
970-224-6050
www.ci.fort-collins.co.us
Laurie Fonken-Joseph, Chair

CONNECTICUT

Federal Information Center
All Locations; 800-688-9889

State Information Office
860-240-0222
http://www.state.ct.us

Department on Aging
Elderly Services
Division of Social Services
25 Sigourney St.
Hartford, CT 06106
860-424-5277
http://www.dss.state.ct.us/

Attorney General's Office
Office of the Attorney General
55 Elm St.
Hartford, CT 06141
860-808-5318
www.cslnet.ctstateu.edu/ attygenl/

Banking Commissioner
Banking Commissioner
260 Constitution Plaza
Hartford, CT 06103
860-240-8229
800-831-7225 (toll free in CT)
http://www.state.ct.us/ dob/

**Child Care and Development
Block Grant Lead Agency**
Office of Child Care
Connecticut Department of Social
Services

25 Sigourney St., 10th Floor
Hartford, CT 06106-5033
860-424-5598
Fax: 860-951-2996
http://www.dss.state.ct.us

**Child Support Enforcement
Agency**
Diane Fray
Bureau of Child Support
Enforcement
Department of Social Services
25 Sigourney St.
Hartford, CT 06106
860-424-5251
860-951-2996
800-228-5437
http://www.dss.state.ct. us/svcs/
csupp.htm

Cooperative Extension Office
Associate Director
Cooperative Extension System
University of Connecticut
1376 Storrs Rd.
Storrs, CT 06269-4036
860-486-6271

Corporation Division Office
Office of Secretary of State
Commercial Recording Division
30 Trinity St.
Hartford, CT 06106
860-509-6001
www.state.ct.us/sots

Day Care Licensing Agency
State of Connecticut Department
of Public Health
Child Day Care Licensing
410 Capital Ave.
MS #12DAC
P.O. Box 340308
Hartford, CT 06134-3038
860-509-8045
http://www.state.ct.us/coc/

Economic Development Office
Economic Resource Center
Department of Economic and
Community Development
805 Brooks St., Bldg. 4
Rocky Hill, CT 06067-3405
860-571-7136
800-392-2122
Fax: 860-571-7150
www.cerc.com

Department of Education
Connecticut Department of
Education
Public Information Office
P.O. Box 2219
Hartford, CT 06145
860-566-5677
http://www.state.ct.us/sde/

Department of Higher Education
Department of Higher Education
61 Woodland Street
Hartford, CT 06105-2326
860-947-1800
Fax: 860-947-1310
http://ctdhe.commnet.edu

Health Department
Connecticut Department of Public
Health
410 Capitol Avenue
P.O. Box 340308
Hartford, CT 06134-0308
860-509-8000
TDD: 860-509-7191
www.state.ct.us/dph/
E-mail: donna.winiarski@
po.state.ct.us

Housing Office
Connecticut Housing Finance
Authority
999 West St.
Rocky Hill, CT 06067
860-721-9501

Insurance Commissioner
Insurance Commissioner
P.O. Box 816
Hartford, CT 06142-0816
860-297-3802
800-203-3447
http://www.state.ct.us/cid/

Labor Department
Connecticut Department of Labor
200 Folly Brook Blvd.
Wethersfield, CT 06109-1114
860-566-7980
www.ctdol.state.ct.us

Licensing Office
Occupational Licensing Division
Department of Consumer
Protection
165 Capitol Ave.

Hartford, CT 06106
860-566-2825
www.dcp.state.ct.us/licensing

One-Stop Career Center
Connecticut Works
Connecticut Department of Labor
200 Folly Brook Boulevard
Wethersfield, CT 06109
860-263-6785
www.ctdol.state.ct.us/ctworks/
ctworks.htm
E-mail: dol.help@po.state.ct.us

Security Regulators
Department of Banking
260 Constitution Plaza
Hartford, CT 06013
860-240-8299
800-831-7225
www.state.ct.us/dob

Small Business Development Center
Connecticut Small Business
Development Center
University of Connecticut
School of Business Administrtion
2 Bourn Place, U-94
Storrs, CT 06269-5094
860-486-4135
Fax: 860-486-1576
E-mail: statedirector@
ct.sbdc.uconn.edu
www.sbdc.uconn.edu

Social Services Offices
Connecticut Department of Social
Services

25 Siqourney Street
Hartford, CT 06106
860-424-5010
www.dss.state.ct.us

Temporary Assistance to Needy Families (TANF)
Temporary Aid To Needy Families
Joyce Thomas
Connecticut Department of Social
Services
25 Sigourney St.
Hartford, CT 06106
860-424-5008
800-842-1508
www.dss.state.ct.us/svcs/
financial.htm

Transportation Department
Lynn DiNallo
Connecticut Department of
Transportation
P.O. Box 317546
2800 Berlin Turnpike
Newington, CT 06131
806-594-2852
www.state.ct.us/dot

Unclaimed Property Office
Unclaimed Property Unit
Office of State Treasurer
55 Elm ST.
Hartford, CT 06106
860-702-3050
www.state.ct.us/ott

Unemployment Insurance Office
State Labor Department
200 Folley Brook Blvd.

Wethersfield, CT 06109
203-566-4280
www.ctdol.state.ct.us/progsupt/
unemplt/unemploy.htm
Weekly benefit range: $15-362
Duration of benefits: 26 weeks

Utility Commission
Department of Public Utility
Control
10 Franklin Square
New Britain, CT 06051
860-827-1553

800-382-4586 (CT only)
http://www.state.ct.us/dpuc/

Women's Commission
Connecticut Permanent Commission of the Status of Women
18-20 Trinity St.
Hartford, CT 06106
860-240-8300
Fax: 860-240-8314
E-mail: pcsw@po.state.ct.us
www.cga.state.ct.us/pcswl/
Leslie Brett, Ph.D, Exec. Director
Barbara DeBaptiste, Chair

DELAWARE

Federal Information Center
All Locations; 800-688-9889

State Information Office
302-739-4000
http://www.state.de.us

Department on Aging
Aging Division
Health and Social Services
Department
1901 N. Dupont Hwy.
New Castle, DE 19720
302-577-4791
http://kidshealth.org/
nhc/divage/index.html

Attorney General's Office
Office of the Attorney General
Carvel State Office Building
820 N. French St.
Wilmington, DE 19801
302-577-3838
www.state.de.us/attgen/ index.htm

Banking Commissioner
State Bank Commissioner
555 E. Lockerman St.
Suite 210
Dover, DE 19901
302-739-4235
800-638-3376 (toll free in DE for
complaints only)
http://www.state.de.us/ banks/

**Child Care and Development
Block Grant Lead Agency**
Social Services Administrator
Delaware Department of Health
and Social Services
P.O. Box 906
New Castle, DE 19720
302-577-4880
Fax: 302-577-4405
http://www.state.de.us/govern/
agencies/ dhss/irm/dhss.htm

**Child Support Enforcement
Agency**
Karryl Hubbard
Division of Child Support
Enforcement
Department of Health and Social
Services
Herman Hallaway Campus
P.O. Box 904
New Castle, DE 19720
302-577-4863
Fax: 302-577-4873
http://www.state.de.us/
govern/agencies/dhss/
irm/dcse/dcsehome.htm

Cooperative Extension Offices
Dr. Richard E. Fowler, Director
Cooperative Extension
131 Townsend Hall
University of Delaware
Newark, DE 19717-1303

302-831-2504
http://www.bluehen.ags.udel.edu/

Dr. Starlene Taylor
Assistant Administrator
Delaware State College
Cooperative Extension Service
1200 N. DuPont Hwy.
Dover, DE 19901
302-739-5157
http://www.dsc.edu

Corporation Division Office
Delaware Department of State
Division of Corporations
Secretary of State
P.O. Box 898
Dover, DE 19903
302-739-3073
www.state.de.us/corp/ index.htm

Day Care Licensing Agency
Department of Health and Social
Services
Office of Child Care Licensing
DSCYF, 1825 Falkland Rd.
Wilmington, DE 19805
302-892-5800
http://www.state.de.us/govern/
agencies/ dhss/irm/dhss.htm

Economic Development Office
Delaware Economic Development
Office
John S. Riley
99 Kings Highway
P.O. Box 1401
Dover, DE 19903
302-739-4271

Fax: 302-739-5749
www.state.de.us/dedo/ index.htm

Department of Education
Delaware Department of Education
Federal and Lockerman Sts.
P.O. Box 1402
Dover, DE 19903-1402
302-739-4601
http://www.doe.state.de.us/reports/r
eports.html

Department of Higher Education
Delaware Higher Education
Commission
820 North French Street
Carvel State Office Building
Wilmington, DE 19801
800-292-7935
302-577-3240
Fax: 302-577-6765
www.doe.state.de.us/high-ed

Health Department
Delaware Division of Public Health
P.O. Box 637
Federal & Water Streets
Dover, DE 19903
302-739-4701
Fax: 302-739-6657
www.state.de.us/govern/
agencies/dhss/irm/dph/
dphhome.htm

Housing Office
Delaware State Housing Authority
Division of Housing and Community
Development
18 the Green

Dover, DE 19901
302-739-4263

Insurance Commissioner
Insurance Commissioner
841 Silver Lake Blvd.
Rodney Bldg.
Dover, DE 19903
302-739-4251
800-282-8611
http://www.state.de.us/govern/
elecoffl/ inscom.htm

Labor Department
Delaware Department of Labor
4425 North Market Street
Wilmington, DE 19802
302-761-8029
www.harvellinteractive.com/dol

Licensing Office
Division of Professional
Regulation
P.O. Box 1401
O'Neil Building
Dover, DE 19903
302-739-4522

One-Stop Career Center
Delaware Career Network
Department of Labor, Employment
and Training
4425 North Market Street
Wilmington, DE 19809-0828
302-761-8102
Fax: 302-761-6617
www.vcnet.net
E-mail: rclarkin@state.de.us

Security Regulators
Delaware Division of Securities
Carvel State Office Building
820 North French St., 8th Floor
Wilmington, DE 19801
302-577-8424

**Small Business Development
Center**
Delaware Small Business
Development Center
University of Delaware
102 MBNA America Hall
Newark, DE 19716-2711
302-831-1555
Fax: 302-831-1423
E-mail: clinton.tymes@
mvs.udel.edu
www.delawaresbdc.org

Social Services Offices
Delaware Department of Health
and Social Services
Health and Social Service
Campus
1901 North DuPont Highway
Main Building
New Castle, DE 19720
302-577-4501
www.state.de.us/govern/
agencies/dhss/irm/dhss.htm

**Temporary Assistance to Needy
Families (TANF)**
Temporary Aid to Needy Families
Nina Licht
Delaware Social Services
Lewis Bldg.
1901 North Dupont Highway

New Castle, DE 19720
302-577-4880, ext. 273
www.state.de.us/govern/
agencies/dhss/irm/dss/
dsshome.htm

Transportation Department
Alton Hillis
Delaware Administration for
Specialized Transit Corp. - DASH
655 Bay Rd.
Blue Hen Mall, Suite 206
Dover, DE 19901
302-739-3278 Ext. 3124

Delaware Department of
Transportation
P.O. Box 778
Dover, DE 19903
800-652-5600
www.state.de.us/deldot/
info/index.html

Unclaimed Property Office
Delaware State Escheater
P.O. Box 8931
Wilmington, DE 19899
302-577-3349

www.state.de.us/govern/
agencies/revenue/escheat.htm

Unemployment Insurance Office
Division of Unemployment
Insurance
P.O. Box 9950
Wilmington, DE 19809
302-761-8350
Weekly benefit range: $20-300
Duration of benefits: 24-26 weeks

Utility Commission
Public Service Commission
861 Silver Lake Blvd.
Suite 100, Cannon Bldg.
Dover, DE 19904
302-739-4247
800-282-8574 (DE only)
http://www.state.de.us

Women's Commission
Delaware Commission for Women
4425 N. Market St.
Wilmington, DE 19802
302-761-8005
Fax: 302-761-6652
E-mail: cgomez@state.de.us
Romona S. Fullman, Esq.,
Director

DISTRICT OF COLUMBIA

Federal Information Center
All Locations; 800-688-9889

District of Columbia Information Office
202-727-6161
http://www.ci.washington. dc.us

Department on Aging
Aging Office
441 4th St., NW, Suite 900
Washington, DC 20001
202-724-5622
http://www.ci.washington.
dc.us/aging/aghome.htm

Attorney General's Office
Office of the Corporation Counsel
441 4th St., NW
Washington, DC 20001
202-727-6248

Banking Commissioner
Superintendent of Banking and
Financial Institutions
717 14th St., NW, Suite 1100
Washington, DC 20005
202-727-1563
http://www.ci.washington.
dc.us/banking/bankhome. htm

Child Care and Development Block Grant Lead Agency
Office of Early Childhood
Development

717 14th St., NW, Suite 730
Washington, DC 20005
202-727-1839
Fax: 202-727-9709

Child Support Enforcement Agency
Donald Brooks
Bureau of Paternity and Child
Support Enforcement
800 9th St., SW, 2nd Floor
Washington, DC 20024
202-645-5301
Fax: 202-645-4102

Cooperative Extension Office
Reginald Taylor, Acting Director
Cooperative Extension Service
University of the District of
Columbia
901 Newton St., NE
Washington, DC 20017
202-274-6900

Corporation Division Office
Corporations Division
Consumer and Regulatory Affairs
614 H St., NW, Room 407
Washington, DC 20001
202-727-7278

Day Care Licensing Agency
Department of Social Services
Consumer and Regulatory Affairs
614 H St., NW, Suite 1003

Washington, DC 20001
202-727-7226

Economic Development Office
Office of Economic Development
441 4th St., NW, Suite 1140
Washington, DC 20001
202-727-6365
www.dchomepage.net

Department of Education
Public Schools
825 North Capitol Street, NE
Washington, DC 20002-4232
202-442-4289
www.K12.dc.us

Department of Higher Education
Office of Postsecondary Education
2100 M.L. King, Jr., Ave., SE
Washington, DC 20020
202-727-3688
www.dhs.washington.dc.us/Prog_
Cit_Service/OPERA/opera.htm

Health Department
District of Columbia Department of
Health
800 9th Street, SW, 3rd Floor
Washington, DC 20024
202-645-5556

Housing Offices
DC Housing Finance Agency
1275 K St., NW, Suite 600
Washington, DC 20005
202-408-0415
http://www.capaccess.org/soc/hfa

District of Columbia Department of
Housing and Community
Development
51 N St., NE
Washington, DC 20002
202-535-1353

Insurance Commissioner
Commissioner of Insurance
441 4th St., NW
8th Floor N.
Washington, DC 20001
202-727-8000

Labor Department
Department of Employment
Services
500 "C" St., NW
Washington, DC 20001
202-754-7054
http://does.ci.washington.dc.us

Licensing Office
Department of Consumer and
Regulatory Affairs
614 H St., NW, Room 108
Washington, DC 20001
202-727-7080

One-Stop Career Center
DOES One-Stop Career Center
Department of Employment
Services
500 "C" Street, NW
Washington, DC 20001
202-724-7100
http://does.ci.washington.dc.us/
one_stop.html

Security Regulators

Securities Bureau of the District of
Columbia
P.O. Box 37378
Washington, DC 20001
202-727-8000

Small Business Development Center

Howard University
Small Business Development
Center
2600 6th Street, NW, Room 125
Washington, DC 20059
202-806-1550
Fax: 202-806-1777
E-mail: husbdc@ cldc.howard.edu
www.cldc.howard.edu/~husbdc

Social Services Offices

Department of Human Services
Martin Luther King Ave., SE
Building 801E
Washington, DC 20032
202-279-6000
http://dhs.washington.dc.us

Temporary Assistance to Needy Families (TANF)

Welfare Reform
Patricia Handy
Washington DC Department of
Human Services
33 N St., NE
Washington, DC 20002
202-727-3444
www.dhs.washington.dc.us/
PublicInfo/WelfareReform/
REFORM.HTM

Transportation Department

Radamese Cabrera
Washington DC Department of
Public Works
2000 14th St., 6th Floor
Washington, DC 20009
202-939-8012
www.ci.washington.dc.us/
transportation.html

Unclaimed Property Office

Office of the Comptroller
Unclaimed Property Unit
415 12th St., NW, Room 408
Washington, DC 20004
202-727-0063

Unemployment Insurance Office

Office of Unemployment
Compensation
Department of Employment
Services
500 C St., NW, Room 515
Washington, DC 20001
202-724-7274
Weekly benefit range: $50-359
Duration of benefits: 20-26 weeks

Utility Commission

Public Service Commission
717 14th St., NW
Suite 200
Washington, DC 20005
202-626-5110

Women's Commission

Women's Bureau
U.S. Department of Labor
200 Constitution Ave., NW

Washington, DC 20210
800-827-5335
202-219-6631
Fax: 202-219-5529

www.dol.gov/dol.wb
Delores L. Crockett, Acting
Director
Lillian M. Long, Chair

FLORIDA

Federal Information Center
All Locations; 800-688-9889

State Information Office
850-488-1234
http://www.state.fl.us

Department on Aging
Department of Elder Affairs
4040 Esplanade Way
Tallahassee, FL 32399-0700
850-414-2108
Elder Helpline:
    800-96-ELDER (in FL)
http://www.state.fl.us/doea/
doea.html

Attorney General's Office
Office of the Attorney General
The Capitol
PL 01
Tallahassee, FL 32399
850-487-1963
http://legal.firn.edu

Banking Commissioner
State Comptroller
Division of Banking
State Capitol Bldg., PL-09
Tallahassee, FL 32399-0350
850-488-0286
800-848-3792 (toll free in FL)
http://www.dbf.state.fl.us

Child Care and Development Block Grant Lead Agency
Chief, Child Care Services
Florida Department of Children
and Families
1317 Windwood Blvd.
Building 7, Room 229
Tallahassee, FL 32399-0700
850-921-4713
Fax: 850-488-9584

Child Support Enforcement Agency
Patricia Piller
Child Support Enforcement
Program
Department of Revenue
P.O. Box 8030
Tallahassee, FL 32314
850-922-9590
Fax: 850-488-4401
http://sun6.dms.state.fl.us/
dor/html/child_support.htm/

Cooperative Extension Offices
Christine Taylor-Stephens, Dean
Florida Cooperative Extension
Service
P.O. Box 110220
University of Florida
Gainesville, FL 32611-0210
352-392-1761
http://www.ifas.ufl.edu

Lawrence Carter, Director
Cooperative Extension Service
215 Perry Paige Building S.
Florida A&M University
Tallahassee, FL 32307
850-599-3546
http://www.famu.edu

Corporation Division Office
Division of Corporations
Secretary of State
P.O. Box 627
Tallahassee, FL 32314
850-488-9000
www.dos.state.fl.us/doc/
index.html

Day Care Licensing Agency
Florida Department of Children
and Families
Family Safety and
Preservation/Child Care
1317 Windwood Blvd.
Building 7, Room 213
Tallahassee, FL 32399-0700
850-488-4900

Economic Development Office
Florida Economic Development
Council
502 East Jefferson Street
Tallahassee, FL 32301
805-222-3000
Fax: 850-222-3019

Enterprise Florida
390 North Orange Avenue
Suite 1300
Orlando, FL 32801

407-316-4600
Fax 407-316-4599
www.floridabusiness.com

Department of Education
Florida Department of Education
Education Information and
Accountability Services
325 W. Gaines St., Room 852
Tallahassee, FL 32399-0400
850-487-2280
http://www.firn.edu/doe/index.html

Department of Higher Education
Florida Office of Student Financial
Assistance
255 Collins Building
325 West Gaines Street
Tallahassee, FL 32399-0400
850-488-4095
Fax: 850-488-3612
www.firn.edu/doe/bin00065/
home0065.htm

Health Department
Florida Department of Health
2020 Capital Circle SE
Tallahassee, FL 32399-1700
850-487-2945
www.doh.state.fl.us
E-mail: Dorothy_Bruce@
doh.state.fl.us
E-mail: JoAnn_Steele@doh.
state.fl.us

Housing Office
Florida Housing Finance Agency
227 N. Bronough St.
Suite 5000

Tallahassee, FL 32301-1329
850-488-4197

Insurance Commissioner
Insurance Commissioner
200 E. Gaines St.
Tallahassee, FL 32399-0300
850-922-3100
800-342-2762
http://www.doi.state.fl.us/

Labor Department
Florida Department of Labor and
Employment Security
2012 Capital Circle SE, Suite 306
Tallahassee, FL 32399-2156
850-481-1927
www.state.fl.us/dles

Licensing Office
Florida Department of business
and Professional Regulation
1940 N. Monroe St.
Tallahassee, FL 32399
850-488-6602
www.state.fl.us/dbpr

One-Stop Career Center
Workforce Florida
Department of Labor and
Employment Security
Division of Jobs and Benefits
2012 Capital Circle SE, Suite 303
Hartman Building
Tallahassee, FL 32399-2152
850-922-7021
www.floridajobs.org/jb/initiatives/
onestop

Security Regulators
Division of Securities
101 East Gaines St.
Tallahassee, FL 32399
850-488-9530
800-848-3792
www.dbf.state.fl.us/index.html

**Small Business Development
Center**
Florida Small Business
Development Center
University of West Florida
19 West Garden Street, Suite 302
Pensacola, FL 32514-5750
850-595-5480
800-644-SBDC
Fax: 850-595-5487
E-mail: fsbdc@uwf.edu
www.sbdc.uwf.edu

Social Services Offices
Florida Department of Children
and Families
1317 Winewood Boulevard
Building 1, Room 206
Tallahassee, FL 32399-0770
904-488-4855
www.state.fl.us\cs_web

**Temporary Assistance to Needy
Families (TANF)**
Temporary Aid to Needy Families
Christy Moore
Florida Department of Health and
Rehabilitation Services
1317 Winewood Blvd.
Tallahassee, FL 32399

850-921-0193
http://fcn.state.fl.us/index.html

Transportation Department
Catherine Kelly
Department of Transportation
605 Suwannee St.
Mail Stop 26
Tallahassee, FL 32399
850-414-4500
www.dot.state.fl.us

Unclaimed Property Office
Department of Banking and
Finance
Abandoned Property Division
101 East Gaines St.
Tallahassee, FL 32399
850-488-0357
www.dbf.state.fl.us/index.html

Unemployment Insurance Office
Division of Unemployment
Compensation
201 Caldwell Building
Tallahassee, FL 32399

904-921-3889
Weekly benefit range: $10-250
Duration of benefits: 10-26 weeks

Utility Commission
Public Service Commission
2540 Shumard-Oak Blvd.
Tallahassee, FL 32399-0850
850-413-6344
800-342-3552 (FL only)
http://www.scri.net/psc

Women's Commission
Florida Commission on the Status
of Women
Office of the Attorney General
The Capitol
Tallahassee, FL 32399-1050
850-414-3300
Fax: 850-921-4131
E-mail: Michele-Manning@
oag.state.fl.us
http://legal.firn.edu/units/fcsw
Kate Gooderham, Chair
Susan Gilbert, Vice Chair

Georgia

Federal Information Center
All Locations; 800-688-9889

State Information Office
404-656-2000
http://www.state.ga.us

Department on Aging
Aging Services Office
2 Peachtree St., NW
Atlanta, GA 30303
404-657-5258
http://www.state.ga.us/
departments/dhr/aging/html

Attorney General's Office
Office of the Attorney General
40 Capitol Square. SW
Atlanta, GA 30334
404-656-3300
http://ganet.org/ago/

Banking Commissioner
Commissioner of Banking and
Finance
2990 Brandywine Rd., Suite 200
Atlanta, GA 30341-5565
707-986-1633
http://www.ganet.org/ services/dbf/
locdepts.htm

*Child Care and Development
Block Grant Lead Agency*
Family Support Unit
Division of Family and Children
Services

Georgia Department of Human
Resources
Two Peachtree St., NW
Suite 12-400
Atlanta, GA 30303-3142
404-657-3438
Fax: 404-657-3489
http://www2.state.ga.us/
Departments/DHR

*Child Support Enforcement
Agency*
Robert Riddle
Child Support Enforcement
Department of Human Resources
P.O. Box 38450
Atlanta, GA 30334
404-657-3851
800-227-7993 (in GA)
Fax: 404-657-3326

Cooperative Extension Offices
Bob Isaac, Interim Director
Cooperative Extension Service
University of Georgia
1111 Conner Hall
Athens, GA 30602
706-542-3824
http://www.ces.uga.edu

Dr. Fred Harrison, Jr., Dir.
Cooperative Extension Service
P.O. Box 4061
Fort Valley State College
Fort Valley, GA 31030

912-825-6269
http://agschool.fvsc.peachnet.edu

Corporation Division Office
Corporations Division
Secretary of State
Suite 306, West Tower #2
Martin Luther King Dr., SE
Atlanta, GA 30334
404-656-2185
www.sos.state.ga.us

Day Care Licensing Agency
Department of Human Resources
Child Care Licensing Unit
2 Peachtree St., NW, 32nd Floor
Atlanta, GA 30303-3142
404-657-5562
http://www2.state.ga.us/
Departments/DHR

Economic Development Office
Office of Economic Development
60 Executive Park South, NE
Suite 250
Atlanta, GA 30329-2231
404-679-4940
Fax: 800-736-1155
www.dca.state.ga.us

Department of Education
Georgia Department of Education
205 Butler St.
Twin Towers East
Suite 1654
Atlanta, GA 30334
404-656-2400
http://www.doe.k12.ga.us/

Department of Higher Education
Student Finance Commission
2082 East Exchange Place
Tucker, GA 30084
800-776-6878
770-414-3000
Fax: 770-724-9089
www.gsfc.org

Health Department
Georgia Division of Public Health
Two Peachtree Street, NW
Atlanta, GA 30303-3186
404-657-2700
www.ph.dhr.state.ga.us/
E-mail: gdphinfo@ dhr.state.ga.us

Housing Office
Georgia Residential Finance
Authority
60 Executive Park South
Suite 250
Atlanta, GA 30329
404-679-4840
http://www.dca.state.ga.us

Insurance Commissioner
Insurance Commissioner
7th Floor West Tower, Floyd Bldg.
2 Martin Luther King, Jr. Dr.
Atlanta, GA 30334
404-656-2070
800-656-2298
http://www2.state.ga.us/gains.
commission/

Labor Department
Georgia Department of Labor
148 International Boulevard

Atlanta, GA 30303-1751
404-656-3028
www.dol.state.ga.us

Licensing Office
Examining Board Division
Secretary of State
166 Pryor St., SW
Atlanta, GA 30303
404-656-3900
www.sos.state.ga.us/ebd/
default.htm

One-Stop Career Center
Department of Labor
Employment Services
148 International Boulevard, NE
Atlanta, GA 30303-1751
404-656-6380
Fax: 404-657-8285
www.state.ga.us/index/gaemp.
html

Security Regulators
Securities and Business
Regulation Division
802 West Tower, Suite 802
2 Martin Luther King Jr. Dr., SE
Atlanta, GA 30334
404-656-2894
www.sos.state.ga.us/Securities

**Small Business Development
Center**
Georgia Small Business
Development Center
University of Georgia
Chicopee Complex
1180 East Broad Street

Athens, GA 30602-5412
706-542-6762
Fax: 706-542-6776
E-mail:SBDCDIR@ sbdc.uga.edu
www.sbdc.uga.edu

Social Services Offices
Georgia Department of Human
Resources
200 Piedmont Avenue
Suite 1504, West Tower
Atlanta, GA 30303
404-656-4937
www.state.ga.us/Departments/
DHR

**Temporary Assistance to Needy
Families (TANF)**
Temporary Aid to Needy Families
Tommy Olmstead
Georgia Department of Human
Resources
2 Peachtree St., NW, Suite 16-200
Atlanta, GA 30303
404-656-5680
www2.state.ga.us/
departments/dhr/tanf.html

Transportation Department
Luke Cousins
Georgia Department of
Transportation
276 Memorial Dr., SW
Atlanta, GA 30303
404-651-9201
www.dot.state.ga.us

Unclaimed Property Office
Department of Revenue

Property Tax Division
Unclaimed Property
270 Washington St.
Room 404
Atlanta, GA 30334
404-656-4244
www2.sate.ga.us/
departments/dor/ptd/

Unemployment Insurance Office
Assistance Commissioner
Unemployment Insurance
Georgia Department of Labor
148 International Blvd.,NE
Suite 718
Atlanta, GA 30303
404-656-3050
Weekly benefit range: $37-205
Duration of benefits: 9-26 weeks

Utility Commission
Public Service Commission
47 Trinity Ave.
Atlanta, GA 30334
404-656-4501
800-282-5813 (GA only)
http://www.psc.state.ga.us

Women's Commission
GA State Commission of Women
148 International Blvd., NE
Atlanta, GA 30303
404-657-9260
Fax: 404-657-2963
E-mail: gawomen@manspring.
com
www.manspring.com/~gawomen
Nellie Duke, Chair
Juliana McConnell, Vice Chair

Hawaii

Federal Information Center
All Locations; 800-688-9889

State Information Office
808-548-6222
http://www.state.hi.us

Department on Aging
Aging Office
205 S. Hotel St., Suite 107
Honolulu, HI 96813-2831
808-586-0100

Attorney General's Office
Office of the Attorney General
425 Queen St.
Honolulu, HI 96813
808-586-1282
www.state.hi.us/ag

Banking Commissioner
Commissioner of Financial
Institutions
P.O. Box 2054
1010 Richards St., Room 602A
Honolulu, HI 96805
808-586-2820

**Child Care and Development
Block Grant Lead Agency**
Hawaii Department of Human
Services
Benefits, Employment and
Support Services Division
Child Care Program Office

1390 Miller St., Room 209
Honolulu, HI 96813
808-586-4888
Fax: 808-586-5180
http://www.hawaii.gov/icsd/
dhs/dhs.html

**Child Support Enforcement
Agency**
Mike Meaney
Child Support Enforcement
Agency
Department of Attorney General
680 Iwilei Rd., Suite 490
Honolulu, HI 96817
808-587-3698
Fax: 808-587-3716
http://www.hawaii.gov/
csea/csea.htm

Cooperative Extension Office
Dr. Po'Yung Lai, Assistant
Director
Cooperative Extension Service
3050 Maile Way
Honolulu, HI 96822
808-956-8397
http://www.hawaii.edu

Corporation Division Office
Business Registration Division
Department of Commerce and
Consumer Affairs
1010 Richards St.
P.O. Box 40

Honolulu, HI 96810
808-586-2727
www.hawaii.gov/dcca/dcca.html

Day Care Licensing Agency
Department of Human Services
Employment/Child Care Program
Office
1390 Miller St., Room 209
Honolulu, HI 96813
808-586-4888
http://www.hawaii.gov/icsd/dhs/
dhs.html

Economic Development Office
Department of Business and
Economic Development and
Tourism
P.O. Box 2359
Honolulu, HI 96804
No. 1 Capitol District Bldg.
250 S. Hotel Street
Honolulu, HI 96813
808-586-2593
Fax: 808-586-2589
www.hawaii.gov/dbedt/index.html

Department of Education
Hawaii Department of Education
Information Branch
P.O. Box 2360
Honolulu, HI 96804
808-832-5880
http://www.k12.hi.us/

Department of Higher Education
Hawaii State Postsecondary
Education Commission
2444 Dole Street, Room 202

Honolulu, HI 96882
808-956-8213

Health Department
Hawaii Department of Health
1250 Punchbowl Street
Honolulu, HI 96813
808-586-4400
Fax: 808-586-4444
www.state.hi.us/health/
E-mail: pijohnst@ health.
state.hi.us

Housing Office
Hawaii Housing Authority
1002 N. School St.
P.O. Box 17907
Honolulu, HI 96817
808-587-0598
http://www.state.hi.us/
hfdc/overview.htm

Insurance Commissioner
Insurance Commissioner
250 S. King Street, 5th Floor
Honolulu, HI 96813
808-586-2790
http://www.state.hi.us/insurance

Labor Department
Hawaii Department of Labor and
Industrial Relations
830 Punchbowl Street
Honolulu, HI 96813
808-586-8842
www.aloha.net/~edpso

Licensing Office
Office of the Director

Department of Commerce and
Consumer Affairs
P.O. Box 3469
Honolulu, HI 96801
808-586-2850
www.hawaii.gov/dcca/dcca.html

One-Stop Career Center
Workforce Development
Department of Labor
Workforce Development Division
830 Punchbowl Street, #112
Honolulu, HI 96813
808-586-8700
Fax: 808-586-8724
http://dlir.state.hi.us/wdd

Security Regulators
Hawaii Corporate & Securities
Commission
P.O. Box 541
Honolulu, HI 96810
808-586-2744

**Small Business Development
Center**
Hawaii Small Business
Development Center Network
University of Hawaii at Hilo
200 West Kawili Street
Hilo, HI 96720-4091
808-974-7515
Fax: 808-974-7683
E-mail: darrylm@interpac.net
www.hawaii-sbdc.org

Social Services Offices
Hawaii Department of Human
Services

P.O. Box 339
Honolulu, HW 96809
808-586-4888
www.hawaii.gov/csd/dhs/dhs.html

**Temporary Assistance to Needy
Families (TANF)**
Temporary Aid to Needy Families
Kathleen Stanley
Hawaii Department of Human
Services
P.O. Box 339
Honolulu, HI 96809
808-586-4999
www.state.hi.us/dhs/index.html

Transportation Department
Harold Lao
Hawaii Department of
Transportation
600 Kapiolani Blvd., Room 306
Honolulu, HI 96813
808-587-1845
www.hawaii.gov/dot/

Unclaimed Property Office
Unclaimed Property Section
P.O. Box 150
Honolulu, HI 96810
808-586-1589

Unemployment Insurance Office
Administrator
Unemployment Insurance Division
Department of Labor and
Industrial Relations
830 Punchbowl Street
Room 325
Honolulu, HI 96813

808-586-9069
www.aloha.net/~edpso/uitext.html
Weekly benefit range: $5-347
Duration of benefits: 26 weeks

Utility Commission
Public Utilities Commission
465 S. King St., Room 103
Honolulu, HI 96813
808-586-2020

Women's Commission
Hawaii State Commission on the
Status of Women
235 S. Beretaniast, Suite 401
Honolulu, HI 96813
808-586-5757
Fax: 808-586-5756
E-mail: hscsw@pixi.com
www.state.hi.us/hscsw
Alicynttikida Tasaka, Executive
Director

Idaho

Federal Information Center
All Locations; 800-688-9889

State Information Office
208-334-2411
http://www.state.id.us

Department on Aging
Aging Office
P.O. Box 83720
Boise, ID 83720-0007
208-334-3833
http://www.state.id.us/icoa/

Attorney General's Office
Office of the Attorney General
Statehouse
Boise, ID 83720
208-334-2400
800-432-3545
www2.state.id.us/ag/index.html

Banking Commissioner
Department of Finance
P.O. Box 83720
700 W. State St.
Boise, ID 83720-0031
208-332-8005
http://www.state.id.us/
finance/dof.htm

**Child Care and Development
Block Grant Lead Agency**
Department of Health and Welfare
Policy
P.O. Box 83720

Boise, ID 83720-0036
208-334-5815
Fax: 208-334-5817
http://www.state.id.us/dhw/
hwgd_www/ home.html

**Child Support Enforcement
Agency**
Jo An Silva
Bureau of Child Support Services
Department of Health and Welfare
P.O. Box 83720
Boise, ID 83720
208-334-5710
800-356-9868
Fax: 208-334-0666

Cooperative Extension Office
Dr. LeRoy D. Luft, Director
Cooperative Extension System
College of Agriculture
University of Idaho
Moscow, ID 83844-2338
208-885-6639
http://www.uidaho.edu/ag/
extension/

Corporation Division Office
Corporate Division
Secretary of State
Room 203, Statehouse
Boise, ID 83720
208-334-2301
www.idsos.state.id.us/corp/
corindex.htm

Day Care Licensing Agency
Department of Health and Welfare
Bureau of Family and Children's
Services
450 W. State St., 10th Floor
Boise, ID 83720-0036
208-334-5500
http://www.state.id.us/dhw/
hwgd_www/ home.html

Economic Development Office
Idaho Department of Commerce
700 West State Street
P.O. Box 83720
Boise, ID 83720-0093
208-334-2470
Fax: 208-334-2631
www.idoc.state.id.us/pages/
businesspage.html

Department of Education
Idaho Department of Education
P.O. Box 83720
Boise, ID 83720-0027
208-332-6800
http://www.sde.state.id.us/dept/

Department of Higher Education
Office of the State Board of
Education
P.O. Box 83720
Boise, ID 83720-0037
208-334-2270
www.sde.state.id.us/osbe/
board.htm

Health Department
Idaho Department of Health &
Welfare

450 W. State St., 10th Floor
P.O. Box 83720
Boise, ID 83720-0036
208-334-5500
Fax: 208-334-6558
TDD: 208-334-4921
www.state.id.us/dhw/
hwgd_www/home.html

Housing Office
Idaho Housing Agency
565 W. Myrtle
P.O. Box 7899
Boise, ID 83707-1899
208-331-4883
http://www.ihfa.org

Insurance Commissioner
Director of Insurance
P.O. Box 83720
Boise, ID 83720-0043
208-334-2250
http://www.doi.state.id.us/

Labor Department
Idaho Department of Labor
317 Main Street
Boise, ID 83735-0600
208-334-6252
www.labor.state.id.us

Licensing Office
State of Idaho
Department of Self-Governing
Agencies
Bureau of Occupational Licenses
Owyhee Plaza, 1109 Main, #220
Boise, ID 83720
208-334-3233

One-Stop Career Center
Idaho Works
Idaho Department of Labor
317 Main Street
Boise, ID 83735-0600
208-334-6303
Fax: 208-332-7417
www.idahoworks.state.id.us

Security Regulators
Idaho Securities Bureau
P.O. Box 83720
Boise, ID 83720
208-332-8004
www2.state.id.us/finance/dof.htm

Small Business Development Center
Idaho Small Business
Development Center
Boise State University
College of Business
1910 University Drive
Boise, ID 83725
208-385-1640
800-225-3815
Fax: 208-385-3877
E-mail: jhogge@bsu.idbsu.edu
www.idbsu.edu/isbdc

Social Services Offices
Idaho Department of Health and
Welfare
450 West State Street
Boise, ID 83720-0036
208-334-5500
www.state.id.us/dhw/
hwgd_www.home.html

Temporary Assistance to Needy Families (TANF)
Temporary Aid to Needy Families
Social Services Block Grant
Linda Caballero
Idaho Department of Health and
Welfare
P.O. Box 83720
Boise, ID 83720
208-334-5500
www.state.id.us/dhw/
hwgd_www/home.html

Transportation Department
Marty Montgomery
Idaho Department of
Transportation
P.O. Box 7129
Boise, ID 83707
208-334-8848
http://www.state.id.us/itd/
itdhmpg.htm

Linda Collins
Idaho Department of
Transportation
P.O. Box 7129
Boise, ID 83707
208-334-8286
http://www.state.id.us/itd/
itdhmpg.htm

Unclaimed Property Office
Unclaimed Property Division
P.O. Box 36
Boise, ID 83722
208-334-7623
www.unclaimed.org/id.htm

Unemployment Insurance Office
Administrator
Unemployment Insurance Division
Department of Employment
317 Main St.
Boise, ID 83735
208-334-6280
www.doe.state.id.us/id-ui.
htm#menu
Weekly benefit range: $44-248
Duration of benefits: 10-26 weeks

Utility Commission
Public Utilities Commission
P.O. Box 83720
Boise, ID 83720-0074

208-334-0300
http://www.puc.state.id.us

Women's Commission
Idaho Commission on the
Women's Program
P.O. Box 83720
Boise, ID 83720-0036
208-334-4673
Fax: 208-334-4646
E_mail: ehurlbudt@
women.state.id.us
www.state.id.us/women
Linda Hurlbudt, Director
Cindy Agidius, Chair

Illinois

Federal Information Center
All Locations; 800-688-9889

State Information Office
217-782-2000
http://www.state.il.us

Department on Aging
Aging Department
421 E. Capitol Ave. #100
Springfield, IL 62701-1789
217-785-2870
http://www.state.il.us/aging/

Attorney General's Office
Office of the Attorney General
100 West Randolph St.
Chicago, IL 60601
312-814-2503
www.ag.state.il.us

Banking Commissioner
Commissioner of Banks and Trust
Companies
500 E. Monroe St.
Springfield, IL 62701
217-782-3000
http://www.state.il.us/obr/

**Child Care and Development
Block Grant Lead Agency**
Office of Child Care and Family
Services
Illinois Department of Human
Services

300 Iles Park Place, Suite 270
Springfield, IL 62762
217-785-2559
Fax: 217-524-6029
http://www.state.il.us/agency/
dhs/Default.htm

**Child Support Enforcement
Agency**
Dianna Durham-McLoud
Child Support Enforcement
Division
Illinois Department of Public Aid
509 South 6th St., 6th Floor
Springfield, IL 62701
217-524-4602
800-447-4278
Fax: 217-524-4608
http://www.state.il.us/ dpa.cse.htm

Cooperative Extension Office
Dennis Campion, Director
University of Illinois
Cooperative Extension Svc.
122 Mumford Hall
1301 W. Gregory Dr.
Urbana, IL 61801
217-333-2660
http://www.ag.uiuc.edu

Corporation Division Office
Department of Business Services
Centennial Building, Room 328
Springfield, IL 62756
217-782-6961

www.sos.state.il.us/depts/
bus_serv/about.html

Day Care Licensing Agency
Department of Children and
Family Services
406 E. Monroe St.
Springfield, IL 62701-1498
217-524-1983
http://www.state.il.us/dcfs/
rules.htm

Economic Development Office
Department of Commerce and
Community Affairs
620 E. Adams,
Springfield, IL, 62602
100 West Randolph St.
Suite 3-400
Chicago, IL 60601
217-782-7500
Fax: 217-524-3701
www.commerce.state.il.us

Department of Education
Illinois State Board of Education
100 N. First St.
Springfield, IL 62777-0001
217-782-3950
http://www.isbe.state.il.us/

Department of Higher Education
Illinois Student Assistance
Commission
1755 Lake Cook Drive
Deerfield, IL 60015
847-948-8550 ext.3503
Fax: 847-831-8519
www.isac-online.org

Health Department
Illinois Department of Public
Health
535 West Jefferson Street
Springfield, IL 62761
217-782-4977
Fax: 217-782-3987
TTY: 800-547-0466
www.idph.state.il.us

Housing Office
Illinois Housing Development
Authority
401 N. Michigan Ave., Suite 900
Chicago, IL 60611
312-836-5200
800-942-8439
http://www.ihda.org

Insurance Commissioner
Director of Insurance
320 W. Washington St., 4th Floor
Springfield, IL 62767-0001
217-782-4515
800-548-9034
http://www.state.il.us/ins/

Labor Department
Illinois Department of Labor
State of Illinois Building
160 North LaSalle, SuiteC-1300
Chicago, IL 60601
312-793-2800
www.state.il.us/agency/idol

Licensing Office
State of Illinois
Department of Professional
Regulations

320 W. Washington, Third Floor
Springfield, IL 62786
217-785-0800
www.state.il.us/dpr

One-Stop Career Center
Illinois Employment and Training
Center (IETC) Network
Dept. of Employment Security
Employment Services
400 West Monroe Street
Springfield, IL 62704
217-785-5069
www.ides.state.il.us/html/
employer.htm

Security Regulators
Illinois Securities Department
Lincoln Tower, Suite 200
520 South Second St.
Springfield, IL 62701
217-782-2256
800-628-7937
www.sos.state.il.us/depts/
securities/sec_home.html

**Small Business Development
Center**
Illinois Small Business
Development Center
Department of Commerce &
Community Affairs
620 East Adams Street, 3rd Floor
Springfield, IL 62701
217-524-5856
217-524-0171
Fax: 217-785-6328
www.commerce.state.il.us/ dcca/
menus/business/ sbdc_hme.htm

Social Services Offices
Illinois Department of Human
Services
Office of Communications
401 South Clinton, 7th Floor
Chicago, IL 60607
312-793-2343
www.state.il.us/agency/dhs

**Temporary Assistance to Needy
Families (TANF)**
Temporary Aid to Needy Families
Howard Peters
Illinois Department of Human
Services
Harris Bldg.
100 South Grand Ave.
Springfield, IL 62762
217-557-1601
www.state.il.us/agency/
dhs/TANF.HTM

Transportation Department
Mr. David Spacek
Illinois Department of
Transportation
310 South Michigan Ave.
Chicago, IL 60604
312-793-2111
www.dot.state.il.us

Neil Ferrari
Illinois Department of
Transportation
310 South Michigan Ave.
Room 1608
Chicago, IL 60604
312-793-2111
www.dot.state.il.us

Unclaimed Property Office
Unclaimed Property Division
Department of Financial
Institutions
500 Iles Park Place
Springfield, IL 62718
217-785-6995
www.state.il.us/dfi/

Unemployment Insurance Office
Unemployment Insurance
Manager
Illinois Department of Employment
Security
401 S. State St., Room 622
Chicago, IL 60605
312-793-1837
http://il.jobsearch.org/html/
worker.htm

Weekly benefit range: $51-269
Duration of benefits: 26 weeks

Utility Commission
Commerce Commission
527 E. Capitol Ave.
P.O. Box 19280
Springfield, IL 62794-9280
217-782-7295
http://www.state.il.us/icc

Women's Commission
Governor's Commission on the
Status of Women
100 W. Randolph, Suite 16-100
Chicago, IL 60601
312-814-5743
Fax: 312-814-3823
Ellen Solomon, Executive Director

Indiana

Federal Information Center
All Locations; 800-688-9889

State Information Office
317-232-1000
http://www.state.in.us

Department on Aging
Aging and Rehabilitative Services
Division
Family and Social Services
Administration
402 W. Washington St.
Room W454
Indianapolis, IN 46207
317-232-7020

Attorney General's Office
Office of the Attorney General
Indiana Government Center South
402 W. Washington St.
Indianapolis, IN 46204
317-232-6201
800-382-5516
www.ai.org/hoosieradvocate/
index.html

Banking Commissioner
Department of Financial Institutions
402 W. Washington, Suite W066
Indianapolis, IN 46204
317-232-3955
800-382-4880 (toll free in IN)
http://www.dfi.state.in.us/

**Child Care and Development
Block Grant Lead Agency**
Indiana Family and Social
Services Administration
Division of Family and Children
402 W. Washington St.
Room W386
P.O. Box 7083
Indianapolis, IN 46204-7083
317-232-1660
Fax: 317-232-4436
http://www.ai.org/fssa/index.html

**Child Support Enforcement
Agency**
Joe Mamlin
Child Support Bureau
402 W. Washington St.
Room W360
Indianapolis, IN 46204
317-232-4894
Fax: 317-233-4925
http://www.ai.org/fssa/ cse/

Cooperative Extension Office
Dr. Wadsworth, Director
1140 AGAD
CES Administration
Purdue University
West Lafayette, IN 47907-1140
317-494-8489
http://www.agcom.purdue.
edu/agcom/extension/ ces.htm

Corporation Division Office
Office of Corporation
Secretary of State
Room E018
302 West Washington St.
Indianapolis, IN 46204
317-232-6576
www.state.in.us/sos/corps/
index.html

Day Care Licensing Agency
Indiana Family and Social
Services Administration
Division of Family and Children
Child Care Licensing Unit
402 W. Washington St.
Room 386
Indianapolis, IN 46204
317-232-4468 for centers
317-232-4521 for family care
http://www.ai.org/fssa/index.html

Economic Development Office
Indiana Department of Commerce
One North Capitol, Suite 700
Indianapolis, IN 46204
317-232-8888
800-463-8081
Fax: 317-233-5123
www.ai.org/bdev/index.html

Department of Education
Indiana Department of Education
Education Information Systems
Room 229, State House
Indianapolis, IN 46204-2798
317-232-0808
http://www.doe.state.in.us/

Department of Higher Education
State Student Assistance
Commission of Indiana
150 West Market Street, Suite 500
Indianapolis, IN 46204
317-232-2350
Fax: 317-232-3260
www.state.in.us/ssaci

Health Department
Indiana State Department of
Health
2 North Meridian Street
Indianapolis, IN 46204
317-233-1325
www.ai.org/doh/index.html
E-mail: OPA@isdh.state.in.us

Housing Office
Indiana Housing Finance Authority
115 W. Washington
South Tower, Suite 1350
Indianapolis, IN 46204-3413
317-232-7777
http://www.ai.org/ihfa

Insurance Commissioner
Commissioner of Insurance
311 W. Washington St., Suite 300
Indianapolis, IN 46204-2787
317-232-2385
800-622-4461
http://www.ai.org/idoi/index.html

Labor Department
Indiana Department of Labor
Indiana Government Center-South
402 W. Washington St.
Room W 195

Indianapolis, IN 46204
317-232-2655
www.state.in.us/labor

Licensing Office
Indiana Professional Licensing
Agency
Indiana Government Center S.
302 W. Washington St.
Room E-034
Indianapolis, IN 46204
317-232-2980
www.state.in.us/pla

One-Stop Career Center
Workforce Development
Indiana Department of Workforce
Development
Indiana Government Center
10 North Senate Avenue
Indianapolis, IN 46204
317-232-4259
Fax: 317-233-4793
www.dwd.state.in.us
E-mail: workone@dwd-
is.state.in.us

Security Regulators
Securities Division
302 W. Washington St.
Room E-111
Indianapolis, IN 46204
317-232-6688
www.ai.org/sos

**Small Business Development
Center**
Small Business Development
Center

One North Capitol, Suite 1275
Indianapolis, IN 46204
317-264-2820
E-mail: sbdc@isbdcorp.org
www.isbdcorp/sbdc

Social Services Offices
Indiana Family and Social
Services Administration
402 West Washington Street
Indianapolis, IN 46204
317-232-4453
www.in.org/fssa/index.html

**Temporary Assistance to Needy
Families (TANF)**
Temporary Aid to Needy Families
James Hmurovich
Indiana Division of Family and
Children
402 West Washington St.
Room W392
Indianapolis, IN 46204
317-232-4705
www.state.in.us/fssa/HTML/
PROGRAMS/dfcfamily.html

Transportation Department
Brian Jones
Indiana Department of
Transportation
100 N. Senate Ave., Room N901
Indianapolis, IN 46204
317-232-1493
http://www.aiorg/dot/

Rebecca Rowley
Indiana Institute for Urban
Transportation

825 East 8th St.
Bloomington, IN 47408
812-855-8143
http://www.indiana.
edu~iutrans.html

Unclaimed Property Office
Attorney General's office
Unclaimed Property Division
402 West Washington St.
Suite C-531
Indianapolis, IN 46204
317-232-6348
www.state.in.us/atty_gen/
index.html

Unemployment Insurance Office
Dept. of Workforce Development
Indiana Government Center South
10 N. Senate Ave., Room 302
Indianapolis, IN 46204

317-233-5724
Weekly benefit range: $87-217
Duration of benefits: 8-26 weeks

Utility Commission
Utility Regulatory Commission
302 W. Washington St.
Suite E306
Indianapolis, IN 46204
317-232-2701
http://www.state.in.us/iurc/
index.html

Women's Commission
Indiana State Commission for
Women
100 N. Senate Ave., N103
Indianapolis, IN 46204
317-233-6303
Fax: 317-232-6580
E-mail: icw@state.in.us
www.state.in.us/icw

Iowa

Federal Information Center
All Locations; 800-688-9889

State Information Office
515-281-5011
http://www.state.ia.us

Department on Aging
Elder Affairs Department
Clemens Building
200 W. 10th St., Third Floor
Des Moines, IA 50309
515-281-5188
http://www.sos.state.ia.us/
register/r4/r4eldaf.htm

Attorney General's Office
Office of the Attorney General
Hoover State Office Building
Des Moines, IA 50319
515-281-5164
515-281-5926 (consumer
advocate)
www.state.ia.us/government/
ag/index.html

Banking Commissioner
Superintendent of Banking
200 E. Grand
Suite 300
Des Moines, IA 50309
515-281-4014
http://www.state.ia.us/
government/com/bank

**Child Care and Development
Block Grant Lead Agency**
Federal Day Care Program
Manager
Iowa Dept. of Human Services
Hoover State Office Bldg., 5th
Floor
Des Moines, IA 50319-0114
515-281-3186
Fax: 515-281-4597
http://www.dhs.state.ia.us/

**Child Support Enforcement
Agency**
Jim Hennessey
Bureau of Collections
Department of Human Services
Hoover Building- 5th Floor
Des Moines, IA 50319
515-281-5580
515-281-8854
800-374-KIDS (in IA)
http://www.state.ia.us/
government/dhs/Home
Pages/DHS/csrunit.htm

Cooperative Extension Office
Nolan R. Hartwig, Interim Director
Cooperative Extension Service
315 Beardshear Hall
Iowa State University
Ames, IA 50011
515-294-9434
http://www.exnet.iastate.edu

Corporation Division Office
Corporate Division
Secretary of State
Hoover State Office building
Des Moines, IA 50319
515-281-5204
www.sos.state.ia.us

Day Care Licensing Agency
Department of Human Services
Child Care Licensing Department
Hoover State Office Bldg.
5th Floor
Des Moines, IA 50319
515-281-4357
http://www.dhs.state.ia.us/

Economic Development Office
Department of Economic
Development
200 East Grand Ave.
Des Moines, IA 50309-1827
515-242-4700
Fax: 515-242-4809
TTY: 800-735-2942
www.state.ia.us/ided

Department of Education
Iowa Department of Education
Grimes State Office Bldg.
Des Moines, IA 50319-0146
515-281-5294
http://www.state.ia.us/educate/
depteduc/

Department of Higher Education
Iowa College Student Aid
Commission
200 Tenth Street, 4th Floor

Des Moines, IA 50309-2036
515-281-3501
www.state.ia.us/collegeaid

Health Department
Iowa Department of Public Health
Lucas Building
321 East 12th Street
DesMoines, IA 50319
517-281-5787
www.idph.state.ia.us

Housing Office
Iowa Finance Authority
100 E. Grand Ave., Suite 250
Des Moines, IA 50309
515-281-4058
http://www.ifahome.com

Insurance Commissioner
Insurance Commissioner
330 E. Maple St.
Des Moines, IA 50319
515-281-5705
800-351-4664
http://www.state.ia.us/
government/com/ ins/ins.htm

Labor Department
Iowa Workforce Development
1000 East Grand Avenue
DesMoines, IA 50319-0209
515-281-5387
www.state.ia.us/iwd

Licensing Office
Bureau of Professional Licensing
Iowa Department of Health
Lucas State Office Building

1918 SE Hulsizer
Ankeny, IA 50021
515-281-3183
www.state.ia.us/government/
com/prof/pdl1.htm

One-Stop Career Center
Workforce Development
Department of Workforce
Development
1000 East Grand Avenue
Des Moines, IA 50319-0209
515-281-5387
800-JOB-IOWA
www.state.ia.us/government/wd/

Security Regulators
Securities Division
340 East Maple St.
Des Moines, IA 50319
515-281-4441
www.state.ia.us/government/
com/ins/security/security.htm

**Small Business Development
Center**
Iowa Small Business
Development Center
Iowa State University
College of Business
Administration
137 Lynn Avenue
Ames, IA 50014
515-292-6351
800-373-7232
Fax: 515-292-0020
E-mail: rmanning@iastate.edu
www.iowasbdc.org

Social Services Offices
Iowa Dept. of Human Services
Hoover Street Office Building
5th Floor NW
1305 East Walnut
DesMoine, IA 50319
515-281-4847
www.dhs.state.ia/us

**Temporary Assistance to Needy
Families (TANF)**
Temporary Aid to Needy Families
Chuck Palmer
Iowa Department of Human
Services
Hoover State Office, Building E
13th and Walnut
Des Moines, IA 50319
515-281-5452
www.dhs.state.ia.us/HomePages/
DHS/serving.htm

Transportation Department
Peter Hallock
Iowa Dept. of Transportation
100 East Euclid St., Suite 7
Park Fair Mall
Des Moines, IA 50313
515-237-3302
www.state.ia.us/government/
dot/index.html

Unclaimed Property Office
Treasurer
Unclaimed Property Division
State Capitol Bldg.
Des Moines, IA 50319
515-281-5367

Unemployment Insurance Office
Bureau Chief of Job Insurance
Dept. of Employment Services
1000 E. Grand Ave.
Des Moines, IA 50319
515-281-5387
www.state.ia.us/government/
wd/ui/index.html
Weekly benefit range: $33-274
Duration of benefits: 11-26 weeks

Utility Commission
Iowa Utilities Board
Lucas State Office Bldg., 5th Floor
Des Moines, IA 50319

515-281-5979
http://www.state.ia.us/
government/com/util/util.htm

Women's Commission
Iowa Commission on the Status of
Women
Lucas State Office Building
Des Moines, IA 50319
515-281-4461
Fax: 515-242-6119
E-mail: icsw@compuserve.com
www.state.ia.us/dhr/sw
Charlotte Nelson, Exec. Director
Kathryn Burt, Chair

Kansas

Federal Information Center
All Locations; 800-688-9889

State Information Office
913-296-0111
http://www.state.ks.us

Department on Aging
Aging Department
915 SW Harrison St., Room 150
Docking State Office Bldg.
Topeka, KS 66612-1500
913-296-4986
http://www.k4s.org/
kdoa/default.htm

Attorney General's Office
Office of the Attorney General
301 SW Tenth St.
Topeka, KS 66612
785-296-2215
http://lawlib.wuacc.edu/ag/
homepage.html

Banking Commissioner
State Bank Commissioner
700 Jackson St., Suite 300
Topeka, KS 66603-3714
785-296-2266
http://www.state.ks.us/bank-dept/

**Child Care and Development
Block Grant Lead Agency**
Coordinator of Child Care
Services

Kansas Department of Social and
Rehabilitation Services
915 SW Harrison, Room 681W
Topeka, KS 66612
785-368-6354
Fax: 785-296-0146
http://www.ink.org/public/srs

**Child Support Enforcement
Agency**
James Robertson
Child Support Enforcement
Program
Department of Social and
Rehabilitation Services
P.O. Box 497
Topeka, KS 66601
913-296-3237
800-432-0152
Fax: 913-296-5206
http://www.ink.org/public/srs/
srslegalservcie.html

Cooperative Extension Office
Mark Johnson, Interim Director
Cooperative Extension Service
Kansas State University
123 Umberger Hall
Manhattan, KS 66506
913-532-5820
http://www.oznet.ksu.edu

Corporation Division Office
Corporate Division
Secretary of State

Capitol Building, Second Floor
Topeka, KS 66612
785-296-7456
www.state.ks.us/public/sos/
corpwelc.html

Day Care Licensing Agency
Kansas Department of Health and
Environment
Child Care Licensing Division
Mills Building, Room 400C
109 SW 9th St.
Topeka, KS 66612-2218
785-296-1270
http://www.kdhe.state.ks.us/
health/

Economic Development Office
Department of Commerce and
Housing
700 SW Harrison Street
Suite 1300
Topeka, KS 66603-3712
785-296-5298
Fax 785-296-3490
TTY 785-296-3487
www.kansascommerce.com

Department of Education
Kansas State Department of
Education
120 SE 10th Ave.
Topeka, KS 66612
785-296-3201
http://www.ksbe.state.ks.us/

Department of Higher Education
Kansas Board of Regents
700 SW Harrison, Suite 1410

Topeka, KS 66603
785-296-3421
Fax: 785-296-0983
www.ukans.edu/~kbor

Health Department
Kansas Division of Health &
Environment
Capitol Tower
400 Eighth Avenue, Suite 200
Topeka, KS 66603-3930
785-296-1500
Fax: 785-368-6368
www.kdhe.state.ks.us

Housing Office
Kansas Office of Housing
Department of Commerce
700 SW Harrison
Suite 1300
Topeka, KS 66603-3712
785-296-3481
http://www.kansas commerce.com

Insurance Commissioner
Commissioner of Insurance
420 SW 9th St.
Topeka, KS 66612-1678
785-296-3071
800-432-2484
http://www.ink.org/public/kid/

Labor Department
Kansas Department of Human
Resources
401 SW Topeka Boulevard
Topeka, KS 66603-3182
785-296-5000
www.hr.state.ks.us

Licensing Office
Governor's Office
State Capitol, 2nd Floor
Topeka, KS 66612
785-296-3232

One-Stop Career Center
Kansas Job Service Career
Centers
Department of Human Resources
Div. of Employment and Training
401 SW Topeka Boulevard
Topeka, KS 66603-3182
913-296-5000
http://entkdhr.ink.org

Security Regulators
Kansas Securities Commission
618 S. Kansas Ave., 2nd Floor
Topeka, KS 66603
785-296-3307
800-232-9580
www.cjnetworks.com/~ksecom/

Small Business Development Center
Fort Hays State University
Kansas Small Business
Development Center
214 SW 6th Street, Suite 205
Topeka, KS 66603
785-296-6514
Fax: 785-291-3261
E-mail: ksbdc@cjnetworks.com
www.pittstate.edu/bti/sbdc.htm

Social Services Offices
Kansas Department of Social and
Rehabilitation Services
915 Harrison Street, 6th Floor

Docking State Office Building
Topeka, KS 66612
785-296-3271
www.ink.org/public/srs

Temporary Assistance to Needy Families (TANF)
Temporary Aid to Needy Families
Rochelle Chronister
Kansas Department of Social and
Rehabilitation Services
Docking State Office Bldg.
915 Harrison St.
Topeka, KS 66612
785-296-3271
http://www.ink.org/public/srs/
srseescomm.html

Transportation Department
James Van Sickel
Kansas Department of
Transportation
217 East 4th St.
Topeka, KS 66603
785-296-5194
http://www.ink.org/public/kdot

Patricia Waver
Kansas University of Kansas
2011 Learned Hall
Lawrence, KS 66045
785-864-5658
www.ukans.edu

Unclaimed Property Office
Unclaimed Property Division
900 Jackson, Suite 201
Topeka, KS 66612
913-296-4165
www.treasurer.state.ks.us

Unemployment Insurance Office
Director
Division of Employment Security
Department of Human Resources
401 Topeka Ave.
Topeka, KS 66603
785-296-5486
www.hr.state.ks.us/ui/html/
enui.htm
Weekly benefit range: $65-260
Duration of benefits: 10-26 weeks

Utility Commission
State Corporation Commission
1500 SW Arrowhead Rd.

Topeka, KS 66604-4027
913-271-3100
800-662-0027 (KS only)
http://www.kcc.state.ks.us

Women's Commission
Wichita Commission on the Status
of Women
Human Services Dept., 2nd Floor
455 North Main St.
Wichita, KS 67202
316-268-4691
Fax: 316-268-4219
Shirley Mast, Contact Person

Kentucky

Federal Information Center
All Locations; 800-688-9889

State Information Office
502-564-3130
http://www.state.ky.us

Department on Aging
Aging Services Division
Cabinet for Families and Children
275 E. Main St., 5th Floor
Frankfort, KY 40621
502-564-6930

Attorney General's Office
Office of the Attorney General
State Capitol, Room 116
Frankfort, KY 40601
502-696-5300
502-692-5389 (consumer protection)
www.law.state.ky.us

Banking Commissioner
Commissioner
Department of Financial Institutions
477 Versailles Rd.
Frankfort, KY 40601
502-573-3390
http://www.dfi.state.ky.us/

Child Care and Development Block Grant Lead Agency
Department for Social Services
Cabinet for Families and Children

275 E. Main St., 6W
Frankfort, KY 40621
502-564-0850
Fax: 502-564-2467
http://cfc-chs.chr.state.ky.us

Child Support Enforcement Agency
Steven Veno
Division of Child Support Enforcement
Cabinet for Human Resources
275 East Main St.
6th Floor East
Frankfort, KY 40621
502-573-4390
800-248-1163
http://www.state.ky.us/
oag/childs.htm

Cooperative Extension Offices
Dr. Absher, Director
Cooperative Extension Service
310 W.P. Garrigus Building
University of Kentucky
Lexington, KY 40546
606-257-1846
http://www.ca.uky.edu

Dr. Harold Benson, Director
Kentucky State University
Cooperative Extension Program
Frankfort, KY 40601
502-227-5905
http://www.kysu.edu

Corporation Division Office
Corporate Division
Secretary of State
Capitol Building, Room 154
Frankfort, KY 40601
502-564-2848
www.sos.state.ky.us/
Busserdiv.html

Day Care Licensing Agency
State Department of Health
Department of Social Services
Child Care Licensing Unit
275 E. Main St., 4E-A
Frankfort, KY 40621
502-564-2800
http://cfc-chs.chr.state.ky.us/

Economic Development Office
Kentucky Cabinet for Economic
Development
2300 Capital Plaza Tower
500 Mero Street
Frankfort, KY 40601
502-564-7670
www.state.ky.us/edc/
cabmain.htm

Department of Education
Kentucky Department of Education
Education Technology Assistance
Center
15 Fountain Place
Frankfort, KY 40601
502-564-2020
http://www.kde.state.ky.us/

Department of Higher Education
Kentucky Higher Education
Assistance Authority

1050 U.S. 127 South, Suite 102
Frankfort, KY 40601-4323
800-928-8926 ext.-3963
502-564-7990

Health Department
Kentucky Cabinet for Health
Services
275 East Main Street
Frankfort, KY 40621
502-564-3970
Fax: 502-564-6533
http://cfc-chs.chr.state.ky.us

Housing Office
Kentucky Housing Corporation
1231 Louisville Rd.
Frankfort, KY 40601
502-564-7630
800-633-8896

Insurance Commissioner
Insurance Commissioner
215 W. Main St.
P.O. Box 517
Frankfort, KY 40602
502-564-3630
800-595-6053
http://www.state.ky.us/agencies/
insur/ default.htm

Labor Department
Kentucky Cabinet for Workforce
Development
500 Mero Street
Frankfort, KY 40601
502-564-6606
www.state.ky.us/agencies/
wforce/index.htm

Licensing Office
Division of Occupations and
Professions
P.O. Box 456
Frankfort, KY 40602
502-564-3296

One-Stop Career Center
One-Stop Career Centers System
Department for Employment
Services
275 East Main Street
Frankfort, KY 40621
502-564-5331
www.state.ky.us/agencies/wforce/
one-stop/oscc.htm

Security Regulators
Kentucky Department of Financial
Institutions
477 Versailles Rd.
Frankfort, KY 40601
502-573-3390
800-223-2579
www.dfi.state.ky.us

Small Business Development Center
Kentucky Small Business
Development Center
University of Kentucky
Center for Entrepreneurship
225 College of Business and
Economics
Lexington, KY 40506-0034
http://gatton.gws.uky.edu/
KentuckyBusiness/ksbdc/
ksbdc.htm

Social Services Offices
Kentucky Cabinet for Families and
Children
275 East Main Street
Frankfort, KY 40621
502-564-6786
http://cfs-chs.chr.state.ky.us/
cfachome.htm

Temporary Assistance to Needy Families (TANF)
Temporary Aid to Needy Families
John Clayton
Department of Social Insurance
275 East Main St.
Third Floor, West
Frankfort, KY 40621
502-564-3703
http://cfc-chs.chr.state.ky.us/
prog.htm

Transportation Department
Vickie Bourne
Kentucky Transportation Cabinet
125 Holmes St., Third Floor
State Office Building- Annex
Frankfort, KY 40622
502-564-7433
www.kytc.state.ky.us

Unclaimed Property Office
Unclaimed Property Branch
Kentucky State Treasury
Department
Suite 183, Capitol Annex
Frankfort, KY 40601
502-564-4722
www.state.ky.us/agencies/
treasury/homepage.htm

Unemployment Insurance Office
Director, Division for
Unemployment Insurance
Dept. of Employment Services
275 E. Main St., 2nd Floor
Frankfort, KY 40621
502-564-2900
www.des.state.ky.us/agencies/
wforce/des/ui/ui.htm
Weekly benefit range: $32-180
Duration of benefits: 15-26 weeks

Utility Commission
Public Service Commission
730 Schenkel Lane
P.O. Box 615

Frankfort, KY 40602
502-564-3940
800-772-4636
http://www.state.ky.us/
agencies/psc/pschome.htm

Women's Commission
Kentucky Commission on Women
614A Shelby St.
Frankfort, KY 40601
502-564-6643
Fax: 502-564-2315
E-mail: gpotter@mail.state.ky.us
www.state.ky.us/agencies/
women/index.html
Genie Potter, Executive Director

Louisiana

Federal Information Center
All Locations; 800-688-9889

State Information Office
504-342-6600
http://www.state.la.us

Department on Aging
Elderly Affairs
412 N. 4th St.
Baton Rouge, LA 70802
504-342-1700

Attorney General's Office
Office of the Attorney General
Department of Justice
P.O. Box 94095
Baton Rouge, LA 70804
504-342-7013
800-351-4889
www.laag.com

Banking Commissioner
Commissioner of Financial
Institutions
8660 United Plaza Blvd., 2nd Floor
P.O. Box 94095
Baton Rouge, LA 70804-9095
504-925-4660
http://www.premier.net/ ~la_ofi

**Child Care and Development
Block Grant Lead Agency**
Child Care Assistance Program
Louisiana Department of Social
Services

P.O. Box 94065
Baton Rouge, LA 70804
504-342-3947
Fax: 504-342-4252
http://www.dss.state.la.us

**Child Support Enforcement
Agency**
Gordon Hood
Support Enforcement Services
Office of Family Support
P.O. Box 94065
Baton Rouge, LA 70804
504-342-4780
504-342-7397
800-256-4650

Cooperative Extension Offices
Dr. Jack Bagent, Director
Cooperative Extension Svc.
Louisiana State University
P.O. Box 25100
Baton Rouge, LA 70894-5100
504-388-4141
http://130.39.57.11/wwwac/
kes.html

Dr. Leadrey Williams
Administrator
Cooperative Extension Program
Southern University and A&M
College
P.O. Box 10010
Baton Rouge, LA 70813
504-771-2242

Corporation Division Office
Commercial Division
Secretary of State
3851 Essen Lane
Baton Rouge, LA 70809
504-925-4704
www.sec.state.la.us/comm-1a.htm

Day Care Licensing Agency
Department of Social Services
Child Care Licensing Division
P.O. Box 3078
Baton Rouge, LA 70821
504-922-0015
http://www.dss.state.la.us/

Economic Development Office
Department of Economic
Development
P.O. Box 94185
Baton Rouge, LA 70804
225-342-3000
www.lded.state.la.us

Department of Education
Louisiana Department of Education
P.O. Box 94064
Baton Rouge, LA 70804
504-342-8841
http://www.doe.state.la.us/

Department of Higher Education
Office of Student Financial
Assistance
P.O. Box 91202
Baton Rouge, LA 70821-9202
225-922-1011
Fax: 225-922-0790
www.osfa.state.la.us

Health Department
Louisiana Department of Health
and Hospitals
1201 Capitol Access Road
P.O. Box 629
Baton Rouge, LA 70821-0629
225-342-9500
Fax: 225-342-5568
www.dhh.state.la.us
E-mail: Webmaster@
dhhmail.dhh.state.la.us

Housing Office
Louisiana Housing Finance Agency
200 Lafayette St., Suite 300
Baton Rouge, LA 70801
504-342-1320

Insurance Commissioner
Commissioner of Insurance
P.O. Box 94214
Baton Rouge, LA 70804-9214
504-342-5900
800-259-5300
http://wwwldi.ldi.state.la.us/

Labor Department
Louisiana Department of Labor
1001 North 23rd
P.O. Box 94094
Baton Rouge, LA 70804
www.ldol.state.la.us

Licensing Office
First Stop Shop
Secretary of State
P.O. Box 94125
Baton Rouge, LA 70804
504-922-2675

800-259-0001
www.sec.state.la.us

One-Stop Career Center
Louisiana Works
Louisiana Occupational
Information Coordinating
Committee (L.O.I.C.C.)
P.O. Box 94094
Baton Rouge, LA 70804
504-342-5149
Fax: 504-342-5115
www.ldol.state.la.us

Security Regulators
Louisiana Securities Commission
3445 N. Causeway, Suite 509
Metairie, LA 70002
504-846-6970

Small Business Development Center
Louisiana Small Business
Development Center
Northeast Louisiana University
College of Business
Administration, Room 2-123
Monroe, LA 71209-6435
318-342-5506
Fax: 318-342-5510
E-mail: esc@alpha.nlu.edu
http://leap.nlu.edu/html/
lsbdc/Nlu/nlu.htm

Social Services Offices
Louisiana Department of Human
Services
P.O. Box 3776
Baton Rouge, LA 70821

504-342-6729
www.dss.state.la.us

Temporary Assistance to Needy Families (TANF)
Temporary Aid to Needy Families
Madlyn Bagneris
Louisiana Dept. of Social Services
P.O. Box 3776
Baton Rouge, LA 70821
504-342-0286
http://www.dss.state.la.us/
offofs/html/family_independence_
temporary_.html

Transportation Department
Emily Callender
Louisiana Department of
Transportation and Development
P.O. Box 94245
Baton Rouge, LA 70804
504-379-1436
www.dotd.state.la.us

Jeanie Boyd
Louisiana Department of
Transportation and Development
P.O. Box 94245
Baton Rouge, LA 70804
504-379-1729
www.dtod.state.la.us

Unclaimed Property Office
Louisiana Department of Revenue
and Taxation
Unclaimed Property Section
P.O. Box 91010
Baton Rouge, LA 70821
504-925-7407
www.rev.state.la.us

Unemployment Insurance Office
Director, Unemployment
Insurance
Louisiana Department of Labor
P.O. Box 94094
Baton Rouge, LA 70804
504-342-3017
www.ldol.state.la.us/faqfoldr/
faqui.html
Weekly benefit range: $10-181
Duration of benefits: 26 weeks

Utility Commission
Public Service Commission
One American Place, Suite 1630

P.O. Box 9115H
Baton Rouge, LA 70825
504-342-4404
800-228-9368 (LA only)

Women's Commission
LA Office of Women's Services
1885 Woodale Blvd., 9th Floor
Baton Rouge, LA 70806
225-922-0960
Fax: 225-922-0959
E-mail: owsbradm@ows.
state.la.us
www.ows.state.la.us/
Vera Clay, Executive Director

Maine

Federal Information Center
All Locations; 800-688-9889

State Information Office
207-582-9500
http://www.state.maine.us

Department on Aging
Elder and Adult Services
Human Services Department
11 State House Station
35 Anthony Ave.
Augusta, ME 04333-0011
207-624-5335
http://www.state.me.us/
beas/dhs_beas.htm

Attorney General's Office
Office of the Attorney General
6 State House Station
Augusta, ME 04333
207-626-8800
www.state.me.us/ag/homepage.
htm

Banking Commissioner
Superintendent of Banking
#36 State House Station
Augusta, ME 04333-0036
207-624-8570
http://www.state.me.us/
pfr/bkg/bkghome2.htm

*Child Care and Development
Block Grant Lead Agency*
Office of Child Care and Head
Start

Maine Dept. of Human Services
221 State St.
Augusta, ME 04333-0011
207-287-5060
Fax: 207-287-5031
http://www.state.me.us/dhs/main/
welcome.htm

*Child Support Enforcement
Agency*
Stephen Hussey
Division of Support Enforcement
and Recovery
Bureau of Income Maintenance
Department of Human Services
State House Station 11
Whitten Rd.
Augusta, ME 04333
207-287-2886
207-287-5096
800-371-3101 (in ME)

Cooperative Extension Office
Vaughn Holyoke, Director
Cooperative Extension Service
University of Maine
5741 Libby Hall, Room 102
Orono, ME 04469-5741
207-581-3188
http://www.umext.maine.edu

Corporation Division Office
Information and Report Section
Bureau of Corporations
Secretary of State

State House Station 101
Augusta, ME 04333
207-287-3676
www.state.me.us/sos/sos.htm

Day Care Licensing Agency
Bureau of Child and Family
Services
221 State St., Station 11
Augusta, ME 04333
207-287-5060
http://www.state.me.us/dhs/main/
welcome.htm

Economic Development Office
Office of Business Development
Department of Economic and
Community Development
59 State House Station
Augusta, ME 04333
207-287-3153
Fax: 207-287-5701
TTY: 207-287-2656
www.econdevmaine.com

Department of Education
Maine Department of Education
Educational Bldg.
Station No. 23
Augusta, ME 04333
207-287-5841
http://www.state.me.us/education/
homepage.htm

Department of Higher Education
Finance Authority of Maine
(FAME)
Maine Education Assistance
Division

83 Western Avenue
P.O. Box 949
Augusta, ME 04332-0949
207-623-3263
TDD: 207-626-2717
Fax: 207-623-0095
www.famemaine.com

Health Department
Maine Department of Human
Services
221 State Street
Augusta, ME 04333
207-287-3707
Fax: 207-626-5555
TTY: 207-287-4479
www.state.me.us/dhs/main/
welcome.htm

Housing Office
Maine State Housing Authority
353 Water St.
Augusta, ME 04330-4633
207-626-4600
800-452-4668
http://www.mainehousing. org

Insurance Commissioner
Superintendent of Insurance
34 State House Station
Augusta, ME 04333
207-624-8475
800-750-5353
http://www.state.me.us/pfr/ins/
inshome2.htm

Labor Department
Maine Department of Labor
Bureau of Employment Services

55 State House Station
Augusta, ME 04333-0055
207-624-6390
www.state.me.us/labor/jsd/
observ.htm

Licensing Office
Department of Professional and
Financial Regulation
State House Station 35
August, ME 04333
207-624-8500
www.state.me.us/pfr/ pfrhome.htm

One-Stop Career Center
Maine Career Centers
Department of Labor
Bureau of Employment Services
55 State House Station
Augusta, ME 04333-0055
888-457-8883
TTY: 800-794-1110
www.state.me.us/labor/jsd/
jobserv.htm

Security Regulators
Maine Securities Division
121 State House Station
Augusta, ME 04333
207-576-6360
www.state.me.us/pfr/sec/
sechome2.htm

**Small Business Development
Center**
Small Business Development
Center
University of Southern Maine
15 Surrenden Street

Portland, ME 04103
MAILING ADDRESS
 96 Falmouth Street
 Portland, ME 04104-9300
207-780-4420
Fax: 207-780-4810
E-mail: msbdc@ portland.
maine.edu
www.usm.maine.edu/~sbdc

Social Services Offices
Maine Dept. of Human Services
221 State Street
Augusta, ME 04333
207-287-2546
www.state.me.us/dhs/main/
welcome.htm

**Temporary Assistance to Needy
Families (TANF)**
Temporary Aid to Needy Families
Kevin Concannon
Maine Department of Human
Services
11 Statehouse Station
Augusta, ME 04333
207-287-2736
www.state.me.us/dhs/main/
welome.htm

Transportation Department
Kim King
Office of Passenger
Transportation
16 Statehouse Station
Augusta, ME 043333
207-287-3318
www.state.me.us/mdot/
homepage.htm

Nathan Moulton
Office of Passenger
Transportation
16 Statehouse Station
Augusta, NE 04333
207-287-3318
www.state.me.us/mdot/
homepage.htm

Unclaimed Property Office
Treasury Department
Abandoned Property Division
39 State House Station
Augusta, ME 043333
207-287-6668

Unemployment Insurance Office
Director, Unemployment
Compensation Division

Maine Department of Labor
P.O. Box 309
Augusta, ME 04332
207-287-3176
www.state.me.us/labor/ucd/
homepag1.htm
Weekly benefit range: $35-303
Duration of benefits: 21-26 weeks

Utility Commission
Public Utilities Commission
18 State House Station
Augusta, ME 04333-0018
207-287-3831
800-452-4699 (ME only)
http://www.state.me. us/mpuc

Women's Commission
Abolished

Maryland

Federal Information Center
All Locations; 800-688-9889

State Information Office
800-449-4347
http://www.state.md.us

Department on Aging
Aging Office
301 W. Preston St., Room 1004
Baltimore, MD 21201-2374
410-767-1100
http://www.inform.umd.edu:8080/
umststate/md_resources/ooa

Attorney General's Office
Office of the Attorney General
200 St. Paul Place
Baltimore, MD 21202
410-576-6300
410-576-6550 (consumer
protection)
www.oag.state.md.us

Banking Commissioner
Bank Commissioner
500 Port Calvert St., Room 402
Baltimore, MD 21202-2272
410-333-6808

**Child Care and Development
Block Grant Lead Agency**
Child Care Administration
Maryland Department of Human
Resources

311 W. Saratoga St., 1st Floor
Baltimore, MD 21201
410-767-7128
Fax: 410-333-8699
http://www.dhr.state.md.us/dhr

**Child Support Enforcement
Agency**
Clifford Layman
Child Support Enforcement
Administration
311 West Saratoga St.
Baltimore, MD 21201
410-767-7674
800-332-3647 (in MD)
Fax: 410-333-0774
http://www.dhr.state.md.
us/srv_csea.htm

Cooperative Extension Offices
Dr. Thomas Fretz
Regional Directors Office
Cooperative Extension Svc.
Room 1104, Simons Hall
University of Maryland
College Park, MD 20742
301-405-2907
http://www.agnr.umd.edu/ces/

Dr. Henry Brookes, Administrator
Cooperative Extension Service,
UMES
Princess Anne, MD 21853
410-651-6206
http://www.umes.umd.
edu/dept/rudept.html

Corporation Division Office
Corporate Charter Division
Department of Assessments and
Taxation
301 W. Preston St.
Baltimore, MD 21201
410-767-1184
www.dat.state.md.us/sdatweb/
index.html

Day Care Licensing Agency
Department of Human Resources
Child Care Administration
Licensing Division
311 W. Saratoga St.
Baltimore, MD 21201
410-767-7805
http://www.dhr.state.md.us/dhr/

Economic Development Office
Department of Business and
Economic Development
217 East Redwood St.
Baltimore, MD 21202
410-767-6300
800-811-0051
Fax: 410-333-6792
TDD/TTY: 410-333-6926
www.dbed.state.md.us/dbed

Department of Education
Maryland Department of Education
Office of Planning
Results and Information
Management
200 W. Baltimore St.
Baltimore, MD 21201
410-767-0073
888-246-0016
http://www.mdse.state.md.us/

Department of Higher Education
Maryland Higher Education
Commission
State Scholarship Administration
The Jeffery Building
16 Francis Street, Suite 209
Annapolis, MD 21401-1781
410-974-5370
Fax: 410-974-5994
www.mhec.state.md.us

Health Department
Maryland Department of Health &
Mental Hygiene
State Office Building Complex
201 West Preston Street
Baltimore, MD 21201-2399
410-767-6860
TDD: 800-735-2258
www.dhmh.state.md.us/index.html

Housing Office
Department of Housing and
Community Development
100 Community Place
Crownsville, MD 21032
410-514-7200
http://dhcd.state.md.us

Insurance Commissioner
Insurance Commissioner
525 St. Paul Place
Baltimore, MD 21202
410-486-2090
800-492-6116
http://www.gacc.com/mia/

Labor Department
Maryland Department of Labor,
Licensing and Regulation

1100 North Eutaw Street
Baltimore, MD 21201-000
410-767-2000
www.dllr.state.md.us

Licensing Office
Division of Occupational and
Professional Licensing
Department of Labor, Licensing
and Regulation
500 N. Calvert St.
Baltimore, MD 21202
410-230-6000
www.dllr.state.md.us/

One-Stop Career Center
CareerNet
Department of Labor, Licensing
and Regulation
Employment Services
500 North Calvert Street
Baltimore, MD 21202-2272
410-767-2400
TTY: 410-767-2986
www.careernet.state.md.us/
CareerNet.html
E-mail: det@dllr.state.md.us

Security Regulators
Maryland Division of Securities
200 St. Paul Place, 20th Floor
Baltimore, MD 21202
410-576-6360
www.oag.state.md.us/Securities

Small Business Development Center
Maryland Small Business
Development Center

7100 Baltimore Avenue
Suite 401
College Park, MD 20740
301-403-8300
Fax: 301-403-8303
E-mail: sbdc@rhsmith.umd.edu
www.mbs.umd.edu/sbdc

Social Services Offices
Maryland Department of Human
Resources
Saratoga State Center
311 West Saratoga Street
Baltimore, MD 21201-1000
410-767-7758
www.dhr.state.md.us/dhr

Temporary Assistance to Needy Families (TANF)
Temporary Aid to Needy Families
Alvin Collins
Maryland Department of Human
Resources
311 West Saratoga St.
Room 1045
Baltimore, MD 21201
410-767-7000
www.dhr.state.md.us/dhr/
services.htm

Transportation Department
Charles Lippy
Maryland Mass Transit
Administration
6 St. Paul St.
Baltimore, MD 21201
410-767-3765
www.mtamaryland.com

Unclaimed Property Office
Unclaimed Property Section
301 West Preston St.
Baltimore, MD 21201
410-225-1700
www.comp.state.md.us/main.htm

Unemployment Insurance Office
Executive Director
Office of Unemployment
Insurance
Department of Labor, Licensing,
and Regulation
1100 N. Eutaw St., Room 501
Baltimore, MD 21201
410-767-2464
www.dllr.state.md.us/employment/
unemployment.html
Weekly benefit range: $25-250
Duration of benefits: 26 weeks

Utility Commission
Public Service Commission
6 St. Paul St.
Baltimore, MD 21202
410-767-8000
800-492-0474 (MD only)
http://www.psc.state.md. us/psc/

Women's Commission
Maryland Commission for Women
311 West Saratoga St., Room 232
Baltimore, MD 21201
410-767-7137
Fax: 410-333-0079
E-mail: lsajardo@dhr.state.md.us
www.dhr.state.md.us/mcw/
index.html
Dr. Carl A. Silberg, Exec. Director
Dr. Fran V. Tracy-Mumsford,
Chair

Massachusetts

Federal Information Center
All Locations; 800-688-9889

State Information Office
617-722-2000
http://www.state.ma.us

Department on Aging
Elder Affairs Department
1 Ashburton Place
5th Floor, Room 506
Boston, MA 02108
617-727-7750

Attorney General's Office
Office of the Attorney General
One Ashburton Place
Boston, MA 02108
617-727-2200
617-727-8400 (consumer information)
www.magnet.state.ma.us/ag/

Banking Commissioner
Commissioner of Banks
100 Cambridge St.
20th Floor, Room 2004
Boston, MA 02202
617-727-3145
800-495-2265
http://www.state.ma.us/ dob/

Child Care and Development Block Grant Lead Agency
Office of Child Care Services

Massachusetts Executive Office of Health and Human Services
One Ashburton Place, Room 1109
Boston, MA 02108
617-626-2000
Fax: 617-626-2028
http://www.magnet.state.ma.us/ eohhs/ agencies/ofc.htm

Child Support Enforcement Agency
Jerry Fay
Child Support Enforcement Division
Department of Revenue
141 Portland St.
Cambridge, MA 02139
617-577-7200
617-621-4991
800-332-2733
http://www.ma-cse.org/

Cooperative Extension Office
Dr. John Gerber
Associate Director
212C Stockbridge Hall
University of Massachusetts
Amherst, MA 01003
413-545-4800
http://www.umass.edu/ umext/

Corporation Division Office
Corporate Division
Secretary of State
1 Ashburton Place

Boston, MA 02108
617-727-9640
www.state.ma.us/sec/cor/
corindx.htm

Day Care Licensing Agency
Department of Health
Office of Child Care Services
Day Care Licensing Division
1 Ashburton Place, 11th Floor
Boston, MA 02108
617-626-2000
http://www.magnet.state.ma.us/
eohhs/ agencies/ofc.htm

Economic Development Office
Massachusetts Office of Business
Development
10 Park Plaza, 3rd Floor
Boston, MA 02116
617-727-3206
800-5-CAPITAL
Fax: 617-727-8797
www.state.ma.us/mobd

Department of Education
Massachusetts Department of
Education
Information and Outreach
350 Main St.
Malden, MA 02148
781-388-3300
http://info.doe.mass.edu/

Department of Higher Education
Board of Higher Education
Scholarship Office
330 Stuart Street
Boston, MA 02116

617-727-9420
www.osfa.mass.edu

Health Department
Massachusetts Department of
Public Health
250 Washington Street
Boston, MA 02108-4619
617-624-5700
Fax: 617-624-5206
www.magnet.state.ma.us/dph/
dphhome.htm

Housing Offices
Massachusetts Housing Finance
Agency
1 Beacon St.
Boston, MA 02108
617-854-1000
http://www.mhfa.com/

Executive Office of Communities
and Development
Commonwealth of Massachusetts
100 Cambridge St.
Room 1804
Boston, MA 02202
617-727-7765

Insurance Commissioner
Commissioner of Insurance
470 Atlantic Ave., 6th Floor
Boston, MA 02210-2223
617-521-7794
800-882-2003

Labor Department
Massachusetts Division of
Employment and Training

19 Stanford Street
Boston, MA 02114
617-727-6560
www.detma.org

Licensing Office
Division of Registration
239 Causeway St.
Boston, MA 02114
617-727-3074
www.state.ma.us/reg

One-Stop Career Center
Massachusetts One-Stop Career
Center Network
Division of Employment and
Training
19 Stanford Street
Boston, MA 02114
617-727-6560
www.masscareers.state.ma.us

Security Regulators
Massachusetts Securities Division
John W. McCormack Bldg.
One Ashburton Place, Room 1719
Boston, MA 02108
617-727-3548
800-269-5428
www.magnet.state.ma.us/sec/
sct/sctidx.htm

**Small Business Development
Center**
Massachusetts Small Business
Development Center
University of Massachusetts
Amherst
205 School of Management

Amherst, MA 01003-4935
413-545-6301
Fax: 413-545-1273
www.umassp.edu/msbdc/

Social Services Offices
Massachusetts Health and Human
Services
1 Ashburton Place, Room 1109
Boston, MA 02108
617-727-7600
www.magnet.state.ma.us/
eohhs/eohhs.htm

**Temporary Assistance to Needy
Families (TANF)**
Temporary Aid to Needy Families
Claire McIntire
Massachusetts Department of
Transitional Assistance
600 Washington St.
Boston, MA 02111
617-348-8500
www.state.ma.us/eohhs/agencies/
dta.htm

Transportation Department
JoAnne Champa
Massachusetts Executive Office of
Transportation and Construction
10 Park Plaza
Boston, MA 02116
617-973-7062
www.eotc.org

Unclaimed Property Office
Abandoned Property Division
1 Ashburton Place, 12th Floor
Boston, MA 02108

617-367-0400
www.magnet.state.ma.us/treasury

Unemployment Insurance Office
Unemployment Insurance Director
Department of Employment and
Training
19 Staniford St., 2nd Floor
Boston, MA 02114
617-727-6560
www.detma.org/claimant.htm
Weekly benefit range: $14-402
Duration of benefits: 10-30 weeks

Utility Commission
Department of
Telecommunications and Energy

100 Cambridge St., 12th Floor
Boston, MA 02202
617-305-3500
http://www.magnet.state.
ma.us/dpu

Women's Commission
Massachusetts Governor's
Advisory Committee on Women's
Issues
Statehouse Governor's Office
Room 360
Boston, MA 02133
617-727-3600
Fax: 617-727-9725
Jennifer Davis Carey, Contact
Joanne Thompson, Chair

Michigan

Federal Information Center
All Locations; 800-688-9889

State Information Office
517-373-1837
http://www.state.mi.us

Department on Aging
Aging Office
P.O. Box 30026
Lansing, MI 48909
517-373-8230
http://mass.iog.wayne.edu/
masshome.html

Attorney General's Office
Office of the Attorney General
P.O. Box 30212
525 West Ottawa St.
Lansing, MI 48909
517-373-1100
517-373-1140 (consumer
protection)
www.ag.state.mi.us

Banking Commissioner
Commissioner of Financial
Institutions Bureau
P.O. Box 30224
Lansing, MI 48909-7724
517-373-3460
http://www.cif.state.mi.us/
fib/home.html

**Child Care and Development
Block Grant Lead Agency**
Office of Children's Services
Michigan Department of Social
Services
235 S. Grand Ave., Suite 1315
P.O. Box 30037
Lansing, MI 48909
517-335-6183
Fax: 517-241-7843

**Child Support Enforcement
Agency**
Wallace Dutkowski
Office of Child Support
Department of Social Services
P.O. Box 30478
Lansing, MI 48909
517-373-7570
517-373-4980

Cooperative Extension Office
Arlen Leholm, Director
Michigan State University
Extension
Room 108, Agriculture Hall
Michigan State University
East Lansing, MI 48824
517-355-2308
http://www.msue.msu.edu/msue

Corporation Division Office
Corporation Division
Corporation and Securities Bureau

Michigan Department of
Commerce
P.O. Box 3004
6546 Mercantile
Lansing, MI 48909
517-334-6302
www.cis.state.mi.us/corp

Day Care Licensing Agency
Division of Child Day Care
Licensing CIS-BRS
7109 W. Saginaw, 2nd Floor
P.O. Box 30650
Lansing, MI 48909-8150
517-373-8300
http://www.cis.state.mi.us/brs/
cdc/rules.htm

Economic Development Office
Michigan Jobs Commission
201 North Washington Square
Victor Office Center, 4th Floor
Lansing MI 48913
517-373-9808
Fax: 517-335-0198
www.mjc.state.mi.us

Department of Education
Michigan Department of Education
Information Center Data Services
P.O. Box 30008
Lansing, MI 48909
517-373-3324
http://www.mde.state.mi.us/

Department of Higher Education
Michigan Department of Treasury
Higher Education Assistance
Authority

1st Floor, Hannah Building
608 West Allegan
Lansing, MI 48901
888-447-2687
517-373-3394
www.treas.state.mi.us/college/
mheaa.htm

Health Department
Michigan Department of
Community Health
Lewis Cass Building-Sixth Floor
320 South Walnut Street
Lansing, MI 48913
517-373-3500
www.mdch.state.mi.us/
E-mail: arias@state.mi.us

Housing Office
Michigan State Housing
Development Authority
Plaza One, Fifth Floor
401 S. Washington Square
P.O. Box 30044
Lansing, MI 48909
517-373-8370
800-327-9158
http://www.voyager.net/
mshda/index.htm/

Insurance Commissioner
Commissioner of Insurance
Insurance Bureau
P.O. Box 30220
Lansing, MI 48909-7720
517-373-9273
800-803-7174
http://www.commerce.state.mi.
us/ins/

Labor Department
Michigan Jobs Commission
201 North Washington Square
Victor Office Center, 4th Floor
Lansing, MI 48913
517-373-9808
www.state.mi.us/mjc/ceo

Licensing Office
Michigan Department of
Consumer and Industry Services
P.O. Box 30650
Lansing, MI 48909
517-373-1820
www.cis.state.mi.us

One-Stop Career Center
Michigan Works!
Michigan Jobs Commission
201 North Washington Square
Victor Office Center, 4th Floor
Lansing, MI 48913
517-373-9808
www.state.mi.us/mjc/ceo/
employ/employ.htm
E-mail: Customer-Assistance@
state.mi.us

Security Regulators
Michigan Corporation & Securities
Bureau
P.O. Box 30222
Lansing, MI 48909
517-334-6215
www.commerce.state.mi.us/corp

Small Business Development Center
Michigan Small Business
Development Center

Wayne State University
2727 Second Avenue, Suite 107
Detroit, MI 48201
313-964-1798
Fax: 313-964-3648
Fax: 313-964-4164
E-mail: ron@misbdc.wayne.edu
http://bizserve.com/sbdc

Social Services Offices
Michigan Family Independence
Agency
235 South Grand Avenue
Lansing, MI 48933
517-373-7394
www.mfia.state.mi.us

Temporary Assistance to Needy Families (TANF)
Temporary Aid to Needy Families
Marva Livingston Hammons
Michigan Family Independence
Agency
P.O. Box 30037
235 South Grand Ave.
Lansing, MI 48909
517-373-2000
http://www.mfia.state.mi.us/
1997fact.htm

Transportation Department
Gus Lluberes
Michigan Department of
Transportation
425 West Ottawa St.
P.O. Box 30050
Lansing, MI 48909
517-373-8820
www.state.mi.us/mdot/index.htm

Al Johnson
Michigan DOT, UPTRAN
P.O. Box 30050
Lansing, MI 48909
517-335-2549
http://www.mdot.state.mi.us/
uptran/uptran.htm

Unclaimed Property Office
Department of Treasury
Abandoned & Unclaimed Property
Division
Lansing, MI 48922
517-335-4327
www.treas.state.mi.us/unclprop/
unclindx.htm

Unemployment Insurance Office
Michigan Employment Security
Commission
7310 Woodward Ave., Room 510
Detroit, MI 48202
313-876-5000

800-638-3995
www.cis.state.mi.us/ua/
homepage.htm
Weekly benefit range: $42-300
Duration of benefits: 15-26 weeks

Utility Commission
Public Service Commission
6545 Mercantile Way
P.O. Box 30221
Lansing, MI 48909
517-334-6445
800-292-9555 (MI only)
http://ermisweb.cis.state.mi.us

Women's Commission
Michigan Women's Commission
741 N. Cedar St., Suite 102
Lansing, MI 48913
517-334-8622
Fax: 517-334-8641
www.mdcr.com
Patti Garrett, Chair

Minnesota

Federal Information Center
All Locations; 800-688-9889

State Information Office
612-296-6013
http://www.state.mn.us

Department on Aging
Aging Program Division
Social Services Department
444 LaFayette Rd.
St. Paul, MN 55155-3843
612-296-2770

Attorney General's Office
Office of the Attorney General
State Capitol, Suite 102
St. Paul, MN 55155
651-296-6196
800-657-3787
www.ag.state.mn.us/home/
default.shtml

Banking Commissioner
Department of Commerce
133 E. 7th St., 4th Floor
St. Paul, MN 55101
612-296-2135
http://commerce.state. mn.us/

**Child Care and Development
Block Grant Lead Agency**
Child Care Program Administrator
Minnesota Children
550 Cedar St., Suite 133

St. Paul, MN 55101-2273
612-296-2030
Fax: 612-297-5695

**Child Support Enforcement
Agency**
Laura Kadwell
Office of Child Support
Enforcement
Department of Human Services
444 Lafayette Rd., 4th Floor
St. Paul, MN 55155
651-296-2542

Cooperative Extension Office
Catherine Fennely, Director
Minnesota Extension Service
University of Minnesota
240 Coffey Hall
1420 Eckles Ave.
St. Paul, MN 55108
612-625-1915
http://www.mes.umn.edu

Corporation Division Office
Business Services Division
Secretary of State
180 State Office Building
St. Paul, MN 55155
612-296-2803
www.sos.state.mn.us/bus/
bus.html

Day Care Licensing Agency
Department of Human Services

Division of Licensing
444 Lafayette Rd.
St. Paul, MN 55155-3842
612-296-3971
http://www.dhs.state.mn.us/

Economic Development Office
Department of Trade and
Economic Development
500 Metro Square Blvd.
121 7th Place East
St. Paul, MN 55101-2146
612-297-1291
800-657-3858
www.dted.state.mn.us

Department of Education
Minnesota Department of Education
Information and Technology Unit
550 Cedar St.
Capitol Square Bldg.
St. Paul, MN 55101
612-296-2751
http://children.state.mn.us/

Department of Higher Education
Minnesota Higher Education
Programs
Capitol Square Building
550 Cedar Street, Suite 400
St. Paul, MN 55101
800-657-3866
612-296-3974
www.heso.state.mn.us

Health Department
Minnesota Department of Health
717 Delaware Street Southeast
Minneapolis, MN 55440-9441

612-676-5000
www.health.state.mn.us
E-mail: webmaster@
health.state.mn.us

Housing Office
Minnesota Housing Finance
Agency
400 Sibley St., Suite 300
St. Paul, MN 55101
612-296-9951
612-296-7608
800-657-3802
http://www.mhfa.state.mn.us

Insurance Commissioner
Commissioner of Commerce
133 E. 7th St.
St. Paul, MN 55101-2362
612-297-7161
800-657-3602
800-657-3978
http://www.commerce.state.mn.us/
mainin.htm

Labor Department
Minnesota Economic Security
390 North Robert Street
St.Paul, MN 55101
651-296-3644
www.des.state.mn.us

Licensing Office
Office of Consumer Services
Office of Attorney General
1400 NCL Tower
445 Minnesota St.
St. Paul, MN 55101
651-296-2331
www.ag.state.mn.us

One-Stop Career Center
Minn WorkForce Center
Department of Economic Security
390 North Robert Street
St. Paul, MN 55101
888-GET-JOBS
www.des.state.mn.us/jseek.htm
E-mail: mdes.webmaster@
des.state. mn.us

Security Regulators
Department of Commerce
133 East Seventh St., 2nd Floor
St. Paul, MN 55101
651-296-2283
www.commerce.state.mn.us

Small Business Development Center
Minnesota Small Business
Development Center
Minnesota Department of Trade
and Economic Development
500 Metro Square
121 Seventh Place East
St. Paul, MN 55101-2145
612-297-5770
Fax: 612-296-1290
E-mail: mary.kruger@dted.
state.mn.us
www.dted.state.mn.us

Social Services Offices
Minnesota Department of Human
Services
444 Lafayette Road
St.Paul, MN 555155
651-296-4416
www.dhs.state.mn.us

Temporary Assistance to Needy Families (TANF)
Temporary Aid to Needy Families
David Doth
Minnesota Department of Human
Services
444 Lafayette Rd. North
St. Paul, MN 55155
612-296-6117
http://www.dhs.state.mn.us/
ecs/Welfare/default.htm

Transportation Department
Teresa Hyde
Minnesota Department of
Transportation
210 Transportation Bldg.
Mail Stop 430
St. Paul, MN 55155
612-282-6754
www.dot.state.mn.us

Deb Fick, CCTM
Minnesota Department of
Transportation
210 Transportation Bldg.
Mail Stop 430
St. Paul, MN 55155
612-296-1610
www.dot.state.mn.us

Unclaimed Property Office
Minnesota Commerce Department
Unclaimed Property Section
133 East 7th St.
St. Paul, MN 55101
612-296-2568
www.commerce.state.mn.us

Unemployment Insurance Office
Assistant Commissioner
Minnesota Department of
Economic Security
Job Services and Reemployment
Insurance
390 N. Robert St.
St. Paul, MN 55101
651-296-3611
888-438-5627
www.des.state.mn.us/
manuals/220.htm
Weekly benefit range: $38-386
Duration of benefits: 10-26 weeks

Utility Commission
Public Utilities Commission
121 7th Place East
St. Paul, MN 55101-2147
612-296-7124
800-657-3782 (MN only)
http://www.puc.state.mn.us

Women's Commission
Minnesota Commission on the
Economic Status of Women
85 State Office Building
St. Paul, MN 55155
651-296-8590
Fax: 651-297-3697
E-mail: lcesw@commissions.
leg.state.mn.us
www.commissions.leg.state.
mn.us/
Aviva Breen, Executive Director
Becky Lourey, Chair

Mississippi

Federal Information Center
All Locations; 800-688-9889

State Information Office
601-359-1000
http://www.state.ms.us

Department on Aging
Aging and Adult Services Division
Human Services Department
P.O. Box 352
Jackson, MS 39205-0352
601-359-4925
http://www.mdhs.state.
ms.us/aas.html

Attorney General's Office
Office of the Attorney General
Department of Justice
P.O. Box 220
Jackson, MS 39205
601-359-3692
800-281-4418
www.ago.state.ms.us

Banking Commissioner
Commissioner of Banking and
Consumer Finance
P.O. Box 23729
Jackson, MS 39225-3729
601-359-1031
800-826-2499
http://www.dbcf.state.ms.us/

**Child Care and Development
Block Grant Lead Agency**
Office for Children and Youth
Mississippi Department of Human
Services
P.O. Box 352
Jackson, MS 39205-0352
601-359-4555
Fax: 601-359-4422
http://www.mdhs.state.ms.us/

**Child Support Enforcement
Agency**
Richard Harris
Division of Child Support
Enforcement
Department of Human Services
P.O. Box 352
Jackson, MS 39205
601-359-4415
800-948-4010 (in MS)
http://www.mdhs.state.
ms.us.cse.htm

Cooperative Extension Offices
Ronald A. Brown, Director
Cooperative Extension Service
Mississippi State University
P.O. Box 9601
Mississippi State, MS 39762
601-325-3034
http://www.ces.msstate.
edu/ces.html

LeRoy Davis, Dean
Co-operative Ext. Service
1000 ASU Dr. #479
Lorman, MS 39096
601-877-6128
http://www.alcorn.edu

Corporation Division Office
Office of Corporations
Secretary of State
P.O. Box 136
Jackson, MS 39205
601-359-1350
www.sos.state.ms.us

Day Care Licensing Agency
Mississippi State Dept. of Health
Child Care Division
750 N. State St.
Jackson, MS 39202
601-359-4994
http://www.mdhs.state.ms.us/
fcs_lic.html

Economic Development Office
Department of Economic and
Community Development
Post Office Box 849
Jackson, MS 39205-0849
601-359-3040
Fax: 601-359-4339
www.decd.state.ms.us

Department of Education
Mississippi Dept. of Education
P.O. Box 771
Jackson, MS 39205-0771
601-359-5615
http://mdek12.state.ms.us/

Department of Higher Education
Mississippi Institution of Higher
Learning
382 Ridgewood Road
Jackson, MS 39211-6453
601-982-6663

Health Department
Mississippi State Dept of Health
2423 North State Street
P.O. Box 1700
Jackson, MS 39215-1700
601-576-7400
Fax: 601-576-7364
www.msdh.state.ms.us/
msdhhome.htm
E-mail: info@msdh.state.ms.us

Housing Office
Mississippi Home Corporation
840 E. River Place, Suite 605
Jackson, MS 39202
601-354-6062
http://www.mshomecorp. com

Insurance Commissioner
Commissioner of Insurance
1804 Walter Sillers Bldg.
P.O. Box 79
Jackson, MS 39205
601-359-3569
800-562-2957
http://www.doi.state.ms.us

Labor Department
Mississippi Employment Security
Commission
MESC P.O. Box 1699
Jackson, MS 31295-1699

601-354-8711
www.mesc.state.ms.us

Licensing Office
Secretary of State
P.O. Box 136
Jackson, MS 39205
601-359-3123
www.sos.state.ms.us

One-Stop Career Center
Workforce, State Board for
Community & Junior Colleges
3825 Ridgewood Road
Jackson, MS 39211
601-982-6439
Fax: 601-982-6365
www.sbcjc.cc.ms.us/workfor.htm

Security Regulators
Securities Division
P.O. Box 136
Jackson, MS 39205
601-359-6371
www.sos.state.ms.us

**Small Business Development
Center**
Mississippi Small Business
Development Center
University of Mississippi
216 Old Chemistry Building
University, MS 38677
601-232-5001
800-725-7232
Fax: 601-232-5650
E-mail: msbdc@olemiss.edu
www.olemiss.edu/depts/mssbdc

Social Services Offices
Mississippi Department of Human
Services
750 North State Street
Jackson, MS 39202
601-359-4480
www.mdhs.state.ms.us

**Temporary Assistance to Needy
Families (TANF)**
Temporary Aid To Needy Families
Sherry Jackson
Department of Human Services
P.O. Box 352
750 State St.
Jackson, MS 39202
601-359-4688
www.mdhs.state.ms.us/
ea_tanf.html

Transportation Department
Charles Car
Mississippi Department of
Transportation
P.O. Box 1850
Jackson, MS 39215
601-359-7781
http://www.mdot.state.us

Unclaimed Property Office
Unclaimed Property Division
P.O. Box 138
Jackson, MS 39205
601-359-3600
www.treasury.state.ms.us

Unemployment Insurance Office
Director, Unemployment
Insurance Division

Employment Security Commission
P.O. Box 1699
Jackson, MS 39215
601-961-7700
www.mesc.state.ms.us
Weekly benefit range: $30-180
Duration of benefits: 13-26 weeks

Utility Commission
Public Service Commission
P.O. Box 1174
Jackson, MS 39215
601-961-5400
http://www.mslawyer.com

Women's Commission
Inactive

Missouri

Federal Information Center
All Locations; 800-688-9889

State Information Office
573-751-2000
http://www.state.mo.us

Department on Aging
Aging Division
P.O. Box 1337
Jefferson City, MO 65102
573-751-3082
http://www.state.mo.us/
dss/da/da.htm

Attorney General's Office
Office of the Attorney General
P.O. Box 899
Jefferson City, MO 65102
573-751-3321
800-392-8222
www.ago.state.mo.us/
homepg.htm

Banking Commissioner
Commissioner of Finance
P.O. Box 716
Jefferson City, MO 65102
573-751-3242
800-722-3321
http://www.ecodev.state.
mo.us/finance/finhome.htm

**Child Care and Development
Block Grant Lead Agency**
Division of Family Services

Missouri Department of Social
Services
P.O. Box 1527
Jefferson City, MO 65102
573-522-1137
Fax: 573-526-4814
http://www.dss.state.mo.us/

**Child Support Enforcement
Agency**
Teresa Kaiser
Division of Child Support
Enforcement
Department of Social Services
3418 Knipp Dr., Suite F
P.O. Box 2320
Jefferson City, MO 65102
573-751-4301
573-751-8450
http://services.state.mo.
us/dss/cse/cse.htm

Cooperative Extension Offices
Ronald J. Turner
Interim Director
Cooperative Extension Service
University of Missouri
309 University Hall
Columbia, MO 65211
573-882-7754
http://outreach.missouri.edu

Dyremple Marsh, Director
Cooperative Extension Service
Lincoln University

110A Allen Hall
P.O. Box 29
Jefferson City, MO 65102-0029
573-681-5550

Corporation Division Office
Business Services Department
Corporate Division
Secretary of State
301 High St.
P.O. Box 778
Jefferson City, MO 65102
573-751-4153
http://mosl.sos.state.mo.us

Day Care Licensing Agency
State Department of Health
Bureau of Child Care, Safey and
Licensure
P.O. Box 570
Jefferson City, MO 65102
573-751-2450
http://www.health.state.mo.us/

Economic Development Office
Department of Economic
Development
Truman Building, Room 720
P.O. Box 118
Jefferson City, MO 65102-0118
573-751-4446
800-523-1434, ext. 4
Fax: 573-526-2416
www.ecodev.state.mo.us

Department of Education
Missouri Department of Education
School Data Section
P.O. Box 480

Jefferson City, MO 65102-0480
573-751-2569
http://services.dese.state.mo.us/

Department of Higher Education
Missouri Department of Higher
Education
P.O. Box 1438
3515 Amazonas Drive
Jefferson City, MO 65109-5717
573-751-2361
Fax: 573-751-6135
www.mocbhe.gov

Health Department
Missouri Department of Health
930 Wildwood
P.O. Box 570
Jefferson, MO 65102-0570
573-751-6001
Fax: 573-751-6041
www.health.state.mo.us
E-mail: info@mail.health.
state.mo.us

Housing Office
Missouri Housing Development
Commission
3435 Broadway
Kansas City, MO 64111-2415
816-759-6600
http://www.mhdc.com

Insurance Commissioner
Director of Insurance
301 W. High St., Room 630
P.O. Box 690
Jefferson City, MO 65102-0690
573-751-4126

800-726-7390
http://services.state.mo.us/
insurance/ mohmepg.htm

Labor Department
Missouri Department of Labor and
Industrial Relations
3315 West Truman Boulevard
P.O. Box 58
Jefferson, MO 65102
573-751-4091
www.dolir.state.mo.us

Licensing Office
Division of Professional
Registration
Department of Economic
Development
3605 Missouri Blvd.
Jefferson City, MO 65109
573-751-0293
www.ecodev.state.mo.us/pr

One-Stop Career Center
Missouri Wins
Workforce Development
Transition Team
P.O. Box 1928
Jefferson City, MO 65102-1928
573-751-7039
Fax: 573-751-0147
www.works.state.mo.us/wfd
E-mail: workforce@works.
state.mo.us

Security Regulators
Securities Division
Missouri State Information Center
P.O. Box 1276

Jefferson City, MO 65101
573-751-4136
http://mosl.sos.state.mo.us/
sos-sec/sossec.html

**Small Business Development
Center**
Missouri Small Business
Development Center
University of Missouri
1205 University Avenue, Suite 300
Columbia, MO 65211
573-882-0344
Fax: 573-884-4297
E-mail: summersm@missouri.edu
http://tiger.bpa.missouri.edu/
Research/Training/sbdc/
homepage.htm

Social Services Offices
Missouri Department of Social
Services
221 West High Street
P.O. Box 1527
Jefferson City, MO 65102-1527
573-751-4815
www.dss.state.mo.us

**Temporary Assistance to Needy
Families (TANF)**
Temporary Aid to Needy Families
Gary Stangler
Missouri Department of Social
Services
P.O. Box 1527
Jefferson City, MO 65102
573-751-4815
www.dss.state.mo.us.dfs.pap.htm

Transportation Department
Don Hall
Missouri Department of
Transportation
P.O. Box 270
Jefferson City, MO 65102
573-526-5500
http://www.modot.state.mo.us

John Rice
Missouri Department of
Transportation
P.O. Box 270
Jefferson City, MO 65102
573-751-7480
http://www.modot.state.mo.us

Unclaimed Property Office
Unclaimed Property Section
P.O. Box 1272
Jefferson City, MO 65102
573-751-0840
www.sto.state.mo.us/ucp/
unclprop.htm

Unemployment Insurance Office
Director
Unemployment Insurance
Division of Employment Security

P.O Box 59
Jefferson City, MO 65104
573-751-3670
www.dolir.state.mo.us/es/
doli.-46_htm
Weekly benefit range: $45-175
Duration of benefits: 11-26 weeks

Utility Commission
Public Service Commission
P.O. Box 360
Jefferson City, MO 65102
573-751-3234
800-392-4211 (MO only)
http://www.ecodev.state.
mo.us/psc

Women's Commission
Missouri Women's Council
P.O. Box 1684
Jefferson City, MO 65102
573-751-0810
Fax: 573-751-8835
E-mail:
wcouncil@mail.state.mo.us
www.womenscouncil.org
Sue P. McDaniel, Executive
Director
Deborah Borchers-Ausmus, Chair

Montana

Federal Information Center
All Locations; 800-688-9889

State Information Office
406-444-2511
http://www.state.mt.us

Department on Aging
Senior and Long Term Care
Division
Department of Public Health and
Human Services
Box 4210
Helena, MT 59604
406-444-5900
http://www.dphhs.mt.gov/
whowhat/sltc.htm

Attorney General's Office
Office of the Attorney General
215 N. Sanders
Helena, MT 59620
406-444-2026
www.doj.mt.gov/ago/index.htm

Banking Commissioner
Commissioner of Banking and
Financial Institutions
P.O. Box 200546
Helena, MT 59620-0546
406-444-2091
http://commerce.mt.gov/
finance/index.htm

**Child Care and Development
Block Grant Lead Agency**
Children's Services
Montana Department of Public
Health and Human Services
P.O. Box 8005
Helena, MT 59604-8005
406-444-1828
Fax: 406-444-2547
http://www.dphhs.mt.gov/

**Child Support Enforcement
Agency**
Mary Ann Wellbank
Child Support Enforcement
Division
Department of Social and
Rehabilitation Services
P.O. Box 202943
Helena, MT 59620
406-442-7278
800-346-5437 (in MT)
Fax: 406-442-1370
http://www.dphhs.mt.
gov/whowhat/csed.htm

Cooperative Extension Office
Vice Provost for Outreach and
Director of Extension
212 Montana Hall
Montana State University
Bozeman, MT 59717
406-994-4371
http://extn.msu.montana.edu

Corporation Division Office
Corporate Department
Secretary of State
Capitol Station
Helena, MT 59620
406-444-3665
www.state.mt.us/sos/biz.html

Day Care Licensing Agency
Department of Health and Human
Services
Division of Child and Family
Services
Child Care Licensing
P.O. Box 202951
Helena, MT 59620-2951
406-444-1742
http://www.dphhs.mt.gov/

Economic Development Office
Department of Commerce
1424 Ninth Ave.
PO Box 200505
Helena, MT 59620-0505
406-444-3814
800-221-8015 (in MT)
Fax: 406-444-1872
commerce.state.mt.us

Department of Education
Montana Office of Public Instruction
Capitol Station
Helena, MT 59620-2501
406-444-3656
http://www.opi.mt.gov/

Department of Higher Education
Office of the Commissioner of
Higher Education

P.O. Box 203101
Helena, MT 59620-3101
406-444-6570
Fax: 404-444-1469
www.montana.edu/wwwoche

Health Department
Montana Department of Public
Health & Human Services
111 North Sanders
Helena, MT 59620
MAILING ADDRESS:
   P.O. Box 4210
   Helena, MT 59604-4210
406-444-2596
Fax: 406-444-1970
www.dphhs.mt.gov
E-mail: kpekoc@mt.gov

Housing Office
Montana Board of Housing
2001 Eleventh Ave.
836 Front St.
Helena, MT 59620-0528
406-444-3040

Insurance Commissioner
Commissioner of Insurance
P.O. Box 4009
Helena, MT 59604-4009
406-444-2040
800-332-6148

Labor Department
Montana Department of Labor and
Industry
P.O. Box 1728
Helena, MT 59624
406-444-9091

http://jsd.dli.state.mt.us/
dli_home/dli.htm

Licensing Office
Professional and Occupational
Licensing, Business Regulation
Department of Commerce
111 N. Jackson St.
Helena, MT 59620
406-444-37373
www.com.state.mt.us/License/
POL/index.htm

One-Stop Career Center
Job Service Centers
Department of Labor and Industry
Workforce Development
Montana Department of Labor and
Industry
P.O. Box 1728
Helena, MT 59624
406-444-4513
http://jsd.dli.state.mt.us
E-mail: kechapman@state.mt.us

Security Regulators
Montana Securities Department
P.O. Box 4009
Helena, MT 59604
406-444-2040
800-332-6148
www.mt.gov/sap

**Small Business Development
Center**
Montana Small Business
Development Center
Montana Dept. of Commerce
1424 Ninth Avenue
Helena, MT 59620

406-444-4780
Fax: 406-444-1872
E-mail: rkloser@mt.gov
www.com.state.mt.us/
economic/sbdc.htm

Social Services Offices
Montana Department of Public
Health and Human Services
111 North Sanders
Helena, MT 59620
406-444-2596
www.dphs.mt.gov

**Temporary Assistance to Needy
Families (TANF)**
Temporary Aid to Needy Families
Laurie Ekanger
Montana Department of Public
Health and Human Services
111 North Sanders St.
P.O. Box 4210
Helena, MT 59604
406-444-5622
www.dphhs.mt.gov/faq/afdc.htm

Transportation Department
Janis Winston
Montana Dept. of Transportation
2701 Prospect Ave.
P.O. Box 201001
Helena, MT 59620
406-444-4210
http://www.mdt.mt.gov

Unclaimed Property Office
Abandoned Property Section
Department of Revenue
Mitchell Bldg.

Helena, MT 59620
406-444-2425
www.state.mt.us/revenue.rev.htm

Unemployment Insurance Office
Administrator
Unemployment Insurance Division
P.O. Box 1728
Helena, MT 59624
406-444-3783
http://jsd.dli.mt.gov/ui/ui.htm
Weekly benefit range: $57-228
Duration of benefits: 8-26 weeks

Utility Commission
Public Service Commission

1701 Prospect Ave.
P.O. Box 202601
Helena, MT 59620-2601
406-444-6199
http://www.psc.mt.gov

Women's Commission
Interdepartmental Coordinating
Committee for Women (ICCW)
P.O. Box 1728
Helena, MT 59624
406-444-1520
E-mail: jbranscum@state.mt.us
www.mdt.state.mt.us/iccw
Jean Branscum, Chair
Jeanne Wolf, Vice Chair

Nebraska

Federal Information Center
All Locations; 800-688-9889

State Information Office
402-471-2311
http://www.state.ne.us

Department on Aging
Aging Department
P.O. Box 95044
Lincoln, NE 68509-5044
402-471-2308
http://www.hhs.state.ne.
us/ags/agsindex.htm

Attorney General's Office
Office of the Attorney General
P.O. Box 98920
Lincoln, NE 68509
402-471-2682

Banking Commissioner
Director of Banking and Finance
P.O. Box 95006
1200 N. Street
Atrium 311
Lincoln, NE 68509-5006
402-471-2171
http://www.ndbf.org

Child Care and Development Block Grant Lead Agency
Child Care and Development
Nebraska Department of Health
and Human Services

P.O. Box 95044
Lincoln, NE 68509-5044
402-471-9676
Fax: 402-471-9455
http://www.hhs.state.ne.us/

Child Support Enforcement Agency
Daryl Wusk
Child Support Enforcement Office
Dept. of Social Services
P.O. Box 95044
Lincoln, NE 68509
402-471-9103
402-471-9455
800-831-4573 (in NE)
http://www.hhs.state.ne.
us/cse/cseindex.htm

Cooperative Extension Office
Randy Cantrell, Director
University of Nebraska
S.E. Research and Extension
Center
Room 211, Mussehl Hall
East Campus
Lincoln, NE 68583-0714
402-472-2966
http://ianrwww.unl.edu/
ianr/coopext/coopext.htm

Corporation Division Office
Corporate Division
Secretary of State
State Capitol

Lincoln, NE 68509
402-471-4079
www.nol.org/home/SOS/

Day Care Licensing Agency
Nebraska Health and Human
Services System
Department of Services
P.O. Box 95044
Lincoln, NE 68509-5044
402-471-9302
http://www.hhs.state.ne.us

Economic Development Office
Department of Economic
Development
P.O. Box 94666
301 Centennial Mall South
Lincoln, NE 68509
402-471-3111
800-426-6505 (in NE)
Fax: 402-471-3365
TDD: 402-471-3441
www.ded.state.ne.us

Department of Education
Nebraska Department of Education
Data Center
P.O. Box 94987
Lincoln, NE 68509
402-471-2295
http://www.nde.state.ne.us/

Department of Higher Education
Nebraska Coordinating
Commission for Postsecondary
Education
140 North Eighth Street, Suite 300
P.O. Box 95005

Lincoln, NE 68509-5005
402-471-2847
Fax: 402-471-2886
http://nol.org/NEpostsecondaryed

Health Department
Nebraska Health & Human
Services System
Department of Services
P.O. Box 95044
Lincoln, NE 68509-5044
402-471-2306
www.hhs.state.ne.us/index.htm
E-mail: hhsinfo@ www.hhs.
state.ne.us

Housing Office
Nebraska Investment Finance
Authority
1230 O St., Suite 200
Lincoln, NE 68508
402-434-3900
http://www.nifa.org

Insurance Commissioner
Director of Insurance
941 O St., Suite 400
Lincoln, NE 68508-3690
402-471-2201
800-833-0920
http://www.nol.org/home/ndoi/

Labor Department
Nebraska Department of Labor
550 South 16th Street
Lincoln, NE 68509-4600
402-471-4189
www.dol.state.ne.us

Licensing Office
Bureau of Examining Boards
Nebraska Department of Health
P.O. Box 95007
Lincoln, NE 68509
402-471-2115

One-Stop Career Center
Nebraska Workforce Development
Centers
Department of Labor
550 South 16th Street
Lincoln, NE 68509
402-471-9928
Fax: 402-471-2318
www.dol.state.ne.us
E-mail: cplager@dol.state.ne.us

Security Regulators
Nebraska Securities Bureau
Department of Banking & Finance
P.O. Box 95006
Lincoln, NE 68509
402-471-3445
www.ndbf.org

Small Business Development Center
Nebraska Small Business
Development Center
University of Nebraska at Omaha
60th & Dodge Streets
College of Business
Administration, Room 407
Omaha, NE 68182-0248
402-554-2521
Fax: 402-554-3473
E-mail: Bob_Bernier/ CBA/UNO/
UNEBR@ unomail.unomaha.edu

Social Services Offices
Nebraska Health and Human
Services System
Department of Services
P.O. Box 95044
Lincoln, NE 68509-5044
402-471-9108
www.hhs.state.ne.us

Temporary Assistance to Needy Families (TANF)
Temporary Aid to Needy Families
Deb Thomas
Nebraska Department of Health
and Human Services
P.O. Box 95026
Lincoln, NE 68509
402-471-3121
http://www.hhs.state.ne.us/
fia/adc.htm

Transportation Department
Jerry Wray
Nebraska Department of Roads
P.O. Box 94759
Lincoln, NE 68509
402-479-4694
www.dor.state.ne.us

Unclaimed Property Office
Unclaimed Property Division
P.O. Box 94788
Lincoln, NE 68509
402-471-2455
www.nebraska.treasurer.org

Unemployment Insurance Office
Unemployment Insurance Director
Nebraska Department of Labor

P.O. Box 94600
550 S. 16th St.
Lincoln, NE 68509
402-471-9979
www.dol.state.ne.us/uihome.htm
Weekly benefit range: $20-184
Duration of benefits: 20-26 weeks

Utility Commission
Public Service Commission
1200 N St.
P.O. Box 94927
Lincoln, NE 68509-4925
402-471-3101

800-526-0017
http://www.nol.org/ home/npsc/

Women's Commission
Nebraska Commission on the
Status of Women
301 Centennial Mall South
Box 94985
Lincoln, NE 65809
402-471-2039
Fax: 402-471-5655
E-mail: ncswmail@mail.
state.ne.us
www.ncsw.org
Toni Gray, Executive Director

Nevada

Federal Information Center
All Locations; 800-688-9889

State Information Office
702-687-5000
http://www.state.nv.us

Department on Aging
Aging Services Division
Human Resources Dept.
340 N. 11th St.
Howard Cannon Center
Las Vegas, NV 89101
702-486-3545
http://www.state.nv.us/ hr/aging/

Attorney General's Office
Office of the Attorney General
100 N. Carson St.
Carson City, NV 89701
702-687-4170
www.state.nv.us/ag

Banking Commissioner
Commissioner of Financial
Institutions
406 E. Second St., Suite 3
Carson City, NV 89701-4758
702-687-4259
http://www.state.nv.us/
busi_industry/fi

**Child Care and Development
Block Grant Lead Agency**
CCDBG Coordinator

Nevada Department of Human
Resources
2527 N. Carson St.
Carson City, NV 89710
702-687-1172
Fax: 702-687-1079

**Child Support Enforcement
Agency**
Leland Sullivan
Child Support Enforcement
Program
Nevada State Welfare Division
2527 North Carson St.
Capitol Complex
Carson City, NV 89710
702-687-4744
702-684-8026
800-922-0900 (in NV)
http://158.96.250.214/ enforce.htm

Cooperative Extension Office
Janet Usinger, Director
Nevada Cooperative Extension
2345 Redrock
Las Vegas, NV 89102
702-222-3130

Corporation Division Office
Office of Corporations
Secretary of State
Capitol Complex
Carson City, NV 89710
702-687-5203
http://sos.state.nv.us

Day Care Licensing Agency
Department of Human Resources
Bureau of Child Care Licensing
3920 E. Idaho St.
Elko, NV 89801
702-753-1237

Economic Development Office
State of Nevada Commission on
Economic Development
5151 South Carson St.
Carson City, NV 89710
775-687-4325
800-336-1600
Fax: 775-687-4450
www.state.nv.us/businessop

555 E. Washington Avenue
Suite 5400
Las Vegas, NV 89101
702-486-2700
Fax: 702-486-2701

Department of Education
Nevada Department of Education
Planning Research and Evaluation
Division
400 W. King St.
Carson City, NV 89710
702-687-3130
http://www.nsn.k12.nv.us/nvdoe/

Department of Higher Education
Nevada Department of Education
Student Incentive Grant Program
700 East 5th Street
Carson City, NV 89701-9050
775-687-9200

Health Department
Nevada State Health Division
505 East King Street, Room 201
Carson City, NV 89710
775-687-3786
Fax: 775-687-3859
www.state.nv.us/health/

Housing Offices
Department of Commerce
Housing Division
1802 N. Carson St., Suite 154
Carson City, NV 89701-1229
702-687-4258
http://www.state.nv.us/
busi_industry/hd

Nevada Rural Housing Authority
2100 California St.
Carson City, NV 89701
702-887-1795

Insurance Commissioner
Commissioner of Insurance
1665 Hot Springs Rd.
Capitol Complex 152
Carson City, NV 89706-0646
702-687-4270
800-992-0900
http://www.state.nv.us/b&i/id/

Labor Department
Nevada Department of
Employment, Training and
Rehabilitation
500 East Third Street
Carson City, NV 89713
702-687-4550
www.state.nv.us/detr/detr.html

Licensing Office
Consumer Affairs Division
Department of Commerce
4600 Kietezke Lane
Bldg. B, Suite 113
Reno, NV 89502
702-688-1800
800-326-5202
www.state.nv.us/st_boards.htm

One-Stop Career Center
Nevada Department of
Employment, Training and
Rehabilitation
500 East Third Street
Carson City, NV 89713
702-687-4550
www.state.nv.us/detr/detr.html
E-mail: detrinfo@govmail.
state.nv.us

Security Regulators
Nevada Securities
555 E. Washington Ave.
Suite 5200
Las Vegas, NV 89101
702-486-2440
http://sos.state.nv.us

Small Business Development Center
Nevada Small Business
Development Center
University of Nevada, Reno
College of Business
Administration/032
Nazir Ansari Business Building
Room 411

Reno, NV 89557-0100
702-784-1717
Fax: 702-784-4337
E-mail: nsbdc@scf.unr.edu
www.scs.unr.edu/nsbdc

Social Services Offices
Nevada Department of Human
Resources
505 East King Street
Carson City, NV 89701-3708
702-687-4356
www.state.nv.us/hr

Temporary Assistance to Needy Families (TANF)
Temporary Aid to Needy Families
Rota Rosaschi
New Employers of Nevada
2527 North Carson St.
Capitol Complex
Carson City, NV 89710
702-687-4143
www.state.nv.us/hr/mission.htm

Transportation Department
Jim Mallery
Nevada Department of
Transportation
1263 South Stewart St.
Carson City, NV 89712
702-888-7464
www.nevadadot.com

Unclaimed Property Office
Unclaimed Property Division
2501 East Sahara Ave.
Suite 304
Las Vegas, NV 89104

702-486-4140
www.state.nv.us/b&i/up/

Unemployment Insurance Office
Unemployment Insurance
Employment Security Department
500 E. Third St.
Carson City, NV 89713
702-687-4510
www.state.nv.us/detr/ui.html
Weekly benefit range: $16-258
Duration of benefits: 12-26 weeks

Utility Commission
Public Service Commission
727 Fairview Dr.
Carson City, NV 89710
702-687-6007
http://www.state.nv.us/puc/

Women's Commission
Nevada Women's Fund
201 W. Liberty
Reno, NV 89501
775-786-2335

New Hampshire

Federal Information Center
All Locations; 800-688-9889

State Information Office
603-271-1110
http://www.state.nh.us

Department on Aging
Elderly and Adult Services
Division
State Office Park South
115 Pleasant St., Annex Bldg. 1
Concord, NH 03301-3843
603-271-4680
http://www.state.nh.us/
dhhs/ofs/ofscstlc.htm

Attorney General's Office
Office of the Attorney General
State House Annex, 25 Capitol St.
Concord, NH 03301
603-271-3658
www.state.nh.us/oag/ag.html

Banking Commissioner
Bank Commissioner
169 Manchester St.
Concord, NH 03301-5127
603-271-3561
http://www.state.nh.us/ banking/

Child Care and Development Block Grant Lead Agency
Child Care Coordinator
New Hampshire Department of
Health and Human Services

Commissioner's Office
6 Hazen Dr.
Concord, NH 03301-6505
603-271-4343
Fax: 603-271-7982
http://webster.state.nh.us/dhhs/

Child Support Enforcement Agency
Kathleen Kerr
Office of Child Support
Office of Program Support
Health and Human Services Bldg.
6 Hazen Dr.
Concord, NH 03301
603-271-4427
800-852-4427 (in NH)
Fax: 603-271-4787
http://www.state.nh.us/
dhhs/ops/chd_supt.htm

Cooperative Extension Office
Peter J. Horne, Dean and Director
UNH Cooperative Ext.
59 College Rd., Taylor Hall
Durham, NH 03824
603-862-1520
http://www.ceinfo.unh.edu/

Corporation Division Office
Corporate Division
Secretary of State
State House, Room 204
Concord, NH 03301
603-271-3244

Day Care Licensing Agency
State Department of Health and
Human Service
Child Care Licensing Unit
6 Hazen Dr.
Health and Human Services
Building
Concord, NH 03301
603-271-4624
http://webster.state.nh.us/dhhs/

Economic Development Office
State of New Hampshire
Department of Resources and
Economic Development
172 Pembroke Road
P.O. Box 1856
Concord, NH 03302-1856
603-271-2341
Fax: 603-271-6784
www.ded.state.nh.us/obid

Department of Education
New Hampshire Department of
Education
Office of Information Services
State Office Park South
101 Pleasant St.
Concord, NH 03301-3860
603-271-2778
http://www.state.nh.us/doe/
education.html

Department of Higher Education
New Hampshire Postsecondary
Education Commission
2 Industrial Park Drive
Concord, NH 03301-8512
603-271-2555

TDD: 800-735-2964
Fax: 603-271-2696
www.state.nh.us/postsecondary

Health Department
New Hampshire Department of
Health & Human Services
6 Hazen Drive
Concord, NH 03301-6505
603-271-4939
www.dhs.state.nh.us/index.htm

Housing Office
Housing Finance Authority
P.O. Box 5087
Manchester, NH 03108
603-472-8623

Insurance Commissioner
Insurance Commissioner
169 Manchester St.
Concord, NH 03301-5151
603-271-2261
800-852-3416
http://www.state.nh.us/insurance/

Labor Department
New Hampshire Dept. of Labor
95 Pleasant Street
Concord, NH 03301
603-271-3177
www.state.nh.us/dol/index.html

Licensing Office
SOICC of New Hampshire
Economic and Labor Market
Information Bureau
New Hampshire Employment
Security

32 S. Main St.
Concord, NH 03301
603-229-4370
www.nhes.state.nh.us

One-Stop Career Center
New Hampshire Works
Department of Employment
Security
32 South Main Street
Concord, NH 03301-3860
603-271-3494
www.nhworks.state.nh.us
E-mail: webmaster@nhes. state.
nh.us

Security Regulators
Bureau of Securities Regulation
State House, Room 204
107 North Main St.
Concord, NH 03301
603-271-1463

Small Business Development Center
New Hampshire Small Business
Development Center
University of New Hampshire
108 McConnell Hall
Durham, NH 03824-3593
603-862-2200
Fax: 603-862-4876
E-mail: gc@christa.unh.edu
www.NHSBDC.org

Social Services Offices
New Hampshire Department of
Health and Human Services
6th Hazen Drive

Concord, NH 03301
603-271-4415
www.dhhs.state.nh.us/

Temporary Assistance to Needy Families (TANF)
Temporary Aid to Needy Families
Mary Anne Broschek
New Hampshire Department of
Health and Human Services
6 Hazen Dr.
Concord, NH 03301
603-271-4442
www.state.nh.us/dhhs/ofs/
ofs_ind.htm

Transportation Department
Kenneth Hazeltine
New Hampshire Department of
Transportation
P.O. Box 483
Concord, NH 03302
603-271-3497
www.state.nh.us/dot

Unclaimed Property Office
Abandoned Property Division
Treasury Department
25 Capitol St., Room 205
Concord, NH 03301
603-271-2649
www.state.nh.us/treasury/

Unemployment Insurance Office
Unemployment Compensation
Bureau
Dept. of Employment Security
32 South Main St.
Concord, NH 03301

603-228-4031
www.nhworks.state.nh.us
Weekly benefit range: $32-216
Duration of benefits: 26 weeks

Utility Commission
Public Utilities Commission
8 Old Suncook Rd., Bldg. #1
Concord, NH 03301
603-271-2431
800-852-3793 (NH only)
http://www.state.nh.us/
puc/puc.html

Women's Commission
New Hampshire Commission on
the Status of Women
State House Annex, Room 334
25 Capitol St.
Concord, NH 03301-6312
603-271-2660
Fax: 603-271-2361
E-mail: kfrey@admin.state.nh.us
www.state.nh.us/csw
Katheryn Frey, Executive Director
Molly Kelly, Chair

New Jersey

Federal Information Center
All Locations; 800-688-9889

State Information Office
609-292-2121
http://www.state.nj.us

Department on Aging
Aging Division
Community Affairs Dept.
101 S. Broad St.
CN 807
Trenton, NJ 08625
609-292-3766
800-792-8820
http://www.state.nj.us/
health/senior/sraffair.htm

Attorney General's Office
Office of the Attorney General
25 Market St., CN 080
Trenton, NJ 08625
609-292-8740
www.state.nj.us/lps

Banking Commissioner
Commissioner of Banking
20 W. State St.
P.O. Box 040
Trenton, NJ 08625
609-292-3420
http://www.naic.org/nj/
div_bank.htm

Child Care and Development Block Grant Lead Agency
Division of Family Development
New Jersey Department of Human Services
P.O. Box 716
Trenton, NJ 08625
609-588-2163
Fax: 609-588-3369
http://www.state.nj.us/
humanservices/ DHSHome.html

Child Support Enforcement Agency
Karen Highsmith
Bureau of Child Support and Paternity Programs
Division of Family Development
Department of Human Services
CN 716
Trenton, NJ 08625
609-588-2406
800-621-5437 (in NJ)
Fax: 609-588-3369
http://www.state.nj.us/
judiciary/prob01.htm

Cooperative Extension Office
Zane Helsel, Director
Rutgers Cooperative Extension
P.O. Box 231
New Brunswick, NJ 08903
732-932-9306
http://www.rce.rutgers.edu

Corporation Division Office
Commercial Recording Division
Secretary of State
820 Bear Tavern Rd.
West Trenton, NJ 08628
609-530-6400
www.state.nj.us/state/dcr/
dcrpg1.html

Day Care Licensing Agency
Division of Youth and Family
Services
Bureau of Licensing
P.O. Box 717
Trenton, NJ 08625-0717
609-292-1018
http://www.state.nj.us/
humanservices/ DHSHome.html

Economic Development Office
New Jersey Economic
Development Authority
P.O. Box 990
Trenton, NJ 08625-0990
609-292-1800
www.njeda.com

Department of Education
New Jersey Dept. of Education
Publications Office
CN 500, 225 E. State St.
Trenton, NJ 08625
609-984-0905
http://www.state.nj.us/education/

Department of Higher Education
New Jersey Department of Higher
Education
Office of Student Assistance

4 Quakerbridge Plaza, CN 540
Trenton, NJ 08625
609-588-3288
www.state.nj.us/treasury/osa

Health Department
New Jersey Department of Health
& Senior Services
P.O. Box 360
John Fitch Plaza
Trenton, NJ 08625-0360
609-292-7836
Fax: 609-633-9601
www.state.nj.us/health/

Housing Office
New Jersey Housing and Mortgage
Finance Agency
637 S. Clinton Ave.
P.O. Box 18550
Trenton, NJ 08650-2085
609-890-8900
800-NJ-HOUSE
http://www.state.nj.us/
dca/progsmor.htm

Insurance Commissioner
Commissioner
Department of Insurance
20 W. State St.
P.O. Box 325
Trenton, NJ 08625-0325
609-292-5316
800-792-8820
http://www.naic.org/nj/div_ins.htm

Labor Department
New Jersey Department of Labor
John Fitch Plaza

P.O. Box 110
Trenton, NJ 08625
609-292-2323
www.state.nj.us/labor

Licensing Office
Division of Consumer Affairs
124 Halsey St.
Newark, NJ 07102
973-504-6200
www.state.nj.us/lps/ca/home.htm

One-Stop Career Center
Workforce New Jersey
Division of Employment and
Training
P.O. Box 005
Trenton, NJ 08625
609-292-5005
www.wnjpin.state.nj.us

Security Regulators
Bureau of Securities
P.O. Box 47029
Newark, NJ 07101
973-504-3600
www.state.nj.us/lps/ca/bos.htm

Small Business Development Center
New Jersey Small Business
Development Center
Rutgers Graduate School of
Management
University Heights
49 Bleeker Street
Newark, NJ 07102-1993
973-353-1927
Fax: 973-353-1110

E-mail: bhopper@andromeda.
rutgers.edu
www.nj.com/njsbdc

Social Services Offices
New Jersey Department of Human
Services
P.O. Box 700
Trenton, NJ 08625
609-292-3703
www.state.nj.us/humanservices/
DHSHome.html

Temporary Assistance to Needy Families (TANF)
Temporary Aid to Needy Families
William Waldman
New Jersey Department of Human
Services
P.O. Box 700
Trenton, NJ 08625
609-292-3717
http://www.state.nj.us/
humanservices/W&W.html

Transportation Department
Bob Koska
New Jersey Transit Corporation
1 Penn Plaza East
Newark, NJ 07105
973-491-7376
http://www.njtransit.state.nj.us

James Holman
New Jersey Transit Corporation
1 Penn Plaza East
Newark, NJ 07105
973-491-7377
www.njtransit.state.nj.us

Unclaimed Property Office
Department of the Treasury
Property Administration
CN 214
Trenton, NJ 08646
609-984-8234
www.state.nj.us/treasury/
taxation/index.html

Unemployment Insurance Office
Director, Division of
Unemployment and Disability
Insurance
New Jersey Department of Labor
CN 058
Trenton, NJ 08625
609-292-2460
www.wnjpin.state.nj.us

Weekly benefit range: $60-390
Duration of benefits: 15-26 weeks

Utility Commission
Board of Public Utilities
Two Gateway Center
Newark, NJ 07102
973-648-2027
800-624-0241 (NJ only)
http://www.njin.net/njbpu/

Women's Commission
New Jersey Department of
Community Affairs
Division of Women
101 South Broad St. CN 808
Trenton, NJ 08625-0801
609-292-8840
Fax: 609-633-6821
Elizabeth L. Cox

New Mexico

Federal Information Center
All Locations; 800-688-9889

State Information Office
505-827-4011
http://www.state.nm.us

Department on Aging
State Agency on Aging
224 E. Palance Ave.
Santa Fe, NM 87501
505-827-7640

Attorney General's Office
Office of the Attorney General
P.O. Drawer 1508
Santa Fe, NM 87504
505-827-6000

Banking Commissioner
Financial Institutions Division
P.O. Box 25101
Santa Fe, NM 87504
505-827-7100
http://www.state.nm.us/
rld/rld_fid.html

**Child Care and Development
Block Grant Lead Agency**
Bureau Chief
Child Care Bureau
Department of Children, Youth
and Families
1120 Paseo Dr.
Peralta, Room 205

Santa Fe, NM 87502
505-827-4033
Fax: 505-827-9978

**Child Support Enforcement
Agency**
Roberto Salazar
Child Support Enforcement
Bureau
Department of Human Services
P.O. Box 25109
Santa Fe, NM 87504
505-827-7200
505-827-7285
800-432-6217 (in NM)
http://www.state.nm.us/
hsd/csed.html

Cooperative Extension Office
Dr. Jerry Schickenanz
New Mexico State University
Box 3AE
Las Cruces, NM 88003
505-646-3016
http://www.cahe.nmsu.
edu/cahe/ces

Corporation Division Office
State Corporation Commission
P.O. Drawer 1269
Santa Fe, NM 87504
505-827-4500
800-947-4722
www.state.nm.us/scc

Day Care Licensing Agency
Department of Health
Child Care Licensing Division
P.O. Drawer 5160
Santa Fe, NM 87502-5160
505-827-7361

Economic Development Office
Economic Development
Department
Joseph M. Montoya Bldg.
1100 St. Francis Drive
Santa Fe, NM 87505-4147
505-827-0170
800-374-3061
Fax: 505-827-0407
www.edd.state.nm.us

Department of Education
New Mexico Department of
Education
Education Bldg.
Data Management
300 Don Gaspar Ave.
Santa Fe, NM 87501-2786
505-827-7354
http://sde.state.nm.us/

Department of Higher Education
New Mexico Commission On
Higher Education
1068 Cerrillos Road
Santa Fe, NM 87501
505-827-7383
Fax: 505-827-7392
www.nmche.org

Health Department
New Mexico Department of Health

1190 St. Francis Drive
Harold Runnels Building
Sante Fe, NM 87504
505-827-2619
Fax: 505-827-2530
www.state.nm.us/state/doh.html

Housing Offices
Mortgage Finance Authority
P.O. Box 2047
Albuquerque, NM 87103
505-843-6880
800-444-6880
http://www.nmmfa.org

New Mexico State Housing
Authority
810 W. San Manteo
Suite D
Santa Fe, NM 87505
505-262-6463

Insurance Commissioner
Superintendent of Insurance
P.O. Drawer 1269
Santa Fe, NM 87504-1269
505-827-4601
800-947-4722

Labor Department
New Mexico Department of Labor
401 Broadway NE
Albuquerque, NM 87102
505-841-8486
www3.state.nm.us/dol

Licensing Office
Regulation and Licensing
Department

2055 Pacheco St., Suite 300
Santa Fe, NM 87504
505-476-6200
www.rld.state.nm.us

One-Stop Career Center
New Mexico Works
Department of Labor
401 Broadway, NE
Albuquerque, NM 87102
505-841-2000
www3.state.nm.us/dol/nmworks/
default.asp
E-mail: jslowen@nm-us.
campus.cwix.net

Security Regulators
New Mexico Securities Division
P.O. Box 25101
Santa Fe, NM 87501
505-827-7140

Small Business Development Center
New Mexico Small Business
Development Center
Santa Fe Community College
6401 Richards Avenue
P.O. Box 4187
Santa Fe, NM 87502-4187
505-438-1343
800-281-7232
Fax: 505-428-1469
www.nmsbdc.org

Social Services Offices
New Mexico Human Services
Department
P.O. Box 2348

Santa Fe, NM 87504
505-827-7750
www.state.nm.us/hsd/home.htm

Temporary Assistance to Needy Families (TANF)
Temporary Aid to Needy Families
Tom Clayton
New Mexico Department of
Human Services
P.O. Box 2348
Santa Fe, NM 87504
505-827-1323
www.state.nm.us/hsd/isd.html

Transportation Department
Brian Ainsworth
New Mexico Highway and
Transportation Department
P.O. Box 1149
1350 Alta Vista St., Building T2
Santa Fe, NM 87504
505-827-1575
www.nmshtd.state.nm.us

Unclaimed Property Office
Department of Revenue &
Taxation
Special Tax Programs and
Services
P.O. Box 25123
Santa Fe, NM 87504
505-827-0767
www.state.nm.us/tax/

Unemployment Insurance Office
Chief, Unemployment Insurance
Bureau
New Mexico Department of Labor

401 Broadway Blvd., NE
P.O. Box 1928
Albuquerque, NM 87103
505-841-8431
www.state.nm.us/dol/
dol_form.html
Weekly benefit range: $42-212
Duration of benefits: 19-26 weeks

Utility Commission
Public Utility Commission
224 E. Palace Ave.
Santa Fe, NM 87501-2013
505-827-6940

800-663-9782
http://www.puc.state.nm.us/

Women's Commission
New Mexico Commission on the
Status of Women
2401 12th St. NW
Albuquerque, NM 87104-2302
505-841-8920
Fax: 505-841-8926
E-mail: rdakota@nm.us.
campuscwix.net
Yolanda Garcia, Info. Officer
Darlene B. Herrera, Vice Chair

New York

Federal Information Center
All Locations; 800-688-9889

State Information Office
518-474-2121
http://www.state.ny.us

Department on Aging
Aging Office
Bldg. 2
Empire State Plaza
Albany, NY 12223-001
518-474-5731
800-342-9871 (NY only)
http://aging.state.ny. us/nysofa/

Attorney General's Office
Office of the Attorney General
Department of Law
The Capitol
2nd Floor
Albany, NY 12224
518-474-7330
800-771-7755
www.oag.state.ny.us

Banking Commissioner
Superintendent of Banks
Two Rector St.
New York, NY 10006-1894
212-618-6553
800-522-3330 (consumer)
800-832-1838 (small business)
http://www.banking.state. ny.us/

Child Care and Development Block Grant Lead Agency
Bureau of Early Childhood
Services
New York State Department of
Family Assistance
40 N. Pearl St., 11B
Albany, NY 12243
518-474-9454
Fax: 518-474-9617
http://www.dfa.state.ny.us/

Child Support Enforcement Agency
Robert Doar
Office of Child Support
Enforcement
Department of Social Services
P.O. Box 14
Albany, NY 12260
518-474-9081
518-486-3127
800-343-8859 (in NY)

Cooperative Extension Office
William Lacy, Director
Cornell Cooperative Ext.
276 Roberts Hall
Ithaca, NY 14853
607-255-2237
http://www.cce.cornell.edu/

Corporation Division Office
New York State
Department of State

Division of Corporations
41 State St.
Albany, NY 12231
518-473-2492
www.dos.state.ny.us

Day Care Licensing Agency
State Department of Family
Assistance
Bureau of Early Childhood
Services
Child Care Licensing Bureau
40 N. Pearl St., 11-B
Albany, NY 12243-0001
518-474-9454
http://www.dfa.state.ny.us/

Economic Development Office
Empire State Development
One Commerce Plaza
Albany, NY 12245
518-474-7756
800-STATE-NY
www.empire.state.ny.us

Department of Education
New York Department of Education
Information Center on Education
Annex, Room 309EB
Albany, NY 12234
518-474-8073
http://www.nysed.gov/

Department of Higher Education
New York Higher Education
Services Corporation
Grants and Scholarship
Information
99 Washington Avenue

Albany, NY 12255
518-474-1137
888-NYSHESC
www.hesc.com

Health Department
New York Department of Health
Corning Tower Building
Empire State Plaza
Albany, NY 12237
518-486-9002
www.health.state.ny.us
E-mail: ljr06@health.state.ny.us

Housing Offices
State of New York
Executive Department
Division of Housing and Community
Renewal
One Fordham Plaza
Bronx, NY 10458
718-563-5700
212-306-3000

New York State Housing Authority
250 Broadway
New York, NY 10007
212-306-3000
http://www.dhcr.state. ny.us

Insurance Commissioner
Superintendent of Insurance
25 Beaver St.
New York, NY 10004
212-480-6400
800-342-3736 (in NY)
http://www.ins.state.ny.us

Labor Department
New York Department of Labor

Building 12
State Campus
Albany, NY 12240
518-457-5519
www.labor.state.ny.us

Licensing Office
New York State Education
Department
Division of Professional Licensing
Cultural Education Center
Empire State Plaza
Albany, NY 12230
518-474-3817
800-442-8106
www.nysed.gov/prof/
profhome.htm

One-Stop Career Center
Workforce Development System
Department of Labor
Workforce Development
Building 12, State Office Campus
Albany, NY 12240
518-457-3584
www.wdsny.org

Security Regulators
New York Bureau of Investment
Protection and Securities
120 Broadway, 23rd Floor
New York, NY 10271
212-416-8222
www.oag.state.ny.us

Small Business Development
Center
New York Small Business
Development Centers

State University of New York
(SUNY)
SUNY Plaza, S523
Albany, NY 12246
518-443-5398
800-732-SBDC
Fax: 518-465-4992
E-mail: kingjl@cc.sunycentral.edu
www.smallbiz.suny.edu/
NYSBDC.HTM

Social Services Offices
New York State Department of
Family Assistance
40 North Pearl Street
Albany, NY 12243
518-486-7545
www.dfa.state.ny.us

Temporary Assistance to Needy
Families (TANF)
Temporary Aid to Needy Families
John Johnson
Office of Children and Family
Services
52 Washington St.
Rensselaer, NY 12144
518-473-8437
www.dfa.state.ny.us/tanf/

Transportation Department
Michael Baker
New York Department of
Transportation
1220 Washington Ave.
Room 115
Albany, NY 12232
518-457-8335
http://www.dot.state.ny.us

Russell DeJarnette
New York State Department of
Transportation
1220 Washington Ave.
Building 4, Room 115
Albany, NY 12023
518-457-8335
http://www.dot.state.ny.us

Unclaimed Property Office
Office of Unclaimed Funds
Alfred E. Smith Bldg., 9th Floor
Albany, NY 12236
518-474-4038
www.osc.state.ny.us

Unemployment Insurance Office
Director, Unemployment
Insurance Division
New York State Department of
Labor
State Campus, Building 12
Albany, NY 12240
518-457-2878

www.labor.state.ny.us/html/
wimdinpg.htm
Weekly benefit range: $40-300
Duration of benefits: 26 weeks

Utility Commission
Public Service Commission
3 Empire State Plaza
Albany, NY 12223
518-474-7080
800-342-3377 (NY only)
http://www.dps.state.ny.us

Women's Commission
New York State Division for
Women
633 Third Ave.
New York, NY 10017
212-681-4547
Fax: 212-681-7626
E-mail: women@women.
state.ny.us
www.women.state.ny.us
Elaine Wingate Conway, Director

North Carolina

Federal Information Center
All Locations; 800-688-9889

State Information Office
919-733-1110
http://www.state.nc.us

Department on Aging
Aging Division
Human Resources Dept.
693 Palmer Dr.
Raleigh, NC 27603
919-733-3983
http://www.state.nc.us/
dhr/doa/home.htm

Attorney General's Office
Office of the Attorney General
Department of Justice
P.O. Box 629
Raleigh, NC 27602
919-716-6400
919-716-6000 (consumer
protection)
www.jus.state.nc.us/Justice

Banking Commissioner
Commissioner of Banks
P.O. Box 10709
Raleigh, NC 27605
919-733-3016
http://www.banking.state. nc.us/

**Child Care and Development
Block Grant Lead Agency**
Program Development
Coordinator

North Carolina Department of
Human Resources
P.O. Box 29553
Raleigh, NC 27626-0553
919-662-4535
Fax: 919-662-4568
http://www.dhr.state.nc.us/DHR/

**Child Support Enforcement
Agency**
Michael Adams
Child Support Enforcement
Section
Division of Social Services
Department of Human Resources
100 East Six Forks Rd.
Raleigh, NC 27609
919-571-4114
919-571-4126
800-992-9457 (in NC)
http://www.cse.state.nc. us/CSE/

Cooperative Extension Offices
Dr. Jon F. Ort, Director
Cooperative Extension Service
North Carolina State University,
Box 7602
Raleigh, NC 27695-7602
919-515-2811
http://www.ces.ncsu.edu/

Dr. Dalton McAfee, Director
Cooperative Extension Program
North Carolina A&T State
University

P.O. Box 21928
Greensboro, NC 27420-1928
910-334-7956
http://www.ncat.edu/~soa

Corporation Division Office
Division of Corporation
Secretary of State
300 N. Salisbury St.
Raleigh, NC 27603
919-733-4201
www.state.nc.us/secstate

Day Care Licensing Agency
Department of Family Assistance
Bureau of Early Childhood
Services
Child Care Licensing
P.O. Box 29553
Raleigh, NC 27626-0553
919-662-4499
http://www.dhr.state.nc.us/DHR/

Economic Development Office
Department of Commerce
Commerce Finance Center
301 N. Wilmington St.
PO Box 29571
Raleigh, NC 27626-0571
919-733-4977
Fax: 919-715-9265
www.commerce.state.nc.us/
commerce

Department of Education
North Carolina Department of
Public Instruction
Information Center
301 N. Wilmington St.
Raleigh, NC 27601-2825

919-715-1018
800-665-1250
http://www.dpi.state.nc.us/

Department of Higher Education
North Carolina State Education
Assistance Authority
P.O. Box 2688
Chapel Hill, NC 27515-2688
919-549-8614
Fax: 919-549-8481
www.ncseaa.edu

Health Department
North Carolina State Center for
Health Statistics
Cotton Classing Building
222 North Dawson Street
Raleigh, NC 27603-1392
MAILING:
   P.O. Box 29538
   Raleigh, NC 27626-0538
919-733-4728
Fax: 919-733-8485
http://hermes.sches.chnr.state.
nc.us/SCHS/main.html

Housing Office
North Carolina Housing Finance
Agency
3801 Lake Boone Trail, Suite 200
Raleigh, NC 27607
919-781-6115
http://www.hfa.state.nc.us

Insurance Commissioner
Commissioner of Insurance
Dobbs Bldg.
P.O. Box 26387

Raleigh, NC 27611
919-733-7349
800-662-7777 (in NC)
http://www.doi.state.nc.us/

Labor Department
North Carolina Dept. of Labor
4 West Edenton Street
Raleigh, NC 27601
919-733-7166
www.dol.state.nc.us/dolhome.htm

Licensing Office
Department of the Secretary of
State
P.O. Box 29622
Raleigh, NC 27626
919-733-4161
www.secstate.state.nc.us/
blio/blocc.htm

One-Stop Career Center
Joblink Career Centers
Governor's Commission on
Workforce Preparedness
NC Department of Commerce
P.O. Box 29571
Raleigh, NC 27626
919-733-4806 ext. 259
Fax: 919-733-1128
www.joblink.state.nc.us

Security Regulators
North Carolina Securities Division
300 N. Salisbury St., Room 302
Raleigh, NC 27603
919-733-3924
800-688-2910
www.state.nc.us/secstate/sec.htm

Small Business Development Center
North Carolina Small Business
Development Center
University of North Carolina
333 Fayetteville Street Mall,
#1150
Raleigh, NC 27601-1742
919-715-7272
800-2580-UNC
Fax: 919-715-7777
E-mail: sdaugherty@sbtdc.org
www.sbtdc.org

Social Services Offices
North Carolina Department of
Health and Human Services
Adams Building, Dix Campus
101 Blair Drive
Raleigh, NC 27603-2041
919-733-9190
www.dhr.state.nc.us/DHR

Temporary Assistance to Needy Families (TANF)
Temporary Aid to Needy Families
Pheon Beal
Division of Social Services
325 North Salisbury St.
Raleigh, NC 27603
919-733-3055
www.dhhs.state.nc.us/dss/
servfami.htm

Transportation Department
Todd Allen
North Carolina Department of
Transportation
P.O. Box 25201

Raleigh, NC 27611
919-733-4713
http://www.dot.state.nc.us/
transit/transitnet

Peter Albrecht
North Carolina Department of
Transportation
P.O. Box 25201
Raleigh, NC 27611
919-733-4713 ext. 233
http://www.dot.state.nc.us/
transit/transitnet

Unclaimed Property Office
Escheat & Unclaimed Property
325 North Salisbury St.
Raliegh, NC 27603
919-733-6876
www.treasurer.state.nc.us/
Treasurer/

Unemployment Insurance Office
Unemployment Insurance Division
Employment Security Commission
of North Carolina

P.O. Box 25903
Raleigh, NC 27611
919-733-3121
www.esc.state.nc.us/html/
wi_division.html
Weekly benefit range: $15-322
Duration of benefits: 13-26 weeks

Utility Commission
Utilities Commission
P.O. Box 29510
Raleigh, NC 27626-0510
919-733-4249
http://www.ncuc.commerce.
state.nc.us

Women's Commission
North Carolina Council for Women
526 North Wilmington St.
Raleigh, NC 27604-1199
919-733-2455
Fax: 919-733-2464
www.doa.state.nc.us/doa/
cfw/cfw.htm
Juanita Bryant, Executive Director
Jane Carver, Chair

North Dakota

Federal Information Center
All Locations; 800-688-9889

State Information Office
701-224-2000
http://www.state.nd.us

Department on Aging
Aging Services Division
Human Services Dept.
600 South 2nd St.
Suite 1-C
Bismarck, ND 58504-5729
701-328-8910

Attorney General's Office
Office of the Attorney General
600 East Boulevard Ave.
Bismarck, ND 58505
701-328-2210
800-472-2600
www.state.nd.us/ndag/

Banking Commissioner
Commissioner of Banking and
Financial Institutions
2000 Schafer St., Suite G
Bismarck, ND 58501-1204
701-328-9933
http://www.state.nd.us/
bank/banking.htm

Child Care and Development Block Grant Lead Agency
Early Childhood Services

North Dakota Department of
Human Services
600 E. Boulevard Ave.
Bismarck, ND 58505-0250
701-328-4809
Fax: 701-328-2359
http://www.state.nd.us/hms/
dhs.htm

Child Support Enforcement Agency
William Strate
Child Support Enforcement
Agency
Department of Human Services
P.O. Box 7190
Bismarck, ND 58507
701-328-3582
701-328-5497
800-755-8530

Cooperative Extension Office
Dr. Sharon Anderson Director
Cooperative Extension Service
North Dakota State University
Morrill Hall, Room 311, Box 5437
Fargo, ND 58105
701-231-8944
http://www.ext.nodak.edu/

Corporation Division Office
Business Info/Registration
Division
Secretary of State
Capitol Building

600 E. Boulevard Ave.
Bismarck, ND 58505
701-328-4284
800-352-0867
www.state.nd.us/sec

Day Care Licensing Agency
Department of Human Services
Early Childhood Services
600 E. Boulevard
Bismarck, ND 58505-0250
701-328-4809
http://www.state.nd.us/hms/
dhs.htm

Economic Development Office
Department of Economic
Development and Finance
1833 East Bismarck Expressway
Bismarck, ND 58504-6708
701-328-5300
Fax: 701-328-5320
TTY: 800-366-6888
www.growingnd.com

Department of Education
North Dakota Department of
Education
Department of Public Instruction
600 E. Boulevard Ave.
Bismarck, ND 58505-0440
701-328-2268
http://www.dpi.state.nd.us/

Department of Higher Education
University Systems
600 East Boulevard
Bismarck, ND 58505-0230
701-328-4114

Health Department
North Dakota Department of
Health
600 East Boulevard Avenue
Bismarck, ND 58505-0200
701-328-2372
Fax: 701-328-4727
www.ehs.health.state.nd.us/ndhd/
E-mail: rfrank@state.nd.us

Housing Office
Housing Finance Agency
P.O. Box 1535
Bismarck, ND 58502-1535
701-328-8080

Insurance Commissioner
Commissioner of Insurance
Capitol Bldg., 5th Floor
600 E. Boulevard Ave.
Bismarck, ND 58505-0320
701-328-2440
800-247-0560 (in ND)

Labor Department
Job Service North Dakota
P.O. Box 5507
Bismarck, ND 58506-5507
701-328-2868
www.state.nd.us/jsnd/lmi.htm

Licensing Office
Consumer Fraud Division
Office of the Attorney General
600 East Boulevard
Bismarck, ND 58505
701-328-3404
800-472-2000
www.state.nd.us/ndag/

One-Stop Career Center
Job Service North Dakota
P.O. Box 5507
Bismarck, ND 58506-5507
800-732-9787
701-328-2868
TTY; 800-366-6888
Fax: 701-328-4193
www.state.nd.us/jsnd/lmi.htm
E-mail: jsndweb@pioneer.
state.nd.us

Security Regulators
North Dakota Securities
Commissioner's Office
State Capitol Building, 5th Floor
600 East Boulevard Ave.
Bismarck, ND 58505
701-328-2910

Small Business Development Center
North Dakota Small Business
Development Center
University of North Dakota
College of Business & Public
Administration
118 Gamble Hall, UND
Box 7308
Grand Forks, ND 58202-7308
701-777-3700
800-445-7232
Fax: 701-777-3225
E-mail: kearns@prairie.nodak.edu
www.und.nodak.edu/dept/
ndsbdc/index.htm

Social Services Offices
Department of Human Services

State Capitol, Judicial Wing
600 E. Boulevard Ave.
Department 325
Bismarck, ND 58505-0250
701-328-2310
www1.state.nd.us/hms/dhs.htm

Temporary Assistance to Needy Families (TANF)
Temporary Aid to Needy Families
John Opp
North Dakota Department of
Economic Assistance
600 East Boulevard Ave.
Bismarck, ND 58505
701-328-2310
http://207.108.104.74/dhs/
dhsweb.nsf/ServicePages/
PublicAssistance

Transportation Department
Bill Weimer
North Dakota Department of
Transportation
608 East Boulevard Ave.
Bismarck, ND 58505
701-328-2194
www.state.nd.us/dot

Unclaimed Property Office
Unclaimed Property Division
State Land Department
P.O. Box 5523
Bismarck, ND 58506
701-328-2805
www.land.state.nd.us

Unemployment Insurance Office
Director, Job Insurance Division

Job Service North Dakota
P.O. Box 5507
Bismarck, ND 58506
701-328-5000
www.state.nd.us/jsnd/uins.html
Weekly benefit range: $43-243
Duration of benefits: 12-26 weeks

Utility Commission
Public Service Commission
State Capitol Bldg., 12th Fl.
Bismarck, ND 58505-0480

701-328-2400
http://www.psc.state.nd.us/

Women's Commission
North Dakota Governor's
Commission on the Status of
Women
600 East Boulevard
Bismarck, ND 58501-0250
701-328-5300
Fax: 701-328-5320
Carol Reed, Chairman

Ohio

Federal Information Center
All Locations; 800-688-9889

State Information Office
614-466-2000
http://www.state.oh.us

Department on Aging
Aging Department
50 W. Broad St., 9th Floor
Columbus, OH 43215-5928
614-466-5500

Attorney General's Office
Office of the Attorney General
30 East Broad St.
Columbus, OH 43266
614-466-4320
800-282-0515
www.ag.ohio.gov

Banking Commissioner
Superintendent of Financial
Institutions
77 S. High St., 21st Floor
Columbus, OH 43266-0121
614-728-8400
http://www.state.oh.us/com/fin/
index.htm

**Child Care and Development
Block Grant Lead Agency**
Bureau of Child Care
Ohio Department of Human
Services

65 E. State St., 5th Floor
Columbus, OH 43215
614-466-1043
Fax: 614-728-6803
http://www.state.oh.us/odhs/

**Child Support Enforcement
Agency**
Loretta Adams
Office of Family Assistance and
Child Support Enforcement
Department of Human Services
30 East Broad St., 31st Floor
Columbus, OH 43266
614-752-6561
614-752-9760
800-686-1556 (in OH)

Cooperative Extension Office
Keith Smith, Director
OSU Extension
2120 Fiffe Rd.
Agriculture Administration Building
Columbus, OH 43210
614-292-6181
http://www.ag.ohio-state.edu/

Corporation Division Office
Corporation Division
Secretary of State
30 East Broad St., 14th Floor
Columbus, OH 43266
614-466-3910
www.state.oh.us/sos

Day Care Licensing Agency
Department of Human Services
Children and Family Services
Child Care Licensing Division
65 E. State St., 5th Floor
Columbus, OH 43215
614-466-3822
http://www.state.oh.us/odhs/cdc/

Economic Development Office
Ohio Department of Development
P.O. Box 1001
Columbus, OH 43216-1001
614-466-5017
800-345-OHIO
Fax: 614-463-1540
www.odod.ohio.gov

Department of Education
Ohio Department of Education
Information Management Services
65 S. Front St.
Columbus, OH 43215-4183
614-466-7000
http://www.ode.ohio.gov/

Department of Higher Education
Ohio Board of Regents
State Grants and Scholarship
Department
P.O. Box 182452
Columbus, OH 43218-2452
888-833-1133
614-466-7420
Fax: 614-752-5903
www.regents.state.oh.us

Health Department
Ohio Department of Health

246 North High Street
P.O. Box 118
Columbus, OH 43266-0118
614-466-3543
www.odh.state.oh.us
E-mail: questions@
gw.odh.state.oh.us

Housing Office
Ohio Housing Finance Agency
77 S. High St., 26th Floor
Columbus, OH 43226-0413
614-466-7970
http://www.odod.ohio. gov/ohfa/

Insurance Commissioner
Director of Insurance
2100 Stella Court
Columbus, OH 43215-1067
614-644-2651
800-686-1526 (consumer)
800-686-1527 (fraud)
800-686-1578 (senior health)
http://www.state.oh.us/ins/

Labor Department
Ohio Bureau of Employment
Services
145 South Front Street
Columbus, OH 43215
614-466-4636
www.state.oh.us/obes

Licensing Office
State of Ohio
State Information Office
30 East Broad St., 40th Floor
Columbus, OH 43215
614-466-2000

One-Stop Career Center
One-Stop Systems
One-Stop Employment and
Training System
Bureau of Employment Services
145 Front Street, 6th Floor
Columbus, OH 43215
614-728-8107
Fax: 614-728-9094
www.state.oh.us/obes/
onestop.html

Security Regulators
Ohio Division of Securities
77 South High St., 22nd Floor
Columbus, OH 43215
614-644-7465
800-788-1194
www.securities.state.oh.us

**Small Business Development
Center**
Ohio Small Business
Development Center
Department of Development
77 South High Street, 28th Floor
Columbus, OH 43216-1001
614-466-2711
Fax: 614-466-0829
www.seorf.ohiou.edu/~xx02/

Social Services Offices
Ohio Department of Human
Services
30 East Broad Street, 32nd Floor
Columbus, OH 43266-0423
614-466-6650
www.state.oh.us/odhs

**Temporary Assistance to Needy
Families (TANF)**
Temporary Aid to Needy Families
Welfare Reform
Issac Palmer
Office of Workforce Development
30 East Broad St., 32nd Floor
Columbus, OH 43266
614-466-4909
http://www.state.oh.us/odhs/
owf/index.htm

Transportation Department
Barbara Piper
Ohio Department of
Transportation
25 South Front St., Room 408
Columbus, OH 43215
614-466-2140
http://www.dot.state.oh.us

Lynn Rathke
Ohio Department of
Transportation
25 South Front St., Room 408
Columbus, OH 43215
614-644-7362
http://www.dot.state.oh.us

Unclaimed Property Office
Division of Unclaimed Funds
77 South High St.
Columbus, OH 43266
614-466-4433
www.com.state.oh.us

Unemployment Insurance Office
Director
Unemployment Insurance

Ohio Bureau of Employment
Services
145 S. Front St.
Columbus, OH 43215
614-466-9755
www.state.oh.us/obes/shared.htm
Weekly benefit range: $66-339
Duration of benefits: 20-26 weeks

Utility Commission
Public Utilities Commission
180 E. Broad St.
Columbus, OH 43215-3793

614-466-3016
800-686-7826 (OH only)
http://www.puc.state.oh.us/

Women's Commission
Ohio Women's Commission
77 S. High St., 24th Floor
Columbus, OH 43266-0920
614-466-5580
Fax: 614-466-5434
Sally Farran Bulford, Executive
Director
Dr. Suzanne Crawford, Chair

Oklahoma

Federal Information Center
All Locations; 800-688-9889

State Information Office
405-521-2011
http://www.state.ok.us

Department on Aging
Aging Services Division
Human Services Dept.
P.O. Box 25352
Oklahoma City, OK 73125
405-521-2327

Attorney General's Office
Office of the Attorney General
State Capitol, Room 112
2300 N. Lincoln Blvd.
Oklahoma City, OK 73105
405-521-3921
405-521-2029 (consumer
protection)
www.oag.state.ok.us/oagweb.nsf

Banking Commissioner
Bank Commissioner
4545 N. Lincoln Blvd., Suite 164
Oklahoma City, OK 73105-3427
405-521-2782
http://www.state.ok.us/ ~sbd/

*Child Care and Development
Block Grant Lead Agency*
Administrator of CCDBG
Office of Child Care

Oklahoma Department of Human
Services
4545 N. Lincoln, Suite 100
Oklahoma City, OK 73105
405-521-3561
Fax: 405-521-0391
http://www.onenet.net/okdhs/

*Child Support Enforcement
Agency*
Herbert Jones
Child Support Enforcement Div.
Department of Human Services
P.O. Box 53552
Oklahoma City, OK 73125
405-522-5871
800-522-2922 (in OK)
Fax: 405-522-2753
http://www.onenet.net/
kodhs/division/cdes/ cseindx.htm

Cooperative Extension Offices
Dr. C.B. Browning, Director
Oklahoma Cooperative Extension
Service
Oklahoma State University
139 Agriculture Hall
Stillwater, OK 74078
405-744-5398
http://www.okstate.edu/
osu_ag/oces

Dr. Ocleris Simpston, Director
Cooperative Research and
Extension

P.O. Box 730
Langston University
Langston, OK 73050
405-466-3836
http://www.lunet.edu/

Corporation Division Office
Corporations
Secretary of State
101 State Capitol Building
Oklahoma City, OK 73105
405-521-3911
www.state.ok.us/~sos/

Day Care Licensing Agency
Department of Human Services
Office of Child Care
P.O. Box 25352
Oklahoma City, OK 73105
405-521-3561
http://www.onenet.net/okdhs

Economic Development Office
Department of Commerce
900 North Stiles
P.O. Box 26980
Oklahoma City, OK 73126-0980
405-815-6552
800-879-6552.
Fax: 405-815-5199
www.locateok.com
www.odoc.state.ok.us/index.html

Department of Education
Oklahoma State Department of
Education
Documents
2500 N. Lincoln Blvd.
Oklahoma City, OK 73105-4599

405-521-2293
http://www.sde.state.ok.us/

Department of Higher Education
Oklahoma State Regents for
Higher Education
500 Education Building
State Capitol Complex
Oklahoma City, OK 73105
405-524-9100
Fax: 405-524-9230
www.okhighered.org

Health Department
Oklahoma State Department of
Health
1000 NE 10th Street
Oklahoma City, OK 73117
405-271-5600
800-522-0203
www.health.state.ok.us
E-mail: webmaster@
health.state.ok.us

Housing Office
Oklahoma Housing Finance
Agency
P.O. Box 26720
Oklahoma City, OK 73126-0720
405-848-1144
800-256-1489
http://www.state.ok.us/
osfdocs/ohfa.html

Insurance Commissioner
Insurance Commissioner
P.O. Box 53408
Oklahoma City, OK 73152-3408
405-521-2828

800-522-0071
http://www.oid.state.ok.us

Labor Department
Oklahoma Department of Labor
4001 North Lincoln Boulevard
Oklahoma City, OK 73105-5212
405-528-1500
www.oklaosf.state.ok.us/~okdol

Licensing Office
Governor's Office
State Capitol
Oklahoma City, OK 73105
405-521-2342

One-Stop Career Center
Oklahoma Workforce Centers
Employment Security Commission
218 Will Rogers Building
Oklahoma City, OK 73152
405-557-7201
www.oesc.state.ok.us

Security Regulators
Oklahoma Dept. of Securities
First National Center
120 North Robinson, Suite 860
Oklahoma City, OK 73102
405-280-7700
www.state.ok.us/~osc/

Small Business Development Center
Oklahoma Small Business
Development Center
Southeastern Oklahoma State
University
517 University

Station A, Box 2584
Durant, OK 74701
580-924-0277
800-522-6154
Fax: 580-920-7471
www.osbdc.org

Social Services Offices
Oklahoma Department of Human
Services
2400 North Lincoln Boulevard
P.O. Box 25352
Oklahoma City, OK 73125
405-521-3027
www.onenet.net/okdhs

Temporary Assistance to Needy Families (TANF)
Temporary Aid to Needy Families
Mary Stalnakger
Oklahoma Department of Human
Service
P.O. Box 25352
Oklahoma City, OK 73125
405-521-4415
www.onenet.net/okdhs/programs/
programs.htm#tanf

Transportation Department
Ken LaRue
Oklahoma Dept. of Transportation
200 N.E. 21st St.
Oklahoma City, OK 73015
405-521-2584
http://www.okladot.state.ok.us

Phil Blue
Oklahoma Department of Human
Services

312 N.E. 28th St.
Oklahoma City, OK 73105
405-521-4214
www.onenet.net/okdhs

Unclaimed Property Office
Oklahoma Tax Commission
Unclaimed Property Section
2501 Lincoln Blvd.
Oklahoma City, OK 73194
405-521-4275
www.kocotv.com/5oys/
fortune.html

Unemployment Insurance Office
Unemployment Insurance Director
Employment Security Commission
2401 North Lincoln
203 Will Rogers Memorial Office
Building
Oklahoma City, OK 73152
405-557-7190
www.desc.state.ok.us/iu/
default.htm
Weekly benefit range: $16-262
Duration of benefits: 20-26 weeks

Utility Commission
Corporation Commission
Jim Thorpe Office Building
P.O. Box 52000-2000

Oklahoma City, OK 73152-2000
405-521-2211
http://www.occ.state.ok.us

Women's Commission
Oklahoma Governor's
Commission on the Status of
Women
101 State Capitol Bldg.
2300 North Lincoln Blvd.
Oklahoma City, OK 73105-4897
918-492-4492
Fax: 918-492-4472
Claudia Tarrington, Chair
Kathi Goebel, Senior Vice Chair

Lawton Mayor's Commission on
the Status of Women
102 SW 5th St.
Lawton, OK 73501
405-581-3260
Janet Childress, Chair
Emma Crowder, Vice Chair

Tulsa Mayor's Commission on the
Status of Women
c/o Department of Human Rights
200 Civic Center
Tulsa, OK 74103
918-582-0558
918-592-7818

Oregon

Federal Information Center
All Locations; 800-688-9889

State Information Office
503-378-3111
http://www.state.or.us

Department on Aging
Senior and Disabled Services
500 Summer St., NE
Salem, OR 97310-1015
503-945-5811
http://www.sdsd.hr.state.or.us/

Attorney General's Office
Office of the Attorney General
Justice Building
1162 Court St., NW
Salem, OR 97310
503-378-6002
503-378-4320 (consumer protection)

Banking Commissioner
Administrator
Division of Finance and Corporate Securities
350 Winter St., NE, Room 21
Salem, OR 97310
503-378-4140
800-722-4134
http://www.cbs.state.or.us/external/dfcs/

Child Care and Development Block Grant Lead Agency
Child Care Division
Department of Employment
875 Union St., NE
Salem, OR 97311
503-947-1400
Fax: 503-947-1428
http://emp.state.or.us/

Child Support Enforcement Agency
Phil Yarnell
Oregon Child Support Program
Adult and Family Services Division
Department of Human Resources
P.O. Box 14170
Salem, OR 97309
503-373-7300
http://www.afs.hr.state.or.us/rss/childsupp.htm

Cooperative Extension Office
Dr. Lila Houghlum, Director
Oregon State Extension Service
Administration
Oregon State University
Ballard Extension Hall #101
Corvallis, OR 97331-3606
541-737-2711
http://wwwagcomm.ads.orst.edu/agcomwebfile/extser/index.html

812

Corporation Division Office
Corporation Division
Secretary of State
255 Capitol St., NE, Suite 151
Salem, OR 97310
503-986-2200
www.sos.state.or.us

Day Care Licensing Agency
Employment Department
Child Care Division
875 Union Street, NE
Salem, OR 97311
503-947-1400
http://emp.state.or.us/

Economic Development Office
Economic Development
Department
775 Summer St., NE
Salem, OR 97310
503-986-0260
Fax: 503-581-5115
www.econ.state.or.us/
javahome.htm

Department of Education
Oregon Department of Education
Data Information Service
Public Service Bldg.
255 Capitol St., NE
Salem, OR 97310-0230
503-378-3310
http://www.ode.state.or.us/

Department of Higher Education
Oregon State Scholarship
Commission
1500 Valley River Drive

Suite 100
Eugene, OR 97401
800-452-8807
503-687-7400
www.ossc.state.or.us

Health Department
Oregon Health Division
800 NE Oregon Street
Portland, OR 97232
503-731-4000
www.ohd.hr.state.or.us
E-mail: ohd.info@state.or.us

Housing Office
Oregon Housing Agency
Housing Division
1600 State St.
Salem, OR 97310
503-986-2046
http://www.hcs.state.or.us

Insurance Commissioner
Insurance Commissioner
440 Labor and Industries Bldg.
330 Winter St., NE
Salem, OR 97310
503-378-4271
800-722-4134
http://www.state.or.us/agencies.ns/
44000/ 00070/index.html

Labor Department
Oregon Employment Department
875 Union Street NE
Salem, OR 97311
503-947-1391
www.emp.state.or.us/agency.htm

Licensing Office
Business Information Center
Corporations Division
255 Capitol St., NW, Suite 151
Salem, OR 97310
503-986-2222
www.sos.state.or.us/corporation/
bic/bic.htm

One-Stop Career Center
Oregon Career Network
Oregon Employment Department
875 Union Street, NE
Salem, OR 97311
503-947-1470
www.emp.state.or.us
E-mail: info@emp.state.or.us

Security Regulators
Oregon Securities Commission
Department of Consumer &
Business Services
350 Winter St., NE
Salem, OR 97310
503-378-4140
www.cbs.state.or.us/external/
dfcs/index.html

Small Business Development Center
Oregon Small Business
Development Center
Lane Community College
44 West Broadway, Suite 501
Eugene, OR 97401-3021
541-726-2250
Fax: 541-345-6006
E-mail: cutlers@lanecc.edu
www.i2m.org/html

Social Services Offices
Oregon Department of Human
Resources
500 Summer Street, NE
Salem, OR 97310-1012
503-945-5738
www.hr.state.or.us/

Temporary Assistance to Needy Families (TANF)
Temporary Aid to Needy Families
Sandie Hoback
Oregon Department of Human
Resources
500 Summer St., NE
Salem, OR 97310
503-945-6116
http://www.afs.hr.state.or.us/
overview.html

Transportation Department
Stephen Fosdick
Oregon Department of
Transportation
555 13th St., NE Annex
Salem, OR 97310
503-986-3410
http://www.odot.state.or.us/tdb/
pubtrans/index.htm

Jean Palmateer
Oregon Department of
Transportation
3313 Brett Clodfelter Way
The Dalles, OR 97058
541-296-2602
http://www.odot.state.or.us/
tdbpubtrans/index.htm

Unclaimed Property Office
Unclaimed Property Unit
775 Summer St., NE
Salem, OR 87310
503-378-3805, ext. 450

Unemployment Insurance Office
Programs and Methods
Employment Department
875 Union St., NE
Salem, OR 97311
503-947-1470
www.emp.state.or.us/benefits/
uiinfo.htm
Weekly benefit range: $70-301
Duration of benefits: 4-26 weeks

Utility Commission
Public Utility Commission
550 Capital St., NE, 2nd Floor
Salem, OR 97310
503-378-6611
800-522-2404 (OR only)
http://www.puc.state.or.us

Women's Commission
Oregon Commission for Women
Portland State University
Smith Center, Room M315
Portland, OR 97207
503-725-5889
Tracy Davis, Contact

Pennsylvania

Federal Information Center
All Locations; 800-688-9889

State Information Office
717-787-2121
http://www.state.pa.us

Department on Aging
Aging Department
400 Market St.
State Office Bldg., 6th Floor
Harrisburg, PA 17101-2301
717-783-1550
http://164.156.7.66/pa_exec/
aging/overview.html

Attorney General's Office
Office of the Attorney General
Strawberry Square
Harrisburg, PA 71720
717-787-3391
800-441-2555
www.attorneygeneral.gov

Banking Commissioner
Secretary of Banking
3333 Market St., 16th Floor
Harrisburg, PA 17101-2290
717-787-6891
800-PA-BANKS (toll free in PA)
http://www.banking.state. pa.us/

**Child Care and Development
Block Grant Lead Agency**
CCDBG Administrator

Bureau of Child Day Care
Services
Office of Children, Youth and
Families
Pennsylvania Dept. of Public
Welfare
Box 2675
Harrisburg, PA 17105-2675
717-787-8691
Fax: 717-787-1529

**Child Support Enforcement
Agency**
Daniel Richard
Bureau of Child Support
Enforcement
Department of Public Welfare
P.O. Box 8018
Harrisburg, PA 17105
717-783-8729
800-932-0211
Fax: 717-787-4936

Cooperative Extension Office
Dr. Ted Alter, Director
Pennsylvania State University
Room 210, A.G. Administration
University Park, PA 16802
814-863-3438
http://www.cas.psu.edu/
docs/coext/coopext.html

Corporation Division Office
Corporation Bureau
Department of State

308 N. Office Building
Harrisburg, PA 17120
717-787-1997
www.dos.state.pa.us/bureau.htm

Day Care Licensing Agency
Bureau of Child Day Care
Office of Children, Youth and
Families
P.O. Box 2675
Harrisburg, PA 17105-2675
717-787-8691

Economic Development Office
Department of Community and
Economic Development
433 Forum Building
Harrisburg, PA
800-379-7448
www.dced.state.pa.us

Governor's Action Team
100 Pine Street, Suite 100
Harrisburg, PA 17101
717-787-8199
Fax: 717-772-5419
www.teampa.com

Department of Education
Pennsylvania Dept. of Education
Office of Data Services
333 Market St.
Harrisburg, PA 17126-0333
717-787-2644
http://www.cas.psu.edu/pde.html

Department of Higher Education
Pennsylvania Higher Education
Assistance Agency
1200 North 7th Street

Harrisburg, PA 17102
717-720-2850
TTY: 800-654-5988
Fax: 717-720-3907
www.pheaa.org

Health Department
Pennsylvania Department of
Health
P.O. Box 90
Health & Welfare Building
Harrisburg, PA 17108
800-692-7254
www.health.state.pa.us
E-mail: webmaster@
heath.state.pa.us

Housing Office
Pennsylvania Housing Finance
Agency
2101 North Front St.
P.O. Box 8029
Harrisburg, PA 17105-8029
717-780-3800
http://www.phfa.org

Insurance Commissioner
Insurance Commissioner
1326 Strawberry Square
Harrisburg, PA 17120
717-787-2317
800-783-7067
http://www.state.pa.us/pa_exec/
insurance/ overview.html

Labor Department
Pennsylvania Department of
Labor and Industry
1700 Labor and Industry Building
Harrisburg, PA 17120

707-787-5279
www.li.state.pa.us

Licensing Office
Bureau of Professional and
Occupational Affairs
618 Transportation and Safety
Building
Harrisburg, PA 17120
717-783-4854
800-822-2113
www.dos.state.pa.us/bpoa/
poa.htm

One-Stop Career Center
Pennsylvania Works
Department of Labor and Industry
1720 Labor and Industry Building
Seventh and Foster Street
Harrisburg, PA 17120
717-783-1115
http://pacareerlink.state.pa.us/
homeframe.asp

Security Regulators
Pennsylvania Securities
Commission
Eastgate Office Building
1010 N. 7th St., 2nd Floor
Harrisburg, PA 17102
717-787-8061
800-600-0007
www.state.pa.us/Pa_Exec/
Securities

**Small Business Development
Center**
Pennsylvania Small Business
Development Center
University of Pennsylvania

The Wharton School
Vance Hall, 4th Floor
3733 Spruce Street
Philadelphia, PA 19104-6374
215-898-1219
Fax: 215-573-2135
E-mail: pasbdc@
wharton.upenn.edu
www.libertynet.org/pasbdc

Social Services Offices
Pennsylvania Department of
Public Welfare
333 Health and Welfare Building
Harrisburg, PA 17105
717-787-4592
www.state.pa.us/PA_Exec/
Public_Welfare/overview.html

**Temporary Assistance to Needy
Families (TANF)**
Temporary Aid to Needy Families
Feather Houston
Pennsylvania Department of
Public Welfare
33 Health and Welfare Building
Harrisburg, PA 17105
717-787-3600
www.state.pa.us/PA_Exec/
Public_Welfare/secletter.html

Transportation Department
Pennsylvania Department of
Transportation
555 Walnut St., 8th Floor
Forum Place
Harrisburg, PA 17101
717-787-7540
http://www.patransit.psu.edu

Jim Grier
Pennsylvania Department of
Transportation
555 Walnut St., 8th Floor
Forum Place
Harrisburg, PA 17101
717-783-3990
http://www.patransit.psu.edu

Unclaimed Property Office
Pennsylvania State Treasury
Office of Unclaimed Property
P.O. Box 1837
Harrisburg, PA 17105
800-222-2046
www.treasury.state.pa.us

Unemployment Insurance Office
Bureau of U.C. Benefits and
Allowances
Department of Labor and Industry
Room 615
Labor and Industry Building
Seventh and Forster Sts.

Harrisburg, PA 17121
717-787-3547
www.li.state.pa.us/ben.html
Weekly benefit range: $33-375
Duration of benefits: 16-26 weeks

Utility Commission
Public Utility Commission
P.O. Box 3265
Harrisburg, PA 17120
717-783-1740
800-782-1110 (PA only)
http://puc.paonline.com/

Women's Commission
Pennsylvania Commission for
Women
Finance Building, Room 205
Harrisburg, PA 17120
888-615-7477
Fax: 717-772-0653
E-mail: lesbn@oa.state.pa.us
Loida Esbri, Executive Director

Rhode Island

Federal Information Center
All Locations; 800-688-9889

State Information Office
401-222-2000
http://www.state.ri.us

Department on Aging
Elderly Affairs Department
160 Pine St.
Providence, RI 02903
401-222-2858
http://www.sec.state.ri.
us/stdept/sd23.htm

Attorney General's Office
Office of the Attorney General
150 South Main St.
Providence, RI 02903
401-274-4400
www.riag.state.ri.us

Banking Commissioner
Director and Superintendent of
Banking
233 Richmond St., Suite 231
Providence, RI 02903-4231
401-222-2405

**Child Care and Development
Block Grant Lead Agency**
Rhode Island Department of
Human Services
Individual and Family Support
Services

Louis Pasteur Bldg. #57
600 New London Ave.
Cranston, RI 02920
401-464-3415
Fax: 401-464-1881
http://www.state.ri.us/stdept/
sd32.htm

**Child Support Enforcement
Agency**
John Murphy
Department of Administration
Division of Taxation
Child Support Enforcement
77 Dorrance St.
Providence, RI 02903
401-222-2847
800-638-5437
Fax: 401-222-2887

Cooperative Extension Office
Marsha Morreira, Director
Cooperative Extension Education
Center
University of Rhode Island
East Alumni Ave.
Kingston, RI 02881-0804
401-874-2900
http://www.edc.uri.edu/

Corporation Division Office
Corporations Division
Secretary of State
100 North Main St.
Providence, RI 02903

401-222-3040
www.state.ri.us/submenus/
corpindex.htm

Day Care Licensing Agency
Department of Children, Youth
and Families
Day Care Licensing Division
Building 3
610 Mount Pleasant Ave.
Providence, RI 02908
401-222-4741

Economic Development Office
Economic Development
Corporation
One West Exchange St.
Providence, RI 02903
401-222-2601
Fax: 401-222-2102
www.riedc.com

Department of Education
Management Information Services
Rhode Island Department of
Education
255 Westminster St.
Providence, RI 02903-3400
401-222-4600, ext. 6
http://instruct.ride.ri.net/ride_
home_page.html

Department of Higher Education
Rhode Island Higher Education
Assistance Authority
560 Jefferson Boulevard
Warwick, RI 02886
401-736-1100
TDD: 401-222-6195

Fax: 401-732-3541
www.riheaa.org

Health Department
Rhode Island Department of
Health
3 Capitol Hill
Providence, RI 02908
401-222-2231
Fax: 401-222-6548
TTY: 800-745-5555
www.health.state.ri.us/
E-mail: library@health.state.ri.us

Housing Office
Rhode Island Housing and
Mortgage Finance Corporation
60 Eddy St.
Providence, RI 02903
401-751-5566
http://www.state.ri.us/
quasisd/qsd12.htm

Insurance Commissioner
Insurance Commissioner
233 Richmond St.
Suite 233
Providence, RI 02903
401-277-2223
800-322-2880

Labor Department
Rhode Island Department of Labor
and Training
101 Friendship Street
Providence, RI 02903-3740
401-277-3600
www.det.state.ri.us

Licensing Office
Rhode Island Occupational
Information Coordinating
Commission
101 Friendship St.
Providence, RI 02903
401-272-0830
www.dlt.state.ri.us/webdev/lmi/
rioicc/rioicchm.html

One-Stop Career Center
NetWorkri
Department of Labor and Training
101 Friendship Street
Providence, RI 02903-3740
401-222-3722
Fax: 401-222-2731
www.networkri.org

Security Regulators
Department of Business
Regulation
233 Richmond St.
Suite 232
Providence, RI 02903
401-222-3048

Small Business Development Center
Bryant College
Small Business Development
Center
1150 Douglas Pike
Smithfield, RI 02197-1284
401-232-6111
Fax: 401-232-6933
E-mil: Admin@RISBDC.org
www.RISBDC.org

Social Services Offices
Rhode Island Department of
Human Services
600 New London Avenue
Cranston, RI 02920
401-464-2121
www.athena.state.ri.us/info/
human.htm

Temporary Assistance to Needy Families (TANF)
Temporary Aid to Needy Families
Edward Sneesby
Field Operations
Aimy Forand Bldg.
Cranston, RI 02920
401-464-2424
www.dhs.state.ri.us

Transportation Department
Robert Letourneau
Rhode Island Department of
Transportation
Two Capitol Hill
Providence, RI 02903
401-222-4203
www.dot.state.ri.us

Unclaimed Property Office
Unclaimed Property Division
P.O. Box 1435
Providence, RI 02901
401-277-6505
www.state.ri.us/treas/
moneylst.htm

Unemployment Insurance Office
Assistant Director
Unemployment Insurance

Department of Employment and
Training
101 Friendship St.
Providence, RI 02903
401-222-3652
www.det.state.ri.us/webdev/ui/
html
Weekly benefit range: $41-404
Duration of benefits: 15-26 weeks

Utility Commission
Public Utilities Commission
100 Orange St.
Providence, RI 02903

401-222-3500
800-341-1000 (RI only)
http://www.state.ri.us/
stdept/sd14.htm

Women's Commission
Rhode Island Advisory
Commission on Women
260 W. Exchange St., Suite 4
Providence, RI 02093
401-222-6105
E-mail: tayers@doa.state.ri.us
Toby Ayers, Ph.D., Director
James M. Anthony, Chair

South Carolina

Federal Information Center
All Locations; 800-688-9889

State Information Office
803-734-1000
http://www.state.sc.us

Department on Aging
Office on Aging
South Carolina Department of
Health and Human Services
P.O. Box 8206
Columbia, SC 29201
803-253-6177

Attorney General's Office
Office of the Attorney General
P.O. Box 11549
Columbia, SC 29211
803-734-3970
www.scattorneygeneral.org

Banking Commissioner
Commissioner of Banking
309 Calhoun Office Bldg.
Columbia, SC 29201
803-734-2001
http://www.lpitr.state.sc.us/
gvtdir97/p225.htm

**Child Care and Development
Block Grant Lead Agency**
South Carolina Health and Human
Services
Bureau of Community Services

P.O. Box 8206
Columbia, SC 29202-8206
803-253-6154
Fax: 803-253-6152
http://www.dhhs.state.sc.us/

**Child Support Enforcement
Agency**
Larry McKeown
Child Support Enforcement
Division
Department of Social Services
P.O. Box 1469
Columbia, SC 29202
803-737-5870
803-737-6032
800-768-5858 (in SC)
http://www.state.sc.us/ css/csed/

Cooperative Extension Offices
Carroll Culvertson, Director
Clemson University
Cooperative Extension Service
P.O. Box 995
Pickens, SC 29671
864-868-2810
http://www.clemson.edu/extension

Director
Cooperative Extension Service
P.O. Box 8103
South Carolina State University
Orangeburg, SC 29117-8103
803-536-8928
http://192.231.63.160/scsu/
state.htm

Information USA, Inc.

Corporation Division Office
Division of Corporations
Secretary of State
P.O. Box 11350
Columbia, SC 29211
803-734-2489

Day Care Licensing Agency
Department of Social Services
Child Care Licensing Division
P.O. Box 1520
Columbia, SC 29202-1520
803-734-5740
http://www.dhhs.state.sc.us/

Economic Development Office
Department of Commerce
P.O. Box 927
Columbia, SC 29202
803-737-0400
800-868-7232
Fax: 803-737-0418
www.state.sc.us/commerce

Department of Education
South Carolina Dept. of Education
Management Information Section
1206 Rutledge Bldg.
1429 Senate St.
Columbia, SC 29201
803-734-8262
http://www.state.sc.us/sde/

Department of Higher Education
South Carolina Commission on
Higher Education
Tuition Grants Commission
1310 Lady Street
Columbia, SC 29211

803-734-1200
Fax: 803-734-1426
www.state.sc.us/tuitiongrants

Health Department
South Carolina Department of
Health & Environmental Control
2600 Bull Street
Columbia, SC 29201
803-898-3432
www.state.sc.us/dhec/
E-mail: menchima@
columb29.dhec.state.sc.us

Housing Office
South Carolina State Housing
Financing and Development
Authority
919 Bluff Rd.
Columbia, SC 29201
803-734-2000
http://www.sha.state.sc.us

Insurance Commissioner
Chief Insurance Commissioner
P.O. Box 100105
Columbia, SC 29202-3105
803-737-6150
800-768-3467
http://www.state.sc.us/doi/

Labor Department
South Carolina Department of
Labor, Licensing and Regulation
Public Information Office
110 Centerview Drive
P.O. Box 11329
Columbia, SC 29211-1329
www.llr.state.sc.us

Licensing Office
South Carolina Department of
Labor, Licensing, and Regulation
P.O. Box 11329
Columbia, SC 29211
803-896-4363
www.llr.state.sc.us/boards.htm

One-Stop Career Center
1 Stop Partnership
Employment Security Commission
P.O. Box 995
1550 Gadsden Street
Columbia, SC 29202
803-737-9935
Fax: 803-737-0202
www.sces.org/1stop/
1stopmain.htm
E-mail: jobs@sces.org

Security Regulators
P.O. Box 11549
Columbia, SC 29211
803-734-9916
www.scattorneygeneral.org

Small Business Development Center
South Carolina Small Business
Development Center
University of South Carolina
College of Business
Administration, Hipp Building
1710 College Street
Columbia, SC 29208
803-777-4907
Fax: 803-777-4403
E-mail:lenti@darla.badm.sc.edu
http://sbdc.web.badmsc.edu

Social Services Offices
South Carolina Department of
Social Services
P.O. Box 1520
Columbia, SC 29202-1520
803-734-6180
www.state.sc.us/dss

Temporary Assistance to Needy Families (TANF)
Temporary Aid to Needy Families
James Clark
South Carolina Department of
Social Services
P.O. Box 1520
Columbia, SC 29202
803-734-5760
www.state.sc.us/dss/
programs.htm

Transportation Department
John Ritner
South Carolina Department of
Transportation
P.O. Box 191
300 Gervais St., Annex 3
Columbia, SC 29202
803-7373-9720
http://www.dot.state.sc.us

Kenny Skenes
South Carolina Department of
Transportation
P.O. Box 191
300 Gervais St., Annex 3
Columbia, SC 29202
803-737-9720
http://www.dot.state.sc.us

Unclaimed Property Office
State Treasurer's Office
Unclaimed Property Division
P.O. Box 11778
Columbia, SC 29211
803-734-2629

Unemployment Insurance Office
Deputy Executive Director
Unemployment Compensation
Employment Security Commission
P.O. Box 995
Columbia, SC 29202
803-737-2787
www.sces.org
Weekly benefit range: $20-238
Duration of benefits: 15-26 weeks

Utility Commission
Public Service Commission
P.O. Drawer 11649
Columbia, SC 29211
803-737-5230
800-922-1531 (SC only)
http://www.psc.state.sc.us

Women's Commission
Governor's Office Commission on
Women
1205 Pendleton St., Suite 306
Columbia, SC 29201
803-734-1609
Fax: 803-734-0241
Rebecca Collier, Executive
Director

South Dakota

Federal Information Center
All Locations; 800-688-9889

State Information Office
605-773-3011
http://www.state.sd.us

Department on Aging
Adult Services on Aging Office.
Social Services Department
700 Governors Dr.
Pierre, SD 57501
605-773-3656
http://www.state.sd.us/state/
executive/social/asa/asa.htm

Attorney General's Office
Office of the Attorney General
500 East Capitol
Pierre, SD 57501
605-773-3215
800-300-1986
www.state.sd.us/state/executive/
attorney/attorney.html

Banking Commissioner
Director of Banking and Finance
State Capitol Bldg.
500 E. Capitol Ave.
Pierre, SD 57501-5070
605-773-3421
http://www.state.sd.us/
executive/dcr/bank/

Child Care and Development Block Grant Lead Agency
Child Care Services
South Dakota Department of
Social Services
700 Governors Dr.
Pierre, SD 57501-2291
605-773-4766
Fax: 605-773-6834
http://www.state.sd.us/state/
executive/ social/social.htm

Child Support Enforcement Agency
Terry Walter
Office of Child Support
Enforcement
Department of Social Services
700 Governors Dr.
Pierre, SD 57501
605-773-3641
Fax: 605-773-6834
http://www.sate.sd.us/state/
executive/social/ CSE/OCSE.htm

Cooperative Extension Office
Mylo Hellickson, Director
SDSU
Box 2207D
AG Hall 154
Brookings, SD 57007
605-688-4792
http://www.abs.sdstate. edu/ces

Corporation Division Office
Corporate Division
Secretary of State
500 East Capitol
Pierre, SD 57501
605-773-4845
www.state.sd.us/sos/sos.htm

Day Care Licensing Agency
Department of Social Services
Child Care Services
Child Care Licensing Division
700 Governors Dr.
Pierre, SD 57501-2291
605-773-4766
http://www.state.sd.us/state/
executive/ social/social.htm

Economic Development Office
Governor's Office of Economic
Development
711 East Wells Ave.
Pierre, SD 57501-3369
605-773-5032
800-872-6190
Fax: 605-773-3256
www.state.sd.us/goed

Department of Education
South Dakota Department of
Education and Cultural Affairs
Office of Finance Management
700 Governors Dr.
Pierre, SD 57501-2291
605-773-3248
605-773-4748
http://www.state.sd.us/state/
executive/deca/

Department of Higher Education
South Dakota Department of
Education and Cultural Affairs
7000 Governors Drive
Pierre, SD 57051
605-773-3134

Health Department
South Dakota Dept. of Health
Health Building
600 East Capitol
Pierre, SD 57501-2563
800-738-2301
Fax: 605-773-5683
www.state.sd.us/state/executive/
doh/doh.html
E-mail: Info@doh.state.sd.us

Housing Office
South Dakota Housing
Development Authority
P.O. Box 1237
Pierre, SD 57501-1237
605-773-3181
http://sdhda.org

Insurance Commissioner
Director of Insurance
Insurance Bldg.
118 W. Capitol St.
Pierre, SD 57501
605-773-3563
800-822-8804
http://www.state.sd.us/insurance/

Labor Department
South Dakota Dept. of Labor
700 Governors Drive

Pierre, SD 57501-2291
605-773-3101
www.state.sd.us/dol/dol.htm

Licensing Office
Department of commerce and
Regulation
118 E. Capitol Ave.
Pierre, SD 57501
605-773-3178
www.state.sd.us/dcr/dcr.html

One-Stop Career Center
Job Service of South Dakota
SD Department of Labor
Kneip Building
700 Governors Drive
Pierre, SD 57501-2291
605-773-3101
Fax: 605-773-4211
www.state.sd.us/dol/sdjob/
js-home.htm
E-mail: infor@dol-pr.state.sd.us

Security Regulators
Division of Securities
118 W. Capitol Ave.
Pierre, SD 57501
605-773-4013
www.state.sd.us/dcr/securities/

**Small Business Development
Center**
South Dakota Small Development
Center
University of South Dakota
School of Business
414 East Clark Street/
Patterson 115

Vermillion, SD 57069-2390
605-677-5287
Fax: 605-677-5427
E-mail: stracy@charlie.usd.edu
www.usd.edu/brbinfo/brb/sbdc/
index.htm

Social Services Offices
South Dakota Department of
Social Services
700 Governors Drive
Pierre, SD 57501-2291
605-773-3165
www.state.sd.us/state/executive/
social/social.html

**Temporary Assistance to Needy
Families (TANF)**
Temporary Aid to Needy Families
Judy Thompson
South Dakota Department of
Social Services
700 Governors Dr.
Pierre, SD 57501
605-773-3493
http://www.state.sd.us/state/
executive/social/TANF/tanf.htm

Transportation Department
Willis McLaughlin
South Dakota Department of
Transportation
700 Broadway Ave., East
Pierre, SD 57501
605-773-3137
http://www.dot.state.sd.us

Lowell Richards
South Dakota Department of
Transportation

700 Broadway Ave., East
Pierre, SD 57501
605-773-3862
http://www.dot.state.sd.us

Unclaimed Property Office
Unclaimed Property Division
500 East Capitol Ave.
Pierre, SD 57501
605-773-3378
www.state.sd.us/state/executive/
treasurer/prop.htm

Unemployment Insurance Office
Director, Unemployment
Insurance Division
Department of Labor
P.O. Box 4730

Aberdeen, SD 57402
605-626-2312
www.state.sd.us/dol/ui/
ui-home.htm
Weekly benefit range: $28-194
Duration of benefits: 15-26 weeks

Utility Commission
Public Utilities Commission
500 E. Capitol Ave.
Pierre, SD 57501
605-773-3201
800-332-1782
http://www.state.sd.us/state/
executive/puc/puc.htm

Women's Commission
Abolished

Tennessee

Federal Information Center
All Locations; 800-688-9889

State Information Office
615-741-3011
http://www.state.tn.us

Department on Aging
Aging Commission
500 Deaderick St., 9th Floor
Nashville, TN 37243-0860
615-741-2056

Attorney General's Office
Office of the Attorney General
500 Charlotte Ave.
Nashville, TN 37243
615-741-6474

Banking Commissioner
Commissioner of Financial
Institutions
500 Charlotte Ave.
John Sevier Bldg., 4th Floor
Nashville, TN 37243-0705
615-741-2236
http://www.state.tn.us/ financialinst/

**Child Care and Development
Block Grant Lead Agency**
Child Care Services
Tennessee Department of Human
Services
Citizens Plaza - 14th Floor
400 Deaderick St.

Nashville, TN 37248
615-313-4778
Fax: 615-532-9956
http://www.state.tn.us/humanserv/

**Child Support Enforcement
Agency**
Joyce McClaran
Child Support Services
Department of Human Services
Citizens Plaza Bldg., 12th Floor
400 Deaderick St.
Nashville, TN 37248
615-313-4880
800-838-6911
http://www.state.tn.us/
humanserv/w2.htm

Cooperative Extension Offices
Dr. Billy G. Hicks, Dean
Agricultural Extension Service
University of Tennessee
P.O. Box 1071
Knoxville, TN 37901-1071
423-974-7114
http://tunnelweb.utcc.
utk.edu/~utext/

Cherry Lane Zon Schmittou,
Extension Leader
Davidson County Agricultural
Service
Tennessee State University
800 Second Ave. N., Suite 3
Nashville, TN 37201-1084
615-254-8734

Corporation Division Office
Office of Secretary of State
Business Services Division
Suite 1800, James K. Polk Bldg.
Nashville, TN 37243
615-741-2286
www.state.tn.us/sos/soshmpg.htm

Day Care Licensing Agency
Department of Human Services
Day Care Licensing Division
400 Deaderick St.
Nashville, TN 37248-9800
615-313-4778
http://www.state.tn.us/humanserv/

Economic Development Office
Department of Economic and
Community Development
Rachel Jackson Bldg., 8th Floor
320 Sixth Avenue North
Nashville, TN 37243-0405
615-741-3282
800-342-8470 (in TN)
800-251-8594
Fax: 615-741-7306
www.state.tn.us

Department of Education
Tennessee Dept. of Education
Office of Accountability
Gateway Plaza
710 James Robertson Parkway
Nashville, TN 37243-0381
615-532-4703
http://www.state.tn.us/education

Department of Higher Education
Tennessee Student Assistance
Corporation

404 James Robertson Pkwy.
Suite 1950
Nashville, TN 37243-0820
615-741-1346
Fax: 615-741-6101
www.state.tn.us/thec/thecp1.hm

Health Department
Tennessee Department of Health
425 5th Avenue North
Nashville, TN 37247
615-741-3111
www.state.tn.us/health
E-mail: DDenton@mail.state.tn.us

Housing Office
Tennessee Housing Development
Agency
404 James Robertson Pkwy.
Suite 1114
Nashville, TN 37243-0900
615-741-4979

Insurance Commissioner
Commissioner of Insurance
500 James Robertson Parkway
Nashville, TN 37243-0565
615-741-2241
800-342-4029
http://www.state.tn.us/commerce

Labor Department
Tennessee Department of Labor
2nd Floor Andrew Johnson Tower
710 James Robertson Parkway
Nashville, TN 37213-0658
615-741-2582
www.state.tn.us/labor

Licensing Office
Division of Regulatory Boards
Department of Commerce and
Insurance
500 James Robertson Parkway
Nashville, TN 37243
615-741-3449
www.state.tn.us/commerce

One-Stop Career Center
Tennessee Career Center
Office of Workforce Development
Andrew Johnson Bldg., 8th Floor
710 James Robertson Parkway
Nashville, TN 37243
615-253-1324
Fax: 615-253-1329
www.owd.state.tn.us/index.html
E-mail: jfite@mail.state.tn.us

Security Regulators
Tennessee Securities Division
Volunteer Plaza
Suite 680
500 James Robertson Pkwy.
Nashville, TN 37243
615-741-5905
www.state.tn.us/commerce/
securdiv.html

Small Business Development Center
Tennessee Small Business
Development Center
University of Memphis
South Campus (Getwell Road)
Building #1
Memphis, TN 38152-0001
901-678-2500

Fax: 901-678-4072
E-mail:gmickle@cc.memphis.edu
www.tsbdc.memphis.edu

Social Services Offices
Tennessee Department of Human
Services
Citizens Plaza Building
400 Deaderick Street
Nashville, TN 37248-0001
615-313-4707
www.state.tn.us/humanserv

Temporary Assistance to Needy Families (TANF)
Temporary Aid to Needy Families
Wanda Moore
Tennessee Department of Human
Services
400 Deaderick St., 12th Floor
Nashville, TN 37248
615-313-4867
www.state.tn.us/humanserv/
fmfirst.htm

Transportation Department
Terry Hayes
Tennessee Department of
Transportation
505 Deaderick
JK Polk Bldg., Suite 400
Nashville, TN 37243
615-741-2781
www.state.tn.us/transport/

Unclaimed Property Office
Unclaimed Property Division
Andrew Jackson Bldg., 9th Floor
Nashville, TN 37243

615-741-6499
www.state.tn.us/treasury/
treasury.htm

Unemployment Insurance Office
Deputy Commissioner
Tennessee Department of
Employment Security
500 James Robertson Pkwy.
12th Floor
Nashville, TN 37245
615-741-2131
www.state.tn.us/empsec/ui/ui.htm

Weekly benefit range: $30-200
Duration of benefits: 12-26 weeks

Utility Commission
Tennessee Regulatory Authority
460 James Robertson Parkway
Nashville, TN 37243
615-741-2904
800-342-8359 (TN only)
http://www.state.tn. us/tra/tra.htm

Women's Commission
Abolished

Texas

Federal Information Center
All Locations; 800-688-9889

State Information Office
512-463-4630
http://www.state.tx.us

Department on Aging
Aging Department
Box 12786
Austin, TX 78711
512-424-6840
http://www.texas.gov/ agency/
340.html

Attorney General's Office
Office of the Attorney General
P.O. Box 12548
Austin, TX 78711
512-463-2100
800-252-8011
www.oag.state.tx.us

Banking Commissioner
Banking Commissioner
2601 N. Lamar Blvd.
Austin, TX 78705
512-475-1300
http://www.banking.state. tx.us

**Child Care and Development
Block Grant Lead Agency**
Texas Workforce Commission
Child Care Services
Work and Family Clearinghouse

101 E. 15th St., Suite 416T
Austin, TX 78778-0001
512-936-3229
Fax: 512-936-3223
http://www.twc.state.tx.us/

**Child Support Enforcement
Agency**
David Vela
Child Support Division
Office of the Attorney General
P.O. Box 12017
Austin, TX 78711
512-460-6000
512-479-6478
800-252-8014
http://www.oag.state.tx. us/
WEBSITE/childsup.htm

Cooperative Extension Offices
Dr. Zerle Carpenter, Director
Texas Agricultural Extension
Service
Administration Bldg. 106-A
Texas A&M University
College Station, TX 77843
409-845-7967
http://agcomwww.tamu.
edu/agcom/taex/taex.htm

Dr. Linda Willis, Director
Cooperative Extension Program
P.O. Box 3059
Prairie View, TX 77446-3059
409-857-2023
http://www.pvamu.edu/

Corporation Division Office
Corporation Section
Statue Filing Division
Secretary of State
P.O. Box 13697
Austin, TX 78711
512-463-5578
http://lamb.sos.state.tx.us/
function/

Day Care Licensing Agency
Department of Protective and
Regulatory Services
Child Care Licensing
P.O. Box 149030
M.C.E-550
Austin, TX 78714-9030
512-438-3267
800-862-5252
http://www.tdprs.state.tx.us/
homepage.html

Economic Development Office
Department of Economic
Development
P.O. Box 12728
Austin, TX 78711
512-936-0260
800-888-0511
www.tded.state.tx.us

Department of Education
Texas Education Agency
Division of Public Information
1701 N. Congress
Austin, TX 78701-1494
MAILING ADDRESS:
  P.O. Box 13817
  Austin, TX 78711-3817

512-463-9734
http://www.tea.state.tx.us/

Department of Higher Education
Texas Higher Education
Coordinating Board
Box 12788, Capitol Station
Austin, TX 78711-2788
512-483-6100
www.thecb.state.tx.us/start/
stu.htm

Health Department
Texas Department of Health
1100 West 49th Street
Austin, TX 78756-3199
512-458-7111
www.tdh.texas.gov/

Housing Office
Texas Housing Agency
507 Saveine St.
Austin, TX 78701
512-475-3800
http://www.tdhca.state. tx.us

Insurance Commissioner
Director
Claims and Compliance Division
State Board of Insurance
P.O. Box 149104
Austin, TX 78714-9104
512-463-6464
800-252-3439
http://www.tdi.state.tx.us

Labor Department
Texas Workforce Commission
101 East 15th Street

Austin, TX 78778
512-463-2222
www.twc.state.tx.us

Licensing Office
Department of Licensing and
Regulation
P.O. Box 12157
Austin, TX 78711
512-463-6599
800-803-9202
www.license.state.tx.us

One-Stop Career Center
Texas Workforce Information
System (TWIST)
Texas Workforce Commission
101 East 15th Street
Austin, TX 78778
512-463-6438
www.twc.state.tx.us
E-mail: ombudsman@twc.
state.tx.us

Security Regulators
State Securities Board
P.O. Box 13167
Austin, TX 78711
512-305-8300
www.ssb.state.tx.us

**Small Business Development
Center**
North Texas Small Business
Development Center
Dallas County Community College
1402 Corinth Street
Dallas, TX 75215
214-860-5831
Fax: 214-860-5813

E-mail: daw1404@dcccd.edu
www.smbizsolutions.uh.edu

Social Services Offices
Texas Department of Human
Services
701 West 51st Street
Austin, TX 78751
512-438-3045
www.dhs.texas.gov

**Temporary Assistance to Needy
Families (TANF)**
Temporary Aid to Needy Families
Eric Bost
Texas Department of Human
Services
P.O. Box 149030
Austin, TX 78714
512-438-3280
http://www.dhs.state.tx.us/dhs/
cssind.htm

Transportation Department
Bobby Killebrew
Texas Department of
Transportation
125 East 11th St.
Austin, TX 78701
512-416-2816
http://www.dot.state.tx.us

Unclaimed Property Office
Comptroller of Public Accounts
Unclaimed Property Section
P.O. Box 12019
Austin, TX 78711
512-463-3120
www.window.state.tx.us/comptrol/
unclprop/unclprop.html

Unemployment Insurance Office
Director
Unemployment Insurance
Texas Workforce Commission
15th and Congress, Room 668
Austin, TX 78778
512-463-0735
www.twc.state.tx.us/ui/bnfts/
benehp.html
Weekly benefit range: $47-287
Duration of benefits: 9-26 weeks

Utility Commission
Public Utility Commission
1701 N. Congress Ave.

Austin, TX 78701
512-936-7000
http://www.puc.state.tx.us

Women's Commission
Texas Governor's Commission for
Women
P.O. Box 12428
Austin, TX 78711
512-463-1782
512-475-2615
Fax: 512-463-1832
www.governor.state.tx.us/women/
Ashley Horton, Executive Director

Utah

Federal Information Center
All Locations; 800-688-9889

State Information Office
801-538-3000
http://www.state.ut.us

Department on Aging
Aging and Adult Services Division
Human Services Dept.
120 North, 200 West
Salt Lake City, UT 84107
801-538-3910
http://www.dhs.state.ut.us/
agency/daas/homeage.htm

Attorney General's Office
Office of the Attorney General
State Capitol, Room 236
Salt Lake City, UT 84114
801-538-9600
801-366-0260
www.attygen.state.ut.us

Banking Commissioner
Commissioner of Financial
Institutions
P.O. Box 89
Salt Lake City, UT 84110-0089
801-538-8830

**Child Care and Development
Block Grant Lead Agency**
Utah Department of Workforce
Services

Policy and Program Unit
140 East 3rd South
Salt Lake City, UT 84111
801-526-4370
Fax: 801-536-7500

**Child Support Enforcement
Agency**
James Kidder
Bureau of Child Support Services
Department of Human Services
P.O. Box 45011
Salt Lake City, UT 84145
801-536-8500/8509
800-257-9156
http://www.dhs.state.ut.us/Agency/
ORS/ Chldsup.htm

Cooperative Extension Office
Dr. Robert Gilliland
Vice President for Extension and
Continuing Education U.M.C.
4900 Old Main Hall
Utah State University
Logan, UT 84322-4900
435-797-2200
http://www.ext.usu.edu/

Corporation Division Office
Corporations and UCC
Division of Business Regulations
P.O. Box 45801
160 East 300 South St., 2nd Floor
Salt Lake City, UT 84145
801-530-4849

Day Care Licensing Agency
Bureau of Licensing
Child Care Unit
288 N. 1460 West
P.O. Box 142003
Salt Lake City, UT 84114-2003
801-538-9299
http://www.dhs.state.ut.us/

Economic Development Office
Business and Economic
Development Division
324 South State St., Suite 500
Salt Lake City, UT 84111
801-538-8800
Fax: 801-538-8889
www.ce.ex.state.ut.us

Department of Education
Utah Board of Education
Department of Finance
250 E. 500 S.
Salt Lake City, UT 84111
801-538-7660
http://www.usoe.k12.ut.us/

Department of Higher Education
Utah System of Higher Education
3 Triad Center, Suite 550
Salt Lake City, UT 84180-1205
801-321-7101
www.state.ut.us/html/
education.htm

Health Department
Utah Department of Health
P.O. Box 1010
Salt Lake City, UT 84114-1010
801-538-5101

http://hlunix.ex.state.ut.us/
E-mail: pwightma@doh.state.ut.us

Housing Office
Utah Housing Finance Agency
554 South, 300 East
Salt Lake City, UT 84111
801-521-6950

Insurance Commissioner
Commissioner of Insurance
3110 State Office Bldg.
Salt Lake City, UT 84114
801-538-3805
800-439-3805
http://www.ins-dept.state.ut.us/

Labor Department
Utah Department of Workforce
Services
P.O. Box 45249
Salt Lake City, UT 84145-0249
801-526-9675
http://dwsa.state.ut.us

Licensing Office
Division of Occupational and
Professional Licensing
Department of Commerce
160 East 300 South
P.O. Box 45802
Salt Lake City, UT 84145
801-530-6628
www.commerce.state.ut.us

One-Stop Career Center
Career Centers
Department of Workforce Services
140 East 300 South

Salt Lake City, UT 84111
801-531-3780
Fax: 801-531-3785
www.dws.state.ut.us/default.htm
E-mail: www@dwsa.state.ut.us

Security Regulators
Securities Division
P.O. Box 146760
Salt Lake City, UT 84114
801-530-6600
www.commerce.state.ut.us/web/
commerce/secint/index.htm

**Small Business Development
Center**
Small Business Development
Center
Salt Lake Community College
1623 South State Street
Salt Lake City, UT 84115
801-957-3480
Fax: 801-957-3489
E-mail: FinnerMi@slcc.edu
www.slcc.edu/utahsbdc

Social Services Offices
Utah Dept. of Human Services
P.O. Box 45500
120 North 200 West
Salt Lake City, UT 84145-0500
801-538-3991
www.dhs.state.ut.us

**Temporary Assistance to Needy
Families (TANF)**
Temporary Aid to Needy Families
Robin Arnold Williams
Utah Dept. of Human Services

120 North 200 West
Suite 319
Salt Lake City, UT 84103
801-538-3998
http://www.dws.state.ut.us

Transportation Department
Glenda Seelos
Utah Department of
Transportation
P.O. Box 143600
4501 South 2700 West
Salt Lake City, UT 84119
801-965-4141
www.sr.ex.state.ut.us

Unclaimed Property Office
State Treasurer's Office
Unclaimed Property Division
341 South Main St., 5th Floor
Salt Lake City, UT 84111
801-533-4101
www.treasurer.state.ut.us

Unemployment Insurance Office
Director Unemployment Insurance
Workforce Services
140 East 300 South
P.O. Box 11249
Salt Lake City, UT 84147
801-536-7423
http://dwsa.state.ut.us/default.htm
Weekly benefit range: $20-284
Duration of benefits: 10-26 weeks

Utility Commission
Public Service Commission
160 East, 300 South
P.O. Box 45585

Salt Lake City, UT 84145
801-530-6716
http://web.state.ut.us/bbs/
psc/html/index.htm

Women's Commission
Utah Governor's Commission for
Women and Families

1160 State Office Bldg.
Salt Lake City, UT 84114
801-538-1736
Fax: 801-538-3027
E-mail: women&families@
gov.state.ut.us
www.governor.state.ut.us/women/
Michael Neider, Chair

Vermont

Federal Information Center
All Locations; 800-688-9889

State Information Office
802-828-1110
http://www.state.vt.us

Department on Aging
Vermont Department of Aging and
Disabilities
103 S. Main St.
Waterbury, VT 05676
802-241-2400
http://www.state.vt.us/
dad/busdir.htm

Attorney General's Office
Office of the Attorney General
109 State St.
Montpelier, VT 05609
802-828-3171
www.state.vt.us/atg/

Banking Commissioner
Commissioner of Banking and
Insurance Securities
89 Main St., Drawer 20
Montpelier, VT 05620-3101
802-828-3301
http://www.state.vt.us/bis

**Child Care and Development
Block Grant Lead Agency**
Child Care Services Division
Vermont Department of Social and
Rehabilitation Services

103 S. Main St., 2nd Floor
Waterbury, VT 05671-2401
802-241-3110
Fax: 802-241-1220
http://www.cit.state.vt.us/srs/
dclic/index.htm

**Child Support Enforcement
Agency**
Jeffery Cohen
Office of Child Support
103 South Main St.
Waterbury, VT 05671
802-241-2319
800-786-3214
Fax: 802-244-1483

Cooperative Extension Office
Dr. Larry Forchier, Dean
Division of Agriculture
Natural Resources, and Extension
University of Vermont
601 Main St.
Burlington, VT 05401-3439
802-656-2990
http://ctr.uvm.edu/ext/

Corporation Division Office
Corporate Division
Secretary of State
109 State St.
Montpelier, VT 05602
802-828-2386
www.sec.state.vt.us

Day Care Licensing Agency
Department of Social and
Rehabilitation Services
Child Care Licensing Unit
103 S. Main St.
Montpelier, VT 05761-2901
802-241-3110
http://www.cit.state.vt.us/srs/
dclic/index.htm

Economic Development Office
Department of Economic
Development
National Life Building, Drawer 20
Montpelier, VT 05620-0501
802-828-3221
800-341-2211
Fax: 802-828-3258
www.state.vt.us/dca/economic/
developm.htm

Department of Education
Vermont Department of Education
School Finance Department
State Office Bldg.
120 State St.
Montpelier, VT 05620-2501
802-828-3147
http://www.state.vt.us/educ/

Department of Higher Education
Vermont Student Assistance
Corporation
P.O. Box 2000
Champlain Mill, 4th Floor
Winooski, VT 05404
800-798-8722
802-655-4050
www.vsac.org

Health Department
Vermont Department of Health
108 Cherry Street
Burlington, VT 05402-0070
800-464-4343
Fax: 802-863-7475
www.state.vt.us/health

Housing Offices
Vermont Housing Finance Agency
One Burlington Sq.
164 St. Paul St.
Burlington, VT 05402-0408
802-864-5743
800-287-8432
http://www.vhfa.org

Vermont State Housing Authority
1 Prospect St.
Montpelier, VT 05602-3556
802-828-3295

Insurance Commissioner
Commissioner of Banking and
Insurance
89 Main St., Drawer 20
Montpelier, VT 05620-3101
802-828-3301
800-642-5119
http://www.state.vt.us/bis/

Labor Department
Vermont Department of
Employment and Training
5 Green Mountain Drive
P.O. Box 488
Montpelier, VT 05601-0488
802-229-1157
www.det.state.ut.us

Licensing Office
Office of Professional Regulation
Secretary of State
Pavilion Office Building
Montpelier, VT 05609
802-828-2363
http://vtprofessionals.org

One-Stop Career Center
One-Stop Career Resource
Department of Employment and
Training
Division of Jobs and Training
5 Green Mountain Drive
P.O. Box 488
Montpelier, VT 05602
802-828-4000
TDD: 802-828-4203
Fax: 802-828-4022
www.det.state.vt.us

Security Regulators
Department of Banking,
Insurance, Securities & Health
Care Administration
Securities Division
89 Main St., Drawer 20
Montpelier, VT 05620
802-828-3301
www.state.vt.us/bis

Small Business Development Center
Vermont Small Business
Devlopment Center
Vermont Technical College
Randolph Center, VT 05060
MAILING: P.O. Box 422
Randolph, VT 05060-0422

802-728-9101
800-464-SBDC
Fax: 802-728-3026
E-mail: dkelpins@vtc.vsc.edu
www.vtsbdc.org

Social Services Offices
Vermont Agency of Human
Services
103 South Main Street
Waterbury, VT 05671-2401
802-241-2220
www.ahs.state.vt.us

Temporary Assistance to Needy Families (TANF)
Temporary Aid to Needy Families
Jane Kitchel
Vermont Department of Social
Welfare
103 South Main St.
Waterbury, VT 05671
802-241-2853
http://www.dsw.state.vt.us/
wrp/tanf_stp.htm

Transportation Department
William Peabody
Vermont Agency of Transportation
133 State St.
Montpelier, VT 05633
802-828-2828
http://www.aot.state.vt.us

Unclaimed Property Office
Abandoned Property Division
State Treasurer's Office
133 State St.
Montpelier, VT 05633

802-828-2301
www.cit.state.vt.us/treasurer/

Unemployment Insurance Office
Unemployment Insurance
Department of Employment and
Training
5 Green Mountain Dr.
P.O. Box 488
Montpelier, VT 05602
802-828-4100
www.det.state.vt.us/~detui/
ui-dir.htm
Weekly benefit range: $25-275
Duration of benefits: 26 weeks

Utility Commission
Public Service Board

112 State St.
Chittenden Bank Bldg.
4th Floor, Drawer 20
Montpelier, VT 05620-2701
802-828-2358
800-622-4496 (VT only)
http://www.state.vt.us/psb

Women's Commission
Vermont Governor's Commission
on the Status of Women
126 State St., Drawer 33
Montpelier, VT 05602
802-828-2851
Fax: 802-828-2930
E-mail: info@women.state.vt.us
www.state.vt.us/wom
Judith Sutphen, Executive Director

Virginia

Federal Information Center
All Locations; 800-688-9889

State Information Office
804-786-0000
http://www.state.va.us

Department on Aging
Aging Department
1600 Forest Ave., Suite 102
Richmond, VA 23229
804-662-9333
http://www.aging.state. va.us/

Attorney General's Office
Office of the Attorney General
900 East Main St.
Richmond, VA 23219
804-786-2071
www.cns.state.va.us/oag

Banking Commissioner
Bureau of Financial Institutions
1300 E. Main St., Suite 800
P.O. Box 640
Richmond, VA 23218-0640
804-371-9657
800-552-7945 (toll free in VA)
http://dit1.state.va.us/scc/
division/banking/index.htm

**Child Care and Development
Block Grant Lead Agency**
Virginia Department of Social
Services

Child Day Care
730 E. Broad St.
Richmond, VA 23219-1849
804-692-1210
Fax: 804-692-2209
http://www.dss.state.va.us/

**Child Support Enforcement
Agency**
Nathaniel Young
Assistant Commissioner for Child
Support Enforcement
Department of Social Services
730 East Broad St.
Richmond, VA 23219
804-692-1428
800-468-8894 (in VA)
Fax: 804-692-1438
http://www.dss.state.va.us/
childspt.html

Cooperative Extension Offices
Dr. Clark Jones, Interim Director
Virginia Cooperative Extension
Virginia Tech
Blacksburg, VA 24061-0402
540-231-5299
http://www.ext.vt.edu/

Lorenza Lyons, Administrator
Cooperative Extension
Virginia State University
Rox 9081
Petersburg, VA 23806-9081
804-524-5961

Corporation Division Office
Clerk of Commission
State Corporation Commission
Secretary of State
P.O. Box 1197
Richmond, VA 23209
804-371-9733
www.state.va.us/scc/index.html

Day Care Licensing Agency
Department of Social Services
Child Care Licensing Division
730 Broad St., 7th Floor
Richmond, VA 23219-1849
804-692-1787
http://www.dss.state.va.us/

Economic Development Office
Economic Development
Partnership
P.O. Box 798
Richmond, VA 23206
804-371-8100
Fax: 804-371-8112
www2.yesvirginia.org/YesVA

Department of Education
Virginia Department of Education
Management Information Office
101 N. 14th St., 22nd Floor
Richmond, VA 23219
804-225-2540
800-292-3820
http://www.pen.k12.va.us/
Anthology/VDOE/

Department of Higher Education
Virginia State Council of Higher
Education
Office of Financial Aid

James Monroe Building
101 North 14th Street, 9th Floor
Richmond, VA 23219
804-225-2137
TDD: 804-371-8017
Fax: 804-225-2604
www.schev.edu

Health Department
Virginia Department of Health
Main Street Station
Richmond, VA 23219
804-786-5916
Fax: 804-371-4110
www.vdh.state.va.us/
E-mail: rnash@vdh.state.va.us

Housing Office
Virginia Housing Development
Authority
601 S. Belvedere St.
Richmond, VA 23220-6504
804-782-1986
800-968-7837
http://www.vhda.com

Insurance Commissioner
Commissioner of Insurance
1300 E. Main St.
P.O. Box 1157
Richmond, VA 23218
804-371-9741
800-552-7945
http://dit1.state.va.us/scc/division/
boi/index.htm

Labor Department
Virginia Department of Labor and
Industry
Powers - Taylor Building

13 South Thirteenth Street
Richmond, VA 23219
804-371-2327
www.dli.state.va.us

Licensing Office
Virginia Dept. of Professional and
Occupational Regulation
3600 W. Broad St.
Richmond, VA 23230
804-367-8500
www.state.va.us/dpor/indexie.html

One-Stop Career Center
Workforce Development System
Employment Commission
P.O. Box 1358
Richmond, VA 23218-1358
804-786-4832
Fax: 804-786-6091
www.vec.state.va.us/seeker/
seeker.htm
E-mail: vaemployment@aol.com

Security Regulators
Virginia Division of Securities
P.O. Box 1197
Richmond, VA 23218
804-371-9051
800-552-7945
www.state.va.us/scc/division/
srf/index.htm

**Small Business Development
Center**
Virginia Small Business
Development Center
Dept. of Economic Development
901 East Byrd Street, Suite 1400
Richmond, VA 23219

804-371-8253
Fax: 804-225-3384
E-mail: rwilburn@dba.state.va.us
www.dba.state.va.us/SBDMain.
htm

Social Services Offices
Virginia Dept. of Social Services
730 East Broad Street
Richmond, VA 23219
804-692-1906

**Temporary Assistance to Needy
Families (TANF)**
Temporary Aid to Needy Families
Marsha Sharpe
Department of Social Services
730 East Broad St., 7th Floor
Richmond, VA 23229
804-692-1730
www.dss.state.va.us/tempasst.
html

Transportation Department
Neil Sherman
Virginia Department of Rail and
Public Transportation
1401 East Broad St., Room 1401
Richmond, VA 23219
804-786-1154
www.state.va.us/drpt/index.html

Metropolitan Planning
Organization
Darrel Feasel
Virginia Department of Rail and
Public Transportation
1401 East Broad St., Room 1401
Richmond, VA 23219

804-786-8089
www.state.va.us/drpt/index.html

Unclaimed Property Office
Division of Unclaimed Property
Department of Treasury
P.O. Box 2478
Richmond, VA 23218
804-225-2393
www.trs.state.va.us/

Unemployment Insurance Office
Field Operations
Virginia Employment Commission
703 E. Main St.
Richmond, VA 23219
804-786-3004
www.vec.state.va.us
Weekly benefit range: $55-228
Duration of benefits: 12-26 weeks

Utility Commission
State Corporation Commission
P.O. Box 1197
Richmond, VA 23218-1197
804-371-9967
800-552-7945 (VA only)
http://www.state.va.us/scc/
index.html

Women's Commission
Alexandria Council on the Status
of Women
110 North Royal St., Suite 201
Alexandria, VA 22314
703-838-5030
Fax: 703-838-4976
http://ci.alexandria.va.us/
alexandria.html
Norma Gattsek, Exec. Director
Tara Hardiman, Chair

Arlington Commission on the
Status of Women
2100 Clarendon Blvd., Suite 310
Arlington, VA 22201
703-228-3257
Fax: 703-228-3295
E-mail: publicaffairs@co.
arlington.va.us
www.co.arlington.va.us/cmo
Katherine Hoffman

Fairfax City Commission for
Women
10455 Armstrong St.
Fairfax, VA 22030
703-385-7894
Fax: 703-385-7811
www.ci.fairfax.va.us
Louise Armitage, Director

Fairfax County Commission for
Women
12000 Government Center Pkwy.,
Suite 318
Fairfax, VA 22035
703-324-5720
Fax: 703-324-3959
TTY: 703-222-3504
Leia Francisco, Executive Director

Richmond Mayor's Committee on
the Concerns of Women
City Hall
900 East Marshall St., Room 302
Richmond, VA 23219
804-646-5987
Nancy Ownes, Admin. Assistant
Caroline Adams, Chair

Washington

Federal Information Center
All Locations; 800-688-9889

State Information Office
360-753-5000
http://www.state.wa.us

Department on Aging
Aging and Adult Services
P.O. Box 45050
Olympia, WA 98504-5600
360-586-8753

Attorney General's Office
Office of the Attorney General
P.O. Box 40100
1125 Washington St., SE
Olympia, WA 98504
360-753-6200
800-551-4636
www.wa.gov/ago

Banking Commissioner
Department of Financial Institutions
Division of Banking
210 11th Ave., SW
Third Floor, Room 300
P.O. Box 41200
Olympia, WA 98504-1200
360-902-8700
800-372-8303
http://www.wa.gov/dfi/

Child Care and Development Block Grant Lead Agency
Office of Child Care Policy

Washington Department of Social and Health Services
P.O. Box 5700
Olympia, WA 98504-5700
360-902-8038
Fax: 360-902-7903
http://www.va.gov/dshs/

Child Support Enforcement Agency
Meg Sollenberger
Division of Child Support, DSHS
P.O. Box 9162
Olympia, WA 98507
360-586-3162
360-586-3274
800-457-6202
http://www.wa.gov/dshs/dce/
csrc.html

Cooperative Extension Office
Dr. Harry Burcalow, Director
Cooperative Extension
411 Hulbert
Washington State University
Pullman, WA 99164-6230
509-335-2811
http://www.cahe.wsu.edu/ce/html

Corporation Division Office
Corporate Division
Secretary of State
Republic Bldg.
505 Union Ave., 2nd Floor
Mail Stop PM-21

Olympia, WA 98504
360-753-7115
www.wa.gov/sec

Day Care Licensing Agency
Office of Child Care Policy
Child Care Licensing Division
P.O. Box 45700
Olympia, WA 98504-5710
360-902-8038
http://www.wa.gov/dshs

Economic Development Office
Department of Community, Trade
and Economic Development
906 Columbia St. SW
P.O. Box 48300
Olympia, WA 98504-8300
800-237-1233
access.wa.gov

Department of Education
Washington Superintendent of
Public Instruction
47200 Old Capitol Bldg.
Olympia, WA 98504-7200
360-753-1700
http://www.ospi.wednet.edu/

Department of Higher Education
Higher Education Coordinating
Board
917 Lakeridge Way
P.O. Box 43430
Olympia, WA 98504-3430
360-753-7800
TTY: 360-753-7809
Fax: 360-753-7808
www.hecb.wa.gov

Health Department
Washington State Department of
Health
1112 SE Quince Street
P.O. Box 47890
Olympia, WA 98504-7890
360-236-4010
www.doh.wa.gov/
E-mail: gkm0303@doh.wa.gov

Housing Office
Washington State Housing Finance
Commission
1000 Second Ave., Suite 2700
Seattle, WA 98104-1046
206-464-7139

Insurance Commissioner
Insurance Commissioner
Insurance Bldg. AQ21
P.O. Box 40255
Olympia, WA 98504-0255
360-753-7301
800-562-6900
http://www.wa.gov/ins/

Labor Department
Washington Workforce Training
and Education Coordinating Board
Building 17 Airdustrial Park
Olympia, WA 98504-3105
360-753-5662
www.wa.gov/wtb/

Licensing Office
Department of Licensing
Department of Health
P.O. Box 9020
Olympia, WA 98507

360-902-3600
www.wa.gov/dol/main.htm

One-Stop Career Center
Washington One-Stop Career
Center System
Employment Security Department
212 Maple Park
P.O. Box 9046
Olympia, WA 98507-9046
360-438-4611
360-438-3224
www.wa.gov/esd/1stop
E-mail: btarrow@esd.wa.gov

Security Regulators
Department of Financial
Institutions
Securities Division
P.O. Box 9033
Olympia, WA 98507
360-902-8760
www.wa.gov/dfi/securities

Small Business Development Center
Washington State Small Business
Development Center
Washington State University
College of Business and
Economics
501 Johnson Tower
MAILING ADDRESS:
  P.O. Box 644851
  Pullman, WA 99164-4851
509-335-1576
Fax: 509-335-0949
E-mail: riesenbe@wsu.edu
www.sbdc.wsu.edu/wsbdc.htm

Social Services Offices
Washington Department of Social
and Health Services
DSHS Constituent Services
P.O. Box 45130
Olympia, WA 98504-5130
360-902-7892
www.wa.gov/dshs

Temporary Assistance to Needy Families (TANF)
Temporary Aid to Needy Families
Roxane Lowe
Department of Social and Health
Services
1009 College St., SE
P.O. Box 45400
Olympia, WA 98504
360-413-3010
www.wa.gov/dshs/workfirst/
tanf.html

Transportation Department
Barbara Savary
Washington State Department of
Transportation
P.O. Box 47387
Olympia, WA 98504
306-705-7919
http://www.wsdot.wa.gov/pubtran/

Unclaimed Property Office
Unclaimed Property Section
Department of Revenue
P.O. Box 448
Olympia, WA 98507
360-586-2736
www.wa.gov/dor/unclaim/

Unemployment Insurance Office
Assistant Commissioner
Employment Security Department
P.O. Box 9046
Olympia, WA 98507
360-902-9303
www.wa.gov/esd/ui.htm
Weekly benefit range: $82-384
Duration of benefits: 10-30 weeks

Utility Commission
Utilities and Transportation
Commission
1300 S. Evergreen Park Dr. SW
Olympia, WA 98504

360-753-6423
800-562-6150 (WA only)
http://www.wutc.wa.gov/

Women's Commission
Seattle Women's Commission
c/o Seattle Office for Civil Rights
700 Third Ave, Suite 250
Seattle WA 98104
206-684-4500
Fax: 206-684-0332
E-mail: diane.pina@ci.seattle.
wa.us
www.ci.seattle.wa.us/seattle/
civil/swc.htm

West Virginia

Federal Information Center
All Locations; 800-688-9889

State Information Office
304-558-3456
http://www.state.wv.us

Department on Aging
Aging Commission
1900 Kanawha Blvd.
State Capitol
Holly Grove
Charleston, WV 25305
304-558-3317
http://www.wvdhhr.org/
pages/bcs/aging.htm

Attorney General's Office
Office of the Attorney General
State Capitol
Charleston, WV 25305
304-558-2021
800-368-8808
www.state.wv.us/wvag

Banking Commissioner
Commissioner of Banking
State Capitol Complex
1900 Kanawha Blvd. East
Bldg. 3, Room 311
Charleston, WV 25305-0240
304-558-2294
800-642-9056

*Child Care and Development
Block Grant Lead Agency*
Day Care and Licensing
DHHR/Bureau of Social Services
Building 6, Room B-850
State Capitol Complex
Charleston, WV 25305
304-558-0938
Fax: 304-558-8800
http://www.wvdhhr.org/

*Child Support Enforcement
Agency*
Jeff Matherly
Child Support Enforcement
Division
Department of Health and Human
Resources
Building 6, Room 817
State Capitol Complex
1900 Kanawa Blvd., East
Charleston, WV 25305
304-558-3780
800-249-3778
Fax: 304-558-2059

Cooperative Extension Office
Robert Maxwell
Interim Director
Cooperative Extension
8th Floor, Knapt Hall
P.O. Box 6031
West Virginia University

Morgantown, WV 26506-6031
304-293-3408
http://www.wvu.edu/~exten

Corporation Division Office
Corporate Division
Secretary of State
Room 139 West, State Capitol
Charleston, WV 25305
304-342-8000
www.state.wv.us/sos

Day Care Licensing Agency
Department of Health and Human
Resources
Day Care Licensing
P.O. Box 2590
Fairmont, WV 26555
304-363-3261
http://www.wvdhhr.org/

Economic Development Office
West Virginia Development Office
1900 Kanawha Blvd., East
Charleston, WV 25305-0311
304-558-2234
800-982-3386
Fax: 304-558-0449
www.wvdo.org

Department of Education
West Virginia Dept. of Education
Department of Statistical
Information
Bldg. 6, Room B-346
1900 Kanawha Blvd. E.
Charleston, WV 25305-0330
304-558-8869
http://wvde.state.wv.us/

Department of Higher Education
State College and University
Systems Central Office
1018 Kanawha Boulevard East
Suite 700
Charleston, WV 25301
304-558-2101
www.scusco.wvnet.edu

Health Department
West Virginia Bureau for Public
Health
Building 3, Room 518
State Capitol Complex
Charelston, WV 25305
304-228-2971
Fax: 304-558-1035
http://wvbph.marshall.edu

Housing Office
West Virginia Housing
Development Fund
814 Virginia St., East
Charleston, WV 25301
304-345-6475
http://www.wvhdf.com/

Insurance Commissioner
Insurance Commissioner
2019 Washington St., E.
P.O. Box 50540
Charleston, WV 25305-0540
304-558-3394
800-642-9004

Labor Department
West Virginia Bureau of
Employment Programs
112 California Avenue

Charleston, WV 25305-0112
304-558-2630
www.state.wv.us/bep

Licensing Office
Secretary of State
State Capitol
Charleston, WV 25305
304-558-6000

One-Stop Career Center
Job Service
Bureau of Employment Programs
Jobs/Job Training
112 California Avenue
Charleston, WV 25305-0112
304-558-1138
Fax: 304-558-1136
www.state.wv.us/bep/jobs/
default.HTM
E-mail: haydep@wvnvm.
wvnet.edu

Security Regulators
West Virginia Securities Division
State Capitol
Kanawha Blvd., East
Room 118 West
Charleston, WV 25305
304-558-2257
www.wvauditor.com

Small Business Development Center
West Virginia Small Business
Development Center
West Virginia Development Office
950 Kanawha Boulevard
Charleston, WV 25301
304-558-2960

Fax: 304-558-0127
E-mail: palmeh@mail.wvnet.edu
www.state.wv.us/wvdev/sbdc/
sb_main.htm

Social Services Offices
West Virginia Department of
Health and Human Resources
State Capital Complex
Building 3, Room 218
Charleston, WV 25305
304-558-8886
www.wvdhhr.org

Temporary Assistance to Needy Families (TANF)
Temporary Aid to Needy Families
Sharon Paterno
West Virginia Department of
Health and Human Resources
Building 6, Room 650
State Capitol Complex
Charleston, WV 25305
304-558-4069
www.wvdhhr.org/pages/bcf/
cf-family.htm

Transportation Department
Toni Boyd
West Virginia Department of
Transportation
1900 Kanawha Boulevard
East Building 5, Room 803
Charleston, WV 25305
304-558-0428
http://www.state.wv.us/wvdot

Unclaimed Property Office
West Virginia State Treasurer

1900 Kanawha Blvd., East
State Capitol Bldg. 1, Room E-145
Charleston, WV 25305
304-558-5000
www.wvtreasury.com

Unemployment Insurance Office
Director, Unemployment
Compensation Division
Bureau of Employment Programs
112 California Ave.
Charleston, WV 25305
304-558-2624
www.state.wv.us/bep/uc/
default.htm
Weekly benefit range: $24-290
Duration of benefits: 26 weeks

Utility Commission
Public Service Commission
201 Brooks St.

P.O. Box 812
Charleston, WV 25323-0812
304-340-0300
800-344-5113 (WV only)
http://www.state.wv.us/psc/
default.htm

Women's Commission
West Virginia Women's
Commission
Building 6, Room 637
Capitol Complex
Charleston, WV 25305
304-558-0070
Fax: 304-558-5767
E-mail: vrobinson@wvdhhr.org
www.state.wv.us/womenscom
Joyce M. Stover, Acting Executive
Director
Sally Riley, Chair

Wisconsin

Federal Information Center
All Locations; 800-688-9889

State Information Office
608-266-2211
http://www.state.wi.us

Department on Aging
Aging and Long Term Care Board
217 S. Hamilton St., Suite 300
Madison, WI 53703
608-266-2536

Attorney General's Office
Office of the Attorney General
State Capitol, Suite 114 East
P.O. Box 7857
Madison, WI 53707
608-266-1221
800-422-7128
www.doj.state.wi.us

Banking Commissioner
Commissioner of Banking
345 W. Washington Ave., 4th Floor
Madison, WI 53703
608-266-1621
800-452-3328
http://badger.state.wi.us/
agencies/bfi/

Child Care and Development Block Grant Lead Agency
Wisconsin Department of
Workforce Development

Office of Child Care
1 West Wilson St.
P.O. Box 7935
Madison, WI 53707-7935
608-267-3708
Fax: 608-261-6968
http://www.dwd.state.wi.us/
notespub/ AboutDwD/1a6.htm

Child Support Enforcement Agency
Mary Southwick
Bureau of Child Support
Division of Economic Support
P.O. Box 7935
Madison, WI 53707
608-266-9909
Fax: 608-627-2824
http://www.dwd.state.wi. us/bcs/

Cooperative Extension Office
Dr. Aeyse Somersan, Director
432 N. Lake St.
Room 601
Madison, WI 53706
608-262-7966
http://www.uwex.edu/ces/

Corporation Division Office
Corporate Division
Secretary of State
P.O. Box 7846
Madison, WI 53707
608-266-3590
www.state.wi.us/agencies/sos/

Day Care Licensing Agency
Department of Health and Social
Services
Child Care Licensing Division
P.O. Box 8916
Madison, WI 53708-8916
608-266-9314

Economic Development Office
Department of Commerce
(COMMERCE)
201 W. Washington Avenue
Madison, WI 53707
Business Helpline:
    1-800-HELP-BUSiness
Fax Request Hotline:
    608-264-6154
Export Helpline:
    1-800-XPORT-WIsconsin
www.commerce.state.wi.us

Department of Education
Wisconsin Department of Public
Instruction
Center for Education Statistics
125 S. Webster
P.O. Box 7841
Madison, WI 53707-7841
608-266-3390
800-441-4563
http://www.dpi.state.wi.us/

Department of Higher Education
State of Wisconsin Higher
Educational Aids Board
P.O. Box 7885
Madison, WI 53707-7885
608-267-2206
Fax: 608-267-2808
http://heab.state.wi.us

Health Department
Wisconsin Department of Health &
Family Services
1 West Wilson Street
Madison, WI 53702-0007
608-266-1865
TTY: 608-267-7371
www.dhfs.state.wi.us

Housing Office
Wisconsin Housing and Economic
Development Authority
P.O. Box 1728
Madison, WI 53701-1728
608-266-7884
800-334-6873
http://www.wheda.state. wi.us

Insurance Commissioner
Commissioner of Insurance
P.O. Box 7873
Madison, WI 53707-7873
608-266-3585
800-236-8517
http://badger.state.wi.us/agencies/
oci/ oci_home.htm

Labor Department
Wisconsin Department of
Workforce Development
201 East Washington Avenue
P.O. Box 7946
Madison, WI 53707-7946
608-267-4400
www.dwd.state.wi.us

Licensing Office
Department of Regulation and
Licensing

P.O. Box 8935
Madison, WI 53708
608-266-7482
http://bager.state.wi.us/
agencies/drl

One-Stop Career Center
Partnership for Full Employment
(PFE)
Department of Workforce
Development
201 East Washington Avenue
P.O. Box 7946
Madison, WI 53707-7946
608-266-3131
Fax: 608-261-7979
www.dwd.state.wi.us/dwepfe/
E-mail: DWDINFO@dwd.
state.wi.us

Security Regulators
Division of Securities
P.O. Box 1768
Madison, WI 53701
608-266-1064
www.wdfi.org

**Small Business Development
Center**
Wisconsin Small Business
Development Center
University of Wisconsin
432 North Lake St., Room 423
Madison, WI 53706
608-263-7794
Fax: 608-262-3878
E-mail: Kauten@admin.uwex.edu
www.uwex.edu/sbdc

Social Services Offices
Wisconsin Department of Health
and Family Services
1 West Wilson Street
Madison, WI 53702
608-266-1683
www.dhfs.state.wi.us

**Temporary Assistance to Needy
Families (TANF)**
Temporary Aid to Needy Families
Linda Stewart
Work Force Development
P.O. Box 7946
Madison, WI 53707
608-266-7553
www.dwd.state.wi.us/desw2/
W2Home.htm

Transportation Department
Elizabeth Trautsch
Wisconsin Bureau of Transit and
Local Roads
P.O. Box 7913
Madison, WI 53606
608-266-0560
www.dot.state.wi.us

Unclaimed Property Office
Unclaimed Property Division
State Treasurer's Office
P.O. Box 2114
Madison, WI 53701
608-267-7977
http://badger.state.wi.us/
agencies/ost

Unemployment Insurance Office
Administrator
Division of Unemployment
Insurance
201 E. Washington Ave.
Room 371
P.O. Box 7905
Madison, WI 53707
608-266-7074
www.dwd.state.wi.us/ui/
Weekly benefit range: $52-274
Duration of benefits: 12-26 weeks

Utility Commission
Public Service Commission
610 North Whitney Way

Madison, WI 53707
608-266-2001
800-225-7729
http://badger.state.wi.us/
agencies/psc

Women's Commission
Wisconsin Women's Council
16 North Carroll St., Suite 720
Madison, WI 53703
608-266-2219
Fax: 608-261-2432
E-mail: Katie.Mnuk@wwc.
state.wi.us
http://wwc.state.wi.us
Katie Mnuk, Executive Director

Wyoming

Federal Information Center
All Locations; 800-688-9889

State Information Office
307-777-7011
http://www.state.wy.us

Department on Aging
Division on Aging
Department of Health
117 Hathaway Bldg.
Room 139
Cheyenne, WY 82002
307-777-7986
http://wdhfs.state.wy.us/
wdh/default.htm

Attorney General's Office
Office of the Attorney General
123 Capitol Bldg.
Cheyenne, WY 82002
307-777-7841
www.state.wy.us/~ag/index.html

Banking Commissioner
Banking Commissioner
Division of Banking
Department of Audit
Herschler Bldg., 3rd Floor E.
Cheyenne, WY 82002
307-777-7797
http://audit.state.wy.us/
banking/banking.htm

**Child Care and Development
Block Grant Lead Agency**
CCDBG Administrator
Wyoming Department of Family
Services
Hathaway Building
2300 Capitol Ave.
Cheyenne, WY 82002-0490
307-777-6848
Fax: 307-777-3693
http://dfsweb.state.wy.us/

**Child Support Enforcement
Agency**
James Mohler
Child Support Enforcement
Program
Department of Family Services
Hathaway Building
2300 Capital Ave.
Cheyenne, WY 82002
307-777-6948
Fax: 307-777-3693
http://dfsweb.state.wy.us/
csehome/cs.htm

Cooperative Extension Office
Darryl Kautzman, Director
CES, University of Wyoming
Box 3354
Laramie, WY 82071-3354
307-766-5124
http://www.uwyo.edu/ag/ces/
ceshome.htm

Corporation Division Office
Corporate Division
Secretary of State
State of Wyoming
Capitol Building
Cheyenne, WY 82002
307-777-5334
http://soswy.state.wy.us

Day Care Licensing Agency
Department of Family Services
Office of Child Care Licensing
Hathaway Building, Room 323
2300 Capitol Ave.
Cheyenne, WY 82002-0490
307-777-6285
http://dfsweb.state.wy.us/

Economic Development Office
Department of Commerce
Cheyenne, WY 82002
307-777-7284
Fax: 307-777-5840
www.state.wy.us/commerce/
decd/index.htm

Department of Education
Wyoming Department of Education
Statistical Department
Hathaway Bldg., 2nd Floor
2300 Capitol Ave.
Cheyenne, WY 82002-0050
307-777-7673
http://www.k12.wy.us/
wdehome.html

Department of Higher Education
Wyoming Department of Higher
Education

Hathaway Building
2300 Capitol Avenue
Cheyenne, WY 82002
307-777-6213

Health Department
Wyoming Department of Health
2300 Capitol Avenue
MAILING ADDRESS:
  117 Hathaway Building
  Cheyenne, WY 82002
307-777-7657
Fax: 307-777-7439
TTY: 307-777-5648
http://wdhfs.state.wy.us/wdh/
E-mail: wdh@missc.state.wy.us

Housing Office
Wyoming Community Development
Authority
123 S. Durbin St.
P.O. Box 634
Casper, WY 82602
307-265-0603

Insurance Commissioner
Commissioner of Insurance
Herschler Bldg. 3 East
122 W. 25th St.
Cheyenne, WY 82002
307-777-7401
800-438-5768

Labor Department
Wyoming Dept. of Employment
122 West 25th Street
Cheyenne, WY 82002
307-777-7672
http://wydoe.state.wy.us/

Licensing Office
Governor's Office
State Capitol
Cheyenne, WY 82002
307-777-7434
www.state.wy.us/governor/
governor_home.html

One-Stop Career Center
Employment Resource Centers
Department of Employment
Employment Resource Division
100 West Midwest
Casper, WY 82602
307-235-3254
http://wydoe.state.wy.us/erd

Security Regulators
Securities Division
Secretary of State
24th Street & State Capitol Ave.
Cheyenne, WY 82002
307-777-7370
http://soswy.state.wy.us

Small Business Development Center
Wyoming Small Business
Development Center
University of Wyoming
P.O. Box 3922
Laramie, WY 82071-3922
307-766-3505
800-348-5194
Fax: 307-766-3406
E-mail: DDW@uwyo.edu
www.uwyo.edu/sbdc

Social Services Offices
Wyoming Department of Family
Services
Hathaway Building
Cheyenne, WY 82002-0490
307-777-3679
www.dfsweb.state.wy.us

Temporary Assistance to Needy Families (TANF)
Temporary Aid to Needy Families
Marianne Lee
Department of Family Services
2300 Capitol Ave.
Hathaway Building, 3rd Floor
Cheyenne, WY 82002
307-777-7531
http://dfsweb.state.wy.us/
updtanf.htm

Transportation Department
John Black
State Highway Department
P.O. Box 1708
Cheyenne, WY 82003
307-777-4181
http://wydotweb.state.wy.us

Unclaimed Property Office
Unclaimed Property Division
State Treasurer's Office
1st Floor West, Herschler Bldg.
122 West 25th St.
Cheyenne, WY 82008
307-777-5590
www.state.wy.us/~sot/
unc_prop.html

Unemployment Insurance Office
Administrator, Division of
Unemployment Insurance
Department of Employment
P.O. Box 2760
Casper, WY 82602
307-235-3254
http://wydoe.state.wy.us/erd/ui/
Weekly benefit range: $18-250
Duration of benefits: 12-26 weeks

Utility Commission
Public Service Commission
2515 Warren Ave.

Hansen Bldg., Suite 300
Cheyenne, WY 82002
307-777-7427

Women's Commission
Wyoming State Government
Commission for Women
c/o Department of Employment
Herschler Building
122 West 25th St.
Cheyenne, WY 82002
307-777-7671
http://wydoe.state.wy.us
Amy McClure, Chair

Index

A

Abortion services, 293
Acid rain, 135
Accounting services, 460
Adoption, 152-153, 296-297, 362
Advocacy groups
    medical, 315, 326-327
Agriculture, U.S. Department of,
    209
Aging, 363
AIDS, 363
AIDS testing, 334
Air and Space Museum, National,
    121
Air courier services, 41
Air Force, 280
Airline discounts, 39, 330-331,
    393-394
Air quality, indoor, 60
Allergies, 363
Alternative medicine, 364
Alzheimer's, 303, 364, 383
American Academy of
    Ophthalmology, 357, 384
American Bar Association, 269
American Business Women's
    Association, 585-586
American Cancer Society, 310,
    384-385
American Civil Liberties Union
    (ACLU), 249
American Heart Association, 351,
    367, 385
American Lung Association, 302
American Optometric Association,
    357

American Savings Council, 190
America's Learning eXchange,
    582
Archeology, 129, 143
Archives and Records, National,
    127-128
Army, 278
Art competitions, 163-165
Art education, 138
Arthritis Foundation, 364, 386
Asthma camps, 302
Attention Deficit Disorder, 306,
    348-349
Attorney General's Offices, 213
Auctions, government, 234-240
Auto Safety Hotline, 27
Automobile loans, 25-26, 42
Automobiles. *See* cars
Automotive Consumer Action
    Program, 22-23
Aviation science, 121

B

Baby Safety Shower How-to-Kit,
    95-96
Backyard conservation, 144, 146
Banking, 263-265
Banks
    choosing, 220, 263-265
    complaints against, 220
Battered women. *See* Domestic
    violence
Bed wetting, 345-346
Bereavement/Compassion Fares,
    39, 330-331

Information USA, Inc.

Oral history guide, 126-127
Osteoporosis, 369

P

Parenting, 105-106, 151
Parkinson's Disease, 343
Parkinson Foundation, United,
386
Peace Corps, 391
Pension Benefit Guaranty
Corporation (PBGC), 222, 240
Pension Search Directory, 240
Pension & Welfare Benefits
Administration Request Line,
188
Pensions, 222-223, 240-241, 381
Pet care, 144
Pilot Dogs, 308
Planned Parenthood, 290-291,
293
Population statistics, 282-284
Postal Service, U.S., 116
Postal vehicles, used, 233-234
Public assistance, 359
Pregnancy and childbirth, 301,
349-350, 352-353, 369
diabetes during, 349
health diaries for, 350
help after, 301
Preschool, 122-123
Prescription drugs, 311
President, contacting the, 115
Presidential Memorial Certificate,
375
President's Council on Physical
Fitness and Sports, 344
Product safety, 227, 370

Q

Qualified Transportation Fringe
Benefit, 43

R

Radon, 75
Railroad Board disability benefits,
358
Real estate, 233, 237-238. *See
also* Home buying
Recalls, car, 26-27
Recycling, 137
Rent assistance, 57-58
Repossession of vehicles, 44-45
Researching
banks, 220-221
businesses, 213-215
money owed, 285-286
occupations, 287
pensions, 240-241
property ownership, 284, 286
Resolve, 342
Respite care, 341
Retirement
estimating needs, 190
pensions, 222, 240-241, 381
saving for, 188-190
Social Security and, 189
Supplemental Security Income
(SSI), 209
taxes and, 223-225
Right to Work Legal Defense
Foundation, 255
Rural Housing Service, 61-63
Rutherford Institute, 259

S

V

Venture capital programs, 464-476

Veterans Affairs, 243, 375, 378

Veterans' services, 375, 378
   National Veterans Legal
     Services Program, 248
   tuition assistance, 530
   Veterans Affairs, 243, 375

Vision care, 292, 357-358, 384, 396

VISION USA, 357

Vital records, obtaining, 276-277, 284-285

Voice mail, free, 202-203

Volcano information, 116-117

Volunteer opportunities
   at National Parks, 389-90
   for business retirees, 389-391
   for seniors, 388-391
   Peace Corps, 391

Voucher programs, 154-155

W

Water quality, 76

Water safety, 124

Water science, 125

Weather education resources, 145

Weatherization Assistance
   Program, 81

Weight loss advertisements, 226

Weight loss programs, 344

Welfare Law Center, 254

Welfare Reform Laws, 487

Wetlands, 136

Wheel chairs, 310

Wheels-to-Work, 13-14, 19

White House, the, 115

Wider Opportunities for Women
   (WOW), 586

Wills, writing, 215-216

Women business owners, 439-440
   government contract awards,
     444-447, 459
   loans for, 423-424, 448-449,
     457
   low-income assistance, 449-451
   mentor programs, 442
   transportation related, 452-455
   websites, 214, 440-441
   Women's Demonstration
     Program, 441-442

Women in Construction, National
   Association of, 587

Women in Trades, Technology &
   Science, 583

Women Work!, 489, 584-585

Women-Owned Business
   Procurement Pilot Program,
   444-446

Women's Demonstration Program,
   441-442

Women's health hotline, 332

Women's Network for
   Entrepreneurial Training
   (WNET), 442

Women, training for, 216, 411

Worker Retraining and
   Readjustment Programs,
   Office of, 566

Y

YWCA, 148-149, 216, 270, 584

Youth Fair Chance, 579-580

Youthbuild, 577-578

REAL WOMEN GET GOVERNMENT MONEY

Margaret Nelson

a clean Chrysler to drive to work and to take the kids to school

Rahsheeda Morrison

a car, repairs and a AAA card

REAL WOMEN GET GOVERNMENT MONEY

Linda Jacobs-Holcomb

$5000 worth of speech therapy for her son

Debra Johnson

$19,000 grant plus low interest mortgage to buy a home

Sally Johnson

over $1 million in contracts for her window cleaning company

Dorothy Hart

$40,000 to pay for her daughter's hospital bills

Mildred Raymond
Mil-Ray Food Company, Inc.

$30,000 to $1 million in contracts for her food distribution business

Sheila Baker

$50,000 in home buying assistance

REAL WOMEN GET GOVERNMENT MONEY

REAL WOMEN GET GOVERNMENT MONEY

Laurie Fasnacht

$39,000 in contracts for her industrial supply company

Jeannyn Ulrich

$28,000 to pay for medical bills

Michelle M. Pannell
Pace Products Dealer

$600,000 for her material supplies business

Linda Swanson-Roshko
Tristate Graphix Sales, LLC

$40,000 in contracts for her printing business

Marissa Pavin

$15,000 in grants, $42,000 at 0%, $15,000 at 3% to buy a home

Sharon Cohen
Globe Trading Company

$50,000 selling beans and cheese to the government

REAL WOMEN GET GOVERNMENT MONEY

REAL WOMEN GET GOVERNMENT MONEY

Lavada Garcia

$8,000 in free medications

Deborah Libby
Libby Window Treatments

*$20,000 selling window
treatments to the government*

Suzzanne Stilwell
Commonwealth Metal Company

*her first contract of $6,000 led
to more for her metal company*

Alice Miller
Alice's Alterations

$60,000 contract for her alterations business

Eileen Connolly
Pennsylvania Gifts & Awards
www.giftspa.com

$12,000 in contracts for her gift and awards business

Patricia Gary

$32,000 grant and $2,500 in closing costs to buy a home

REAL WOMEN GET GOVERNMENT MONEY